Major Problems in the Era of the American Revolution, 1760–1791

MAJOR PROBLEMS IN AMERICAN HISTORY SERIES

GENERAL EDITOR
THOMAS G. PATERSON

Major Problems
in the Era of the
American Revolution,
1760–1791

DOCUMENTS AND ESSAYS

SECOND EDITION

EDITED BY
RICHARD D. BROWN
UNIVERSITY OF CONNECTICUT

HOUGHTON MIFFLIN COMPANY
Boston   New York

Editor in Chief: Jean L. Woy
Senior Associate Editor: Frances Gay
Project Editor: Rebecca Bennett
Associate Production/Design Coordinator: Jodi O'Rourke
Associate Manufacturing Coordinator: Andrea Wagner
Senior Marketing Manager: Sandra McGuire

Cover Image: John Trumbull, *The Death of General Warren at the Battle of Bunker Hill,*
June 1775, Yale University Art Gallery, Trumbull Collection.

Back Cover Photo: Peter Morenus/UConn

Printed in the U.S.A.

Library of Congress Catalog Card Number: 98-72005

ISBN: 0-395-90344-0

3456789-CRS-03 02 01 00

For my students

Contents

CHAPTER 6
Fighting for Independence
Page 189

CHAPTER 7
Outsiders and Enemies: Native Americans and the Loyalists
Page 224

CHAPTER 8
Are All Men Equal? The African-American Challenge
Page 256

CHAPTER 9
Gender and Citizenship in a Revolutionary Republic
Page 287

CHAPTER 10
Toleration Versus Religious Freedom in a Protestant Republic
Page 311

C H A P T E R   1 1

*Peacetime Government Under the
Articles of Confederation*

Page 341

C H A P T E R   1 2

Making the Constitution of 1787

Page 389

Preface

As we begin a new century in a new millennium, the American Revolution and the formation of the Constitution remain central in the history of the United States because they continue to influence our understanding of American government, society, and culture. Although historians agree that the events of the decades from 1760 to 1790 were seminal for American development, when historians explore the meaning of these events and their causes and consequences, agreement yields to controversy. Because the Revolution and the Constitution stand at the foundation of the history of the United States and are essential to establishing the legitimacy of American political and social viewpoints, Americans of all regions, classes, and origins have argued about their significance for generations. The events themselves are complex and multifaceted; moreover, they have been susceptible to diverse interpretations that are at once reasonable yet conflicting. For the student, this may be a source of confusion or, worse, cynicism. If, after all, scholars cannot agree, and if the meaning of history itself changes from one decade to the next, why bother?

Why bother? This is a serious question that every teacher and student must confront. The first reason is that knowledge of the foundation of the United States is an essential part of being an educated citizen. By studying classic American historical texts such as the Declaration of Independence and the First Amendment, a citizen can begin to master the vocabulary of American culture and to understand the issues that face Americans today.

A second, even more important reason to study the Revolution and the Constitution is to position oneself to evaluate the public claims that politicians, journalists, lawyers, the clergy, educators, and others make regarding the meaning of these historical events. Anyone who listens to public discussion will find aspects of the Revolution and the Constitution employed to justify a wide range of current domestic policies—abortion rights, affirmative action, gun control, school busing, tax support for private schools, censorship questions, environmental protection, and national programs for health and old age insurance. In the realm of foreign policy, human rights, democracy, and freedom are regularly invoked to justify the giving or withholding of foreign aid and to support decisions of war and peace. Anyone who seeks to judge the legitimacy of these claims—or who wants to draw on the reservoir of principles expressed in the Revolution and Constitution to defend their own arguments—must possess a genuine familiarity with what happened.

A third and more personal reason for studying the Revolutionary origins of the United States is to locate oneself better in the moving stream of American history. Because the study of the Revolution and Constitution permits one to grasp some of the essential features of American politics, society, and culture, it enables us to make informed judgments about where we stand personally in relation to the past. As with all other historical study, it enables us to distinguish what is fundamental and durable from what is transitory.

This new, second edition differs from the old edition in two important ways. First, it opens up a wider variety of interpretations of the Revolutionary era by using Gordon S. Wood's *Radicalism of the American Revolution* (1992) as a point of departure and by concluding with new essays by Rosemarie Zagarri, Alfred F. Young, and Edward Countryman that consider the long-range consequences of the Revolution for American society. Second, the new edition devotes more space to culture and society in the Revolutionary era. One new chapter treats colonial society on the eve of the Revolution (Chapter 2). In addition, new chapters on women and African Americans supply fuller consideration of the complex ways in which the Revolution generated change in some ways but reinforced continuity in others (Chapters 8 and 9). Throughout, new essays have been added to introduce students to the leading scholarship of the field.

Among the essays new to this second edition are works by Barbara Clark Smith and Gordon S. Wood in a follow-up discussion of *Radicalism of the American Revolution* in Chapter 1. Also in Chapter 1, T. H. Breen recognizes the power of ideology and economic interest in the independence movement. In Chapter 2, Richard R. Beeman writes on the emergence of popular politics on the eve of the Revolution. Fred Anderson investigates the friction between colonial troops and British regulars in Chapter 3, where P. J. Marshall explores ways the colonies helped define the British Empire. Pauline Maier explains the complicated interplay of external events and political manuevering that produced the Declaration of Independence (Chapter 5). In Chapter 7, Gregory Evans Dowd explains the impact of the interplay of warfare and diplomacy on the Indians of the Ohio region, and Robert M. Calhoon considers the Loyalist dimension of the fighting. Sylvia R. Frey explains the conflicts over slavery and the different meanings of the Revolution generated by the war and its politics in Chapter 8. Chapter 9 includes Linda K. Kerber, who shows how deeply unsettling the Revolution was for the politics of the sexes and the home, and Jan Lewis who suggests the Revolution opened a path toward equality for women and African Americans that was later closed. Jack N. Rakove analyzes the national political issues of the 1780s that led from reform of the Articles of Confederation to a new Constitution, while John L. Brooke tackles local and state politics in Massachusetts during the 1780s that provided a catalyst for constitutional reform (Chapter 11). Lastly, in Chapter 12, Rakove focuses on the profound conflicts over federalism that the delegates to the Constitutional Convention faced. The pathbreaking work of these scholars stimulates fresh understanding and interpretation.

Like the other volumes in the series, *Major Problems in the Era of the American Revolution, 1760–1791* approaches its subject in two ways: through primary sources and through the interpretations of distinguished scholars. In both cases, head notes provide background information to enhance the reader's understanding of the documents and essays. Enabling students to confront documents from the period directly is essential for grasping control of the subject. Nothing is so empowering, for by reading the sources, students can form their own opinions and measure the explanations of others against their own first-hand knowledge of the subject. The essays supply interpretive possibilities. Because they are written by scholars who have conducted research and read widely and deeply, they bring a sophistication to their topics that enables students to appreciate the complexity of events and to form discriminating judgments. Such active challenges between students, the primary sources, and the secondary texts encourage students to reach a lasting level of mastery of the Revolution and Constitution. When hour exams and finals have long faded from memory, knowledge of key texts such as *Common Sense,* the Declaration of Independence, and the Bill of Rights endures, as does the understanding that the Revolution and the Constitution represent more than simple statements of democracy and freedom. Finally, further reading lists at the end of each chapter will provide guidance for students who want to explore this period in more depth.

I am grateful to the following reviewers for suggestions on revising the table of contents for this new edition: Michael A. Bellesiles, Emory University; Holly Brewer, North Carolina State University; Eric Hinderaker, University of Utah; and Dane Morrison, Salem State College. Their ideas and those of Series Editor Thomas G. Paterson and Editor in Chief Jean Woy helped shape the direction of this second edition. I would also like to thank those who helped with the first edition: Fred Anderson, Lance Banning, Bernard Bailyn, Richard R. Beeman, Richard Buel, Richard L. Bushman, Paul Bowers, Robert M. Calhoon, Jere R. Daniell, Linda Grant De Pauw, Robert L. Ganyard, Paul A. Gilje, Robert Gilmore, Robert A. Gross, Donald R. Hickey, Ronald Hoffman, Richard R. Johnson, Pauline Maier, Gary B. Nash, David W. Robson, James Ronda, Thomas P. Slaughter, Alan Taylor, Gordon S. Wood, and Alfred F. Young. Regarding the actual preparation of the text, Frances Gay of Houghton Mifflin's College Division has been a model editor. She and her colleagues, Rebecca Bennett, project editor, and Maria Leon Maimone, permissions editor, have been cordial, constructive, and competent at every step.

Finally, I am grateful to my students, both graduate and undergraduate. They have taught me more than they imagine about teaching and about history through their questions, their smiles, their frowns, and even their blank stares. I dedicate the book to them because they make it a pleasure to walk into the classroom.

R. D. B.

Major Problems in the Era of the
American Revolution, 1760–1791

CHAPTER

1

Interpreting the American Revolution

The meaning of the American Revolution, and even a precise definition of what it was, can never be established with absolute finality. The movement to independence and for the creation of the national republic—which lasted a full generation, from about 1763 to about 1789—was too rich in its variety of events, too intricate in its workings, and too heterogeneous in its participants and their motives to allow for a single incontestable and definitive interpretation. Moreover, because the Revolution was the crucial event for the formation of American nationality, our current sense of the United States must always influence the ways in which we see and understand the Revolution. Americans, who have most often and most thoroughly investigated the Revolution, cannot view it with complete detachment. We can and do learn more about what happened, but we cannot expect to fix the meaning of events permanently.

Yet certain coherent schools of general interpretation have been widely accepted during the past two centuries. A brief synopsis of them reveals the continuing vitality of some themes and helps us to place present-day interpretations in perspective. It is reasonable to begin with the "Whig" interpretation because it was the earliest, most durable viewpoint and has shaped debate over the Revolution from the era of its first appearance in the early republic.

The Whig view was initially articulated by victorious participants in the independence movement like David Ramsay, the South Carolina clergyman, and Mercy Otis Warren, the Massachusetts writer and a relative of patriot partisans. Their writings presented the Revolution as a movement for liberty in opposition to British tyranny. In the Whig interpretation's most full-blown, mid-nineteenth-century expression, the historian and Jacksonian Democrat George Bancroft explained the Revolution as a heroic struggle in which hardy yeoman farmers and idealistic merchants and planters took arms so as to defend their political liberty. In the process, they fashioned a democratic republic that became a model of free government for the rest of the world. This interpretation of the Revolution lay at the foundation of American nationalism and has been closely associated with patriotism. Until the beginning of the twentieth century, it was the standard interpretation, favored by scholars, schoolteachers, journalists, and politicians alike.

1

Although the Whig view has never been wholly swept away from popular culture, it was effectively challenged at the turn of the twentieth century by university scholars such as George Louis Beer and Charles McLean Andrews, who, together with their students, most notably Lawrence Henry Gipson, formulated a new "imperial" interpretation based on British archival sources. They "discovered" that Britain had never intended to impose tyranny in the colonies, and they agreed with eighteenth-century British officials that in fact the colonists were a free people flourishing under imperial rule. Independence, these scholars explained, resulted from transatlantic misunderstandings and bureaucratic and parliamentary mismanagement. Although Britain was generally well intentioned, its system was haphazard, and its officials were clumsy. This interpretation did not erase notions of patriotic idealism or heroics, but it made them incidental. The key to understanding the Revolution, according to this school, lay in grasping British political culture on both sides of the Atlantic and the inadequacies of the imperial system for responding to changing issues and demands.

About the same time that the imperial school took root among American scholars, a new, critical viewpoint was articulated by political scientists, essayists, and historians, among them Charles A. Beard, Carl M. Becker, and Arthur M. Schlesinger. Their views, which came to be labeled "Progressive," focused on economic and political self-interest as the central motives propelling the Revolution. Indeed, the dynamic forces that shaped the movement for independence and the formation of state and national government were conflicts between merchants and farmers, easterners and westerners, city dwellers and country folk, aristocrats and democrats, creditors and debtors. Pulling patriotic icons like Washington, Hamilton, and Jefferson down from their pedestals, Progressive interpreters maintained that the same kinds of flesh-and-blood political contests characteristic of their own era were also operating at the nation's founding.

During the 1930s and 1940s this interpretation became widely established, in both academe through the writings of such scholars as Merrill M. Jensen and popular culture, where the novelist Kenneth Roberts used Progressive ideas in several best-selling novels about the Revolution. This interpretation made the Revolution relevant to contemporary political struggles. Like the older Whig interpretation, it has retained vitality and is particularly attractive to critics of national complacency and the status quo. But during the generation following World War II and in the 1950s especially, it was effectively challenged by scholars such as the political scientist Louis M. Hartz and the historian Richard E. Hofstadter.

Their works, influenced by a more global perspective and by a comparison of the American Revolution with the revolutions of France, Russia, and China, emphasized the broad republican consensus that the Revolutionaries shared, their commitment to pragmatic politics, and their affinity for practical compromises. Here there was no significant right-wing party that favored a hereditary system, just as there was no substantial support for social leveling and attacks on private property. American Revolutionaries might argue over tactics, but they were, it was said, generally united around the liberal, Lockean idea of a republic grounded on widespread property ownership and a state committed to fostering individual rights and opportunities. Because a mood of national unity prevailed during the postwar and cold war eras, this "consensus" interpretation had an appeal that made it popular far beyond the campus. As with the older Whig interpretation, it was popular among journalists, politicians, and schoolteachers.

During the past generation, starting in the 1960s, various scholars have challenged this consensus view. One group, whose criticism of the consensus interpretation is oblique, has been labeled "neo-Whig." In the neo-Whig view, both the

Progressive and consensus schools failed to take Revolutionary ideology seriously. Both regarded ideas as secondary, as mere propaganda or rationalization, subject to manipulation in a political struggle where the real issues—concrete material and political advantages—were settled by pragmatic deals. NeoWhigs, among whom the historian Bernard Bailyn has been most influential, accept a role for material interests and practical politics but emphasize the power of ideology. Ideas, they maintain, shaped the Revolutionaries' understanding of events and thus guided their actions. Like the first Whig interpreters of the Revolution, neo-Whigs regard its rhetoric as expressing the actual beliefs of Revolutionaries, not as a "public relations" smokescreen intended to mask their real objectives.

A second challenge to the consensus school has been frontal and has often targeted the neo-Whigs as well. Labeled "neo-Progressive," this view, which the historian Gary B. Nash has most powerfully articulated, accepts both the reality of a republican consensus in the Revolutionary era and an influential role for ideology. But the crux of the Revolution, neo-Progressives believe, was social conflict—struggles rooted in the material interests first identified by Beard, Becker, Schlesinger, and Jensen. When it came to mobilizing common men and women, they argue, ideas did not suffice. And the movement for republicanism, they maintain, comprehended an ongoing battle between democratic and elitist forces. As neo-Progressives see it, the consensus interpretation is too placid and the neoWhig too cerebral to portray accurately the blood, sweat, tears, and hard interests that the Revolution encompassed.

In the 1990s, Gordon S. Wood proposed an interpretation of the Revolution that creatively combined themes from both neo-Whig and neo-Progressive interpretations. His synthesis re-cast the time span of the Revolution, stretching it from the 1760s to the 1830s. Wood's two-stage argument—first republicanism, then democracy—was challenged immediately as being too narrowly focused on white men and too provincial, inasmuch as it was constructed from the perspective of the winners. Yet it is a measure of Wood's achievement that if his synthesis is not the final word, it serves as the point of departure for many interpreters.

There is no agreement about how best to interpret the Revolution. In addition to new perspectives, elements of all the earlier interpretations are still current and are expressed in books, speeches, and dramatic performances. Individual experience and judgment, not only information, shape opinion. Readers of this book are invited to fashion their own interpretation of the Revolution as they reflect on the documents and essays that follow.

ESSAYS

Gordon S. Wood, a professor at Brown University, won a Pulitzer Prize for his interpretive synthesis, *The Radicalism of the American Revolution* (1992). The work has been widely praised, but it has also been criticized because, in the judgment of some scholars, it takes a celebratory view of a revolution that laid the foundation for competitive capitalism and imperial expansion, while perpetuating patriarchy and slavery. In 1994 the leading journal of early American history, the *William and Mary Quarterly,* published a discussion by several scholars of Wood's *Radicalism of the American Revolution,* and the essays by Barbara Clark Smith, a curator at the National Museum of American History, and Wood are drawn from that publication. The final essay, by T. H. Breen, a distinguished early American historian who heads the Center for the Humanities at Northwestern University, presents a fresh interpretation of the independence movement that recognizes the power of ideology and economic interest. According to Breen, the boycott movement created a new, inclusive American revolutionary community.

The Revolution Preserved Social Inequality

BARBARA CLARK SMITH

The Radicalism of the American Revolution is a powerful and ambitious work, a synthesis that aspires to reinterpret events that Americans have long seen as central to their identity as a nation. Gordon Wood states his purpose in the title: his book will explicate ways in which the American Revolution was radical, establishing that it was, in fact, "as radical and as revolutionary as any [such unheaval] in history." But if the radicalism of the era is crucial to Wood, it remains in his hands an elusive and unsatisfying characterization. Seventeenth-century English revolutionaries toppled a king and embraced startling, leveling, and millennial ideas. Eighteenth-century French revolutionaries went so far as to abolish slavery and consider the rights of women as citizens of the republic. And in early nineteenth-century Peru, an anticolonial revolution produced the impulse to include Native Americans as "Peruvians." In the light of such events, how are we to understand Wood's repeated emphasis on the radicalism of the American case? . . .

What were the characteristics that made the Revolution radical? Most obviously, perhaps, Wood means that it was extensive and sweeping. No quick explosion of colonial resentment, American Independence had roots deep in the colonial past and came to fruition in the experience of subsequent generations. As Wood constructs it, the American Revolution consisted of more than the two decades of turmoil that consume a full semester in many college courses. His synthetic account, he suggests, will offer a larger view. Some historians cite John Adams, who said that the Revolution took place well before Independence in the hearts and minds of the American people; others quote Benjamin Rush, who declared that the Revolution would not be complete until the institutions of American society were transformed in accordance with the premises of liberty. Wood deftly and ambitiously incorporates both emphases; his revolution is a long revolution, and it happens twice.

It happens first to a society steeped in the principles of monarchy. Colonial America was obsessed with dependencies, premised on patriarchal authority, caught up with degrees and subordinations, organized around personal connections and political influence, committed above all to hierarchy. That society had republican aspects nonetheless, for the colonies suffered from a weak aristocracy, unruly commoners, and a mobile population increasingly given to commerce and consuming. These elements of republicanism became so pronounced that the Revolutionaries were able to slough off monarchy rather effortlessly when the time came. . . . But Wood's revolution occurs decades later as well, in a democratic phase, as republicanism (which, after all, was already pervasive in American society and, as such, is not easily posed as an agent of sweeping change) yielded to democracy, as the pretensions of aristocracy fell and the defense of gentlemanly merit increasingly fell on deaf ears. In this moment Wood finds the "real revolution," a transformation that took place in the nineteenth century. . . .

As to what was radical about this, readers receive various and conflicting indications. Patriot leaders, Wood points out, adopted a radically new way of seeing themselves and their world. Born in a society that reserved political authority for men of birth and breeding, they imagined and dared to embrace the notion that men of humble origins might merit political rule. . . .

Within pages, however, those patriots' achievement melts into air. Readers learn that the Revolution was not republican at all. . . . In the aftermath of the Revolution, with the coming of the Jacksonian age, Americans faced the limits of human virtue, dismissed their utopian ideals, and accepted the invisible hand of self-interest as the basis for social and political life. The radicalism of the Revolution, it emerges, was not republicanism but its abandonment. . . .

Reserving the term "revolutionaries" for an elite makes it possible, even necessary, for Wood to leave out significant parts of the resistance movement. There is a gap at the middle, at the heart, of his dual revolution. If he offers more than the usual college course on Revolutionary America, he also offers less. A section entitled "Revolution" occupies twenty out of 369 pages of text. Neither there nor elsewhere do readers learn substantial amounts about these topics and events: the Boston Tea Party, the Boston Massacre; the gathering of Sons of Liberty; women mobilizing to disuse tea and take up the spinning wheel; merchants and artisans negotiating over terms of nonimportation; committees of correspondence feverishly linking inland villages and seaports; committees of inspection cementing a cross-class patriot coalition by enforcing the Continental Association of 1774; wartime antitory mobs and struggles against monopolists and price gougers. In this revolution there is no heroism, delinquency, or treason; no one fought this revolution (save George Washington, who took no salary for it). Although the federal Constitution comes in for discussion, the bulk of what counts as "the Revolution" in many courses and monographs is barely here.

Readers receive no picture of the unfolding of resistance, the moves and countermoves of different actors, the reluctance of merchants and the energy of artisans; the fears of indebted slaveholders as they faced fervent evangelicals and unruly African-American workers. Wood doesn't march us through the familiar course of events, and for that we might well be grateful, save for this effect: he has thereby omitted the means by which the patriot coalition, a coalition across region, rank, interest, and belief, was achieved. . . .

There is too little here, for example, about popular ideas of liberty and popular political forms. Wood does not consider whether the relatively humble patriots who joined the Revolution actively shaped the coalition and contributed their own understanding of events. If there was something radical about the era, it seems, it could not be the plebeian capacity for interracial alliance, for running away, rising up, contesting the law, and otherwise presuming their own competence to occupy a public terrain. If there was something radical about patriot leaders, it could not be their capacity to ally themselves and hence negotiate with those beneath them on the social scale. So the long sweep of Wood's Revolution, from colonial society to Jacksonian America, takes place at the surface, absent a careful account of revolutionary events, absent the agency of artisans, sailors, and foot soldiers, absent the full daring of elite patriots, who staked their all on their inferiors' competence to resist constituted authority and to commit themselves to liberty. . . .

. . . To accept much of Wood's argument, to follow his use of terms, readers must absorb an imperative: although many things have happened in this history, we allow only some of them to count. . . .

Indeed, it is noteworthy that what interests Wood most about African-American slavery is whether that institution was conspicuous to eighteenth-century Euro-Americans. . . . Most slaveholders and others saw no evil, Wood tells us, as if that were all we need to know about them or as if theirs were the only subjectivities that mattered. Surely African-American slavery was conspicuous to some Americans: it depends on who was looking. . . .

We might imagine a radical revolution in the eighteenth century, centered in the vision and the acts of those Americans—patriot and tory, black and white—who extended the imperatives of liberty from the imperial controversy to relationships at home. The radical moment in some Americans' revolution came when they looked anew at slavery. Although some Founding Fathers would still figure as revolution-aries in this story and although the narrative would still unfold in the nineteenth cen-tury, its center would substantially shift outside elite hands and elite vision.

One is left with the impression that Wood's purpose is less to discover Ameri-can radicalism than to avoid acknowledging radicalisms of the wrong kind. He plays down historical reservations about the market to suggest an unproblematic relationship between ordinary people and consumption. . . . Yet in one crucial decade, from 1765 to 1775, colonists high and low sought liberty by rallying around a critique of consumption and withdrawing from the British market. . . . Antebellum Americans were strongly evangelical, Wood says, but he does not note that many looked to religion—as to trade unionism, political participation, and social reform—precisely to give their individualistic, consuming society some moral compass. Instead, Wood resolves the Revolution into a comfortable, democractic nineteenth-century society that was, after all, good enough for everyone. What, in the end, does Wood means when he characterizes the American Revolution as radi-cal? At heart, I think, he means that it was adequate.

Edmund S. Morgan once noted that most Americans seem to think that the American Revolution was "a good thing." Morgan's characteristic understatement contains a wealth of insight. Few historians or others approach the Revolution freshly. . . . Revolutionary ideas and events lay claim to Americans' loyalty. . . . Americans do not have to accord sacred status to the intentions of the Founders to feel implicated in the American Revolution or obligated by its commitments and aspirations. . . . In this culture, the Revolution has claims.

It is because of that context, I think, that *The Radicalism of the American Revo-lution* remains insistent that for Revolutionaries we look to the Founders and for rad-icalism we ultimately look to impersonal demographic and commercial forces. . . . This book invokes the American Revolution as a powerful legitimating narrative and attaches it to the socioeconomic changes of the early nineteenth century. There is more to this than harnessing our approval of the Revolution to nineteenth-century capitalism, making mobile, competitive, and individualistic elements of the Jackson-ian era not just revolutionary but American Revolutionary, hence worthy of celebra-tion and deference. . . .

. . . Wood commits himself to overstating the impact of Revolution, constructing a unidimensional, fully adequate revolutionary legacy. That commitment renders the relationship between the Revolution and the freedom of people not initially included in its blessing far too transparent, linear, and simple than it was and remains. Wood's revolution takes too much credit. It slights the agency of those who did struggle to end slavery and makes it difficult to comprehend or even credit those who opposed abolition. "American now recognized that slavery in a republic of workers was an aberration, 'a peculiar institution,' and that if any Americans were to retain it, as southern Americans eventually did, they would have to explain and justify it in new racial and anthropological ways. . . . The Revolution in effect set in motion ideological and social forces that doomed the institution of slavery in the North and led inexorably to the Civil War." But Revolutionaries and their followers defended slavery too. Those who believed that slavery was the bedrock of the republic were drawing on their Revolutionary heritage every bit as surely as those who cast the Constitution as a compact with the devil. . . .

Wood silently rejects the argument that slavery and freedom were less coincident, contradictory growths than two formations that implied and assumed each other, phenomena "joined at the hip." . . . Wood does not attend to the ways that the bonds of slavery loosened and then tightened again in the late eighteenth and early nineteenth centuries. . . . [M]aking a defense of slavery necessary was not the same as making a defense of slavery impossible.

Yet Wood persists in constructing a Revolution and a Jacksonian society sufficient to all. In his account, women of any circumstance figure largely as an absence. The Revolution failed to liberate women in this period, he notes, although it would do so later. But the Revolution was not a transhistorical agent that could go marching through the ages to bestow economic, social, or political rights on waiting womankind. Women's inequality was a presence in the nineteenth century, and present with it were ideological versions of women's nature that have profoundly affected female Americans for over a century. Take women's responsibility for virtue. As Wood himself notes, having adopted self-interest as the basis of politics and society, American culture did not dispense with virtue but placed it under the custodial care of middle-class women. At the same time that self-interest became what participation in public life was about, women were given the virtue that made it crucial that they not participate.

Thus neither women nor enslaved African Americans were left out of American freedom; both were included in it within critical, unfree, and arguably necessary roles. . . . This Revolution did not bring "a full-scale assault on dependency" so much as a reformulation of dependence that banished it from the consciousness of the public world, set apart African Americans, children, women, tenants, and other poor people, remade the American state, recast forms of participation, and constructed a narrative of the Revolution and of American-ness without their aspirations, experiences, and agency. Such omission was necessary and real, in part as a denial of the dependence of the heads of households, the supposedly independent and sometimes even self-made men of the nineteenth century, who in fact relied on the labor they controlled and denied in the home, the fields, and the mills.

For Wood, I think, such arguments appear to be quibbling, stressing the things the Revolution did not do, when in fact it accomplished so much. The Revolution made possible later movements for abolition and women's rights "and in fact all our current egalitarian thinking," he writes. Others would suggest that those movements and that thinking have also taken place against the weight of the American past, for the Revolution extended *and contained* liberty. It offered a particular heritage of participation, particular possibilities for public life, but not others . . . .

The Revolution Destroyed Monarchy and Paved the Way for Democracy

GORDON S. WOOD

Smith, like other neo-Progressive or New Left historians, believes that radicalism means "substantive change in the lot of those who were most oppressed, subjugated, or marginal in the society." In her opinion, these most oppressed, subjugated, or marginal were African-American slaves, women, and other "have-nots" on the very bottom of American society.

No one denies that these groups were oppressed in various ways, as most people were in premodern times, and that black slaves especially endured a subjugation rarely duplicated in the history of the world. . . . I do not ignore issues of slavery and gender or of ethnicity. . . . To be sure, I do not repeat . . . dozens of monographs on race and gender over the past few decades, but I believe I have set these issues in their proper context for fully understanding them . . . and have correctly set forth the essential challenges the Revolution made to the position of women and to slavery, including explaining the origins of the first emancipation and the abolition movement. . . .

No doubt I spent less time than Smith . . . would have liked or expected on the lot of slaves and women in the Revolution. . . . But I never intended merely to synthesize contemporary scholarship. Of course, my book does rely heavily on the writing of many historians. . . . But it tries to be much more than a simple summing up of existing scholarship; it also aims to say something new and original about the Revolution, to see it from an unconventional, if not unfashionable, perspective— which is why . . . "the bulk of what counts as 'the Revolution' in many courses and monographs is barely here."

What I hoped to do was press beyond the issues of contemporary scholarship, which often deal with past oppressions of women and blacks in a very present-minded manner, to retrieve a kind of oppression that has been lost to us. There existed in the premodern world another, more general sort of oppression that I believe the Revolution eliminated, a comprehensive oppression that subsumed the oppression of both slaves and women and in which all ordinary people had a stake.

This oppression involved all common ordinary Americans, including not only blacks and women but white males as well. This oppression was, of course, scarcely comparable to the particular degradation suffered by African-American slaves; nevertheless, its elimination had to precede the elimination of the oppression of blacks and women. The age-old humiliation felt by all commoners in the premodern world is by no means as well known today as that experienced by black slaves and women, and for that reason I thought it was worth emphasizing. . . . Because this oppression of all ordinary people is not an issue of our own time in the way race, gender, and ethnicity are, it is not easy to get present-minded historians . . . to

From Gordon S. Wood, "Equality and Social Conflict in the American Revolution," *William and Mary Quarterly,* 3d Series, Vol. 51, 1994, pp. 703–716. Reprinted by permission.

understand it. In fact, so absorbed in the present cultural wars are they that it is inconceivable to them that any white males in the past, unless they were sailors or homeless or very poor, could ever have been oppressed or have felt oppressed. They imply that only those who are oppressed or marginalized in our own time were capable of being oppressed two centuries ago. If the Revolution did not totally abolish slavery and fundamentally change the lot of women, then it could not possibly have been radical. In other words, there is something profoundly anachronistic about their conception of the Revolution, as far as it is expressed in their critiques: they indict the Americans of the past for not thinking as we think and for not behaving as we would behave today. Consequently, they are unable to understand a document as fundamental to the Revolution as the Declaration of Independence.

We cannot appreciate the radical significance in 1776 of the Declaration's ringing affirmation that all men were created equal and had certain inalienable rights unless we understand the earlier presumptions of inequality and the contempt in which ordinary people, white as well as black, were held throughout previous history. What was radical about the Declaration in 1776? We know it did not mean that blacks and women were created equal to white men (although it would in time be used to justify those equalities too). It was radical in 1776 because it meant that all white men were equal. . . . In my book I wanted to get that point clear; for once the claim of equality by all white males was established in the eighteenth century (no mean feat since it took a few thousand years of Western history to accomplish), then the other claims to equality could follow and, relative to the total span of Western history, although not to our brief American past, follow rather rapidly.

So when Smith says that developments concerning social leveling are not central to my story, or . . . that I exclude from my account the ideals and passions of ordinary Americans, they could not be more mistaken. Central to my story is the struggle of ordinary people to emerge into consciousness and prominence; indeed, their emergence ultimately is what the radicalism of the Revolution is all about.

Contrary to what these critics say, my account is not written out of elite archives and is not merely a reflection of northeastern aristocrats. They assume that I am taking the point of view only of the Revolutionary leaders and the better sort and ignoring that of common ordinary people because I do not talk about Jack Tars or women in food riots or the homeless. The only ordinary people they can really conceive of are those on the very bottom of the society, usually the society's victims, whom they sentimentalize and wrap in a nostalgic mantle of romantic communalism. Common farmers, artisans, shopkeepers, petty merchants, protobusinessmen—those whom today we might label "lower-middle class" or "middle class"—these ordinary people have no real place in their consciousness.

Yet these sorts of ordinary people are the major actors in the Revolution and the major actors in my story. . . . The demographic and economic forces that I talked about are not some superhuman entities. They are merely shorthand terms for the actions of hundreds of thousands of these ordinary workaday people.

These common people did have spokesmen among the Revolutionary elite. . . . Jefferson was the most important of these spokesmen. Better than anyone else ever had, Jefferson articulated our basic American ideology—our belief in liberty and equality, our confidence in education, and our faith in the common sense of ordinary people. But Jefferson was not an ordinary working person—he was a slave-owning aristocrat who never really worked a day in his life—and consequently he never fully saw the explosive implications of what he was saying. His words outran many of his intentions, and his common people became far more money-loving and religious than he ever imagined. Certainly, he had little awareness of the commercial nature of the popular forces he was leading.

But ordinary people themselves also became spokesmen for their cause, and they spoke with a degree of anger and feeling that the liberal intellectual Jefferson could never muster. I am thinking of middling men like William Findley, Matthew Lyon, and William Manning, men to whom I devote a good deal of attention in my book. These Scots-Irish immigrants, ex-weavers, ex-servants, uneducated farmers, and all the hundreds of thousands of lowly and middling folk they spoke for— these are the real heroes and principal agents of my story. . . . These men were intelligent and tough-minded exponents of the emerging democractic ideology. . . . They were the principal actors in Jefferson's democratic assault on the Federalist establishment and other remnants of an older hierarchical society. These ordinary people did not need the French Revolution to give their democratic movement its momentum. They had enough indigenous rage and resentment to make their revolution without the aid of a foreign model. They were determined to destroy the social pretensions of so-called or would-be aristocrats like Hugh Henry Brackenridge or Nathaniel Chipman or James Bowdoin and to establish the moral superiority of their hitherto despised labor. . . .

. . . But Smith . . . can scarcely admit the existence of men like Findley, Lyon, and Manning because such white males do not fit the modern definition of oppressed people. Since the Revolution did not totally abolish black slavery or free women from patriarchal dependency, it could not have been radical; it could only have been, in Smith's word, "adequate."

How the Revolution could have been merely adequate if it transformed something as important as people's sense of equality and self-worth and their conceptions of property and labor is not addressed by these critics. . . . The British historian and socialist R. H. Tawney, for example, realized that America "is marked indeed by much economic inequality; but it is also marked by much social equality." In his classic 1906 account *Why Is There No Socialism in the United States?* German economist Werner Sombart illustrated this social equality by contrasting the American worker with the European one: "He carries his head high, walks with a lissom stride, and is as open and cheerful in his expression as any member of the middle class. There is nothing oppressed or submissive about him." More important than equality of wealth, says [Mickey] Kaus, is this social equality, this equal sense of self-worth and dignity among people, a feeling of equality that allows people, regardless of differences of wealth, to look others in the eye and treat them as equals and to expect to be treated as equals in return. Americans generally have had more of this feeling of equality than other peoples, and the Revolution was crucial in creating it.

Correspondingly important were changes that the Revolution brought about in people's conceptions of property and labor. These changes were linked and were based on substantial transformations in the society. . . . Eighteenth-century gentry were eager to acquire landed property or any other form of property that would give them the desired independence. . . . Such wealth was composed of static forms of property that generated what we might call "unearned income"—rents from tenants, returns on bonds, interest from money out on loan—sufficient to allow its holders not to have to work for a living so that they had leisure to assume the burdens of public office without expecting high salaries. . . . Their static proprietary wealth was of course very vulnerable to inflation, which is why the printing of paper money was so frightening to these gentry: inflation threatened not simply their livelihood but their very identity and social position. . . .

Not only was this kind of proprietary wealth very hard to come by in America, where, compared to England, land was so plentiful and rent-paying tenants so rare, but commerce and trade were creating new forms of property that gave wealth and power to new sorts of people. The Revolution accelerated the creation of this kind of property. This new property was anything but static: it was risk-taking, entrepreneurial capital—not money out on loan, but money borrowed; it was in fact all the paper money that enterprising people clamored for in these years. . . . This was the property of businessmen and protobusinessmen—of commercial farmers, artisan-manufacturers, traders, shopkeepers, and all who labored for a living and produced and exchanged things, no matter how poor or wealthy they might be.

Unlike proprietary wealth, this new kind of dynamic, fluid, and evanescent property could not create personal authority or identity; it was, said Joseph Story, "continually changing like the waves of the sea." Hence it could not be relied on as a source of independence. Once this was understood, then property qualifications for participation in public life either as voters or as officerholders lost their relevance and rapidly fell away.

This radical change in people's idea of property during the Revolution is linked with similarly radical changes that took place in their conception of labor. But this seems to be the wrong kind of radicalism for my critics. . . .

In a world where aristocratic leisure was valued above all—leisure being defined as the freedom from the need to labor or to have an occupation—the necessity of earning a livelihood and working directly for money was traditionally seen as contemptible. In fact, this need of common people to work, particularly to work with their hands, was what lay behind their degraded and oppressed position throughout history. Even Native American males had an aristocratic contempt for common labor; they hunted and fought and regarded ordinary work as belonging exclusively to their women. Before the American Revolution, labor, as it had been for ages in Western culture, was still widely associated with toil, trouble, and pain (which is why women's experience of childbirth was called labor in all European languages). To be sure, industriousness and the need for a calling were everywhere extolled in the colonies, and the Puritan ethic was widely preached—but only for ordinary people, not for the aristocratic gentry, and only for moral reasons, not for the sake of increasing an individual's prosperity or the society's productivity. Hard work was good for common people; it lifted them out of idleness and barbarism and kept them out of trouble. . . . People labored out of necessity, out of poverty, it was said, and necessity and poverty bred the contempt in which working people had been held for centuries. But changes had long been in the air, and enlightened eighteenth-century aristocrats condescended to extol the value of labor much as they condescended to celebrate the equality of all men. Just as the Revolution became the occasion for the wholesale expression of the new importance to be granted to equality, so too was it the occasion for the full expression of this new moral value to be given to labor. . . .

This transformation in the meaning of labor is a major part of what I mean by the radicalism of the Revolution. Suddenly, all who worked for a living were no longer willing to put up with their hitherto degraded and oppressed condition. The Revolution became an important expression of their strenuous and angry struggle to establish their moral superiority over those they labeled leisured aristocrats— over those who did not have to work for a living or have occupations, over those whose income came from proprietary wealth, came, in other words, without exertion or manual labor: landed gentry, rentiers, and those we today would call professionals. Many of these leisured aristocrats, having themselves so recently praised the virtues of labor and equality, were in no position to resist this assault, and in the North they were overwhelmed.

This struggle was what the farmer William Manning and the rich manufacturer Matthew Lyon meant when they said the essential social conflict was between "those that Labour for a Living and those that git a Living without Bodily Labour" or between "the industrious part of the community" and those brought up in "idleness, dissipation, and extravagance." Manning and Lyon are not yet talking about the later nineteenth-century class conflict between a modern proletariat and businessmen. In the eighteenth century, hard as it may be for us to accept, rich businessmen like Lyon with many employees and struggling single shoemakers like William Brewster of Connecticut saw themselves in a similar category as laborers, sharing a common resentment of a genteel aristocratic world that had humiliated and disdained them since the beginning of time because of their need to work. Eventually, of course, this common category of laborers would break apart into employers and employees, into manual and nonmanual, and into blue-collar and white-collar workers—into, in other words, the modern categories and classes that New Left historians like Smith are more comfortable with. . . . Presentist prejudices . . . prevent them from seeing that my book is all about social and class conflict; it is just not the social and class conflict that they have been conditioned to expect.

They are unable to see the social conflict and the radicalism of the Revolution that I describe because the Findleys, Lyons, and Mannings and other ordinary white males who are featured in my story were not opposed to the development of capitalism, and everyone today knows that one has to be opposed to capitalism in order to be truly radical. This assumption that the eighteenth-century proponents and practitioners of capitalism could never have been radical is probably the ultimate anachronism. . . . There was a time, however, . . . when the development of capitalism was regarded as very radical indeed. But to link the Revolution, which, as Smith says, was "a good thing," with capitalism, which is "a bad thing"—well, that's going too far: this "harnessing our approval of the Revolution to nineteenth-century capitalism" is to make "mobile, competitive, and individualistic elements of the Jacksonian era not just revolutionary but American Revolutionary, hence worthy of celebration and deference." Smith needs to . . . realize that what Americans thought about politics and the economy in 1800 is no longer much with us in the late twentieth century. It is quite possible for us to recognize that the Revolution and capitalism were linked and that early nineteenth-century contemporaries considered both to be good things, and yet at the same time for us to believe that capitalism today might need controlling by the government. That is what doing history is all about—recovering different, lost worlds and showing how they developed into our present. . . .

The democratic world of the early nineteenth century that I attempted to describe was not a world only of crass material strivings and obsessive consumers. Throughout the book I was concerned with the different ways people related to one another. By the early nineteenth century, it is my opinion that, with the general de-nunciation of the monarchial adhesives of blood, family, and patronage and with the perceived weakness of republican virtue and sociability as a means of trying people together, many people had come to rely on interest as the principal and strongest source of attachment between people. This is not the same thing as saying that they cared only about money or consumer goods. . . .

This new liberal society of the early nineteenth century may have been held together largely by interest, which was no mean adhesive, but interest was not the only adhesive. Not only did the older bonds, both monarchical and republican, linger on into the nineteenth century and even into our own day, but the Revolu-tionary explosion of evangelical religious passion worked to tie people together in new ways and to temper and control the scramble for private wealth—a point my book spends some time on, despite Smith's statement to the contrary. Most evangelicals were not unworldly and anticapitalist. Quite the contrary: there is considerable evidence that religion increased people's energy as it restrained their liberty, got them on with their work as it disciplined their acquisitive urges, and gave them confidence that even self-interested individuals subscribed to absolute standards of right and wrong and thus could be trusted in market exchange and contractual relationships. . . .

In the three decades between the 1760s and the 1790s the religious landscape of America was transformed. The older state churches that had dominated colonial society for a century and a half—the Anglican, Congregational, and Presbyterian—were surrounded or supplanted by new and in some cases unheard of religious de-nominations and sects. By 1790 the Baptists had already become the largest denomination in the country, and the Methodists, who had no adherents in America in 1760, were moving up fast, soon to outstrip every group. . . .

These religious changes represented a radical shift in the American people's social relationships and cultural consciousness. Because religion (and not the ideas of Bacon, Locke, and Newton as issued from the heights of Monticello) was still the major means by which most ordinary people made sense of the world, these startling religious changes are some of the best signs we have of the radically social and class-ridden character of the Revolution. But there is more work to be done, particularly on this matter of religion. I have no doubt that the more we explore the social and cultural history of the Revolution, the more we will discover just what a radically transforming event it was. And it is not over yet.

Boycotts Made the Revolution Radical

T. H. BREEN

On the eve of Independence, . . . Parliament aggressively asserted its sovereignty by taxing the colonists at about the same time that a flood of British manufactured items transformed the American marketplace. . . .

By reconstructing the mental framework that informed one of the central narra-tives of the mid-eighteenth century—in this case, an elaborate story of misunderstood

T. H. Breen, "Boycotts Made the Revolution Radical," *William and Mary Quarterly,* 3d Series, Vol. L, No. 3, July 1993. Copyright 1993. Reprinted by permission of *William and Mary Quarterly.*

American consumers—we shall better understand how the colonists came to imagine themselves within an expanding empire of trade, how at a moment of extreme political crisis a bundle of popular ideas and assumptions about commerce suggested specific styles of resistance, and finally, how a boycott movement organized to counter British policy allowed scattered colonists to reach out to each other and to reimagine themselves within an independent commercial empire.

In 1763, no one could have foreseen that the translation of a "Genius of Commerce" into political protest would produce radical new forms of liberal community in America. It was the unintended consequences of commercial ideas that made the Revolution genuinely revolutionary. We shall look initially at the evolution of a popular narrative of commercial life and then explore the broad experiential and ideological context in which this bizarre account briefly but powerfully flourished. . . .

The first troubled response appeared in Boston. Although the author of an anonymous pamphlet of 1764 entitled *Considerations Upon the Act of Parliament* did not proclaim a full-blown conspiracy, he suggested that American themselves bore responsibility for deteriorating relations with England. During the Seven Years' War, the colonists not only have lived too well but had done so too publicly. Their opulent consumption of British manufactures strongly impressed "the gentlemen of the army and others at present and lately residing in the maritime towns." These outsiders learned that the Americans "spend full as much [on] the luxurious British imports as prudence will countenance, and often much more."

The next year, the commercial interpretation of parliamentary taxation acquired fuller definition. John Dickinson, a respected Pennsylvania lawyer, traced the imperial crisis in part to a stunning misinterpretation in Great Britain of American consumer habits. "We are informed," Dickinson noted in *The Late Regulations,* "that an opinion has been industriously propagated in *Great-Britain* that the colonies are wallowing in wealth and luxury." That conclusion, he insisted, represented a pernicious misreading of colonial culture. . . . Americans, Dickinson claimed, were ordinarily and mostly quite poor. British observers had been misled because the colonists, "having a number of strangers among us," were too generous and hospitable for their own good. The Americans had "indulged themselves in many uncommon expenses." This "imprudent excess of kindness" was simply an ill-conceived attempt to impress British visitors.

Other writers took up the narrative of commercial life, adding innovative elements of their own. In 1768, for example, an anonymous New York pamphleteer situated Anglo-American consumption within a larger historical framework. . . . Like other colonial authors, the New Yorker described the Seven Years' War as the crucial moment in the development of an empire of goods. In its aftermath, Britain turned the ingenuity of American consumers into a justification for parliamentary taxation, based on the reports of visitors "who saw a great display of luxury, arising from the wealth, which many had suddenly acquired during the wars." . . .

In 1768, William Hicks of Philadelphia heightened the conspiratorial element in this broad folk discourse. It was no accident, he announced, that ordinary English people accepted inflated estimates of colonial prosperity as truth, for unnamed sources had systematically distorted reports of economic conditions in America. Hicks protested that "the estimates of our wealth which have been received from ignorant or prejudiced persons, are, in every calculation, grossly erroneous. These misrepresentations, which have been so industriously propagated, are very possibly the offspring of political invention, as they form the best apology for imposing upon us burthens to which we are altogether unequal." This interpretive framework—what was becoming for Hicks as conspiracy of commerce—carried extremely sinister implications for the colonists' happiness within a commercial empire. Boldly linking consumption and politics, Hicks asked Americans to remember exactly how Parliament had first reacted to the false reports of wealth. Had that body not immediately imposed new taxes? Were not these revenue acts an ominous hint of future assaults? Without money, what would the colonists be able to afford? The plot was obvious. The British wanted to keep the Americans poor, marginal consumers just able to pay the rising taxes but never "suffered to riot in a superfluity of wealth." . . .

Narratives of commercial life—a fluid assemblage of popular notions about consumption and politics—echoed through the colonial newspapers, indicating that the tale of hospitable American consumers and bemused British visitors, of luxury and poverty in a changing economy, had become a staple of popular culture on the eve of Independence. . . . By 1771, the argument for disjuncture between appearance and reality had become standard fare. "A Friend of the Colony of Connecticut" explained in the *New-Haven Post-Boy* that "a large consumption of unnecessary foreign articles . . . has given us the false and deceitful appearance of riches, in buildings, at or tables, and on our bodies. Which has attracted the attention if not raised the envy of our neighbours, and perhaps had its influence in making the late grievous unconstitutional revenue acts."

Even as the contest with Great Britain intensified and the possibility of armed conflict loomed, Americans maintained that the political crisis was somehow related to their own participation in a new Anglo-American marketplace. One example appeared in 1774. The Reverend Ebenezer Baldwin of Danbury, Connecticut, published a short sermon explicitly directed to ordinary farmers living in isolated communities. . . .

. . . "In a country like this," Baldwin reminded the farmers, "where property is so equally divided, every one will be disposed to rival his neighbour in goodness of dress, sumptuousness of furniture, &c. All our little earnings therefore went to Britain to purchase mainly the superfluities of life." Economic leveling in the colonies stimulated status competition; consumer goods were the primary means by which men and women sorted themselves out in society. "Hence the common people here make a show, much above what they do in England," Baldwin asserted. Here was the source of a profound cultural misunderstanding. "The luxury and superfluities in which even the lower ranks of people here indulge themselves," the Connecticut minister observed, "being reported in England by the officers and soldiers upon their return, excited in the people there a very exalted idea of the riches of this country, and the abilities of the inhabitants to bear taxes." . . . Americans could still save the political situation. All they had to do was reform their buying habits, putting aside the imported goods that had made them seem richer than they actually were. . . .

The narrative of commercial life gained what may have been a final reformulation in David Ramsay's *History of the American Revolution* [1789]. . . . The South Carolina physician and army veteran found it difficult to understand why Parliament decided to tax the Americans in the first place. He located the answer in Britain's willingness to accept "exaggerated accounts" of Americans' wealth. "It was said," Ramsay explained, " 'that the American planters lived in affluence, and with inconsiderable taxes, while the inhabitants of Great-Britain were borne down.' " The culprits again seem to have been British soldiers serving in America. "Their observations were founded on what they had seen in cities, and at a time, when large sums were spent by government, in support of fleets and armies, and when American commodities were in great demand." Kind Americans spared no expense in feting their British allies in the great struggle against France. "To treat with attention those, who came to fight for them," Ramsay asserted, "and also to gratify their own pride, the colonists had made a parade of their riches, by frequently and sumptuously entertaining the gentlemen of the British army." The visitors mistakenly concluded that the colonists lived very well. It was a natural error. These officers "judging from what they saw, without considering the general state of the country, concurred in representing the colonists, as very able to contribute, largely, towards defraying the common expenses of empire."

These various versions of the commercial narrative joined other discourses that Americans invented to explain to themselves why relations with England had soured so suddenly. Although other tales circulated widely throughout the colonies during this period—for example, stories of massive political corruption in Great Britain—this largely overlooked account of eager, misunderstood colonial consumers possesses unusual interest. It represents an imaginative, often entirely plausible response to two distinct crises in the Anglo-American world of the mid-eighteenth century. The colonists had to accommodate not only the demands of a new consumer marketplace that inundated the homes of free men and women with alluring goods but also the aggressive Parliament that threatened to destroy a delicate commercial system that made it possible to pay for these goods.

The commercial narrative that enjoyed popularity for over two decades effectively linked these separate challenges. For one thing, it established a shared chronology. Change accelerated during the Seven Years' War, setting the stage for a cultural misinterpretation so profound that the Americans could never again persuade Parliament that they were in fact poor. The interpretation turned on the consumption of English manufactures by Americans who were overly hospitable, remarkably self-indulgent, and socially insecure. Versions of the story came from all regions of the continent, from different classes and backgrounds, from people who seemed in retrospect to have felt a little guilty that their own excesses had given off such confusing signals. The narrative of commercial life explained that it was not the goods that had hurt the Americans but, rather, their misuse; not the purchase, but the vulgarity.

Historians have failed to give the commercial perspective proper interpretive standing. Another body of thought has long dominated the search for the ideological origins of the American Revolution. According to Bernard Bailyn, who more than any other has set the terms of this debate, eighteenth-century colonists subscribed to a controlling set of "assumptions, beliefs, and ideas—the articulated world view—that lay behind the manifest events of the time." This complex mental framework, often labeled "republican" marginalized the language and experience of commercial capitalism. In this interpretive perspective, colonial Americans were not trying to accommodate to a rapidly changing world economic system; instead, they resisted it. They condemned the modern commercial mentality. They were backward looking, suspicious of trade and banking, fearful of spreading political corruption produced by financial revolution in Great Britain. . . .

Historians critical of this dominant interpretation have argued that the colonists' political ideology before the Revolution was more liberal and Lockean than we had been led to believe. Others have tried to restore elements of traditional Protestant theology to the ideological mix, but . . . few seem comfortable with a political discourse that owed much to the experiences of ordinary men and women in a new consumer marketplace. To construct a persuasive explanation of the dialectic between experience and ideology on the eve of Independence, one would need to address two separate interpretive problems about which current historiography has little to say.

First, we should focus on the elusive relation between the events of everyday life and the stories that contemporaries invented to make sense of those events. . . .

Second, we should consider how artisans and farmers—the sort of folk who may have heard the Reverend Baldwin—confronted a mid-eighteenth-century world that impinged ever more insistently on their sense of self. . . .

Local analysis, however, cannot be its own reward. Throughout recorded history, ordinary people have found that they must express agency within larger frameworks, such as capitalism and nationalism—forces that puzzled and frightened, that demanded personal response, and that presented an unprecedented range of choice. In mid-eighteenth-century America, the outside world often spoke most seductively through imported consumer goods, and because they imagined themselves within an empire of commerce, colonists who had previously not had much to do with each other came to see it a matter of common sense to respond to the disruption of their economic and political lives through specific commercial strategies such as an ever-wider boycott movement. Political actions grew out of popular ideology. What no one anticipated was that mass political mobilization within a consumer marketplace would radically transform how Americans construed community so that by the 1770s their experience provoked them to imagine a powerful commercial empire of their own.

Americans brought to the final political crisis a complex bundle of ideas about the British empire that were products of long commercial experience. This set of popular assumptions provided an interpretive lens through which the colonists viewed parliamentary claims to absolute sovereignty. . . .

On one point Americans expressed near universal agreement. They believed that the empire owed its ascendance almost entirely to international commerce, that trade was the indispensable source of national wealth and military power, and that trade even sustained political liberty. . . .

Colonial newspapers regularly reaffirmed the lesson. Commerce distinguished the British empire from other empires, from despotic systems that could never deliver the peace, security, and coherence that eighteenth-century Americans now took for granted. "Commerce is the most solid foundation of civil society," the *Boston Evening-Post* announced in 1764. "By this our necessities, conveniencies, and pleasures are supplied from distant shores; every region is amazed to find itself abounding in foreign productions, and enriched with a thousand commodities unknown to itself, and promoting its welfare and serving to make life more agreeable."

Mid-century Americans imagined themselves within a great circulation of money and goods, a practically Newtonian marketing system connecting them in mutually beneficial ways to strangers throughout the empire. . . .

While the commercial model assumed balance and fairness within the empire, the colonists—even before the crisis over parliamentary taxation—routinely betrayed a sense of their own vulnerability. American rhetoric often sounded more anxious than descriptive. Writers seemed overly eager to persuade the British—perhaps their fellow colonists also—that trade did in fact benefit the metropolitan core as well as the distant peripheries. The key to any positive assessment of imperial trade was the Americans' rising consumption of manufactured goods. In 1764, for example, Governor Thomas Fitch lectured the people of Connecticut that "the Colonies and Plantations in *America* are, indeed, of great Importance to their Mother Country and an Interest worthy of her most tender Regard." The provinces were partners, not competitors. "The more they prosper and increase in Number, Riches and Commerce," Fitch noted defensively, "the greater will be the Advantage not only to them but also to the Nation at Home." . . .

Colonial observers understood something fundamental about the imperial connection that modern historians have generally ignored: mid-century Americans confronted a situation that was genuinely new. Before the 1740s, few would have described their relation with Great Britain within the framework of a rapidly expanding consumer marketplace. After that date, the commercial connection became much more invasive, more manifest—a development demanding adjustment and accommodation and one that touched the lives of people living in all parts of America.

Contemporaries were fully aware of the changes that had dramatically transformed the face of a provincial material culture. A quotidian world had taken on a different appearance. People dressed more opulently and more colorfully. They purchased more manufactured items that made them feel happier, warmer, or better looking. . . . "I am now forty-four years old," a "Countryman" told the readers of the *Boston Gazette* in 1769, "and to see the difference in the times really astonishes me. I never had, Mr. Printers, believe me, nothing better to go to meeting in, than a pair of sheepskin breeches, a felt hatt, and homespun-made coat with horn buttons." According to the Countryman, his neighbors now demanded "English-made cloth that cost . . . a guinea a yard."

Statistical evidence abundantly supports contemporary impressions. Trade figures compiled for the eighteenth century reveal that England's exports to the mainland colonies increased over 50 percent between 1720 and 1770. The sharpest rise occurred between 1750 and 1770. . . .

Increasing opportunities to consume triggered intense print controversies about the character and limits of luxury, the moral implications of credit, the role of personal choice in a liberal society, and the relevance of traditional status hierarchies in a commercial world that encouraged people to fashion protean public identities. Heated debates on these issues represented an initial effort by large numbers of Americans throughout the colonies to gain intellectual control over the marketplace, to make sense of their new experiences, and to bring ideology into line with a commercial system that they found inviting as well as intimidating. . . .

This developing commercial mentality was neither premodern nor anticapitalist. Americans welcomed improved living standards, and they would have regarded calls to restore an earlier, largely subsistence economy as sheer lunacy. . . . In 1761 [James] Otis observed that "luxury is a very vague & loose term, [and] if by it is meant the important of many foreign commodities, the more we have the better. . . . I know it is the maxim of some, that the common people in this town and country lie too well; however I am of a quite different opinion, I do not think they live half well enough."

During the 1760s, Parliament revised the rules of empire in an effort to reduce a huge national debt. For Americans, the revenue acts came as a shock. They could see no compelling reason to tinker with a commercial system that seemed to be working well enough. . . .

The escalating dispute raised fundamental constitutional issues, and while Americans passionately defended their positions on rights and representation, they also worried about their continued participation in the consumer marketplace. In their attempts to comprehend the sudden shift in British policy, they drew as much on their own recent commercial experience as they did on abstract theories of republican governance. The stories they told themselves about prodigal American consumers entertaining British soldiers were a part of this general response. So, too, were decisions about specific forms of political mobilization. The colonists evolved instruments of protest within a mental framework that was largely a product of living in a commercial empire.

The most striking aspect of the Revolutionary boycotts is their utter novelty. No previous popular rebellion had organized itself so centrally around the consumer. That the Americans did so is an additional indication of their modernity. Yet historians have not viewed the boycott movement as problematic: it just happened; it was a reflexive response to taxation without representation. And so it must have seemed to most colonial Americans. . . .

The first boycotts of 1765–1766 contested the Stamp Act. Similar protests occurred in 1768–1770 and 1774–1776. Over time, the nonimportation movement grew larger, more successful, and more democratic. Groups of local merchants usually planned and executed the initial efforts, but the driving force behind the various committees and associations gradually passed to the people. Throughout the colonies, extralegal bodies seized control of the boycott movement; as they did so, their members increasingly spoke in the name of a newly constituted American public.

While the boycott was rapidly becoming the distinctive signature of American political protest, colonists began to resituate themselves in an evolving commercial discourse. Their focus shifted away from reciprocity, away from a mutually beneficial exchange with Great Britain, to outright claims of American preeminence. "I think it may justly be said," boldly declared a Philadelphia writer, "that THE FOUNDATION OF THE POWER AND GLORY OF GREAT BRITAIN ARE LAID IN AMERICA." . . .

If riots in the Midlands of England failed to win parliamentary concessions, American had another card to play: they could go into manufacturing themselves. This had not been a topic of broad colonial interest before the passage of the Stamp Act, but once it became part of a general commercial conversation, it opened up new creative possibilities. Insistence that Americans were capable of satisfying their own consumer demand—something that they would not achieve for many decades—made it easier for people to imagine genuine economic independence. . . .

Such plausible, though exaggerated, economic claims fed the boycott movement, continuously strengthening the political resolve of individual consumers. Local associations organized to promote nonimportation and manufacturing represented initial, often tentative steps toward a radical reconstitution of civil society. For in point of fact, Americans of the time were experimenting with new forms of community, founded not on traditional religious affiliations but on shared commercial interests. Only those who insist that preindustrial capitalism inevitably sparked destructive individualism will be surprised by popular attempts to construct interpretive communities around a temporary withdrawal from an Atlantic marketplace.

The truth of the matter is that a liberal market ideology proved capable of . . . mobilizing ordinary men and women into associations unequivocally dedicated to the common good. As a "Tradesman" writing for the *Pennsylvania Chronicle* in 1770 well understood, civil society in America could develop from sources other than republicanism. He explained that "as we form a considerable, independent, and respectable Body of the People, we certainly have an *equal Right* to enter into Agreements and Resolutions *with others* for the public Good, in a sober, orderly Manner, becoming Freemen and loyal Subjects. . . . [L]et us determine, *for the Good of the Whole,* to strengthen the Hands of the Patriotic Majority, by agreeing not to purchase *British Goods.*" . . .

The nonimportation movement—in effect, a communal experiment in applied ideology—exposed a radical egalitarian strand within the commercial discourse. To appreciate this development one must remember that the consumer market of the mid-eighteenth century was open to almost any white person able to pay the price. Generous credit, paper currency, and newspaper advertisements encouraged broad participation. Usually, free producers were also consumers. And on the eve of Revolution, the success of the colonial boycotts depended on all these consumers temporarily deciding to become nonconsumers. The argument for the liberating possibilities of agency in the new Anglo-American marketplace is not intended to mitigate the exploitative and oppressive effects of eighteenth-century capitalism. The development of an Atlantic economy meant that African-American slaves and indentured servants—indeed, unfree people of all sorts—worked very hard, often under extremely harsh conditions. New forms of self-fashioning were built on the suffering of laborers in England and America who made mass consumption possible.

Since in the politicization of private economic choice every free voice counted, it is not surprising that the promoters of the boycott movement tried to legitimate their activities through appeals to the popular will. They presumed to speak for the majority, however defined. Exclusiveness ran counter to the spirit of this powerful mobilizing discourse, and it was a happy moment when a town could report—as did Norwich, Connecticut, in September 1770–that "there was as full a Town Meeting as [was] ever known when the Town voted, almost unanimously, to adhere to their . . . Non-Importation Agreement."

The so-called subscription lists also testify to the egalitarian thrust of eighteenth-century commercial thought. These instruments extended the boycott movement to large numbers of people who normally would not have had a voice in public affairs. The lists presented individual consumers with a formal declaration of purpose, followed by an oath or pledge. The goal of subscription was in part indoctrination. The forms reviewed a growing catalogue of grievances and announced that in the short term only nonimportation could preserve liberty and property. More significant, the ritual of signing gave birth to new collectivities. The ordinary consumer who accepted the logic of the argument and signed the paper thereby volunteered to support a community protest.

Surviving subscriptions resonate with religious as well as contractual language. A Boston agreement drafted in 1767 announced that all signers: "DO promise and engage, to and with each other, that we will encourage the Use and Consumption of all Articles manufactured in any of the British American Colonies, and more especially in this Province; and that we will not . . . purchase . . . Articles from abroad." A 1773 South Carolina subscription sounded remarkably similar to that of Boston. . . .

The subscription campaign caught the public interest. Numbers provide an index of political success. . . .

One person's signature seems to have been as desirable an another's. In 1767, Boston town officials specifically urged "Persons of all Ranks" to come forward, and in Annapolis, Maryland, people circulating "our Association-Paper" predicted that colonists of "every Degree" would sign it. The *South-Carolina Gazette* even reported that in New York, "The Sense of the People was taken by Subscription, and near 800 Names got, about 300 of the People without a single Shilling Property."

Even more significant, the subscription movement actively involved women. It was as consumers participating in new interpretive communities that American women first gained a political voice. Although men amy have pushed women to the margins of formal protest, so that they had to organize their own subscriptions, women made the most of this opportunity. In 1770, for example, a group of Boston women drew up an agreement "against drinking foreign TEA." One hundred twenty-six "young Ladies" announced: "We the Daughters of those Patriots who have and now do appear for the public Interest . . . do with Pleasure engage with them in denying ourselves the drinking of Foreign Tea, in hopes to frustrate a Plan that tends to deprive the whole Community of their all that is valuable in Life." Another Boston subscription gained the signatures of 300 "Mistresses of their respective families." The next week, 110 more names appeared. In 1774, the women of Charleston, South Carolina, formed an association and, according to the local newspaper, "are subscribing to it very fast."

These innovative efforts to bring people into the boycott remind us that consumer-based actions were inherently more open than were the traditional political ones accessible only to white males with property. Peter Oliver, the Boston loyalist . . . claimed that "it was highly diverting, to see the names & marks, to the Subscription, of Porters & Washing Women." Oliver ridiculed such activities. How could persons outside politics ever hope to have their opinions on important issues taken seriously? But the poor laborers of Boston—women as well as men—knew what they were doing. Their "names & marks" testify to their membership in a new volitional community that people of Oliver's status could never comprehend.

Subscription should be seen, therefore, as an instrument through which the colonists explored the limits of democratic participation. Appearing on the margins of mainstream political discourse, the popular lists raised the issue of political exclusivity. Did the men and women who signed the papers, for example, necessarily represent the people? If they did not, then for whom did they speak? . . .

During the summer of 1770, the New York boycott movement hotly debated the issue of democratic participation. After Parliament repealed the Townshend duties, thus dropping all taxes except that on tea, the major import merchants of the city agitated to renew trade as soon as possible. Delays in reestablishing English contacts might give competitors in Philadelphia or Boston a huge advantage. But however much the New York merchants wanted to turn a profit, they could not bring themselves unilaterally to break the local nonimportant agreement. What they needed at this decisive moment was authorization from the people, and this they determined to obtain through a public opinion poll of consumers—perhaps the first such effort conducted in America. If they could demonstrate with quantitative evidence that the public wanted to rescind the boycott, the merchants knew they would be safe. The tactic worked. Polling papers carried though the city wards revealed that a majority of the people of New York supported a greatly modified boycott that allowed the merchants to import virtually everything except British tea.

The radical leaders of New York found themselves confronted with a quandary that has haunted democratic theorists since ancient Greece. How does a minority respond when it is certain that the majority has made a mistake? The obvious ploy was to declare the poll a fraud, and over several months the supporters of a continued total boycott did just that. They happened away at the merchants' sham democracy. The author of "A Protest" in the *New-York Mercury* argued that the reported numbers were not credible. "It appears from the Ward-Lists," the writer charged, "that only 794 Persons in this populous City, including all Ranks, and both Sexes; declared for the Affirmative of the Question." It is particularly significant for my argument that this writer assumed that a true canvass of colonial consumers—even one involving complex political issues—required inclusiveness, full participation by women as well as men, the poor as well as the rich. . . .

During this contest, "A Citizen" produced a pointed defense of open, egalitarian procedures in a politicized consumer marketplace. To appreciate fully his contribution to the liberal discourse, we must remember that A Citizen was discussing civic responsibility within a commercial public sphere of quite recent invention—in other words, within a popular political arena that was just beginning to express itself apart from traditional institutions of governance. The merchant canvass of New York brought theory into contact with events, helping ordinary men and women better to appreciate the interdependence of liberty and commerce. "Will it excuse this City to the rest of the World," A Citizen asked, "if it should appear that a Majority of the Inhabitants concurred in desiring to break thro' the [nonimportation] Agreement?" He argued through interrogation, with hard questions leading to harder ones until the logic of the performance seemed irrefutable. "Supposing there is a Majority, (which is not admitted)," he inquired of the merchants,

> was it fairly and properly obtained? Was that Opinion given and subscribed with due Deliberation, Knowledge and Freedom? Or were not a very considerable Number of the Subscribers, influenced and determined, by your Persuasions and Representations, or by submitting their Opinions to be guided by your Advice and superior Judgment? Can opinions so given and obtained, properly be called the Voice of the People, or given a Sanction to the Dissolution of an Agreement of such immense Weight and Importance? . . .

Americans of different backgrounds and regions regularly insisted that without "virtue" their cause had no chance whatsoever. Virtue was the social glue that kept the newly formed liberal communities from fragmenting. Colonists who signed the subscriptions, supported the boycotts of British goods, and marched the streets carrying banners proclaiming "Liberty and Non-Importation" assumed that their protests mobilized virtuous people.

Eighteenth-century virtue claims two distinguished genealogies. J. G. A. Pocock traces it back to the Florentine world of Niccolò Machiavelli, arguing that the virtuous citizen was a man whose landed wealth enabled him to rise above the corrupting influences of commerce and thereby preserve the purity of republican government. Such historians as Edmund S. Morgan associate eighteenth-century virtue with the so-called Protestant Ethic. While both positions possess merit—indeed, political discourse on the eve of the Revolution seems to have drawn on both traditions—the virtue that resonated through the entire boycott movement was closer to what T. A. Horne provocatively labels "bourgeois virtue."

When advocates of nonimportation spoke of virtue, they referred primarily to a personal attribute. A virtuous man or woman was one who voluntarily exercised self-restraint in the consumer marketplace. Such behavior represented a sacrifice. No one denied the desirability of the new manufactured items. But however appealing the British imports were, the virtuous person exercised self-control for the common good. . . .

This rather straightforward sense of market virtue that developed throughout the colonies before Independence had important implications for political mobilization. Anyone who regularly purchased manufactured goods from Great Britain could become virtuous simply by controlling consumption. The concept thus linked everyday experience and behavior with a broadly shared sense of the common good. What one did with one's money mattered very much to the entire community, for in this highly charged atmosphere, economic self-indulgence became a glaring public vice. Unlike Cincinnatus, the bourgeois patriot did not reach immediately for the sword. He first examined the household budget. . . . The *Boston Gazette* translated market virtue into a direct all to action: "Save your Money and you save your Country." . . .

For all their insistence on voluntarism, the proponents of nonimportation developed a potentially coercive understanding of political obligation. To be sure, the individual consumer could exercise his or her free will and ignore appeals from those who supported the boycotts. But one thereby surrendered one's right to blame others for the destruction of political liberty. Membership in a commercial society implied responsibilities to the larger collectivity. . . .

Within the framework of bourgeois virtue, organizers of local boycotts and subscription drives created a new political abstraction that would be of great significance in the coming of the American Revolution. The nonimportation movement constructed a "public," an imagined body of people who demonstrated virtue by renouncing British goods and thus earned the right to judge the behavior of the less virtuous. In the American colonies this may have been as close as people came to creating what Jürgen Habermas calls the "public sphere." For him, this imagined space was an arena in which intellectuals—writers who published largely in the pages of the newly founded urban journals of the eighteenth century—criticized the absolutist state. These independent critics addressed a growing audience of literate men and women in the name of the public. The public—an abstract body that never actually assembled—was composed of reasonable persons, individuals open to liberal argument and hostile to the arbitrary exercise of power. . . .

When vicious consumers were caught with British manufactured goods, it was bourgeois virtue that held them accountable, often demanding full confession and restitution. A New York City merchant, Alexander Robertson, who violated the boycott, had to publish a broadside addressed specifically "To the PUBLICK." A chastened Robertson stated, "As I have justly incurred the Resentment of my Fellow Citizens, from my Behaviour, as set forth in an Advertisement, *of great Importance to the Publick,* assuring them that I am truly sorry for the Part I have acted; declare and promise that I never will again attempt an Act contrary to the true Interest and Resolutions of the People zealous in the Cause of *Virtue* and *Liberty*." He closed with a pathetic appeal to "the Publick in general to believe me."

Such local conversations—however painful for the likes of Robertson—encouraged virtuous consumers to imagine even larger collectivities. The process was slow, halting, punctuated by self-doubt and mutual recrimination, but during the run-up to Independence, Americans living in scattered communities managed to reach out convincingly to distant strangers, to persons not directly known but assumed to share in the development of a new consumer marketplace. The initial boycott experiments of the 1760s persuaded the colonists of the need for broader, more effective alliances. They learned about each other through the weekly newspapers that were themselves both a product and a voice of expanding commerce. . . .

The collapse of nonimportation in 1770 left Americans in a sour mood. As they assessed the failure to wean themselves from British goods, they momentarily doubted their moral ability to create a truly virtuous state. Their self-deprecatory statements during this period seem to echo the anticommercial rhetoric of republican discourse, persuading some modern historians, at least, that preindustrial capitalism and the public good were in fact incompatible. What, inquired one newspaper essay, can the colonists learn from recent defection from the boycott?

> That self-interest is irresistible.
> That liberty and public good can stand no change among men when self-interest is its rival.
> That self-interest recommends the most underhanded schemes to every man's good conscience. . . .

Such statements—and they were common—should not be interpreted as evidence that Americans rejected either preindustrial capitalism or the consumer marketplace. The renunciation of excess in the market made sense only in a society that took consumption for granted. The challenge for Revolutionary Americans was to negotiate between extreme self-indulgence and primitive simplicity. It involved mediation, not repudiation. . . .

In any case, the cries of the pessimists were unfounded. They misread the commercial changes sweeping American society and therefore underestimated the capacity of men and women to translate individual market behavior into mass political protest. The delegates to the First Continental Congress did not make that mistake. They appreciated the centrality of consumption in mobilizing persons of different regions and social backgrounds. On October 20, 1774, Congress authorized the Association, a broad network of local elected committees entrusted with the total enforcement of nonimportation. These bodies became in effect, "committees of public safety." At the moment of decision about ultimate political loyalties, the colonists' friends and neighbors were busy monitoring commercial behavior and enforcing bourgeois virtue in the name of the common good. "We need only fight our Own selves," announced "A Carolinian" in 1774, "suppress for a while our Luxury and Corruption, and wield the Arms of Self Denial in our own Houses, to obtain the Victory. . . . And the Man who would not refuse himself a fine Coat, to save his Country, deserves to be hanged."

We have traced a complex flow of ideas into actions, of shared assumptions about a commercial empire into forms of political resistance. This was most certainly not the only route from experience and ideology to revolution. Other, more celebrated political discourses helped Americans make sense out of rapidly changing social and economic conditions within the British empire. In this particular exploration, however, we have reconstituted a frame of reference that defined itself around participation in a newly established consumer marketplace. This focus powerfully illuminates how the great shaping forces of history—commercial capitalism, for example—impinged on the lives of ordinary men and women, compelling them to reimagine themselves within a larger polity. For consuming Americans, the mental process had unintended results: the creation of political instruments open to persons of "all ranks," the development of a concept of virtue that included any man or woman capable of economic self-restraint, and the formation of new intrepetive communities based on shared, secular interests.

F U R T H E R   R E A D I N G

Bernard Bailyn, *Faces of Revolution: Personalities and Themes in the Struggle for American Independence* (1990)

————, *The Ideological Origins of the American Revolution* (1967)

Thomas C. Barrow, "The American Revolution Considered as a Colonial War for Independence," *William and Mary Quarterly,* 3d ser., 25 (1968), 452–464

Richard Buel Jr., "Democracy and the American Revolution: A Frame of Reference," *William and Mary Quarterly,* 3d ser., 21 (1964), 165–190

Edwin G. Burrows and Michael Wallace, "The American Revolution: The Ideology and Practice of National Liberation," *Perspectives in American History* 6 (1972), 167–306

Edward Countryman, *The American Revolution* (1985)

Jay Fliegelman, *Prodigals and Pilgrims: The American Revolution Against Patriarchal Authority* (1982)

William M. Fowler, Jr., and Wallace Coyle, eds., *The American Revolution: Changing Perspectives* (1979)

Jack P. Greene, ed., *The American Revolution: Its Character and Limits* (1987)

Ronald Hoffman and Peter J. Albert, *The Transforming Hand of Revolution: Reconsidering the American Revolution as a Social Movement* (1995)

J. Franklin Jameson, *The American Revolution Considered as a Social Movement* (1926)

Merrill Jensen, "The American People and the American Revolution," *Journal of American History* 57 (1970), 5–35

————, "Historians and the Nature of the American Revolution," in *The Reinterpretation of Early American History,* R. A. Billington, ed. (1966)

Stephen G. Kurtz and James H. Hutson, eds., *Essays on the American Revolution* (1973)

Jesse Lemisch, "The American Revolution Seen from the Bottom Up," in *Towards a New Past,* Barton Bernstein, ed. (1968)

Kenneth A. Lockridge, "Social Change and the Meaning of the American Revolution," *Journal of Social History* 4 (1973), 403–439

Michael McGiffert, ed., "Forum: Rethinking the American Revolution," *William and Mary Quarterly,* 3d Ser., 53 (1996), 341–386

Edmund S. Morgan, *The Challenge of the American Revolution* (1976)

Richard B. Morris, *The American Revolution Reconsidered* (1967)

Gary B. Nash, *The Urban Crucible: Social Change, Political Consciousness, and the Origins of the American Revolution* (1979)

Robert R. Palmer, "The Revolution," in *The Comparative Approach to American History,* C. Vann Woodward, ed. (1968)

Frederick B. Tolles, "The American Revolution Considered as a Social Movement: A Re-Evaluation," *American Historical Review* 60 (1954–55), 1–12

Gordon S. Wood, *The Radicalism of the American Revolution* (1992)

————, "Rhetoric and Reality in the American Revolution," *William and Mary Quarterly,* 3d ser., 23 (1966), 3–32

Alfred F. Young, ed., *The American Revolution: Explorations in the History of American Radicalism* (1993)

Society and Politics

on the

Eve of the Revolution

Colonial American society in the 1760s and 1770s was neither serene nor static, and in retrospect scholars have identified long-standing tensions that propelled the conflict with Britain. Yet most people of the time did not recognize that theirs was an unusual era, at least not until 1773, or even as late as 1775. Concerned chiefly with their own well-being, their families, and their communities, they thought more often and more deeply about religion and the next world than they did about imperial politics. Only men who were directly involved in frontier or transatlantic trade or military affairs gave their attention to the empire. Most free people occupied themselves with earning a livelihood, keeping a home, raising children, and making a career in communities where birth, sex, race, wealth, education, and manners mostly determined one's social role and rank.

The model for colonial society was mainly English. English culture and customs supplied much of the content as well as the ideals that colonists admired. In their speech, dress, tastes, and living arrangements the free population re- sembled the people of provincial England. But there were important new world differences: property in land was far more widely distributed in America than Britain; there was no single, established national church that dominated the colonies; and where Britain had a large class of tenants and farm laborers, all the colonies had slave labor—a labor force that from Maryland to Georgia num- bered in the hundreds of thousands. As early as the 1750s, Benjamin Franklin, who saw Pennsylvania thronged with Germans and Scots-Irish immigrants, had pointed out the heterogeneity of the colonial population and the rapid pace of growth. By the 1770s, the thirteen mainland colonies were populated by about 3 million inhabitants (one-third the population of Britain), and the numbers were doubling every generation. Sooner or later the imperial leaders would need to adjust the empire to the dynamic societies that were emerging in their North American possessions.

DOCUMENTS

The personal writings excerpted here provide some clues about the values and structure of colonial society, especially from the perspective of the "better sort" on the eve of the Revolution. Such private documents are quite scarce, especially for African Americans, women, and common people generally. The first selection, taken from the only known account by a long-time colonial slave, Venture Smith, gives us a glimpse of New England slave experiences. The passage from John Adams's diary when he was a young, unknown lawyer, offers an insider's perspective on the same society. The Boston schoolgirl's experiences reveal genteel female socialization in a commercial center that resembled New York and Philadelphia in many respects. Philip V. Fithian was a New Jersey native who, upon graduation from Princeton, worked in Virginia as a tutor in the highest echelon of colonial American society. Because personal documents are necessarily highly individual, they do not lead us to easy generalizations. Yet at the same time they cannot escape the influences of the time and place of their origin, and so they often express indirectly some of the widely shared characteristics of that society.

1. Venture Smith, a Connecticut Slave, Earns His Freedom, 1729–1766

I was born at Dukandarra, in Guinea, about the year 1729. My father's name was Saungm Furro, Prince of the Tribe of Dukandarra. My father had three wives. Polygamy was not uncommon in that country, especially among the rich, as every man was allowed to keep as many wives as he could maintain. By his first wife he had three children. The eldest of them was myself, named by my father, Broteer. The other two were named Cundazo and Soozaduka. My father had two children by his second wife, and one by his third. I descended from a very large, tall and stout race of beings, much larger than the generality of people in other parts of the globe, being commonly considerable above six feet in height, and every way well proportioned.

The first thing worthy of notice which I remember was, a contention between my father and mother, on account of my father's marrying his third wife without the consent of his first and eldest, which was contrary to the custom generally observed among my countrymen. In consequence of this rupture, my mother left her husband and country, and traveled away with her three children to the eastward. I was then five years old. [He then relates how he was captured in warfare.] . . . On a certain time I and other prisoners were put on board a canoe, under our master, and rowed away to a vessel belonging to Rhode Island, commanded by capt. Collingwood, and the mate Thomas Mumford. While we were going to the vessel, our master told us all to appear to the best possible advantage for sale. I was bought on board by one Robert Mumford, steward of said vessel, for four gallons of rum, and a piece of calico, and called Venture, on account of his having purchased me with his own private venture. Thus I came by my name. All the slaves that were bought for that vessel's cargo, were two hundred and sixty. . . .

From [Venture Smith], *A Narrative of the Life and Adventures of Venture, A Native of Africa, But resident above sixty years in the United States of America* (New London, 1798), 3–24.

After all the business was ended on the coast of Africa, the ship sailed from thence to Barbadoes. After an ordinary passage, except great mortality by the small pox, which broke out on board, we arrived at the island of Barbadoes: but when we reached it, there were found out of the two hundred and sixty that sailed from Africa, not more than two hundred alive. These were all sold, except myself and three more, to the planters there. The vessel then sailed for Rhode Island [ca. 1736]. . . .

At my master's own place, I was pretty much employed in the house at carding wool and other household business. [Venture was now 8 years old.] In this situation I continued for some years, after which my master put me to work out of doors. After many proofs of my faithfulness and honesty, my master began to put great confidence in me. My behavior to him had as yet been submissive and obedient. I then began to have hard tests imposed on me. Some of these were to pound four bushels of ears of corn every night in a barrel for the poultry, or be vigorously punished. At other seasons of the year I had to card wool unit a very late hour. These tasks I had to perform when I was about nine years old. . . .

After I had lived with my master thirteen years, being then about twenty-two years old, I married Meg, a slave of his who was about my age. . . . At the close of that year [1752 or 1753] I was sold to a Thomas Stanton, and had to be separated from my wife and one daughter, who was about one month old. He resided at Stonington point. To this place I brought with me from my late master's, two johannes, three old Spanish dollars, and two thousand of coppers, besides five pounds of my wife's money. This money I got by cleaning gentlemen's shoes and drawing boots, by catching muskrats and minks, raising potatoes and carrots, &c. and by fishing in the night, and at odd spells.

All this money amounting to near twenty-one pounds York currency, my master's brother, Robert Stanton, hired of me, for which he gave me his note. About one year and a half after that time, my master purchased my wife and her child, for seven hundred pounds old tenor. . . .

Towards the close of the time that I resided with this master, I had a falling out with my mistress. This happened one time when my master was gone to Long Island a gunning. At first the quarrel began between my wife and her mistress. I was then at work in the barn, and hearing a racket in the house, induced me to run there and see what had broken out. When I entered the house, I found my mistress in a violent passion with my wife, for what she informed me was a mere trifle; such a small affair that I forbear to put my mistress to the shame of having it known. I earnestly requested my wife to beg pardon of her mistress for the sake of peace, even if she had given no just occasion for offence. But whilst I was thus saying my mistress turned the blows which she was repeating on my wife to me. She took down her horsewhip, and while she was glutting her fury with it, I reached out my great black hand, raised it up and received the blows of the whip on it which were designed for my head. Then I immediately committed the whip to the devouring fire.

When my master returned from the island, his wife told him of the affair, but for the present he seemed to take no notice of it, and mentioned not a word about it to me. Some days after his return, in the morning as I was putting on a log in the fire place, not suspecting harm from any one, I received a most violent stroke on the crown of my head with a club two feet long and as large round as a chair post. This blow very badly wounded my head, and the scar of it remains to this day. The first blow made me have my wits about me you may suppose, for as soon as he went to renew it, I snatched the club out of his hands and dragged him out of the door. He then sent for his brother to come and assist him, but I presently left my master, took the club he wounded me with, carried it to a neighboring Justice of the Peace, and complained of my master. He finally advised me to return to my master, and live contented with him till he abused me again, and then complain. I consented to do accordingly. But before I set out for my master's, up he come and his brother Robert after me. The Justice improved this convenient opportunity to caution my master. He asked him for what he treated his slave thus hastily and unjustly, and told him what would be the consequence if he continued the same treatment towards me. After the Justice had ended his discourse with my master, he and his brother set out with me for home, one before and the other behind me. When they had come to a bye place, they both dismounted their respective horses, and fell to beating me with great violence. I became enraged at this and immediately turned them both under me, laid one of them across the other, and stamped both with my feet what I would.

This occasioned my master's brother to advise him to put me off. A short time after this I was taken by a constable and two men. They carried me to a blacksmith's shop and had me handcuffed. When I returned home my mistress enquired much of her waiters, whether Venture was handcuffed. When she was informed that I was, she appeared to be very contented and was much transported with the news. In the midst of this content and joy, I presented myself before my mistress, showed her my handcuffs, and gave her thanks for my gold rings. For this my master commanded a negro of his to fetch him a large ox chain. This my master locked on my legs with two padlocks. I continued to wear the chain peaceably for two or three days, when my master asked me with contemptuous hard names whether I had not better be freed from my chains and go to work. I answered him, No. Well then, said he, I will send you to the West Indies or banish you, for I am resolved not to keep you. I answered him I crossed the waters to come here, and I am willing to cross them to return.

For a day or two after this not any one said much to me, until one Hempsted Miner, of Stonington, asked me if I would live with him. I answered him that I would. He then requested me to make myself discontented and to appear as unreconciled to my master as I could before that he bargained with him for me; and that in return he would give me a good chance to gain my freedom when I came to live with him. I did as he requested me. Not long after Hempsted Miner purchased me of my master for fifty six pounds lawful. He took the chain and padlocks from off me immediately after. . . .

A short time after my master carried me to Hartford, and first proposed to sell me to one William Hooker of that place. . . .

My master next offered me to Daniel Edwards, Esq. of Hartford, for sale. But not purchasing me, my master pawned me to him for ten pounds, and returned to Stonington. After some trial of my honesty, Mr. Edwards placed considerable trust and confidence in me. He put me to serve as his cupbearer and waiter. When there was company at his house, he would send me into the cellar and other parts of his house to fetch wine and other articles occasionally for them. When I had been with him some time, he asked me why my master wished to part with such an honest negro, and why he did not keep me himself. I replied that I could not give him the reason, unless it was to convert me into cash, and speculate with me as with other commodities. I hope that he can never justly say it was on account of my ill conduct that he did not keep me himself. Mr. Edwards told me that he should be very willing to keep me himself, and that he would never let me go from him to live, if it was not unreasonable and inconvenient for me to be parted from my wife and children; therefore he would furnish me with a horse to return to Stonington, if I had a mind for it. As Miner did not appear to redeem me I went, and called at my old master Stanton's first to see my wife, who was then owned by him. As my old master appeared much ruffled at my being there, I left my wife before I had spent any considerable time with her, and went to Colonel O. Smith's. Miner had not as yet wholly settled with Stanton for me, and had before my return from Hartford given Col. Smith a bill of sale of me. These men once met to determine which of them should hold me, and upon my expressing a desire to be owned by Col. Smith, . . . it was agreed that I should live with Col. Smith. This was the third time of my being sold, and I was then thirty-one years old [1760]. As I never had an opportunity of redeeming myself whilst I was owned by Miner, though he promised to give me a chance, I was then very ambitious of obtaining it. I asked my master one time if he would consent to have me purchase my freedom. He replied that he would. I was then very happy, knowing that I was at that time able to pay part of the purchase money, by means of the money which I some time since buried. This I took out of the earth and tendered to my master, having previously engaged a free negro man to take his security for it, as I was the property of my master, and therefore could not safely take his obligation myself. What was wanting in redeeming myself, my master agreed to wait on me for, until I could procure it for him. I still continued to work for Col. Smith. There was continually some interest accruing on my master's note to my friend the free negro man above named, which I received, and with some besides which I got by fishing, I laid out in land adjoining my old master Stanton's. By cultivating this land with the greatest diligence and economy, at times when my master did not require my labor, in two years I laid up ten pounds. This my friend tendered my master for myself, and received his note for it.

Being encouraged by the success which I had met in redeeming myself, I again solicited my master for a further chance of completing it. The chance for which I solicited him was that of going out to work the ensuing winter. He agreed to this on condition that I would give him one quarter of my earnings. On these terms I worked the following winter, and earned four pounds sixteen shillings, one quarter of which went to my master for the privilege, and the rest was paid him on my own account. This added to the other payments made up forty four pounds, eight shillings, which I had paid on my own account. I was then about thirty five years old [1764].

The next summer I again desired he would give me a chance of going out to work. But he refused and answered that he must have my labor this summer, as he did not have it the past winter. I replied that I considered it as hard that I could not have a chance to work out when the season became advantageous, and that I must only be permitted to hire myself out in the poorest season of the year. He asked me after this what I would give him for the privilege per month. I replied that I would leave it wholly with his own generosity to determine what I should return him a month. Well then, said he, if so two pounds a month. I answered him that if that was the least he would take I would be contented. Accordingly I hired myself out at Fisher's Island, and earned twenty pounds; thirteen pounds six shillings of which my master drew for the privilege, and the remainder I paid him for my freedom. This made fifty-one pounds two shillings which I paid him. In October following I went and wrought six months at Long Island. In that six month's time I cut and corded four hundred cords of wood, besides threshing out seventy-five bushels of grain, and received of my wages down only twenty pounds, which left remaining a larger sum. Whilst I was out that time, I took up on my wages only one pair of shoes. At night I lay on the hearth, with one coverlet over and another under me. I returned to my master and gave him what I received of my six months labor. This left only thirteen pounds eighteen shillings to make up the full sum for my redemption. My master liberated me, saying that I might pay what was behind if I could ever make it convenient, otherwise it would be well. The amount of the money which I had paid my master towards redeeming my time, was seventy-one pounds two shillings. The reason of my master for asking such an unreasonable price, was he said, to secure himself in case I should ever come to want. Being thirty-six years old, I left Col. Smith once for all [1765]. I had already been sold three different times, made considerable money with seemingly nothing to derive it from, been cheated out of a large sum of money, lost much by misfortunes, and paid an enormous sum for my freedom.

2. John Adams, a College Graduate, Views Rural Massachusetts, 1760

May 30 1760. Friday.

Rose early. Several Country Towns, within my observation, have at least a Dozen Taverns and Retailers. Here The Time, the Money, the Health and the Modesty, of most that are young and of many old, are wasted; here Diseases, vicious Habits, Bastards and Legislators, are frequently begotten.

Nightingale, Hayden, Saunders, J. Spear, N. Spear, Benoni Spear, would vote for any Man for a little Phlip, or a Dram. N. Belcher, John Spear, O. Gay, James Brackett, John Mills, Wm. Veasey &c. voted for T[hayer]. for other Reasons. . . .

Saturday. [June] 7th.

Arose late, again. When shall I shake off the shackells of morning slumbers, and arise with the sun? Between sun rise, and Breackfast, I might write, or read, or contemplate, a good deal. I might, before Breakfast, entirely shake off the Drowziness of the Morning, and get my Thoughts into a steady Train, my Imagination raised, my Ambition inflamed, in short every Thing within me and without, into a Preparation for Improvement.—I have some Points [of] Law to examine to day. . . .

1760 Aug. 19th.

I began Popes Homer, last Saturday Night was a Week, and last Night, which was Monday night I finished it. Thus I found that in seven days I could have easily read the 6 Volumes, Notes, Preface, Essays, that on Homer, and that on Homers Battles

"John Adams Views Rural Massachusetts, 1760." As found in *The Diary and Autobiography of John Adams,* ed. L. H. Butterfield et al. (Cambridge: Harvard University Press, 1961), vol. 1, pp. 130–133, 152–153, 168–173, 176–177, 181–184.

and that on the funeral Games of Homer and Virgil &c. Therefore I will be bound that in 6 months I would conquer him in Greek, and make myself able to translate every Line in him elegantly.

[*Benjamin*] *Prat.* It is a very happy Thing to have People superstitious. They should believe exactly as their Minister believes. They should have no Creeds and Confessions ⟨*of Faith*⟩. They should not so much as know what they believe. The People ought to be ignorant. And our Free schools are the very bane of society. They make the lowest of the People infinitely conceited. (These Words I heard Prat utter. They would come naturally enough from the mouth of a Tyrant or of a K[ing] or Ministry about introducing an Arbitrary Power; or from the mouth of an ambitious or avaricious Ecclesiastic, but they are base detestable Principles of slavery. He would have 99/100 of the World as ignorant as the wild Beasts of the forest, and as servile as the slaves in a Galley, or as oxen yoked in a Team. He a friend to Liberty? He an Enemy to slavery? He has the very Principles of a Frenchman—worse Principles than a Frenchman, for they know their Belief and can give Reasons for it.)

Prat. It grieves me to see any sect of Religion extinguished. I should be very sorry, to have the Quaker Society dissolved, so I should be sorry to [have] Condy's Anabaptist Society dissolved. I love to see a Variety. A Variety of Religions has the same Beauty in the Moral World, that a Variety of flowers has in a Garden, or a Variety of Trees in a forrest.

This fine speech was Prats. Yet he is sometimes of opinion that all these Sectaries ought to turn Churchmen, and that a Uniform Establishment ought to take a place through the whole Nation. I have heard him say, that We had better all of us come into the Church, than pretend to overturn it &c. Thus it is, that fine Speechmakers are sometimes for Uniformity, sometimes for Variety, and Toleration. They don't speak for the Truth or Weight but for the Smartness, and Novelty, singularity of their speech. However I heard him make two Observations, that pleased me much more. One was that People in Years never suppose that young People have any Judgment. . . .

Novr. 14th. 1760.

Another Year is now gone and upon Recollection, I find I have executed none of my Plans of study. I cannot Satisfy my self that I am much more knowing either from Books, or Men, from this Chamber, or the World, than I was at least a Year ago. . . . Most of my Time has been spent in Rambling and Dissipation. Riding, and Walking, Smoking Pipes and Spending Evenings, consume a vast Proportion of my Time, and the Cares and Anxieties of Business, damp my Ardor and scatter my attention. But I must stay more at home—and commit more to Writing. A Pen is certainly an excellent Instrument, to fix a Mans Attention and to inflame his Ambition. I am therefore beginning a new literary Year, with the 26th. of my life.

1760. Novr. 14th. Friday.

I am just entered on the 26th Year of my Life, and on the fifth Year of my studies in Law, and I think it is high Time for a Reformation both in the Man, and the Lawyer. 25 Years of the Animal Life is a great Proportion to be spent, to so little Purpose, and four Years, the Space that we spend at Colledge is a great deal of Time to spend for no more Knowledge in the science and no more Employment in the Practice of Law. Let me keep an exact Journal therefore of the Authors I read, in this Paper.

This day I am beginning my Ld. Hales History of the Common Law, a Book borrowed of Mr. Otis, and read already once, Analysis and all, with great Satisfaction. I wish I had Mr. Blackstones Analysis, that I might compare, and see what Improvements he has made upon Hale's. . . .

Wednesday [19 November].

Dined at Badcocks, with McKenzie. He pretends to Mechanicks, and Manufactures. He owns the snuff Mill, and he is about setting up some Machine to hull our Barley. One Welsh dined with us, who he said was the best, most ingenious Tradesman, that ever was in this Country. McKenzie and Welsh were very full of the Machinery, in Europe, the Fire Engines, the Water Works, the silk Machines, the Wind Mills, in Holland &c. McKenzie says there are 27,000 Wheels, and 90,000 Movements in the silk Machine. You may see 10,000 Wind Mills going at once in Holland. Thus he tells Wondrous Things, like other Travellers.—I suspect he would be unable to describe the fire Engine or the Water Works. Had I been Master of my self I should have examined him, artfully, but I could not recollect any one Particular of the fire Engine, but the Receiver, and that he says is no Part of the Engine. But he talks about a Center Cylinder.

This conceited Scotchman has been a Rambler I believe. He set up Merchandize in New London. He married a Cunningham, sister to Otis's Wife.—These restless Projectors, in Mechanicks, Husbandry, Merchandize, Manufactures, seldom succeed here. No Manufactury has succeeded here, as yet. And I believe Franklins Reasoning is good, and the Causes he mentions will hinder the growth of Manufactures here in America, for a great While yet to come. . . .

[November] 1760.

Pater [Father] was in a very sociable Mood this Evening. He told 3 or 4 merry stories of old Horn. Old Horn, a little crooked old Lawyer in my fathers Youth, who made a Business of Jest and Banter, attacked an old Squaw one Day upon the Neck. The old Squaw made answer, "You poor smitten Boy, you with your Knife in your Tail and your Loaf on your Back, did your Mother born you so?"

A Man, whom he assaulted at another Time, with his Jests, asked him "Did you come straight from Boston?" And upon being answered yes, replied you have been miserably warped by the Way then.

A Market Girl whom he overtook upon the Neck, and asked to let him jigg her? answered by asking what is that? What good will that do? He replied it will make you fat! Pray be so good then says the Girl as to Gigg my Mare. She's miserably lean.

Novr. 25th. 1760.

Rode to the Iron Works Landing to see a Vessell launched. And after Launching went to smoke a Pipe, at Ben. Thayers, where the Rabble filled the House. Every Room, kitchen, Chamber was crowded with People. Negroes with a fiddle. Young fellows and Girls dancing in the Chamber as if they would kick the floor thro. Zab Hayward, not finding admittance to the Chamber, gathered a Circle round him in the lower Room. There He began to shew his Tricks and Postures, and Activity. He has had the Reputation, for at least fifteen Years, of the best Dancer in the World in these Towns. Several attempted, but none could equal him, in nimbleness of heels.

But he has no Conception of the Grace, the Air nor the Regularity of dancing. His Air is absurd and wild, desultory, and irregular, as his Countenance is low and ignoble. In short the Air of his Countenance, the Motions of his Body, Hands, and Head, are extreamly silly, and affected and mean.

When he first began, his Behaviour and Speeches were softly silly, but as his Blood grew warm by motion and Liquor, he grew droll. He caught a Girl and danced a Gigg with her, and then led her to one side of the Ring and said, "Stand there, I call for you by and by." This was spoke comically enough, and raised a loud laugh. He caught another Girl, with light Hair, and a Patch on her Chin, and held her by the Hand while he sung a song, describing her as he said. This tickled the Girls Vanity, for the song which he applied to her described a very fine Girl indeed.

One of his witty droll sayings he thought, was this. I am a clever fellow, or else the Devil is in me. That is a Clever Girl or else the Devil is in her. Wm. Swan is such another Funmaking animal of diverting Tricks.

Hayward took one Girl by the Hand, and made a Speech to her. "I must confess I am an old Man, and as father Smith says hardly capable of doing my Duty." This raised a broad Laugh too.

Thus, in dancing, singing songs, drinking flip, running after one Girl, and married Woman and another, and making these affected, humorous Speeches, he spent the whole Afternoon.—And Zab and I were foolish enough to spend the whole afternoon in gazing and listening.

Gurney danced, but was modest and said nothing. E. Turner danced not, but bawled aloud.—God dam it, and dam it, and the Devil, &c.—And swore he'd go to Captn. Thayers, and be merry and get as drunk as the Devil. He insisted upon it, drunk he would get. And indeed, not 2 pence better than drunk he was.

Fiddling and dancing, in a Chamber full of young fellows and Girls, a wild Rable of both sexes, and all Ages, in the lower Room, singing dancing, fiddling, drinking flip and Toddy, and drams.—This is the Riot and Revelling of Taverns And of Thayers frolicks. . . .

1760. Decr. 2d.

Spent the Evening at Coll. [Josiah] Q[uincy].'s with Captn. Freeman. About the middle of the Evening Dr. Lincoln and his Lady came in. The Dr. gave us an ample Confirmation of our Opinion of his Brutality and Rusticity. He treated his Wife, as no drunken Cobler, or Clothier would have done, before Company. Her father never gave such Looks and Answers to one of his slaves in my Hearing. And he contradicted he Squibd, shrugged, scouled, laughd at the Coll. in such a Manner as the Coll. would have called Boorish, urgentlemanly, unpolite, ridiculous, in any other Man. More of the Clown, is not in the World. A hoggish, ill bred, uncivil, haughty, Coxcomb, as ever I saw. His Wit is forced and affected, his Manners to his father, Wife, and to Company are brutally rustic, he is ostentatious of his Talent at Disputation, forever giving an History, like my Uncle Hottentot, of some Wrangle he has had with this and that Divine. Affects to be thought an Heretic. Disputes against the Eternity of Hell, torments &c. His treatment of his Wife amazed me. Miss Q. asked the Dr. a Question. Miss Lincoln seeing the Dr. engaged with me, gave her Mother an Answer, which however was not satisfactory. Miss Q. repeats it. "Dr. you did not hear my Question."—"Yes I did, replies the Dr., and the Answer to it, my Wife is so pert, she must put in her Oar, or she must blabb, before I could speak." And then shrugged And affected a laugh, to cow her as he used to, the freshmen and sophymores at Colledge.—She sunk into silence and shame and Grief, as I thought.—After supper, she says "Oh my dear, do let my father see that Letter we read on the road." Bela answers, like the great Mogul, like Nero or Caligula, "he shant."—Why, Dr., do let me have it! do!—He turns his face about as stern as the Devil, sour as Vinegar. "I wont."—Why sir says she, what makes you answer me so sternly, shant and wont?—Because I wont, says he. Then the poor Girl, between shame and Grief and Resentment and Contempt, at last, strives to turn it off with a Laugh.—"I wish I had it. Ide shew it, I know."—Bela really acts that Part of the Tamer of the Shrew in Shakespear. Thus a kind Look, an obliging Air, a civil Answer, is a boon that she cant obtain from her Husband. Farmers, Tradesmen, Soldiers, Sailors, People of no fortune, Figure, Education, are really more civil, obliging, kind, to their Wives than he is.—She always is under Restraint before me. She never dares shew her endearing Airs, nor any fondness for him. . . .

1760 Decr. 18th. Thursday.

Yesterday spent in Weymouth, in settling the Disputes between old Thos. White and young Isaac French. White has the Remainders of his habitual Trickish lying, cheating Disposition, strongly working to this Day—an infinity of jesuitical Distinctions, and mental Reservations.

He told me he never lost a Cause at Court in his Life—which James White and Mr. Whitmarsh say is a down right Lye.

He owned to me that his Character had been that of a Knave and a Villain: and says ever Man of Wit and sense will be called a Villain.—My Principle has been, to deal upon Honour with all men, so long as they deal upon Honour with me, but as soon as they begin to trick me, I think I ought to trick them.

Thus every Knave thinks others, as knavish or more knavish than himself.

What an Intrenchment, is this against the Attacks of his Conscience, is this, "the Knavery of my Neighbours, is superiour to mine."

An old withered, decripit Person, 87 years of Age with a Head full of all the Wiles, and Guile and Artifice of the Infernal serpent, is really a ⟨*Phenomenon*⟩ melancholly sight. Ambition of appearing sprightly, cunning, smart, capable of outwitting younger Men. In short I never saw that Guile and subtilty in any Man of that Age. Father Niles has a little of that same serpentine Guile. I never felt the meaning of the Words, Stratagem, Guile, Subtilty, Cunning, Wiles &c. that Milton applies to the Devil [in?] his Plan to effect the Ruin of our first Parents so forcibly, as since I knew that old Man, and his grandson Isaac, who seems to have the same subtilty, and a worse Temper, under a total secresy, and dissembled Intention. He has a smiling face, and a flattering Tongue with a total Concealment of his Designs, tho a devilish malignant, fiery temper appears in his Eyes. He's a Cassius, like Ben. Thayer. Sees thro the Characters of Men, much further, and clearer, than ordinary, never laughs, now and then smiles, or half smiles. Father White, with all his subtilty and Guile, may be easily over reached by Men like him self. He is too open, too ostentatious of his Cunning, and therefore is generally, out witted, and worsted. . . .

There is every Year, some new and astonishing scene of Vice, laid open to the Consideration of the Public. Parson [Nathaniel] Potters Affairs, with Mrs. Winchester, and other Women, is hardly forgotten. A Minister, famous for Learning, oratory, orthodoxy, Piety and Gravity, discovered to have the most debauched and polluted of Minds, to have pursued a series of wanton Intrigues, with one Woman and another, to have got his Maid with Child and all that.—Lately Deacon Savils Affair has become public. An old Man 77 Years of Age, a Deacon, whose chief Ambition has always been Prayer, and religious Conversation, and sacredotal Company, discovered to have been the most salacious, rampant, Stallion, in the Universe—rambling all the Town over, lodging with this and that Boy and Attempting at least the Crime of Buggery.

1760. Decr. 18.

Justice Dyer says there is more Occasion for Justices than for Lawyers. Lawyers live upon the sins of the People. If all Men were just, and honest, and pious, and Religious &c. there would be no need of Lawyers. But Justices are necessary to keep men just and honest and pious, and religious.—Oh sagacity!

But, it may be said with equal Truth, that all Magistrates, and all civil officers, and all civil Government, is founded and maintained by the sins of the People. All armies would be needless if Men were universally virtuous. Most manufacturers and Tradesmen would be needless. Nay, some of the natural Passions and sentiments of human Minds, would be needless upon that supposition. Resentment, e.g. which has for its object, Wrong and Injury. No man upon that supposition would ever give another, a just Provocation. And no just Resentment could take Place without a just Provocation. Thus, our natural Resentments are founded on the sins of the People, as much as the Profession of the Law, or that of Arms, or that of Divinity. In short Vice and folly are so interwoven in all human Affairs that they could not possibly be wholly separated from them without tearing and rending the whole system of human Nature, and state. Nothing would remain as it is.

3. Anna Green Winslow, a Schoolgirl, Learns About Growing Up in Boston, 1771

April 9.—. . . Yesterday afternoon I visited Miss Polly Deming & took her with me to Mr Rogers' in the evening where Mr Hunt discours'd upon the 7th question of the catechism viz what are the decrees of God? I remember a good many of his observations, which I have got set down on a loose paper. But my aunt says that a Miss of 12 year's old cant possibly do justice to the nicest subject in Divinity, & therefore had better not attempt a repetition of perticulars, that she finds lie (as may be easily concluded) somewhat confused in my young mind. She also says, that in her poor judgment, Mr Hunt discours'd soundly as well as ingeniously upon the subject, & very much to her instruction & satisfaction. My Papa inform'd me in his last letter that he had done me the honor to read my journals & that he approv'd of some part of them, I suppose he means that he likes some parts better than other,

"Anna Green Winslow, a Schoolgirl, Learns About Growing Up in Boston, 1771." As found in *Diary of Anna Green Winslow: A Boston School Girl of 1771,* ed. Alice Morse Earle (Boston: Houghton Mifflin, 1894), 56–70.

indeed it would be wonderful, as aunt says, if a gentleman of papa's understanding & judgment cou'd be highly entertain'd with *every little* saying or observation that came from a girl of my years & that I ought to esteem it a great favour that he notices any of my simple matter with his *approbation.* . . .

April 14ᵗʰ.—I went a visiting yesterday to Col. Gridley's with my aunt. After tea Miss Becky Gridley sung a minuet. Miss Polly Deming & I danced to her musick, which when perform'd was approv'd of by Mrs Gridley, Mrs Deming, Mrs Thompson, Mrs Avery, Miss Sally Hill, Miss Becky Gridley, Miss Polly Gridley & Miss Sally Winslow. Colⁿ Gridley was out o' the room. Colⁿ brought in the talk of Whigs & Tories & taught me the difference between them. . . .

April 16ᵗʰ.—I dined with Aunt Storer yesterday & spent the afternoon very agreeably at Aunt Suky's. Aunt Storer is not very well, but she drank tea with us, & went down to Mr Stillman's lecture in the evening. I spent the evening with Unkle & Aunt at Mrs Rogers's. Mr Bacon preach'd his fourth sermon from Romans iv. 6. My cousin Charles Storer lent me Gulliver's Travels abreviated, which aunt says I may read for the sake of perfecting myself in reading a variety of composures. she sais farther that the piece was desin'd as a burlesque upon the times in which it was wrote,—& Martimas Scriblensis & Pope Dunciad were wrote with the same design & as parts of the same work, tho' wrote by three several hands. . . .

April 18ᵗʰ.—Some time since I exchang'd a piece of patchwork, which had been wrought in my leisure intervals, with Miss Peggy Phillips, my schoolmate, for a pair of curious lace mitts with blue flaps which I shall send, with a yard of white ribbon edg'd with green to Miss Nancy Macky for a present. I had intended that the patchwork should have grown large enough to have cover'd a bed when that same live stock which you wrote me about some time since, should be increas'd to that portion you intend to bestow upon me, should a certain event take place. I have just now finish'd my Letter to Papa. I had wrote to my other correspondents at Cumberland, some time ago, all which with this I wish safe to your & their hand. I have been carefull not to repeat in my journal any thing that I had wrote in a Letter either to papa, you, &c. Else I should have inform'd you of some of Bet Smith's abominations with the deserv'd punishment she is soon to meet with. But I have wrote it to papa, so need not repeat. I guess when this reaches you, you will be too much engag'd in preparing to quit your present habitation, & will have too much upon your head & hands, to pay much attention to this scrowl. But it may be an amusement to you on your voyage—therefore I send it.

Pray mamma, be so kind as to bring up all my journal with you. My Papa has promised me, he will bring up my baby house with him. I shall send you a droll figure of a young lady, in or under, which you please, a tasty head Dress. It was taken from a print that came over in one of the last ships from London. After you have sufficiently amused yourself with it I am willing . . .

Boston April 20, 1772.—Last Saterday I seal'd up 45 pages of Journal for Cumberland. This is a very stormy day—no going to school. I am learning to knit lace.

April 21.—Visited at uncle Joshua Green's. I saw three funerals from their window poor Capⁿ Turner's was one.

April 22ⁿᵈ.—I spent this evening at Miss Rogers as usual. Mr. Hunt continued his discourse upon the 7ᵗʰ question of the catechism & finish'd what he had to say upon it.

April 23ᵈ.—This mornᵍ early our Mr Bacon set out upon a tour to Maryland, he proposed to be absent 8 weeks. He told the Church that brother Hunt would supply the pulpit till his return. I made a visit this afternoon with cousin Sally at Dr. Phillip's. . . .

May 16.—Last Wednesday Bet Smith was set upon the gallows. She behav'd with great impudence. Thursday I danc'd a minuet & country dances at school, after which I drank tea with aunt Storer. To day I am somewhat out of sorts, a little sick at my stomach. . . .

June 1ˢᵗ.—All last week till saterday was very cold & rainy. Aunt Deming kept me within doors, there were no schools on account of the Election of Councellers, & other public doings; with one eye (for t'other was bound up) I saw the governer & his train of life guard &c. ride by in state to Cambridge. I form'd Letters last week to suit cousin Sally & aunt Thomas, but my eyes were so bad aunt would not let me coppy but one of them. Monday being Artillery Election I went to see the hall, din'd at aunt Storer's, took a walk in the P. M. Unkle laid down the commission he took up last year. Mr Handcock invited the whole company into his house in the afternoon & treated them very genteelly & generously, with cake, wine, &c. There were 10 corn baskets of the feast (at the Hall) sent to the prison & almshouse.

4ᵗʰ.—From June 1 when I wrote last there has nothing extraordinary happen'd till today the whole regiment muster'd upon the common. Mr Gannett, aunt & myself went up into the common, & there saw Capᵗ Water's, Capᵗ Paddock's, Capᵗ Peirce's, Capᵗ Eliot's, Capᵗ Barret's, Capᵗ Gay's, Capᵗ May's, Capᵗ Borington's & Capᵗ Stimpson's company's exercise. From there, we went into King street to Col Marshal's where we saw all of them prettily exercise & fire. Mr. Gannett din'd with us. On Sabbath-day evening 7 June My Honᵈ Papa, Mamma, little Brother, cousin H. D. Thomas, Miss Jenny Allen, & Mrs Huston arriv'd here from Cumberland, all in good health, to the great joy of all their friends, myself in particular—they sail'd from Cumberland the 1ˢᵗ instant, in the evening.

Aug. 18.—Many avocations have prevented my keeping my journal so exactly as heretofore, by which means a pleasant visit to the peacock, my Papa's & mamma's journey to Marshfield &c. have been omitted. The 6 instant Mr Samˡ Jarvis was married to Miss Suky Peirce, & on the 13th I made her a visit in company with mamma & many others. The bride was dress'd in a white satin night gound.

27.—Yesterday I heard an account of a cat of 17 years old, that has just recovered of the meazels. This same cat it is said had the small pox 8 years ago!

28.—I spent the P. M. & eve at aunt Suky's very agreeably with aunt Pierce's young ladies viz. Miss Johnson, Miss Walker, Miss Polly & Miss Betsey Warton, (of Newport) Miss Betsey is just a fortnight wanting 1 day older than I am, who I became acquainted with that P. M. Papa, Mamma, Unkle & aunt Storer, Aunt Pierce & Mr & Mrs Jarvis was there. There were 18 at supper besides a great many did not eat any. Mrs Jarvis sang after supper. My brother Johny has got over the measels.

Sept. 1.—Last evening after meeting, Mrs Bacon was brought to bed of a fine daughter. But was very ill. She had fits.

September 7.—Yesterday afternoon Mr Bacon baptiz'd his daughter by the name of Elizabeth Lewis. It is a pretty looking child. Mrs Whitwell is like to loose her Henry Harris. He is very ill. . . .

14.—Very busy all day, went into the common in the afternoon to see training. It was very pretty perform'd. . . .

20.—Sabbath day. I went to hear Mr Stilman all day, I like him very much. I don't wonder so many go to hear him.

21st.—Mr. Sawyer, Mr Parks, & Mrs Chatbourn, din'd at aunt Storer's. I went to dancing in the afternoon. Miss Winslow & Miss Allen visited there.

22d.—The king's coronation day. In the evening I went with mamma to Coln Marshal's in King Street to see the fireworks.

23d.—I din'd at aunt Suky's with Mr & Mrs Hooper of Marblehead. In the afternoon I went over to see Miss Betsy Winslow. When I came back I had the pleasure to meet papa. I came home in the evening to see aunt Deming. Unkle Winslow sup'd here.

24.—Papa cal'd here in the morng. Nothing else worth noticeing.

25.—Very pleasant. Unkle Ned cal'd here. Little Henry Harris was buried this afternoon.

28.—My papa & unkle Winslow spent the evening here.

29. 30.—Very stormy. Miss Winslow & I read out the Generous Inconstant, & have begun Sir Charles Grandison. . . .

4. Philip Vickers Fithian, a New Jersey Tutor, Admires the Tidewater Gentry, 1773

Monday August 9 [1773]

Waited on Dr Witherspoon [President of Princeton College] about nine o Clock, to hear his proposal for my going to *Virginia*—He read me a Letter which he receivd from Col: Carter, & proposed the following Terms—To teach his Children, five Daughters, & three Sons, who are from five to seventeen years Old—The young Ladies are to be taught the English Language. And the Boys are to study the English Language carefully; & to be instructed in the Latin, & Greek—And he proposes to give thirty five Pounds Sterling, which is about Sixty Pounds currency; Provide all Accommodations; Allow him the undisturbed Use of a Room; And the Use of his own Library; find Provender for a Horse; & a Servant to Wait—

—By the Advice of the Dr & his Recommendation of the Gentleman, & the Place, I accepted the Offer, & agreed to go in the Fall into *Virginia*— . . .

Thursday 28. [October 1773]

Rode after Breakfast to the Honorable Rob: Carters the End of my Journey; 12 Miles, by two o-Clock in the Afternoon. Both Myself, and my Horse seem neither tired nor Dispirited—Occasional Expences on the Road. In Baltimore for some *Buff-Ball, 1/6.* In Blandensburg for having straps put to my Saddle-Bags *3/.* In Colchester for Shaving and Dressing *1/3.* The whole *5/9.* So that my whole Distance

"Philip Vickers Fithian, a New Jersey Tutor, Admires the Tidewater Gentry, 1773." As found in Philip Vickers Fithian, *Journal and Letters of Philip Vickers Fithian, 1773–1774: A Plantation Tutor of the Old Dominion* (Williamsburg: University Press of Virginia, 1943), 8–9, 24–27, 34–39, 41–56.

appears to be *260 Miles,* perform'd in seven Days. And my whole Expence appears to be 3£ 6S 6D. . . .

[Letter to the Reverend Enoch Green]

Decemr 1st 1773.

REVD SIR.

As you desired I may not omit to inform you, so far as I can be a letter, of the business in which I am now engaged, it would indeed be vastly agreeable to me if it was in my power to give you particular intelligence concerning the state and plan of my employment here.

I set out from home the 20th of Octr and arrived at the Hon: Robert Carters, of Nominy, in Westmorland County, the 28th I began to teach his children the first of November. He has two sons, and one Nephew; the oldest Son is turned of seventeen, and is reading Salust and the greek grammer; the others are about fourteen, and in english grammer, and Arithmetic. He has besides five daughters which I am to teach english, the eldest is turned of fifteen, and is reading the spectator; she is employed two days in every week in learning to play the Forte-Piana, and Harpsicord— The others are smaller, and learning to read and spell. Mr Carter is one of the Councellors in the general court at Williamsburg, and possest of as great, perhaps the clearest fortune according to the estimation of people here, of any man in Virginia: He seems to be a good scholar, even in classical learning, and is remarkable one in english grammar; and notwithstanding his rank, which in general seems to countenance indulgence to children, both himself and Mrs Carter have a manner of instructing and dealing with children far superior, I may say it with confidence, to any I have ever seen, in any place, or in any family. They keep them in perfect subjection to themselves, and never pass over an occasion of reproof; and I blush for many of my acquaintances when I say that the children are more kind and complaisant to the servants who constantly attend them than we are to our superiors in age and condition. Mr Carter has an overgrown library of Books of which he allows me the free use. It consists of a general collection of law books, all the Latin and Greek Classicks, vast number of Books on Divinity chiefly by writers who are of established Religion; he has the works of almost all the late famous writers, as Locke, Addison, Young, Pope, Swift, Dryden, &c. in Short, Sir, to speak moderately, he has more than eight times your number—His eldest Son, who seems to be a Boy of genius and application is to be sent to Cambridge University, but I believe will go through a course either in Philadelphia or Princeton College first. As to what is commonly said concerning Virginia that it is difficult to avoid being corrupted with the manners of the people, I believe it is founded wholly in a mistaken notion that persons must, when here frequent all promiscuous assemblies; but this is so far from truth that any one who does practise it, tho' he is accused of no crime, loses at once his character; so that either the manners have been lately charged, or the report is false, for he seems now to be best esteemed and most applauded who attends to his business, whatever it be, with the greatest diligence. I believe the virginians have of late altered their manner very much, for they begin to find that their estates by even small extravagance, decline, and grow involved with debt, this seems to be the spring which induces the People of fortune who are the pattern of all behaviour here, to be frugal, and moderate.

Sunday 12. [December 1773]

Rode to Nominy-Church, parson Smith preached 15 minutes—Advertisement at the Church door dated Sunday Decemr 12th Pork to be sold to-morrow at 20/. per Hundred—dined with us to day Captain Walker. Colonel Richd Lee; & Mr Lanclot Lee. sat after Dinner till Sunset, drank three Bottles of Medaira, two Bowls of Toddy!—

Monday 13. [December]

Mr Carter is preparing for a Voyage in his Schooner, the Hariot, to the Eastern Shore in Maryland, for Oysters: there are of the party, Mr *Carter,* Captain *Walker* Colonel *Richd Lee,* & Mr *Lancelot Lee.* With Sailors to work the vessel—I observe it is a general custom on Sundays here, with Gentlemen to invite one another home to dine, after Church; and to consult about, determine their common business, either before or after Service—It is not the Custom for Gentlemen to go into Church til Service is beginning, when they enter in a Body, in the same manner as they come out; I have known the Clerk to come out and call them in to prayers.—They stay also after the Service is over, usually as long, sometimes longer, than the Parson was preaching—Almost every Lady wears a red Cloak; and when they ride out they tye a white handkerchief over their Head and face, so that when I first came into Virginia, I was distress'd whenever I saw a Lady, for I thought She had the Tooth-Ach!—The People are extremely hospitable, and very polite both of which are most certainly universal Characteristics of the Gentlemen in Virginia—some swear bitterly, but the practise seems to be generally disapproved—I have heard that this Country is notorious for Gaming, however this be, I have not seen a Pack of *Cards,* nor a *Die,* since I left home, nor gaming nor Betting of any kind except at the Richmond-Race. Almost every Gentleman of Condition, keeps a Chariot and *Four*; many drive with six Horses—I observe that all the Merchants & shopkeepers in the Sphere of my acquaintance and I am told it is the Case through the Province, are young Scotch-Men; Several of whom I know, as *Cunningham, Jennings, Hamilton, Blain*;—And it has been the custom heretofore to have all their Tutors, and Schoolmasters from Scotland, tho' they begin to be willing to employ their own Countrymen—Evening Ben Carter and myself had a long dispute on the practice of fighting—He thinks it best for two persons who have any dispute to go out in good-humour & fight manfully, & says they will be sooner and longer friends than to brood and harbour malice—Mr *Carter* is practising this Evening on the *Guittar* He begins with the *Trumpet Minuet.* He has a good Ear for Music; a vastly delicate Taste: and keeps good Instruments, he has here at Home a *Harpsichord, Forte-Piano, Harmonica, Guittar, Violin,* & *German Flutes,* & at Williamsburg, has a good *Organ,* he himself also is indefatigable in the Practice. . . .

Wednesday 15. [December]

Busy in School—To day Dined with us Mrs Turburville, & her Daughter Miss Letty Miss Jenny Corbin, & Mr Blain. We dined at three. The manner here is different from our way of living. . . . In the morning so soon as it is light a Boy knocks at my Door to make a fire; after the Fire is kindled, I rise which now in the winter is commonly by Seven, or a little after, By the time I am drest the Children commonly enter the School-Room, which is under the Room I sleep in; I hear them round one lesson, when the Bell rings for eight o-Clock (for Mr Carter has a large good Bell of up-wards of 60 Lb. which my be heard some miles, & this is always rung at meal Times;) the Children then go out; and at half after eight the Bell rings for Break-fast, we then repair to the Dining-Room; after Breakfast, which is generally about half after nine, we go into School, and sit til twelve, when the Bell rings, & they go out for noon; the dinner-Bell rings commonly about half after two, often at three, but never before two.—After dinner is over, which in common, when we have no Company, is about half after three we go into School, & sit til the Bell rings at five, when they separate til the next morning; I have to myself in the Evening, a neat Chamber, a large Fire, Books, & Candle & my Liberty, either to continue in the school room, in my own Room or to sit over at the great House with Mr & Mrs Carter—We go into Supper commonly about half after eight or at nine & I usually go to Bed between ten and Eleven. Altho the family in which I live, is certainly under as good political Regulations, and every way as suitable & agreeable as I can expect, or even could desire. . . .

Saturday 18. [December]

Rose by Seven, Sent for Mr Carters Barber and was drest for Breakfast—We went in to Breakfast at ten;—. . . There were present of Grown persons Mr & Mrs *Carter,* Mrs *Lee,* & Miss *Jenny Corbin*; young Misses about Eleven: & Seven young Fel-lows, including myself;—After Breakfast, we all retired into the Dancing-Room, & after the Scholars had their Lesson singly round Mr Christian, very politely, re-quested me to step a *Minuet*; I excused myself however, but signified my peculiar pleasure in the Accuracy of their performance—There were several Minuets danced with great ease and propriety; after which the whole company Joined in country-dances, and it was indeed beautiful to admiration, to see such a number of young persons, set off by dress to the best Advantage, moving easily, to the sound of well performed Music, and with perfect regularity, tho' apparently in the utmost Disorder—The Dance continued til two, we dined at half after three—soon after Dinner we repaired to the Dancing-Room again; I observe in the course of the lessons, that Mr Christian is punctual, and rigid in his discipline, so strict indeed that he struck two of the young Misses for a fault in the course of their performance, even in the presence of the Mother of one of them! And be rebuked one of the young Fellows so highly as to tell him he must alter his manner, which he had observed through the Course of the Dance, to be insolent, and wanton, or absent himself from the School—I thought this as sharp reproof, to a young Gentleman of seven-teen, before a large number of Ladies!—When it grew too dark to dance, the young Gentlemen walked over to my Room, we conversed til half after six; Nothing is now to be heard of in conversation, but the *Balls,* the *Fox-hunts,* the fine *entertainments,* and the *good fellowship,* which are to be exhibited at the approaching *Christmas.* . . .

When the candles were lighted we all repaired, for the last time, into the dancing Room; first each couple danced a Minuet; then all joined as before in the country Dances, these continued till half after Seven when Mr Christian retired; and at the proposal of several, (with Mr Carters approbation) we played *Button,* to get Pauns for Redemption; where I could join with them, and indeed it was carried on with sprightliness, and Decency; in the course of redeeming my Pauns, I had several Kisses of the Ladies!—Early in the Evening cam colonel Philip Lee, in a travelling

Chariot from Williamsburg—Half after eight we were rung in to Supper; The room looked luminous and splendid; four very large candles burning on the table where we supp'd, three others in different parts of the Room; a gay, sociable Assembly, & four well instructed waiters!—So soon as we rose from supper, the Company form'd into a semicircle round the fire, & Mr Lee, by the voice of the Company was chosen *Pope,* and Mr Carter, Mr Christian, Mrs *Carter,* Mrs *Lee,* and the rest of the company were appointed Friars, in the Play call'd "break the Popes neck"—Here we had great Diversion in the respective Judgments upon offenders, but we were all dismiss'd by ten, and retired to our several Rooms. . . .

Monday 20. [December]

Rose at half after Seven; the Morning extremely cold—We had in School to Day as visitors Miss Betsy, and Miss Matilda Lee. Mr Carter gave me for his Daughter Nancy to Read, the "Compleat Letter-writer"—Also he put into my hands for the use of the School, "the British-Grammar."

Wednesday 22. [December]

Mr *Cunningham* came last Evening and staid the Night.—There is a Report that he is making suit to Miss *Jenny Corbin.*

To day I finished my Sermon for the Presbitery—I read *Pictete,* The *Spectator, Salust, History of England, English Grammar, Arithmetic,* and the *Magazines* by turns. Miss *Priscilla,* and Miss *Nancy* rode this morning in the Chariot over to Mr *Turburvills*—Bob, every day at twelve o-Clock, is down by the River Side with his Gun after Ducks, Gulls &c.—Ben is on his Horse a Riding, Harry, is either in the Kitchen, or at the Blacksmiths, or Carpenters Shop. They all find places of Rendesvous so soon as the Beell rings, and all seem to choose different Sports!—To day dined with us Mr Cox the Gentleman at whose House I breakfasted the Day after I came first.—Evening Mr Carter spent in playing on the Harmonica; It is the first time I have heard the Instrument. The music is charming! He play'd, Water parted from the Sea!—The Notes are clear and inexpressibly Soft, they swell, and are inexpressibly grand; & either it is because the sounds are new, and therefore please me, or it is the most captivating Instrument I have Ever heard. The sounds very much resemble the human voice, and in my opinion they far exceed even the swelling Organ.

Thursday 23. [December]

Rose at eight—Rains this morning, the weather is also warmer. Mr Carter has sent his son Ben to his head *Overseer,* to take notice and account of the measuring the Crop of Corn—For the Planters now have just gathered in their Summers Crop! . . .

At Dinner Mr & Mrs *Carter* gave their opinion concering what they thought pleasing and agreeable in a person; Mrs Carter said she loved a sociable open, chatty person; that She could not bear Sullenness, and stupidity—Mr Carter, on the other-hand, observed that it is just which Solomon says, that there is a "time for all things under the Sun"; that it discovers great Judgment to laugh in Season, and that, on the whole, he is pleased with Taciturnity—pray which of the two should I suit?— It is a custom with our *Bob* whenever he can coax his *Dog* up stairs, to take him into his Bed, and make him a companion; I was much pleased this morning while he and *Harry* were reading in Course a Chapter in the Bible, that they read in the 27th

Chapter of Deuteronomy the Curses threatened there for Crimes; Bob seldom, perhaps never before, read the verse, at last read that "Cursed be he that lyeth with any manner of Beast, and all the People shall say Amen." I was exceedingly Pleased, yet astonished at the Boy on two accounts.—1st At the end of every verse, befor he came to this, he would pronounce aloud, "Amen." But on Reading this verse he not only omitted the "Amen," but seem'd visibly struck with confusion!—2d And so soon as the Verse was read, to excuse himself, he said at once, Brother *Ben* slept all last winter with his Dog, and learn'd me!—Thus ready are Mankind always to evade Corection!—This Evening, after I had dismiss'd the Children, & was sitting in the School-Room cracking Nuts, none present but Mr *Carter Clerk,* a civil, inoffensive, agreeable young Man, who acts both in the character of a Clerk and Steward, when the Woman who makes my Bed, asked me for the key of my Room, and on seeing the young Man sitting with me, she told him that her Mistress had this afternoon given order that their Allowance of Meat should be given out to them to-morrow.— She left us; I then asked the young man what their allowance is? He told me that excepting some favourites about the table, their weekly allowance is a peck of Corn, & a pound of Meat a Head!—And Mr Carter is allow'd by all, & from what I have already seen of others, I make no Doubt at all but he is, by far the most humane to his Slaves of any in these parts! Good God! are these Christians?—When I am on the Subject, I will relate further, what I heard Mr George Lees Overseer, one Morgan, say the other day that he himself had often done to Negroes, and found it useful; He said that whipping of any kind does them no good, for they will laugh at your greatest Severity; But he told us he had invented two things, and by several experiments had proved their success.—For Sulleness, Obstinacy, or Idleness, says he, Take a Negro, strip him, tie him fast to a post; take then a sharp Curry-Comb, & curry him severely til he is well scrap'd; & call a Boy with some dry Hay, and make the Boy rub him down for several Minutes, then salt him, & unlose him. He will attend to his Business, (said the inhuman Infidel) afterwards!—But savage Cruelty does not exceed His next diabolical Invention—To get a Secret from a Negro, says he, take the following Method—Lay upon your Floor a large thick plank, having a peg about eighteen Inches long, of hard wood, & very Sharp, on the upper end, fixed fast in the plank—then strip the Negro, tie the Cord to a staple in the Ceiling, so as that his foot may just rest on the sharpened Peg, then turn him briskly round, and you would laugh (said our informer) at the Dexterity of the Negro, while he was releiving his Feet on the sharpen'd Peg!—I need say nothing to these seeing there is a righteous God, who will take vengeance on such Inventions! . . .

Fryday 24. [December]

. . . In the Evening I read the two first Books of *pope Homer.* Dr Jones supped with us, & is to stay the Night. The conversation at supper was on Nursing Children; I find it is common here for people of Fortune to have their young Children suckled by the Negroes! Dr Jones told us his first and only Child is now with such a Nurse; & Mrs Carter said that Wenches have suckled several of hers—Mrs Carter has had thirteen Children. She told us to night and she has nine now living; of which seven are with me. Guns are fired this Evening in the Neighbourhood, and the Negroes seem to be inspired with new Life. The Day has been serene and mild, but the Evening is hazy.

Supp'd on Oysters.

Saturday 25. [December]

I was waked this morning by Guns fired all round the House. The morning is stormy, the wind at South East rains hard Nelson the Boy who makes my Fire, blacks my shoes, does errands &c. was early in my Room, drest only in his shirt and Breeches! He made me a vast fire, blacked my Shoes, set my Room in order, and wish'd me a joyful Christmas, for which I gave him half a Bit.—Soon after he left the Room, and before I was Drest, the Fellow who makes the Fire in our School Room, drest very neatly in green, but almost drunk, entered my chamber with three or four profound Bows, & made me the same salutation; I gave him a *Bit,* and dismissed him as soon as possible.—Soon after my Cloths and Linen were sent in with a message for a Christmas *Box,* as they call it; I sent the poor Slave a Bit, & my thanks.—I was obliged for want of small change, to put off for some days the Barber who shaves & dresses me.—I gave *Tom* the Coachman, who Doctors my Horse, for his care two Bits, & am to give more when the Horse is well.—I gave to *Dennis* the Boy who waits at Table half a *Bit*—So that the sum of my Donations of the Servants, for this Christmas appears to be five Bits, a Bit is a pisterene bisected; or an English six-pence, & passes here for seven pence Halfpenny. the whole is *3S..1½ D.—*

At Breakfast, when Mr Carter entered the Room, he gave us the compliments of the Season. He told me, very civilly, that as my Horse was Lame, his own riding Horse is at my Service to ride when & where I Choose.

Mrs Carter was, as always, cheerful, chatty, & agreeable; She told me after Breakfast several droll, merry Occurrences that happened while she was in the City Williamsburg.—

This morning came from the Post-office at Hobbes-Hole, on the Rappahan-nock, our News-papers. Mrs Carter takes the Pennsylvania Gazette, which seems vastly agreeable to me, for it is like having something from home—But I have yet no answer to my Letter. We dined at four o-Clock—Mr Carter kept in his Room, be-cause he breakfasted late, and on Oysters—There were at Table Mrs Carter & her five Daughters that are at School with me—Miss *Priscilla, Nancy, Fanny, Betsy,* and *Harriot,* five as beautiful delicate, well-instructed Children as I have ever known!— *Ben* is abroad; *Bob & Harry* are out; so there was no Man at Table but myself.—I must carve—Drink the Health—and talk if I can! Our Dinner was no otherwise than common, yet as elegant a *Christmas Dinner* as I ever sat Down to—The table Dis-course was Marriage; Mrs *Carter* observ'd that was she a Widow, she should scruple to marry any man alive; She gave a reason, that She did not think it probable a man could love her grown old when the world is thronged with blooming, ripening Vir-gins; but in fact Mrs Carter looks & would pass for a younger Woman than some un-married Ladies of my acquaintance, who would willingly enough make us place them below twenty!—We dined at four; when we rose from table it was growing dark—The wind continues at South East & is stormy and muddy.

Mr *Randolph* the Clerk told me this Evening a Circumstance concerning *Bob* which tho it discovered stupidity, yet at the same time discovered great thoughtfulness.—It was about his sleeping with the *Dog;* Mr *Randolph* told me *Bob* asked him with great solemnity if he thought *God Almighty* knew it!—While we supped Mr *Carter* as he often does played on the *Forte-Piano.* He almost never sups. Last Night and to night I had large clear, & very elegant Spermaceti Candles sent into my Room;

Sunday 26. [December]

I rose at eight—The morning is fair; all seem quite—I went to the window before I was drest, having only a Gown thrown about me & enjoy'd a beautiful Prospect of the high Banks of the River Nomini gilded by the morning Sun—I could not help casting my Eyes with eagerness over the blue Potowmack and look homewards.— After having paid my morning secret Devotion to the King of Kings, I sat myself to the correcting and transcribing my Sermon—I had the pleasure to wait on Mrs *Carter* to Church. She rode in the Chariot, & Miss Prissy and Nancy; Mr Carter chose to stay at Home—The Sacrament was to have been administred but there was so few people that he thought it improper, and put of til Sunday fortnight. He preach'd from Isaiah 9.6. For unto us a child is Born &c. his Sermon was fifteen Minutes long! very fashionable—He invited me very civilly to Dine & spend the Evening with him, but I could not leave the Ladies! He made me almost promise, however to call some Day this Week.

E S S A Y S

Jack P. Greene of the Johns Hopkins University, one of the most eminent contemporary scholars of colonial America, is the author of many works, among them *Pursuits of Happiness* (1988) and *The Intellectual Construction of America* (1993). His essay, "The Preconditions of the American Revolution" excerpted here, identifies chronic tensions in the imperial system that lay beneath the surface of order and harmony prior to 1763. Richard R. Beeman, a professor at the University of Pennsylvania, has long studied society and politics in the southern backcountry of the 18th century. His essay "The Emergence of Popular Politics," offers a perspective on colonial affairs rooted in local rather than imperial experience.

The Preconditions of the American Revolution

JACK P. GREENE

I

To a question about "the temper of America towards Great-Britain before the year 1763," Benjamin Franklin, in his famous "examination" before the House of Commons during the debates over the repeal of the Stamp Act in early 1766, replied that it was the "best in the world." The colonies, he said,

> submitted willingly to the government of the Crown, and paid, in all their courts, obedience to acts of parliament. Numerous as the people are in the several old provinces, they cost you nothing in forts, citadels, garrisons or armies, to keep them in subjection. They were governed by this country at the expense only of a little pen, ink, and paper. They were led by a thread. They had not only a respect, but an affection, for Great Britain, for its laws, its customs and manners, and even a fondness for its fashions, that

greatly increased the commerce. Natives of Britain were always treated with particular regard; to be an Old-England man was, of itself, a character of some respect, and gave a kind of rank among us.

That Franklin was correct in this assessment was widely seconded by his contemporaries and has been the . . . judgment of the most sophisticated students of the problem. . . .

So persuaded have modern historians been that the relationship between Britain and the colonies prior to the Stamp Act crisis was basically satisfactory to both parties that they have . . . organized their continuing search for an adequate explanation of the American Revolution around a single, overriding question: why in less than a dozen years after 1763 the colonists became so estranged from Britain as to take up arms against her and, a little more than a year later, to declare for independence. The focus of their inquiries has thus been primarily upon the colonial response to the pre-Revolutionary controversy and upon the many medium-range issues and conditions that contributed to the creation of a revolutionary situation in the colonies between 1764 and 1774 and the short-run developments that touched off armed conflict in 1775 and led to the colonial decision to seek independence in 1776.

A result of this preoccupation with the immediate origins of the Revolution has been the neglect of two other, interrelated questions also raised by Franklin's remarks: first, whether the relationship between Britain and the colonies actually was so satisfactory prior to 1763, and, second, if the existing imperial system worked as well for Britain as Franklin contended, why the British government would ever undertake—much less persist in—measures that would . . . impair such a . . . beneficial arrangement. . . . Neither of these questions is new. They were widely canvassed . . . on both sides of the Atlantic in the 1760s and 1770s, and they provided a focus for most of the early students of the causes of the Revolution. . . . But no recent historian has dealt with both of these questions systematically. . . . This essay seeks . . . to provide a comprehensive discussion of the preconditions—the long-term, underlying causes—of the Revolution. . . .

II

When one looks closely at the relationship between Britain and the colonies during the century from 1660 to 1760, one discovers . . . that it was in many respects an uneasy connection . . . through the middle decades of the eighteenth century as a result of several important structural changes taking place in both the colonies and Britain. Throughout these decades, contemporaries on both sides of the Atlantic conventionally described the imperial-colonial relationship in terms of the familiar parent-child metaphor with Britain as the mother country and the colonies as its infant offspring. The clear implication of this usage was, of course, that the colonies had by no means yet reached a state of competency. . . . However, by the middle of the eighteenth century in most of the colonies, the colonists themselves were already handling a substantial portion of their internal affairs with an impressive . . . efficiency: to an extraordinary degree, the several colonies had become . . . "pockets of approximate independence" within the transatlantic imperial polity. In all save the newest colonies of Georgia and Nova Scotia, they possessed by 1750 virtually all of the conditions necessary for self-governing states.

The first of these conditions was the emergence of stable, coherent, effective, and acknowledged local political and social elites. . . . By the middle of the century, there existed in virtually every colony authoritative ruling groups with great social and economic power, extensive political experience, confidence in their capacity to govern, and broad public support. Indeed, the direction of colonial political life throughout the middle of the eighteenth century was probably toward more and more public deference to these ruling elites; certainly, their willingness to mobilize various groups of marginal members of political society in the protests against the Stamp Act as well as at later stages of the pre-Revolutionary conflict strongly suggests not a fear of such groups but a confidence in their ability to control them. . . .

A second and complementary condition was the development of . . . centers and institutions in which authority was concentrated and from which it was dispersed outward through a settled network of local urban administrative centers and institutions to the outermost perimeters of colonial society. Whether merely small administrative centers such as Annapolis or Williamsburg or large, central trading places such as Philadelphia, Boston, New York, and Charleston, the colonial capitals supplied the colonists with internal foci to which they customarily looked for political leadership and models for social behavior.

Perhaps even more important was the emergence of a set of viable governing institutions . . . in the towns and the counties and, especially significant, at the colony level in the form of the elected lower houses of assembly. More than any other political institution . . . the lower houses were endowed with charismatic authority both because, as the representatives of the colonists, they were thought to hold in trusteeship all of the sacred rights and privileges of the public and to be the sole giver of internal public law and because of their presumed—and actively cultivated—equivalence to the British Parliament, that emporium of British freedom and embodiment of all that was most sacred to Englishmen everywhere. As powerful, independent, self-confident institutions . . . the lower houses were potentially effective mechanisms for crystallizing and expressing grievances against Great Britain. Together with the elites who spoke through them, the local centers and institutions, particularly the lower houses, . . . provided authoritative symbols for the colony at large and thereby served as a preexisting local alternative to imperial authority.

A third and closely related condition was the development of remarkably elastic political systems. . . . First, they were inclusivist rather than exclusivist. For analytic purposes, one may divide the potential participants in the political process, that is, the free adult male population, into three categories: the elite, including both colony-wide and local officeholders; a broader "politically relevant strata or mobilized population" that participated with some regularity in the political process; and a passive or underlying population that took little part in the political system, in some cases because they were legally excluded by racial or property qualifications and in others because they had no interest in doing so. . . . The first two groups were relatively large and the third group relatively small. The elite seems . . . to have taken in as much as 3 percent to 5 percent of the free adult males, while the second category may have included as many as 60 percent to 90 percent of the same group. This wide diffusion of offices and extensive participation in the political process meant that colonial Americans—leaders and followers alike—had very wide training in politics and self-government and were thoroughly socialized to a . . . tested political system.

A second sense in which the political systems of the colonies were elastic was in their capacity to permit the resolution of internal conflict. Indeed, they were early forced to develop that capacity. The expansive character of American life prevented any group from obtaining a long-standing monopoly of political power, economic opportunity, or social status; new groups were constantly springing up demanding parity with the old. . . . The capacity of the political systems of the colonies to absorb new and diverse groups was steadily expanding during the middle of the century as a result of severe pressures created by a combination of rapid demographic and economic growth and increasing social, cultural, and religious diversity.

The rising competence of the colonies in nonpolitical or semipolitical spheres during the eighteenth century was a fourth condition that had prepared them for self-government. This competence was made possible by the dramatic enlargement of internal and external trade, travel, and migration; the increasing availability of knowledge through a broad spectrum of educational, cultural, social, economic, and religious institutions and through a rising number of books, magazines, and newspapers of colonial, British, and European origin accessible to the colonists; the development of more efficient means and networks of communication within and among the colonies and between the colonies and Great Britain; and the emergence of relatively large numbers of men with the technical skills, especially in law, trade, and finance, requisite for the successful functioning of an autonomous society. These developments not only provided the colonists with some of the technical wherewithal—for example, lawyers and newspapers—that turned out to be of crucial importance in resisting Britain and creating a new nation; they also helped to free the colonies from total dependence upon Britain for certain kinds of essential skills, to raise levels of literacy and education within the colonies, to liberate them from their former isolation and rusticity, to widen their "range of perception and imagination," and to create a potential for cooperation, for overcoming the "inherent localism" and traditional disunity they had stubbornly . . . manifested. . . .

A fifth and final condition was the tremendous increase in the size and wealth of the colonies in terms of the number of people, the amount of productive land, labor, and skills, and the extent of settled territory. The wealth of the colonies had become sufficient to give them a potential for economic and military resistance, while the sheer vastness of all of the continental colonies, taken together, constituted a formidable obstacle to suppressing any large-scale or broadly diffused movement of resistance. Indeed, this condition may well have been the most important of all, because it is the only one of the five not shared to a large degree by the British West Indian colonies, which did not revolt.

It is thus clear in retrospect that the colonies had achieved a high degree of competency by the 1750s and 1760s. . . . By 1760 the colonies were thus not only able to meet most of the objective conditions necessary for self-government but even had to a significant degree been governing themselves, maintaining internal civil order, prospering, and building an ever more complex and closely integrated society for at least three-quarters of a century and in some cases much longer. Equally important, such a large measure of de facto autonomy at every level and in all sectors of colonial society—with all of the responsibilities it required—had prepared them psychologically for self-government and independence.

The corollary of this impressive increase in colonial competency was the continued weakness of British power in the colonies. The bureaucratic structures organized, for the most part during the Restoration, to . . . control . . . the colonies had never been adequate. . . . There was no central governing agency within Britain with effective authority to deal quickly and efficiently with colonial matters until 1768, on the very eve of the Revolution. The Board of Trade, which had primary responsibility for the colonies after 1696, had only advisory powers, and its history is essentially one of failure to obtain the ministerial and parliamentary support necessary for its many and repeated attempts to establish a more elaborate and effective system of colonial administration. . . .

The counterpoint of this continuing weakness of British power in the colonies was the dramatic increase in the importance of the colonies to Britain's economy during the first seven decades of the eighteenth century. The population of the continental colonies soared from 257,060 in 1700 to 635,083 in 1730 and 1,593,625 in 1760. . . . As the population increased, the colonies not only supplied Britain at extremely favorable rates with a growing variety of raw materials, many of which were subsequently reexported at a considerable profit to British middlemen, but also provided a growing stimulus to British manufacturers by taking an ever-rising amount of British finished products. Indeed, during the eighteenth century, the colonial trade became "the most rapidly growing section"—and accounted for a significant proportion of the total volume—of British overseas trade. Imports from the colonies (including the West Indies) accounted for 20 percent of the total volume of English imports in 1700–1701 and 36 percent in 1772–1773, while exports to the colonies rose from 10 percent of the total volume of English exports during the former year to 37 percent during the latter. . . . The colonial trade thus constituted a large and critical segment of the British economy and was becoming more important every decade. . . . To a considerable degree, the growing awareness of how much the economic well-being of Britain actually did depend upon the colonies . . . accounts for Parliament's willingness to contribute substantial sums toward the expenses of settling Georgia beginning in the 1730s and Nova Scotia starting in 1749 and to make such enormous outlays of money and men in defense of them during the Seven Years' War. Such profitable possessions could never be permitted to fall into the hands of Britain's Continental rivals.

III

In itself, no one of these structural features—not the growing competence of the colonies, the continued weakness of British power in the colonies, or the increasing importance of the colonies to Britain's economy—was productive of sufficient strain to make the possibility of revolution very great; in combination, however, they contributed to the development of two fundamental discrepancies within the imperial-colonial relationship, discrepancies that made the potential for dysfunction within the empire extremely high. The first was the obvious discrepancy between theory and fact, between what imperial authorities thought the colonies should be and what they actually were. The increasing competency of the colonies during the eighteenth century obviously called for some adjustment in imperial behavior and attitudes towards the colonies, and such an adjustment appeared to have been made during the long ministry of Sir Robert Walpole from 1721 to 1742. Under Walpole, an informal accommodation between imperial authorities and the colonies had been achieved that permitted the colonies a generous amount of de facto self-government and economic freedom. . . .

A far more compelling foundation for [the British political nation's] illusion [that imperial authorities continued to hold control over the colonies] was the over-powering conviction . . . of the inherent superiority of Britain, of its political institutions and its culture. . . . Following the Glorious Revolution, it was widely believed within the British political nation that the British constitution as it had been restored by the Revolutionary Settlement represented the ultimate political achievement of all time, permitting the enjoyment of so many liberties and at the same time preserving a high degree of political order. . . .

Nor were Britain's superiority and glory limited to the political realm. The prose and poetry of Addison, Defoe, Gay, Pope, Steele, Swift, and a host of lesser writers during the first half of the eighteenth century were widely heralded as evidence that Britain had achieved its "Augustan Age" in literature. And, despite a number of temporary setbacks, the economic picture, especially as measured by a rising volume of foreign trade and a quickening pace in domestic economic activity, seemed to be especially bright, so bright, in fact, that it was thought in Britain and feared on the Continent that Britain would eventually outstrip all of its traditional Continental rivals in wealth and power. . . .

In the face of such achievements, . . . who could doubt that Britain was in every respect superior to its colonies overseas? . . . As imperial usage of the parent-child metaphor so clearly revealed, the colonies were by definition thought to be subordinate and dependent, bound by their position within the imperial family order to yield obedience to their mother country and unable, like children, either to control their own passions—were they not forever squabbling among themselves?—or to protect themselves from external aggression. . . . Acknowledgment of colonial competency on the part of British authorities was virtually impossible, for competency carried with it the hint of an equivalence between the colonies and Britain. In view of . . . British convictions of superiority, such a hint would have been a . . . violation of the national self-image.

The second discrepancy within the imperial-colonial relationship was between two divergent conceptions of what the relationship actually was. This discrepancy may be discussed in terms of a question raised by much of the previous discussion: if British coercive power over the colonies was so weak and colonial competence so high, what was it that continued to bind the colonies to Britain? Part of the answer, as we have already suggested, is to be found in the very real utilitarian benefits they derived from the connection. . . . [T]he colonies had prospered during the first half of the eighteenth century and had a strong vested interest in maintaining their economic ties with Britain. Far more important than these utilitarian benefits, however, were, as Franklin underscored in his *Examination,* the vital and deeply rooted customary bonds of allegiance and affection that tied the colonies very tightly to their parent state, ties whose strength had increased enormously through the middle decades of the eighteenth century as a result of the growing involvement of the colonies with Britain, the emergence of colonial elites intent upon reproducing in the colonies a society that resembled that of Britain as closely as possible, and the increasing Anglicization of colonial life in both form and substance. . . .

Britain also served the colonies as a source of pride and self-esteem as well as of moral authority. To have a share, if often largely only a peripheral share, in the achievements of Britain during the eighteenth century . . . was an exhilarating experience that operated to heighten British patriotism in the colonies and to strengthen still further the psychological bonds between them and Britain. . . .

But . . . strong as it was, the colonial attachment to Britain . . . was conditional. If it was true, as John Dickinson later remarked, that the "Dependence" of the colonists could not "be retained but by preserving their affections," it was also true, as he so strongly emphasized, that "their affections" could not "be preserved, but by treating them in such a manner, as they think consistent with Freedom and Justice." If to British authorities the parent-child metaphor meant that the colonies were to be dependent and subordinate, to the colonists it meant that Britain was to be nurturant and protective. . . . They expected Britain to provide a favorable political and economic climate in which they could pursue with a minimum amount of anxiety their own, specifically colonial and individual, ends, while it also continued to provide a praiseworthy example by which they could measure their own achievements. . . .

But the voluntary attachment of the colonies to Britain depended upon something far more fundamental than the careful observation by British authorities of these traditional imperatives: it depended as well upon their willingness not to violate a basic substructure of expectations among the colonists that those imperatives were thought to protect. . . . The most obvious and explicit element in this substructure of expectations was that the imperial government would not . . . violate the sanctity of the elected lower houses of assembly and other institutions and symbols of self-government in each colony, institutions and symbols that, as we remarked earlier, had come to assume such extensive authority within the colonies that they, rather than Parliament, had . . . come to be regarded by the colonists as the . . . primary guardians of their rights and property.

A second . . . component of this substructure of . . . assumptions was the expectation that the imperial government would place as few impediments as possible in the way of the colonists' free pursuit of their own social and economic interests. . . . What the actions of the colonists seemed to assume, in fact, is that political society was a human device not only . . . for the maintenance of orderly relations among the men who composed it . . . but also . . . for the protection of the individual's property in his land, goods, and person, in which one's property in person included the right . . . of pursuing . . . one's interests, of seeking to alter one's place on the scale of economic well-being, social status, or political power. . . .

A third, related . . . component of this . . . structure of expectations was the assumption that the imperial government would not interfere with the capacity of the colonists as individuals to maintain their personal autonomy. . . . The implicit expectation of the colonists was thus that the British government would continue to provide a stable external background that would not call into question their accustomed autonomy, their ability—so crucial to their self-esteem and their continuing capacity to function as successful individuals in colonial society—to act in accordance with the mandates of virtue and independence. . . .

The voluntary attachment of the colonists to Britain thus depended . . . upon . . . assumptions that it was the moral obligation of the *mother* country to provide nurturance and protection for the colonies. What nurturance and protection had come to mean for the colonists . . . were: first, that the imperial government would not undermine . . . the colonists' self-esteem as defined by their capacity as individuals to act . . . with a high degree of autonomy . . . in the colonial environment; second, that it would interfere as little as possible with their ability to pursue whatever . . . activity seemed to them to be in their best interests; third, that it would respect the sanctity of the local self-governing institutions on which they depended for the . . . protection of the property, in person as well as in goods, they had acquired; . . . and, fourth, that in its dealings with the colonies it would continue to manifest respect for all of those central imperatives of Anglo-American political culture that were thought by Englishmen everywhere to be essential for the preservation of liberty and property.

This cluster of . . . expectations on the part of the colonists suggested a conception of the imperial-colonial connection that was fundamentally different from that held by imperial authorities. The divergency is most clearly revealed in the different meanings attached to the parent-child metaphor in Britain and in the colonies, in the explicit British emphasis upon the disciplinary implications of the metaphor and the colonial stress upon the nurturant and facilitative. The British emphasis implied a relationship of perpetual dependency of the colonies upon the mother country, while the colonial suggested an eventual equivalence. . . .

The existence of these two related and overlapping discrepancies, the one between imperial theory and colonial reality and the other between imperial and colonial ideas about the nature of the imperial-colonial connection, . . . gave the British Empire a latent potential for revolution through the middle decades of the eighteenth century. I say *latent* potential because these discrepancies had first to be clearly defined and their implications fully explored before they could actually . . . cause the disruption . . . of the empire. So long as they were only dimly perceived and not explicitly confronted, these discrepancies actually functioned as an essential . . . component of stability with the empire, because they permitted the colonists to exercise a considerable amount of autonomy without requiring imperial officials explicitly to abandon their traditional notions about the character of the empire. So long as the imperial government did not attempt to remove these discrepancies by enforcing those notions or acting in a sustained or systematic way upon them, the potential for any large-scale revolt by the colonies was not extremely high. . . .

Given the potential for dysfunction produced by these two discrepancies in the imperial-colonial relationship, there was a strong possibility that some serious . . . transgression of the existing moral order as it was conceived by one party or the other would shatter it beyond repair. But . . . such a transgression was necessary before any of the preconditions we have been describing could become causes of revolution or imperial disintegration. Some structural conditions had pointed the colonists toward equivalence and independence and, in doing so, had undermined the traditional bonds between Britain and the colonies and made the relationship . . . fragile. But these preconditions did no more than make the creation of a dysfunctional situation possible. Whether . . . such a situation would be created would be determined by other kinds of intervening causes.

IV

What began the process by which the old British Empire acquired . . . a marked susceptibility to disintegration or revolution, what, in fact, was the salient precondition of the American Revolution, was the decision by colonial authorities in Britain to abandon Walpole's policy of accommodation and to attempt to bring the colonies under much more rigid controls. This decision was taken, not abruptly in 1763, . . . but gradually in the decade beginning in 1748. Neither this general decision nor the many specific policy decisions of which it was composed constituted any sharp ideological break with the past. On the contrary, they merely represented another attempt to implement the traditional goals of English colonial policy . . . in accord with the guiding assumptions behind the British conception of the meaning of the parent-child metaphor. But the situation differed markedly from the one that had obtained during the Restoration or in the decades immediately following the Glorious Revolution, the two periods during which similarly systematic attempts had been made. The differences arose out of the conjoint facts that the colonies were infinitely more competent and correspondingly less dependent upon Britain . . . and that the attempt followed a long period of over a quarter of a century during which the imperial government appeared to have abandoned most of the goals it suddenly once again seemed bent upon achieving. . . .

If the rapid growth of the colonies with the consequent increase in their value to Britain was the single most important precondition behind the shift in British policy beginning in the late 1740s, there were two short-run conditions that, in combination, accounted for its timing. The first was the end of the era of internal domestic political instability in Britain that had begun in 1739 and was intensified by the vigorous competition for power through the mid-1740s following the fall of Sir Robert Walpole in 1742. . . .

An even more important short-run condition that helped to determine the timing of this shift in policy and that itself contributed to intensify the . . . heightened sense of urgency that lay behind it was the simultaneous eruption of . . . severe political and social disturbances in many of the colonies. During the late 1740s and early 1750s, there were so many problems . . . in so many colonies that the empire seemed to authorities . . . in London to be on the verge of disintegration. Violent factional disputes had thrown New Jersey into civil war, put an end to all legislative activity in New Hampshire and North Carolina, and seriously weakened the position of the royal administration in Jamaica, Bermuda, and New York. From New York, South Carolina, New Jersey, Bermuda, Jamaica, North Carolina, and New Hampshire— from all of the royal colonies except Massachusetts, Virginia, Barbados, and the Leeward Islands—governors complained that they were powerless to carry out imperial directions against the opposition of local interests and the exorbitant power of the local lower houses of assembly. From Bermuda there came reports that the status of the king's governor had sunk so low that one member of the assembly had even offered a reward for his assassination. So desperate was the situation throughout all the colonies that it became exceedingly difficult for imperial authorities to maintain their illusion of control over them. . . .

Under the guidance of Halifax, who continued in office until 1761, the Board of Trade systematically set about the task of shoring up imperial authority in the colonies. It presided over a major effort to strengthen the defenses of the British colonies against French Canada by turning Nova Scotia, hitherto only a nominal British colony inhabited almost entirely by neutral and even hostile French, into a full-fledged British colony. Much more important, it prepared a series of long reports on the difficulties in most of the major trouble spots in the colonies, and the recommendations in these reports clearly revealed that, despite the long era of accommodation and easy administration since the advent of Walpole, the members of the Board and other colonial officials had not altered their long-standing conceptions about the proper relationship between the mother country and the colonies and that they were intent upon enforcing the traditional, but hitherto largely unachieved, goals of British colonial policy. Except for the Nova Scotia enterprise, which received strong backing from the administration and large sums of money from Parliament, none of the Board's recommendations received the necessary support from the administration, though colonial affairs did receive far more attention from the Privy Council and administration than they had in the past few decades. However desperate the situation in the colonies might appear to those best informed about it, existing procedures were too cumbersome and the preoccupation with domestic matters too great to permit effective action on most colonial problems. In part to remedy this situation, Halifax pushed very hard to have himself appointed a separate secretary of state with broad jurisdiction and full responsibility for the colonies. Although he failed in this effort . . . he did succeed in securing enlarged powers for the Board of Trade in April 1752. . . .

Although the Board of Trade's programs were greeted in many places with enthusiasm by royal officeholders and others who had long been alarmed by the imbalance of the colonial constitutions in favor of the representative assemblies, they were, in general, adamantly opposed by the lower houses and other powerful local interest groups, whose members considered them a violation of the traditional relationship between mother country and colonies . . . and, in many instances, an attack upon the established constitutions of the colonies. Even with its enlarged authority and its new assertiveness, the Board could not effectively meet such opposition. The Board could and did intimidate the governors into a strict observance of their instructions, but that only reduced their room for maneuver when they needed all the latitude possible to accomplish the impossible tasks assigned to them. Thus, the Board succeeded in its objectives only in New Hampshire, where Gov. Benning Wentworth had put together a powerful political combination that monopolized all political power and stifled opposition, and in the new civil governments in Nova Scotia and Georgia, where the Board took extraordinary pains "to check all Irregularities and unnecessary Deviations from the Constitution of the Mother Country in their Infancy." By the time the outbreak of the Seven Years' War forced it to suspend its reform activities in 1756, the Board had realized that its general campaign was a failure. . . .

Collectively, the efforts of Halifax and his colleagues between 1748 and 1756 represented a major reversal in the tone and quality of imperial behavior toward the colonies. . . . It amounted to a shift on the part of imperial authorities from a posture . . . that was essentially permissive to one that was basically restrictive . . . [and dependent] upon coercion. These years witnessed . . . the attempted imposition of a whole series of . . . policies that . . . threatened . . . the . . . structure of colonial expectations about the nature of the imperial-colonial relationship and the proper modes of imperial behavior. . . . The vast majority of those policies that colonials found so objectionable between 1759 and 1776 were, in fact, either worked out or proposed in one form or another during these years, and attempts were actually made to implement many of them. . . .

In terms of the causal significance of this change in . . . policy for the American Revolution, the fact that it yielded only minimal results is . . . as important as the fact that it was undertaken in the first place and much more important than the isolated and transitory pockets of discontent it created among the colonists. For the abject failure of most of . . . this early effort at reform served both to heighten imperial fears that the colonies would sooner or later get completely out of hand and to increase—almost to the point of obsession—imperial determination to secure tighter control over the colonies and to channel the colonists' expansive energies into forms . . . more acceptable to Britain. . . .

Although the Seven Years' War forced the temporary abandonment of the reform program, the war experience only intensified the impulses that had lain behind it, as the weakness of British authority over the colonies was more fully exposed than ever before. Throughout the war, aggressive lower houses openly used the government's need for defense funds to pry still more authority away from the governors; many colonial traders flagrantly violated the navigation acts, in many cases with the implicit connivance of the colonial governments and even of imperial customs officials; and many of the colonial legislatures failed to comply with imperial requisitions for men and money for the war effort—even with the promise of reimbursement by Parliament. The war experience thus reinforced . . . imperial fears of loss of control over and potential rivalry from the colonies, deepened their suspicions that the colonists harbored secret desires for independence, and intensified their determination for reform. As soon as the British and colonial armies had defeated the French in Canada in 1759 and 1760 and colonial support for the war effort was no longer vital, imperial authorities . . . undertook a variety of new restrictive measures to bolster imperial authority over the colonies. . . . The new measures of 1759 to 1764 were merely a renewal and an extension of the earlier reform program.

But they were an extension within a significantly different—and far more fragile—context. The war had been a liberating and (psychologically) reinforcing experience for the colonists. That so much of the war was fought on American soil and that the British government made such an enormous effort to defend the colonies contributed to an expanded sense of colonial self-importance. Moreover, . . . the war . . . produced a surge of British patriotism among the colonists and . . . created among them heightened expectations for a larger role within the empire, a role that would raise the status of the colonies . . . to . . . a near equivalence with the mother country. By contrast, the war left many members of the British political nation with feelings of bitterness and resentment towards the colonists and a determination to restore them to a proper state of dependence. Having incurred an enormous debt and a heavy tax burden in defense of the colonies and having had exaggerated reports of American opulence and the low level of taxation in the colonies, they regarded colonial failures to comply with royal requisitions and . . . violations of imperial regulations as evidences of extreme ingratitude that could not go unremarked, lest such excessive behavior rob Britain of the large investment it had made in protecting and securing the colonies.

If the experience of the war caused the expectations of men on opposite sides of the Atlantic about the relationship between Britain and the colonies in the postwar world to veer off in such different directions, the war itself altered the very structure of that relationship. . . . The expulsion of the French and Spanish from eastern North America removed the need for the last absolutely essential nurturing element the British had to offer the mainland colonies—protection against the French and Spanish—and thereby presumably removed a major . . . remaining block that had helped to keep whatever fantasies the colonists may have had about equivalence and independence in an unconscious and unarticulated state. . . . More important, . . . by destroying their rivals and thus making it less necessary to pacify the colonies, the British victory left imperial authorities with a much freer hand to go ahead with their program of colonial reform. Moreover, for the first time during and after the war, the British had significant coercive resources in the colonies in the form of a large number of royal troops. By giving them an excessive confidence in their ability to suppress potential colonial opposition, the presence of these troops may well have made imperial officials less cautious in dealing with the colonies than they had been a decade earlier.

In combination, the psychological consequences and structural changes produced by the war made the relationship between Britain and the colonies much more volatile. . . . The colonists now had heightened expectations about their position in the empire and less need for Britain's protection, while British officials were bitter about colonial behavior during the war, more determined than ever to bring the colonies under closer control, persuaded that they would have to use the authority of Parliament to do so, and possessed of an army to back them up if it should be needed. Given this set of . . . conditions, it was highly predictable that British officials in the 1760s would take some action, probably even by bringing parliamentary authority to bear upon the colonies in new, unaccustomed, and hence, for the colonists, illegitimate ways, that could be interpreted . . . as a fundamental violation of the existing relationship between them and Great Britain. . . .

VI

The assumption behind this essay has been that any satisfactory analysis of the causes of the American Revolution has to consider not only the nature and content of colonial opposition to Britain after 1763 but also the long-term conditions that made the imperial-colonial relationship, however satisfactory it may have seemed on the surface, so fragile; and we must also consider when and why British authorities altered their traditional posture towards the colonies. What I have tried to suggest is that the change in posture began in the late 1740s and that the explanation for it is to be found primarily in the dramatic rise of the economic importance of the colonies to Britain and the attendant fears within the British political nation that the colonies would shake off their dependence and leave Britain to sink slowly back into its former undifferentiated state among the nations of western Europe. Fed by developments in the 1750s and 1760s, these fears underlay British behavior throughout the years of controversy from 1763 to 1776. Ironically, . . . the measures taken by imperial authorities to prevent these fears from coming true helped to bring about the very thing they most wished to prevent.

The Emergence of Popular Politics

RICHARD R. BEEMAN

The eighteenth-century poet James Thomson, in a panegyric to England's glory, identified the three essential virtues in the classical republican prescription for public liberty: "independent life; / Integrity in office; and o'er all / Supreme, a passion for the commonweal." . . . For virtually all the political leaders of mid-eighteenth-century America—from Pinckneys in South Carolina to Randolphs in Virginia To Adamses and Hutchinsons in Massachusetts—the message was the same: the difference between rightful, virtuous rulers and unworthy parvenus was the ability to subordinate private interest to the common good.

United in venerating the ideal, Americans faced the problem of how best to identify and certify men who had a rightful claim to the public trust. Although the mechanisms for selecting public officials were shifting from hereditary right to some form of popular election, the personal criteria deemed necessary—property, education, lineage—were more resistant to change. Persistence of traditional attitudes toward political authority was reflected, we are told, in a "deferential" ethic, a belief among the ordinary citizens of colonial America that they were obliged to exhibit, in John Adams's formulation, "a Decency, and Respect, and Veneration . . . for Persons in Authority."

This emphasis on disinterested public service was useful not only to suppress unacceptable forms of private interest but also, and more subtly, to advance the interests of wealthy and well-born men whose access to political power was facilitated by an ideology that preached the deference of the many to the virtuous few. That the promotion of a deferential ethic could be self-serving is not in itself proof that those who invoked it were anything but sincere in their attachment to the ideal of public virtue. There is ample evidence that the rhetorical power of classical republican ideology was on at least some occasions sufficient to command appropriate behavior on the part of both the few who claimed political authority and the many who submitted to that authority. Yet our full comprehension of eighteenth-century American life requires that we do not too readily assume a correspondence between political rhetoric and reality but look closely at the relationship between the two. . . .

This essay seeks to comprehend the connections between rhetoric and reality in eighteenth-century politics and to chart the changing relationship between political leaders and ordinary citizens whose interests were becoming recognized as a necessary and legitimate part of the public good. That relationship was not everywhere the

Richard R. Beeman, "The Emergence of Popular Politics." Reprinted by permission of *William and Mary Quarterly.*

same; the polities of the colonies displayed a remarkable diversity of styles and structures. The dominant trend, however, was unmistakable; increasingly, politics was marked by open and aggressive protection, promotion, and mobilization of interests. However eloquent or impassioned the republican language accompanying those interests, American politics was moving toward a very different future. . . .

The Discovery of Deference

Electoral practices in the colonies ranged from coercive, as on some New York manors, to occasionally polite and genteel modes, in Virginia, to aggressive and popular, as in southeastern Pennsylvania and Rhode Island. The direction in which the politics of all of the colonies was moving was a popular one, but the dominant condition was neither democracy nor aristocracy nor oligarchy nor deference but diversity. The colonies, on the eve of the Revolution, lacked a common political culture; the rules of politics—of electoral politics in particular—varied widely not only from one locality to another but also among groups within the same locality. Indeed, so great were the differences that Americans found themselves without a common language capable of describing and comprehending their political behavior. To be sure, they often drew from the rhetorical stockpile of classical republicanism, but the meanings they attached to some of the most oft-used words in the republican lexicon—words such as "interest," "influence," "representation," and "virtue"—varied enormously. Republican language, employed in selective and often contradictory ways in America's diverse and fragmented political cultures, indicated more confusion than cohesion.

The discussion that follows illustrates some of the confusion that Americans—both the many and the few—were experiencing as they engaged in electoral politics. The evidence comes from locales with widely differing political structures and styles. In every case, close examination suggests that it was becoming ever more difficult for men to base their claims to political leadership on traditional assumptions about social and political authority. In practice, the process of recruiting votes was frequently so laborious as to indicate that voters were not simply deciding who among the competitors was the most worthy. Similarly a close look at the candidates reveals that most of them fell far short of the ideal of a natural aristocrat. We can see, too, that considerations of interest, as calculated by both candidates and constituents, often played a far greater role in political contests that anyone in those contests would have frankly acknowledged. And finally, as we recognize the fragile, often artificial character of the deference paid to the ostensibly virtuous political leaders of eighteenth-century America, we can also identify the inadequacies of republican ideology as a guide to political behavior in that society.

Varieties of Political Behavior

If . . . Virginia . . . is the most often cited example of a deferential society, Puritan New England runs a close second. . . .

Even though many New England political leaders enjoyed notable longevity in their posts, they had to work diligently . . . to maintain their privileged positions. Nowhere was this more striking than among the "River Gods" of Massachusetts's Connecticut Valley. Among the River Gods, none had greater political power than Israel Williams of Hampshire County. Born into one of the wealthiest families in the valley, Williams was able to consolidate social power through skillful use of an intricate web of kin relations with the two other prominent families of the region, the Stoddards and the Hawleys. After graduating from Harvard in 1727 (Williams's rank, determined by the Harvard College officials' reckoning of social status, was tenth in a class of thirty-seven; his classmate and future political ally Thomas Hutchinson was third), he became a farmer, merchant, land speculator, and politician and involved himself in virtually every aspect of every business transacted in Hampshire County. Starting with an inheritance of a house, a home lot, and 109 acres, Williams systematically acquired land in Massachusetts and New York until he owned over 3,000 acres, a substantial amount by New England standards. The principal merchant and manufacturer in his region, he supplied his county not only with a large portion of its imported goods but also with most of the potash and linseed oil it exported.

Williams began his political career as selectman for the town of Hatfield in 1732; the town elected him its representative to the General Court the following year, and he subsequently added positions as justice of the peace, judge of the Hampshire court of common pleas, colonel in the local militia, and member of the governor's council. As a resident of Massachusetts, where plural officeholding was commonplace, he occupied many of these positions simultaneously. So great were his power and influence that his fellow townspeople called him the "monarch of Hampshire."

Williams's behavior as a businessman and politician was hardly a model of disinterestedness: he spent his whole life in battles, petty and grand, in which he aggressively used his influence to promote his interests. When the General Court was not dealing with issues of concern to Williams or to Hampshire County, he often skipped the session; when there were such issues—a bill to give him a ten-year monopoly on the manufacture of linseed oil, for example, or one relating to the distribution of political patronage in the Connecticut Valley—he worked hard to insure that his prerogatives were respected.

In country politics, Williams rewarded his friends and punished his enemies. When a fellow townsman, Gideon Lyman, campaigning for the General Court, identified himself as one of the "honest Plowmen" in opposition to one of the "great men," Williams—who certainly considered himself a great man—did not let the challenge pass. He formally requested Governor Francis Bernard to remove Lyman as justice of the peace on the ground that "he made it his business, in a low private way, to slander and abuse those of the County who were noted for supporting Government." Though Williams lost that fight, he did not lose many others. From 1733 to the Revolution few candidates gained seats in the General Court or on the county bench in Hampshire who had not joined interests with Israel Williams.

Williams's dominance was not based purely on the interested respect of his fellow citizens. His use of power and patronage as colonel and commander in chief of the Hampshire militia during the Seven Years' War—when escalating conflict on the frontier made high office in the militia more than merely honorific—provides a striking case in point. Williams's personnel decisions in reviving the county's weakened militia forces consistently consolidated the network of men loyal to him; his procurement practices in refurbishing disused frontier posts achieved a similar result; and many of his strategic choices for the defense of the Connecticut Valley benefitted some communities while hurting others. When neighbors opposed his policies, he did not hestitate to marshall support from powerful allies in the legislature and from the governor himself. Accordingly, as the toll of war mounted, citizens voiced complaints about Williams's strategic decisions and self-serving practices.

By the end of the war Williams was still entrenched as "monarch" of Hampshire, but the seeds of popular dissatisfaction had been sown. As resistance to British policy surfaced during the 1760s and early 1770s, Williams's close associations with Bernard and Hutchinson were crucial in making Hatfield one of a handful of Massachusetts towns that usually sided with the royal governors. But after passage of the Coercive Acts, even the combined forces of a received tradition of obedience to authority and the entrenched power of Israel Williams were not enough to withstand the popular fury: in February 1775, Williams was seized by a mob, placed in a smokehouse, and smoked all night long until he emerged the next morning, smudged and disheveled, apparently ready to condemn the Coercive Acts. Deference, even when buttressed by great social and economic power, had its limits.

Matthew Marrable of Lunenburg County would have loved to become known as the "monarch of Lunenburg." The son of a middling tobacco planter in Virginia's Southside, he could boast neither an impressive family background nor a college education. But he possessed abundant ambition. Through hard work and adroit land speculation, beginning in the early 1750s, he built an estate of 3,700 acres and sixteen slaves. He served as a justice on the county bench and as a vestryman of his Anglican parish, the two main requisites for political advancement. Marrable understood the importance of marshaling influence and interest in order to establish claims to superior social status and political power, but he lacked the politesse and the power to exercise those claims without experiencing substantial challenge. Campaigning for the House of Burgesses in 1758, he bid for votes in ways that separated a parvenu from a natural aristocrat. He treated the voters on several occasions, including feasts of seven roasted lambs and thirty gallons of rum. Although he warned recipients of his election-day treat "to take care they should not intoxicate themselves, least a Riot might ensure at the Election," the Burgesses' Committee on Privileges and Elections found that his use of food and drink far exceeded the bounds of propriety. More serious, the committee noted that Marrable had written a letter to David Caldwell, "a man of Great Interest in the County, strongly soliciting his Interest, in which is contained the following Words: 'This shall be my obligation to be liable and answerable to you, and all who are my Friends, in the Sum of five hundred pounds, if I do not use the Utmost of my Endeavors (in case I should be a Burgess) to divide this our county of Lunenburg in the following manner, to wit, Beginning at Byrd's Mill, running a straight line to the Head of the Nottoway.'" Caldwell, principal agent for William Byrd III's land dealings in the area, was indeed a man of great interest whose opinion of the rival candidates could affect the election, but the attempt to win his support by pledging a vote on a bill or, worse still, by promising money, went far beyond any permissible definition of the deference code. . . . The House of Burgesses declared Marrable's election void, but the ambitious Lenenburg politician did not give up. Having learned a lesson about a proper joining of interests, Marrable cultivated sufficient support among the local worthies to gain a seat in the Burgesses in 1760 and held it for most of the next decade. For Matthew Marrable, the pathway to power was neither straight nor smooth.

If there was an eighteenth-century American whom we might expect to have been a paragon of disinterested public service and therefore to have commanded the suffrages of his fellow citizens, that person was George Washington. And certainly at some point—perhaps by the mid-1760s, after he had distinguished himself in the Seven Years' War, and more assuredly after the Revolution—Washington ascended to archetypal status as the republican statesman. More revealing is the situation the aspiring colonel faced earlier in his career. His lineage was respectable but not pre-eminent; some even in his home county of Fairfax could claim more distinguished family connections. Washington found his path to power temporarily blocked by better-placed Fairfax neighbors.

Washington also owned land in Frederick County, immediately west of Fairfax, and in 1775, at the last minute, friends of the twenty-three-year-old colonel entered his name for burgess in that county against the two incumbents, Hugh West and Thomas Swearingen. Washington was not yet well known in Frederick, and he played no part in the campaign; moreover, none of his backers expended any effort in his behalf. In consequence, he ran a distant third in the race for the two vacant seats, attracting only 40 votes to West's 271 and Swearingen's 270. While we lack explicit commentary about the outcome from Washington himself, it is notable that he took the pains to copy from the poll book the names of the forty who had cast their votes for him.

Three years later, his reputation as a military leader rising, Washington made another bid from Frederick, and this time he took an active role in the campaign. He declared his candidacy several months before the balloting and assiduously cultivated the support of men of influence. When military duties called him to Fort Cumberland—some forty miles away—on election day, he made certain that his interests were well represented at the poll. He asked his friend Colonel James Wood, founder and leading citizen of Winchester, the county seat, to appear on his behalf and to thank the electors for their votes. He also saw to it that other influential men displayed their support in a timely and visible fashion.

Four candidates vied for the county's two seats. The incumbents West and Swearingen were running for reelection; Colonel Thomas Bryan Martin, related to the powerful Fairfax family, joined Washington in challenging them. Assembled at a table at the Frederick County courthouse were the sheriff, his clerks, and the candidates (in Washington's case, the candidate's representative). The first voter to approach the table was the most eminent man in the region, Thomas, Lord Fairfax, proprietor of the Northern Neck, county lieutenant, and senior justice of the peace of the county court. Lord Fairfax cast his votes for Martin and Washington. The next to appear, also voting for Washington, was William Meldrum, rector of Frederick Parish. Washington's designated representative, Colonel Wood, then cast his ballots for Washington and West. Another colonel in the militia and a leading merchant, John Carlyle, followed, casting his for Washington and Martin. As the balloting progressed, it became apparent that virtually all of the men of influence in the county had swung their support to Washington. Every voter identified on the poll sheets as "gentleman" voted for Washington, as did the county's three ministers—Presbyterian, Baptist, and Anglican. This strategy of pre-arranging prominent support was highly successful; Washington took an early lead that grew as the day wore on. When the poll closed, the vote stood Washington 310, Martin 240, West 199, and Swearingen 45.

While Washington owed his victory in part to the highly visible support of local worthies at the election, he had also taken pains to woo the voters before the balloting began. He spent £39. 6s. out of his own pocket on 28 gallons of rum, 50 gallons and one hogshead of rum punch, 34 gallons of wine, 46 gallons of "strong beer," and 2 gallons of cider royal—a total of 160 gallons of liquor to be served to the 391 voters of the district. Washington made clear that he was not trying to buy votes with food and drink. He wrote to an associate that "I hope no exception were taken to any that voted against me but that all were alike treated and all had enough; it is what I much desird—my only fear is that you spent with too sparing a hand." The young Washington knew that hospitality and liberality were defining traits of a gentleman, and this display of generosity, in combination with mobilization of men of interest and influence, marked the successful beginning of his political career. . . .

In subsequent years, as his reputation grew, Washington did not need to go to such lengths to win the public trust, but at this early stage it was not sufficient merely to announce his willingness to serve. The young colonel, like many other Virginia gentry, could not rely on the automatic deference of his neighbors; rather, it was necessary to join interests with prominent local men in order to command the support required to gain office. While this joining was not inconsistent with a conception of deference as "persuasion in a tangible shape," it was, in the extent to which Washington had to exert himself to gain votes, far removed from classical notions of deference. Indeed, what we find in Washington's experience is that the popular impulses in American politics, though certainly not articulated or structured in a shape that we can call "democratic," were changing the conduct of politics in local communities.

The Emergence of Popular Politics in America

Political leaders such as Williams, Marrable, and even Washington were learning that ordinary citizens could assert themselves in an active and independent fashion. In some cases their assertion amounted to a judgment about the personal capacities of their political leaders, . . . but more and more the voters were pressing and defending their own vision of their interests and voting for candidates who appeared best able to serve those interests. Accordingly, the number of contested elections whose outcomes were not considered either preordained or meaningless by the participants was steadily increasing.

While popular impulses remained subdued in most parts of New England, in Rhode Island they became a regular part of politics by the mid-eighteenth century. . . . About three-quarters of Rhode Island's free adult male population probably met the property qualifications for voting, and the voters elected more of their public officials than was the custom anywhere else in America. They elected members of the lower house of assembly—by far the most powerful agency of government in the colony—twice a year and balloted annually for a group of ten assistants who together with the governor and deputy governor composed the upper house. And, in marked contrast to every other colony except Connecticut, the voters elected annually virtually all of the members of the executive branch—governor, deputy governor, secretary, treasurer, and attorney general. Rhode Islanders also possessed a tradition of local government that was activist and popular. . . . The annual election for governor provided a focus for political opinion that encouraged high rates of turnout, rates that by the late 1750s and 1760s regularly reached 40–50 percent of free adult males, the highest average turnout in America.

The high rates occurred during the contest for the governorship and control of the assembly between Samuel Ward and Stephen Hopkins over the period

1757–1767. The Ward-Hopkins rivalry has been variously interpreted as a class struggle between the commercial interests of Newport and the agrarian interests of northern Rhode Island, as a division between Quakers and Anglicans on the one side and Baptists and Congregationalists on the other, and, most commonly, as a clash among men of similar class background and economic interests from the two principal seaports of the colony, with Ward favoring Newport and Hopkins speaking for Providence. These elements were all present in the electoral contests, but more striking is the extent to which the citizens of Rhode Island entered into the fray. Some of their involvement was orchestrated from above. Backers of the competing candidates held caucuses to plan strategy and raised campaign war chests amounting to several thousand pounds. To organize the electorate, they distributed tickets with a slate of recommended candidates. But by almost every standard—the percentage of the populace voting, the volume and vituperation of published broadsides and newspapers articles, and the extent to which the voters were aware of the nature of the choices they were making—the Rhode Island gubernatorial elections between 1757 and 1767 were popular contests. They were also close; Hopkins won six times, Ward three, but in no election did the victor gain more than 54.5 percent of the vote, and on several occasions the margin was less than a percentage point. . . .

The involvement of provincial American governments in the making and financing of war from the mid-eighteenth century onward brought more and more Americans into direct contact with their governments, nowhere more so than in Rhode Island. As the colony's seaport towns became enmeshed in the military conflict of the Great War for the Empire, citizens discovered that government policies were not simply the business of a few distinguished leaders. A variety of actions—issuing of flags of truce to merchants to allow them to trade with the West Indies; decisions about which merchant ships might be fitted out as privateers; granting monopolies to businessmen; currency reform; allocation of tax monies or, more commonly, authorization of lotteries for the construction of buildings, bridges, or schools—all fell within the sphere of the provincial government. . . .

This combination of a set of structural preconditons favorable to popular involvement and activist government that elicited such involvement was not everywhere present in the colonies. In Virginia and South Carolina, for example, members of the ruling elite went to great lengths to avoid factional quarrels that might lead to a popular challenge to their power. The political cultures in which they operated were ones that prized attributes of civility and gentility precisely for their usefulness in muting political conflict. In New York, where relations among members of the elite could be decidedly uncivil and ungenteel, members of the traditional ruling class were nevertheless able to prevent their differences from becoming an entering wedge for popular insurgency. That they were able to control electoral politics so effectively is testimony not only to the strength of their determination but also to the economic power they were able to muster to enforce that determination. As the New York manor lords discovered during the Revolution, however, their relatively effective suppression of popular sentiment in electoral politics was hardly a guarantee of popular consensus or contentment.

Mid-eighteenth-century Pennsylvania exhibited tendencies that stand midway between Rhode Island's popular politics and New York's popular discontent. The Pennsylvania Charter of Privileges of 1701 stipulated that representatives to the

Generally Assembly by elected by secret ballot each year. . . . William Penn had an explicitly popular vision of political representation: "Every representative may be called the creature of the people, because the people make them, and to them they owe their being. Here is no transessentiating, or transubstantiating of being, from people to a representative; no more than there is an absolute transferring of a title in a letter of attorney. the very term representative is enough to the contrary."

The provincial leaders of Pennsylvania, while adept at using Penn's ideas about representative government to justify weakening proprietary prerogative, were nevertheless, unwilling to enter into the sort of attorney-client relationship with their constituents that Penn envisioned. A small group of "weighty" Quakers and their non-Quaker allies came to dominate Pennsylvania's unicameral legislature; the secret of their success, according to Alan Tully, lay in a combination of the continuing deferential relationship between leaders and constituents, the unpopularity of the principal alternative source of political power in Pennsylvania politics—those in the circle of patronage of the proprietor—and, at lest in the period 1726–1755— their ability to respond to the basic needs of the people they served, Quakers and non-Quakers alike.

Tully's description of a generally stable and consensual political climate obscures occasions when portions of the electorate abandoned a deferential posture and mobilized forcefully to protect their interests. The main site was the city of Philadelphia. In the beginning, political mobilization was a top-down affair, as leaders of the Quaker or proprietary factions periodically attempted to broaden their political bases in order to gain advantage over their legislative rivals. Weighty Quakers were particularly skilled at recruiting voters; they had the advantage of being the most prominent and respected members of their communities, while their opposition to the proprietors enabled them to appear to be aligned with "popular" forces. Recruitment of the people was a dangerous game, since the leaders of both Quaker and proprietary factions were committed to elite control of politics, but in the early decades of the century, with a population overwhelmingly English and middling in wealth, it was a game that could be fairly easily managed. By midcentury, however, after two decades of massive German and Scots-Irish immigration and in the context of a differentiated and stratified economic order, traditional leaders began to see the consequence more clearly.

Popular interest in Philadelphia elections rose steadily from the early 1740s through the mid-1760s. While upswings in popular participation during the 1740s were largely the products of elite manipulation unconnected with substantive issues, the mobilizations for assembly elections of the mid-1760s suggest that popular awareness of policy issues was developing and that elite control of the political arena was declining. The contenders were the same—Quakers in control of the assembly versus wealthy and socially prominent politicians dependent on proprietary patronage. By the 1760s, however, popular confidence in the assembly, which had dragged its feet on defense of the frontier, was sinking. Moreover, the Quaker faction's attempt to put its proprietary opponents out of business once and for all by persuading the crown to convert Pennsylvania into a royal colony destabilized the political scene; many traditional constituents of the assembly faction— Germans in particular—viewed royal rule with apprehension. Finally, leaders of the proprietary faction, previously unwilling to look beyond the circle of a few wealthy and well-born Anglicans, took the bold step in 1764 of including on their eight-man assembly slate two Germans and a Scots-Irishman.

The 1764 campaign was innovative. First, both sides went to unusual lengths in making face-to-face appeals to the voters. Benjamin Franklin, a stalwart of the assembly faction, organized a mass meeting in Philadelphia at which he and Joseph Galloway promoted the scheme for royal government. . . . Second, there was a marked growth in both the quantity and the vituperative quality of the printed campaign literature. The opposing sides produced no fewer than forty-four pamphlets and broadsides, many of them in German. If a deferential attitude toward Philadelphia's "natural aristocracy" had ever been a factor in Philadelphia elections, it certainly was not much in evidence in 1764. Proprietary leader William Smith, an Anglican clergyman and provost of the University of Pennsylvania, was castigated as a "consummate Sycophant" with a head full of "*flatulent Preachments,*" and even such a civic paragon as Franklin became the target of abuse. To his proprietary opponents he was a person of "ingrate Disposition and Badness of Heart" who "By assuming the merit / Of other mens *discoveries* . . . obtain'd the name of / A PHILOSOPHER." One publicist took aim at Franklin's sexual habits, berating him as "a Letcher" who "Needs nothing to excite him, / But is too ready to engage, / When younger Arms envite him." He was also called a schemer, a squanderer of public funds, and a corrupt politician familiar with "every Zig Zag Machination." . . .

The 1764 campaign also engaged religious interests that allowed for a more far-reaching appeal to the electorate than had been possible earlier. Ministers and lay leaders of the contending religious groups of the city—Anglicans, Presbyterians, and Lutherans as well as Quakers—enlisted on one side or the other during this election. Perhaps most important, the campaign did not simply turn on questions relating to the personal honor of the leaders of the factions. The issue of royal versus proprietary government was a real one, and citizens made rational calculations as to how their interests would be affected by the imposition of royal control. Coming just when the crown was beginning to tighten its hold on the colonies, the questions stirred fears among artisans, mechanics, and sailors in addition to affluent merchants that the revocation of the proprietary charter would mean a loss of liberty. Presbyterians and Quakers alike were concerned with threats to their liberty from an established Anglican Church should the colony be placed under royal control.

Election day brought an unprecedented popular upsurge. According to one observer, "never before in the history of Pennsylvania . . . have so many people assembled for an election." In Philadelphia, a line of voters jammed the stairway of the courthouse from nine in the morning on October 1 until three in the afternoon the following day, with balloting continuing all through the night. In the end, aided by a substantial block of votes from Presbyterians and German Reformed, the proprietary party captured five of the eight assembly seats from Philadelphia county. . . .

Statistics bear out . . . the popular character of the election. Both sides made unusual efforts to recruit voters; the forty-four pamphlets and broadsides represented the culmination of an upward trend. Between 1755 and 1764, 109 campaign pamphlets were printed in Philadelphia, more than six times the number distributed in either of the previous two decades. The intensified campaigns in the public prints and in face-to-face encounters led to an unprecedented expansion in voter participation. Voter turnout among the taxable male population of Philadelphia County—an expanse stretching well beyond the city itself—had bounced back and forth between 10 and 35 percent during the years from 1727 to 1760; in 1764 it rose to 45.7 percent and in 1765, when many of the same issues were replayed, it rose to 51.2 percent. In the city itself, the percentage of taxables voting soared to 54.5 in 1764 and 65.1 in 1765.

Citizen involvement in Philadelphia elections decreased after 1765. What the elections of 1764 and 1765 showed was the potential for popular mobilization in eighteenth-century America. Philadelphia in particular—with electoral laws that were broadly inclusive, diverse population groups attuned to the need to work aggressively to promote their interests and identities, and a ruling elite insufficiently responsive to those realities—was especially ripe for a popular insurgence. Although that mobilization was initially orchestrated from the top, political leaders soon discovered that the populist impulse was difficult to contain.

Republican Ideology and the Emergence of Popular Politics

Classical republican language, borrowed from the country party tradition of English politics, always conveyed a double message in the American context. On the one hand, fear of the aggressive and oppressive tendencies of power, joined to concern for the fragile and vulnerable state of liberty, could lead to efforts to shift political power from the few to the many. On the other, the tradition's overriding commitment to the preservation and cultivation of virtue—an attribute for which every member of society should strive but which was particularly likely to be found among the natural aristocracy—provided the basis for all of the defenses of a deferential political and social order. . . .

These recitations of the libertarian aspects of republican ideology were nearly always used defensively, in the face of some direct threat to the political power and autonomy of provincial leaders. They were almost never employed to justify popular government at home in the absence of such threats. Indeed, the *Pennsylvania Gazette,* in the same breath that it warned of despotism at home, averred that such attempts at consolidation of arbitrary power "constituted a design almost as wicked as was the attempt to change the English *constitution* into a *democracy.*" Republican language, as it was used in the sporadic but often intense jockeying for position that characterized Anglo-American imperial relations in the eighteenth century, was the staple substance of a secular jeremiad, an ideological tradition on which provincial leaders could draw whenever things did not go their way.

While few American were willing to invoke the libertarian side of republicanism as a positive justification for democracy, a good many political leaders—especially when they came out on the short end of an election—embraced the elitist, virtue-oriented side of republicanism in attacking populist politics at home. Indeed, they assailed their opponents as rogues and demagogues, guilty of stirring the passions of the people, at least as often as they bemoaned the demise of popular government at the hands of a corrupt "Robinocracy" of royal placemen. James Logan, smarting from a series of political setbacks from Sir William Keith in Pennsylvania in the late 1720s, complained that "Keith was so mad, as well as wicked, most industriously to sett up the lowest part of the People; through a vain expectation that he should always be able to steer and influence them as his own Will. But he weakly forgot how soon the minds of such Peoples are changed by any new Accident and how licentious force, when the Awe of Government . . . is thrown off, has been turned against those who first taught them to throw it off." Logan had access to some of the power and patronage that America's leaders so feared, but his provincial opponents, once they had tasted the bitter fruit of popular defeat, sang very much the same tune. Galloway in 1764 played both sides of the classical republican record, accusing his opponents of being corrupted by their passion for "arbitrary Power" while denouncing their popular excesses, which he believed to be fueled by the "Passion of Ambition." Everywhere the story was the same. In Massachusetts, Israel Williams decried the conduct of upstart politicians who, unimpressed by the importance of electing men of virtue, declaimed on the hustings against the conduct of the "great men." In Virginia, wealthy planter gentry such as Landon Carter, convinced of their own superior virtue but nevertheless occasional victims of popular disfavor, railed against the "Adultress Popularity" as the greatest threat to good republican government.

The rhetoric of republican virtue, like that of republican liberty, was . . . trotted out when one's opponents were using popular electioneering devices and organizing in a partisan fashion. What is remarkable, however, is the extent to which politicians, when faced with competition for election, routinely availed themselves of those popular and partisan electioneering tools. Williams, though quick to denounce the presumption of upstart politicians, worked aggressively among the populace to aggrandize his power. The same Galloway who attributed democratic excess to the passion of ambition, . . . not only engaged in vigorous, behind-the-scenes politicking but also wrote pamphlets and delivered speeches at rallies where he denounced his opponents as "proprietary hireling[s]" operating in "total disregard for the Rights of the People." Even that model of disinterested virtue, Washington, when facing a tough election, instructed his friends not to stint on the rum, beer, and cider.

One should not be too cynical, but the decision on when and how to employ the rhetoric of classical republicanism in pre-Revolutionary America often depended on whose ox was being gored. We should therefore perhaps pay less attention to the whining of the losers—for whom declarations about the declining state of republican virtue came easily and offered a helpful does of self-justification and solace—and watch more carefully the behavior of the winners. The winners were concerned not with maintaining republican virtue but with winning elections.

Equally important, winners and losers alike were discovering that voter support frequently depended less on their personal qualities as disinterested public servants than on active and faithful advocacy of their constituents' interests. Political men were learning, however dimly and reluctantly, that the process of political transformation was not going to be controlled wholly from the top. While the transformation of American politics was never simply a struggle between the many and the few, it was a process in which the few would be engaged in alternating relationships of consensus, accommodation, tension, and sometimes outright conflict with the many. In the final analysis, it was the active advocacy and assertion by the many—not the voluntary abandonment of deferential politics by the few—that made democratic government in America a reality.

F U R T H E R   R E A D I N G

Richard R. Beeman, *The Evolution of the Southern Backcountry: A Case Study of Lunenburg County, Virginia, 1746–1832* (1984)

Patricia U. Bonomi, *A Factious People: Politics and Society in Colonial New York* (1971)

———, *Under the Cope of Heaven: Religion, Society and Politics in Colonial America* (1986)

T. H. Breen, *Tobacco Culture: The Mentality of the Great Tidewater Planters on the Eve of the Revolution* (1985)

Richard L. Bushman, *King and People in Provincial Massachusetts* (1985)

———, *The Refinement of America: Persons, Houses, Cities* (1992)

David W. Conroy, *In Public Houses: Drink and the Revolution of Authority in Colonial Massachusetts* (1995)

Bruce C. Daniels, ed., *Power and Status: Officeholding in Colonial America* (1986)

Toby L. Ditz, *Property and Kinship: Inheritance in Early Connecticut, 1750–1820* (1986)

Thomas M. Doerflinger, *A Vigorous Spirit of Enterprise: Merchants and Economic Development in Revolutionary Philadelphia* (1986)

David Galenson, *White Servitude in Colonial America: An Economic Analysis* (1981)

Robert A. Gross, *The Minutemen and Their World* (1976)

Ronald Hoffman, et al., eds. *The Economy of Early America: The Revolutionary Period, 1763–1790* (1988)

Rhys Isaac, *The Transformation of Virginia, 1740–1790* (1982)

Christopher Jedry, *The World of John Cleveland: Family and Community in Eighteenth-Century New England* (1979)

Allan Kulikoff, *Tobacco and Slaves: the Development of Southern Cultures in the Chesapeake, 1680–1800* (1986)

James T. Lemon, *The Best Poor Man's Country: A Geographical Study of Early Southeastern Pennsylvania* (1972)

Gary Nash, *The Urban Crucible: Social Change, Political Consciousness, and the Origins of the American Revolution* (1979)

Gregory H. Nobles, *Divisions throughout the Whole: Politics and Society in Hampshire County, Massachusetts, 1740–1775* (1983)

Edward C. Papenfuse, *In Pursuit of Profit: The Annapolis Merchants in the Era of the American Revolution, 1763–1805* (1975)

Sharon V. Salinger, *"To Serve Well and Faithfully": Labor and Indentured Servants in Pennsylvania, 1692–1800* (1987)

Daniel Blake Smith, *Inside the Great House: Planter Life in Eighteenth-Century Chesapeake Society* (1980)

John W. Tyler, *Smugglers and Patriots: Boston Merchants and the Advent of the American Revolution* (1986)

Gordon S. Wood, *The Radicalism of the American Revolution* (1992)

Michael Zuckerman, *Peaceable Kingdoms: New England Towns in the Eighteenth Century* (1970)

The British Empire
and the War for
North America

To understand the British imperial system and Britain's relationship to the colonies, it is important to recognize that the British government did not found any of the colonies. Indeed, the earliest colonies in the Chesapeake region and New England were settled and organized a generation or two before the British government made any attempt to develop a central policy on settlement or trade. Such efforts were begun intermittently in the 1650s and 1660s and thereafter, but domestic political instability prevented London authorities from establishing a comprehensive or consistent colonial policy. As a result, British imperial arrangements were never as logical, orderly, and coherent in practice as royal officials would have liked. Moreover, because most of the colonies had experienced generations of semiautonomous government under seventeenth-century charters, the goal of central control was a difficult, long-term challenge for eighteenth-century British administrators. In their domestic politics, military defense, and commercial activities, the colonies had operated largely on their own.

Europe's Seven Years' War (known in the colonies as the French and Indian War), which ended in 1763, marked a turning point in British imperial history. For the first time, Britain had concentrated its military resources in North America; with colonial help, the British conquered French Canada. In the process, cabinet-level British officials became concerned with the serious political and administrative defects of the imperial system they were supposed to rule. Britain meanwhile had run up a huge public debt by financing the war on the high seas and in Europe and America. After a century of operating an imperial policy sometimes described as "salutary neglect," British leaders believed they had to find a better way to run the empire. But to colonial Americans, who shared in the glory of British victories and welcomed the expulsion of French power from North America, there was no better way. In their view, the empire had simply entered a new era of peace, prosperity, and growth; the imperial system wasn't broken and didn't need fixing.

Benjamin Franklin (1706–1790), the Boston native who made his career in Philadelphia, London, and Paris, in the 1750s and 1760s was deeply interested in the success of the British Empire. When war with France loomed in 1754 he was, with fellow-Bostonian Thomas Hutchinson, one of the delegates sent to Albany, New York to plan a co-ordinated colonial and imperial military policy. Though the plan went nowhere and was later viewed in London as a symbol of intercolonial divisions, in retrospect it also appears to be a precursor to the Continental Congress, the Articles of Confederation, and the Constitution. First Franklin drafted the plan, as documented in the first selection in this chapter, and then he realistically predicted its failure in the second document.

The third document, the Order in Council, was a key London approach to improve imperial administration by making a temporary wartime reform permanent. Colonial un-concern regarding imperial reform and such administrative measures, in the context of the victory over France, is suggested by the celebratory sermon of a Massachusetts clergyman, Thomas Barnard. In 1763 he brought a millenialist enthusiasm to the glorification of the British Empire, though later he would support American independence.

1. Benjamin Franklin, *et al.,* Devise Albany Plan of Colonial Union, 1754

[July 10, 1754]

Plan of Proposed Union of the Several Colonies of Massachusets-bay, New Hampshire, Coneticut, Rhode Island, New York, New Jerseys, Pensilvania, Maryland, Virginia, North Carolina, and South Carolina. For their Mutual Defence and Security, and for Extending the British Settlements in North America.

That humble Application be made for an Act of the Parliament of Great Britain by Virtue of which, one General Government may be formed in America, including all the said Colonies, within and under which Government, each Colony may retrain its present Constitution, except in the Particulars wherein a Change may be directed by the said Act, as hereafter follows.

President General Grand Council.	That the said General Government be administred by a President General, To be appointed and Supported by the Crown, and a Grand Council to be Chosen by the Representatives of the People of the Several Colonies, met in their respective Assemblies.
Election of Members.	That . . . The House of Representatives in the Several Assemblies . . . Shall Choose Members for the Grand Council in the following Proportions, that is to say.

The Papers of Benjamin Franklin, Vol. 5, pp. 387–393; 453–454, Leonard W. Labaree et al., eds., New Haven and London: Yale University Press, 1962.

Masachusets-Bay	7.
New Hampshire	2.
Conecticut	5.
Rhode-Island	2.
New-York	4.
New-Jerseys	3.
Pensilvania	6.
Maryland	4.
Virginia	7.
North-Carolina	4.
South-Carolina	4.
	48.

Place of first meeting.

Who shall meet for the first time at the City of Philadelphia . . . being called by the President General. . . .

New Election.

That there shall be a New Election of Members for the Grand Council every three years; . . .

Proportion of Members after first 3 years.

That after the first three years, when the Proportion of Money arising out of each Colony to the General Treasury can be known, The Number of Members to be Chosen, for each Colony shall from time to time in all ensuing Elections be regulated by that proportion (yet so as that the Number to be Chosen by any one Province be not more than Seven nor less than Two).

Meetings of Grand Council. Call.

That the Grand Council shall meet once in every Year, and oftner if Occasion require, at such Time and place as they shall adjourn to at the last preceeding meeting, or as they shall be called to meet at by the President General, on any Emergency. . . .

Speaker.

That the Grand Council have Power to Chuse their Speaker, and shall neither be Dissolved, prorogued nor Continue Sitting longer than Six Weeks

Continuance.

at one Time without their own Consent, or the Special Command of the Crown.

Member's Allowance

That the Members of the Grand Council shall be Allowed for their Service ten shillings Sterling per Diem, during their Sessions or Journey to and from the Place of Meeting; Twenty miles to be reckoned a days Journey.

Assent of President General. His Duty.

That the Assent of the President General be requisite, to all Acts of the Grand Council, and that it be His Office, and Duty to cause them to be carried into Execution.

Power of President and Grand Council. Peace and War.

That the President General with the Advice of the Grand Council, hold or Direct all Indian Treaties in which the General Interest or Welfare of the Colony's may be Concerned; And make Peace or

Declare War with the Indian Nations. That they make such Laws as they Judge Necessary for regulating all Indian Trade. That they make all Purchases from Indians for the Crown, of Lands not within the Bounds of Particular Colonies. . . . That they make New Settlements on such Purchases, by Granting Lands in the Kings Name, reserving a Quit Rent to the Crown, for the use of the General Treasury. That they make Laws for regulating and Governing such new Settlements, till the Crown shall think fit to form them into Particular Governments.

Indian Purchases.

New Settlements.

Laws to Govern them.

That they raise and pay Soldiers, and build Forts for the Defence of any of the Colonies, and equip Vessels of Force to Guard the Coasts and Protect the Trade on the Ocean, Lakes, or Great Rivers; But they shall not Impress Men in any Colonies, without the Consent of its Legislature. That for these purposes they have Power to make Laws And lay and Levy such General Duties, Imposts, or Taxes, as to them shall appear most equal and Just, . . . and such as may be Collected with the least Inconvenience to the People, rather discouraging Luxury, than Loading Industry with unnecessary Burthens. That they may Appoint a General Treasurer and a Particular Treasurer in each Government, when Necessary. . . .

Raise Soldiers &c.
Lakes.
Not to Impress.

Power to make Laws
Duties &c.

Treasurer.

That a Quorum of the Grand Council impower'd to Act with the President General, do consist of Twenty-five Members, among whom there shall be one, or more from a Majority of the Colonies. That that Laws made by them for the Purposes aforesaid, shall not be repugnant but near as may be agreeable to the Laws of England, and Shall be transmitted to the King in Council for Approbation, as Soon as may be after their Passing and if not disapproved within Three years after Presentation to remain in Force.

Quorum.

Laws to be Transmitted.

That in case of the Death of the President General The Speaker of the Grand Council for the Time Being shall Succeed, and be Vested with the Same Powers, and Authority, to Continue until the King's Pleasure be known.

Death of President General.

That all Military Commission Officers Whether for Land or Sea Service, to Act under this General Constitution, shall be Nominated by the President General But the Approbation of the Grand Council, is to be Obtained before they receive their Commissions, And all Civil Officers are to be Nominated,

Officers how Appointed.

by the Grand Council, and to receive the President General's Approbation, before they Officiate. . . . That the Particular Military as well as Civil Establishments in each Colony remain in their present State, this General Constitution Notwithstanding. And that on Sudden Emergencies any Colony may Defend itself, and lay the Accounts of Expence thence Arisen, before the President General and Grand Council, who may allow and order payment of the same As far as they Judge such Accounts Just and reasonable.

Each Colony may defend itself on Emergency.

2. Franklin Predicts the Plan of Union Will Fail, 1754

To Peter Collinson

Boston, Dec. 29. 1754

Dear Sir

. . . As to the State of Colonies, a pretty full Representation of it was drawn up by the Commissioners at Albany, and was sent home to the Ministry with the Proceedings. However, as you perhaps have not seen it, I send you herewith the whole Treaty, [and] as, I have no other Copy, I must beg you would return it after Perusal. All the Assemblies in the Colonies have, I suppose, had the Union Plan laid before them; but it is not likely, in my Opinion, that any of them will act upon it so as to agree to it, or to propose any Amendments to it. Every Body cries, a Union is absolutely necessary; but when they come to the Manner and Form of the Union, their weak Noddles are presently distracted. So if ever there be an Union, it must be form'd at home by the Ministry and Parliament. I doubt not but they will make a good one, and I wish it may be done this Winter. . . .

With the Treaty at Albany, I send you a Paper I drew up containing the Motives on which the Commissioners at Albany proceeded in forming their Plan. . . . Some Things in the Plan may perhaps appear of too popular a Turn, the Commissioners from the 2 popular Governments, having a considerable Weight at the Board: When I give the Reasons on which each Article was settled as it stands, I would not be understood as expressing every where my own Opinion: For tho' I projected the Plan and drew it, I was oblig'd to alter some Things contrary to my Judgment, or should never have been able to carry it through.

With great Esteem and Affection, I am, Dear Sir, Your most obedient humble Servant

B Franklin

Benjamin Franklin to Peter Collinson, Boston, December 29, 1754. As found in *The Papers of Benjamin Franklin,* ed. Leonard W. Labaree et al. (New Haven: Yale University Press, 1959), vol. 5, pp. 453–454.

3. Order in Council on the Reform of the Customs Service, 1763

We, the Commissioners of your Majesty's Treasury beg leave humbly to represent to your Majesty that having taken into consideration the present state of the duties of customs imposed on your Majesty's subjects in America and the West Indies, we find that the revenue arising therefrom is very small and inconsiderable, having in no degree increased with the commerce of those countries, and is not yet sufficient to defray a fourth part of the expense necessary for collecting it. We observe with concern that through neglect, connivance, and fraud, not only the revenue is impaired, but the commerce of the colonies is diverted from its natural course and the . . . provisions of many wise laws to secure it to the mother country are in great measure defeated. Attention to objects of so great importance . . . is more indispensable when the military establishment necessary for maintaining these colonies requires a large revenue to support it, and when their vast increase in territory and population makes the proper regulation of their trade of immediate necessity lest the continuance and extent of the dangerous evils above-mentioned may render all attempts to remedy them hereafter . . . utterly impracticable. We have endeavoured therefore to discover, and . . . remove the causes, to which the deficiency of this revenue and the contraband trade with other European nations are owing. For this purpose we have ordered all the officers belonging to the customs in America and the West Indies to be fully instructed in their duty to repair forthwith to their respective stations and constantly to reside there for the future; and where we find that a sufficient number of proper officers are not yet established, it is intended to supply the deficiency by the appointment of others. We have directed that all the officers of the revenue in your Majesty's plantations should be furnished with new and ample instructions, enforcing in the strongest manner the strictest attention to their duty, and requiring that by regular and constant correspondence they give an account, as well of their own proceedings as of the conduct of the officers under them, and inform us likewise of any obstructions they may meet. . . . We have ordered them to transmit exact amounts of the imports and exports in their several districts, of the state of the revenue, and of the illicit commerce with other European states, . . . with such observations as may occur to them in regard either to the efficacy . . . of . . . regulations, or to such alterations as they may judge conducive to the . . . improvement of the revenue, to the prevention of those frauds by which it is impaired, and to the suppression of the contraband trade which has been . . . carried on with too much impunity; and we have directed the Commissioners of your Majesty's Customs immediately to dismiss every officer that shall fail to pay obedience to these instructions or be any way deficient in his duty. . . . We are further . . . of opinion that it will greatly contribute to the same salutary ends, and to the carrying of the several laws and regulations into execution with success, if all officers, both civil and military, are strictly commanded to give their assistance upon all proper occasions, and if the commanders-in-chief of your Majesty's ships and troops in America and the West

"Order in Council on the Reform of the Customs Service, 1763." As found in *Acts of the Privy Council of England, Colonial Series,* ed. W. L. Grant and J. Munro (London: 1908–1912), vol. IV, pp. 569–572.

Indies are directed to attend to this object with the utmost care, and to make sure a disposition of the force under their respective commands as will be most serviceable in suppressing these dangerous practices, and in protecting the officers of the revenue from the violence of any desperate and lawless persons.

4. Rev. Thomas Barnard Looks to Future Glories, 1763

Britain, favoured of God, has hitherto maintained her Liberty; Freedom has subsisted in Health and Vigour, overcome all Opposition; recovered of every Disorder: There may she ever flourish, and "under her Shadow we shall be safe." Not all the Vicissitudes of human Affairs have afforded Opportunity for the Destruction of the Freedom of our Nations. Intestine Frauds and Treasons, the Weakness and Wickedness of Princes, foreign Invasions, have all in Event ('tis wonderful!) but they have all, in Event, served to fix Liberty more firmly, to mark out her Path, determine her Bounds, extend her Influence.

Look back, my Hearers, to the most distant Times. . . . *England* was frequently in Jeopardy from Abroad; sometimes ready in Despair to subject herself to foreign Power, that she might free herself from domestic Tyranny, as in the Case of King *John*; once at the Brink of being swallowed up by an invincible *Armada* of *Spain*; once nigh remediless Confusion, thro' the infernal Arts of *Rome,* in the infamous Powder-Plot; and for a Century past, constantly endangered by the insidious Arts of *France,* the unceasing Enemy of her Tranquillity—an Enemy, at one Time tampering with her indolent, profuse, superstitious Princes; at another, abetting vagrant Pretenders to her Crown: At length, this aspiring Power rightly judged that her future Efforts of this Kind would be vain, if the *British* Plantations on the Continent of *America* should flourish and extend, and derive Wealth and Strength for their Mother-Country: Her Ministry therefore, with Craft and Perfidy, laid a Plan for first stinting their Growth (as they found the inhuman stimulating the Savages to their Destruction, would not effect the Purpose) that they might by and by overwhelm them. This brought on the late bloody War, . . . to distress and weaken *Britain.* . . .

The Exaltation of *Great-Britain* to the Summit of earthly Grandeur and Glory, was reserved in the Counsels of God for the Age and Reign of GEORGE the *Third.* . . .

We see a King on the Throne (succeeding his royal Grandfather, of immortal Memory) rejoicing, that, to every other Motive, this of Birth is added, to endear his Subjects to him, to attach him to their Laws and Constitutions, and engage him to Vigilance and Zeal for their Protection. While the venerable Foundations of all we hold dear, are guarded with the strictest Care, while the lowest Subject is safe as the highest, in every Enjoyment he can desire; the most powerful Enemies, the most formidable Combination of them, have fallen into "the Pit which they themselves digged."

"Rev. Thomas Barnard Looks to Future Glories, 1763." In Thomas Barnard, *A Sermon Preached Before His Excellency Francis Bernard, Esq.; Governor and Commander in Chief, the Honourable House of Representatives, of the Province of the Massachusetts-Bay in New-England, May 25th, 1763: Being the Anniversary for the Election of His Majesty's Council for said province* (Boston, 1763), 36–45.

Auspicious Day! when Britain, the special Care of Heaven, blessed with a patriot-Sovereign, served by wise and faithful Councellors, brave Commanders, successful Fleets and Armies, seconded in her Efforts by all her Children, and by none more zealously than by those of *New-England, . . .* has it in her Power to demand Peace of the most powerful Enemies, on Terms, just and equal, safe, highly advantageous and glorious, beyond what were expected or even fought for, through a Deluge of Blood.

Happy Sovereign of such a People, generous Olive-Tree; whose Branches spread out, whose Fruit is dispersed for the Healing of the Nations! Happy Island of his Nativity; blessed the Womb that bare him! It is GEORGE the *Third,* who gives Peace to half the World. How can Faction but be dumb, contending Parties but melt into gentle Harmony.

In these Events, the Lord God hath spoken, who can but prophecy, "In his Days shall the Righteous flourish, and Abundance of Peace so long as the Moon endureth: He shall have Dominion from Sea to Sea: They that dwell in the Wilderness shall bow before him, and his Enemies shall lick the Dust. . . .

America, mayest well rejoice, the Children of *New-England* may be glad and triumph, in Reflection on Events past, and Prospect of the future. Encompassed with native Savages, our Fathers having escaped from Oppression, deepest felt by pious Minds, carried their Lives in their Hands, subjected to Captivities, to inhuman Cruelties and Massacres: Encompassed with crafty, faithless *Europeans,* who sought their Ruin, what Prospect could they have before them? The dearer and more valuable the Rights they had earned, the more gloomy the Fore-thought of losing them. And if we their Offspring, call to Mind the Ideas which possessed us in the Year 1756, with what Exultation must we sing, "The Snare is broken and we are escaped."

Now commences the Era of our quiet Enjoyment of those Liberties, which our Fathers purchased with the Toil of their whole Lives, their Treasure, their Blood. Safe from the Enemy of the Wilderness, safe from the griping Hand of arbitrary Sway and cruel Superstition; Here shall be the late founded Seat of Peace and Freedom. Here shall our indulgent Mother, who has most generously rescued and protected us, be served and honoured by growing Numbers, with all Duty, Love and Gratitude, till Time shall be no more. Here shall be a perennial Source of her Strength and Riches. Here shall Arts and Sciences, the Companions of Tranquility, flourish. Here shall her new Subjects and their Posterity, bless the Day, when their imagined Enemies Victories proved to them the Beginning of the most valuable Freedom. Here shall dwell uncorrupted Faith, the pure Worship of God in its primitive Simplicity, unawed, uninterrupted; here shall it extend itself and its benign Influences among those who have hitherto "sat in Darkness, in the Region and under the Shadow of Death." "Truth shall spring out of the Earth, and Righteousness shall look down from Heaven; yea the Lord shall give that which is good; Righteousness shall go before him; and shall set us in the Way of his Steps."

ESSAYS

Fred Anderson, a professor of history at the University of Colorado, Boulder, has investigated the social and political ramifications for colonists of imperialism, warfare, and military service. The selection that follows comes from his *A People's Army: Massachusetts*

Soldiers and Society in the Seven Years' War (1984). It explains some of the reasons why, even in victory, joint military operations produced tension in the colonial relationship with Britain. The second essay, by the British scholar P. J. Marshall, explores the ways in which the colonies helped to define British national identity in the 18th century. Clearly, colonial America was more than a commercial asset to Britons.

Friction Between Colonial Troops and British Regulars

FRED ANDERSON

One of the most important legacies of the Seven Years' War was the creation among the provincials of this general sense of what could be expected of redcoats. The war offered New Englanders and Britons a chance to take each other's measure with an intimacy and on a scale unprecedented in colonial history. Such intercultural contact—for that is what it was—largely took place through the operation of the British military justice system, and it gave the colonial soldiers an unflattering, disturbing impression of their comrades in arms.

I

When provincial enlisted men had direct contact with redcoat officers, it was the regulars' mercilessness and haughtiness that they were most likely to note. Joseph Nichols recorded with distaste an example of regular mistreatment of provincial troops and the provincials' reactions, which occurred at the close of the 1758 campaign. . . . On 31 October, the day that the men of the regiment understood to be the very last of their enlistments, at "about sunrise, the chief officer of the fort came to our regiment and ordered all our men up to the falls to meet the wagons and teams. Our men seemed to be loath to go before they eat. Those that refused to turn out, he drove out, and some he struck with his staff, which caused a great uproar among us. Our people in general declare in case we are so used tomorrow, blows shall end the dispute." As it turned out, the regiment was dismissed later in the day, and the crisis was averted. The incident only reinforced impressions of the British that already existed among the provincials. . . .

Even more than did their enlisted men, provincial officers resented the regular leaders' hauteur. . . . By the end of the campaign of 1755, the New England officers' early enthusiasm had been transformed into animosity. The estimate they had formed of regular behavior contributed heavily to the New England assemblies' insistence upon strict division between regular and provincial force in the campaign proposed for the following year.

The distaste of provincials for haughty regulars runs like a litany through officers' diaries during the rest of the war. Caleb Rea retailed story after story of provincial officers who had been affronted, slighted, or abused by regulars. . . . Rea also resented the way in which regular leaders consistently ignored their provincial colleagues and failed to include them in councils of war. On 23 August, for example, he noted: "This day at a general council, Colonels Lyman and Preble was called as members. Mark, two provincials with perhaps twice or thrice the number of regulars." In the same vein the Reverend John Cleaveland grumbled in a letter to his wife from Lake George that provincial colonels were never consulted "and know no more what is a-going to be done than a sergeant till the orders come out." Both Rea and Cleaveland, along with other provincial officers, came to worry before the end of the1758 campaign that the regulars—who were responsible for the failure of the expedition against Ticonderoga—would contrive a means of blaming the defeat on the provincials. . . .

The differences between British and New England goals, expectations, and views of military service all tended to strain relations between the groups when the regulars were exercising their authority. There were other kinds of interactions, too, between redcoats and provincials, interactions not complicated by the exercise of authority and the envy or resentment that it generated. These situations, as much as any, were the ones by which the provincials took the measure of the British. Insofar as most New Englanders, before the war, had had little opportunity to observe Britons at first hand, military service provided them with their first real chance to form immediately verifiable impressions. Provincials' diaries allow us in effect to watch as they form their images of the regulars—perceptions both favorable and unfavorable, by which the New Englanders came to know more about the British and more about themselves.

Many of the interactions between the groups consisted merely of curious observation, as when Joseph Nichols strolled around the encampment of Gage's regiment, whom he identified as "the Leather Caps who are called the Light Infantry." They were, he noted, "a mixed nation, even of all sorts." Sometimes what the New Englanders saw was more disturbing than that: one observer noted that the redcoats of the Fiftieth Regiment were "Scotch Irish and English and by their manners and behavior we suppose[d] were convicts." . . . Provincials noted other redcoat peculiarities, too: their officers fought duels, for instance, a practice in which New Englanders seem not to have engaged. Regulars were also known to commit suicide—an act that was evidently rare or unknown among provincials. Insofar as the recorded suicides were committed by men awaiting punishment, it seems likely that this tendency was a consequence of the harshness of regular discipline.

Provincials found much to admire in the redcoats and noted especially their courage under fire, their ability to remain healthy on campaign, and their greater disposition to orderliness and teamwork—all functions of their more effective discipline. Provincials were also aware that they were being unfavorably compared to regulars, apparently a habit of British officers. . . . The provincials' consciousness of such comparisons led them to compete avidly with the regulars. . . . Such impromptu contests, which included shooting matches and wrestling ("the Lobsters and our men hopped and wrestled together to see which would beat, and our men beat"), reflected the provincials' desire to prove themselves the equals of the redcoats in strength and skill. The provincials' evident interest in these events perhaps betrays a certain anxiousness to establish their prowess as soldiers, even as it suggests that they regarded the regulars as martial models, of a sort. But it is also clear that the New Englanders entertained no doubt that they were the moral superiors of the redcoats, and this conviction colors most of their perceptions of the British.

The most common depiction of the redcoats, officers and men alike, was as inveterate breakers of the Second and Third Commandments, matters of no small concern to many provincials. "Sad! sad! is it to see how the Sabbath is profaned in the camp!" mourned Caleb Rea, who went on to observe that "many that seem pious" did their best to rebuke the defilers of the day, even though they could do little because the real problem lay with the regular leaders, who refused to enforce proper Sabbath order. . . . Following the defeat of Abercromby's army at Ticonderoga in 1758, Caleb Rea was moved to reflect on what "horrid cursing and swearing there is in the camp, more especially among the regulars; and," he shuddered, "as a moral cause I can't but charge our defeat on this sin, which so much prevails, even among the chief commanders." Joseph Nichols commented repeatedly on the language of his comrades and noted, typically, that he "observed but little profaneness among our provincials, but among the regulars, much profaneness."

Such comments illustrate a point of cultural divergence between the two groups. . . . Most New England soldiers had grown up in a land where those who took the Lord's name in vain or who traveled on Sundays could be—and often were—brought to book for misdemeanor before the local justice of the peace. As soldiers, the natives of the Bay Colony not only found it disturbing that such flagrant breaches of good order occurred; they were bothered even more by the fact that the leaders of the army did nothing to stop them. . . . Profanity does not seem to have bothered the regular leaders at all. . . . [T]he regulars' attitudes toward casual oaths and amusement on the Sabbath derived from a cultural milieu that was unexpectedly alien to the colonists. . . .

Other aspects of redcoat behavior excited similarly adverse reactions. The provincials found, for example, that they were lewd. Unlike New Englanders, who did not permit women to follow their regiments into the field, regulars were accompanied by, and consistently identified with, camp women. Female camp followers in fact performed valuable services to the army, including laundry and care of the sick. Some were undoubtedly prostitutes, but this was by no means true of all, or even many of them. Camp women were regulated by general orders, were subject to military justice, and were provisioned by the command, along with the soldiers; thirty or forty were allowed to accompany each regiment. As far as the provincials were concerned, however, they were loose women. . . . In a typical reference one soldier noted on 18 October 1758 that "this afternoon there was a Lobster corporal married to a Rhode Island whore." At least the event was a peaceful one; David Holdin's account of an altercation involving regulars and a camp woman was altogether more violent and sinister. "A mighty discord amongst the regulars this night," he wrote in 1760, "disputing who had the best right to a woman and who should have first go at her, even until it came to blows, and their hubbub raised almost the whole camp." Other incidents that the New Englanders set down, like the explusion of women for carrying "an infectious distemper . . . very common to the sex in these parts," the involvement of women in violent wrangles, and the subjection of women to whipping for various infractions, indicate that the provincials saw regulars and their consorts as equally unsavory beings.

Aggressiveness was the final touch in the provincials' portrait of the redcoats. As long as the war went on, violence punctuated relations between the groups, and if the provincials are to be believed, it was the regulars who started fights. There is no

reason to suppose that it was so one-sided; the antagonism was mutual and expressed itself in escalating intensity from name-calling to fistfights to riots. *Lobster*
was a favorite provincial epithet, and the British seem to have responded in kind. . . .

Although the provincials' impression of redcoat aggressiveness was probably
exaggerated, British soldiers were an unlovely lot, and the New Englanders' opinion of them was unquestionably founded in reality. Within the British army itself
the assumption ran that the typical enlisted man was at best a rascal, at worst a
brute. . . . The ferocious disciplinary system through which regular leaders attempted to control the men under their command was the principal medium
through which provincials had contact with redcoat officers. Provincial soldiers
consistently commented on the harsh physical punishments of the British army—
particularly so after 1756, when provincial troops who served jointly with the regulars were subject to the British Rules and Articles of War—the code of military
justice that the provincials called "the martial law."

II

The ability of regular officers to inflict drastic punishments on enlisted men who
had violated military law was the basic fact of life for the eighteenth-century redcoat. It provided the means by which leaders secured obedience to their commands
and rested on the assumption that soldiers had to be made certain that, however
much they might fear the enemy, they had more to fear from their own leaders if
they disobeyed orders. Regular officers enjoyed a reputation for disciplinary rigor
that was clearly deserved, one which struck awe in the hearts of the provincials. Yet
regular officers, although they administered an intentionally harsh system of military justice, were not sadists. English military law and its application during the
Seven Years' War reflected the suppositions that underlay the English criminal law
in general. Like civilian courts, military tribunals emphasized capital punishment
as the mainstay of order. . . .

. . . Yet the army had at its disposal a wide range of auxiliary punishments, too,
by which it could compel submissive behavior among the common soldiers. Insubordination, for example, a uniquely military crime that was defined ad hoc by officers using personal, subjective criteria, could be punished as severely as theft, with
hundreds of lashes from a cat-o'-nine-tails. Outright defiance of a superior officer
carried the death penalty.

The function of courts-martial in maintaining order, like that of civilian courts,
depended upon the trinity of justice, terror, and mercy. The second element carried
particular weight in the military context, since punishments were swiftly meted out
after sentencing, appeals were impossible, and soldiers were compelled to witness
the administration of the lash or noose at punishment parades. Mercy, too, was dispensed with a practiced hand: Jeffery Amherst pardoned half of the men sentenced
to heavy flogging by courts-martial under his command in 1759 and commuted the
sentences of just under a third of the men sentenced to death. Under the closer control commanders could exercise over the administration of justice, pardons could
be withheld until the very last instant and create an especially touching spectacle as
the condemned man broke down and sobbed in gratitude. Such a situation could be
exploited for immediately practical ends as well. Lord Loudoun once observed that

a properly managed pardon provided the ideal means of inducing a man to enlist for life or to volunteer for service in the West Indies as a token of his appreciation.

Regular officers thus used military justice to promote discipline in the army in much the same way that civilian magistrates in England employed the law to promote social order, protect the interests of property, and provide justice as they understood it. But New Englanders did not share the regular officers' assumptions; nor was the distinctive structure and composition of provincial armies, which fostered close ties between leaders and enlisted men, conducive to the exercise of British-style military justice. Following Loudoun's unification of regular and provincial commands in 1757, Massachusetts provincials were governed by the Rules and Articles of War and by the British Mutiny Act, just as the regulars were. In the years before 1757, however, and in certain isolated commands thereafter, Massachusetts soldiers served under their own version of military law—a system that reflected, as surely as Britain's did, the structure and suppositions of the surrounding society.

The cornerstone of provincial military justice was a brief law, the 1754 Mutiny Act. Mutiny acts were passed by the General Court only in wartime and were limited in operation to one year, or until the year's provincials were discharged from service. The act dealt with offenses which were strictly military: mutiny, sedition, and desertion, as well as incitement to any of those three crimes. It authorized specially convened eleven-member courts-martial to impose capital sentences on those guilty of such offenses. . . . In case a court-martial should actually hand down a death sentence, the penalty had to be approved by the governor of the province, acting as commander in chief, before it could be carried out. The assumption behind the Mutiny Act . . . was that minor aberrations in discipline would be adjudged by courts-martial and "punished by riding the wooden horse, running the gauntlet, and other like military punishment." Soldiers who committed major crimes, as comprehended in the law of the province, might be whipped, expelled from the army, and bound over the civilian authorities; but further punishment could only be exacted by magistrates. Although the traditional military punishment of flogging was not specifically covered, the law of the Bay Colony was understood to govern the permissible number of strokes. Under all but extraordinary circumstances the civil and Biblical limit of thirty-nine lashes was observed by provincial courts-martial until the junction with the regulars in 1757. . . .

By eighteenth-century professional standards, such punishments were ridiculously mild. While riding the wooden horse for an hour and suffering thirty lashes from a cat-o'-nine-tails were painful and humiliating experiences, they were comparatively nothing beside the savage floggings handed out by regular courts-martial. Thirty lashes, at any rate, was not sufficient to deter Private William Mitchell from indulging his penchant for "sauciness to his officers and . . . profane cursing and swearing" only a week after he had been whipped twenty strokes for the same offense." There was, then, comparatively little terror in the provincial punishments; but there was not much mercy either. In no case during 1775 was a man pardoned after sentencing—the standard British means of keeping soldiers both grateful and submissive. Far from creating the climactic scene in a drama of magisterial justice and mercy, provincial punishments were predictable, workaday penalties. . . .

Maintaining order in the camps was a major concern of both regular and provincial officers, but they employed very different methods to do so. Whenever a regular commander wanted to correct a breach of camp discipline, he would issue an order identifying the practice he wanted to suppress and specifying the punishment that would be levied on offenders if they did not immediately desist. These orders were terse and peremptory. The following examples, issued at Fort Edward in 1758, are typical:

> [3 June.] All soldiers and followers of the army who are found gaming in camp, shall immediately receive three hundred lashes without a court martial.
>
> [3 June.] The Article of War, which forbids, on pain of death or such other punishment as shall be ordered by a general court martial, if any person [is] to occasion false alarms in camp by discharging of firearms, by drawing of swords, by beating of drums, or by any other means whatsoever, will, for the future, be strictly put in execution.
>
> [15 June.] Any sutler who is convicted of selling or giving any rum to a soldier will immediately receive two hundred lashes, [have] his liquors seized, and [be] banished [from] the camp.

Provincial orders. on the other hand, took the form of admonitions, and rarely included the explicit threat of punishment. In 1755, for example, when Winslow's men began to violate restrictions on leaving their encampment at Grand Pré, Winslow did not threaten; instead, he issued an order "to remind the soldiers of this camp of the former orders" against passing beyond the picquet line without permission. . . .

Joseph Frye's orders demonstrate the persistent provincial assumption that discipline did not necessarily require the free application of physical coercion. Instead of linking promises of punishment to his directives, Frye tried to explain the reasons behind them. He addressed his men paternally, as if their refractoriness was somehow the product of childishness or misinformation. His mildness cannot be explained as the consequence of inexperience, stupidity, or weakness. Frye had led troops in the previous war; he had served in Acadia in 1755 as a combat commander and had fulfilled his duties with great coolness and competence at the siege of Fort William Henry in 1757. He was obviously intelligent: his account of the atrocities that followed the capitulation of Fort William Henry stands as a model of clarity and precision. And he was not incapable of applying force, since he did approve at least one whipping—a fifty-lash sentence for a member of his artillery train, on 8 June 1759. The only satisfactory explanation of his aversion to threatening physical punishment is that he did not believe such a policy was necessary to secure the cooperation of his troops. . . . At any rate he never became sufficiently disillusioned with his persuasive, paternalist methods to abandon them. He evidently assumed to the very last that the men under his command were susceptible of instruction, that once they came to understand what was expected of them, and why, they would do their duty. . . .

The difference between the provincial and the regular approach to disciplining habitual offenders emerges in an exchange between John Winslow and Lord Loudoun in 1756. In September Winslow found himself faced with a minor dilemma: a provincial general court-martial, acting under the authority of the Massachusetts Mutiny Act, had condemned an infamous deserter to death at Fort William Henry. Normally Winslow would have ordered the man to be drummed out of the camp with a noose about his neck to symbolize his commission of a capital crime. Now, because of his new subordinate relationship to Loudoun, he was unsure whether he had the authority to grant a pardon. He decided to ask for guidance: "I am not clear in hanging matters and, if your lordship thinks proper, in lieu thereof will drum the fellow out of the regiment as he is, it seems, a common disturber of the camp." Loudoun was astonished at Winslow's proposal. Merely to expel the man, he replied, would be looked on by the soldiers "as no punishment at all" and would set a bad example. He suggested that Winslow go ahead with the reprieve, but to manage it in such a way as to induce the man to enlist for life in a regular regiment, thus providing a salutary example for the other soldiers even as he secured a new soldier for the king's troops. . . .

Provincial disciplinary practices and the assumptions that underlay them reflected traditional New England ideals of community life—that men ought to be knit together as one in the common pursuit of God's will. Nothing could have been less consistent with British conceptions of military order, or less understandable to most redcoat officers. The common soldiers of New England viewed the operation of the regulars' disciplinary system with equal incomprehension—bafflement alloyed, naturally enough, with the anxiety that they might at any time become the system's next victims.

III

The enlisted men who were the principal subjects of the disciplinary system did not see military justice from the vantage point of a court-martial board. For them it was a levy of pain: soldiers like themselves being flogged in a daily succession, irregularly punctuated by executions. Soldiers who served in 1757 and thereafter were intensely conscious of the coercive aspects of military discipline. It had not always been so: provincials who kept diaries in 1754–1756 rarely mentioned physical punishments. No soldier in the early years of the war, in fact, referred to corporal punishment more than a single time in his journal, and several made no mention at all. . . .

By comparison, at Ford Edward between 10 May and 3 November 1757, Private Luke Gridley recorded eighty-two punishments, including seventy-one floggings and six executions—on average, three to four sentences carried out per week. In his almost adverb-free diary, Gridley wrote of men being "whipped cruelly" and described this relatively mild punishment, one of the first he witnessed:

> Day 25th [of May]. There was one Daniel Boake, one of Captain Gallup's men, run the gauntlet through thirty men for sleeping on guard. [He] cried "Lord God have mercy on me," the blood flying every stroke. This was a sorrowful sight.

As the campaign wore on, Gridley grew accustomed to such sights, and the entries in his journal became less graphic, but with ritual precision he went on recording every punishment he saw and others that he heard about.

The eighty-odd instances of disciplinary action that Gridley noted probably did not exceed what the average soldier would have seen or heard described during a single campaign. . . .The total of all public punishments in Amherst's expeditionary army was . . . at least as great as that which Gridley recorded at Fort Edward two years earlier.

From the soldiers' point of view, corporal punishment was one of the constants of life; moreover, they saw capital sentences exacted every month or two. Officers, not personally threatened by the noose or the cat, could observe the goings-on with a kind of sympathetic detachment. "There is almost every day more or less whipped or picqueted or some other ways punished," wrote Caleb Rea. For the enlisted men, however, the fall of the lash and "the shrieks and cries" of the afflicted were more than the accuse of pity: they were perpetual reminders that soldiers under British discipline lived under a reign of terror. Punishments of provincials and regulars alike distressed New Englanders, for both groups were equally at risk. Even the most dispassionate observers among the New England soldiers were appalled to see a man "whipped cruelly" or "whipped till the blood came out at the knee of his breeches." Diaries indicate that the horror of the floggings formed part of the currency of camp rumor: "This Day," wrote Samuel Morris on Sunday, 2 September 1759, "there was a man whipped to death belonging to the Light Infantry. They say he had twenty-five lashes after he was dead."

The feelings of resentment, fear, and powerlessness aroused by such punishments burned the sight into witnesses' memories. David Perry was looking back across almost sixty years when he recalled an episode that took place near Halifax, Nova Scotia, in 1762:

> Three men, for some trifling offense which I do not recollect, were tied up to be whipped. One of them was to receive eight hundred lashes, the others five hundred apiece. By the time they had received three hundred lashes, the flesh appeared to be entirely whipped from their shoulders, and they hung as mute and motionless as though they had been long since deprived of life. But this was not enough. The doctor stood by with a vial of sharp stuff, which he would ever and anon apply to their noses, and finding, by the pain it gave them, that some signs of life remained, he would tell them, "d——mn you, you can bear it yet"—and then the whipping would commence again. It was . . . by far worse than death. I felt at the time as though I could have taken summary vengeance on those who were the authors of it, on the spot, had it been in my power to do it.

Hideous as eight hundred lashes was, it was far from being the worst a man could receive: a thousand stripes was the standard punishment for desertion, and sentences of as many as fifteen hundred were awarded for theft.

But even more than floggings, executions exercised fascination and horror for the provincials. This was of course what the commanders who signed the death warrants intended, assuming that the drama of the gallows would deter potential criminals from mischief-making. The reactions of the witnesses, in their length and detail, bear out the commanders' expectations, for the provincials were paying close attention indeed. . . .

> This forenoon, about nine o'clock, one of the regulars was hanged for thefts. He confessed on the ladder that gaming, robbery, theft, whoring, bad company-keeping, etc. were [the] sins which brought him to this shameful untimely death, and warned his fellow soldier[s] against such vices. He desired the prayers of the people standing by for his poor soul, and [was] praying for himself [as he] was hove off the ladder. The Lord makes this sad spectacle a means of warning effectually all from the sad [sins] that the soldiery are much addicted to.

It might be added that no commander could have wished for a more exemplary performance than that rendered by the hanged man. . . . When the convict did not cooperate, however, the effect on the observer was no less powerful:

> The 20th [of July, 1759]. This morning the criminal that was condemned yesterday [a redcoat, and a notorious thief] was brought forth . . . to be shot. . . . When he came to the place of execution, he was very loath to die. They could not persuade him to kneel down to be shot. They then tied him hand and foot but could not make him stand still. They then took and tied [him] to an old log and he hung down underside the log. They then fired and killed him.

The soldier who described this pathetic episode, Lemuel Wood, had witnessed his first firing squad execution just seven days earlier. He had described that event with equal precision:

> The 13 [th of July, 1759]. This morning at six o'clock a court-martial set for the trial of the deserter that was brought in yesterday. He was sentenced . . . to be shot today at twelve o'clock in the front of the quarter guard of Forbes's Regiment. Accordingly all the picquets of the lines was drawn up for the execution of the above prisoner. The provost guard brought forth the prisoner and marched him round before all the regulars' regiments [and] from thence to the place of execution. There was drawn out of the regiment to which the prisoner belonged [two] platoons of six men each. The prisoner was brought and set before one of the platoons and kneeled down upon his knees. He clinched his hand. The platoon of six men each of them fired him through the body. The other platoon then came up instantly and fired him through the head and blowed his head all to pieces. They then dug a grave by his side and tumbled him in and covered him up, and that was an end of the whole.

Lemuel Wood was not yet eighteen when he described this scene. His clarity in depicting this ritual promenade of the prisoner, the size of the firing squads, and the last gesture of the condemned man's "clinched" hand all suggest the strength of the impression that the execution, and especially the gratuitous violence of the second volley, made upon him. If he did not remember these details into his old age—and he died an old man—all he needed to do was consult this diary to bring back the images. One suspects, however, that Wood had no need to refresh his memory: like David Perry's recollection of the barbarous floggings at Halifax, these were sights burned into his consciousness, memories that would live as long as the man.

Such descriptions vividly convey the effects of regular-style discipline on New England provincials. Punishments were unarguable successful in striking awe into the hearts of New Englanders; at the same time, however, they created a vigorously unfavorable impression of the regular officers. When David Perry recounted the brutal whipping at Halifax, he remembered it not just as an example of cruel treatment but as "a specimen of *British* cruelty." Gibson Clough, as he arrived at Louisbourg, noted darkly that "there is no spare here of the whip." When he realized later that he would be detained beyond his enlistment, Clough reflected that we now see what it is be under martial law and to be with the regulars, who are but little better than slaves to their officers." As the provincials realized, the regulars' unyielding disciplinary system forged an effective, efficient, fighting force, the product of a society and culture more different from New England's than the New Englanders had ever suspected. The provincials, who had only the most rudimentary understanding of cultural differences, could hardly have failed to explain the disparity between regular behavior and their own expectations in moral terms. When the New Englanders weighed their allies in the moral balance, they could only find the redcoats wanting.

Britain Defined by Its Empire

P. J. MARSHALL

In the last years of the Seven Years War British fleets and armies ranged across the world, dismembering the colonial empires of France and Spain. Yet, as tension rose in the early 1750s and undeclared war gave way to open war, British ministers viewed the prospect of defending the British Isles and Britain's European and world-wide interests with dismay. There seemed to be far too many points of danger. . . .

On the American continent, the peoples of New England could be presumed to be willing and able to defend themselves. The Virginians might do so after a fashion. Elsewhere, however, there were glaring weaknesses. Nova Scotia was taken to be a particularly acute problem. There the so-called "neutral" French and their Indian allies would let in the French of New France. Once Halifax had fallen, so alarmist scenarios went, the northern colonies would be rolled up. Pennsylvania was seen as an open incitement to French attack. Its Quaker politicians would do nothing for their own defence and there was a large population of unassimilated Germans whose loyalty seemed questionable. South Carolina and Georgia could not effectively defend themselves against the Cherokees, let alone against a European enemy. In the Caribbean the great wealth of Jamaica was thought to lie open for the picking. The disproportion between slaves and whites was so great that the Jamaica militia was hard pressed to contain slave revolts; it could do nothing to ward off a French or a Spanish attack. The East India Company was appealing for help against French reinforcements on the coast of Coromandel [in India] at the moment when a quite different thunderbolt struck them, as the Nawab of Bengal's troops overwhelmed Calcutta.

This brief summary indicates that mid-eighteenth-century Britain felt itself threatened, not just by the Bourbon enemy from without but by many possible enemies from within: Highland Scots, Irish Catholics, the Indians of the North American continent, non-British settlers in the colonies, the successor states to the Mughal Empire, and African slaves might all turn against Britain. Yet events were soon to show that potential enemies within could be turned into loyal subjects and allies. Highlanders became the flower of the British army. The first very tentative steps were taken towards tapping the resources of Catholic Irish manpower for the forces of the Crown. Pennsylvania Germans were recruited into regiments of Royal Americans. Colonial Americans, if never as many as was hoped, were enlisted into royal regiments, while some 21,000 American Provincial troops were mobilised for the 1758 campaign in North America. By the end of the war the British had engaged on their side most of the Indian peoples in the area of the conflict in America. Within a year of the end of the war, General Amherst was even proposing that a corps of French Americans should be raised for British service. The East India Company enlisted very large numbers of Indian sepoys for the war and informed them into a permanent part of its army, paid for by resources extracted from Indian rulers who were now its docile allies. The Jamaica maroons had been invaluable in suppressing

From P. J. Marshall, "A Nation Defined by Empire, 1755–1776," in Alexander Grant and Keith J. Stringer, eds., *Uniting the Kingdom? The Making of British History.* Copyright © 1955. Reprinted by permission of the publisher. Taylor & Francis Books Ltd.

the 1760 slave revolt, and there was a project for raising a regiment of free blacks for the attack on Havana in 1762.

War had thus forced the British greatly to widen the base of their military manpower. . . . Even the king's own electoral Hanoverian troops were regarded as "foreign." The involvement of other troops in British service was, however, part of important processes of change, bringing about the closer integration both of the British Isles and of that complex network of overseas interests which contemporaries were coming to call the British Empire. These two developments were linked. Successful war overseas did much to cement the Union between England and Scotland. . . . It both provided a focus for a British triumphalism and offered great rewards to the Scots. War overseas also had significant implications for Ireland's relations with Britain. But if war helped to consolidate Britain within the British Isles, it also helped to set limits to any wider Britain. The lesson of war for Britain's rulers was that empire required the effective exercise of authority. Whatever the actual scale of their contributions, colonial Americans were judged to have questioned authority. When efforts were made to strengthen the exercise of authority over the colonies after 1763, American questioning escalated into outright resistance. By their resistance, in the eyes of the majority of British people, Americans forfeited their right to be counted as British. So my theme is both the integration of the United Kingdom and the Empire, and the contradiction of the nation.

British forces were committed outside Europe, above all in North America, on a scale that was entirely new. The size of this commitment both focused an overwhelming public attention on empire in America and exposed very many British people to service in that Empire. The extent to which the forces deployed in America were British in the widest sense was brought out by a survey ordered by Lord Loudoun of the troops assembled in 1757 at Halifax for the aborted attack on Louisbourg. Returns were required for the nationality of the men from the British Isles, which was defined as English, 'Scotch' or Irish. English—3,426—and Irish—3,138—were almost equal, with Scots markedly lower at 1,390. Irish officers actually outnumbered the English by 166 to 131, with 71 Scots. . . . Since a return for the Highland regiments in America is not included in the Halifax contingent, the Scottish element is certainly too low to represent the Scottish contribution to the army as a whole. A return for Montgomery's Highlanders in South Carolina shows that the regiment was exactly what its name would suggest. All the officers were Scottish and the rank and file were described as 1,001 Highland and 59 Lowland Scots. . . .

. . . There is much evidence suggesting that Scottish soldiers enlisted very readily for America, and there seems little doubt that they did so as a form of emigration. . . .

Although prohibitions on the recruiting of Irish Catholic soldiers were not officially lifted until 1771, it seems realistic to suppose that there were Catholics among the large number of soldiers classified as Irish. The Lord Lieutenant believed that any regiment recruited in Ireland was likely to contain Papists. . . . Loudoun tried to hunt Catholics out of his army, but the British government could not for long ignore their potential contribution as manpower. . . . With the outbreak of the American War . . . [a] full-scale programme of Catholic recruiting was initiated. Lord George Germain commented in 1775 that ministers would not listen to any proposals for raising new corps, 'so long as they flatter themselves with being able to recruit the regiments from Irish Roman Catholics.' Formal relaxation of parts of the penal laws [against Catholics] was to follow later in the war.

The needs of war pulled the United Kingdom closer together. The war also brought about very significant changes in relations between Britain and her overseas possessions. These changes gave definition to empire. . . . Much has been written about the strains put on relations between Britain and the Thirteen Colonies by questions of the raising of provincial regiments and the authority to be exercised over them by British commanders, the quartering of troops, British intervention in Indian affairs, the requisition of labour and transport, and many other issues. Had Lord Loudoun had his way he would have forced a showdown with some of the provinces in 1757. In recalling him Pitt publicly upbraided him for "exerting too much authority over the people of the country [and] not treating the provincial troops as well as they deserved." For the rest of the war the colonies were treated with great indulgence as more or less equal partners in war, but the reckoning was only put off. In the eyes of most British commanders, the colonies had not been partners; they had been not altogether willing subordinates. . . .

I would like to . . . illustrate strikingly the way in which the nature of the British Empire was being reassessed: the cases of the Pennsylvania Germans and of the French and the Indians of British North America. They show how metropolitan authority was responding to the 'strangers withing the realm.' . . .

"Foreign Protestants" had become an almost universal panacea for any imperial problem. It was assumed that Germany and Switzerland offered a limitless supply of suitable colonists—docile, industrious people with martial qualities. To encourage their settlement in America, the British Parliament had passed acts offering them naturalisation on very easy terms. By the 1750s, however, the concentration of Germans in Pennsylvania—Franklin's estimate of 100,000 out of a provincial population of 190,000 circulated widely—was causing concern. Questions were raised as to how thoroughly they had been assimilated. They gave offence by seeming to vote regularly for Quakers. Doubts were even expressed as to whether they might not "be led away from the British interest by French emissaries." To try to turn the Germans into good British subjects, a Society of Nobility and Gentry was formed in London in 1753 with full royal and ministerial support to set up schools to teach English to young Germans in America. . . . Under the pressures of war, however, British ministers looked at the Pennsylvania Germans in a different light. "An hundred thousand Germans and Swiss, animated by the most amiable principles, zeal for religion, passion for liberty, and a spirit of industry" were described in Parliament as "a providential resource." They were to be recruited into special Royal American regiments under foreign officers sent to America from Europe. After the war . . . virtually every colony continued to encourage the unrestricted import of foreign Protestants.

At the beginning of the war Catholic French were regarded as enemies rather than subjects. In 1755, 6,000 French were expelled from Acadia. They were to be distributed throughout other British colonies where it was hoped they would be subjected to unremitting anglicisation. . . . After the capture of Louisbourg in 1758, the destruction of Canadian settlements and the deportation of their inhabitants continued around the estuary of the St Lawrence.

Two years later a marked change in attitudes became apparent. Amherst brought his army into Montreal in 1760, not as the agents of vengeance, . . . but as the bringers of a new order of justice and benevolence. . . . He was commended by British ministers and told that Britain did not wish to lose its new French subjects, "who being now equally his Majesty's subjects are consequently equally entitled to his protection." They must be allowed to "enjoy the full benefits of that indulgent and benign government which constitutes the peculiar happiness of all who are subjects of the British Empire." They should not even be subjected to "uncharitable reflections on the errors of that mistaken religion, which they unhappily profess." The line forward to the Quebec Act of 1774 and the official recognition of the Catholic Church in Canada was clear.

The war had forced a serious British reappraisal of the foreign "strangers within the realm." Anglicisation had been advocated but tacitly shelved. The British Empire needed manpower, both for war and for settlement. An even greater deployment of British manpower overseas was ruled out. . . . Continental Europeans must be accepted, Protestants for choice, but even Catholics, if need be. . . . But necessity was also being embellished by rhetoric, and pride was being taken in a cosmopolitan empire living in prosperity under a benevolent British rule.

The war also forced consideration of non-Europeans strangers. . . . During and immediately after the war . . . American Indians affairs . . . obsessed the British ministers and a wider public. The success of the French in constructing Indian alliances, together with horrifying stories of massacres along the British American frontier, led to imperial intervention in the appointing of Indian superintendents and to the laying down of rules for the treatment of Indians. . . . In his brief of 1762 for charitable collections for the new colleges in New York and Philadelphia, George III wrote of his satisfaction at the prospect of bringing "barbarous nations within the pale of religion and civil life." Much money was raised for the purpose by the Anglican Society for the Propagation of the Gospel, by the Church of Scotland Society for Propagating Christian Knowledge, by the New England Company, and by Presbyterians and Moravians. By 1769 more money was said to be being raised in England and Scotland than could actually be spent on available missionaries and school-masters.

Any kind of systematic theorising about the nature of the "Empire" which Britain had acquired lagged far behind the fact of acquisition and the need to resolve practical problems in very diverse situations. . . . The simplest model for empire was an old but still extremely powerful one. Colonies were dominions of the Crown and the Empire was united by common allegiance to the king. "The [American] provinces seem to be falling off from their duty to their King in not raising the number of men his Majesty has been pleased to require of them," Amherst lamented in 1761. He attributed this to "a want of a due sense of the war being carried on to the general good of his Majesty's subjects." New peoples could easily be incorporated into the Empire on these principles. They became the king's subjects by right of conquest. This doctrine was immediately applied to the French of North America and Grenada. Indians living in the king's dominions in America were also his subjects, although this was not at first clearly spelled out for the Indians in the vast new territories acquired in 1763; they were said to be peoples "with whom we are connected and who live under our protection." Whether Indians who lived in the new provinces of the East India Company were subjects of the Crown was a complex question. In theory they were still subjects of the Mughal emperor, who had delegated his authority to the East India Company. Legal opinion considered, however, that the sovereignty of the Crown extended over conquests made by or grants awarded to British subjects. In 1773 the House of Commons resolved that the Company's possessions belonged to the British state. By then the concept that the British Crown had "subjects in Asia, as well as those in America" was losing some of its novelty. Burke was to take pleasure in referring to "our fellow subjects" in India.

For all its apparent simplicity, the doctrine of an empire based on obedience to the Crown had much wider implications by the mid-eighteenth century. When Americans like Franklin took the doctrine literally and proclaimed that their allegiance to Britain was analogous to that of Hanover, that is that it rested solely on obedience owed to a common sovereign, they were reminded that their obedience was, in the words of the Declaratory Act of 1766, to "the imperial Crown and Parliament of Great Britain," which had full power to make laws binding on them "in all cases whatsoever."

Yet even with this most portentous elaboration that obedience to the Crown meant obedience to Parliament, the doctrine of an empire based on a common link of obedience binding together the different subjects of the Crown was an admirably flexible one that could accommodate all sorts of diversity. In return for protection subjects owed obedience, but they did not have to conform in any other way. . . .

Throughout the rest of Britain's imperial history many British people have taken pride in the concept of a diverse empire of many "races," as they usually put it, differing in religion, language, law and custom, but united in obedience to one sovereign. Yet to many others, just as the United Kingdom was more than a mere union of separate peoples under a common Crown, the Empire embodied a diffusion of Britishness, which made it a distinctly British empire. Such aspirations were very much alive in the eighteenth century, as attempts to anglicise Acadians or Pennsylvania Germans or to bring Indians within the fold of Christian civilisation clearly indicate. Arthur Young's *Political Essays Concerning the Present State of the British Empire* of 1772 began with a characteristic statement of such aspirations.

> The British dominions consist of Great Britain and Ireland, divers colonies and settlements in all parts of the world and there appears not any just reason for considering these countries in any other light than as a part of a whole . . . The clearest method is to consider all as forming one nation, united under one sovereign, speaking the same language and enjoying the same liberty, but living in different parts of the world.

Contemporaries were no doubt as puzzled as historians are by the omission of religion from language and liberty as the elements that constitute a nation, but the implications are clear: Young conceived of empire as more than different peoples "united under one sovereign." It was an extension of the British nation overseas. . . .

In Young's time, as in later periods, such aspirations of course embodied a highly selective view of empire. In postulating a world-wide nation, Young took no account of ethnic and linguistic diversity in America, let alone of the East India Company's dominions. Nevertheless, his belief that the British colonies overseas constituted one nation in terms of language and liberty and, others would have added, of religion would have been very widely shared by people of British origin on both sides of the Atlantic in 1772. Yet within three years the supposed nation began to split apart at Lexington and Concord. It became clear, at least in retrospect, that within the parameters that seemed to unite Britons there were crucial differences. If there was a Britishness that could sustain a union of England, Wales and Scotland and which might . . . have been extended to Ireland, it could not be extended indefinitely.

About language there was virtually no disagreement throughout the British world. The eighteenth century was the age of the triumphant march of English. It was propagated in the Highlands with official support. The Society for Promoting English Protestant Schools attempted to do the same thing in Ireland. Although the London Society for Schools in Pennsylvania ran out of money, the German communities in the American colonies on their own acquired the English that enabled them to participate in public and commercial life. . . .

Convention assumed that common ideals of religion and liberty united British of all sorts and conditions. Yet interpretations of what constituted these ideals were beginning to differ.

For the generation of the Seven Years War the British Empire was defined by Protestantism and the war was fought in defence of Protestantism. . . . In such an emergency Protestants needed to sink their differences. Lord Loudoun, although he thought Quakers unfit for any position of responsibility, tried to rally all shades of Protestant opinion in the colonies. At Boston he attended the Anglican King's Chapel in the morning, went to Dr Sewall's meeting house in the afternoon, and invited a Presbyterian to say Grace at dinner. . . .

Pitt was a strong upholder of the alliance of all Protestants:

> The Presbyterian dissenters in general, must ever deserve to be considered in opposition to the Church of Rome, as a very valuable branch of the Reformation, and that with regard to their civil principles that respectable body have, in all times, shewed themselves, both in England and in Ireland, firm and zealous supporters of the glorious revolution under King William, and the present happy establishment.

The people of New England were said almost to "idolise" Pitt, and he continued to praise "the loyal free and Protestant Americans' when it was ceasing to be fashionable to do so.

Official British policy was generally even-handed in its dealings with all denominations of colonial Protestants. . . . A Pennsylvania Quaker was present when the British Friends delivered their address of loyalty on the accession of George III and received the king's assurance of his "protection." Moravians were given recognition by an Act of Parliament in 1749. The London Society for German Schools paid subsidies to Calvinist and Lutheran ministers in Pennsylvania. American Anglicans, especially from the northern Provinces, were increasingly assertive with the growth of their numbers, but they were generally disappointed by the attitude of British ministers. . . .

In 1761 Samuel Davies, the Virginian Presbyterian, delivered a eulogy on George II. "In his reign the state had been the guardian of Christians in general . . . the defence of the Dissenter as well as of the Conformist: of TOLERATION as well as of the ESTABLISHMENT." The British state never formally abandoned its patronage of Dissent, but the relationship was to fray somewhat in the years ahead. . . . Outright opposition to government authority appeared among the Congregationalists of Massachusetts, some of whose ministers were reported to be abetting riot from the mid-1760s, and among the Presbyterians of Ulster in the agrarian disorders of the early 1770s. . . . From 1775 opposition in England to Lord North's government over America was identified with Dissent, with good reason. . . . "Dissenters provided the dominant ideology of opposition and the charismatic leadership for the pro-American agitation." On their side, British governments seemed to be consorting with High Anglicans but, most reprehensibly from the American point of view, to be extending their indulgence to Catholics, first of all in Grenada, then in Canada, and ultimately in Britain itself.

With the ending of the Seven Years War many Americans began to fear that the association between Britishness and Protestant ecumenism was breaking down. Their fears were exaggerated, but not without some foundation. Anglicanism was gaining a greater degree of official patronage in the Empire, as the establishment of the first colonial bishoprics after the American war was to confirm, while imperial Britain was becoming less and less fasitidious as to the faiths, not just Catholicism, but Islam and Hinduism as well, with which it would have dealings.

Arthur Young described the British Empire as a single nation, enjoying "the same liberty." By 1772 there were of course sharp disputes as to what constituted British liberty. . . . It is sufficient to note that the bulk of British opinion did indeed believe that the British Empire was unique among modern European empires in resting on liberty, but that liberty also required obedience to the duly authorised prerogatives of the executive government and to the will of a sovereign parliament. War had reinforced the need for obedience. Americans, on the other hand, had a long record of disobeying their Governors and had recently taken to disregarding Acts of Parliament as well. "Republican" and "levelling" principles seemed to be rife among them. For its part, colonial opinion was convinced that Britain was disregarding the common heritage of liberty that had kept the Empire united, and that there was a conspiracy to destroy this on both sides of the Atlantic. Again, of course, they exaggerated greatly, but . . . the mainstream of British political beliefs was becoming increasingly authoritarian. . . .

There were significant differences across the Atlantic as to what British Protestantism and British liberty implied. How seriously did these differences threaten any sense of a single "nation"? The evidence from the writings of the colonial elites leaves little doubt that they thought of themselves as part of a British nation until very late in the conflict. The concepts of "country" and "nation" constantly recur in their writings. These appear to have had meanings that were clearly distinct. For Washington, for instance, his "country" was Virginia, but his "nation" was Britain. "American" was very widely used as a descriptive term, but it seems only slowly to have been invested with significance as a references point for identity. One of Franklin's correspondents told him of an encounter in London in 1771, when his describing himself as an "American" led his British companion to say: "I hope you don't look on yourself as an American. I told him yes I did and gloried in the name." But he still felt it necessary to add: "for that I look'd upon a good Englishman and a good American to be synonymous terms it being impossible to be one without being the other also." Many of those who called themselves "Americans" in the 1770s seem to have implied that they were doing so because they had been deprived of their Britishness.

There were innumerable links, such as kinship, religious denomination or business dealings, tying people in Britain to people in the colonies. But whether opinion in Britain itself generally thought of colonial Americans as belonging to a single nation with them is doubtful. . . . Historians of Ireland have pointed out that the eighteenth-century English were not good at distinguishing: all Irish people were simply "Irish" to them and invested with the same qualities. So it was with Americans, who were lumped together and also invested with certain qualities. This implied that they were a distinct people. Lord Halifax made this point explicitly when he commented in 1763 that: "The people of England seem to consider the inhabitants of these provinces, though H. M.'s subjects, as foreigners." In the correspondence of Americans in Britain there are many references to the ignorance of British people about the colonies but also to a certain pride of possession over a supposedly subject people. James Fothergill, the London Quaker, warned his American correspondent that, at least until the Stamp Act crisis, "not one half of this nation knew what country their American brothers sprang from, what language they spoke, whether they were black or white," but "that American talk of resistance" aroused "the mastif spirit of John Bull," and "pride and passion" would "carry him headlong into battle and to violence." . . .

Some colonial Americans came to view the rise of the new cosmopolitan British Empire with dismay. "They are arming every hand, Protestant and Catholic, English, Irish, Scotch, Hanoverians, Hessians, Indians, Canadians against the devoted colonies," Arthur Lee wrote in anguish in 1775. Yet for most British people the two concepts of empire that I have tried to identify overlapped, rather than competed with, one another. On the one hand, Britain conceived herself as being at the centre of a diversity of peoples tied by obligations of obedience to the British state in return for protection from it. . . . The British were coming to define themselves as a people who ruled over other peoples.

Yet the eighteenth-century Empire and the Empire in all its future incarnations amounted to more than the exercise of rule over other people. Through empire the British aspired to be a world-wide people. The experience of the eighteenth century showed how difficult such aspirations would be to fulfill. It made it clear that Britishness was not a set of immutable principles about religion, language and liberty, but was specific to time and place and had evolved on different historical trajectories in different situations. In crucial respects, the practice of Britishness in America and that in the British Isles had come to deviate from one another, as the Seven Years War and its aftermath were to make clear. The eighteenth-century experience also revealed that "imagined communities" of Britishness were parochial. English people could perhaps envisage a common community with the Welsh and, often with much difficulty, with the Scots, but they failed to incorporate the Irish or colonial Americans into their idea of nation. Under hard necessity and by what still seems a very extraordinary feat of creative imagination, citizens of individual colonial "countries" could eventually extend their loyalties to an idea of America, even while the self-images of many of them probably remained locked in an idealised English nation. . . .

The lesson, for the future of the British Empire, of the war of Britishnesses that broke out in 1775 was that aspirations for the British to be one worldwide people would never be realised. With greater dexterity of imperial management than was shown in the 1760s and 1770s, a loose-joined Empire and later Commonwealth of more or less British peoples closely allied with one another would certainly endure from the nineteenth century into the twentieth, but "Greater Britons," merging Canadians, Australians, New Zealanders and white South Africans with Britons, would not come about, however much enthusiasts might desire them. The conventional wisdom that these aspirations were incompatible with colonial nationalism is no doubt true, but they were also incompatible with that deep-rooted plant that was British parochialism.

FURTHER READING

Fred Anderson, *The Crucible of War: The Seven Years' War and the Fate of Empire in North America, 1754–1766* (2000)

———, *A People's Army: Massachusetts Soldiers and Society in the Seven Years' War* (1984)

George Louis Beer, *British Colonial Policy, 1754–1765* (1907)

John Brewer, *Party Ideology and Popular Politics at the Accession of George III* (1976)

———, *The Sinews of Power: War, Money and the English State, 1688–1783* (1989)

John Brooke, *King George III* (1972)

Ian R. Christie, *Crisis of Empire: Great Britain and the American Colonies, 1754–1783* (1967)

Lawrence H. Gipson, "The American Revolution as an Aftermath of the Great War for the Empire, 1754–1763," *Political Science Quarterly* 65 (1950), 86–104

———, *The Great War for the Empire: The Years of Defeat, 1754–1757* (1946)

———, *The Great War for the Empire: The Victorious Years, 1758–1760* (1949)

———, *The Great War for the Empire: The Culmination, 1760–1763* (1953)

Alexander Grant and Keith J. Stringer, eds., *Uniting the Kingdom? The Making of British History* (1995)

Jack P. Greene, *Peripheries and Center: Constitutional Development in the Extended Politics of the British Empire and the United States, 1607–1788* (1986)

Edward P. Hamilton, *The French and Indian Wars: The Story of Battles and Forts in the Wilderness* (1962)

Michael Kammen, *Empire and Interest: The American Colonies and the Politics of Mercantilism* (1970)

Nancy F. Koehn, *The Power of Commerce: Economy and Governance in the First British Empire* (1994)

Paul E. Kopperman, *Braddock at the Monongahela* (1977)

Leonard W. Labaree, "Benjamin Franklin and the Defense of Pennsylvania, 1754–1757," *Pennsylvania History* 29 (1962), 7–23

———, *Royal Government in America: A Study of the British Colonial System Before 1783* (1930)

Douglas Edward Leach, *Roots of Conflict: British Armed Forces and Colonial Americans, 1677–1763* (1986)

Jack D. Marietta, "Conscience, the Quaker Community, and the French and Indian War," *Pennsylvania Magazine of History and Biography* 95 (1971), 3–27

John M. Murrin, "The French and Indian War, the American Revolution, and the Counterfactual Hypotheses: Reflections on Lawrence Henry Gipson and John Shy," *Reviews in American History* 1 (1973), 307–318

Curtis P. Nettels, "British Mercantilism and the Economic Development of the Thirteen Colonies," *Journal of Economic History* 12 (1952), 105–114

Alison Gilbert Olson, *Making the Empire Work: London and American Interest Groups, 1690–1790* (1992)

Francis Parkman, *Montcalm and Wolfe* (1884)

William Pencak, *War and Politics and Revolution in Provincial Massachusetts* (1981)

G. A. Rawlyk, *Yankees at Louisbourg* (1967)

Alan Rogers, *Empire and Liberty: American Resistance to British Authority, 1775–1763* (1974)

O. A. Sherrard, *Lord Chatham: Pitt and the Seven Years' War* (1955)

John Shy, *Toward Lexington: The Role of the British Army in the Coming of the American Revolution* (1965)

Jack M. Sosin, *Whitehall and the Wilderness: The Middle West in British Colonial Policy, 1760–1775* (1961)

C. P. Stacey, *Quebec, 1759: The Siege and the Battle* (1959)

British Reforms
and Colonial Resistance

When, in the aftermath of the French and Indian War, Britain sought to
reform its imperial system, it employed both administrative and legislative
measures. Colonial administration was tightened by regulations such as the
Orders in Council, which ended absentee office-holding in the colonies and
provided lucrative incentives for customs enforcement; in addition, the Royal
Proclamation of 1763 curtailed settlement west of the Appalachians. Even
more important for enlarging British political power, as well as crystallizing
American resistance, was new legislation: the Currency and Revenue (or Sugar)
acts of 1764 and the Stamp Act of March 22, 1765. While all these measures
sparked colonial protest, it was the Stamp Act that set off a wave of resistance
of unprecedented breadth, intensity, and intercolonial coordination. This law
extended to America a broadly based form of direct taxation long used in Britain.
It required the colonists to pay a tax, in silver, on a long list of legal documents
and printed materials. Every paper filed in a legal proceeding, every deed and
land survey, every will, all licenses and diplomas, as well as all bonds written
to secure loans were included. Colonists in all walks of life were affected,
because the Stamp Act also taxed every indenture and apprenticeship paper,
all newspapers and newspaper advertisements, pamphlets, almanacs, and even
playing cards.

Protests, both verbal and violent, erupted all over the colonies. Some emphasized the absolute constitutional right to taxation by representatives; others complained of the adverse economic effects of the Stamp Act; and some asserted that
while Parliament had the right to regulate colonial trade through legislation, it
could not legally enact taxes for the colonies.

American opposition succeeded, but only in part. In 1766, Lord Rockingham,
the new prime minister, persuaded Parliament to repeal the Stamp Act as a matter
of expedience, but at the same time, Parliament passed the Declaratory Act, asserting its full legislative powers. In the following year, 1767, it would enact the
Townshend Duties to raise revenues on the importation of nearly all kinds of
paper, on the widely used commodity tea, on window glass, painters' colors, and
red and white lead (also used in paint). The new taxes provoked new protests, a

*nonimportation movement, and the further development of constitutional argu-
ments. Finally, in 1770, the Townshend Acts were repealed except for the duty on
tea, which Britain retained as a matter of principle.*

D O C U M E N T S

The first three documents—the Virginia Resolves of 1765 (proposed by Patrick Henry),
Governor Francis Bernard's account of the Boston riot of August 14, 1765, and the Declarations of the Stamp Act Congress—show the ideas and actions of a politically awakened
colonial population. The several following documents, comprising the "William Pym"
newspaper essay, the interrogation of Benjamin Franklin on colonial affairs before the
House of Commons, Lord Camden's speech, the Stamp Act repeal, and the Declaratory
Act of 1766, afford insights into British interpretations of colonial views, as well as
general British assumptions and expectations. The eighth document is an excerpt from John
Dickinson's *Letters from a Farmer in Pennsylvania,* which first appeared serially in colonial newspapers in 1767–1768. *Letters,* the most widely read discussion of the constitutional issues in the colonies at the time, provided a theoretical foundation for colonial
opposition, including nonimportation, as is illustrated by the final selection, Charleston
merchants' agreement in 1769 on nonimportation.

1. Virginia Stamp Act Resolutions, 1765

Whereas, the honourable House of Commons in England, have of late draw[n] into
question how far the General Assembly of this colony hath power to enact laws for
laying of taxes and imposing duties payable by the people of this, his Majesty's
most ancient colony: . . . .

Resolved, that the first adventurers, settlers of this his Majesty's colony and
dominion of Virginia, brought with them and transmitted to their posterity, and all
other his Majesty's subjects since inhabiting in this his Majesty's colony, all the
privileges and immunities that have at any time been held, enjoyed, and possessed
by the people of Great Britain.

Resolved, that by two royal charters granted by King James the first, the
colonists aforesaid are declared and entitled to all privileges and immunities of natural born subjects, to all intents and purposes as if they had been abiding and born
within the realm of England.

Resolved, that the taxation of the people by themselves, or by persons chosen
by themselves to represent them, who can only know what taxes the people are
able to bear, or the easiest method of raising them, and must themselves be affected
by every tax laid on the people, is the only security against a burdensome taxation,
and the distinguishing characteristic of British freedom, without which the ancient
constitution cannot exist.

"Virginia Stamp Act Resolutions, 1765." As found in *Journals of the House of Burgesses, 1761–1765,*
ed. H. R. McIlwaine (Birmingham, AL: Colonial Press, 1906), 360.

Resolved, that his Majesty's liege people of this ancient colony have enjoyed the right of being thus governed by their own Assembly in the article of taxes and internal police, and that the same have never been forfeited, or any other way yielded up, but have been constantly recognized by the king and people of Great Britain. [The next three resolutions were not passed but circulated widely in colonial newspapers.]

Resolved, therefore, that the General Assembly of this colony, together with his Majesty or his substitutes, have in their representatives capacity, the only exclusive right and power to lay taxes and imposts upon the inhabitants of this colony; and that every attempt to vest such power in any other person or persons whatever than the General Assembly aforesaid, is illegal, unconstitutional, and unjust, and has a manifest tendency to destroy British as well as American liberty.

Resolved, that his Majesty's liege people, the inhabitants of this colony, are not bound to yield obedience to any law or ordinance whatever, designed to impose any taxation whatsoever upon them, other than the laws or ordinances of the General Assembly aforesaid.

Resolved, that any person who shall, by speaking or writing, assert or maintain that any person or persons other than the General Assembly of this colony, have any right or power to impose or lay any taxation on the people here, shall be deemed an enemy to his Majesty's colony.

2. Governor Francis Bernard Describes the Boston Riot, 1765

Castle William August 15, 1765

My Lords,

I am extremely concerned, that I am obliged to give your Lordships the Relation that is to follow; as it will reflect disgrace upon this Province, and bring the Town of Boston under great difficulties. Two or three months ago, I thought that this People would have submitted to the Stamp Act without actual Opposition. Murmurs indeed were continually heard, but they seemed to be such as would in time die away; But the publishing the Virginia Resolves proved an Alarm bell to the disaffected. From that time an infamous weekly Paper, which is printed here, has swarmed with libells of the most atrocious kind. These have been urged with so much Vehemence and so industriously repeated, that I have considered them as preludes to Action. But I did not think, that it would have commenced so early, or be carried to such Lengths, as it has been.

Yesterday Morning at break of day was discovered hanging upon a Tree in a Street of the Town an Effigy, with inscriptions, shewing that it was intended to represent Mr. Oliver, the Secretary, who had lately accepted the Office of Stamp Distributor. Some of the Neighbours offered to take it down, but they were given to know, that would not be permitted. Many Gentlemen, especially some of the Council,

Governor Francis Bernard to Lord Halifax, Boston, August 15, 1765. As found in *Prologue to Revolution: Sources and Documents on the Stamp Act Crisis, 1764–1766,* ed. Edmund S. Morgan (New York: W. W. Norton, 1973), 106–108.

treated it as a boyish sport, that did not deserve the Notice of the Governor and Council. But I did not think so however I contented myself with the Lt. Governor, as Chief Justice, directing the Sheriff to order his Officers to take down the Effigy; and I appointed a Council to meet in the Afternoon to consider what should be done, if the Sheriff's Officers were obstructed in removing the Effigy.

Before the Council met, the Sheriff reported, that his Officers had endeavoured to take down the Effigy: but could not do it without imminent danger of their lives. The Council met I represented this Transaction to them as the beginning in my Opinion, of much greater Commotions. I desired their Advice, what I should do upon this Occasion. A Majority of the Council spoke in form against doing anything but upon very different Principles: some said, that it was trifling Business, which, if let alone, would subside of itself, but, if taken notice of would become a serious Affair. Others said, that it was a serious Affair already; that it was a preconcerted Business, in which the greatest Part of the Town was engaged; that we had no force to oppose to it, and making an Opposition to it, without a power to support the Opposition, would only inflame the People; and be a means of extending the mischief to persons not at present the Objects of it. Tho' the Council were allmost unanimous in advising, that nothing should be done, they were averse to having such advice entered upon the Council Book. But I insisted upon their giving me an Answer to my Question, and that it should be entered in the Book; when, after a long altercation, it was avoided by their advising me to order the Sheriff to assemble the Peace Officers and preserve the peace which I immediately ordered, being a matter of form rather than of real Significance.

It now grew dark when the Mob, which had been gathering all the Afternoon, came down to the Town House, bringing the Effigy with them, and knowing we were sitting in the Council Chamber, they gave three Huzzas by way of defiance, and passed on. From thence they went to a new Building, lately erected by Mr Oliver to let out for Shops, and not quite finished: this they called the Stamp Office, and pulled it down to the Ground in five minutes. From thence they went to Mr Oliver's House; before which they beheaded the Effigy; and broke all the Windows next the Street; then they carried the Effigy to Fort hill near Mr Oliver's House, where they burnt the Effigy in a Bonfire made of the Timber they had pulled down from the Building. Mr Oliver had removed his family from his House, and remained himself with a few friends, when the Mob returned to attack the House. Mr Oliver was prevailed upon to retire, and his friends kept Possession of the House. The Mob finding the Doors barricaded, broke down the whole fence of the Garden towards fort hill, and coming on beat in all the doors and Windows of the Garden front, and entered the House, the Gentlemen there retiring. As soon as they had got Possession, they searched about for Mr Oliver, declaring they would kill him; finding that he had left the House, a party set out to search two neighbouring Houses, in one of which Mr Oliver was, but happily they were diverted from this pursuit by a Gentleman telling them, that Mr Oliver was gone with the Governor to the Castle. Otherwise he would certainly have been murdered. After 11 o'clock the Mob seeming to grow quiet, the (Lt. Governor) Chief Justice and the Sheriff ventured to go to Mr Oliver's House to endeavour to perswade them to disperse. As soon as they began to speak, a Ringleader cried out, The Governor and the Sheriff! to your Arms, my boys! Presently after a volley of Stones followed, and the two Gentlemen narrowly escaped thro' favour of the Night, not without some bruises. I should have mentioned before, that I sent a written order to the Colonel of the Regiment of Militia, to beat an Alarm; he answered, that it would signify nothing, for as soon as the drum was heard, the drummer would be knocked down, and the drum broke; he added, that probably all the drummers of the Regiment were in the Mob. Nothing more being to be done, The Mob were left to disperse at their own Time, which they did about 12 o'clock.

3. The Declarations of the Stamp Act Congress, 1765

The members of this congress, sincerely devoted, with the warmest sentiments of affection and duty to his Majesty's person and government; inviolably attached to the present happy establishment of the Protestant succession, and with minds deeply impressed by a sense of the present and impending misfortunes of the British colonies on this continent; . . . make the following declarations, of our humble opinion, respecting the most essential rights and liberties of the colonists, and of the grievances under which they labour, by reason of several late acts of Parliament.

I. That his Majesty's subjects in these colonies, owe the same allegiance to the Crown of Great Britain, that is owing from his subjects born within the realm, and all due subordination to that august body, the Parliament of Great Britain.

II. That his Majesty's liege subjects in these colonies are entitled to all the inherent rights and liberties of his natural born subjects within the kingdom of Great Britain.

III. That it is inseparably essential to the freedom of a people, and the undoubted right of Englishmen, that no taxes should be imposed on them, but with their own consent, given personally, or by their representatives.

IV. That the people of these colonies are not, and from their local circumstances, cannot be represented in the House of Commons in Great Britain.

V. That the only representatives of the people of these colonies, are persons chosen therein, by themselves; and that no taxes ever have been, or can be constitutionally imposed on them, but by their respective legislature.

VI. That all supplies to the Crown, being free gifts of the people, it is unreasonable and inconsistent with the principles and spirit of the British constitution, for the people of Great Britain to grant to his Majesty the property of the colonists.

VII. That trial by jury is the inherent and invaluable right of every British subject in these colonies.

VIII. That the late Act of Parliament, entitled, An Act for granting and applying certain Stamp Duties, . . . by imposing taxes on the inhabitants of these colonies, and the said Act, and several other Acts, by extending the jurisdiction of the courts of admiralty beyond its ancient limits, have a manifest tendency to subvert the rights and liberties of the colonists.

IX. That the duties imposed by several late Acts of Parliament, from the peculiar circumstances of these colonies, will be extremely burdensome and grievous, and from the scarcity of specie, the payment of them absolutely impracticable.

"The Declarations of the Stamp Act Congress, 1765." As found in *English Historical Documents,* ed. David C. Douglas (London: E. Methuen, 1979), vol. IX, pp. 642–673.

X. That as the profits of the trade of these colonies ultimately centre in Great Britain, to pay for the manufactures which they are obliged to take from thence, they eventually contribute very largely to all supplies granted there to the Crown.

XI. That the restrictions imposed by several late Acts of Parliament, on the trade of these colonies, will render them unable to purchase the manufactures of Great Britain.

XII. That the increase, prosperity and happiness of these colonies, depend on the full and free enjoyment of their rights and liberties, and an intercourse with Great Britain, mutually affectionate and advantageous.

XIII. That it is the right of the British subjects in these colonies, to petition the king or either house of Parliament.

Lastly, that it is the indispensable duty of these colonies to the best of sovereigns, to the mother country, and to themselves, to endeavour by a loyal and dutiful address to his Majesty, and humble applications to both houses of Parliament, to procure the repeal of the Act for granting and applying certain stamp duties, of all clauses of any other Acts of Parliament, whereby the jurisdiction of the admiralty is extended as aforesaid, and of the other late Acts for the restriction of American commerce.

4. "William Pym" Asserts Parliamentary Supremacy, 1765

The people in our American colonies lay a very great stress upon the importance of their charters, and imagine that the privileges granted to their ancestors, at the time of their original establishment, must infallibly exempt them from participating in the least inconvenience of the Mother country, though the Mother country must share in every inconvenience of theirs. This mode of reasoning is however no less new than it is extraordinary: and one would almost be tempted to imagine that the persons, who argue in this manner, were alike unacquainted with the nature of the colonies and the constitution of this kingdom.

I shall very readily grant, that the colonies at the time of their first settling might receive particular indulgences from the Crown, to encourage adventurers to go over; and I will also grant, that these charters should be as inviolably adhered to as the nature of public contingencies will admit. But at the same time let me inform my fellow subjects of America, that a resolution of the British parliament can at any time set aside all the charters that have ever been granted by our monarchs; and that consequently nothing can be more idle than this pompous exclamation about their charter exemptions, whenever such a resolution has actually passed.

The great business of the British Legislative power is, to consult upon what new laws may be necessary for the general good of the British dominions, and to remove any casual inconveniences which may arise from the existence of their former acts. In the prosecution of this important end, they cannot expect but what the most salutary laws will prove oppressive to some part of the people. However

"'William Pym' Asserts Parliamentary Supremacy," *London General Evening Post*, August 20, 1765. As found in Edmund S. Morgan, ed., *Prologue to Revolution: Sources and Documents on the Stamp Act Crisis, 1764–1766* (New York: W. W. Norton, 1973), 97–99.

no injury, which may be sustained by individuals, is to prevent them from promoting the welfare of the community; for if they debated till they framed an ordinance agreeable to the wishes of every body, 'twould be utterly impossible for them ever to frame any ordinance at all.

If then the Legislative power of this country have a right to alter or annul those public acts which were solemnly passed by former princes and former parliaments; it must be a necessary consequence that they have an equal right to annul the private charters of former princes also; and that these charters, which are by no means to be set in the same degree of importance with our laws, are at least every whit as subject to their jurisdiction and authority. This is a circumstance which the assembly of Virginia in particular should have attended to before their late unaccountable resolutions; and 'tis what I hope the assemblies of our other settlements will judiciously attend to, if they find the least propensity to follow the extraordinary example of their Sister-colony.

The people of Ireland, though they have a parliament of their own (and a parliament, I will take the liberty of saying, composed of people to the full as eminent for their fortune and abilities, as any of our American assemblies) are nevertheless under the immediate subjection of the British Legislature. The vote of an English Senate can in an instant abrogate all the laws of that kingdom; and surely none of the plantations can possibly plead a greater share either of merit or privileges than our Irish fellow subjects; who nevertheless behave with an uncommon degree of respect to our decisions; and never presume to blame the hand which increases their burdens, however they may groan beneath the heaviness of the load.

I am very well aware that the present impatience, which the whole kingdom feels at the least increase of taxes, will naturally create a number of friends for the colonies: but at the same time let us consider that the propriety of the tax, which has excited such a ferment among our American fellow-subjects, is not now the foundation of dispute. The question now is, Whether those American subjects are, or are not, bound by the resolutions of a British parliament? If they are *not,* they are entirely a separate people from us, and the mere reception of officers appointed in this kingdom, is nothing but an idle farce of government, which it is by no means our interest to keep up, if it is to produce us no benefit but the honour of protecting them whenever they are attacked by their enemies. On the other hand, if the people of America *are* bound by the proceedings of the English legislature, what excuse can the Virginians possibly make for the late indecent vote (to give it no harsher appellation) of their assembly. The present crisis, Sir, is really an alarming one; and after all the blood and treasure which we have expended in defence of the colonies, it is now questioned, whether we have any interest in those colonies at all.

If the people of Virginia were offended either with the tax itself, or with the mode of taxation, the proper method of proceeding would have been to petition the parliament, to point out the grievances arising from it, and to solicit the necessary redress. This is the invariable manner in which all the rest of their fellow-subjects (at least the European part of their fellow subjects) have acted in cases of a like nature. But to think of bullying their King, and the august Council of the Mother country, into an acquiescence with their sentiments, by a rash and hot headed vote; not only must expose them to the ridicule, but to the resentment of every considerate man who wishes well either to their interest or to the prosperity of this kingdom.

The people of the colonies know very well that the taxes of the Mother country are every day increasing; and can they expect that no addition whatsoever will be made to theirs? They know very well that a great part of our national debt was contracted in establishing them on a firm foundation, and protecting them from the arbitrary attempts of their implacable enemies.—Can anything then be so unreasonable, as a refusal of their assistance to wipe a little of it off? For my own part I am as much astonished at their want of justice, as I am surprized at their want of gratitude; and cannot help declaring it as my opinion, that we ought to shew but a very small share of sensibility for the circumstances of those people who are so utterly regardless of ours. To be sure, Sir, in assisting the colonies we had an eye to our own interest. It would be ridiculous otherwise to squander away our blood and our treasure in their defence. But certainly the benefit was mutual; and consequently the disadvantage should be mutual too. If we reap emoluments from the existence of the colonies, the colonies owe every thing to our encouragement and protection. As therefore we share in the same prosperity, we ought to participate of the same distress; and nothing can be more inequitable, than the least disinclination to bear a regular portion of those disbursements, which were applied to support the general interest both of the mother-country and themselves.

5. The House of Commons Questions Benjamin Franklin, 1766

Q. What is your name, and place of abode?

A. Franklin, of Philadelphia.

Q. Do the Americans pay any considerable taxes among themselves?

A. Certainly many, and very heavy taxes.

Q. What are the present taxes in Pennsylvania, laid by the laws of the colony?

A. There are taxes on all estates real and personal, a poll tax, a tax on all offices, professions, trades and businesses, according to their profits; an excise on all wine, rum, and other spirits; and a duty of Ten Pounds per head on all Negroes imported, with some other duties.

Q. For what purposes are those taxes laid?

A. For the support of the civil and military establishments of the country, and to discharge the heavy debt contracted in the last war.

Q. How long are those taxes to continue?

A. Those for discharging the debt are to continue till 1772, and longer, if the debt should not be then all discharged. The others must always continue. . . .

Q. Are not the Colonies, from their circumstances, very able to pay the stamp duty?

A. In my opinion, there is not gold and silver enough in the Colonies to pay the stamp duty for one year. . . .

Q. Do you think it right that America should be protected by this country, and pay no part of the expence?

The Papers of Benjamin Franklin, Vol. 13, pp. 129–137; 139–140; 142–145; 147–150; 153–154; 156; 158–159. Leonard W. Labaree et al., eds., New Haven and London: Yale University Press, 1969.

A. That is not the case. The Colonies raised, cloathed and paid, during the last war, near 25000 men, and spent many millions.

Q. Were you not reimbursed by parliament?

A. We were only reimbursed what, in your opinion, we had advanced beyond our proportion, or beyond what might reasonably be expected from us; and it was a very small part of what we spent. Pennsylvania, in particular, disbursed about 500,000 Pounds, and the reimbursements, in the whole, did not exceed 60,000 Pounds.

Q. You have said that you pay heavy taxes in Pennsylvania; what do they amount to in the Pound?

A. The tax on all estates, real and personal, is Eighteen Pence in the Pound, fully rated; and the tax on the profits of trades and professions, with other taxes, do, I suppose, make full Half a Crown in the Pound. . . .

Q. Do not you think the people of America would submit to pay the stamp duty, if it was moderated?

A. No, never, unless compelled by force of arms. . . .

Q. How is the assembly composed? Of what kinds of people are the members, landholders or traders?

A. It is composed of landholders, merchants and artificers.

Q. Are not the majority landholders?

A. I believe they are. . . .

Q. What was the temper of America towards Great-Britain before the year 1763?

A. The best in the world. They submitted willingly to the government of the Crown, and paid, in all their courts, obedience to acts of parliament. Numerous as the people are in the several old provinces, they cost you nothing in forts, citadels, garrisons or armies, to keep them in subjection. They were governed by this country at the expence only of a little pen, ink and paper. They were led by a thread. They had not only a respect, but an affection, for Great-Britain, for its laws, its customs and manners, and even a fondness for its fashions, that greatly increased the commerce. Natives of Britain were always treated with particular regard; to be an Old Englandman was, of itself, a character of some respect, and gave a kind of rank among us.

Q. And what is their temper now?

A. O, very much altered.

Q. Did you ever hear the authority of parliament to make laws for America questioned till lately?

A. The authority of parliament was allowed to be valid in all laws, except such as should lay internal taxes. It was never disputed in laying duties to regulate commerce. . . .

Q. In what light did the people of America use to consider the parliament of Great-Britain?

A. They considered the parliament as the great bulwark and security of their liberties and privileges, and always spoke of it with the utmost respect and veneration. Arbitrary ministers, they thought, might possibly, at times, attempt to oppress them; but they relied on it, that the parliament, on application, would always give redress. They remembered, with gratitude, a strong instance of this, when a bill was brought into parliament, with a clause to make royal instructions laws in the Colonies, which the house of commons would not pass, and it was thrown out.

Q. And have they not still the same respect for parliament?

A. No; it is greatly lessened.

Q. To what causes is that owing?

A. To a concurrence of causes; the restraints lately laid on their trade, by which the bringing of foreign gold and silver into the Colonies was prevented; the prohibition of making paper money among themselves; and then demanding a new and heavy tax by stamps; taking away, at the same time, trials by juries, and refusing to receive and hear their humble petitions.

Q. Don't you think they would submit to the stamp-act, if it was modified, the obnoxious parts taken out, and the duty reduced to some particulars, of small moment?

A. No; they will never submit to it. . . .

Q. What is your opinion of a future tax, imposed on the same principle with that of the stamp-act; how would the Americans receive it?

A. Just as they do this. They would not pay it.

Q. Have you not heard of the resolutions of this house, and of the house of lords, asserting the right of parliament relating to America, including a power to tax the people there?

A. Yes, I have heard of such resolutions.

Q. What will be the opinion of the Americans on those resolutions?

A. They will think them unconstitutional, and unjust.

Q. Was it an opinion in America before 1763, that the parliament had no right to lay taxes and duties there?

A. I never heard any objection to the right of laying duties to regulate commerce; but a right to lay internal taxes was never supposed to be in parliament, as we are not represented there. . . .

Q. You say the Colonies have always submitted to external taxes, and object to the right of parliament only in laying internal taxes; now can you shew that there is any kind of difference between the two taxes to the Colony on which they may be laid?

A. I think the difference is very great. An external tax is a duty laid on commodities imported; that duty is added to the first cost, and other charges on the commodity, and when it is offered to sale, makes a part of the price. If the people do not like it at that price, they refuse it; they are not obliged to pay it. But an internal tax is forced from the people without their consent, if not laid by their own representatives. The stamp-act says, we shall have no commerce, make no exchange of property with each other, neither purchase nor grant, nor recover debts; we shall neither marry, nor make our wills, unless we pay such and such sums, and thus it is intended to extort our money from us, or ruin us by the consequences of refusing to pay it.

Q. But supposing the external tax or duty to be laid on the necessaries of life imported into your Colony, will not that be the same thing in its effects as an internal tax?

A. I do not know a single article imported into the Northern Colonies, but what they can either do without, or make themselves.

Q. Don't you think cloth from England absolutely necessary to them?

A. No, by no means absolutely necessary; with industry and good management, they may very well supply themselves with all they want.

Q. Will it not take a long time to establish that manufacture among them? and must they not in the mean while suffer greatly?

A. I think not. They have made a surprising progress already. And I am of opinion, that before their old clothes are worn out, they will have new ones of their own making. . . .

Q. Did the Americans ever dispute the controling power of parliament to regulate the commerce?

A. No.

Q. Can any thing less than a military force carry the stamp-act into execution?

A. I do not see how a military force can be applied to that purpose.

Q. Why may it not?

A. Suppose a military force sent into America, they will find nobody in arms; what are they then to do? They cannot force a man to take stamps who chooses to do without them. They will not find a rebellion; they may indeed make one.

Q. If the act is not repealed, what do you think will be the consequences?

A. A total loss of the respect and affection the people of America bear to this country, and of all the commerce that depends on that respect and affection.

Q. How can the commerce be affected?

A. You will find, that if the act is not repealed, they will take very little of your manufactures in a short time.

Q. Is it in their power to do without them?

A. I think they may very well do without them. . . .

Q. Suppose an act of internal regulations, connected with a tax, how would they receive it?

A. I think it would be objected to.

Q. Then no regulation with a tax would be submitted to?

A. Their opinion is, that when aids to the Crown are wanted, they are to be asked of the several assemblies, according to the old established usage, who will, as they always have done, grant them freely. And that their money ought not to be given away without their consent, by persons at a distance, unacquainted with their circumstances and abilities. The granting aids to the Crown, is the only means they have of recommending themselves to their sovereign, and they think it extremely hard and unjust, that a body of men, in which they have no representatives, should make a merit to itself to giving and granting what is not its own, but theirs, and deprive them of a right they esteem of the utmost value and importance, as it is the security of all their other rights.

Q. But is not the post-office, which they have long received, a tax as well as a regulation?

A. No; the money paid for the postage of a letter is not of the nature of a tax; it is merely a quantum meruit for a service done; no person is compellable to pay the money, if he does not chuse to receive the service. A man may still, as before the act, send his letter by a servant, a special messenger, or a friend, if he thinks it cheaper and safer. . . .

Q. You say they do not object to the right of parliament in laying duties on goods to be paid on their importation; now, is there any kind of difference between a duty on the importation of goods, and an excise on their consumption?

A. Yes; a very material one; an excise, for the reasons I have just mentioned, they think you can have no right to lay within their country. But the sea is yours; you maintain, by your fleets, the safety of navigation in it; and keep it clear of pirates; you may have therefore a natural and equitable right to some toll or duty on merchandizes carried through that part of your dominions, towards defraying the expence you are at in ships to maintain the safety of that carriage. . . .

Q. What do you think a sufficient military force to protect the distribution of the stamps in every part of America?

A. A very great force; I can't say what, if the disposition of America is for a general resistance. . . .

Q. If the stamp act should be repealed, would not the Americans think they could oblige the parliament to repeal every external tax law now in force? . . .

A. I suppose they will think that it was repealed from a conviction of its inexpediency; and they will rely upon it, that while the same inexpediency subsists, you will never attempt to make such another. . . .

Q. If the act should be repealed, and the legislature should shew its resentment to the opposers of the stamp-act, would the Colonies acquiesce in the authority of the legislature? What is your opinion they would do?

A. I don't doubt at all, that if the legislature repeal the stamp-act, the Colonies will acquiesce in the authority.

Q. But if the legislature should think fit to ascertain its right to lay taxes, by any act laying a small tax, contrary to their opinion, would they submit to pay the tax?

A. The proceedings of the people in America have been considered too much together. The proceedings of the assemblies have been very different from those of the mobs, and should be distinguished, as having no connection with each other. The assemblies have only peaceably resolved what they take to be their rights; they have taken no measures for opposition by force; they have not built a fort, raised a man, or provided a grain of ammunition, in order to such opposition. The ringleaders of riots they think ought to be punished; they would punish them themselves, if they could. Every sober sensible man would wish to see rioters punished; as otherwise peaceable people have no security of person or estate. But as to any internal tax, how small soever, laid by the legislature here on the people there, while they have no representatives in this legislature, I think it will never be submitted to. They will oppose it to the last. They do not consider it as at all necessary for you to raise money on them by your taxes, because they are, and always have been, ready to raise money by taxes among themselves, and to grant large sums, equal to their abilities, upon requisition from the Crown. . . . America has been greatly misrepresented and abused here, in papers, and pamphlets, and speeches, as ungrateful, and unreasonable, and unjust, in having put this nation to immense expence for their defence, and refusing to bear any part of that expence. The Colonies raised, paid and clothed, near 25000 men during the last war, a number equal to those sent from Britain, and far beyond their proportion; they went deeply into debt in doing this, and all their taxes and estates are mortgaged, for many years to come, for discharging that debt. Government here was at that time very sensible of this. The Colonies were recommended to parliament. Every year the King sent down to the house a written message to this purpose, That his Majesty, being highly sensible of the zeal and vigour with which his faithful subjects in North-America had exerted themselves, in defence of his Majesty's just

rights and possessions, recommended it to the house to take the same into consideration, and enable him to give them a proper compensation. You will find
those messages on your own journals every year of the war to the very last, and
you did accordingly give 200,000 Pounds annually to the Crown, to be distributed
in such compensation to the Colonies. This is the strongest of all proofs that the
Colonies, far from being unwilling to bear a share of the burthen, did exceed their
proportion; for if they had done less, or had only equalled their proportion, there
would have been no room or reason for compensation. Indeed the sums reimbursed them, were by no means adequate to the expence they incurred beyond
their proportion; but they never murmured at that; they esteemed their Sovereign's
approbation of their zeal and fidelity, and the approbation of this house, far beyond any other kind of compensation; therefore there was no occasion for this act,
to force money from a willing people; they had not refused giving money for the
purposes of the act; no requisition had been made; they were always willing and
ready to do what could reasonably be expected from them, and in this light they
wish to be considered. . . .

Q. If the stamp-act should be repealed, would it induce the assemblies of
America to acknowledge the rights of parliament to tax them, and would they erase
their resolutions?

A. No, never.

Q. Is there no means of obliging them to erase those resolutions?

A. None that I know of; they will never do it unless compelled by force of arms.

Q. Is there a power on earth that can force them to erase them?

A. No power, how great soever, can force men to change their opinions. . . .

Q. What used to be the pride of the Americans?

A. To indulge in the fashions and manufactures of Great-Britain.

Q. What is now their pride?

A. To wear their old cloaths over again, till they can make new ones.

6. Lord Camden (Charles Pratt) Exhorts Parliament
to Change Direction, 1766

I find that I have been very injuriously treated; have been considered as the
broacher of new-fangled doctrines, contrary to the laws of this kingdom, and subversive of the rights of parliament. . . . As the affair is of the utmost importance,
and in its consequences may involve the fate of kingdoms, I took the strictest review
of my arguments; I re-examined all my authorities; fully determined, if I found
myself mistaken, publicly to own my mistake, and give up my opinion: but my
searches have more and more convinced me, that the British parliament have no
right to tax the Americans. I shall not therefore consider the Declaratory Bill now
lying on your table . . . the very existence of which is illegal, absolutely illegal,

From *The Parliamentary History of England* (London, 1813), vol. 16, pp. 177–181.

contrary to the fundamental laws of nature, contrary to the fundamental laws of this constitution? A constitution grounded on the eternal and immutable laws of nature; a constitution whose foundation and centre is liberty, which sends liberty to every subject, that is or may happen to be within any part of its ample circumference. Nor, my lords, is the doctrine new, it is as old as the constitution; it grew up with it; indeed it is its support; taxation and representation are inseparably united; God hath joined them, no British parliament can separate them; to endeavour to do it, is to stab our very vitals. Nor is this the first time this doctrine has been mentioned; 70 years ago, my lords, a pamphlet was published, recommending the levying a parliamentary tax on one of the colonies; this pamphlet was answered by two others, then much read; these totally deny the power of taxing the colonies; and why? Because the colonies had no representatives in parliament to give consent; no answer, public or private, was given to these pamphlets, no censure passed upon them; men were not startled at the doctrine as either new or illegal, or derogatory to the rights of parliament. I do not mention these pamphlets by way of authority, but to vindicate myself from the imputation of having first broached this doctrine.

My position is this—I repeat it—I will maintain it to my last hour,— taxation and representation are inseparable;—this position is founded on the laws of nature; it is more, it is itself an eternal law of nature; for whatever is a man's own, is absolutely his own; no man hath a right to take it from him without his consent, either expressed by himself or representative; whoever attempts to do it, attempts an injury; whoever does it, commits a robbery; he throws down and destroys the distinction between liberty and slavery. Taxation and representation are coeval with and essential to this constitution. . . . As to Ireland, my lords, before that kingdom had a parliament as it now has, if your lordships will examine the old records, you will find, that when a tax was to be laid on that country, the Irish sent over here representatives; and the same records will inform your lordships, what wages those representatives received from their constituents. In short, my lords, from the whole of our history, from the earliest period, you will find that taxation and representation were always united; so true are the words of that consummate reasoner and politician Mr. Locke. I before alluded to his book; I have again consulted him; and finding what he writes so applicable to the subject in hand, and so much in favour of my sentiments, I beg your lordships' leave to read a little of this book.

"The supreme power cannot take from any man, any part of his property, without his own consent;" and B. 2. p. 136-139, particularly 140. Such are the words of this great man, and which are well worth your serious attention. His principles are drawn from the heart of our constitution, which he thoroughly understood, and will last as long as that shall last; . . . For these reasons, my lords, I can never give my assent to any bill for taxing the American colonies, while they remain unrepresented; for as to the distinction of a virtual representation, it is so absurd as not to deserve an answer; I therefore pass it over with contempt. The forefathers of the Americans did not leave their native country, and subject themselves to every danger and distress, to be reduced to a state of slavery: they did not give up their rights; they looked for protection, and not for chains, from their mother country; by her they expected to be defended in the possession of their property, and not to be deprived of it: for, should the present power continue, there is nothing which they can call their own; or, to use the words of Mr. Locke, "What property have they in that, which another may, by right, take, when he pleases, to himself ?"

7. Parliament Repeals the Stamp Act but Declares Its Authority, 1766

Repeal Act, March 18, 1766

Whereas an Act was passed in the last session of Parliament entitled, An Act for granting and applying certain stamp duties, and other duties in the British colonies and plantations in America towards further defraying the expenses of defending, protecting, and securing the same; and for amending such parts of the several Acts of Parliament relating to the trade and revenues of the said colonies and plantations as direct the manner of determining and recovering the penalties and forfeitures therein mentioned; and whereas the continuance of the said Act would be attended with many inconveniencies, and may be productive of consequences greatly detrimental to the commercial interests of these kingdoms; . . . be it enacted by the king's most excellent Majesty, by and with the advice and consent of the Lords Spiritual and Temporal, and Commons, . . . that . . . the above-mentioned Act . . . is . . . hereby repealed.

The Declaratory Act of March 18, 1766

Whereas several of the houses of representatives in his Majesty's colonies and plantations in America, have of late, against law, claimed to themselves, or to the general assemblies of the same, the sole and exclusive right of imposing duties and taxes upon his Majesty's subjects in the said colonies and plantations; and have, in pursuance of such claim, passed certain votes, resolutions, and orders, derogatory to the legislative authority of Parliament, and inconsistent with the dependency of the said colonies and plantations upon the Crown of Great Britain: may it therefore . . . be declared, . . . in this present Parliament assembled, . . . that the said colonies and plantations in America have been, are, and of right ought to be, subordinate unto, and dependent upon the imperial Crown and Parliament of Great Britain; and that the . . . Parliament assembled, had, hath, and of right ought to have, full power and authority to make laws and statutes of sufficient force and validity to bind the colonies and people of America, subjects of the Crown of Great Britain, in all cases whatsoever.

II. And be it further declared and enacted by the authority aforesaid, that all resolutions, votes, orders, and proceedings, in any of the said colonies or plantations, whereby the power and authority of the Parliament of Great Britain, to make laws and statutes as aforesaid, is denied, or drawn into question, are, and are hereby declared to be, utterly null and void to all intents and purposes whatsoever.

"Parliament Repeals the Stamp Act but Declares Its Authority, 1766." In Danby Pickering, ed., *The Statutes at Large from the Magna Charta, to the end of the eleventh Parliament of Great Britain, anno 1761* (London: J. Bentham, 1762–1807), vol. 27, pp. 19–20.

8. John Dickinson Exhorts the Colonists to Opposition,
1767–1768

My Dear Countrymen,

[A] late act of parliament, which appears to me to be unconstitutional, and . . . destructive to the liberty of these colonies . . . is the act for granting the duties on paper, glass, etc.

The parliament unquestionably possesses a legal authority to *regulate* the trade of *Great Britain,* and all her colonies. Such an authority is essential to the relation between a mother country and her colonies; and necessary for the common good of all. He who considers these provinces as states distinct from the *British Empire,* has very slender notions of *justice,* or of their *interests.* We are but parts of a *whole;* and therefore there must exist a power somewhere, to preside, and preserve the connection in due order. This power is lodged in the parliament; and we are as much dependent on *Great Britain,* as a perfectly free people can be on another.

I have looked over *every statute* relating to these colonies, from their first settlement to this time; and I find every one of them founded on this principle, till the *Stamp Act* administration. *All before,* are calculated to regulate trade, and preserve or promote a mutually beneficial intercourse between the several constituent parts of the empire; and though many of them imposed duties on trade, yet those duties were always imposed *with design* to restrain the commerce of one part, that was injurious to another, and thus to promote the general welfare. The raising of a revenue thereby was never intended. . . . Never did the *British* parliament, till the period above mentioned, think of imposing duties in *America* FOR THE PURPOSE OF RAISING A REVENUE. Mr. *Greenville* first introduced this language. . . .

A few months after came the *Stamp Act.* . . .

The last act, granting duties upon paper, etc. carefully pursues these modern precedents. The preamble is, "Whereas it is expedient THAT A REVENUE SHOULD BE RAISED IN YOUR MAJESTY S DOMINIONS IN AMERICA." . . .

This I call an innovation; and a most dangerous innovation. It may perhaps be objected, that *Great Britain* has a right to lay what duties she pleases upon her exports, and it makes no difference to us, whether they are paid here or there.

To this I answer. These colonies require many things for their use, which the laws of *Great Britain* prohibit them from getting any where but from her. Such are paper and glass. . . .

Our great advocate, Mr. *Pitt,* in his speeches on the debate concerning the repeal of the *Stamp Act,* acknowledged, that *Great Britain* could restrain our manufactures. His words are these—"This kingdom, as the supreme governing and legislative power, has ALWAYS bound the colonies by her regulations and RESTRICTIONS in trade, in navigation, in MANUFACTURES—in everything, *except that of taking their money out of their pockets* WITHOUT THEIR CONSENT." Again he says, "We may bind their

"John Dickinson Exhorts the Colonists to Opposition, 1767–1768." In John Dickinson, *Letters from a Farmer in Pennsylvania* (Philadelphia: Hall and Sellers, 1768), 7–15, 58–85.

trade, CONFINE THEIR MANUFACTURES, and exercise every power whatever, *except that of taking their money out of their pockets* WITHOUT THEIR CONSENT."

Here then, my dear countrymen, ROUSE yourselves, and behold the ruin hanging over your heads. If you ONCE admit, that *Great Britain* may lay duties upon her exportations to us, *for the purpose of levying money on us only,* she then will have nothing to do, but to lay those duties on the articles which she prohibits us to manufacture—and the tragedy of *American* liberty is finished. . . . If *Great Britain* can order us to come to her for necessaries we want, and can order us to pay what taxes she pleases before we take them away, or when we land them here, we are as abject slaves as *France* and *Poland* can show in wooden shoes and with uncombed hair. . . .

A Farmer

My Dear Countrymen,

. . . We feel too sensibly, that *any ministerial measures* relating to these colonies, are soon carried successfully through the parliament. Certain prejudices operate there so strongly against us, that it may be justly questioned, whether *all* the provinces united, will ever be able effectually to call to an account before the parliament, any minister who shall abuse the power by the late act given to the crown in *America.* He may divide the spoils torn from us in what manner he pleases, *and we shall have no way of making him responsible.* If he should order, that every *governor* shall have a yearly salary of 5,000£ sterling; every *chief justice* of 3,000£; every inferior officer in proportion; and should then reward the most profligate, ignorant, or needy dependents or himself or his friends, with places of the greatest trust, because they were of the greatest profit, this would be called an arrangement in consequence of the "adequate provision for defraying the charge of the administration of justice, and the support of the civil government": And if the taxes should prove at any time insufficient to answer all the expenses of the numberless offices, which ministers may please to create, surely the members of the house of commons will be so *"modest,"* as not to "contradict a minister" who shall tell them, it is become necessary to lay a new tax upon the colonies, for the laudable purposes of defraying the charges of the "administration of justice, and support of civil government" among them. Thus, in fact, we shall be taxed by ministers. In short, it will be in their power to settle upon us any CIVIL, ECCLESIASTICAL, or MILITARY establishment, which they choose.

We may perceive, by the example of *Ireland,* how eager ministers are to seize upon any settled revenue, and apply it in supporting their own power. Happy are the men, and *happy the people who grow wise by the misfortunes of others.* Earnestly, my dear countrymen, do I beseech the author of all good gifts, that you may grow wise in this manner; and if I may be allowed to take such a liberty, I beg leave to recommend to you in general, as the best method of attaining this wisdom, diligently to study the histories of other countries. You will there find all the arts, that can possibly be practiced by cunning rulers, or false patriots among yourselves, so fully delineated, that, changing names, the account would serve for your own times.

It is pretty well known on this continent, that *Ireland* has, with a regular consistency of injustice, been cruelly treated by ministers in the article of *pensions.* . . .

Besides the burden of *pensions* in *Ireland,* which have enormously increased within these few years, almost all the *offices* in that poor kingdom, have been, since the commencement of the present century, and now are bestowed upon *strangers.* For tho' the merit of persons born there, justly raises them to places of high trust when they go abroad, as all *Europe* can witness, yet he is an uncommonly lucky *Irishman,* who can get a good post *in his* NATIVE *country.* . . .

In the same manner shall we unquestionably be treated, as soon as the late taxes laid upon us, shall make posts in the "government," and the "administration of justice" *here,* worth the attention of persons of influence in *Great Britain.* We know enough already to satisfy us of this truth. But this will not be the worst part of our case.

The *principals,* in all great offices, will reside in *England,* making some paltry allowance to deputies for doing the business *here.* Let any consider what an exhausting drain this must be upon us, when ministers are possessed of the power of creating what posts they please, and of affixing to such posts what salaries they please, and he must be convinced how destructive the late act will be. The injured kingdom lately mentioned, can tell us the mischiefs of ABSENTEES; and we may perceive already the same disposition taking place with us. The government of *New York* has been exercised by a deputy. That of *Virginia is* now held so; and we know of a number of secretaryships, collectorships, and other offices, held in the same manner. . . .

Surely therefore, those who wish the welfare of their country, ought seriously to reflect, what may be the consequence of such a new creation of offices, in the disposal of the crown. The *army,* the *administration of justice,* and the *civil government* here, with such salaries as the crown shall please to annex, will extend *ministerial influence* as much beyond its former bounds, as the late war did the *British* dominions.

But whatever the people of *Great Britain* may think on this occasion, I hope the people of these colonies will unanimously join in this sentiment, that the late act of parliament is injurious to their liberty, and that this sentiment will unite them in a firm opposition to it, in the same manner as the dread of the *Stamp Act* did.

Some persons may imagine the sums to be raised by it, are but small, and therefore may be inclined to acquiesce under it. A conduct more dangerous to freedom, as before has been observed, can never be adopted. Nothing is wanted at home but a PRECEDENT, the force of which shall be established, by the tacit submission of the colonies. With what zeal was the statute erecting the post office, and another relating to the recovery of debts in *America,* urged and tortured, as *precedents* in support of the *Stamp Act,* tho' wholly inapplicable. If the parliament succeeds in this attempt, other statutes will impose other duties. Instead of taxing ourselves, as we have been accustomed to do, from the first settlement of these provinces, all our usual taxes will be converted into parliamentary taxes on our importations; and thus the parliament will levy upon us such sums of money as they choose to take, *without any other* LIMITATION, *than their* PLEASURE. . . .

In short, if the late act of parliament takes effect, these colonies must dwindle down into "COMMON CORPORATIONS," as their enemies, in the debates concerning the repeal of the *Stamp Act, strenuously insisted they were;* and it seems not improbable that some future historian may thus record our fall. . . .

Remember your ancestors and your posterity.

A Farmer

My Dear Countrymen,

Some states have lost their liberty by *particular accidents:* But this calamity is generally owing to the *decay of virtue.* A *people is* travelling fast to destruction, when *individuals* consider *their* interests as distinct from *those of the public.* Such notions are fatal to their country, and to themselves. Yet how many are there, so *weak* and *sordid* as to *think* they perform *all the offices of life,* if they earnestly endeavor to increase their own *wealth, power,* and *credit,* without the least regard for the society, under the protection of which they live; who, if they can make an *immediate profit to themselves,* by lending their assistance to those, whose projects plainly tend to the injury of their country, rejoice in their *dexterity,* and believe themselves entitled to the character of *able politicians.* Miserable men! Of whom it is hard to say, whether they ought to be most the objects of *pity* or *contempt:* But whose opinions are certainly as *detestable,* as their practices are *destructive.*

Though I always reflect, with a high pleasure, on the integrity and understanding of my countrymen, . . . yet when I consider, that in every age and country there have been bad men, my heart, at this threatening period, is so full of apprehension, as not to permit me to believe, but that there may be some on this continent, *against whom you ought to be upon your guard*—Men, who either hold, or expect to hold certain advantages, by setting examples of servility to their countrymen.—Men, who trained to the employment, or self taught by a natural versatility of genius, serve as decoys for drawing the innocent and unwary into snares. It is not to be doubted but that such men will diligently bestir themselves on this and every like occasion, to spread the infection of their meanness as far as they can. On the plans *they* have adopted, this is *their* course. *This* is the method to recommend themselves to their *patrons.* . . .

Our *vigilance* and our *union* are *success* and *safety.* Our *negligence* and our *division* are *distress* and *death.* They are *worse*—They are *shame* and *slavery.* Let us equally shun the benumbing stillness of *overweening sloth,* and the feverish activity of that *ill informed zeal,* which busies itself in maintaining *little, mean* and *narrow* opinions. Let us, with a truly wise *generosity* and *charity,* banish and discourage all *illiberal distinctions,* which may arise from differences in *situation,* forms of *government,* or modes of *religion.* Let us consider ourselves as MEN—FREEMEN—CHRISTIAN FREEMEN—*separated from the rest of the world, and firmly bound together* by the *same rights, interests* and *dangers.* Let *these* keep our attention inflexibly fixed on the GREAT OBJECTS, which we must CONTINUALLY REGARD, in order to *preserve those rights, to promote those interests,* and to *avert those dangers.*

Let these *truths* be indelibly impressed on our minds—*that* we *cannot be* HAPPY, *without being* FREE—that we cannot be free, *without being secure in our property*—that *we* cannot be secure in our property, *if, without our consent, others may, as by right, take it away*—that *taxes imposed on us by parliament,* do thus take it away—that *duties laid for the sole purpose of raising money,* are taxes—that *attempts* to lay such duties *should be instantly and firmly opposed*—that this opposition can never be effectual, *unless it is the united effort of these provinces*—that therefore BENEVOLENCE *of temper towards each other,* and UNANIMITY *of counsels,* are essential to the welfare of the whole—and lastly, that for this reason, every man among us, who in any manner would encourage either *dissension, dissidence,* or *indifference,* between these colonies, is an enemy to *himself,* and *to his country. . . .*

Let us take care of our *rights,* and we *therein* take care of *our prosperity.* "SLAVERY IS EVER PRECEDED BY SLEEP." *Individuals* may be *dependent* on ministers, if they please. STATES SHOULD SCORN IT. . . .

You are assigned by divine providence, in the appointed order of things, the *protectors of unborn ages,* whose *fate* depends upon your *virtue.* Whether *they* shall arise the *generous* and *indisputable heirs* of the noblest patrimonies, or the *dastardly and hereditary drudges* of imperious task-masters, YOU MUST DETERMINE. . . .

For my part, I am resolved to contend for the liberty delivered down to me by my ancestors, but whether I shall do it effectually or not, depends on you, my countrymen. . . .

A Farmer

9. Charleston Merchants Propose a Plan of Nonimportation, 1769

We, his Majesty's dutiful and loving subjects, the inhabitants of South Carolina, being sensibly affected with the great prejudice done to Great Britain, and the abject and wretched condition to which the British colonies are reduced by several Acts of Parliament lately passed; by *some of which* the moneys that the colonists usually and cheerfully spent in the purchase of all sorts of goods imported from Great Britain, are now, to their great grievance, wrung from them, without their consent, or even their being represented, and applied by the ministry, in prejudice of, and without regard to, the real interest of Great Britain, or the manufactures thereof, almost totally, to the support of new-created commissioners of customs, placemen, parasitical and novel ministerial officers; and *by others of which acts* we are not only deprived of those invaluable rights, trial by our peers and the common law, but are also made subject to the arbitrary and oppressive proceedings of the civil law, justly abhorred and rejected by our ancestors, the freemen of England; and finding that the most dutiful and loyal petitions from the colonies alone, for redress of those grievances, have been rejected with contempt so that no relief can be expected from that method of proceedings; and being fully convinced of the absolute necessity of stimulating our fellow subjects and sufferers in Great Britain to aid us in this our distress, and of joining the rest of the colonies in some other loyal and vigorous methods that may most probably procure such relief, which we believe may be most effectually promoted by strict economy, and by encouraging the manufactures of America in general, and of this province in particular: we therefore, whose names are underwritten, do solemnly promise, and agree to and with each other, that, until the colonies be restored to their former freedom by the repeal of the said Acts, we will most strictly abide by the following[:]

"Charleston Merchants Propose a Plan of Nonimportation, 1769." In *Publications of the Colonial Society of Massachusetts, XIX,* 217–219.

Resolutions

I. That we will encourage and promote the use of North American manufactures in general, and those of this province in particular. And any of us who are vendors thereof, do engage to sell and dispose of them at the same rates as heretofore.

II. That we will upon no pretence whatsoever, either upon our own account or on commission, import into this province any of the manufactures of Great Britain, or any other European or East India goods, either from Great Britain, Holland, or any other place, other than such as may have been shipped in consequence of former orders; excepting only Negro cloth, commonly called white and coloured plains, not exceeding one shilling and six pence sterling per yard, canvas, bolting cloths, drugs and family medicines, plantation and workmen's tools, nails, firearms, bar steel, gunpowder, shot, lead, flints, wire cards and card-wire, mill and grindstones, fishhooks, printed books and pamphlets, salt, coals, and saltpeter. And exclusive of these articles, we do solemnly promise and declare that we will immediately countermand all orders to our correspondents in Great Britain for shipping any such goods, wares, and merchandise; and we will sell and dispose of the goods we have on hand, or that may arrive in consequence of former orders at the same rates as heretofore.

III. That we will use the utmost economy in our persons, houses, and furniture; particularly, that we will give no mourning, or gloves, or scarves at funerals.

IV. That from and after the 1st day of January, 1770, we will not import, buy, or sell any Negroes that shall be brought into this province from Africa; nor after the 1st day of October next, any Negroes that shall be imported from the West Indies, or any other place excepting from Africa as aforesaid; and that if any goods or Negroes shall be sent to us contrary to our agreement in this subscription, such goods shall be re-shipped or stored, and such Negroes re-shipped from this province, and not by any means offered for sale therein.

V. That we will not purchase from, or sell for, any masters of vessels, transient persons, or non-subscribers, any kind of European or East India goods whatever, excepting coals and salt, after the 1st day of November next.

VI. That as wines are subject to a heavy duty, we agree not to import any on our account or commission, or purchase from any master of vessel, transient person, or non-subscriber, after the 1st day of January next.

VII. Lastly, that we will not purchase any Negroes imported, or any goods or merchandise whatever, from any resident in this province, that refuses or neglects to sign this agreement within one month from the date hereof; excepting it shall appear he has been unavoidably prevented from doing the same. And every subscriber who shall not strictly and literally adhere to this agreement, according to the true intent and meaning hereof, ought to be treated with the utmost contempt.

E S S A Y S

The Stamp Act and the Townshend Acts provided the political foundations for the central issues of the imperial crisis. As the following essays demonstrate, the basic conflict between parliamentary rule and colonial rights had emerged by 1765, although a full realization of the depth of the division became clear only after repeated political maneuvers and tests of will.

Edmund S. Morgan, a Pulitzer Prize–winning Yale professor emeritus, and his late wife Helen M. Morgan argue in the first essay that Prime Minister George Grenville deviously used the Stamp Act to establish the authority of Parliament in the colonies. Conciliatory Americans who wished to supply revenues to Britain by their own means were first encouraged but then brushed aside in a way that provoked stern resistance. The Morgans also go on to explain how, following the repeal of the Stamp Act in 1766 and the simultaneous reassertion of Parliament's right to legislate for the colonies "in all cases whatsoever," the conflict was renewed over the Townshend Acts, a series of customs duties intended to achieve the same objectives as the Stamp Act but by a slightly more indirect route. Although the fundamental issue—Parliament's assertion of the right of taxation—remained unchanged, Pauline Maier, a William R. Kenan, Jr., Professor of History at Massachusetts Institute of Technology, argues in the third essay that this sequel to the Stamp Act changed the character of resistance, because the Townshend Acts dashed remaining colonial hopes for fairness. Although colonial leaders continued to intimidate their adversaries, Maier reports, they still normally regarded violence as an unnecessary and illegitimate tactic. At the same time, she shows that their non-importation associations became ever more ready to assert quasi-governmental authority. A pattern of mutual alienation, first evident in 1765–1766, came to characterize relations between imperial authorities and the leaders of colonial legislatures. As a result, though a kind of peace would be restored in 1770 by the repeal of most of the Townshend Acts, Britain and the colonies in fact were even further apart politically than when the Declaratory Act had been issued.

The Assertion of Parliamentary Control and Its Significance

EDMUND S. AND HELEN M. MORGAN

When George Grenville tightened up the administration of the colonial customs service and revised the rates to make them produce a revenue, he knew that he was only beginning, that the colonies could and should contribute more to the cost of their defence. During the summer of 1763 he had already begun to consider the possibility of a stamp tax, and had assigned two different individuals to prepare drafts of an American Stamp Act. When these were presented to him on September 30, 1763, and October 10, 1763, respectively, he found neither satisfactory. The men who drew them up simply did not know the details of American judicial procedures well enough to name and describe the documents upon which a tax should be collected. In fact it is unlikely that anyone in the offices at Whitehall knew enough. Consequently, although Grenville was anxious to increase the revenue as rapidly as possible, a stamp tax would have to wait until the necessary information could be gathered.

Since he could not present Parliament with an American Stamp Act in the spring of 1764, why did Grenville offer his resolution that one might be proper in the future? Why not wait until he had it ready, before introducing the subject? . . . Grenville was worried, though probably not greatly, about the reaction to a stamp tax both in Parliament and in the colonies. . . . Legislative bodies are not fond of

"Voices of the System" from *The Stamp Act Crisis: Prologue to Revolution* by Edmund S. and Helen M. Morgan. Published for the Institute of Early American History and Culture, Williamsburg, VA. © 1962 The University of North Carolina Press.

setting limits on their own competence, and Parliament had long since accustomed itself to the idea of its own omnipotence. Yet Grenville had heard hints dropped outside Parliament. Perhaps he knew that his great brother-in-law did not share the general view, and a view which William Pitt did not share was possibly not so general after all. One way to establish its acceptance, however, was by a Parliamentary resolution. Once Parliament agreed that it had the right to levy stamp duties in the colonies, it was not likely to reverse its opinion when asked to exercise the right. . . .

There was also the question of how a stamp act would be received in the colonies. Grenville saw a way to take care of this problem too with his advance resolution: when introducing it to Parliament he managed to maneuver the colonists into a position where a stamp act would appear to be the result of their own failure to come to the assistance of the mother country in an hour of need. . . . There is no official record of what he said in Parliament on March 9, 1764, and in the several accounts by private hands most of the space is devoted to his remarks on the deplorable condition of English finances and his explanation of the resolutions which were to form the basis of the Sugar Act. With regard to the fifteenth resolution (which affirmed that a stamp tax might be necessary), the accounts are meager, but a few facts stand out: Grenville announced that he wished no action on this subject until the next session, that his reason for delay was a desire to consult the ease, the interest (or the quiet), and the good will of the colonies, and that the colonies might take advantage of the delay to offer any objections they might have to the tax, or to suggest some more satisfactory tax, or—and here was the most misleading suggestion—to raise the money themselves in any way they saw fit. . . .

Grenville definitely proposed in his speech of March 9, that the colonies might avert the stamp tax. If they would prefer to tax themselves rather than be taxed by Parliament they had a year in which to take action. Having made this magnanimous gesture, Grenville put in motion the machinery for drawing up a stamp bill to present to the next session of Parliament. For reasons that will become apparent Grenville was probably certain that the colonies would do nothing, and he wanted to have his bill ready by 1765. He gave to Thomas Whately in the treasury office the task of preparing it, and Whately wrote to persons he knew in America to get the necessary information. . . .

While Thomas Whately was busy preparing the Stamp Act, the colonial agents, to say nothing of the colonists, were puzzling over the meaning of the alternative proposal that Grenville had made in his speech of March 9. For a reason which is obvious enough if we assume that Grenville had already made up his mind to have a stamp tax, he had not communicated the proposal to the colonial assemblies through the channel normally used. Had he really intended to allow the colonies a chance to raise the money themselves, he would have made his offer in the regular manner by having the Secretary of State for the Southern Department write to the governors of the colonies. . . .

Yet in spite of the fact that Grenville did not make the offer in proper form, he did make it, and the agents did report it to their constituents. . . . The agents, before they could have had time to hear from their constituents about it, decided to have a talk with the Minister. He met them on May 17, 1764, in a conference which was afterwards described in some detail by three of the participants.

Grenville opened by stating that he had not changed his mind, but he then proceeded to propose something he had not so much as mentioned in his speech. The agents were trying to find out "the sort of proposition, which would probably be accepted from them to Parliament," in other words how much he wanted the colonies to raise. But Grenville, rather than stating the sum he wanted from them, now proposed that they assent in advance to the Parliamentary tax and thereby set a precedent for being consulted about any future taxes! He also spoke strongly of the difficulties which "would have" attended any scheme of letting them tax themselves, as though that issue were closed. But he did not expressly repudiate his offer; and the agents, although they could not help seeing that he was discouraging action by the colonies, apparently did not recognize that he was precluding it. They did not, however, press for a statement of the exact sum with which the colonies might satisfy him. Grenville had steered the conference beyond that subject, and they probably feared to upset his evident good humor by insisting on a matter so obviously distasteful. They must prolong the conference and find out, if possible, the terms of the act he expected to bring in if the colonies did not raise the money themselves. They must know the terms, one of the agents explained, "in order that our respective constituents might have the whole, both substance and form under their deliberation, when they would be far better able to determine whether or how far, to approve or disapprove." But the details of the act were, of course, unknown to Grenville himself, for it had not yet been drawn up. Israel Mauduit [Massachusetts' agent] pointed out that to ask the colonies to assent in advance to a bill without giving the provisions of it was asking them "to assent to they did not know what." To this Grenville answered simply that it was not necessary to bother with details, "That everyone knew the stamp laws here; and that this Bill is intended to be formed upon the same plan." He did agree to consult with the agents on this matter just before the meeting of Parliament, provided that in the meantime the colonial assemblies should signify their assent to the general idea of a stamp tax. He warned that any protests based on the financial inability of the colonies to pay would carry little weight in Parliament. In his speech of March 9 he had already made it plain that he would listen to nothing which called in question the right of Parliament to levy the tax, so that he left the colonies very little room either for criticism or for constructive action.

It is evident from this conference that Grenville was determined upon a stamp tax. Though he was willing to make magnanimous gestures, he had no intention of allowing the colonies to prevent passage of his measure either by objections to it or by raising an "equivalent" sum. They would not thwart him by levying a substitute tax themselves: by withholding the necessary information he made sure of that. . . .

It was only when a colony set about to tax itself that the hollowness of Grenville's offer became apparent. Massachusetts made the attempt. Though Governor Bernard was convinced that the Ministry really intended to let the colonies raise all internal taxes themselves, yet when several members of the Assembly approached him in the summer of 1764, asking for a special session in order that the colony might tax itself to avoid being taxed by Parliament, Bernard refused, because he saw that nothing could be done without more information from Grenville. He related the entire incident to his friend Richard Jackson, in a letter dated at Boston, August 18, 1764. . . .

This letter shows plainly enough why the colonies did not take advantage of Grenville's offer to let them tax themselves. Not only was the offer never made them in a regular manner by letters from the Secretary of State, but it was never couched in terms that were definite enough to permit of action. Several colonies signified their willingness to contribute if requested in a regular manner for a specific sum, but such a request was never made.

What the colonies did do was to take up the challenge which Grenville had thrown to Parliament and which Parliament had endorsed and passed on to them. The Americans read the fifteenth resolution correctly, as a declaration of Parliament's right to tax them. And since the challenge was no more than a declaration, albeit by a body which regarded its own declarations as final, they replied in the mode, infuriating to omnipotence, of talking back. In the petitions to Parliament and letters to their agents . . . they denied that Parliament had any right to tax them. This denial was by no means limited to the dusky halls of legislative assemblies. The people at large were as much concerned over the measure as their representatives. Jared Ingersoll, in answer to Thomas Whately's inquiries, warned the man who was drafting the Stamp Act, that the minds of the people "are filled with the most dreadfull apprehensions from such a Step's taking place, from whence I leave you to guess how Easily a tax of that kind would be Collected; tis difficult to say how many ways could be invented to avoid the payment of a tax laid upon a Country without the Consent of the Legislature of that Country and in the opinion of most of the people Contrary to the foundation principles of their natural and Constitutional rights and Liberties. Dont think me impertinent, Since you desire Information, when I tell you that I have heard Gentlemen of the greatest property in Neighbouring Governments say, Seemingly very Cooly, that should such a Step take place they would immediately remove themselves with their families and fortunes into some foreign Kingdom." Ingersoll also told Whately, much as Bernard had told Jackson, that "If the King should fix the proportion of our Duty, we all say we will do our parts in the Common Cause, but if the Parliament once interpose and Lay a tax, tho' it may be a very moderate one . . . what Consequences may, or rather may not, follow?" . . .

If Parliament was not as aware as Grenville that its authority in America needed support, the colonists themselves completed the awakening. As the protests from across the ocean poured into England, Parliamentary hackles rose, and the Minister could rejoice, for, as he had calculated, the members reacted to the denial of their authority with the wrath of injured dignity. The unfortunate colonial agents, fighting frantically to stave off the coming blow, saw that because of their clients' declarations the battle was being transformed into a test of Parliament's authority. The main issue was no longer raising a revenue, but putting the Americans in their place. . . .

By this time the situation was becoming desperate. Parliament was due to open, and though a good deal of propaganda had been published, most of it probably at the instigation of the agents, there was no organized opposition in the House of Commons to contest the bill when Grenville should bring it in. The agents decided to make one last attempt to stop the tax at its source and deputed four of their number to call on the Minister again and point out to him that most of the colonies had expressed their willingness to contribute to the British Treasury if called upon to do so in a regular, constitutional manner. The agents . . . met with Grenville on February 2, 1765. . . .

When the conference of February 2 was over the agents must have realized at last that Grenville's offer had never been made in good faith, that a year ago, even while making the offer, he had already made up his mind to levy a stamp tax. The willingness he had then expressed to let the colonies tax themselves or offer objections was nothing more than a rhetorical gesture, designed to demonstrate his own benevolence. In the conference of February 2, 1765, he even told the agents that "he had pledged his Word for Offering the Stamp Bill to the house." What he had given the colonies was not an opportunity to tax themselves but an opportunity to refuse to tax themselves.

In the time that was left the agents continued their preparation for the ensuing battle in Parliament, but the impudence of the Americans had so irritated the lawmakers, that the issue was a foregone conclusion. . . . Even the most eloquent opponents of the tax spoke in terms of equity and expediency and did not venture to deny the absolute authority of Parliament.

The staunchest supporter of the colonies in this first debate was Colonel Isaac Barré, a veteran of the French and Indian War. According to one observer, "He most strongly recommended that if there must be a tax laid, tho' he could wish there was to be none, that the Provinces might be indulged with the liberty as heretofore of furnishing their quotas of any sums required and colecting it in their own modes." Barré, in other words, advocated the proposal that Grenville himself had first made but failed to carry through. Charles Townshend, author-to-be of the Townshend Duties, spoke with some warmth in the debate, asking on one occasion: "And now will these Americans, Children planted by our Care, nourished up by our Indulgence untill they are grown to a Degree of Strength and Opulence, and protected by our Arms, will they grudge to contribute their mite to relieve us from the heavy weight of that burden which we lie under?" To this Barré answered with words that would soon make him famous throughout the American Colonies:

They planted by your Care? No! your Oppressions planted em in America. They fled from your Tyranny to a then uncultivated and unhospitable Country—where they exposed themselves to almost all the hardships to which human Nature is liable, and among others to the Cruelties of a Savage foe, the most subtle and I take upon me to say the most formidable of any People upon the face of Gods Earth. And yet, actuated by Principles of true english Lyberty, they met all these hardships with pleasure, compared with those they suffered in their own Country, from the hands of those who should have been their Friends.

They nourished by *your* indulgence? they grew by your neglect of Em: as soon as you began to care about Em, that Care was Exercised in sending persons to rule over Em, in one Department and another, who were perhaps the Deputies of Deputies to some Member of this house—sent to Spy out their Lyberty, to misrepresent their Actions and to prey upon Em; men whose behaviour on many Occasions has caused the Blood of those Sons of Liberty to recoil within them; men promoted to the highest Seats of Justice, some, who to my knowledge were glad by going to a foreign Country to Escape being brought to the Bar of a Court of Justice in their own.

They protected by *your* Arms? they have nobly taken up Arms in your defence, have Exerted a Valour amidst their constant and Laborious industry for the defence of a Country, whose frontier, while drench'd in blood, its interior Parts have yielded all its little Savings to your Emolument. And believe me, remember I this Day told you so, that same Spirit of freedom which actuated that people at first, will accompany them still.—But prudence forbids me to explain myself further. God knows I do not at this Time speak from motives of party Heat, what I deliver are the genuine Sentiments of my heart.

Even Barré's eloquence, which did not, after all, deny the authority of Parliament, could not alter the determination of the members to prove their unlimited authority by taxing the colonies. . . . The sentiment in favor of the tax was so strong that the opposition, instead of bringing the matter to a vote on the immediate question, tried to get through a vote to adjourn. . . . The motion was lost by a vote of 245 to 49, taken at about midnight, and on the following day the House of Commons passed, without a division, the fifty-five resolutions which formed the basis of the Stamp Act.

Grenville, having thus secured the approval of Parliament, brought in the bill itself on February 13. It received its first reading then and its second on February 15. This was the crucial reading, and the opposition prepared to present petitions against it. . . .

The refusal of Parliament to hear these petitions did not pass without debate. General Conway . . . was the principal defender of the colonies at this juncture. He made a telling point when he reminded the members that they had postponed the Stamp Act the preceding year in order to give the colonies time to send messages representing their objections to it. "This time has been given," said Conway. "The Representations are come from the Colonies; and shall we shut our Ears against that Information, which, with an Affectation of Candour, we allotted sufficient Time to reach us? . . . [F]rom whom, unless from themselves, are we to learn the Circumstances of the Colonies, and the fatal Consequences that may attend the imposing of this Tax?"

Conway's plea on February 15 was no more effective than Barré's had been on February 6; . . . and by March 22 the Stamp Act was a statute of the realm. It remained to be seen whether it would establish, or destroy, the authority of Parliament in America. . . .

One of the principal arguments which the opposition had used against repeal of the Stamp Act was that the colonies would interpret it as a sign of weakness, that whatever reason Parliament assigned for repeal, the Americans would believe that their own resistance had been the real cause. The friends of the colonies took care to inform their correspondents in America that the violence against the stamp distributors had prolonged the struggle for repeal and had even threatened to prevent it entirely. Letters sent by the committee of merchants in London to the merchants of the principal towns and cities of North America urged the Americans not to exult in the victory as a point gained over Parliamentary authority. Any such attitude would surely strengthen the hand of Grenville and his followers, who might still return to power and undo the great work of reconciliation. The merchants had had a hard fight, in which they had "pawned their words" for the colonies, and "I hope," one of them wrote, "nothing will be done, that may make them ashamed of the assurances they have given, that all would return to quiet and good humour. A contrary behaviour will hurt the present ministry, who are your true friends; and if they fall, your enemies will succeed, from whom you have everything to fear." In order to prevent such a catastrophe, the committee urged the Americans to send over expressions of "filial duty and gratitude to your parent country."

These words were made more pointed by two protests issuing from the minority in the House of Lords against repeal of the Stamp Act. . . . Repeal of the Stamp Act, they said, was a surrender of Parliament's supreme jurisdiction. The reasons the Americans had assigned for disobedience to the Act would extend "to all other laws, of what nature soever, which that Parliament had enacted, or shall enact, to bind them in times to come, and must, if admitted, set them absolutely free from any obedience to the power of the British legislature." By the Declaratory Act, they said, Parliament only "more grievously injured its own dignity and authority by verbally asserting that right which it substantially yields up to its opposition." The total effect would be to push the colonies in the direction toward which they were already verging—independence. In the protests of the Lords the Americans could read the narrowness of their escape as well as their future peril, and they hastened to comply with the advice of the merchants, which had been seconded by Secretary Conway in sending official notice of the repeal. The assemblies of the various colonies drew up addresses of thanks to King and Parliament for their parental solicitude and gave assurance of their loyalty to the King and their submission to the authority of Parliament— though none of them specifically acknowledged that this authority included the right to tax them.

In spite of the loyal sentiments of their addresses, the colonists would have been a little more than human if they had not given themselves some of the credit for repeal. "Had we tamely submitted," they asked themselves, "would the Justice of our Cause have procured us Relief?" Probably few could find it in their hearts to say yes. . . . Thomas Hutchinson, looking back upon the period some years later thought that repeal was interpreted throughout the colonies, not as an act of favor, but as a concession to the colonial view that taxation was the power only of a representative body. The celebrations with which repeal was greeted were decent and orderly, as the committee of merchants had urged. . . . Up and down the Atlantic coast, houses were illuminated; paintings and verses composed for the occasion were exhibited; and toasts were drunk publicly to William Pitt and the other men who had championed the cause of the colonies in Parliament; but the most significant thing about the celebrations was that they were directed by the Sons of Liberty, the men responsible for the violent proceedings which according to the Committee of Merchants had hindered repeal. The Sons of Liberty showed no contrition for their sins. Not only did they direct celebrations of repeal in 1766, but they also staged celebrations upon the anniversary of repeal every year thereafter, until the Revolution began. In Boston they even celebrated the anniversary of August 14, the night of the first riot. Thus the Sons of Liberty kept alive the memory of the glorious days when Americans had risen up against the threat of tyranny and had successfully asserted their rights. . . .

There is no evidence that the Americans, in rejoicing over repeal of the Stamp Act, accepted the right of Parliament to tax them. Many of their loyal addresses of thanks upon the repeal, were phrased so as to reject any such admission. . . . The vague terms of the Declaratory Act enabled them to accept it as a statement of their own position: that Parliament had supreme legislative authority, but that taxation was not a part of legislation.

William Pitt himself had spectacularly supported the American position in Parliament, and the American press like the British press gave to Pitt the credit for carrying the repeal. He had asserted plainly the power of Parliament in all branches of legislation whatsoever, but he had stoutly denied Parliament's right to tax. Upon reading his speech of January 14, John Adams wrote in his diary: "What has been said in America which Mr. Pitt has not confirmed? Otis, Adams, Hopkins, &c. have said no more." Since they believed that repeal was the work of Pitt many Americans must have found it hard to believe that the Declaratory Act should be interpreted as a denial of everything he had said. George Mason of Virginia observed that the Act asserted the "legislative authority" of Great Britain in all cases whatsoever, but he remembered that "a just and necessary Distinction between Legislation and Taxation hath been made by the greatest and wisest men in the Nation," for surely Pitt was one of the greatest and wisest. . . .

When the Americans did come to realize that the Declaratory Act was intended to affirm the right of taxation, they were by no means ready to accept it. . . .

Those who perceived the true meaning of the Declaratory Act also perceived that the Americans had small reason to display the gratitude which the merchants had insisted upon, for both Parliament and the merchants had been motivated by a concern for the welfare of England rather than America. . . . George Mason ridiculed the merchants for speaking to the colonists like schoolboys, as if to say:

> We have with infinite difficulty and fatigue got you excused this one time; pray be a good boy for the future, do what your papa and mama bid you, and hasten to return them your most grateful acknowledgments for condescending to let you keep what is your own; and then all your acquaintance will love you, and praise you, and give you pretty things; . . . Is not this a little ridiculous, when applied to three millions of as loyal and useful subjects as any in the British dominions, who have been only contending for their birth-right, and have now only gained, or rather kept, what could not, with common justice, or even policy, be denied them?

Not all Americans were able to see . . . the implications of what Parliament had done, and even they missed the larger significance of the Declaratory Act. Perhaps even Rockingham failed to understand that his Act assigned a greater authority to Parliament than Grenville had originally claimed with his Stamp Act. Grenville had justified taxing the colonies on the ground that they were represented—virtually—in Parliament. Repeal of the Stamp Act, unaccompanied by the Declaratory Act, could have been utilized as a demonstration that virtual representation worked. Though the Americans did not elect a single member, Parliament had been sufficiently sensitive to their interests, as expressed through the British merchants, to repeal a measure they disliked. What better answer than this to the American claim that virtual representation could not cross the ocean? But the Declaratory Act precluded such an interpretation of repeal, for it rendered unnecessary the pretense of linking taxation and representation, and rested the authority of Parliament on a simple declaration of that body's sovereignty. . . . Officially there was no longer any doubt that Parliament had authority to tax the colonies, and there was no longer any need to justify that authority by the doctrine of virtual representation. The British government had abandoned the constitutional position which linked them with the Americans and had retreated to the heights of arbitrary declaration. . . .

As the years went by the government fell more and more into the grasp of men who believed with George Grenville that the Stamp Act should have been enforced instead of repealed. . . .

In the eyes of these men the Americans had been aiming at independence ever since the Peace of Paris. It was a common observation in the mid-eighteenth century that the colonies would not forever remain as dependencies of Great Britain. No one who considered the extent of the North American continent and the rate at which its population was increasing could doubt the truth of the observation, though the separation was scarcely expected to take place in the eighteenth century. Many Englishmen had warned before the Peace of Paris that if Canada were not returned to the French the Americans would no longer feel the need of the British army and navy to protect them and would turn their faces toward independence. When these warnings were ignored and the French menace was ended by the Peace of Paris, the prophets of doom saw their fears justified in the ensuing American resistance to the Stamp Act. . . .

As the English thought that they saw the Americans inching their way toward independence, the Americans thought that they saw a sinister party in England seeking by gradual degrees to enslave them. There had been rumors of a plan to reorganize the colonies ever since the fall of Quebec, and Governor Bernard had intimated that the Stamp Act was a part of that plan. Even so reasonable a man as William Samuel Johnson thought that the ministry must have had a "formal design" constantly in view for several years. "Fortunately," he wrote in January, 1766, "they have of late precipitated their Measures and by that means opened our Eyes. Had they proceeded by slow and sensible degrees as they have been wont to do perhaps in a course of years they might have effected their baneful purpose. But by pressing it too much and making more haste than good speed they have defeated the whole design and given such an Alarm as will forever keep America upon her guard."

With the repeal of the Stamp Act many Americans, misinterpreting the meaning of the Declaratory Act, believed that the plot had been foiled, and when Rockingham was replaced by Pitt, they rejoiced that their fastest friend was now in control. When the attempt to tax them was renewed under a ministry with Pitt at the head, they could see that the repeal was only a pause in the relentless advance of the plot to enslave them, and the vagueness of the Declaratory Act an effort to lull them into delusions of security, while stronger claims were fastened about them. . . .

Unfortunately the Stamp Act period had not merely created illusions about the aims of both Englishmen and Americans but had also impaired the disposition to compromise in both countries and had in some cases discredited the men who would have been willing to do so. The circumstances that enabled Lord North to retain power from 1770 to 1782 were complex, but undoubtedly one reason was the conviction of most members of Parliament after 1768 that the repeal of the Stamp Act had been a mistake. Certainly this conviction was expressed again and again on the floor of the House of Commons, and the Whigs felt obliged to apologize for the measure which had staved off revolution in 1766.

In America too the Stamp Act had discredited moderates and enabled extremists to gain greater influence than they had ever enjoyed before. . . . The withdrawal of these men from public life was accompanied by the rise of bolder and more aggressive politicians who had made their reputation in resistance to the Stamp Act. . . . It seems particularly significant that the parties which brought on the revolution in the two leading colonies, Massachusetts and Virginia, gained their ascendancy at the time of the Stamp Act. . . .

Besides disposing the colonies to accept radical leadership the Stamp Act period furnished those leaders with a method for bringing pressure to bear in England. Hitherto the colonies had never been able to unite for any purpose, not even for their own defense against the French and Indians. The Stamp Act, much to their own surprise, enabled them to act together. . . . The most spectacular achievement in unity was of course the Stamp Act Congress, but the non-importation agreements adopted by the merchants of Boston, New York, and Philadelphia were equally surprising and more effective. . . .

The colonies remembered the strength of union well enough, as they demonstrated later in their non-importation agreements against the Townshend Duties, in their continental congresses, and finally in their formation of a continental army. Yet in the last analysis the significance of the Stamp Act crisis lies in the emergence, not of leaders and methods and organizations, but of well-defined constitutional principles. The resolutions of the colonial and intercolonial assemblies in 1765 laid down the line on which Americans stood until they cut their connections with England. Consistently from 1765 to 1776 they denied the authority of Parliament to tax them externally or internally; consistently they affirmed their willingness to submit to whatever legislation Parliament should enact for the supervision of the empire as a whole. . . .

The Townshend Acts and the Consolidation of Colonial Resistance

PAULINE MAIER

Repeal of the Stamp Act did not, of course, finally resolve the Anglo-American conflict. Colonial opposition reawoke . . . over the Townshend Revenue Act of 1767. Never again, however, did the Americans relapse to the consternation of 1765 when they had lamented that "no similar Examples from former Times" existed to guide them. Colonists now simply revived and developed the tactics first evolved during the Stamp Act crisis and articulated by the Sons of Liberty. It was clear that legitimate resistance must involve the body of the people, must prefer peaceful over violent forms of action, and must confine whatever force was necessary within defined limits. Yet even as these limitations upon agitation were honored, colonial resistance moved beyond the model of 1765–6 toward a more serious threat to British authority as nonimportation associations increasingly assumed the functions of civil government. The portents of revolution in the final months of the Townshend agitation reflected, moreover, an important corrosion of that ultimate faith in British rule which had characterized the Stamp Act resistance, and which had survived even into the opening years of opposition to the Townshend Act.

I

In 1766, Jonathan Mayhew already grasped the potential significance of the Stamp Act resistance. Should a similar occasion recur, he said, the colonists' "late experience and success will teach them how to act in order to obtain the redress of grievances." He referred to the peaceful methods gradually settled upon in the course of the Stamp Act agitation: "joint, manly and spirited, yet respectful and loyal petitioning," backed up by commercial sanctions. The strategy of petition and non-importation reappeared a year later in John Dickinson's "Letters from a Farmer in Pennsylvania." First published between December 1767 and February 1768, the Farmer's Letters rallied colonists against the new British legislation and more than any other source defined guidelines for the Americans' subsequent opposition to Britain. All "excesses and outrages" were condemned by Dickinson in 1767 just as they had been in 1766 by Mayhew. To talk of defending rights as if they could be upheld only by arms or by riots and tumults was "as much out of the way," Dickinson said, "as if a man having a choice of several roads to reach his journey's end, should prefer the worst for no other reason but because it *is* the worst." Free men should be spirited, ready to maintain their rights; but such efforts should for the time be channeled into "constitutional methods of seeking Redress," such as petitions or nonimportation, modes of opposition proposed as conscious alternatives to violence.

Accordingly, the colonists first petitioned Britain for relief from the Townshend Revenue Act. But during 1769, as it became clear that their petitions were unsuccessful, Americans gradually united behind nonimportation agreements similar to those already initiated in New England and New York. There were, however, significant local variations in the various nonimportation associations. In the Northern and middle colonies, merchants alone formed the covenant; while in the plantation colonies, which lacked so pre-eminent a commercial class, broader-based public bodies endorsed the agreements. . . . The lists of goods proscribed for importation also varied from colony to colony, and in the South agreements tended to emphasize nonconsumption more than nonimportation. . . .

Nonimportation was thus the successor of the Stamp Act resistance. . . . Continuity was evident in strategy, such as the nonimporters' concern for widening their base of support throughout the population. In the South, this goal was often explicit from the outset: Virginia's association of May 18, 1769, for example, invited "all Gentlemen, Merchants, Traders, and other Inhabitants of this Colony" to sign subscription lists. In the Northern colonies, however, the nonimportation associations only gradually involved the nonmercantile population. Massachusetts developments illustrated the slow widening of the movement. The original Boston agreement of March 1768 was drafted and signed only by merchants. In the fall of 1769, however, merchants circulated another subscription paper through the town, asking other inhabitants to pledge not to purchase goods imported contrary to the association and to support patriotic traders. . . . By April 1770, Thomas Hutchinson estimated that the representatives of seven-eighths of the provincial towns favored the agreement, and that "the majority of every order of men in government" had united with "the body of the people" on that issue. . . .

The effort to unite the people against Britain's "unconstitutional" legislation encouraged also the creation of popular institutions where none had previously existed. The virtues of the New England town meeting for "uniting the whole body of the people in the measures taken to oppose the Stamp Act induced other Provinces to imitate their example," Philadelphia's Charles Thomson later testified. Large public meetings provided important support for nonimportation in New York and Philadelphia. . . . In 1770, the South Carolinians sought to hold meetings as *"full . . . as possible"* so that their resolutions could be announced as *"the Sense of the Whole Body."*

At the outset of the nonimportation effort, economic considerations encouraged widespread participation. A commercial depression afflicted the continent. Colonists suffered in part from a scarcity of hard currency, which, they said, had been drained from America by customs payments. New Englanders were particularly aware that trade law reform and economic retrenchment were necessary for recovery. In the South, nonimportation conferred an additional benefit, as George Washington understood, for it gave debt-ridden planters an honorable excuse for cutting back upon extravagant display. Meanwhile merchants could use the curtailment of imports to reduce their inventories of less desirable goods. Yet by late 1769 it had become clear that the association involved—as the town of Abington, Massachusetts, expressed it—"self-denial and public virtue" more than self-indulgence. Even artisans, who might have gained by the new emphasis upon domestic manufacturing, frequently suffered. Too often their trades depended upon imported materials, while occasional public efforts to support American manufacturing were for the most part limited to the production of essential articles such as paper or cloth.

The enduring arguments for nonimportation were, then, above all political. It offered the "wisest and only peaceable method" for Americans to recover their liberty, one, moreover, that was legal and seemed to promise success. As during the Stamp Act crisis, colonists argued that economic retrenchment would awaken the attention of [the] British. . . .

The claims for effectiveness were never disproven in the period through 1770. The movement's disintegration indicated only that any future nonimportation association would have to be more carefully designed—preferably with one identical plan for all the colonies—and less dependent upon the merchants than its predecessor. . . . Hence there was justification enough for the Continental Congress to revive the policy in 1774.

The notion that nonimportation afforded a peaceful and legal means to redress did, however, come into question. Proponents considered nonimportation peaceful in that it was nonviolent. But force was not condemned in general; even the docile John Dickinson considered the resort to forceful resistance in 1765, when there was no alternative but submission to the Stamp Act, "prudent and glorious." Admittedly, force was "always to be the very last means thought of, when every things else fails," and as of 1768 and 1769 it seemed possible to avoid it. . . .

Once again, as during the Stamp Act period, those who ignored or violated the patriotic agreements were coerced by social and economic boycotts which became harsher as the movement itself gained strength and intensity. . . . Whole colonies might be indicted: when Georgia failed to enforce its agreement, patriots in Charleston resolved that the colony ought "to be amputated from the rest of their brethren, as a rotten part that might spread a dangerous infection"; and attempts in Providence and Newport to withdraw from the agreement in May 1770 were cut short after New York, Philadelphia, and Boston imposed an absolute boycott on Rhode Island merchants. A mass of resolutions to boycott New York was also passed after that city finally defected from the movement in 1770.

The architects of nonimportation hoped that the movement could remain peaceful and still be effective. By publishing the names of those who violated the agreement or patronized violators as enemies of their country and greeting them with "every mark of infamy and reproach," Virginia's George Mason argued, associators could effectively play upon men's "sense of shame and fear of reproach." . . . More direct intimidation came only from the "indiscreet Zeal" of individuals and was by no means characteristic of the nonimporters as a whole.

Nonviolence was rarely if ever a passive achievement. In Boston, active efforts to contain popular exuberance were as necessary as they had been during the Stamp Act agitation. As early as 1767, Thomas Hutchinson understood that those who had been "very forward" in promoting the tumults of 1765 had decided to use other means against the Townshend duties. Mobbish incidents were successfully avoided that year. . . .

When violence did break out—in June 1768 during the *Liberty* riot—it was not a result of nonimportation. The incident culminated weeks of mounting tension over impressment between townsmen and the King's ship *Romney,* and was sparked off by the customsmen's method in seizing John Hancock's sloop *Liberty.* From the outset, leading Bostonians tried to stop the disorder. A mob pelting the comptroller's house with stones withdrew "by the advice of some prudent gentlemen that interposed"; and as the crowd burned a pleasure boat belonging to the customs collector, Joseph Harrison, "some gentlemen who had influence" with the mob— allegedly John Hancock, Samuel Adams, and Joseph Warren—persuaded the rioters to disperse. . . . Within the week William Molineux, the radical nonimportation supporter, wrote a letter of sympathy to Harrison, blaming the collector's losses upon a local minority of "such Sort of People" as inhabited "Every Great City perhaps in the World." . . .

Although violence was everywhere curtailed, coercion was not universally eschewed. Fear of mob reprisals forced Simon Cooley to confess his political sins and vow to honor the association at New York in July 1769, and a scaffold erected near Liberty Tree brought the submission of a jeweler, Thomas Richardson, in September. . . .

About [this] time . . . the Bostonians, it seems, began to use more forceful methods against importing merchants. One observer complained in October 1769 that the means taken to induce compliance were "really infamous." The nonsubscribers, he thought, were "in real danger of their Lives. Their property was actually unsafe, their Signs, Doors and Windows were daub'd over in the Night time with every kind of Filth, and one of them particularly had his person treated in the same manner." On October 28, the crowd turned against John Mein, publisher of the *Boston Chronicle* and leading opponent of the association, whom impending social stigma and economic ruin had failed to silence. Mein was first attacked by ten to twelve persons "of some considerable Rank." . . . Later, these assailants were joined by a mob of over a thousand persons which had gathered earlier to tar and feather a suspected customs informer. Mein received an ugly wound from an iron shovel . . . but managed to escape into the guardhouse, where he was shielded by royal troops.

In December, Lieutenant Governor Hutchinson reported that the province was "in a very calm state" although "discontents" continued in Boston. Then, in January, a group of merchants that included Hutchinson's sons Elisha and Thomas, Jr., decided to resume the sale of imported goods. The entire association was brought into peril and agitation revived. Association meetings voted to visit the offenders *en masse,* but these official visits were, as Hutchinson admitted, "without any degree of tumult." Committees were chosen before each visit, and the crowd normally marched to the offender's house with great order, then remained outside the gate while its leaders negotiated with its host. . . .

With the failure of peaceful mass pressure, more virulent forms of mob pressure were again revived. On three successive Thursdays—February 8, 15, and 22—signs and effigies mysteriously appeared pointing out "importers," particularly William Jackson and Theophilus Lillie. Crowds of boys and country people gathered, for it was marketing day, when schools were closed. Customers were intimidated from entering proscribed shops and sometimes pelted with dirt. During those weeks, importers' signs were defaced and their windows broken or "besmeared . . . with tar & feathers." On each occasion, efforts to remove the "importer" signs were repulsed: on the eighth, Jackson was turned back by "a Number of Idle people . . . standing by, with Clubs and sticks in their Hands"; soldiers who made a similar effort on the fifteenth were "beat of[f] and some of them much Hurt"; and finally, on the twenty-second, an attempt to remove an effigy over Lillie's door by Ebenezer Richardson, an ex-customs informer who was considered particularly obnoxious in Boston, resulted in bloodshed. Richardson was chased to his nearby home and besieged by a rock-throwing crowd until he fired shots into the street, hitting an eleven-year-old boy, Christopher Sneider. At that the crowd seized Richardson, dragged him through the streets, and some tried "to put a rope about his Neck and . . . execute him themselves."

Even within this surge of violence the hand of restraint was apparent. A line was usually drawn at lesser forms of harassment: window breaking, the "besmearing" of signs, suggestions of impending violence. . . . On other occasions, leaders intervened to curtail violence and to protect the persons of their enemies. In June 1770, for example, a mob was dissuaded from tarring and feathering Patrick McMasters when it became clear that he could not survive the ordeal. More important, Richardson was saved from his would-be murderers by William Molineux, who was probably responsible for turning the crowd against importers in the first place. Molineux in fact personified the ambiguity that persisted even in the extremes of Boston radicalism. He was the arch demagogue of nonimportation, believed to be "the first Leader of Dirty Matters," whose violence was a divisive factor even within the nonimportation movement in 1770; yet it was he who saved Richardson and also consoled Joseph Harrison after the *Liberty* riot. . . .

Basic to Molineux's behavior there was, it seems, a distinction drawn between violence and coercion. While the destruction of persons and property was condemned as criminal, the resort to lesser forms of harassment for political purposes might be justifiable under criteria of collective necessity. Once force was used against importers, however, the immediate legality of nonimportation came increasingly into question. From the outset, proponents argued that the associations were lawful because their aims were lawful: no statute required colonists to purchase imported goods or to patronize importing merchants and their supporters. . . . If, however, the associations could be linked with illegal violence, all members would be in grave danger: since, as Hutchinson warned in January 1770, "their professed design [was] to reform the law by effecting the repeal of the revenue acts"—a public aim, beyond their personal grievances—"any violence from any of the inferior people who were among them would in my opinion involve them all in the guilt of high treason." . . .

The colonists' concern for acting within the law indicated a continued respect for British institutions. Like the Sons of Liberty during the Stamp Act crisis, the nonimporters insisted that their opposition to British authority was limited. The various associations usually provided for their own dissolution once the Townshend Revenue Act was repealed. An effort by Boston to extend the agreements to work for the repeal of earlier review acts as well, particularly that of 1764, failed completely. Even where royal control faced the greatest resistance, at Boston, the ligaments of British authority were loosened in only limited areas. "In other matters which have no relation to this dispute between the Kingdom and the Colonies," Hutchinson wrote as late as February 28, 1770, "Government retains its vigour and the administration of it is attended with no unusual difficulty."

Nonetheless, by 1770 the American agitation had clearly reached a stage of seriousness far beyond that of three years earlier. Escalation was marked by the increasing severity of reprisals: from mild economic boycotts, through public advertisements of importers as "enemies of their country" who deserved the contempt of their countrymen, to the violence of Boston, which was itself an act of desperation. The town's disorder, Hutchinson testified, came from a "general disposition . . . to favour the measures of the Merchants as the *only means* to preserve the Rights of the people and bring about the Repeal of the Revenue Acts and other Acts called unconstitutional." . . .

The inflamed rhetoric, the assertions that Parliament's unconstitutional acts justified colonial resistance, were reminiscent of the Stamp Act crisis. But even while precautions were taken to maintain the general framework of legal authority, resistance to the Townshend duties became a more serious threat to British authority than that to the Stamp Act. By nature, nonimportation committed partisans to a wider share of administrative responsibilities than had been exercised by the Sons of Liberty of 1765–6. In short, the associations increasingly exercised functions normally reserved to a sovereign state. Committees regularly demanded the right to inspect merchants' invoices and papers, to judge the guilt of suspected violators of the association, and to impose sanctions against the unyielding. . . .

As the number of adherents increased, and nonimporters could claim to speak for the body of the people, the various associations came to serve as social compacts, analogous to the formal constitutions that would be set up by the various colonies in the mid-1770's. The Virginia Association of June 1770, for example, outlined the structure and procedures of that colony's enforcement mechanisms. It took the form of a solemn agreement or compact among the subscribers—described simply as "his Majesty's most dutiful and loyal subjects of *Virginia*"—to adhere to its provisions, which were "binding on all and each" of them. Although their sphere of activity was limited, within that sphere the associations had, as Drayton charged in South Carolina, set up a new legislative power. . . .

As committees increasingly assumed the right to speak and act for the people, the associations' right to coerce nonconformers seemed ever more justified. The personal rights of opponents were not denied, but put in perspective. "The hardships of particulars are not to be considered," Christopher Gadsden wrote, "when the good of the whole is the object in view; as evidently it is, in the case before us." Eighteenth-century political thought had never emphasized individual rights so much as the corporate rights of the community; and patriotism itself was said to involve at core a willingness to sacrifice private interest for the public good. As such nonimportation, with its demand of self-sacrifice for the general welfare, seemed to institutionalize public virtue: "the little conveniences and comforts of life," George Mason wrote, "when set in competition with our liberty, ought to be rejected, not with reluctance, but with pleasure." Importers were, . . . as the Virginia Association of June 1770 put it, men who "preferred their own private emolument, by importing or selling articles prohibited by this association, to the destruction of the dearest rights of the people of this colony." . . .

Samuel Adams similarly compared the authority of the nonimportation supporters with that of regular institutions when he defended the Bostonians' actions against importer Patrick McMasters, who was banished from Boston by a mob in June 1770. In all states, Adams said, individuals were bound to act according to the common will of their fellow citizens or to leave. And in exceptional situations, like the present, the "will and pleasure of the society" was not "declared in its laws," but had to be imposed directly.

II

For most royal observers, the careful legal distinctions that colonial leaders tried to maintain were of no significance. The associators' claim that nonimportation was lawful seemed at best a pretense. In Boston, the fanatical Tory Peter Oliver later claimed, inhabitants armed themselves with homemade "massy Clubs," since "Guns they imagined were Weapons of Death in the Eye of the Law, which the meanest of them was an Adept in; but Bludgeons were only Implements to beat out Brains with." Such constructions seemed only to circumvent the law. . . .

The royal officials' insistence on the authority of Parliament and the Americans' criminality acquired particular shrillness and rigidity as they saw their own authority disintegrate. The failure of local magistrates and militias to support them during the Stamp Act period was not easily forgotten, particularly since the same situation was re-enacted during later incidents. Nor was the success of colonial political leaders in repressing or subduing violence of any consolation. Such authority was not their own; it was at the disposal of powers outside the legal British establishment, and as such seemed unreliable . . . .

As the dominant opinion in the colonies turned toward the radicals rather than toward London, royal officials had a ready explanation. They argued, as Thomas Jefferson later put it, "that the whole ferment has been raised and constantly kept up by a few principal men in every colony, and that it might be expected to subside in a short time either of itself, or by the assistance of a coercive power." The theory was readily adopted in England, where some Members of Parliament clamored for the arrest and punishment of the principal troublemakers. The argument appealed also to the King, who considered Parliament's right to bind the colonists "in all cases whatsoever, as essential to the dignity of the crown, and a right appertaining to the state, which it was his duty to preserve entirely enviolate." He was therefore "greatly displeased" with colonial petitions and remonstrances that denied

Parliament's absolute supremacy, and regretted that his subjects were so "misled"—again, by a handful of factious leaders. In retrospect this rhetoric of conspiracy, which the colonists themselves gradually adopted to explain England's actions, belied the gap between English and American political assumptions, for neither side could recognize the other as acting honestly upon legitimate principles different from its own. . . .

Sometimes haunted by fears for their own safety, conscious that the King's and Parliament's authority was at stake in their own persons, the governors and officials reverted to an old solution for their problems. Troops were necessary, not only to execute individual laws, but, as Georgia's Governor Wright wrote, to support His Majesty's authority from insults. . . . This call for soldiers became a standard theme, not only for governors, but for customs officials, particularly those on the American Board of Customs Commissioners, who arrived in November 1767 and within a year convinced London to send a contingent of troops—uncalled for by local officials—to Boston. . . .

British suppositions also hindered any confident and effective use of troops against the colonists. Traditional ideas about the proper role of the army in a free country were as vivid for military commanders like Sir Jeffery Amherst or Thomas Gage as for John Adams, and even British ministers shared the Americans' misgivings. When Governor Wright of Georgia managed briefly to distribute stamps with the aid of regular troops, he earned not the thanks of his superiors but a word of admonition from Secretary of State Shelburne. . . . The secretary's sentiments here were not far different from those of New York's radical printer John Holt. In commenting upon a letter that anticipated the day when mobs would be suppressed and a proper respect for the laws impressed upon "the lower rank," Holt said simply that *"Not force, but justice will do it."*

Out of this impossibility of military rule arose in good part the peculiar conditions that gave the American Revolution its distinctive character. British authority could not be imposed upon an unwilling people. To be effective it had to be administered by men "reverenced and beloved by the people," as the *Boston Gazette* once said; its power had to flow directly from the governed who, when the laws seemed to promote their welfare, would both obey and enforce them. As these conditions ceased to be true, royal authority disintegrated; imperial officials became incapable of restraining hostility and disorderly outbreaks. But simultaneously, the function of maintaining order was assumed by their opponents. Both sides shared a respect for orderly, lawful procedures; they differed in their definitions of order and their conceptions of legitimacy. The colonists' progressive assumption of power paralleled their increasing conviction that Britain aspired to despotic power. Yet, ironically, it was not only British inability but also her remaining liberal traditions that prevented a simple forceful suppression of the American agitation.

III

The basic guidelines for American opposition to Britain were defined already during the Stamp Act crisis; but the nature of the Anglo-American conflict changed radically within the next decade. Signs of this transformation were already apparent in the nonimportation effort by 1770. The fixation of 1765–6 with buttressing British authority beyond the regions affected by the Stamp Act had to some extent been replaced by a conscious assumption of extralegal political power. More important, the old Sons of Liberty's faith in Britain, her rulers and institutions had given way to a new desperation for American liberty, which was marked by a willingness to resort to ever more extreme methods to maintain the nonimportation association. By 1770, in short, the colonists had begun to advance along the road from resistance to revolution.

Disillusionment with Britain did not immediately follow the Declaratory Act of 1766, which asserted Parliament's sovereign right "to make Laws . . . to bind the Colonists and People of America . . . in all Cases whatsoever." Most colonists apparently interpreted the enactment as a face-saving device upon which Parliament did not intend to act. Colonists remained strongly confident of British justice in late 1767, when John Dickinson's "Letters from a Farmer in Pennsylvania" were readily accepted as expressing the views of his countrymen. In words strikingly like those of Jonathan Mayhew a year earlier, Dickinson stressed that the Americans had "an excellent prince" in whose "good dispositions they could confide"; they had a "generous, sensible and humane nation" to whom they could apply for redress from their newest grievances. Separation was the least desirable outcome of the conflict—
"Torn from the body, to which we are united by religion, liberty, laws, affections, relation, language and commerce, we must bleed at every vein."

Attitudes toward Britain changed, in short, most dramatically only after 1767. . . .

In assigning responsibility for continued "oppressive" policies, the colonists tended to accuse . . . familiar figures. . . . Newspapers of 1765 and 1766 continually repeated rumors that the Stamp Act had been proposed and promoted by British agents on the American continent. . . . Gradually, misrepresentations from "this side the water" became the entire explanation of British policy, as King and Parliament were allegedly led into ill-considered decisions by false information from the colonies. . . .

A belief in misrepresentation was, however, insufficient to transform American opposition from resistance to revolution. Its implications were reformist, not revolutionary. . . . Moreover, misrepresentation absolved officials in London of any guilt for their actions. This was true for the dispatch of troops to Boston. . . . The protraction of grievances was "not to be imputed to an unkind disposition in Lord Hillsborough towards us," it said, "but altogether to the malicious and false representations of an infamous faction on this side the water."

For the radical movement to become revolutionary, more extreme conclusions were necessary. The Americans must become convinced, as John Dickinson put it, that "mistake or passion" could not explain Britain's wrongheaded actions. It had to appear "UNDOUBTED that an inveterate resolution is formed to annihilate the liberties of the governed," one that involved the King, Parliament, and ministry as centrally as their servants in the colonies. And to arrive at such a conclusion, colonists had to turn their eyes from their own continent to London, to examine the actions of King, Parliament, and ministry. In that fact lay the truth of a statement continually repeated by colonists during the frenetic days of the Stamp Act crisis—that only Great Britain could force America toward independence.

FURTHER READING

John Brooke, *The Chatham Administration, 1766–1768* (1956)

John L. Bullion, *The Great and Necessary Measure, George Grenville and the Genesis of the Stamp Act* (1982)

Robert J. Chaffin, "The Townshend Acts of 1767," *William and Mary Quarterly,* 3d ser., 27 (1970), 90–121

Oliver M. Dickerson, *The Navigation Acts and the American Revolution* (1951)

Joseph A. Ernst, "The Currency Act Repeal Movement: A Study of Imperial Politics and Revolutionary Crisis, 1764–1767," *William and Mary Quarterly,* 3d ser., 25 (1968), 177–211

Lawrence H. Gipson, "The Great Debate in the Committee of the Whole House of Commons on the Stamp Act, 1766, as Reported by Nathaniel Ryder," *Pennsylvania Magazine of History* 86 (1962), 10–41

———, *The Triumphant Empire: The Rumbling of the Coming Storm, 1766–1770* (1965)

———, *The Triumphant Empire: Thunder-Clouds Gather in the West, 1763–1766* (1961)

Michael Kammen, *A Rope of Sand: The Colonial Agents, British Politics, and the American Revolution* (1968)

Bernard Knollenberg, *Origin of the American Revolution, 1759–1766* (1960)

Jesse Lemisch, "Radical Plot in Boston (1770): A Study in the Use of Evidence," *Harvard Law Review* (1970), 485–504

Pauline Maier, *From Resistance to Revolution: Colonial Radicals and the Development of American Opposition to Britain, 1765–1776* (1972)

Edmund S. Morgan, "Colonial Ideas of Parliamentary Power, 1764–1766," *William and Mary Quarterly,* 3d ser., 5 (1948), 311–341

———, ed., *Prologue to Revolution: Sources and Documents on the Stamp Act Crisis, 1764–1766* (1959)

———, and Helen M. Morgan, *The Stamp Act Crisis: Prologue to Revolution* (1953)

Arthur M. Schlesinger, *The Colonial Merchants and the American Revolution, 1763–1776* (1918)

Glenn C. Smith, "An Era of Non-Importation Associations, 1768–1773," *William and Mary Quarterly,* 2d ser., 20 (1940), 84–98

Neil R. Stout, *The Royal Navy in America: A Study of Enforcement of Colonial Policy in the Era of the American Revolution* (1973)

Peter D. G. Thomas, *British Politics and the Stamp Act Crisis: The First Phase of the American Revolution, 1763–1767* (1975)

———, *The Townshend Duties Crisis: The Second Phase of the American Revolution, 1767–1773* (1987)

Carl Ubbelohde, *The Vice-Admiralty Courts and the American Revolution* (1960)

John J. Waters and John A. Schutz, "Patterns of Colonial Politics: The Writs of Assistance and the Rivalry Between the Otis and Hutchinson Families," *William and Mary Quarterly,* 3d ser., 24 (1967), 543–567

Derek Watson, "The Rockingham Whigs and the Townshend Duties," *English Historical Review* 84 (1969), 561–565

Robert M. Weir, "North Carolina: Reaction to the Currency Act of 1764," *North Carolina Historical Review* 40 (1963), 183–199

Hiller B. Zobel, *The Boston Massacre* (1970)

The Imperial Crisis: From the Tea Act to the Declaration of Independence

When Parliament passed the Tea Act on May 10, 1773, it unwittingly supplied the catalyst that would revive united colonial resistance to British rule. The law aimed to relieve the East India Company's huge oversupply of tea by enabling the company to market the popular consumer product directly in America and Ireland at a reduced price. Members of Parliament never supposed that by providing tea—which had been taxed since 1767—more cheaply to America, they would cause a storm of protest. But when patriot leaders explained the meaning of the Tea Act, colonists from Charleston, South Carolina, to Boston, Massachusetts, became convinced that the new law was a deceptive scheme intended to enforce the collection of taxes in America. By giving the East India Company a monopoly on the importation of tea into the colonies, Parliament was pushing out untaxed tea from Dutch sources that enterprising colonists previously had smuggled in. And whereas taxes on East India Company tea formerly had been paid by shippers in England, now revenues would be collected in America by the East India Company's loyal, hand-picked agents. With the principle of collecting taxes in America thus established, patriots argued that Parliament might not only raise the tea duty at some later point but impose similar taxes on other commodities, and even on land. Because of these threats, patriots were able to mobilize effective resistance to the landing of the tea in all the major colonial ports. Everywhere, colonists returned the tea to Britain before it was unloaded on shore or taxed—everywhere, that is, except Boston. There Governor Thomas Hutchinson, whose son was an East India Company agent, refused to allow the tea ship to sail back to England with its savory cargo. So in a carefully executed protest, patriots disguised as Indians dumped the tea into the harbor.

As John Adams among others recognized immediately, the patriots' "tea party" was a critical action. Parliament retaliated with the Coercive Acts, by which it intended to establish control over Massachusetts while sending a stern message to the other colonies. Americans' subsequent decision to treat

Massachusetts as suffering in the common cause led to the creation of the Continental Congress, which not only supported Massachusetts but, in October 1774, enacted a trade embargo (the Continental Association) against Britain. Later, after fighting broke out at Lexington and Concord, the Congress would back Massachusetts.

Reconciliation now receded further and further from the reach of leaders on both sides of the Atlantic. As imperial politics became polarized and positions hardened, in the colonists' eyes, an open break from England seemed more and more necessary. The king effectively declared war on the colonists as rebels by proclaiming America in rebellion in August 1775. In response, the colonists turned to independence as a reasonable policy. Although it was never possible for the colonists as a whole to achieve unanimity—too many different interests and too much diversity prevailed among them—in the Continental Congress the tide of opinion swept rapidly toward independence.

D O C U M E N T S

In the first document, John Adams's private response to the Tea Party, the patriot leader reveals the depth of colonial resistance to the Tea Act, whereas the parliamentary debates reprinted in the second selection show how differently the same event was viewed in Britain. The colonists had a few friends in Parliament—Sir George Saville and General Conway, for example—but the weight of parliamentary opinion and numbers favored restrictions, if not outright punishment, for Boston and the rest of Massachusetts. Britain's considered response was the Coercive Acts, excerpted here as the third selection. This legislation so threatened all the colonies that they banded together in the Continental Congress to protest.

Virginia, along with Massachusetts, emerged as an advocate of vigorous resistance. The reasoning of the Virginia patriots is set forth in Jefferson's *Summary View* (the fourth document), a tract that anticipated Thomas Paine's *Common Sense* and the *Declaration of Independence*. Later that year, in October 1774, the First Continental Congress declared that "by the immutable laws of nature" and "the principles of the English constitution," as well as their individual colony charters, Parliament had no right to legislate for the American colonies. By the time of the battles of Lexington and Concord in April 1775 and Bunker Hill in June 1775, few politicians on either side believed in conciliation. After blood was shed, both sides hardened. Indeed, Parliament and Lord North's ministry supported King George's proclamation that the colonies had now entered into rebellion which must be suppressed. In America objections to independence were being swept aside by powerful arguments such as those expressed in *Common Sense,* which is excerpted in document seven. This pamphlet, published in January 1776 by an anonymous English immigrant, rapidly circulated among tens of thousands of households and gave the once-frightening idea of independence legitimacy. A few colonies, most importantly New York and Pennsylvania, were divided on the question and so argued for delay. But in June the Congress decided to act, and in July 1776 adopted and proclaimed the Declaration of Independence, document eight, which Thomas Jefferson, in committee with John Adams, Benjamin Franklin, John Jay, and Roger Sherman, had drafted. Grounding the Declaration on both natural rights and the rights of Englishmen under the British Constitution, they asserted American independence on a broad but legalistic basis quite different from Thomas Paine's sweeping rejection of monarchy and the whole corrupt British system.

1. John Adams Reflects on the Boston Tea Party, 1773

Last Night 3 Cargoes of Bohea Tea were emptied into the Sea. This Morning a Man of War sails.

This is the most magnificent Movement of all. There is a Dignity, a Majesty, a Sublimity, in this last Effort of the Patriots, that I greatly admire. The People should never rise, without doing something to be remembered—something notable And striking. This Destruction of the Tea is so bold, so daring, so firm, intrepid and inflexible, and it must have so important Consequences, and so lasting, that I cant but consider it as an Epocha in History.

This however is but an Attack upon Property. Another similar Exertion of popular Power, may produce the destruction of Lives. Many Persons wish, that as many dead Carcasses were floating in the Harbour, as there are Chests of Tea:—a much less Number of Lives however would remove the Causes of all our Calamities. . . .

What Measures will the Ministry take, in Consequence of this?—Will they resent it? will they dare to resent it? will they punish Us? How? By quartering Troops upon Us?—by annulling our Charter?—by laying on more duties? By restraining our Trade? By Sacrifice of Individuals, or how.

The Question is whether the Destruction of this Tea was necessary? I apprehend it was absolutely and indispensably so.—They could not send it back, the Governor, Admiral and Collector and Comptroller would not suffer it. It was in their Power to have saved it—but in no other. It could not get by the Castle, the Men of War &c. Then there was no other Alternative but to destroy it or let it be landed. To let it be landed, would be giving up the Principle of Taxation by Parliamentary Authority, against which the Continent have struggled for 10 years, it was loosing all our labour for 10 years and subjecting ourselves and our Posterity forever to Egyptian Taskmasters—to Burthens, Indignities, to Ignominy, Reproach and Contempt, to Desolation and Oppression, to Poverty and Servitude.

But it will be said it might have been left in the Care of a Committee of the Town, or in Castle William. To this many Objections may be made.

Deacon Palmer and Mr. Is. Smith dined with me, and Mr. Trumble came in. They say, the Tories blame the Consignees, as much as the Whiggs do—and say that the Governor will loose his Place, for not taking the Tea into his Protection before, by Means of the Ships of War, I suppose, and the Troops at the Castle.

2. Parliament Debates the Coercive Acts, 1774

Sir George Saville said . . . that the measure now before the house was a very doubtful and dangerous one; doubtful as to the propriety of regulation, and dangerous as to its consequence; that charters by government were sacred things, and are only to be taken away by a due course of law, either as a punishment for an offence,

Reprinted by permission of the publisher from *The Diary and Autobiography of John Adams,* Volumes II and IV, edited by L. H. Butterfield, Cambridge, Mass.: The Belknap Press of Harvard University Press, Copyright © 1961 by the President and Fellows of Harvard College.

"Parliament Debates the Coercive Acts, 1774." In Hezekiah Niles, ed., *Principles and Acts of the Revolution in America: or, An Attempt to Collect and Preserve some of the Speeches, Orations, and Proceedings, with Sketches and Remarks on Men and Things and other Fugitive or Neglected Pieces, belonging to the Revolutionary Period in the United States* (Baltimore: W. O. Niles, 1822), 189–197.

or for a breach of the contract, and that can only be by evidence of the facts; nor could he conceive that in either of those cases there could be any such thing as proceeding without a fair hearing of BOTH parties. This measure before us seems to be a most extraordinary exertion of legislative power. . . . You are now going to alter the charter because it is convenient. In what manner does the house mean to take away this charter, when in fact they refuse to hear the parties, or to go through a legal course of evidence of the facts. Chartered rights have, at all times, when attempted to be altered or taken away, occasioned much bloodshed and strife. . . .

Mr. Welbore Ellis. . . . I differ from the honorable gentleman who spoke last; . . . I think, sir, that chartered rights are by no means those sacred things which never can be altered; they are vested in the crown as a prerogative, for the good of the people at large; if the supreme legislature find that those charters so granted, are both unfit and inconvenient for the public utility, they have a right to make them fit and convenient. . . . Is a charter, not consistent with the public good, to be continued? . . .

General Conway. What I intend to say will not delay the house long. . . . The consequence of this bill will be very important and dangerous. Parliament cannot break into a right without hearing the parties. The question then is simply this:— Have they been heard? What! because the papers say a murder had been committed, does it follow they have proved it? . . . Gentlemen will consider, that this is not only the charter of Boston, or of any particular part, but the charter of ALL America. Are the Americans not to be heard? . . . I do think, and it is my sincere opinion, that we are the AGGRESSORS and INNOVATORS, and NOT THE COLONIES. We have IRRITATED and FORCED laws upon them for these six or seven years last past. We have enacted such a variety of laws, with these new taxes, together with a refusal to repeal the *trifling* duty on tea; all these things have served no other purpose but to *distress* and *perplex*. I think the Americans have done *no more* than *every* subject *would* do in an *arbitrary* state, where laws are imposed against their will. In my conscience, I think, *taxation* and *legislation* are in this case *inconsistent*. Have you not a legislative right over Ireland? And yet no one will dare to say we have a right to tax. These acts respecting America, will *involve* this country and its ministers in *misfortunes,* and I wish I may not add, in *ruin*.

Lord North. I do not consider this matter of regulation to be taking away their charters in such manner as is represented; it is a regulation of government to assist the crown; it appears to me not to be a matter of political expediency, but of necessity. If it does not stand upon that ground, it stands on nothing. . . . Gentlemen say, let the colony come to your bar, and be heard in their defence; though it is not likely that they will come, when they deny your authority in every instance, can we remain in this situation long? We must effectually take some measures to correct and amend the defects of that government. . . . The Americans have tarred and feathered your subjects, plundered your merchants, burnt your ships, denied all obedience to your laws and authority; yet so clement and forbearing has our conduct been, that it is incumbent upon us now to take a different course. Whatever may be the consequence, we must risque something; if we do not, all is over. . . .

Sir George Young. It remains to me, sir, . . . that the parties should be heard, though even at a twelve-month hence. Nothing, sir, but *fatal* necessity can countenance this measure. No body of men ought to be proceeded against without being heard, much less ought the regulation of a whole government to take place, without the parties attending in their defence against such alterations. . . .

Mr. C. Jenkinson. I rise, sir, only to observe, that if the colony has not that power within itself to maintain its own peace and order, the legislature should, and ought to have. Let me ask, sir, whether the colony took any step, in any shape, to quell the riots and disturbances? No, they took none. . . . It is not only in the late proceedings, but in all former, that they have denied your authority over them; they have refused protection to his majesty's subjects, and in every instance disobeyed the laws of this country; either let this country forsake its trade with America, or let us give that due protection to it which safety requires.

Mr. Harris. I cannot see, sir, any reason for so wide a separation between America and England as other gentlemen are apt to think there ought to be; that country, sir, was hatched from this, and I hope we shall always keep it under the shadow of our wings. It has been said, no representation, no taxation. This was the system formerly adopted, but I do not find it authorised in any book of jurisprudence, nor do I deem it to be a doctrine either reasonable or constitutional. I insist upon it, they are bound to obey both the crown and parliament. The last twelve years of our proceedings have been a scene of lenity and inactivity. Let us proceed and mend our method. . . .

Governor Pownal. . . . Things are now come to action; and I must be free to tell the house, that the Americans will resist these measures: they are prepared to do it. I do not mean by arms, but by the conversation of public town meetings; they now send their letters by couriers, instead of the post, from one town to another; and I can say your post office will very soon be deprived of its revenue. With regard to the officers who command the militia of that country, they will have them of their own appointment, and not from government; but I will never more give an opinion concerning America in this house; those I have given have been disregarded.

Mr. Rigby. Upon my word, sir, what was just now said, is very worthy the consideration of this house; . . . it appears, *that America is preparing to arms; and that the deliberations of their town meetings tend chiefly to oppose the measures of this country by force.* He has told you, sir, that the Americans will appoint other officers than those sent by government to command their troops. He has told you that the post office is established on their account from town to town, in order to carry their traitorous correspondence from one to another. He has told you the post office revenue will soon be annihilated. If these things are true, sir, I find we have been the aggressors, by continually doing acts of lenity for these twelve years last past. . . . I think this country has a right to tax America; but I do not say that I would put any new tax on at this particular crisis; but when things are returned to a peaceable state, I would then begin to exercise it. And I am free to declare my opinion, that I think we have a right to tax Ireland, if there was a necessity so to do, in order to help the mother country. If Ireland was to rebel and resist our laws, I would tax it. The mother country has an undoubted right and controul over the whole of its colonies. Again, sir, a great deal has been said concerning requisition. Pray, in what manner is it to be obtained? Is the king to demand it, or are we, the legislative power of this country, to send a very *civil polite gentleman* over to treat with their assemblies? . . . Is he to tell the speaker that we have been extremely ill used by our neighbors the French; that they have attacked us in several quarters; that the finances of this country are in a bad state; and therefore we desire you will be *kind* enough to assist us, and give us some money? Is this to be the language of this country to that; and are we thus to go cap in hand? I am of opinion, that if the administration of this country had not been changed soon after passing the stamp-act, that tax would have been collected with as much ease as the land-tax is in Great Britain. . . .

Mr. C. Fox. I am glad to hear from the honorable gentleman who spoke last, that *now* is not the time to tax America; that the only time for that is, when all these disturbances are quelled, and they are returned to their duty; so, I find taxes are to be the reward of obedience; and the Americans, who are considered to have been in open rebellion, are to be rewarded by acquiescing to their measures. When will be the time when America ought to have heavy taxes laid upon it? The honorable gentleman (Mr. Rigby) tells you, that that time will be when the Americans are returned to peace and quietness. The hon. gentleman tells us also, that we have a right to tax Ireland; however I may agree with him in regard to the principle, it would not be policy to exercise it; I believe we have no more right to tax the one than the other. I believe America is wrong in resisting against this country, with regard to legislative authority. . . . But, sir, there has been a constant conduct practised in this country, consisting of violence and weakness; I wish those measures may not continue; nor can I think that the stamp-act would have been submitted to without resistance, if the administration had not been changed; the present bill before you . . . irritates the minds of the people, but does not correct the deficiencies of that government.

Sir Gilbert Elliot arose to answer Mr. C. Fox, which he did in a very masterly manner, by stating that there was not the least degree of absurdity in taxing your own subjects, over whom you have declared you had an absolute right; though that tax should, through necessity, be enacted at a time when peace and quietness were the reigning system of the times; you declare you have that right, where is the absurdity in the exercise of it?

Sir Richard Sutton read a copy of a letter, relative to the government of America, *from a governor in America,* to the board of trade, shewing that, at the most quiet times, the dispositions to oppose the laws of this country were strongly ingrafted in them, and that all their actions conveyed a spirit and wish for independence. If you ask an American who is his master? he will tell you he has none, nor any governor but Jesus Christ. I do believe it, and it is my firm opinion, that the opposition to the measures of the legislature of this country, is a determined prepossession of the idea of total independence.

3. The Coercive Acts, 1774

1. The Boston Port Act

Whereas dangerous commotions and insurrections have been fomented and raised in the town of Boston, in the province of Massachusetts Bay in New England, by divers ill-affected persons, to the subversion of his Majesty's government and to the utter destruction of the public peace and good order of the said town; in which commotions and insurrections certain valuable cargoes of teas, being the property of the East India Company and on board certain vessels lying within the bay or harbour of

"The Coercive Acts, 1774." In Danby Pickering, ed., *The Statutes at Large from the Magna Charta, to the end of the eleventh Parliament of Great Britain, anno 1761* (London: J. Bentham, 1762–1807), vol. 30, pp. 336–341, 381–390, 367–371, 410.

Boston, were seized and destroyed; and whereas, in the present condition of the said town and harbour the commerce of his Majesty's subjects cannot be safely carried on there, nor the customs payable to his Majesty duly collected; and it is therefore expedient that the officers of his Majesty's customs should be forthwith removed from the said town: . . . be it enacted . . . [that it is unlawful to load on any vessel goods for shipment to any other part of the province or to any other colony or country, and that it is unlawful to unload goods from any other part of the province or any other colony or country in the town of Boston and in the bay called the harbour of Boston. Penalty for violation is forfeiture of ship and goods] . . . until it shall be certified to his Majesty in Council by the governor or lieutenant-governor of the said province, that reasonable satisfaction hath been made to the officers of his Majesty's revenue, and others, who suffered by the riots and insurrections above mentioned, in the months of November and December, in the year one thousand seven hundred and seventy-three, and in the month of January, in the year one thousand seven hundred and seventy-four.

2. The Massachusetts Government Act

Whereas [the Massachusetts Bay Charter of 1692 provides that the twenty-eight members of the Governor's Council should be chosen by the Assembly each year, and that method] has been so far from contributing to the attainment of the good ends and purposes thereby intended, and to the promoting of the internal welfare, peace, and good government of the said province, or to the maintenance of the just subordination to, and conformity with, the laws of Great Britain that the manner of exercising the powers, authorities, and privileges aforesaid, by the persons so annually elected, hath for some time past been such as had the most manifest tendency to obstruct, and, in great measure, defeat, the execution of the laws; to weaken the attachment of his Majesty's well-disposed subjects . . . and to encourage the ill-disposed among them to proceed even to acts of direct resistance to, and defiance of, his Majesty's authority; and it hath accordingly happened that an open resistance to the execution of the laws hath actually taken place in the town of Boston and the neighbourhood thereof, within the said province; and whereas it is, under these circumstances, become absolutely necessary, in order to the preservation of the peace and good order of the said province, the protection of his Majesty's well-disposed subjects therein resident, the continuance of the mutual benefits arising from the commerce and correspondence between this kingdom and the said province, and the maintaining of the just dependence of the said province upon the Crown and Parliament of Great Britain that the said method of annually electing the councillors or assistants of the said province should no longer be suffered to continue but that the appointment of the said councillors or assistants should henceforth be put upon the like footing as is established in such other of his Majesty's colonies or plantations in America. . . . Be it therefore enacted . . . that . . . the council or court of assistants of the said province for the time being, shall be composed of such of the inhabitants or proprietors of lands within the same as shall be thereunto nominated and appointed by his Majesty, . . . agreeable to the practice now used in respect to the appointment of councillors in such of his Majesty's other colonies in America. . . .

II. And it is hereby further enacted, that the said assistants or councillors, so to be appointed as aforesaid, shall hold their offices respectively, for and during the pleasure of his Majesty. . . .

III. And be it further enacted, . . . that . . . it shall and may be lawful for his Majesty's governor . . . to nominate and appoint, under the seal of the province, from time to time, and also to remove, without the consent of the council, all judges of the inferior courts of common pleas, commissioners of oyer and terminer, the attorney general, provosts, marshals, justices of the peace, and other officers to the council or courts of justice belonging. . . .

V. And be it further enacted . . . that . . . it shall and may be lawful for his Majesty's governor . . . to nominate and appoint the sheriffs without the consent of the council, and to remove such sheriffs with such consent, and not otherwise.

VI. And be it further enacted . . . that upon every vacancy of the offices of chief justice and judges of the Superior Court . . . the governor . . . shall have full power and authority to nominate and appoint the persons to succeed to the said offices, who shall hold their commissions during the pleasure of his Majesty. . . .

VII. And whereas, . . . [town meetings have been called at the discretion of local officials] and whereas a great abuse has been made of the power of calling such meetings, and the inhabitants have, contrary to the design of their institution, been misled to treat upon matters of the most general concern, and to pass many dangerous and unwarrantable resolves; for remedy whereof, be it enacted, that from and after the said first day of August, one thousand seven hundred and seventy-four, no meeting shall be called by the selectmen, or at the request of any number of freeholders of any township, district, or precinct, without the leave of the governor . . . in writing, expressing the special business of the said meeting, first had and obtained, except the annual meeting in the months of March or May, for the choice of selectmen, constables, and other officers, . . . and that no other matter shall be treated of at such meetings, except the election of their aforesaid officers or representatives, nor at any other meeting, except the business expressed in the leave given by the governor. . . .

VIII. And whereas the method at present used in the province of Massachusetts Bay in America, of electing persons to serve on grand juries, and other juries, by the freeholders and inhabitants of the several towns, affords occasion for many evil practices, and tends to pervert the free and impartial administration of justice; for remedy whereof, be it further enacted . . . that . . . jurors . . . shall not be elected, nominated, or appointed, by the freeholders and inhabitants of the several towns within the said respective counties, nor summoned or returned by the constables of the said towns; but that, from thenceforth, the jurors . . . shall be summoned and returned by the sheriffs of the respective counties within the said province. . . .

3. The Administration of Justice Act

Whereas in his Majesty's province of Massachusetts Bay, in New England, an attempt has lately been made to throw off the authority of the Parliament of Great Britain over the said province, and an actual and avowed resistance by open force, to the execution of certain Acts of Parliament, has been suffered to take place, uncontrolled and unpunished, in defiance of his Majesty's authority, and to the utter subversion of all lawful government; and whereas, in the present disordered state of the said province it is of the utmost importance to the general welfare thereof, and to the re-establishment of lawful authority throughout the same, that neither the magistrates acting in support of the laws, nor any of his Majesty's subjects aiding and assisting them therein, or in the suppression of riots and tumults raised in opposition to the execution of the laws and statutes of this realm, should be discouraged from the proper discharge of their duty by an apprehension that in case of their being questioned for any acts done therein, they may be liable to be brought to trial for the same before persons who do not acknowledge the validity of the laws, in the execution thereof, or the authority of the magistrate in the support of whom such acts had been done: in order therefore to remove every such discouragement from the minds of his Majesty's subjects, and to induce them, upon all proper occasions, to exert themselves in support of the public peace of the province, and of the authority of the king and Parliament of Great Britain over the same, be it enacted . . . that if any inquisition or indictment shall be found, or if any appeal shall be sued or preferred against any person for murder, or other capital offence, in the province of Massachusetts Bay, and it shall appear by information given upon oath to the governor, . . . that the fact was committed by the person . . . either in the execution of his duty as a magistrate for the suppression of riots, or in the support of the laws of revenue, or in acting in his duty as an officer of revenue, or in acting under the direction and order of any magistrate for the suppression of riots, or for the carrying into effect the laws of revenue, or in aiding and assisting in any of the cases aforesaid; and if it shall also appear to the satisfaction of the said governor . . . that an indifferent trial cannot be had within the said province; in that case it shall and may be lawful for the governor . . . to direct, with the advice and consent of the council, that the inquisition, indictment, or appeal shall be tried in some other of his Majesty's colonies, or in Great Britain. . . .

4. The Quartering Act

Whereas doubts have been entertained, whether troops can be quartered otherwise than in barracks . . . within his Majesty's dominions in North America; and whereas it may frequently happen, from the situation of such barracks that, if troops should be quartered therein they would not be stationed where their presence may be necessary and required: be it therefore enacted . . . that, in such cases it shall and may be lawful . . . to cause any officers or soldiers in his Majesty's service to be quartered and billeted in such manner as is now directed by law, where no barracks are provided by the colonies.

II. And be it further enacted . . . that . . . it shall and may be lawful for the governor of the province to order and direct such and so many uninhabited houses, outhouses, barns, or other buildings, as he shall think necessary to be taken (making a reasonable allowance for the same) and make fit for the reception of such officers and soldiers, and to put and quarter such officers and soldiers therein for such time as he shall think proper. . . .

4. Thomas Jefferson Asserts American Rights, 1774

Resolved, that . . . when assembled in general congress with the deputies from the other states of British America, . . . an humble and dutiful address be presented to his majesty, begging leave to lay before him, as chief magistrate of the British empire, the united complaints of his majesty's subjects in America; complaints which

"Thomas Jefferson Asserts American Rights, 1774." In Thomas Jefferson, *A Summary View of the Rights of British America* (Williamsburg, 1774), 257–276.

are excited by many unwarrantable encroachments and usurpations, attempted to be made by the legislature of one part of the empire, upon those rights which God and the laws have given equally and independently to all. To represent to his majesty that these his states have often individually made humble application to his imperial throne to obtain, through its intervention, some redress of their injured rights, to none of which was ever even an answer condescended; humbly to hope that this their joint address, penned in the language of truth, and divested of those expressions of servility which would persuade his majesty that we are asking favours, and not rights, shall obtain from his majesty a more respectful acceptance. And this his majesty will think we have reason to expect when he reflects that he is no more than the chief officer of the people, appointed by the laws, and circumscribed with definite powers, to assist in working the great machine of government, erected for their use, and consequently subject to their superintendence. And in order that these our rights, as well as the invasions of them, may be laid more fully before his majesty, to take a view of them from the origin and first settlement of these countries.

To remind him that our ancestors, before their emigration to America, were the free inhabitants of the British dominions in Europe, and possessed a right which nature has given to all men, of departing from the country in which chance, not choice, has placed them, of going in quest of new habitations, and of there establishing new societies, under such laws and regulations as to them shall seem most likely to promote public happiness. That their Saxon ancestors had, under this universal law, in like manner left their native wilds and woods in the north of Europe, had possessed themselves of the island of Britain, then less charged with inhabitants, and had established there that system of laws which has so long been the glory and protection of that country. Nor was ever any claim of superiority or dependence asserted over them by that mother country from which they had migrated; and were such a claim made, it is believed that his majesty's subjects in Great Britain have too firm a feeling of the rights derived to them from their ancestors, to bow down the sovereignty of their state before such visionary pretensions. And it is thought that no circumstance has occurred to distinguish materially the British from the Saxon emigration. America was conquered, and her settlements made, and firmly established, at the expence of individuals, and not of the British public. Their own blood was spilt in acquiring lands for their settlement, their own fortunes expended in making that settlement effectual; for themselves they fought, for themselves they conquered, and for themselves alone they have right to hold. Not a shilling was ever issued from the public treasures of his majesty, or his ancestors, for their assistance, till of very late times, after the colonies had become established on a firm and permanent footing. That then, indeed, having become valuable to Great Britain for her commercial purposes, his parliament was pleased to lend them assistance against an enemy, who would fain have drawn to herself the benefits of their commerce, to the great aggrandizement of herself, and danger of Great Britain. Such assistance, and in such circumstances, they had often before given to Portugal, and other allied states, with whom they carry on a commercial intercourse; yet these states never supposed, that by calling in her aid, they thereby submitted themselves to her sovereignty. . . .

That the exercise of a free trade with all parts of the world, possessed by the American colonists, as of natural right, and which no law of their own had taken away or abridged, was next the object of unjust encroachment. . . . The trade of the colonies was laid under such restrictions, as shew what hopes they might form from the justice of a British parliament, were its uncontrouled power admitted over the states. History has informed us that bodies of men, as well as individuals, are susceptible of the spirit of tyranny. A view of these acts of parliament for regulation, as it has been affectedly called, of the American trade, if all other evidence were removed out of the case, would undeniably evince the truth of this observation. . . . That these acts prohibit us from carrying in quest of other purchasers the surplus of our tobaccoes remaining after the consumption of Great Britain is supplied; so that we must leave them with the British merchant for whatever he will please to allow us, to be by him reshipped to foreign markets, where he will reap the benefits of making sale of them for full value. That to heighten still the idea of parliamentary justice, and to shew with what moderation they are like to exercise power, where themselves are to feel no part of its weight, we take leave to mention to his majesty certain other acts of British parliament, by which they would prohibit us from manufacturing for our own use the articles we raise on our own lands with our own labour. By an act passed in the 5th Year of the reign of his late majesty king George the second, an American subject is forbidden to make a hat for himself of the fur which he has taken perhaps on his own soil; an instance of despotism to which no parallel can be produced in the most arbitrary ages of British history. . . . The true ground on which we declare these acts void is, that the British parliament has no right to exercise authority over us. . . .

That thus have we hastened through the reigns which preceded his majesty's, during which the violations of our right were less alarming, because repeated at more distant intervals than that rapid and bold succession of injuries which is likely to distinguish the present from all other periods of American story. Scarcely have our minds been able to emerge from the astonishment into which one stroke of parliamentary thunder has involved us, before another more heavy, and more alarming, is fallen on us. Single acts of tyranny may be ascribed to the accidental opinion of a day; but a series of oppressions, begun at a distinguished period, and pursued unalterably through every change of ministers, too plainly prove a deliberate and systematical plan of reducing us to slavery.

That the act passed in the 4th year of his majesty's reign, intitled "An act for granting certain duties in the British colonies and plantations in America, &c."

One other act, passed in the 5th year of his reign, intitled "An act for granting and applying certain stamp duties and other duties in the British colonies and plantations in America, &c."

One other act, passed in the 6th year of his reign, intitled "An act for the better securing the dependency of his majesty's dominions in America upon the crown and parliament of Great Britain;" and one other act, passed in the 7th year of his reign, intitled "An act for granting duties on paper, tea, &c." form that connected chain of parliamentary usurpation, which has already been the subject of frequent applications to his majesty, and the houses of lords and commons of Great Britain; and no answers having yet been condescended to any of these, we shall not trouble his majesty with a repetition of the matters they contained.

But that one other act, passed in the same 7th year of the reign, having been a peculiar attempt, must ever require peculiar mention; it is intitled "An act for suspending the legislature of New York." One free and independent legislature hereby takes upon itself to suspend the powers of another, free and independent as itself;

thus exhibiting a phœnomenon unknown in nature, the creator and creature of its own power. Not only the principles of common sense, but the common feelings of human nature, must be surrendered up before his majesty's subjects here can be persuaded to believe that they hold their political existence at the will of a British parliament. Shall these governments be dissolved, their property annihilated, and their people reduced to a state of nature, at the imperious breath of a body of men, whom they never saw, in whom they never confided, and over whom they have no powers of punishment or removal, let their crimes against the American public be ever so great? Can any one reason be assigned why 160,000 electors in the island of Great Britain should give law to four millions in the states of America, every in-dividual of whom is equal to every individual of them, in virtue, in understanding, and in bodily strength? Were this to be admitted, instead of being a free people, as we have hitherto supposed, and mean to continue ourselves, we should suddenly be found the slaves, not of one, but of 160,000 tyrants, distinguished too from all others by this singular circumstance, that they are removed from the reach of fear, the only restraining motive which may hold the hand of a tyrant.

That by "an act to discontinue in such manner and for such time as are therein mentioned the landing and discharging, lading or shipping, of goods, wares, and merchandize, at the town and within the harbour of Boston, in the province of Massachusetts Bay, in North America," which was passed at the last session of British parliament; a large and populous town, whose trade was their sole subsis-tence, was deprived of that trade, and involved in utter ruin. Let us for a while sup-pose the question of right suspended, in order to examine this act on principles of justice: An act of parliament had been passed imposing duties on teas, to be paid in America, against which act the Americans had protested as inauthoritative. The East India company, who till that time had never sent a pound of tea to America on their own account, step forth on that occasion the assertors of parliamentary right, and send hither many ship loads of that obnoxious commodity. The masters of their several vessels, however, on their arrival in America, wisely attended to admoni-tion, and returned with their cargoes. In the province of New England alone the re-monstrances of the people were disregarded, and a compliance, after being many days waited for, was flatly refused. Whether in this the master of the vessel was governed by his obstinacy, or his instructions, let those who know, say. There are extraordinary situations which require extraordinary interposition. An exasperated people, who feel that they possess power, are not easily restrained within limits strictly regular. A number of them assembled in the town of Boston, threw the tea into the ocean, and dispersed without doing any other act of violence. If in this they did wrong, they were known and were amenable to the laws of the land, against which it could not be objected that they had ever, in any instance, been obstructed or diverted from their regular course in favour of popular offenders. They should therefore not have been distrusted on this occasion. But that ill fated colony had formerly been bold in their enmities against the house of Stuart, and were now de-voted to ruin by that unseen hand which governs the momentous affairs of this great empire. On the partial representations of a few worthless ministerial depen-dents, whose constant office it has been to keep that government embroiled, and who, by their treacheries, hope to obtain the dignity of the British knighthood, without calling for a party accused, without asking a proof, without attempting a distinction between the guilty and the innocent, the whole of that antient and wealthy town is in a moment reduced from opulence to beggary. Men who had spent their lives in extending the British commerce, who had invested in that place the wealth their honest endeavours had merited, found themselves and their families thrown at once on the world for subsistence by its charities. Not the hundredth part of the inhabitants of that town had been concerned in the act complained of; many of them were in Great Britain and in other parts beyond sea; yet all were involved in one indiscriminate ruin, by a new executive power, unheard of till then, that of a British parliament. A property, of the value of many millions of money, was sacrificed to revenge, not repay, the loss of a few thousands. This is administering justice with a heavy hand indeed! and when is this tempest to be arrested in its course? . . .

By the act for the suppression of riots and tumults in the town of Boston, passed also in the last session of parliament, a murder committed there is, if the governor pleases, to be tried . . . in the island of Great Britain. . . . And the wretched criminal, if he happen to have offended on the American side, stripped of his privilege of trial by peers of his vicinage, removed from the place where alone full evidence could be obtained, without money, without counsel, without friends, without exculpatory proof, is tried before judges predetermined to condemn. The cowards who would suffer a countryman to be torn from the bowels of their society, in order to be thus offered a sacrifice to parliamentary tyranny, would merit that everlasting infamy now fixed on the authors of the act! . . .

That these are the acts of power, assumed by a body of men, foreign to our constitutions, and unacknowledged by our laws, against which we do, on behalf of the inhabitants of British America, enter this our solemn and determined protest; and we do earnestly entreat his majesty, as yet the only mediatory power between the several states of the British empire, to recommend to his parliament of Great Britain the total revocation of these acts, which, however nugatory they be, may yet prove the cause of further discontents and jealousies among us.

That we next proceed to consider the conduct of his majesty, as holding the executive powers of the laws of these states, and mark out his deviations from the line of duty: By the constitution of Great Britain, as well as of the several American states, his majesty possesses the power of refusing to pass into a law any bill which has already passed the other two branches of legislature. His majesty, however, and his ancestors, conscious of the impropriety of opposing their single opinion to the united wisdom of two houses of parliament, while their proceedings were unbiassed by interested principles, for several ages past have modestly declined the exercise of this power in that part of his empire called Great Britain. But by change of circumstances, other principles than those of justice simply have obtained an influence on their determinations; the addition of new states to the British empire has produced an addition of new, and sometimes opposite interests. It is now, therefore, the great office of his majesty, to resume the exercise of his negative power, and to prevent the passage of laws by any one legislature of the empire, which might bear injuriously on the rights and interests of another. Yet this will not excuse the wanton exercise of this power which we have seen his majesty practise on the laws of the American legislatures. For the most trifling reasons, and sometimes for no conceivable reason at all, his majesty has rejected laws of the most salutary tendency.

The abolition of domestic slavery is the great object of desire in those colonies, where it was unhappily introduced in their infant state. But previous to the enfranchisement of the slaves we have, it is necessary to exclude all further importations from Africa; yet our repeated attempts to effect this by prohibitions, and by imposing duties which might amount to a prohibition, have been hitherto defeated by his majesty's negative: Thus preferring the immediate advantages of a few African corsairs to the lasting interests of the American states, and to the rights of human nature, deeply wounded by this infamous practice. Nay, the single interposition of an interested individual against a law was scarcely ever known to fail of success, though in the opposite scale were placed the interests of a whole country. That this is so shameful an abuse of a power trusted with his majesty for other purposes, as if not reformed, would call for some legal restrictions.

With equal inattention to the necessities of his people here has his majesty permitted our laws to lie neglected in England for years, neither confirming them by his assent, nor annulling them by his negative; so that such of them as have no suspending clause we hold on the most precarious of all tenures, his majesty's will. . . .

That in order to enforce the arbitrary measures before complained of, his majesty has from time to time sent among us large bodies of armed forces, not made up of the people here, nor raised by the authority of our laws: Did his majesty possess such a right as this, it might swallow up all our other rights whenever he should think proper. But his majesty has no right to land a single armed man on our shores, and those whom he sends here are liable to our laws made for the suppression and punishment of riots, routs, and unlawful assemblies; or are hostile bodies, invading us in defiance of law. . . .

To render these proceedings still more criminal against our laws, instead of subjecting the military to the civil powers, his majesty has expressly made the civil subordinate to the military. But can his majesty thus put down all law under his feet? Can he erect a power superior to that which erected himself? He has done it indeed by force; but let him remember that force cannot give right.

That these are our grievances which we have thus laid before his majesty, with that freedom of language and sentiment which becomes a free people claiming their rights, as derived from the laws of nature, and not as the gift of their chief magistrate: Let those flatter who fear; it is not an American art. . . . Kings are the servants, not the proprietors of the people. Open your breast, sire, to liberal and expanded thought. Let not the name of George the third be a blot in the page of history. You are surrounded by British counsellors, but remember that they are parties. You have no ministers for American affairs, because you have none taken from among us, nor amenable to the laws on which they are to give you advice. It behoves you, therefore, to think and to act for yourself and your people. The great principles of right and wrong are legible to every reader; to pursue them requires not the aid of many counsellors. The whole art of government consists in the art of being honest. Only aim to do your duty, and mankind will give you credit where you fail. No longer persevere in sacrificing the rights of one part of the empire to the inordinate desires of another; but deal out to all equal and impartial right. Let no act be passed by any one legislature which may infringe on the rights and liberties of another. This is the important post in which fortune has placed you, holding the balance of a great, if a well poised empire. . . .

5. Declaration and Resolves of the First Continental Congress, 1774

Whereas, since the close of the last war, the British parliament, claiming a power of right to bind the people of America by statute in all cases whatsoever, hath, in some acts expressly imposed taxes on them, and in others, under various pretences, but in fact for the purpose of raising a revenue, hath imposed rates and duties payable in these colonies, established a board of commissioners with unconstitutional powers, and extended the jurisdiction of courts of Admiralty not only for collecting the said duties, but for the trial of causes merely arising within the body of a county.

And whereas, in consequence of other statutes, judges . . . have been made dependent on the Crown alone for their salaries, and standing armies kept in times of peace. And it has lately been resolved in Parliament, that . . . colonists may be transported to England, and tried there upon accusations for treasons . . . committed in the colonies. . . .

And whereas, in the last session of Parliament, three statutes were made . . . [the Boston Port Act, the Massachusetts Government Act, the Administration of Justice Act], and another statute was then made [the Quebec Act] . . . All which statutes are impolitic, unjust, and cruel, as well as unconstitutional, and most dangerous and destructive of American rights.

And whereas, Assemblies have been frequently dissolved, contrary to the rights of the people, when they attempted to deliberate on grievances; and their dutiful, humble, loyal, & reasonable petitions to the crown for redress, have been repeatedly treated with contempt, by His Majesty's ministers of state:

The good people of the several Colonies of New-hampshire, Massachusetts-bay, Rhode-island and Providence plantations, Connecticut, New-York, New-Jersey, Pennsylvania, Newcastle Kent and Sussex on Delaware, Maryland, Virginia, North-Carolina, and South-Carolina, justly alarmed at these arbitrary proceedings of parliament and administration, have severally elected constituted, and appointed deputies to meet, and sit in general Congress, in the city of Philadelphia, . . . that their religion, laws, and liberties, may not be subverted:

Whereupon the deputies so appointed being now assembled, in a full and free representation of these Colonies, taking into their most serious consideration the best means of attaining the ends aforesaid, do in the first place, as Englishmen their ancestors in like cases have usually done, for asserting and vindicating their rights and liberties, declare,

That the inhabitants of the English Colonies in North America, by the immutable laws of nature, the principles of the English constitution, and the several charters or compacts, have the following Rights:

1. That they are entitled to life, liberty, and property, & they have never ceded to any sovereign power whatever, a right to dispose of either without their consent.

"Declaration and Resolves of the First Continental Congress, 1774." As found in *Journals of the Continental Congress, 1774–1789*, ed. W. C. Ford (Washington, DC, 1904–1937), vol. 1, pp. 63–74.

2. That our ancestors, who first settled these colonies, were at the time of their emigration from the mother country, entitled to all the rights, liberties, and immunities of free and natural-born subjects within the realm of England.

3. That by such emigration they by no means forfeited, surrendered, or lost any of those rights, but that they were, and their descendants now are entitled to the exercise and enjoyment of all such of them, as their local and other circumstances enable them to exercise and enjoy.

4. That the foundation of English liberty, and of all free government, is a right in the people to participate in their legislative council: and as the English colonists are not represented, and from their local and other circumstances, cannot properly be represented in the British parliament, they are entitled to a free and exclusive power of legislation in their several provincial legislatures, where their right of representation can alone be preserved, in all cases of taxation and internal polity, subject only to the negative of their sovereign, in such manner as has been heretofore used and accustomed. But, from the necessity of the case, and a regard to the mutual interest of both countries, we cheerfully consent to the operation of such acts of the British parliament, as are bona fide restrained to the regulation of our external commerce, for the purpose of securing the commercial advantages of the whole empire to the mother country, and the commercial benefits of its respective members excluding every idea of taxation, internal or external, for raising a revenue on the subjects in America without their consent.

5. That the respective colonies are entitled to the common law of England, and more especially to the great and inestimable privilege of being tried by their peers of the vicinage, according to the course of that law.

6. That they are entitled to the benefit of such of the English statutes, as existed at the time of their colonization; and which they have, by experience, respectively found to be applicable to their several local and other circumstances.

7. That these, his majesty's colonies, are likewise entitled to all the immunities and privileges granted and confirmed to them by royal charters, or secured by their several codes of provincial laws.

8. That they have a right peaceably to assemble, consider of their grievances, and petition the King; and that all prosecutions, prohibitory proclamations, and commitments for the same, are illegal.

9. That the keeping a Standing army in these colonies, in times of peace, without the consent of the legislature of that colony in which such army is kept, is against law.

10. It is indispensably necessary to good government, and rendered essential by the English constitution, that the constituent branches of the legislature be independent of each other; that, therefore, the exercise of legislative power in several colonies, by a council appointed during pleasure, by the crown, is unconstitutional, dangerous, and destructive to the freedom of American legislation.

All and each of which the aforesaid deputies, in behalf of themselves, and their constituents, do claim, demand, and insist on, as their indubitable rights and liberties; which cannot be legally taken from them, altered or abridged by any power whatever, without their own consent, by their representatives in their several provincial legislatures.

In the course of our inquiry, we find many infringements and violations of the foregoing rights, . . . and proceed to state such acts and measures as have been adopted since the last war, which demonstrate a system formed to enslave America.

Resolved, That the following acts of Parliament are infringements and violations of the rights of the colonists; and that the repeal of them is essentially necessary, in order to restore harmony between Great Britain and the American colonies, . . . viz.:

The several Acts . . . which impose duties for the purpose of raising a revenue in America, extend the powers of the admiralty courts beyond their ancient limits, deprive the American subject of trial by jury, . . .

Also . . . "An act for the better preserving his Majesty's dockyards, . . . which declares a new offense in America, and deprives the American subject of a constitutional trial by jury of the vicinage, by authorizing the trial of any person charged . . . in any shire or county within the realm.

Also the three acts passed in the last session of parliament, for stopping the port and blocking up the harbour of Boston, for altering the charter & government of the Massachusetts-bay, and that which is entitled "An Act for the better administration of Justice," &c.

Also the act . . . for establishing the Roman Catholick Religion in the province of Quebec, abolishing the equitable system of English laws, and erecting a tyranny there, to the great danger, from so great a dissimilarity of Religion, law, and government, of the neighbouring British colonies. . . .

Also the act . . . for the better providing suitable quarters for officers and soldiers in his Majesty's service in North America.

Also, that the keeping a standing army in several of these colonies, in time of peace, without the consent of the legislature of that colony in which the army is kept, is against law.

To these grievous acts and measures Americans cannot submit, but in hopes that their fellow subjects in Great-Britain will, on a revision of them, restore us to that state in which both countries found happiness and prosperity, we have for the present only resolved to pursue the following peaceable measures: 1st. To enter into a non-important, non-consumption, and non-exportation agreement or association. 2. To prepare an address to the people of Great-Britain, and a memorial to the inhabitants of British America, & 3. To prepare a loyal address to his Majesty, agreeable to resolutions already entered into.

6. King George Proclaims America in Rebellion, 1775

Whereas many of our subjects in divers parts of our Colonies and Plantations in *North America,* misled by dangerous and ill designing men, and forgetting the allegiance which they owe to the power that has protected and supported them; after various disorderly acts committed in disturbance of the publick peace, to the obstruction of lawful commerce, and to the oppression of our loyal subjects carrying

---

"King George Proclaims America in Rebellion, 1775." In *American Archives,* ed. Peter Force (Washington, DC: M. St. Clair and Peter Force, 1837–1853), Fourth Series, vol. 3, p. 240.

on the same; have at length proceeded to open and avowed rebellion, by arraying themselves in a hostile manner, to withstand the execution of the law, and traitorously preparing, ordering and levying war against us: And whereas, there is reason to apprehend that such rebellion hath been much promoted and encouraged by the traitorous correspondence, counsels and comfort of divers wicked and desperate persons within this realm: To the end therefore, that none of our subjects may neglect or violate their duty through ignorance thereof, . . . we do accordingly strictly charge and command all our Officers, as well civil as military, and all others our obedient and loyal subjects, to use their utmost endeavours to withstand and suppress such rebellion, and to disclose and make known all treasons and traitorous conspiracies which they shall know to be against us, our crown and dignity; . . . in order to bring to condign punishment the authors, perpetrators, and abetters of such traitorous designs.

Given at our Court at *St. James's* the twenty-third day of *August,* one thousand seven hundred and seventy-five, in the fifteenth year of our reign.

GOD *save the* KING.

7. Thomas Paine Calls for Common Sense, 1776

Introduction

Perhaps the sentiments contained in the following pages, are not *yet* sufficiently fashionable to procure them general favor; a long habit of not thinking a thing *wrong,* gives it a superficial appearance of being *right,* and raises at first a formidable outcry in defence of custom. But the tumult soon subsides. Time makes more converts than reason. . . .

The cause of America is in a great measure the cause of all mankind. Many circumstances hath, and will arise, which are not local, but universal, and through which the principles of all Lovers of Mankind are affected, and in the Event of which, their Affections are interested. The laying a Country desolate with Fire and Sword, declaring War against the natural rights of all Mankind, and extirpating the Defenders thereof from the Face of the Earth, is the Concern of every Man to whom Nature hath given the Power of feeling; of which Class, regardless of Party Censure, is the

AUTHOR.

**Of the Origin and Design of Government in General.
With Concise Remarks on the English Constitution**

Some writers have so confounded society with government, as to leave little or no distinction between them; whereas they are not only different, but have different origins. Society is produced by our wants, and government by our wickedness; the former promotes our happiness *positively* by uniting our affections, the latter

From Thomas Paine, *Common Sense* (Philadelphia, 1776), 11–52.

negatively by restraining our vices. The one encourages intercourse, the other creates distinctions. The first is a patron, the last a punisher.

Society in every state is a blessing, but government even in its best state is but a necessary evil; in its worst state an intolerable one; for when we suffer, or are exposed to the same miseries *by a government,* which we might expect in a country *without government,* our calamity is heightened by reflecting that we furnish the means by which we suffer. Government, like dress, is the badge of lost innocence; the palaces of kings are built on the ruins of the bowers of paradise. For were the impulses of conscience clear, uniform, and irresistibly obeyed, man would need no other lawgiver; but that not being the case, he finds it necessary to surrender up a part of his property to furnish means for the protection of the rest; and this he is induced to do by the same prudence which in every other case advises him out of two evils to choose the least. *Wherefore,* security being the true design and end of government, it unanswerably follows, that whatever *form* thereof appears most likely to ensure it to us, with the least expence and greatest benefit, is preferable to all others.

In order to gain a clear and just idea of the design and end of government, let us suppose a small number of persons settled in some sequestered part of the earth, unconnected with the rest, they will then represent the first peopling of any country, or of the world. In this state of natural liberty, society will be their first thought. A thousand motives will excite them thereto, the strength of one man is so unequal to his wants, and his mind so unfitted for perpetual solitude, that he is soon obliged to seek assistance and relief of another, who in his turn requires the same. Four or five united would be able to raise a tolerable dwelling in the midst of a wilderness, but *one* man might labour out the common period of life without accomplishing any thing; when he had felled his timber he could not remove it, nor erect it after it was removed; hunger in the mean time would urge him from his work, and every different want call him a different way. Disease, nay even misfortune would be death, for though neither might be mortal, yet either would disable him from living, and reduce him to a state in which he might rather be said to perish than to die.

Thus necessity, like a gravitating power, would soon form our newly arrived emigrants into society, the reciprocal blessings of which, would supersede, and render the obligations of law and government unnecessary while they remained perfectly just to each other; but as nothing but heaven is impregnable to vice, it will unavoidably happen, that in proportion as they surmount the first difficulties of emigration, which bound them together in a common cause, they will begin to relax in their duty and attachment to each other; and this remissness will point out the necessity of establishing some form of government to supply the defect of moral virtue.

Some convenient tree will afford them a State-House, under the branches of which, the whole colony may assemble to deliberate on public matters. It is more than probable that their first laws will have the title only of REGULATIONS, and be enforced by no other penalty than public disesteem. In this first parliament every man, by natural right, will have a seat.

But as the colony increases, the public concerns will increase likewise, and the distance at which the members may be separated, will render it too inconvenient for all of them to meet on every occasion as at first, when their number was small, their habitations near, and the public concerns few and trifling. This will point out the convenience of their consenting to leave the legislative part to be managed by a select number chosen from the whole body, who are supposed to have the same concerns at stake which those have who appointed them, and who will act in the same manner as the whole body would act, were they present. If the colony continue increasing, it will become necessary to augment the number of the representatives, and that the interest of every part of the colony may be attended to, it will be found best to divide the whole into convenient parts, each part sending its proper number; and that the *elected* might never form to themselves an interest separate from the *electors,* prudence will point out the propriety of having elections often; because as the *elected* might by that means return and mix again with the general body of the *electors* in a few months, their fidelity to the public will be secured by the prudent reflexion of not making a rod for themselves. And as this frequent interchange will establish a common interest with every part of the community, they will mutually and naturally support each other, and on this (not on the unmeaning name of king) depends the *strength of government, and the happiness of the governed.*

Here then is the origin and rise of government; namely, a mode rendered necessary by the inability of moral virtue to govern the world; here too is the design and end of government, viz. freedom and security. And however our eyes may be dazzled with show, or our ears deceived by sound; however prejudice may warp our wills, or interest darken our understanding, the simple voice of nature and of reason will say, it is right.

I draw my idea of the form of government from a principle in nature, which no art can overturn, viz. that the more simple any thing is, the less liable it is to be disordered, and the easier repaired when disordered; and with this maxim in view, I offer a few remarks on the so much boasted constitution of England. That it was noble for the dark and slavish times in which it was erected, is granted. When the world was overrun with tyranny the least remove therefrom was a glorious rescue. But that it is imperfect, subject to convulsions, and incapable of producing what it seems to promise, is easily demonstrated.

Absolute governments (tho' the disgrace of human nature) have this advantage with them, that they are simple; if the people suffer, they know the head from which their suffering springs, know likewise the remedy, and are not bewildered by a variety of causes and cures. But the constitution of England is so exceedingly complex, that the nation may suffer for years together without being able to discover in which part the fault lies; some will say in one and some in another, and every political physician will advise a different medicine.

I know it is difficult to get over local or long standing prejudices, yet if we will suffer ourselves to examine the component parts of the English constitution, we shall find them to be the base remains of two ancient tyrannies, compounded with some new republican materials.

First.—The remains of monarchical tyranny in the person of the king.

Secondly.—The remains of aristocratical tyranny in the persons of the peers.

Thirdly.—The new republican materials in the persons of the commons, on whose virtue depends the freedom of England. . . .

That the crown is this overbearing part in the English constitution, needs not be mentioned, and that it derives its whole consequence merely from being the giver of places and pensions, is self-evident, wherefore, though we have been wise enough to shut and lock a door against absolute monarchy, we at the same time have been foolish enough to put the crown in possession of the key.

The prejudice of Englishmen in favour of their own government by king, lords and commons, arises as much or more from national pride than reason. Individuals are undoubtedly safer in England than in some other countries, but the *will* of the king is as much the *law* of the land in Britain as in France, with this difference, that instead of proceeding directly from his mouth, it is handed to the people under the more formidable shape of an act of parliament. For the fate of Charles the First hath only made kings more subtle—not more just.

Wherefore, laying aside all national pride and prejudice in favour of modes and forms, the plain truth is, that *it is wholly owing to the constitution of the people, and not to the constitution of the government,* that the crown is not as oppressive in England as in Turkey. . . .

Of Monarchy and Hereditary Succession

Mankind being originally equals in the order of creation, the equality could only be destroyed by some subsequent circumstance; the distinctions of rich, and poor, may in a great measure be accounted for, and that without having recourse to the harsh, ill-sounding names of oppression and avarice. Oppression is often the *consequence,* but seldom or never the *means* of riches; and though avarice will preserve a man from being necessitously poor, it generally makes him too timorous to be wealthy.

But there is another and greater distinction, for which no truly natural or religious reason can be assigned, and that is, the distinction of men into KINGS and SUBJECTS. Male and female are the distinctions of nature, good and bad the distinctions of heaven; but how a race of men came into the world so exalted above the rest, and distinguished like some new species, is worth inquiring into, and whether they are the means of happiness or of misery to mankind.

In the early ages of the world, according to the scripture chronology, there were no kings; the consequence of which was, there were no wars; it is the pride of kings which throw mankind into confusion. Holland without a king hath enjoyed more peace for this last century than any of the monarchical governments in Europe. Antiquity favours the same remark; for the quiet and rural lives of the first patriarchs hath a happy something in them, which vanishes away when we come to the history of Jewish royalty.

Government by kings was first introduced into the world by the Heathens, from whom the children of Israel copied the custom. It was the most prosperous invention the Devil ever set on foot for the promotion of idolatry. The Heathens paid divine honors to their deceased kings, and the Christian world hath improved on the plan, by doing the same to their living ones. How impious is the title of sacred majesty applied to a worm, who in the midst of his splendor is crumbling into dust!

As the exalting one man so greatly above the rest cannot be justified on the equal rights of nature, so neither can it be defended on the authority of scripture; for the will of the Almighty, as declared by Gideon and the prophet Samuel, expressly disapproves of government by kings. All antimonarchical parts of scripture have been very smoothly glossed over in monarchical governments, but they undoubtedly merit the attention of countries which have their governments yet to form. *"Render unto Caesar the things which are Caesar's"* is the scripture doctrine of courts, yet it is no support of monarchical government, for the Jews at that time were without a king, and in a state of vassalage to the Romans.

Near three thousand years passed away from the Mosaic account of the creation, till the Jews under a national delusion requested a king. Till then their form of government (except in extraordinary cases, where the Almighty interposed) was a kind of republic administered by a judge and the elders of the tribes. Kings they had none, and it was held sinful to acknowledge any being under that title but the Lord of Hosts. And when a man seriously reflects on the idolatrous homage which is paid to the persons of kings, he need not wonder that the Almighty, ever jealous of his honor, should disapprove of a form of government which so impiously invades the prerogative of heaven.

Monarchy is ranked in scripture as one of the sins of the Jews, for which a curse in reserve is denounced against them. The history of that transaction is worth attending to.

The children of Israel being oppressed by the Midianites, Gideon marched against them with a small army, and victory, thro' the divine interposition, decided in his favour. The Jews, elate with success, and attributing it to the generalship of Gideon, proposed making him a king, saying, *Rule thou over us, thou and thy son's son.* Here was temptation in its fullest extent; not a kingdom only, but an hereditary one, but Gideon in the piety of his soul replied, *I will not rule over you, neither shall my son rule over you*, THE LORD SHALL RULE OVER YOU. Words need not be more explicit; Gideon doth not decline the honor, but denieth their right to give it; neither doth he compliment them with invented declarations of his thanks, but in the positive stile of a prophet charges them with disaffection to their proper Sovereign, the King of heaven. . . .

That the almighty hath here entered his protest against monarchical government, is true, or the scripture is false. And a man hath good reason to believe that there is as much of king-craft, as priest-craft, in withholding the scripture from the public in Popish countries. For monarchy in every instance is the Popery of government.

To the evil of monarchy we have added that of hereditary succession; and as the first is a degradation and lessening of ourselves, so the second, claimed as a matter of right, is an insult and an imposition on posterity. For all men being originally equals, no *one* by *birth* could have a right to set up his own family in perpetual preference to all others for ever, and though himself might deserve *some* decent degree of honors of his contemporaries, yet his descendants might be far too unworthy to inherit them. One of the strongest *natural* proofs of the folly of hereditary right in kings, is, that nature disapproves it, otherwise she would not so frequently turn it into ridicule by giving mankind an *Ass for a Lion.*

Secondly, as no man at first could possess any other public honors than were bestowed upon him, so the givers of those honors could have no power to give away the right of posterity. And though they might say, "We choose you for *our* head," they could not, without manifest injustice to their children, say "that your children and your childrens children shall reign over *ours* for ever." Because such an unwise, unjust, unnatural compact might (perhaps) in the next succession put them under the government of a rogue or a fool. Most wise men, in their private sentiments, have ever treated hereditary right with contempt; yet it is one of those evils, which when once established is not easily removed; many submit from fear, others from superstition, and the more powerful part shares with the king the plunder of the rest.

This is supposing the present race of kings in the world to have had an honorable origin; whereas it is more than probable, that could we take off the dark covering of antiquity, and trace them to their first rise, that we should find the first of them nothing better than the principal ruffian of some restless gang, whose savage manners or pre-eminence in subtilty obtained him the title of chief among plunderers. . . .

England, since the conquest, hath known some few good monarchs, but groaned beneath a much larger number of bad ones; yet no man in his senses can say that their claim under William the Conqueror is a very honorable one. A French bastard landing with an armed banditti, and establishing himself king of England against the consent of the natives, is in plain terms a very paltry rascally original.—It certainly hath no divinity in it. However, it is needless to spend much time in exposing the folly of hereditary right; if there are any so weak as to believe it, let them promiscuously worship the ass and lion, and welcome. I shall neither copy their humility, nor disturb their devotion.

Yet I should be glad to ask how they suppose kings came at first? The question admits but of three answers, viz. either by lot, by election, or by usurpation. If the first king was taken by lot, it establishes a precedent for the next, which excludes hereditary succession. . . . If the first king of any country was by election, that likewise establishes a precedent for the next; for to say, that the *right* of all future generations is taken away, by the act of the first electors, in their choice not only of a king, but of a family of kings for ever, hath no parallel in or out of scripture but the doctrine of original sin, which supposes the free will of all men lost in Adam; and from such comparison, and it will admit of no other, hereditary succession can derive no glory. For as in Adam all sinned, and as in the first electors all men obeyed; as in the one all mankind were subjected to Satan, and in the other to Sovereignty; as our innocence was lost in the first, and our authority in the last; and as both disable us from reassuming some former state and privilege, it unanswerably follows that original sin and hereditary succession are parallels. Dishonorable rank! Inglorious connexion! Yet the most subtile sophist cannot produce a juster simile.

As to usurpation, no man will be so hardy as to defend it; and that William the Conqueror was an usurper is a fact not to be contradicted. The plain truth is, that the antiquity of English monarchy will not bear looking into.

But it is not so much the absurdity as the evil of hereditary succession which concerns mankind. Did it ensure a race of good and wise men it would have the seal of divine authority, but as it opens a door to the *foolish,* the *wicked,* and the *improper,* it hath in it the nature of oppression. Men who look upon themselves born to reign, and others to obey, soon grow insolent; selected from the rest of mankind their minds are early poisoned by importance; and the world they act in differs so materially from the world at large, that they have but little opportunity of knowing its true interests, and when they succeed to the government are frequently the most ignorant and unfit of any throughout the dominions.

Another evil which attends hereditary succession is, that the throne is subject to be possessed by a minor at any age; all which time the regency, acting under the cover of a king, have every opportunity and inducement to betray their trust. The same national misfortune happens, when a king, worn out with age and infirmity, enters the last stage of human weakness. In both these cases the public becomes a prey to every miscreant, who can tamper successfully with the follies either of age or infancy.

The most plausible plea, which hath ever been offered in favour of hereditary succession, is, that it preserves a nation from civil wars; and were this true, it would be weighty; whereas, it is the most barefaced falsity ever imposed upon mankind. The whole history of England disowns the fact. Thirty kings and two minors have reigned in that distracted kingdom since the conquest, in which time there have been (including the Revolution) no less than eight civil wars and nineteen rebellions. Wherefore instead of making for peace, it makes against it, and destroys the very foundation it seems to stand on. . . .

In short, monarchy and succession have laid (not this or that kingdom only) but the world in blood and ashes. 'Tis a form of government which the word of God bears testimony against, and blood will attend it. . . .

In England a king hath little more to do than to make war and give away places; which in plain terms, is to impoverish the nation and set it together by the ears. A pretty business indeed for a man to be allowed eight hundred thousand sterling a year for, and worshipped into the bargain! Of more worth is one honest man to society and in the sight of God, than all the crowned ruffians that ever lived.

Thoughts on the Present State of American Affairs

In the following pages I offer nothing more than simple facts, plain arguments, and common sense; and have no other preliminaries to settle with the reader, than that he will divest himself of prejudice and prepossession, and suffer his reason and his feelings to determine for themselves; that he will put *on,* or rather that he will not put *off* the true character of a man, and generously enlarge his views beyond the present day.

Volumes have been written on the subject of the struggle between England and America. Men of all ranks have embarked in the controversy, from different motives, and with various designs; but all have been ineffectual, and the period of debate is closed. Arms, as the last resource, decide the contest; the appeal was the choice of the king, and the continent hath accepted the challenge. . . .

The sun never shined on a cause of greater worth. 'Tis not the affair of a city, a county, a province, or a kingdom, but of a continent—of at least one eighth part of the habitable globe. 'Tis not the concern of a day, a year, or an age; posterity are virtually involved in the contest, and will be more or less affected, even to the end of time, by the proceedings now. Now is the seed-time of continental union, faith and honor. The least fracture now will be like a name engraved with the point of a pin on the tender rind of a young oak; the wound will enlarge with the tree, and posterity read it in full grown characters.

By referring the matter from argument to arms, a new æra for politics is struck; a new method of thinking hath arisen. All plans, proposals, &c. prior to the nineteenth of April, *i.e.,* to the commencement of hostilities, are like the almanacks of the last year; which, though proper then are superseded and useless now. Whatever was advanced by the advocates on either side of the question then, terminated in one and the same point, viz. a union with Great-Britain; the only difference between the parties was the method of effecting it; the one proposing force, the other friendship; but it hath so far happened that the first hath failed, and the second hath withdrawn her influence.

As much hath been said of the advantages of reconciliation, which, like an agreeable dream, hath passed away and left us as we were, it is but right, that we should examine the contrary side of the argument, and inquire into some of the many material injuries which these colonies sustain, and always will sustain, by being connected with, and dependent on Great-Britain: To examine that connexion and dependence, on the principles of nature and common sense, to see what we have to trust to, if separated, and what we are to expect, if dependent.

I have heard it asserted by some, that as America hath flourished under her former connexion with Great-Britain, that the same connexion is necessary towards her future happiness, and will always have the same effect. Nothing can be more fallacious than this kind of argument. We may as well assert that because a child has thrived upon milk, that it is never to have meat, or that the first twenty years of our lives is to become a precedent for the next twenty. But even this is admitting more than is true, for I answer roundly, that America would have flourished as much, and probably much more, had no European power had any thing to do with her. The commerce, by which she hath enriched herself, are the necessaries of life, and will always have a market while eating is the custom of Europe.

But she has protected us, say some. That she has engrossed us is true, and defended the continent at our expence as well as her own is admitted, and she would have defended Turkey from the same motive, viz. the sake of trade and dominion.

Alas, we have been long led away by ancient prejudices, and made large sacrifices to superstition. We have boasted the protection of Great-Britain, without considering, that her motive was *interest* not *attachment;* that she did not protect us from *our enemies* on *our account,* but from *her enemies* on *her own account,* from those who had no quarrel with us on any *other account,* and who will always be our enemies on the *same account.* Let Britain wave her pretensions to the continent, or the continent throw off the dependence, and we should be at peace with France and Spain were they at war with Britain. The miseries of Hanover last war ought to warn us against connexions. . . .

But Britain is the parent country, say some. Then the more shame upon her conduct. Even brutes do not devour their young, nor savages make war upon their families; wherefore the assertion, if true, turns to her reproach; but it happens not to be true, or only partly so, and the phrase *parent* or *mother country* hath been jesuitically adopted by the king and his parasites, with a low papistical design of gaining an unfair bias on the credulous weakness of our minds. Europe, and not England, is the parent country of America. This new world hath been the asylum for the persecuted lovers of civil and religious liberty from *every part* of Europe. Hither have they fled, not from the tender embraces of the mother, but from the cruelty of the monster; and it is so far true of England, that the same tyranny which drove the first emigrants from home, pursues their descendants still.

In this extensive quarter of the globe, we forget the narrow limits of three hundred and sixty miles (the extent of England) and carry our friendship on a larger scale; we claim brotherhood with every European Christian, and triumph in the generosity of the sentiment. . . .

Much hath been said of the united strength of Britain and the colonies, that in conjunction they might bid defiance to the world. But this is mere presumption; the fate of war is uncertain, neither do the expressions mean any thing; for this continent would never suffer itself to be drained of inhabitants, to support the British arms in either Asia, Africa, or Europe.

Besides what have we to do with setting the world at defiance? Our plan is commerce, and that, well attended to, will secure us the peace and friendship of all Europe; because, it is the interest of all Europe to have America a *free port*. Her trade will always be a protection, and her barrenness of gold and silver secure her from invaders.

I challenge the warmest advocate for reconciliation, to shew, a single advantage that this continent can reap, by being connected with Great Britain. I repeat the challenge, not a single advantage is derived. Our corn will fetch its price in any market in Europe, and our imported goods must be paid for buy them where we will.

But the injuries and disadvantages we sustain by that connection, are without number; and our duty to mankind at large, as well as to ourselves, instruct us to renounce the alliance: Because, any submission to, or dependence on Great-Britain, tends directly to involve this continent in European wars and quarrels; and sets us at variance with nations, who would otherwise seek our friendship, and against whom, we have neither anger nor complaint. As Europe is our market for trade, we ought to form no partial connection with any part of it. It is the true interest of America to steer clear of European contentions, which she never can do, while by her dependence on Britain, she is made the make-weight in the scale of British politics.

Europe is too thickly planted with kingdoms to be long at peace, and whenever a war breaks out between England and any foreign power, the trade of America goes to ruin, *because of her connection with Britain.* . . . Every thing that is right or natural pleads for separation. The blood of the slain, the weeping voice of nature cries, 'TIS TIME TO PART. Even the distance at which the Almighty hath placed England and America, is a strong and natural proof, that the authority of the one, over the other, was never the design of Heaven. The time likewise at which the continent was discovered, adds weight to the argument, and the manner in which it was peopled encreases the force of it. The reformation was preceded by the discovery of America, as if the Almighty graciously meant to open a sanctuary to the persecuted in future years, when home should afford neither friendship nor safety. . . .

It is the good fortune of many to live distant from the scene of sorrow; the evil is not sufficient brought to *their* doors to make *them* feel the precariousness with which all American property is possessed. But let our imaginations transport us for a few moments to Boston, that seat of wretchedness will teach us wisdom, and instruct us for ever to renounce a power in whom we can have no trust. . . .

Men of passive tempers look somewhat lightly over the offences of Britain, and, still hoping for the best, are apt to call out, *"Come, come, we shall be friends again, for all this."* But examine the passions and feelings of mankind, bring the doctrine of reconciliation to the touchstone of nature, and then tell me, whether you can hereafter love, honor, and faithfully serve the power that hath carried fire and sword into your land? If you cannot do all these, then are you only deceiving yourselves, and by your delay bringing ruin upon posterity. Your future connexion with Britain, whom you can neither love nor honor, will be forced and unnatural, and being formed only on the plan of present convenience, will in a little time fall into a relapse more wretched than the first. But if you say, you can still pass the violations over, then I ask, Hath your house been burnt? Hath your property been destroyed before your face? Are your wife and children destitute of a bed to lie on, or bread to live on? Have you lost a parent or a child by their hands, and yourself the ruined and wretched survivor? If you have not, then are you not a judge of those who have? But if you have, and still can shake hands with the murderers, then are you unworthy the name of husband, father, friend, or lover, and whatever may be your rank or title in life, you have the heart of a coward, and the spirit of a sycophant.

This is not inflaming or exaggerating matters, but trying them by those feelings and affections which nature justifies, and without which, we should be incapable of discharging the social duties of life, or enjoying the felicities of it. I mean not to exhibit horror for the purpose of provoking revenge, but to awaken us from fatal and unmanly slumbers, that we may pursue determinately some fixed object. It is not in the power of Britain or of Europe to conquer America, if she do not conquer herself by *delay* and *timidity*. The present winter is worth an age if rightly employed, but if lost or neglected, the whole continent will partake of the misfortune; and there is no punishment which that man will not deserve, be he who, or what, or where he will, that may be the means of sacrificing a season so precious and useful.

It is repugnant to reason, to the universal order of things, to all examples from former ages, to suppose, that this continent can longer remain subject to any external power. The most sanguine in Britain does not think so. The utmost stretch of human wisdom cannot, at this time, compass a plan short of separation, which can promise the continent even a year's security. Reconciliation is *now* a fallacious dream. Nature hath deserted the connexion, and Art cannot supply her place. For, as Milton wisely expresses, "never can true reconcilement grow, where wounds of deadly hate have pierc'd so deep."

Every quiet method for peace hath been ineffectual. Our prayers have been rejected with disdain; and only tended to convince us, that nothing flatters vanity, or confirms obstinacy in Kings more than repeated petitioning—and nothing hath contributed more than that very measure to make the Kings of Europe absolute: Witness Denmark and Sweden. Wherefore, since nothing but blows will do, for God's sake, let us come to a final separation, and not leave the next generation to be cutting throats, under the violated unmeaning names of parent and child.

To say, they will never attempt it again is idle and visionary, we thought so at the repeal of the stamp-act, yet a year or two undeceived us; as well may we suppose that nations, which have been once defeated, will never renew the quarrel.

As to government matters, it is not in the power of Britain to do this continent justice: The business of it will soon be too weighty, and intricate, to be managed with any tolerable degree of convenience, by a power so distant from us, and so very ignorant of us; for if they cannot conquer us, they cannot govern us. To be always running three or four thousand miles with a tale or a petition, waiting four or five months for an answer, which when obtained requires five or six more to explain it in, will in a few years be looked upon as folly and childishness—There was a time when it was proper, and there is a proper time for it to cease.

Small islands not capable of protecting themselves, are the proper objects for kingdoms to take under their care; but there is something very absurd, in supposing a continent to be perpetually governed by an island. In no instance hath nature made the satellite larger than its primary planet, and as England and America, with respect to each other, reverses the common order of nature, it is evident they belong to different systems; England to Europe, America to itself.

I am not induced by motives of pride, party, or resentment to espouse the doctrine of separation and independence; I am clearly, positively, and conscientiously persuaded that it is the true interest of this continent to be so; that every thing short of *that* is mere patchwork, that it can afford no lasting felicity,—that it is leaving the sword to our children, and shrinking back at a time, when, a little more, a little farther, would have rendered this continent the glory of the earth. . . .

No man was a warmer wisher for reconciliation than myself, before the fatal nineteenth of April 1775,* but the moment the event of that day was made known, I rejected the hardened, sullen tempered Pharaoh of England for ever; and disdain the wretch, that with the pretended title of FATHER OF HIS PEOPLE can unfeelingly hear of their slaughter, and composedly sleep with their blood upon his soul.

But admitting that matters were now made up, what would be the event? I answer, the ruin of the continent. And that for several reasons.

First. The powers of governing still remaining in the hands of the king, he will have a negative over the whole legislation of this continent. And as he hath shewn himself such an inveterate enemy to liberty, and discovered such a thirst for arbitrary power; is he, or is he not, a proper man to say to these colonies, *"You shall make no laws but what I please."* . . .

America is only a secondary object in the system of British politics, England consults the good of *this* country, no farther than it answers her *own* purpose. Wherefore, her own interest leads her to suppress the growth of *ours* in every case which doth not promote her advantage, or in the least interferes with it. A pretty state we should soon be in under such a secondhand government, considering what has happened! Men do not change from enemies to friends by the alteration of a name: And in order to shew that reconciliation *now* is a dangerous doctrine, I affirm, *that it would be policy in the king at this time, to repeal the acts for the sake of reinstating himself in the government of the provinces;* in order, that HE MAY ACCOMPLISH BY CRAFT AND SUBTILTY, IN THE LONG RUN, WHAT HE CANNOT DO BY FORCE AND VIOLENCE IN THE SHORT ONE. Reconciliation and ruin are nearly related.

Secondly. That as even the best terms, which we can expect to obtain, can amount to no more than a temporary expedient, or a kind of government by guardianship, which can last no longer than till the colonies come of age, so the general face and state of things, in the interim, will be unsettled and unpromising. . . .

But the most powerful of all arguments, is, that nothing but independence, i.e., a continental form of government, can keep the peace of the continent and preserve it inviolate from civil wars. I dread the event of a reconciliation with Britain now, as it is more than probable, that it will be followed by a revolt somewhere or other, the consequences of which may be far more fatal than all the malice of Britain. . . .

If there is any true cause of fear respecting independence, it is because no plan is yet laid down. Men do not see their way out—Wherefore, as an opening into that business, I offer the following hints; at the same time modestly affirming, that I have no other opinion of them myself, than that they may be the means of giving rise to something better. Could the straggling thoughts of individuals be collected, they would frequently form materials for wise and able men to improve into useful matter.

---

* Massacre at Lexington.

Let the assemblies be annual, with a President only. The representation more equal. Their business wholly domestic, and subject to the authority of a Continental Congress.

Let each colony be divided into six, eight, or ten, convenient districts, each district to send a proper number of delegates to Congress, so that each colony send at least thirty. The whole number in Congress will be at least 390. . . . And in order that nothing may pass into a law but what is satisfactorily just, not less than three fifths of the Congress to be called a majority—He that will promote discord, under a government so equally formed as this, would have joined Lucifer in his revolt.

But as there is a peculiar delicacy, from whom, or in what manner, this business must first arise, and as it seems most agreeable and consistent, that it should come from some intermediate body between the governed and the governors, that is, between the Congress and the people, let a CONTINENTAL CONFERENCE be held. . . .

. . . [L]et their business be to frame a CONTINENTAL CHARTER, or Charter of the United Colonies; (answering to what is called the Magna Charta of England) fixing the number and manner of choosing members of Congress, members of Assembly, with their date of sitting, and drawing the line of business and jurisdiction between them: (Always remembering, that our strength is continental, not provincial:) Securing freedom and property to all men, and above all things, the free exercise of religion, according to the dictates of conscience; with such other matter as is necessary for a charter to contain. Immediately after which, the said Conference to dissolve, and the bodies which shall be chosen conformable to the said charter, to be the legislators and governors of this continent for the time being: Whose peace and happiness may God preserve, Amen. . . .

But where, says some, is the King of America? I'll tell you. Friend, he reigns above, and doth not make havoc of mankind like the Royal Brute of Britain. Yet that we may not appear to be defective even in earthly honors, let a day be solemnly set apart for proclaiming the charter; let it be brought forth placed on the divine law, the word of God; let a crown be placed thereon, by which the world may know, that so far we approve of monarchy, that in America THE LAW IS KING. For as in absolute governments the King is law, so in free countries the law *ought* to be King; and there ought to be no other. But lest any ill use should afterwards arise, let the crown at the conclusion of the ceremony, be demolished, and scattered among the people whose right it is.

A government of our own is our natural right: And when a man seriously reflects on the precariousness of human affairs, he will become convinced, that it is infinitely wiser and safer, to form a constitution of our own in a cool deliberate manner, while we have it in our power, than to trust such an interesting event to time and chance. . . . Ye that oppose independence now, ye know not what ye do; ye are opening a door to eternal tyranny, by keeping vacant the seat of government. There are thousands, and tens of thousands, who would think it glorious to expel from the continent that barbarous and hellish power, which hath stirred up the Indians and Negroes to destroy us; the cruelty hath a double guilt, it is dealing brutally by us, and treacherously by them. . . .

Ye that tell us of harmony and reconciliation, can ye restore to us the time that is past? Can ye give to prostitution its former innocence? Neither can ye reconcile Britain and America. The last cord now is broken, the people of England are presenting addresses against us. There are injuries which nature cannot forgive; she would cease to be nature if she did. As well can the lover forgive the ravisher of his mistress, as the continent forgive the murders of Britain. The Almighty hath implanted in us these unextinguishable feelings for good and wise purposes. They are the guardians of his image in our hearts. They distinguish us from the herd of common animals. The social compact would dissolve, and justice be extirpated the earth, or have only a casual existence were we callous to the touches of affection. The robber, and the murderer, would often escape unpunished, did not the injuries which our tempers sustain, provoke us into justice.

O ye that love mankind! Ye that dare oppose, not only the tyranny, but the tyrant, stand forth! Every spot of the old world is overrun with oppression. Freedom hath been hunted round the globe. Asia, and Africa, have long expelled her— Europe regards her like a stranger, and England hath given her warning to depart. O! receive the fugitive, and prepare in time an asylum for mankind.

Of the Present Ability of America, with Some Miscellaneous Reflexions

I have never met with a man, either in England or America, who hath not confessed his opinion, that a separation between the countries, would take place one time or other: And there is no instance, in which we have shewn less judgment, than in endeavouring to describe, what we call the ripeness or fitness of the Continent for independence.

As all men allow the measure, and vary only in their opinion of the time, let us, in order to remove mistakes, take a general survey of things, and endeavour, if possible, to find out the *very* time. But we need not go far, the inquiry ceases at once, for, the *time hath found us*. The general concurrence, the glorious union of all things prove the fact.

It is not in numbers, but in unity, that our great strength lies; yet our present numbers are sufficient to repel the force of all the world. The Continent hath, at this time, the largest body of armed and disciplined men of any power under Heaven; and is just arrived at that pitch of strength, in which no single colony is able to support itself, and the whole, when united, can accomplish the matter, and either more, or, less than this, might be fatal in its effects. Our land force is already sufficient, and as to naval affairs, we cannot be insensible, that Britain would never suffer an American man of war to be built, while the continent remained in her hands. Wherefore, we should be no forwarder an hundred years hence in that branch, than we are now; but the truth is, we should be less so, because the timber of the country is every day diminishing, and that, which will remain at last, will be far off and difficult to procure.

Were the continent crowded with inhabitants, her sufferings under the present circumstances would be intolerable. The more seaport towns we had, the more should we have both to defend and to lose. Our present numbers are so happily proportioned to our wants, that no man need be idle. The diminution of trade affords an army, and the necessities of an army create a new trade.

Debts we have none; and whatever we may contract on this account will serve as a glorious memento of our virtue. Can we but leave posterity with a settled form of government, an independent constitution of its own, the purchase at any price will be cheap. But to expend millions for the sake of getting a few vile acts repealed, and routing the present ministry only, is unworthy the charge, and is using posterity with the utmost cruelty; because it is leaving them the great work to do, and a debt upon their backs, from which they derive no advantage. Such a thought is unworthy a man of honor, and is the true characteristic of a narrow heart and a peddling politician.

The debt we may contract doth not deserve our regard, if the work be but accomplished. No nation ought to be without a debt. A national debt is a national bond; and when it bears no interest, is in no case a grievance. Britain is oppressed with a debt of upwards of one hundred and forty millions sterling, for which she pays upwards of four millions interest. And as a compensation for her debt, she has a large navy; America is without a debt, and without a navy; yet for the twentieth part of the English national debt, could have a navy as large again. . . .

No country on the globe is so happily situated, or so internally capable of raising a fleet as America. Tar, timber, iron, and cordage are her natural produce. We need go abroad for nothing. Whereas the Dutch, who make large profits by hiring out their ships of war to the Spaniards and Portuguese, are obliged to import most of their materials they use. We ought to view the building a fleet as an article of commerce, it being the natural manufactory of this country. It is the best money we can lay out. A navy when finished is worth more than it cost. And is that nice point in national policy, in which commerce and protection are united. Let us build; if we want them not, we can sell; and by that means replace our paper currency with ready gold and silver.

In point of manning a fleet, people in general run into great errors; it is not necessary that one fourth part should be sailors. . . . A few able and social sailors will soon instruct a sufficient number of active landmen in the common work of a ship. Wherefore, we never can be more capable to begin on maritime matters than now, while our timber is standing, our fisheries blocked up, and our sailors and shipwrights out of employ. Men of war of seventy and eighty guns were built forty years ago in New-England, and why not the same now? Ship-building is America's greatest pride, and in which she will in time excel the whole world. . . .

The English list of ships of war, is long and formidable, but not a tenth part of them are at any one time fit for service, numbers of them not in being; yet their names are pompously continued in the list, if only a plank be left of the ship: and not a fifth part of such as are fit for service, can be spared on any one station at one time. The East and West Indies, Mediterranean, Africa, and other parts over which Britain extends her claim, make large demands upon her navy. From a mixture of prejudice and inattention, we have contracted a false notion respecting the navy of England, and have talked as if we should have the whole of it to encounter at once, and for that reason, supposed, that we must have one as large; which not being instantly practicable, have been made use of by a set of disguised Tories to discourage our beginning thereon. Nothing can be farther from truth than this; for if America had only a twentieth part of the naval force of Britain, she would be by far an overmatch for her; because, as we neither have, nor claim any foreign dominion, our whole force would be employed on our own coast, where we should, in the long run, have two to one the advantage of those who had three or four thousand miles to sail over, before they could attack us, and the same distance to return in order to refit and recruit. . . .

In almost every article of defence we abound. Hemp flourishes even to rankness, so that we need not want cordage. Our iron is superior to that of other countries. Our small arms equal to any in the world. Cannon we can cast at pleasure. Saltpetre and gunpowder we are every day producing. Our knowledge is hourly improving. Resolution is our inherent character, and courage hath never yet forsaken us. . . .

Another reason why the present time is preferable to all others, is, that the fewer our numbers are, the more land there is yet unoccupied, which instead of being lavished by the king on his worthless dependents, may be hereafter applied, not only to the discharge of the present debt, but to the constant support of government. No nation under heaven hath such an advantage as this.

The infant state of the Colonies, as it is called, so far from being against, is an argument in favor of independence. We are sufficiently numerous, and were we more so, we might be less united. . . .

Youth is the seed time of good habits, as well in nations as in individuals. It might be difficult, if not impossible, to form the Continent into one government half a century hence. The vast variety of interests, occasioned by an increase of trade and population, would create confusion. Colony would be against colony. Each being able might scorn each other's assistance: and while the proud and foolish gloried in their little distinctions, the wise would lament, that the union had not been formed before. Wherefore, the *present time* is the *true time* for establishing it. The intimacy which is contracted in infancy, and the friendship which is formed in misfortune, are, of all others, the most lasting and unalterable. Our present union is marked with both these characters: we are young, and we have been distressed; but our concord hath withstood our troubles, and fixes a memorable æra for posterity to glory in.

The present time, likewise, is that peculiar time, which never happens to a nation but once, *viz.* the time of forming itself into a government. Most nations have let slip the opportunity, and by that means have been compelled to receive laws from their conquerors, instead of making laws for themselves. First, they had a king, and then a form of government; whereas, the articles or charter of government, should be formed first, and men delegated to execute them afterward: but from the errors of other nations, let us learn wisdom, and lay hold of the present opportunity—*To begin government at the right end.* . . .

To Conclude, however strange it may appear to some, or however unwilling they may be to think so, matters not, but many strong and striking reasons may be given, to shew, that nothing can settle our affairs so expeditiously as an open and determined declaration for independence. Some of which are,

First.—It is the custom of nations, when any two are at war, for some other powers, not engaged in the quarrel, to step in as mediators, and bring about the preliminaries of a peace: but while America calls herself the Subject of Great-Britain, no power, however well disposed she may be, can offer her mediation. Wherefore, in our present state we may quarrel on for ever.

Secondly.—It is unreasonable to suppose, that France or Spain will give us any kind of assistance, if we mean only, to make use of that assistance for the purpose of repairing the breach, and strengthening the connection between Britain and America; because, those powers would be sufferers by the consequences.

Thirdly.—While we profess ourselves the subjects of Britain, we must, in the eye of foreign nations, be considered as rebels. The precedent is somewhat dangerous to *their peace,* for men to be in arms under the name of subjects; we, on the spot, can solve the paradox: but to unite resistance and subjection, requires an idea much too refined for common understanding.

Fourthly.—Were a manifesto to be published, and despatched to foreign courts, setting forth the miseries we have endured, and the peaceable methods we have in-effectually used for redress; declaring, at the same time, that not being able, any longer, to live happily or safely under the cruel disposition of the British court, we had been driven to the necessity of breaking off all connections with her; at the same time, assuring all such courts of our peaceable disposition towards them, and of our desire of entering into trade with them: Such a memorial would produce more good effects to this Continent, than if a ship were freighted with petitions to Britain.

Under our present denomination of British subjects, we can neither be received nor heard abroad: The custom of all courts is against us, and will be so, until, by an independence, we take rank with other nations.

These proceedings may at first appear strange and difficult; but, like all other steps which we have already passed over, will in a little time become familiar and agreeable; and, until an independence is declared, the Continent will feel itself like a man who continues putting off some unpleasant business from day to day, yet knows it must be done, hates to set about it, wishes it over, and is continually haunted with the thoughts of its necessity.

8. The Declaration of Independence, 1776

When, in the course of human events, it becomes necessary for one people to dis-solve the political bands which have connected them with another, and to assume, among the powers of the earth, the separate and equal station to which the laws of nature and of nature's God entitle them, a decent respect to the opinions of mankind requires that they should declare the causes which impel them to the separation.

We hold these truths to be self-evident, that all men are created equal; that they are endowed by their Creator with certain unalienable rights; that among these are life, liberty, and the pursuit of happiness. That, to secure these rights, governments are instituted among men, deriving their just powers from the consent of the gov-erned; that, whenever any form of government becomes destructive of these ends, it is the right of the people to alter or to abolish it, and to institute a new government, laying its foundation on such principles, and organizing its powers in such form, as to them shall seem most likely to effect their safety and happiness. Prudence, in-deed, will dictate that governments long established should not be changed for light and transient causes; and, accordingly, all experience hath shown, that mankind are more disposed to suffer, while evils are sufferable, than to right themselves by abolishing the forms to which they are accustomed. But, when a long train of abuses and usurpations, pursuing invariably the same object, evinces a design to reduce them under absolute despotism, it is their right, it is their duty, to throw off such government, and to provide new guards for their future security. Such has

From The Declaration of Independence, 1776.

been the patient sufferance of these colonies, and such is now the necessity which constrains them to alter their former systems of government. The history of the present King of Great Britain is a history of repeated injuries and usurpations, all having, in direct object, the establishment of an absolute tyranny over these states. To prove this, let facts be submitted to a candid world:

He has refused his assent to laws the most wholesome and necessary for the public good.

He has forbidden his governors to pass laws of immediate and pressing importance, unless suspended in their operation till his assent should be obtained; and, when so suspended, he has utterly neglected to attend to them.

He has refused to pass other laws for the accommodation of large districts of people, unless those people would relinquish the right of representation in the legislature; a right inestimable to them, and formidable to tyrants only.

He has called together legislative bodies at places unusual, uncomfortable, and distant from the depository of their public records, for the sole purpose of fatiguing them into compliance with his measures.

He has dissolved representative houses repeatedly, for opposing, with manly firmness, his invasions on the rights of the people.

He has refused, for a long time after such dissolutions, to cause others to be elected; whereby the legislative powers, incapable of annihilation, have returned to the people at large for their exercise; the state remaining, in the meantime, exposed to all the danger of invasion from without, and convulsions within.

He has endeavored to prevent the population of these States; for that purpose, obstructing the laws for naturalization of foreigners, refusing to pass others to encourage their migration hither, and raising the conditions of new appropriations of lands.

He has obstructed the administration of justice, by refusing his assent to laws for establishing judiciary powers.

He has made judges dependent on his will alone, for the tenure of their offices, and the amount and payment of their salaries.

He has erected a multitude of new offices, and sent hither swarms of officers to harass our people, and eat out their substance.

He has kept among us, in time of peace, standing armies, without the consent of our legislatures.

He has affected to render the military independent of, and superior to, the civil power.

He has combined, with others, to subject us to a jurisdiction foreign to our Constitution, and unacknowledged by our laws; giving his assent to their acts of pretended legislation:

For quartering large bodies of armed troops among us:

For protecting them by a mock trial, from punishment, for any murders which they should commit on the inhabitants of these States:

For cutting off our trade with all parts of the world:

For imposing taxes on us without our consent:

For depriving us, in many cases, of the benefit of trial by jury:

For transporting us beyond seas to be tried for pretended offenses:

For abolishing the free system of English laws in a neighboring province, establishing therein an arbitrary government, and enlarging its boundaries, so as to render it at once an example and fit instrument for introducing the same absolute rule into these colonies:

For taking away our charters, abolishing our most valuable laws, and altering, fundamentally, the forms of our governments:

For suspending our own legislatures, and declaring themselves invested with power to legislate for us in all cases whatsoever.

He has abdicated government here, by declaring us out of his protection, and waging war against us.

He has plundered our seas, ravaged our coasts, burnt our towns, and destroyed the lives of our people.

He is, at this time, transporting large armies of foreign mercenaries to complete the works of death, desolation, and tyranny, already begun, with circumstances of cruelty and perfidy scarcely paralleled in the most barbarous ages, and totally unworthy the head of a civilized nation.

He has constrained our fellow-citizens, taken captive on the high seas, to bear arms against their country, to become the executioners of their friends and brethren, or to fall themselves by their hands.

He has excited domestic insurrections amongst us, and has endeavored to bring on the inhabitants of our frontiers, the merciless Indian savages, whose known rule of warfare is an undistinguished destruction of all ages, sexes, and conditions.

In every stage of these oppressions, we have petitioned for redress, in the most humble terms; our repeated petitions have been answered only by repeated injury. A prince, whose character is thus marked by every act which may define a tyrant, is unfit to be the ruler of a free people.

Nor have we been wanting in attention to our British brethren. We have warned them, from time to time, of attempts by their legislature to extend an unwarrantable jurisdiction over us. We have reminded them of the circumstances of our emigration and settlement here. We have appealed to their native justice and magnanimity, and we have conjured them, by the ties of our common kindred, to disavow these usurpations, which would inevitably interrupt our connections and correspondence. They, too, have been deaf to the voice of justice and consanguinity. We must, therefore, acquiesce in the necessity which denounces our separation, and hold them, as we hold the rest of mankind, enemies in war, in peace, friends.

We, therefore, the representatives of the United States of America, in general Congress assembled, appealing to the Supreme Judge of the world for the rectitude of our intentions, do, in the name, and by the authority of the good people of these colonies, solemnly publish and declare, that these united colonies are, and of right ought to be, free and independent states; that they are absolved from all allegiance to the British Crown, and that all political connection between them and the state of Great Britain is, and ought to be, totally dissolved; and that, as free and independent states, they have full power to levy war, conclude peace, contract alliances, establish commerce, and to do all other acts and things which independent states may of right do. And, for the support of this declaration, with a firm reliance on the protection of Divine Providence, we mutually pledge to each other our lives, our fortunes, and our sacred honour.

No two colonies responded to the crisis in imperial affairs in exactly the same way. Although elite leadership prevailed in every colony, economic interests, political circumstances, and cultural traditions varied. In the first essay, Thomas M. Doerflinger, a securities analyst and the author of *A Vigorous Spirit of Enterprise: Merchants and Economic Development in Revolutionary Philadelphia* (1986), examines the variety of factors that influenced the men who led Pennsylvania into the Revolution at a more gradual pace than Massachusetts or Virginia. In the second selection, drawn from her *American Scripture: Making the Declaration of Independence* (1997), Pauline Maier, a William R. Kenan, Jr., Professor of History at M.I.T., explains the complicated interplay of external events and political maneuvering that produced the Declaration.

The Mixed Motives of Merchant Revolutionaries

THOMAS M. DOERFLINGER

Philadelphia merchants before the Revolution . . . genuinely feared British encroachments on American rights and were willing to make real financial sacrifices to oppose them. Yet their opposition was qualified and inconsistent, their attitudes complex and conflicted; the merchants never offered sustained, united support for the resistance and Revolutionary movements. They neither strenuously lobbied against the Sugar Act, nor led the opposition to the Stamp Act, nor initiated the boycott of 1769–1770, nor supported strongly the convening of the Continental Congress. If it had been left to the city's merchants, the Revolutionary movement would have been more circumspect and cautious, more judicious and temperate, less eager to make the final break with Britain. In short, it would not have been a revolutionary movement at all. One reason for this ambivalence was that Philadelphia's economy was not especially disordered or depressed between 1760 and 1775, as some neo-Progressive historians have suggested; indeed, the period offered notable entrepreneurial opportunities. The merchants thus had no compelling financial reason to break with England. Quite to the contrary, they were restrained by a variety of countervailing factors. They had close commercial and personal ties with England; they wished to avoid disruption of their trade by boycotts and protests; and the Quakers among them not only discountenanced tumultuous extralegal protests but also feared that the Revolutionary movement would sweep Pennsylvania's turbulent Presbyterian faction into power.

The merchants' ambivalence is significant, first, because it shows that they did not propel the Revolutionary movement forward, and, second, because it illuminates the complex relationship in the pre-war years between ideas and interest—between the merchants' conception of their constitutional rights and their specific economic, social, and religious concerns. Although some scholars have attempted to identify the socioeconomic roots of Revolutionary ideologies, it seems more useful in the present case to explore how financial self-interest, religious affiliation, and social conservatism inhibited the emergence of a radical commitment

From "Philadelphia Merchants and the Logic of Moderation, 1760–1775," by Thomas Doerflinger from *William and Mary Quarterly,* 80, 1983. Reprinted by permission of the author.

among most merchants. This pattern is of more than local interest, because it throws light on an important regional dynamic of the Revolutionary era—that the Middle Atlantic area was consistently a center of political conservatism.

Historians have recently identified Philadelphia's dry goods trade with England as the center of a pre-Revolutionary economic crisis. It has been suggested that "English capital and English decisions increasingly dominated the colonial economy," as aggressive English firms sold huge quantities of merchandise on credit and undercut American merchant firms by selling directly to American shopkeepers and auction houses. The weight of evidence suggests that the dry goods trade was indeed overstocked during the period 1760–1775, following a profitable boom during the Seven Years' War. . . .

Although the relevant data are not fully consistent, it appears that the years 1764–1768 were indeed ones of severe commercial stagnation. Dry goods imports drifted in these years; the West Indies trade was unprofitable; and the volume of shipping activity in the port was low. In addition, merchants were frustrated by a serious "shortage of cash" caused by the withdrawal of provincial paper money from circulation and the movement of specie to England to finance the heavy wartime imports. As a result of these problems, the amount of shipping tonnage registered by merchants plunged in the second half of the 1760s, and the number of bankruptcies in Philadelphia peaked in 1767.

This downturn ended decisively in 1769, however, when flour and bread exports to the West Indies and southern Europe surged 128 percent above their 1768 levels. Philadelphia's provision trade continued to prosper until 1776. . . .

What we have, then, is a mixed picture: a dry goods market that was glutted as usual, but a strong housing market and a generally buoyant provision trade. The commercial downturn in the mid-1760s was followed by impressive expansion after 1768. This hardly adds up to a structural economic crisis that would have turned conservative businessmen into revolutionaries. The merchants, in fact, fared relatively well in this period, as a number of documents show. The number of carriage owners in Philadelphia increased from twenty-nine in 1761 to eighty-four in 1772, and in the latter year forty-four of them were merchants. Shipping records tell a similar story. . . .

Thus, despite the downturn of the mid-1760s, the pre-Revolutionary period offered good opportunities for the shrewd trader. This assessment does not imply that Philadelphia society was free from inequality and social strain in the decade and a half before Independence. It is, in fact, consistent with the argument that the distribution of wealth became increasingly unequal during the later colonial period. How else than through an expansion of commercial profits could merchants have financed the "urban mansions built during the 1760s" or purchased the "four-wheeled coaches and carriages imported from London"?

As the favorable commercial outlook in Philadelphia tended to moderate the merchants' attitudes toward the Revolutionary crisis, so too did their political orientation. Although they viewed encroachments of British power with as much dismay as other Philadelphians, politics was not the major concern of most traders. Moreover, the merchants feared that radical initiatives might sever their close and valuable ties with England and the empire.

There is a plethora of evidence, both private and public, that Philadelphia's merchants sincerely believed that parliamentary taxation of Americans was unconstitutional. In 1768 a committee of Philadelphia traders wrote to a group of leading English merchants that "the Statutes imposing Duties on Paper, Glass, Tea, &c. being a Tax on the Americans, without their Consent, we look upon, [as] Unconstitutional and destructive of our Rights, as your Brethren and Subjects." When the English merchants admitted that the Townshend duties might be "inexpedient," the Philadelphians pointedly insisted that they were unconstitutional as well. This belief was repeated again and again in the private correspondence not only of leading whig traders but of merchants who were loyalist or neutral during the Revolution. . . .

Grounded in the merchants' conceptions of their rights as Englishmen, these constitutional fears were sharpened by their problems as businessmen. The tightening of the customs administration after 1763 greatly complicated life for Philadelphia's smugglers, and both the Sugar Act and the Stamp Act required payment of taxes in specie at just the moment when the Currency Act of 1764 forbade colonial legislatures to issue legal tender paper money. All three of these acts coincided with the commercial downturn of the mid-1760s, when exchange rates were high and large amounts of specie were shipped to England to extinguish sterling debts. The result was a severe shortage of money in Pennsylvania. . . .

Even in the absence of an economic crisis, one might have expected these constitutional grievances to have aligned the merchants unambiguously behind the radical cause. A major task facing the historian, then, is to discern the factors that tended to moderate their political stance. Certainly one factor was the speed with which some of the merchants' major complaints were defused. The Stamp Act was never enforced; the Sugar Act was greatly revised in 1766. The Currency Act did not wreck Pennsylvania's paper currency but allowed the legislature to keep outstanding paper in circulation until its regular expiration date, and the colony was able to issue £102,000 of new money that was not legal tender. This was enough to meet most, though not all, of the colony's monetary needs.

A second reason for the merchants' caution may have been that they were more apolitical than the concept of a "merchant aristocracy" implies. To be sure, such traders as Charles Thomson, Thomas Mifflin, George Clymer, Thomas Wharton, and George Bryan were political activists, and many others had clear political affiliations. But before the Revolution merchants did not dominate political life. The men who articulated the colonists' constitutional position in pamphlets, broadsides, and newspaper articles usually were not active merchants, and Pennsylvania's party chieftains were generally wealthy lawyers, clerics, and landed gentlemen, rather than traders. . . .

It is clear that many merchants, whether or not politically oriented, identified closely with the British Empire, which was, after all, a commercial construct. Merchants were the engineers of commerce who took risks to move goods across the Atlantic; without them, the empire was only an inert bureaucratic entity. As the Philadelphia traders wrote to their English colleagues, "We consider the Merchants here and in England as the Links of the Chain that binds both Countries together. They are deeply concerned in preserving the Union and Connection." . . .

This identification with the empire was challenged by a key instrument of the Revolutionary movement, the boycotts of 1765–1766, 1768–1770, and 1774–1776. Although the stated aim of nonimportation was to exert pressure for the repeal of particular measures, its actual reach was far wider. It was in fact a tentative declaration of American economic independence, and its enforcement by local committees gave rise to some of the earliest extralegal Revolutionary governments in the colonies. The boycotts played an important ideological role as well, for they translated into action the moral component of a republican ideology that rejected the debilitating vices and luxuries of the Old World. Nonimportation thus provided a means of atoning for the sins of avarice and materialism in an increasingly secular age.

Philadelphia dry goods merchants, particularly the Quakers, did not necessarily reject these attitudes *in toto*. In 1769 John Reynell donned a leather jacket and set his wife to turning out homespun. . . . But the merchants could hardly overlook the fact that they were the conduit by which pernicious luxuries poured into the Delaware Valley and that not a few of the choicest extravagances ended up in their own parlors and pantries. If fully executed, nonimportation entailed nothing less than repudiation of their profession and destruction of the elaborate trading networks they had laboriously constructed. In this respect the merchants viewed the imperial connection quite differently from Virginia planters, who found that they were increasingly financing their expensive tastes with debt rather than tobacco shipments.

The merchants' moderate outlook was also fostered by the interrelated issues of religion and social control, for the Revolutionary movement in Pennsylvania was shaped at every step by bitter antagonism among religious groups, especially between Quakers and Presbyterians. Anglicans and Quakers each composed over a third of the merchant community, and they dominated its upper stratum even more. . . . Presbyterians, on the other hand, accounted for less than a fifth of the merchants and included few traders of the first rank. Thus the economic muscle of the merchant group, the power to make or break a boycott, rested with the conservative congregations of the Friends' Meeting House and of Christ and St. Peter's churches.

The principles of the Society of Friends were ill-suited to governing during an era of war and revolution, for the Quaker peace testimony not only forbade military activity but discouraged riots, rallies, boycotts, and smuggling. . . . Many years of control of Pennsylvania's government, together with their commercial prominence and civic leadership, gave the Friends a conservative, rather complacent outlook. In this respect they resembled many Anglican merchants, who favored the status quo because they had close political and family ties with the colony's proprietors, British descendants of William Penn. The Anglicans' connections with England were also strong because the ministers of the church were ordained in London, and because the church in America depended on financial support from England.

The colony's Presbyterians, on the other hand, were of Scottish descent and had long resisted English domination. They traced their political lineage back to the Civil Wars, which had overthrown both bishop and king, and they felt little love for either. Indeed, Presbyterian ministers, especially those of a New Light persuasion, preached a distinctly republican message, emphasizing "the idea of a fundamental constitution based on law, of inalienable rights which were God-given and therefore natural, of government as a binding compact made between rulers and peoples, of the right of people to hold their rulers to account and to defend their rights against all oppression." The concentration of Presbyterians in Pennsylvania's underrepresented frontier counties minimized their influence in the assembly, but they hoped that their political power would grow as their share of the colony's population increased. . . .

The march of the Paxton Boys [a group of Scotch-Irish frontiersmen who marched on Philadelphia in order to reverse Pennsylvania policy friendly to the Indians] triggered a vicious political battle in Pennsylvania. To many Quakers, William Penn's once peaceful province seemed to be lurching toward anarchy as unruly Presbyterians tried to overrun the colony. These fears were heightened in 1765 when a band of Scotch-Irishmen in Cumberland County seized and destroyed a large shipment of goods that a Quaker mercantile firm was sending to Pittsburgh. Fundamental structural change—elimination of proprietary control of the colony—seemed to offer the only solution to the crisis. Therefore in 1765 the assembly dispatched Benjamin Franklin to London to persuade the British ministry that order could be maintained in Pennsylvania in no other way than by making it a royal colony. . . .

Fear of Presbyterian hegemony was a major factor in the Quaker merchants' view of the Revolutionary movement. They perceived an inexorable logic to the Revolutionary process that had nothing to do with commercial problems, parliamentary taxation, or ministerial tyranny. Like their forebears of the seventeenth century, the Presbyterians were evidently using discontent over constitutional issues to seize power for themselves and deny their fellow Christians freedom of conscience.

The prosperity of most merchants, a habitual detachment from political affairs, close ties with England, and fear of a rising Presbyterian faction all combined to moderate the merchants' political stance between 1764 and 1776. Although they clearly disliked the Sugar Act, their response to it was very restrained, perhaps in part because they were absorbed by the local political tumults of 1764. The Stamp Act crisis of the following year was powerfully shaped by the contingencies of provincial politics. . . .

Since the attacks on stamp agents constituted the chief form of resistance to the tax, it cannot be said that merchants as a group led the opposition to parliamentary taxation in 1765, as has been suggested. In reality, the trading community was split: Quaker merchants generally did not oppose the Stamp Act, while Anglican and Presbyterian merchants of the proprietary faction did. The one instance in which merchants united to oppose the act was the boycott of British imports, organized in November 1765. Even here, there is evidence that some merchants joined the boycott under duress. . . .

Despite their divisions in 1765, the merchants could have played a major role in opposing the Townshend Acts of 1767. . . . Primary opposition to the duties took the form, not of riots, but of a major commercial boycott from March 1769 to September 1770, in which the traders actively participated. According to some analysts, the merchants' causal role was indeed central. Neo-Progressive historians have argued that . . . the merchants initiated the boycott primarily to gain an eighteen-month respite from the relentless cascade of British capital and goods, during which they could sell off inventories, pay debts to English suppliers at favorable exchange rates, and build up cash reserves. Such a formulation is elegantly logical, and there is enough evidence to demonstrate that this consideration definitely was in the minds of some traders. At issue, however, is the causation of a revolution: the question is whether these concerns determined the pace and pattern of events.

The answer to this question is an unequivocal "no," for the neo-Progressives have overlooked one devastating detail. Far from leading the nonimportation movement in Philadelphia, dry goods merchants stubbornly opposed it throughout 1768, steadfastly ignoring the increasingly vituperative demands of radicals that they place the public welfare above private interests. Pressure steadily mounted on importers to join the boycott, which Boston and New York had already agreed to start. In pamphlets, speeches, and newspaper articles the Philadelphia radicals, led by John Dickinson, showered the merchants with abuse. They even tried to force the issue by enlisting individual merchants, but the intransigence of "eight or ten" wealthy importers scotched the effort. Although questioning the constitutionality of the Townshend Acts, conservative merchants evidently opposed precipitate action that would violate the Quaker peace testimony and offend valuable correspondents in England. . . .

Nonimportation shows clearly how patriotism was shaded by self-interest and by the circumspection of the mercantile mind. Anxious not to offend their correspondents in England, the merchants took their time in entering the boycott. Once the initiative was under way, however, they supported it to the point of foregoing profits as their inventories dwindled during 1770. But sacrifice had its limits; when other colonies abandoned the boycott and some of the Townshend duties were repealed, they became eager to get on with their trade. Of course the radicals in Philadelphia accused the moderates of being motivated by crass self-interest. To this charge the moderates replied, with some justice, that wet goods merchants were pressing for extension of a boycott that did not affect their own business even as they paid into the royal treasury duties on wine and rum. And their major allies in Philadelphia, the mechanics, benefited tremendously from the suspension of trade with England. Republican ideology was thus tempered and twisted by the realities of the marketplace.

Merchants approached with similar ambivalence the British East India Company's plan to unload its huge supply of tea in America. Many undoubtedly viewed it as a trick to seduce Americans into importing a dutied commodity, but it is apparent that some merchants had financial reasons for attacking the tea scheme. In addition to injuring directly those few traders who smuggled Dutch tea into Philadelphia, the company's plan concentrated power in the hands of a small number of prominent traders who had good connections in England. . . .

When news of the Coercive Acts reached Philadelphia in May 1774, wealthy Anglican and Quaker merchants attempted, as one said, "to keep the transactions of our City within the limits of Moderation and not Indecent or offensive to our parent State." They insisted that Boston should pay for the ruined tea and strongly opposed resumption of nonimportation, knowing by now that a boycott was far easier to start than to stop. The convening of the Continental Congress in September 1774, however, deprived them of the power to shape events as they had in the past. In particular, they could not delay the third boycott of the Revolutionary movement, the Association formulated by Congress, which banned imports after December 1, 1774, and exports after September 10, 1775.

Some traders—Charles Thomson, Thomas Mifflin, and George Clymer, for instance—enthusiastically promoted the Revolutionary cause as it moved forward in 1774 and 1775. Yet many wealthy merchants looked on with dismay as Independence drew near and the familiar social and political landscape was transformed. . . . Religious antagonisms continued to be a potent concern, especially for Quakers. James and Drinker discerned a common Presbyterian spring to events in Philadelphia and Boston in 1773: had not the "hasty and violent resolves" of Charles Thomson and other local Presbyterians inspired the intransigence of the Bostonians that led to the destruction of the tea? If Presbyterians finally managed to seize control of Pennsylvania, the freedom of conscience that had long graced the colony's constitution would disappear. . . . In the past, Quakers had battled in the political arena to hold back the Presbyterian tide, but by 1775 the forces of change were too strong, the political environment too turbulent, to justify this approach, and Friends defiantly retired from politics. For these various reasons—economic, social, religious, and political—a substantial proportion of the Philadelphia merchant community refused to enlist in the patriot cause.

The case of Philadelphia's merchants reminds us that interest may temper rather than intensify ideological commitment. While socioeconomic concerns may have made some Americans particularly receptive to a republican ideology, such factors had the opposite effect in Philadelphia's trading community. In the first place, the merchants did not face an economic crisis in the 1760s and 1770s. Despite the nearly chronic glut of the dry goods market and the stagnation of the provision trade between 1764 and 1768, the merchants were reasonably prosperous in the fifteen years before the War for Independence. They resented and feared English efforts to tax Americans and were willing to make sacrifices to defend their liberties, but these sentiments did not turn them into Revolutionaries because other factors intervened. Contingencies of local politics, close personal and commercial ties with England, fear of Presbyterian hegemony, and economic self-interest all conspired to moderate their stance. While the merchants did not mirror public opinion throughout the colony, neither were they an isolated group of rich reactionaries. A great many other Pennsylvanians viewed the prospect of Independence with equal misgiving. As late as May 1776, for instance, an election in Philadelphia that amounted to a referendum on the question of Independence favored the conservative position by a small margin.

The behavior of the merchants illustrates the limits of an ideological or intellectual explanation of the origins of the Revolution. By itself, such an approach explains too much; it lacks the specificity intrinsic to the problem at hand. The ideas of John Trenchard and Thomas Gordon, John Locke, and James Harrington were widely publicized throughout the colonies, yet they had far greater resonance in some colonies than in others. To understand fully the origins of the Revolution, we must determine what specific local and regional factors made particular areas more or less receptive to these ideas. The relative prosperity of the Middle Colonies, for example, in conjunction with a substantial Quaker influence and the presence of a large non-English-speaking population, may have predisposed this section toward conservatism. . . .

Regional differences continued to operate after 1776. The same pragmatism, elitism, and materialism that had hitherto made Philadelphia merchants reluctant Revolutionaries predisposed some of them to lead the Revolution in its later, more conservative phase. . . .

Declaring Independence

PAULINE MAIER

Why was the decision for Independence so difficult? Fear played a role. Could the colonists stand up against the power of Britain? A full-scale war would bring more death and devastation; and an alliance with France, which would help the colonies hold out militarily, itself seemed extremely dangerous. For most colonists, France was an old enemy whose defeat in the French and Indian War had freed North America from the threat of Catholic absolutism. Was France any more trustworthy in 1776 than it had been fifteen or twenty years earlier? Louis XVI would not help America for reasons of benevolence, or from any dedication to the cause of freedom: France would act only to serve its own best interests. Suppose, then, that Britain, once it despaired of keeping all its colonies, offered to partition them, much as Poland had been partitioned in 1772, returning Canada to France and Florida to Spain, if they kept out of the Anglo-American conflict. Would France refuse? Or suppose that France and America did form an alliance and succeeded in defeating Britain. Who would then protect America from French domination? "We shall weep at our victories," John Dickinson predicted. Even British tyranny seemed preferable to French rule.

Americans with special ties to the British government often planted themselves most firmly in the opposition: British officeholders, from royal governors of colonial birth down through justices of the peace, became Loyalists well out of proportion to their incidence in the population. But virtually all colonists, some recent European immigrants excepted, found the prospect of Independence troubling because they thought of themselves as British, and their pride in that identity, which had risen to a feverish height with Britain's victory in the French and Indian War, remained strong. . . .

Americans took particular pride in being governed under Britain's unwritten constitution, which they considered the most perfect form of government ever invented "by the wit of man"—a judgment with which, they often added, every major writer on politics agreed. Power in Britain was entrusted not to any one man or group of men, but was divided and balanced among King, Lords, and Commons, which curbed the ambitions of rulers and so preserved freedom. Under the "mildness and equity of the *English* Constitution," members of the Maryland Convention recalled on January 12, 1776, they and their ancestors had experienced a remarkable state of happiness because "of all known systems" British government was "best calculated to secure the liberty of the subject." Their felicity had lapsed when the "grounds of the present controversy were laid by the Ministry and Parliament of *Great Britain*," but Maryland wanted above all else to recover the remembered peace and freedom of times past. Even the news of early January failed to shake that desire: the Convention instructed its Congressional delegates to do all they could to secure reconciliation with the Mother Country, and also explicitly precluded their voting for Independence or for measures that might lead toward Independence without its previous consent.

In the closing months of 1775 and early 1776, as the crisis mounted, several other provincial assemblies, congresses, and conventions, particularly those in the "middle colonies" between New England and Virginia, also adopted instructions that prohibited their Congressional delegates from consenting to separation from the Mother Country or, as Pennsylvania and New Jersey added, any change in the form of American government. In part those instructions reflected strategic maneuvers on the part of moderate delegates, particularly Dickinson, to strengthen their position in Congress. But resistance to political change was by no means confined to the middle colonies: everywhere reverence for the inherited institutions of British government inhibited the movement toward separate nationhood. Throughout their conflict with Britain, colonists had rarely questioned the British system of government but directed their suspicions toward particular men within it. . . . Soon, however, Americans throughout the Continent would be reading a powerful treatise that challenged assumptions deeply bound up with the colonists' pride in being British.

On January 9, the same day James Wilson proposed that Congress once again disavow any desire for Independence, the Philadelphia press of Robert Bell distributed the first copies of *Common Sense.* The pamphlet was published anonymously, but in time it became known as the work of Thomas Paine, a largely self-educated Englishman of no particular previous distinction, who had first arrived in America on November 30, 1774. . . .

American freedom would never be secure under British rule, Paine argued, because "the so much boasted Constitution of England" was deeply flawed. The problem lay in two major *"constitutional errors"*—monarchy and hereditary rule. . . . The problem, then, was not just that evil persons were exercising power. It was systemic, in the very design of British government, which, like all governments, was incapable of constraining the power of hereditary rulers. The only way to solve that problem was to redesign the machine of government, eliminating monarchy and hereditary rule and expanding the "republican" element of British government which derived power not from birth but from the ballot. The solution, in short, was revolution.

Americans were afraid to embrace Independence, Paine said, not only because they thought better of the old regime than it deserved, but also because they had no plans for a new one. So he offered some suggestions guided by a "maxim" that "the more simple any thing is, the less liable it is to be disordered, and the easier repaired when disordered. . . . Out went the complex divisions and balancing of the British constitution. State governments, he suggested, should consist of annually elected assemblies with a president or presiding officer—not altogether unlike the extra-legal provincial congresses and conventions of the time—and be "subject to the authority of a Continental Congress." . . . The precise institutions of the American republic could be determined only through debate and experimentation. Paine promised, however, that by eliminating monarchy and hereditary rule and founding government entirely on popular choice, the Americans could "form the noblest, purest constitution on the face of the earth," one free of errors that had dogged mankind for centuries. "We have it in our power to begin the world over again," he wrote; and what the Americans did would affect the future of "all mankind."

Paine confronted the fears that kept many colonists from embracing Independence. Could the Americans hold out against Britain? Yes, since they had sufficient men and materials, a strength that came from political unity, and the prospect of foreign aid. Could America's economy thrive outside the British trade system? American products, he said, "will always have a market while eating is the custom of Europe." He cited the King's use of Indians and slaves against the Americans and his rejection of their petitions for redress and reconciliation. Later editions noted that news of the King's speech of October 26, 1775, had providentially arrived in America just as *Common Sense* was first published, such that "the bloody-mindedness of the one" showed "the necessity of pursuing the doctrine of the other." Above all, however, Paine insisted that the war made Independence necessary. "No man was a warmer wisher for reconciliation than myself, before the fatal nineteenth of April, 1775," he wrote, "but the moment the event of the day was made known, I rejected the hardened, sullen-tempered Pharaoh of England for ever; and disdain the wretch, that with the pretended title of FATHER OF HIS PEOPLE can unfeelingly hear of their slaughter, and composedly sleep with their blood upon his soul." War bred feelings of resentment and hatred that God had planted in peoples' hearts "for good and wise purposes," and that made reconciliation "a fallacious dream." The "blood of the slain, the weeping voice of nature cries, 'TIS TIME TO PART." Any settlement would be "mere patchwork" with no prospect of "lasting felicity," a temporary solution purchased at an enormous price in blood and treasure when by going "a little more, a little further," the Americans could have "rendered this continent the glory of the earth."

. . . Certainly much of Paine's case against monarchy had been made in the colonial press or pulpits at one point or another over the previous six years. *Common Sense,* however, gathered those arguments together and used them not to persuade Congress, which was already moving apace toward Independence, but the people whose support Congress needed. Within days of the pamphlet's publication, the New Hampshire delegate Josiah Bartlett reported that it was "greedily bought up and read by all ranks of people." Further editions soon issued from rival presses in Philadelphia and then in other cities until Paine estimated that some 150,000 copies had been sold in America alone, which he proudly described as "the greatest sale that any performance ever had since the use of letters." . . . The pamphlet's style also contributed to its popularity, and it appeared just as breaking news—of the burning of Norfolk, the King's speech of October 1775, and soon also the Prohibitory Act—seemed to close off alternatives to Independence. . . . "The country was ripe for independence, and only needed somebody to tell the people so, with decision, boldness, and plausibility." . . .

Paine's plans of government awoke more opposition than his arguments for Independence. By its "crude, ignorant Notion of a Government by one assembly," *Common Sense* would "do more Mischief, in dividing the Friends of Liberty, than all the Tory Writings together," John Adams lamented. Paine was "a keen Writer, but very ignorant of the Science of Government." Adams expressed his own views in *Thoughts on Government* (1776), which advocated the retention of complexity and balance in American republican institutions. However, Adams's challenge to *Common Sense* served to confirm that pamphlet's success. Paine wanted to shift the focus of public debate from evaluations of British rulers and the prospects for reconciliation to deciding how an independent America should be governed. And that he did.

Among those still hesitant on Independence, the idea of founding a republic gave another good reason for delay. In 1776, there were no regular, "republican" governments of the sort Paine advocated, in which all authority rested on popular choice and none on hereditary title. The best-known republics of past times—Athens and Rome, for example, or England's own Commonwealth of the 1650s—had not survived, and in general republics were said to be so short-lived that the wisdom of founding another was questionable. . . .

Republics, in short, were "fraught with all the tumult and riot incident to simple Democracy." . . .

In truth, those who held back had reason to fear that Independence would bring "Intestine Wars and Convulsions" and so leave the Americans worse off than they were under a hostile King and Parliament. They saw a republican future in the threat of rebellion by poor whites, Loyalists, and slaves on Maryland's eastern shore; restive slaves elsewhere who read their own meaning into the cause of liberty; mobs that freed debtors from jail, or the ordinary people who claimed seats in Virginia's provincial convention, one of whom, Landon Carter reported, defined independency as "a form of Government that, by being independent of the rich men, every man would then be able to do as he pleased." And what about the acrimonious and sometimes bloody disputes over land rights in the western reaches of Virginia and Pennsylvania or between New York and the settlers of Vermont? Surely such conflicts should be resolved, or at least a firm confederation formed to replace the supervising power of Britain, before Independence was declared. New Englanders were by no means free of such doubts. Not even [John] Adams expected that new governments founded on the authority of the people would be "so quiet as I could wish," or "that harmony, confidence, and affection" would bind the colonies before a "long time" had passed. Independence would require "toil and blood and treasure" more surely than it would bring "happiness and halcyon days." In the end, he could only pray that "Heaven prosper the new-born Republick, and make it more glorious than any former Republicks have been!" . . .

Finally, on May 10, 1776, the Continental Congress recommended to "the respective assemblies and conventions of the United Colonies, where no government sufficient to the exigencies of their affairs has been hitherto established," that they "adopt such government as shall, in the opinion of the representatives of the people, best conduce to the happiness and safety of their constituents in particular and America in general." Then it appointed a committee consisting of John Adams, Richard Henry Lee, and Edward Rutledge to compose a preface for the resolution. Three days later the committee proposed a draft that Adams had written. It was even more radical than the resolution it introduced.

> Whereas his Britannic Majesty, in conjunction with the lords and commons of Great Britain, has, by a late act of Parliament, excluded the inhabitants of these United Colonies from the protection of his crown; And whereas, no answer, whatever to the humble petitions of the colonies for redress of grievances and reconciliation with Great Britain, has been or is likely to be given; but, the whole force of that kingdom, aided by foreign mercenaries, is to be exerted for the destruction of the good people of these colonies; And whereas, it appears absolutely irreconcilable to reason and good Conscience, for the people of these colonies now to take the oaths and affirmations necessary for the support of any government under the crown of Great Britain, and it is necessary that the exercise of every kind of authority under the said crown should be totally suppressed, and all the powers of government exerted, under the authority of the

people of the colonies, for the preservation of internal peace, virtue, and good order, as well as for the defence of their lives, liberties, and properties, against the hostile invasions and cruel depredations of their enemies; therefore, resolved, &c.

Congress approved the preface on May 15, but only after two days of acrimonious debate and desire—despite its practice of seeking consensus on important issues—by a divided vote, with six or seven colonies in favor, four opposed, and at least one and perhaps two states abstaining. New York's instructions, as James Duane made clear, prevented its delegates from approving anything that did not further a restoration of harmony between Great Britain and its colonies, and the Pennsylvania delegation, James Wilson noted, was under a similar restraint. Maryland's delegates in fact left Congress once the preface was passed. . . . For all practical purposes, Adams wrote his wife, Abigail, the preface and resolution together effected "a total, absolute Independence" of America not only from Britain's Parliament but from her Crown. The document was not, however, a formal Declaration of Independence, which Adams understood would still be necessary.

In the preface of May 15 Congress for the first time publicly assigned responsibility for American grievances to the King. That was highly significant. . . . Accusations were extended to the King only when grievances had become so general, and evidence of his complicity so unmistakable, that the authority of his government had come into dispute. To attack the King was, in short, a constitutional form. It was the way Englishmen announced revolution.

The specific charges that Congress brought against the King on May 15 were few but powerful: he had consented to the Prohibitory Act, which formally removed the Americans from his protection; refused to answer their petitions for redress; and was bringing against them "the whole Force of the Kingdom, aided by foreign Mercenaries." The reference to "foreign mercenaries" was new. Early in the year Congress had received reports that the King was attempting to hire troops from other countries, but only in early May did it learn, from a Cork newspaper, that Britain was sending some 40,000 additional soldiers to America, including substantial numbers of "Hessians, Hanoverians, Mechlenburghers, Scotch Hollanders, & Scotch Highlanders." . . . On May 16, John Hancock wrote Massachusetts that "the best Intelligence from Europe" indicated that "the British Nation have proceeded to the last Extremity, and have actually taken into a pay a Number of foreign Troops," who were probably "on their Passage to America at this very Time." Five days later Congress received—through a mysterious emissary who came from London with documents sewn in his clothes—copies of the treaties George III had concluded with the Duke of Brunswick, the Landgrave of Hesse Cassel, and the Count of Hanau, each of which specified the terms on which German-speaking soldiers would be supplied for the King's service in America. Within a week the treaties were published in Pennsylvania newspapers.

The effect was electrifying, in part because the treaties' arrival coincided with alarming news from Canada. . . .

Accounts of the unfolding catastrophe provoked enormous concern. If American troops were forced to evacuate that province, John Hancock wrote General John Thomas in late May, not only would Canada be lost, but the northern frontiers of New York and New England would be exposed to the "ravages" of both Indians and the British forces. Congress sent more troops to salvage the situation, but all efforts to reserve the downward spiral failed. . . . Before long even Arnold, who bore some responsibility for initiating the Canadian fiasco, understood that there was no point in going on, that it was best to leave the northland "and secure our own country before it is too late."

In fact, the colonies' home territory needed all the defenders it could gather. After finally evacuating Boston on March 17, 1776, the British Army had regrouped at Halifax, Nova Scotia, from which it was expected to mount a major offensive somewhere along the Atlantic coast in the spring or summer of 1776. If the British were recruiting German and Scottish soldiers to reinforce that campaign, surely the Americans would have to solicit foreign aid on their own behalf. But would any European power consent to support a people who remained subjects of the British Crown? Hopes of help from imperial France were specious in any case, the opponents of Independence insisted; why should Louis XVI help sustain the struggle of a revolution republican America? Their argument that the friendship of Catholic France was a worse danger to American freedom than the enmity of George III made some sense to colonists for whom France had long been the enemy and an incarnation of absolutism.

Once again events in England undercut the arguments of those colonists most committed to preserving the empire. In late May, colonists learned that the King had rejected a petition from the City of London that asked him to define the terms of a just and honorable peace before turning the full force of British arms against the colonists. In reply, George III expressed regret for the miseries his American subjects had "brought upon themselves by an unjustifiable resistance to the constitutional authority of this Kingdom," and said he would be "ready and happy to alleviate those miseries, by acts of mercy and clemency, whenever that authority is established, and the now existing rebellion is at an end." . . . Robert Morris, who had done his best to hold off a decision for separation, conceded that George III's response to London "totally destroyed all hopes of reconciliation" and made a "declaration of Independency" inevitable. For that event, he said, Great Britain could thank only herself."

The Continental Congress had a full schedule on Friday, June 7. It began by agreeing to compensate a Mr. Charles Walker for a sloop and other goods. . . . Next it considered a committee report on resolutions passed by the convention of South Carolina. . . . Then "certain resolutions" were moved by Richard Henry Lee on the instructions of the Virginia Convention and seconded by John Adams:

> That these United Colonies are, and of right ought to be, free and independent States, that they are absolved from all allegiance to the British Crown, and that all political connection between them and the State of Great Britain is, and ought to be, totally dissolved.
>
> That it is expedient forthwith to take the most effectual measures for forming foreign Alliances.
>
> That a plan of confederation be prepared and transmitted to the respective Colonies for their consideration and approbation.

Since Congress was "obliged to attend at that time to some other business," . . . it put off debate on Lee's resolutions until the next morning. . . .

When Congress returned to Lee's motion on June 8, it resolved itself into a Committee of the Whole and . . . "passed that day & Monday the 10th. in debating on the subject." One group of Congressmen, including Pennsylvania's Dickinson, his colleague James Wilson, Edward Rutledge of South Carolina, and New York's Robert R. Livingston, admitted that it was impossible for the colonies "ever again [to] be united with Gr[eat] Britain" and said they were "friends" to Lee's resolutions, but opposed adopting them at that time. In the past, Congress had followed the "wise & proper" policy of "deferring to take any capital step till the voice of the people drove us into it" since "they were our power, & without them our declarations could not be carried into effect." At present, however, the delegates of several colonies, including Maryland, Pennsylvania, Delaware, New Jersey, and New York, had not been empowered by their home governments to vote for Independence. If the vote was taken immediately, those delegates would necessarily "retire" from Congress, and "possibly their colonies might secede from the Union," which would hurt the American cause more than a foreign alliance would help it. Division, in fact, would make foreign powers less willing "to join themselves to our fortunes," or allow them to insist on hard terms for their help. Delaying the decision would avoid that contingency since opinion in the middle colonies was "fast ripening & in a short time [the people there] would join in the general voice of America." The proponents of putting off Independence also questioned whether France or Spain would help the Americans, concerned as those nations were for the continued subjection of their own colonies. It was more likely, they argued, that France would form an alliance with Britain to divide the North American colonies between them. . . .

The proposition's supporters—particularly Lee, John Adams, and Virginia's George Wythe—responded that Lee's first resolution called on Congress only to "declare a fact which already exists." The Americans had always been independent of the British people and Parliament, they argued, and were now absolved from their obligation of allegiance to the King by his own act in declaring them out of his protection and waging war against them. Until the colonists declared their Independence, no European power could negotiate with them, receive an ambassador, or even allow American ships to enter their ports. It was surely in France's interest to help sever the connection between the American colonies and Britain; but if, as their opponents alleged, France proved unwilling to support the Americans, "we shall be but where we are; whereas without trying we shall never know whether they will aid us or not." On the other hand, France could be of considerable help in the coming military campaign, if only by interrupting the shipment of British military supplies, or by obliging Britain to divert some of its forces to the protection of its possessions in the West Indies. The surest way to prevent a partition treaty by which they American colonies would be divided among European powers much as Poland had been partitioned was to declare Independence and secure an alliance with France before Britain could raise that possibility. As for opposition to Independence in the middle colonies, . . . the supporters of Lee's resolutions were willing to abandon Congress's longstanding struggle for consensus, as they had on May 15 in pushing through Adams's call for the repression of all authority under the Crown. It would be "vain to wait either weeks or months for perfect unanimity," they said, "since it was impossible that all men should ever become of one sentiment on any question."

This time Congress was more prudent. It decided to give the laggard colonies time to accept Independence, and postponed the question for three weeks, until the first of July. So no time would be lost if Congress then approved Lee's motion, on June 11 it appointed a committee to prepare a declaration of Independence. That committee had five members: Thomas Jefferson, John Adams, Benjamin Franklin, Roger Sherman of Connecticut, and Robert R. Livingston of New York. Seventeen days later, on June 28, the committee presented its draft to Congress, which promptly tabled the report. By then only Maryland and New York had failed to allow their delegates to vote for Independence. That night Maryland fell into line.

The war did not wait for Congress's decision. . . . [O]n June 29 Washington reported the arrival of some fifty British ships of sail at Sandy Hook on the New Jersey shore near the entrance to New York harbor. Their number doubled within a few days. Washington was making "every preparation" for the impending attack, but reported that the American army was "extremely deficient in arms . . . and in great distress for want of them." By July 1 Congress also learned that another fifty-three British ships were outside Charleston, South Carolina, and that the American army had been forced to evacuate Canada. Urgent military issues consequently competed for the delegates' attention and haunted their deliberations as Congress turned again to Lee's resolution. The outcome of the war, they understood, would decide whether they would be remembered as the founders of a nation or be hanged by the British as traitors. . . .

On July 1, Congress again resolved itself into a Committee of the Whole "to take into consideration the resolution respecting independency." The debates went on through most of the day, but they were, John Adams claimed, a waste of time, since nothing was said "but what had been repeated and hackneyed in that Room before an hundred Times, for Six Months past." . . .

When Congress reconvened on July 2, it received correspondence from Washington and others, mostly relating to the military situation. . . . Congress then received from the Committee of the Whole the resolutions Richard Henry Lee had first proposed almost a month earlier. When the vote was put, the nine affirmative votes of the previous day had grown to twelve: not only South Carolina voted in favor, but also Delaware—the arrival of Caesar Rodney broke the tie in that delegation's vote—and Pennsylvania. Because John Dickinson and Robert Morris abstained on July 2, the four-to-three vote of Pennsylvania delegates against Independence on the previous day became a three-to-two vote in favor of Independence. A week later New York's Provincial Congress convention allowed its delegates to add the colony's approval to that of the other twelve colonies. The politics of patience—of slackening the pace of the "fleetest sailors" until they kept pace with "the dullest and slowest," that all might arrive at their destiny together—had triumphed. Public unanimity disguised differences of judgment on timing but not on Independence itself. In the end, there was no alternative; even the most hesitant agreed on that.

With Independence itself adopted, Congress again resolved itself into a Committee of the Whole to consider the document written to "declare the causes" of the colonies' separation from Britain. Other issues kept interrupting the Committee's discussions. . . . And yet, as the British began to bring the greatest fleet and the largest army ever assembled in North America into action against the Americans, Congress devoted the better part of two days to revising the draft declaration of Independence. Wars, it understood, were not won by ships and sailors and arms alone. Words, too, had power to serve the cause of victory.

FURTHER READING

David Ammerman, *In the Common Cause: American Response to the Coercive Acts of 1774* (1974)

Bernard Bailyn, *The Ideological Origins of the American Revolution* (1967)

Richard D. Brown, *Revolutionary Politics in Massachusetts: The Boston Committee of Correspondence and the Towns, 1772–1774* (1970)

Roger Champagne, "New York and the Intolerable Acts, 1774," *New-York Historical Society Quarterly* 45 (1961), 195–207

Cecil B. Currey, *Road to Revolution: Benjamin Franklin in England, 1765–1775* (1968)

David Hackett Fischer, *Paul Revere's Ride* (1994)

Eric Foner, *Tom Paine and Revolutionary America* (1976)

Lawrence H. Gipson, *The Triumphant Empire: Britain Sails into the Storm, 1770–1776* (1965)

Robert A. Gross, *The Minutemen and Their World* (1976)

Ira D. Gruber, "The American Revolution as a Conspiracy," *William and Mary Quarterly,* 3d ser., 26 (1969), 360–372

Richard M. Ketchum, *Decisive Day: The Battle for Bunker Hill* (1974)

Benjamin W. Labaree, *The Boston Tea Party* (1964)

William R. Leslie, "The Gaspee Affair: A Study of Its Constitutional Significance," *Mississippi Valley Historical Review 39* (1952–1953), 233–256

Pauline Maier, *From Resistance to Revolution: Colonial Radicals and the Development of American Opposition to Britain* (1972)

Jerrilyn Greene Marston, *King and Congress: The Transfer of Political Legitimacy, 1774–1776* (1987)

Charles H. Metzger, *The Quebec Act: A Primary Cause of the American Revolution* (1936)

John A. Neunschwander, *The Middle Colonies and the Coming of the Revolution* (1973)

John Phillip Reid, *In Defiance of the Law: The Standing-Army Controversy, the Two Constitutions, and the Coming of the American Revolution* (1981)

———, *In a Rebellious Spirit: The Argument of Facts, the Liberty Riot, and the Coming of the American Revolution* (1979)

Richard Alan Ryerson, *The Revolution Is Now Begun: The Radical Committees of Philadelphia, 1765–1776* (1978)

Peter Shaw, *American Patriots and the Rituals of Revolution* (1981)

Peter D. G. Thomas, *Tea Party to Independence: the Third Phase of the American Revolution, 1773–1776* (1991)

Robert E. Toohey, *Liberty and Empire: British Radical Solutions to the American Problem, 1774–1776* (1978)

Arthur Bernon Tourtellot, *William Diamond's Drum* (1959)

Robert W. Tucker and David C. Hendrickson, *The Fall of the First British Empire: Origins of the War of American Independence* (1982)

John W. Tyler, *Smugglers and Patriots: Boston Merchants and the Advent of the American Revolution* (1986)

Robert M. Weir, *"A Most Important Epocha": The Coming of the Revolution in South Carolina* (1970)

Garry Wills, *Inventing America: Jefferson's Declaration of Independence* (1978)

Fighting for Independence

In July 1776 opposition to British control came to a climax with the Declaration of Independence, but the challenge of defending the Revolution and creating a viable nation was only beginning. Facing the thirteen former colonies—now states—was the most formidable military power in the world, the British nation, with a navy so huge that it could deploy tens of thousands of well-provisioned and well-equipped professional troops anywhere along the Atlantic seaboard. No American port was safe; indeed, most settlements were within striking distance from the coast and inland waterways.

Their own military legacy and the influence of Whig political theory had led the colonists to rely on locally raised militia companies, citizen-soldiers who could rise swiftly in defense of their communities, as they had done at Lexington and Concord. And it was militiamen alone who enabled the Revolution to muster large armies at Bunker Hill in 1775 and Saratoga in 1777. But during most military operations, these part-time amateurs had limited value. In training and discipline they were deficient, and, most important, they could not be trusted to stay for the weeks, months, and even years that campaigning against Britain required. They would rise briefly to defend their own localities, but they were unwilling to travel long distances to fight away from home, nor would they leave their families, farms, and workshops for prolonged, indefinite periods. As a result, the Continental Congress had to turn away from colonial tradition. Working through the state governments, which possessed exclusive power to tax, it had to raise, equip, provision, and train a regular army that could go anywhere to fight, year after year.

This was an immense practical challenge of great political and financial complexity. It would occupy Congress's best energies until 1782. And it would be closely connected to the formation of American foreign policy. From the beginning of the war, Congress recognized that outside help was crucial and that the traditional enemy, France, was the nation most likely to supply assistance because of its eagerness to harass and humiliate Britain. The Catholic monarchy that Americans had excoriated during the French and Indian wars of the 1740s and 1750s could supply money, military equipment, and ultimately troops and a naval squadron. It could also threaten Britain directly and thus divert forces from America and raise Britain's military expenses. Moreover, a long-term commercial connection with France would be mutually advantageous. Thus, even before the colonists declared independence, they had begun secret talks with France—negotiations that were encouraged immediately by covert French material support.

But as eager as the Americans were for open military and commercial treaties with France, for a time French policymakers were reluctant to commit France publicly to the United States. Not only did a reconciliation between the British and the American colonists still seem possible, but there was a great chance that the American fight for independence would collapse. Under these circumstances France, not Britain, would taste humiliation. So the French government continued its covert assistance, avoiding any public commitments.

The victory at Saratoga and France's entry into the war as a U.S. ally in 1778 were great triumphs, but they did not win the war. The British government remained unyielding, while in America war weariness set in. Perhaps, Americans hoped, France would now carry the major burden. As a consequence of such wishful thinking, the army continued near starvation, and recurrent unrest stirred among the troops. After Saratoga, the British shifted the main theater of warfare to the south, where, if anything, Americans faced an even more difficult military challenge than before. Here, not only were settlers more thinly scattered through the countryside, but the revolutionary governments were threatened by Native American attacks, loyalist troops, and slave unrest in addition to British invasions.

As in the north earlier, the course of the fighting was generally inconclusive. Although the Americans scored a few notable victories and defeated the Native American and loyalist threats, the British army succeeded in moving through the southern states, capturing any town it wished. True, the British often paid a high price in casualties and supplies, but in most battles the redcoats won the field. As a result, during 1779, 1780, and 1781, the battle for independence became a war of attrition—a test of British, American, and French willpower as well as material resources.

In the summer and fall of 1781, Washington finally fashioned the crucial victory at Yorktown, thanks to French military assistance on land and sea. Now, for the first time in the war, Washington attacked a British army with superior numbers, while a French fleet under DeGrasse cut off its escape route. At Yorktown there were more French troops under Rochambeau and Lafayette than there were Americans under Washington—and for the moment the sea belonged to France—yet this campaign proved to be the decisive American triumph. After London learned of the loss of a second army—Burgoyne's had been the first—the North ministry fell, and Britain sought to negotiate a peace with the United States.

The peace negotiations were complicated. The United States Congress was not entirely united in its priorities as to boundaries, trade, and fishing rights. France, now bound to honor the objectives of its other ally, Spain, also had multiple, and not always compatible, goals. And Britain maneuvered so that it could retain as much as possible or at least prevent the shift of any advantages to France or Spain. Under these circumstances the negotiations took time. Ultimately the American diplomats Benjamin Franklin, John Adams, and John Jay used their discretion to negotiate terms with Britain, leaving France and its Spanish ally to accept American realpolitik. In light of the United States' pledge to France not to sign a separate treaty, this was not the most elegant or idealistic note on which to end the war for American independence; but the United States, like other nations, faced hard realities at home and abroad that made an early peace imperative. To most Americans, the 1783 Treaty of Paris was cause for celebration.

The difficulty of forming a national army—a challenge in both practical and theoretical terms—is illustrated in the correspondence of John Adams, General George Washington, and the Congress that composes the first three documents in this chapter. Such efforts permitted the United States to respond effectively to the British invasion from Canada led by General Burgoyne. Nevertheless, during much of the war supplies and enlistments lagged. Although patriotic legend emphasizes only the heroism of Revolutionary soldiers, late in the war when supplies and pay were short—as they often were—officers as well as enlisted men might be mutinous. A soldier's vantage point is expressed in the fourth document; whereas the commander's assessment is revealed in Washington's plea for help. The veteran's account of one of the Saratoga battles, in the sixth document, reminds us that warfare is not an abstract chess game but a grim, bloody, human experience in which individuals, as well as nations, pay the price of victory and defeat. In the final pair of documents, a young Massachusetts officer and a soldier's wife, who worked as an army cook and washerwoman, describe the Yorktown battle.

1. John Adams Discusses Military Preparations, 1776

John Adams to Henry Knox

Philadelphia August 25, 1776

Dear Sir . . .

Able Officers, are the Soul of an Army. Gentlemen of Sense, and Knowledge, as well as valour, must be advanced. I wish you would give me in Confidence a List of the best Officers from the Massachusetts, with their Characters. . . . Pray give me, your Sentiments frankly, and candidly. We have been delicate too long. Our Country, is too much interested, in this Subject. Men of Genius and Spirit, must be promoted, wherever they are. . . .

I am a constant Advocate for a regular Army, and the most masterly Discipline, because, I know, that without these We cannot reasonably hope to be a powerfull, a prosperous, or a free People, and therefore, I have been constantly labouring to obtain an handsome Encouragement for inlisting a permanent Body of Troops. But have not as yet prevailed, and indeed, I despair of ever Succeeding, unless the General, and the Officers from the Southward, Should convince Gentlemen here; or unless two or three horrid Defeats, Should bring a more melancholly Conviction, which I expect and believe will one day, or other be the Case.

Reprinted by permission of the publisher from *The Diary and Autobiography of John Adams,* Volumes II and IV, edited by L. H. Butterfield, Cambridge, Mass.: The Belknap Press of Harvard University Press, Copyright © 1961 by the President and Fellows of Harvard College.

Samuel Holden Parsons Reports to John Adams on Massachusetts Officers, 1776

I know I may write in Confidence to you, and therefore will endeavor to give the Characters of your [Massachusetts] Officers as I am able from my Acquaintance, tho' I think the Task hard and not the most agreable.

Colonels

Whitcomb	has no Trace of an Officer, his Men under no Government
Reed	A good Officer not of the most extensive Knowledge but far from being low or despicable
Prescot	A Good Soldier to fight no Sense after Eight o'Clock A.M.
Little	A Midling Officer and of tolerable Genius, not great
Serjeant	has a pretty good Character but I have no Acquaintance
Glover	is said to be a good Officer but am not acquainted
Hutchinson	An easy good Man not of great Genius
Baley	is Nothing
Baldwin	a Personable Man but not of the first Character
Learned	Was a good Officer, is old, Superanuated and Resigned
Greaton	An excellent Disciplinarian his Courage has been questioned, but I dont know with what Justice
Bond	I dont know him
Patterson	A Good Officer of a liberal Education, ingenious and Sensible

Lt. Colonels

Shephard	an excellent Officer none before him, of good Understanding and good common Learning
Jacobs	is less than Nothing
Wesson	An Able Officer
Clap	Pretty good
Reed	Pretty good
Moulton	Am not acquainted
Henshaw	Am not acquainted
Johonnot	Very good a fine Soldier and an extensive Acquaintance

Majors

Sprout	a good, able, Officer
Brooks	an Officer, Soldier, Gentleman and Scholar of the first Character
Smith	a midling Officer
Haydon	a good Officer faithful and prudent not of the most Learning or great Knowledge of the World

Lt. Col. Nixon I had forgot he is a discreet good Officer not of the greatest Mind.

Col. Ward is a diligent faithful Man and a good Soldier.

These are all the Field Officers from your State which I at present recollect with whom I have any Acquaintance; amongst them all tis my Opinion Lt. Col. Shephard would make as good an Officer as any at the Head of a Regiment and that Major Brooks would Honor any Command he Should be appointed to, he is now a Major of Col. Wibb's Regiment and as fit to command a Regiment as any Man in the Lines. Thus you have my Opinion without disguise and I am sure you will make no improper Use of it.

John Adams to Joseph Hawley

Philadelphia Aug. 25, 1776

Dear Sir . . .

We have been apt to flatter ourselves, with gay Prospects of Happiness to the People Prosperity to the State, and Glory to our Arms, from those free Kinds of Governments, which are to be erected in America.

And it is very true that no People ever had a finer opportunity to settle Things upon the best Foundations. But yet I fear that human Nature will be found to be the Same in America as it has been in Europe, and that the true Principles of Liberty will not be Sufficiently attended to.

Knowledge is among the most essential Foundations of Liberty. But is there not a Jealousy or an Envy taking Place among the Multitude of Men of Learning, and, a Wish to exclude them from the public Councils and from military Command? I could mention many Phenomena, in various Parts of these States, which indicate such a growing Disposition. To what Cause Shall I attribute the Surprizing Conduct of the Massachusetts Bay? How has it happened that such an illiterate Group of General and Field Officers, have been thrust into public View, by that Commonwealth which as it has an indisputable Superiority of Power to every other, in America as well as of Experience and Skill in War, ought to have set an Example to her sisters, by sending into the Field her best Men. Men of the most Genius Learning, Reflection, and Address. Instead of this, every Man you send into the Army as a General or a Collonell exhibits a Character, which nobody ever heard of before, or an aukward, illiterate, ill bred Man. . . .

This Conduct is Sinking the Character of the Province, into the lowest Contempt, and is injuring the service beyond description. Able Officers are the Soul of an Army. Good Officers will make good Soldiers, if you give them human Nature as a Material to work upon. But ignorant, unambitious, unfeeling unprincipled Officers, will make bad soldiers of the best Men in the World. . . .

If this is the Effect of popular Elections it is but a poor Pangyrick, upon such Elections. I fear We shall find that popular Elections are not oftener determined, upon pure Principles of Merit, Virtue, and public Spirit, than the Nominations of a Court, if We dont take Care. I fear there is an infinity of Corruption in our Elections already crept in. All kinds of Favour, Intrigue and Partiality in Elections are as real, Corruption in my Mind, as Treats and Bribes. A popular Government is the worse

Curse, to which human Nature can be devoted when it is thoroughly corrupted. Despotism is better. A Sober, conscientious Habit, of electing for the public good alone must be introduced, and every Appearance of Interest, Favour, and Partiality, reprobated, or you will very soon make wise and honest Men wish for Monarchy again, nay you will make them introduce it into America.

There is another Particular, in which it is manifest that the Principles of Liberty have not sufficient Weight in Mens Minds, or are not well understood.

Equality of Representation in the Legislature, is a first Principle of Liberty, and the Moment, the least departure from such Equality takes Place, that Moment an Inroad is made upon Liberty. Yet this essential Principle is disregarded, in many Places, in several of these Republicks. Every County is to have an equal Voice altho some Counties are six times more numerous, and twelve times more wealthy. The Same Iniquity will be established in Congress. R.I. will have an equal Weight with the Mass. The Delaware Government with Pensilvania and Georgia with Virginia. Thus We are sowing the Seeds of Ignorance Corruption, and Injustice, in the fairest Field of Liberty, that ever appeared upon Earth, even in the first Attempts to cultivate it.

2. General George Washington Asks Congress for an Effective Army, 1776

To John Hancock, the President of Congress

Colonel Morris's, on the Heights of Harlem,

September 24, 1776

Sir:

From the hours allotted to Sleep, I will borrow a few Moments to convey my thoughts on sundry important matters to Congress. . . .

We are now as it were, upon the eve of another dissolution of our Army; . . . unless some speedy, and effectual measures are adopted by Congress, our cause will be lost.

It is in vain to expect, that any (or more than a trifling) part of this Army will again engage in the Service on the encouragement offered by Congress. When Men find that their Townsmen and Companions are receiving 20, 30, and more Dollars, for a few Months Service, (which is truely the case) it cannot be expected; without using compulsion; and to force them into the Service would answer no valuable purpose. When Men are irritated, and the Passions inflamed, they fly hastely and chearfully to Arms; but after the first emotions are over, to expect, among such People, as compose the bulk of an Army, that they are influenced by any other principles than those of Interest, is to look for what never did, and I fear never will happen; the Congress will deceive themselves therefore if they expect it.

"General George Washington Asks Congress for an Effective Army, 1776." As found in George Washington, *The Writings of George Washington,* ed. John C. Fitzpatrick (Washington, DC: US Government Printing Office, 1932), 106–116.

A Soldier reasoned with upon the goodness of the cause he is engaged in, and the inestimable rights he is contending for, hears you with patience, and acknowledges the truth of your observations, but adds, that it is of no more Importance to him than others. The Officer makes you the same reply, with this further remark, that his pay will not support him, and he cannot ruin himself and Family to serve his Country, when every Member of the community is equally Interested and benefitted by his Labours. The few therefore, who act upon Principles of disinterestedness, are, comparatively speaking, no more than a drop in the Ocean. It becomes evidently clear then, that as this Contest is not likely to be the Work of a day; as the War must be carried on systematically, and to do it, you must have good Officers, there are, in my Judgment, no other possible means to obtain them but by establishing your Army upon a permanent footing; and giving your Officers good pay; this will induce Gentlemen, and Men of Character to engage; and till the bulk of your Officers are composed of such persons as are actuated by Principles of honour, and a spirit of enterprize, you have little to expect from them.—They ought to have such allowances as will enable them to live like, and support the Characters of Gentlemen; and not be driven by a scanty pittance to the low, and dirty arts which many of them practice, to filch the Public of more than the difference of pay would amount to upon an ample allowe. Besides, something is due to the Man who puts his life in his hands, hazards his health, and forsakes the Sweets of domestic enjoyments. . . . There is nothing that gives a Man consequence, and renders him fit for Command, like a support that renders him Independant of every body but the State he Serves.

With respect to the Men, nothing but a good bounty can obtain them upon a permanent establishment; and for no shorter time than the continuance of the War, ought they to be engaged; as Facts incontestibly prove, that the difficulty, and cost of Inlistments, increase with time. When the Army was first raised at Cambridge, I am persuaded the Men might have been got without a bounty for the War: after this, they began to see that the Contest was not likely to end so speedily as was imagined, and to feel their consequence, by remarking, that to get the Militia In, in the course of last year, many Towns were induced to give them a bounty. . . . I shall therefore take the freedom of giving it as my opinion, that a good Bounty be immediately offered, aided by the proffer of at least 100, or 150 Acres of Land and a suit of Cloaths and Blankt, to each non-Comd. Officer and Soldier; as I have good authority for saying, that however high the Men's pay may appear, it is barely sufficient in the present scarcity and dearness of all kinds of goods, to keep them in Cloaths, much less afford support to their Families. If this encouragement then is given to the Men, and such Pay allowed the Officers as will induce Gentlemen of Character and liberal Sentiments to engage; and proper care and precaution are used in the nomination (having more regard to the Characters of Persons, than the Number of Men they can Inlist) we should in a little time have an Army able to cope with any that can be opposed to it, as there are excellent Materials to form one out of: but while the only merit an Officer possesses is his ability to raise Men; while those Men consider, and treat him as an equal; and (in the Character of an Officer) regard him no more than a broomstick, being mixed together as one common herd; no order, nor no discipline can prevail; nor will the Officer ever meet with that respect which is essentially necessary to due subordination.

To place any dependance upon Militia, is, assuredly, resting upon a broken staff. Men just dragged from the tender Scenes of domestick life; unaccustomed to the din of Arms; totally unacquainted with every kind of Military skill, which being followed by a want of confidence in themselves, when opposed to Troops regularly train'd, disciplined, and appointed, superior in knowledge, and superior in Arms, makes them timid, and ready to fly from their own shadows. Besides, the sudden change in their manner of living, (particularly in the lodging) brings on sickness in many; impatience in all, and such an unconquerable desire of returning to their respective homes that it not only produces shameful, and scandalous Desertions among themselves, but infuses the like spirit in others. Again, Men accustomed to unbounded freedom, and no controul, cannot brook the Restraint which is indispensably necessary to the good order and Government of an Army; without which, licentiousness, and every kind of disorder triumphantly reign. To bring Men to a proper degree of Subordination, is not the work of a day, a Month or even a year; and unhappily for us, and the cause we are Engaged in, the little discipline I have been labouring to establish in the Army under my immediate Command, is in a manner done away by having such a mixture of Troops as have been called together within these few Months.

Relaxed, and unfit, as our Rules and Regulations of War are, for the Government of an Army, the Militia (those properly so called, for of these we have two sorts, the Six Months Men and those sent in as a temporary aid) do not think themselves subject to 'em, and therefore take liberties, which the Soldier is punished for; this creates jealousy; jealousy begets dissatisfaction, and these by degrees ripen into Mutiny; keeping the whole Army in a confused, and disordered State; rendering the time of those who wish to see regularity and good Order prevail more unhappy than Words can describe. Besides this, such repeated changes take place, that all arrangement is set at nought, and the constant fluctuation of things, deranges every plan, as fast as adopted.

These Sir, Congress may be assured, are but a small part of the Inconveniences which might be enumerated and attributed to Militia; but there is one that merits particular attention, and that is the expence. Certain I am, that it would be cheaper to keep 50, or 100,000 Men in constant pay than to depend upon half the number, and supply the other half occasionally by Militia. The time the latter is in pay before and after they are in Camp, assembling and Marching; the waste of Ammunition; the consumption of Stores, which in spite of every Resolution, and requisition of Congress they must be furnished with, or sent home, added to other incidental expences consequent upon their coming, and conduct in Camp, surpasses all Idea, and destroys every kind of regularity and œconomy which you could establish among fixed and Settled Troops; and will, in my opinion prove (if the scheme is adhered to) the Ruin of our Cause.

The Jealousies of a standing Army, and the Evils to be apprehended from one, are remote; and in my judgment, situated and circumstanced as we are, not at all to be dreaded; but the consequence of wanting one, according to my Ideas, formed from the present view of things, is certain, and inevitable Ruin. . . .

Another matter highly worthy of attention, is, that other Rules and Regulations may be adopted for the Government of the Army than those now in existence, otherwise the Army, but for the name, might as well be disbanded. For the most attrocious offences, (one or two Instances only excepted) a Man receives no more than 39 Lashes; and these perhaps (thro' the collusion of the Officer who is to see it inflicted), are given in such a manner as to become rather a matter of sport than punishment. . . . Of late, a practice prevails . . . of Plundering, for under the Idea of Tory property, or property which may fall into the hands of the Enemy, no Man is secure in his effects, and scarcely in his Person; for in order to get at them, we have several Instances of People being frightned out of their Houses under pretence of those Houses being ordered to be burnt, and this is done with a view of seizing the Goods; nay, in order that the villany may be more effectually concealed, some Houses have actually been burnt to cover the theft.

I have with some others, used my utmost endeavours to stop this horrid practice, but under the present lust after plunder, and want of Laws to punish Offenders, I might almost as well attempt to remove Mount Atlas.—I have ordered instant corporal Punishment upon every Man who passes our Lines, or is seen with Plunder. . . .

An Army formed of good Officers moves like Clock-Work; but there is no Situation upon Earth, less enviable, nor more distressing, than that Person's who is at the head of Troops, who are regardless of Order and discipline; and who are unprovided with almost every necessary.

3. Congress Calls on States to Support Continental Army, 1776

PHILADA. Sept. 24th, 1776.

Gentlemen,

You will perceive by the inclosed Resolves, which I have the honor to forward, in obedience to the Commands of Congress, that they have come to a determination to augment our Army, and to engage the Troops to serve during the War. As an Inducement to enlist on these Terms, the Congress have agreed to give, besides a Bounty of twenty dollars, a Hundred Acres of Land to each soldier; and in Case he should fall in Battle, they have resolved that his children, or other Representatives, shall succeed to such Land. . . .

The heavy and enormous expences consequent upon calling for the Militia, the Delay attending their Motions, and the Difficulty of keeping them in the Camp, render it extremely improper to place our whole dependence upon them. Experience hath uniformly convinced us of this, some of the Militia having actually deserted the Camp, at the very moment their services were most wanted. In the mean time the strength of the British Army which is great is rendered much more formidable by the Superior Order and Regularity which prevail in it.

Under these circumstances, and in this Situation of our affairs, it is evident that the Only Means left us of preserving our Liberties, is the Measure which the Congress have now adopted, and which I am ordered most earnestly to recommend

"Congress Calls on States to Support Continental Army, 1776." As found in *Letters of Members of the Continental Congress,* ed. Edmund Cody Burnett (Washington, DC: The Carnegie Institute of Washington, 1921–1936), vol. 1, pp. 98–99.

to you, to carry into immediate effect. Without a well disciplined Army, we can never expect success agst veteran Troops; and it is totally impossible we should have a well disciplined Army, unless our Troops are engaged to serve during the war. To attain therefore this most desirable End, I am to request you will at once, and without a moments delay, bend all your attention to raise your Quota of the American army. . . .

4. A Soldier Views Mutiny Among American Troops, 1780

We left Westfield [New Jersey] about the twenty-fifth of May and went to Basking Ridge to our old winter cantonments. . . . The men were now exasperated beyond endurance; they could not stand it any longer. . . . What was to be done? Here was the army starved and naked, and there their country sitting still and expecting the army to do notable things while fainting from sheer starvation. All things considered, the army was not to be blamed. . . .

We had borne as long as human nature could endure, and to bear longer we considered folly. Accordingly, one pleasant day, the men spent the most of their time upon the parade, growling like soreheaded dogs. At evening roll call they began to show their dissatisfaction by snapping at the officers and acting contrary to their orders. After their dismissal from the parade, the officers went, as usual, to their quarters, except the adjutant, who happened to remain, giving details for next day's duty to the orderly sergeants, or some other business, when the men, none of whom had left the parade began to make him sensible that they had something in train. He said something that did not altogether accord with the soldiers' ideas of propriety, one of the men retorted; the adjutant called him a mutinous rascal, or some such epithet, and then left the parade. This man, then stamping the butt of his musket upon the ground, as much as to say, I am in a passion, called out, "Who will parade with me?" The whole regiment immediately fell in and formed.

We had made no plans for our future operations, but while we were consulting how to proceed, the Fourth Regiment, which lay on our left, formed, and came and paraded with us. We now concluded to go in a body to the other two regiments [the Third and Sixth] that belonged to our brigade and induce them to join with us. These regiments lay forty or fifty rods in front of us, with a brook and bushes between. We did not wish to have anyone in particular to command, lest he might be singled out for a court-martial to exercise its clemency upon. We therefore gave directions to the drummers to give certain signals on the drums; at the first signal we shouldered our arms, at the second we faced, at the third we began our march to join with the other two regiments, and went off with music playing.

By this time our officers had obtained knowledge of our military maneuvering and some of them had run across the brook, by a nearer way than we had taken, it

---

"A Soldier Views Mutiny Among American Troops, 1780." As found in Joseph Plumb Martin, *Private Yankee Doodle: Being a Narrative of Some of the Adventures, Dangers, and Sufferings of a Revolutionary Soldier,* ed. George F. Scheer (Boston: Little, Brown, 1962), 183–187.

being now quite dark, and informed the officers of those regiments of our approach and supposed intentions. The officers ordered their men to parade as quick as possible *without* arms. When that was done, they stationed a camp guard, that happened to be near at hand, between the men and their huts, which prevented them from entering and taking their arms, which they were very anxious to do. Colonel [Return Jonathan] Meigs, of the Sixth Regiment, exerted himself to prevent his men from obtaining their arms until he received a severe wound in his side by a bayonet in the scuffle, which cooled his courage at the time. He said he had always considered himself the soldier's friend and thought the soldiers regarded him as such, but had reason now to conclude he might be mistaken. Colonel Meigs was truly an excellent man and a brave officer. The man, whoever he was, that wounded him, doubtless had no particular grudge against him; it was dark and the wound was given, it is probable, altogether unintentionally. . . .

When we found the officers had been too crafty for us we returned with grumbling instead of music, the officers following in the rear growling in concert. One of the men in the rear calling out, "Halt in front," the officers seized upon him like wolves on a sheep and dragged him out of the ranks, intending to make an example of him for being a "mutinous rascal," but the bayonets of the men pointing at their breasts as thick as hatchel teeth, compelled them quickly to relinquish their hold of him. We marched back to our own parade and then formed again. The officers now began to coax us to disperse to our quarters, but that had no more effect upon us than their threats. One of them slipped away into the bushes, and after a short time returned, counterfeiting to have come directly from headquarters. Said he, "There is good news for you, boys, there has just arrived a large drove of cattle for the army." But this piece of finesse would not avail. All the answer he received for his labor was, "Go and butcher them," or some such slight expression. The lieutenant colonel of the Fourth Regiment now came on to the parade. He could persuade *his* men, he said, to go peaceably to their quarters. After a good deal of palaver, he ordered them to shoulder their arms, but the men taking no notice of him or his order, he fell into a violent passion, threatening them with the bitterest punishment if they did not immediately obey his orders. After spending a whole quiver of the arrows of his rhetoric, he again ordered them to shoulder their arms, but he met with the same success that he did at the first trial. He therefore gave up the contest as hopeless and left us and walked off to his quarters, chewing the cud of resentment all the way, and how much longer I neither knew nor cared. The rest of the officers, after they found that they were likely to meet with no better success than the colonel, walked off likewise to their huts. . . .

After our officers had left us to our own option, we dispersed to our huts and laid by our arms of our own accord, but the worm of hunger gnawing so keen kept us from being entirely quiet. We therefore still kept upon the parade in groups, venting our spleen at our country and government, then at our officers, and then at ourselves for our imbecility in staying there and starving in detail for an ungrateful people who did not care what became of us, so they could enjoy themselves while we were keeping a cruel enemy from them. . . .

Our stir did us some good in the end, for we had provisions directly after, so we had no great cause for complaint for some time.

5. General George Washington Explains Army Problems and Calls for Help, 1780

Gen. George Washington's Circular to the States

Head Quarters, near the Liberty Pole, in
Bergen County, August 27, 1780.

Sir:

The Honble: the Committee of Co-operation having returned to Congress, I am under the disagreeable necessity of informing you that the Army is again reduced to an extremity of distress for want of provision. The greater part of it had been without Meat from the 21st. to the 26th. To endeavour to obtain some relief, I moved down to this place, with a view of stripping the lower parts of the County of the remainder of its Cattle, which after a most rigorous exaction is found to afford between two and three days supply only, and those, consisting of Milch Cows and Calves of one or two years old. When this scanty pittance is consumed, I know not what will be our next resource, as the Commissary can give me no certain information of more than 120 head of Cattle expected from pennsylvania and about 150 from Massachusetts. I mean in time to supply our immediate wants. Military coercion is no longer of any avail, as nothing further can possibly be collected from the Country in which we are obliged to take a position, without depriving the inhabitants of the last morsel. This mode of subsisting, supposing the desired end could be answered by it, besides being in the highest degree distressing to individuals, is attended with ruin to the Morals and discipline of the Army; during the few days which we have been obliged to send out small parties to procure provision for themselves, the most enormous excesses have been committed.

It has been no inconsiderable support of our cause, to have had it in our power to contrast the conduct of our Army with that of the enemy, and to convince the inhabitants that while their rights were wantonly violated by the British Troops, by ours they were respected. This distinction must unhappily now cease, and we must assume the odious character of the plunderers instead of the protectors of the people, the direct consequence of which must be to alienate their minds from the Army and insensibly from the cause. We have not yet been absolutely without Flour, but we have *this* day but *one* days supply in Camp, and I am not certain that there is a single Barrel between this place and Trenton. I shall be obliged therefore to draw down one or two hundred Barrels from a small Magazine which I have endeavoured to establish at West point, for the security of the Garrison in case of a sudden investiture.

From the above state of facts it may be foreseen that this army cannot possibly remain much longer together, unless very vigorous and immediate measures are taken by the States to comply with the requisitions made upon them. The Commissary General has neither the means nor the power of procuring supplies; he is only to receive them from the several Agents. Without a speedy change of circumstances,

---

"General George Washington Explains Army Problems and Calls for Help, 1780." As found in *Letters of Members of the Continental Congress,* ed. Edmund Cody Burnett (Washington, DC: The Carnegie Institute of Washington, 1921–1936), vol. 5, pp. 402–451.

this dilemma will be involved; either the Army must disband, or what is, if possible, worse, subsist upon the plunder of the people. . . . Altho' the troops have upon every occasion hitherto borne their wants with unparralled patience, it will be dangerous to trust too often to a repetition of the causes of discontent.

6. A Veteran Remembers the Battle of Saratoga, 1777

About the tenth day of August, 1777, he was enrolled as a volunteer soldier in a military company under the command of said Capt. Asa Bray at said Southington [in Connecticut] and marched with them through Albany to Saratoga. . . . He would further state that while in this service at Saratoga he was engaged in the battle fought by the hostile armies on the seventh of October, the following particulars of which, together with many others which might be related, he distinctly remembers: viz., that about eleven o'clock in the forenoon of that day, the British troops advanced under the command of General Fraser, who led up the grenadiers, drove in our pickets and advanced guards, and made several unsuccessful charges with fixed bayonets upon the line of the Continental troops at the American redoubts on Bemis Heights, near the headquarters of General Gates. But meeting a repulse at this point of attack, the grenadiers commenced a slow but orderly retreat, still keeping up a brisk fire. After falling back two or three hundred yards, this part of the hostile army met and joined with the main body of the royal troops commanded by Lord Balcarres and General Riedesel. Here, on a level piece of ground of considerable extent called Freeman's Farms, thinly covered with yellow pines, the royal army formed an extensive line with the principal part of their artillery in front. By this time the American line was formed, consisting of Continentals, state troops, and militia. The fire immediately became general through the line with renewed spirit, and nearly the whole force on both sides was brought into action. General Fraser, mounted on a gray horse a little to the right of their center and greatly distinguishing himself by his activity, received a rifle shot through his body (supposed to be from one of Colonel Morgan's sharpshooters), of which he died the next morning at eight o'clock at the Smith house, then the headquarters of General Burgoyne. Soon after this occurrence, the British grenadiers began reluctantly to give ground, and their whole line, within a few minutes, appeared broken. Still, they kept up a respectable fire, both of artillery and musketry.

At about this stage in the action, General Arnold, while galloping up and down our line upon a small brown horse which he had that day borrowed of his friend Leonard Chester of Wethersfield, received a musket ball which broke his leg and killed the horse under him. He was at that moment about forty yards distant from this applicant and in fair view. Isaac Newell of said Southington, since deceased, and one or two others assisted this applicant to extricate Arnold from his fallen horse, placed him on a litter, and sent him back to the headquarters of General Gates.

A regiment of the royal grenadiers, with the brave Major Ackland at their head, in conducting the retreat came to a small cultivated field enclosed by a fence. Here they halted, formed, and made a stand, apparently determined to retrieve what they

"A Veteran Remembers the Battle of Saratoga, 1777." As found in *The Revolution Remembered: Eyewitness Accounts of the War for Independence,* ed. John C. Dann (Chicago: University of Chicago Press, 1980), 240–245.

had lost by their repulse at the redoubts in the commencement of the action. They placed in their center and at each flank a strong battery of brass fieldpieces. The carnage became frightful, but the conflict was of short duration. Their gallant major received a musket ball through both legs, which placed him hors de combat. Retreat immediately ensued, leaving their killed and some of their wounded with two brass fieldpieces on the ground. Ackland, leaning upon a stump of a tree in the corner of the fence, was made prisoner by Adjutant General Wilkinson and his servant, who were passing by. They dismounted from their horses and, placing the major on the servant's horse, sent him to General Gates's headquarters to have his wounds dressed.

The retreat, pursuit, and firing continued till eight o'clock. It was then dark. The royal army continued their retreat about a mile further and there bivouacked for the night. Ours returned to camp, where we arrived between nine and ten o'clock in the evening. About two hundred of our wounded men, during the afternoon, and by that time in the evening, were brought from the field of battle in wagons, and for want of tents, sheds, or any kind of buildings to receive and cover them, were placed in a circular row on the naked ground. It was a clear, but cold and frosty, night. The sufferings of the wounded were extreme, having neither beds under them nor any kind of bed clothing to cover them. Several surgeons were busily employed during the night extracting bullets and performing other surgical operations. This applicant, though greatly fatigued by the exercise of the day, felt no inclination to sleep, but with several others spent the whole night carrying water and administering what other comforts were in our power to the sufferers, about seventy of whom died of their wounds during the night.

The next day (October 8th), this applicant was detached from our company to assist others detached from other companies in burying the dead remaining on the field of battle. This was a sad and laborious day's work. On the cleared field already mentioned and within the compass of a quarter of an acre of ground we found and assisted to bury between twenty and thirty dead bodies of the royal grenadiers. The brigade in which this term of service was performed was commanded by Gen. Oliver Wolcott [one of Connecticut's signers of the Declaration of Independence] of Litchfield. . . .

7. Two Views of the Battle of Yorktown, 1781

Letters from an American Soldier (Benjamin Gilbert)

To His Father and Stepmother

Maubin Hills [Malvern Hill, Va.] 18 July 1781

Honoured Parents

Since writing my last, the Army under Marquis de la fayatte moved towards James Town, where Cornwallis encamped his Troops and on the 6th Instant, a small

---

"Two Views of the Battle of Yorktown, 1781." As found in Benjamin Gilbert, *Winding Down: The Revolutionary War Letters of Lieutenant Benjamin Gilbert of Massachusetts, 1780–1783*, ed. John Shy (Ann Arbor: University of Michigan Press, 1989), 46–49; *The Revolution Remembered: Eyewitness Accounts of the War for Independence*, ed. John C. Dann (Chicago: University of Chicago Press, 1980), 240–245.

part of our army, Detached as a front Guard, fell in with the Enemies Piquet, and drove them into their lines, on which their whole army formed for Action, began the attackt on our detachments. Our Army being at that time from Eight to fifteen miles from the field of action, no immediate support could be lent them, but they maintaining their ground with unexampled Braverey, kept the Enemy at such a distance, as gave time for six Hundred of Pensilvania line to come to their assistance. The Enemies front line at that time conssisted of 2100, our 700 often changing 4 or 5 shots of a side. The Enemy made a violent charge with Bayonetts, and being 3 to 1 they flanked our troops to that degree, that they gave way, and retreated with the loss of all their Dead and two field peices. Our killed, wounded, and missing is 111, some of which Deserted to the enemy in time of Action. The Enemies loss we are not able to assertain, but are informed it is very considerable.* Next Day they crossed the river, leaving all our wounded that fell into their hands on the place of Action. After they had Crossed the River the foot marched toward Portsmouth, and the Horse thro the Center of the Country towards Carolina, where we are in Daily expectations of marching. But I dread the march, our men having not more than one pair of shoes or Hose to Eight men, and the sands are so hot in the middle of the Day that it continually raises Blisters on the mens feet.

To Lieutenant Park Holland

[August 1781]

Dear Park

I shall not attempt to give you any perticular account of the strength or situation of the Enemy. They ly at York[town] and in its Vicinity. Our army are lying in different parts of Kings County upwards of thirty miles from them, and are daily marching. Our Provision is very Indifferent but the duty is not hard. We are Ragged and destitute of Cash which prevents our makeing so great an aquaintence as we should do, were we other ways provided for. The Inhabitints are Exceeding polite and Hospitable which ennables us to make more acquaintence than could be expected with persons in our situation. The Ladies are exceeding Amouris but not So Beautifull as at the Northward, tho there is some rare Beauties amongst them. Amouris Intrigues and Gallantry are every where approved of in this State, and amongst the Vulgar any man that is given to concupcience may have his fill. The Ladies are Exceeding fond of the Northern Gentleman, Esspecially those of the Army. Daily Invitations are given by the Inhabitints for our Gentleman to dine and dring grogg with them where they are generally entertained with musick and the conversation of the Ladies. Yet notwithstanding these diversions, my want of Clothes and Cash and the unwholesomeness of the Climent makes me anxious to return to Head Quarters where I shall Injoye the Company and agreable conversation of my old friends.

---

* This action is known as the Battle of Green Spring. Howard H. Peckham (ed.), *The Toll of Independence* (Chicago, 1974), p. 87, gives the American losses as 28 killed, 99 wounded, and 12 missing, British losses as 75 killed and wounded.

To His Father

Camp near Williamsburg September 19th 1781

Honoured Sir,

Military affairs in this Quarter bears a more favourable Aspect than it has for some time passt. Count De Grass has arived from the West Indias with Twenty eight sail of the line and five Thousand two Hundred french Troops. His Excellency [General Washington] has Arived from Whites plains with Count Rochambeau and has Eight Thousand Troops French and Americans on their way for this place, some of which are arived, the others hourly Expected. Nine Ships of the line with six Hundred french Troops and a large Quantity of Artillerey have arived in the James River. What Troops Pensilvania Maryland and Virginia have Raised this sumer are with us so that a morderate computation makes our strength sixteen Thousand Regulars beside Artilerey Cavalry and Militia. The French fleet has shut Lord Cornwallis into York River and he is fortifying himself in york Town wheir we shall soon lay seige to him. If the French fleet continues long enough and the smile of Providence we shall give as good an account of him as we did of Burgoyine. Nothing but the warmest Expectations of capturing Cornwallis keeps my spirits hight, my Cloths being almost worne out, and no money to get new ones, having Received but 25 Dollars since March Eighty which passed six for one and no expectations of getting any sone.

Recollections of an Army Cook and Washerwoman (Sarah Osborne)

They [the American troops], however, marched immediately for a place called Williamsburg, as she thinks, deponent [Sarah Osborn] alternately on horseback and on foot. There arrived, they remained two days till the army all came in by land and then marched for Yorktown, or Little York as it was then called. The York troops were posted at the right, the Connecticut troops next, and the French to the left. In about one day or less than a day, they reached the place of encampment about one mile from Yorktown. . . . Deponent's attention was arrested by the appearance of a large plain between them and Yorktown and an entrenchment thrown up. She also saw a number of dead Negroes lying round their encampment, whom she understood the British had driven out of the town and left to starve, or were first starved and then thrown out. Deponent took her stand just back of the American tents, say about a mile from the town, and busied herself washing, mending, and cooking for the soldiers, in which she was assisted by the other females; some men washed their own clothing. She heard the roar of the artillery for a number of days, and the last night the Americans threw up entrenchments, it was a misty, foggy night, rather wet but not rainy. Every soldier threw up for himself, as she understood, and she afterwards saw and went into the entrenchments. Deponent's said husband was there throwing up entrenchments, and deponent cooked and carried in beef, and bread, and coffee (in a gallon pot) to the soldiers in the entrenchment.

On one occasion when deponent was thus employed carrying in provisions, she met General Washington, who asked her if she "was not afraid of the cannonballs?"

She replied, "No, the bullets would not cheat the gallows," that "It would not do for the men to fight and starve too."

They dug entrenchments nearer and nearer to Yorktown every night or two till the last. While digging that, the enemy fired very heavy till about nine o'clock next morning, then stopped, and the drums from the enemy beat excessively. Deponent was a little way off in Colonel Van Schaick's or the officers' marquee and a number of officers were present, among whom was Captain Gregg, who, on account of infirmities, did not go out much to do duty.

The drums continued beating, and all at once the officers hurrahed and swung their hats, and deponent asked them, "What is the matter now?"

One of them replied, "Are not you soldier enough to know what it means?"

Deponent replied, "No."

They then replied, "The British have surrendered."

Deponent, having provisions ready, carried the same down to the entrenchments that morning, and four of the soldiers whom she was in the habit of cooking for ate their breakfasts.

Deponent stood on one side of the road and the American officers upon the other side when the British officers came out of the town and rode up to the American officers and delivered up [their swords, which the deponent] thinks were returned again, and the British officers rode right on before the army, who marched out beating and playing a melancholy tune, their drums covered with black handkerchiefs and their fifes with black ribbands tied around them, into an old field and there grounded their arms and then returned into town again to await their destiny. Deponent recollects seeing a great many American officers, some on horseback and some on foot, but cannot call them all by name. Washington, Lafayette, and Clinton were among the number. The British general at the head of the army was a large, portly man, full face, and the tears rolled down his cheeks as he passed along. She does not recollect his name, but it was not Cornwallis. She saw the latter afterwards and noticed his being a man of diminutive appearance and having cross eyes.

E S S A Y S

The question of why men fight is crucial in every war, and especially when a representative government relies on volunteers. In the first essay, John W. Shy, the distinguished University of Michigan scholar of war and American society, explores the interplay of interests confronting Congress and American soldiers during the war. By comparing myths and realities in his essay on "Long Bill" Scott, Shy reveals that the question of motive—why men fought—may be answered at several levels. In the second essay, the much celebrated and much maligned role of the militia is assessed by Professor Don Higginbotham, a leading scholar on the Revolutionary War, who teaches at the University of North Carolina, Chapel Hill.

Hearts and Minds: The Case of "Long Bill" Scott

JOHN W. SHY

Armed force, and nothing else, decided the outcome of the American Revolution. . . . Crude, obvious, and unappealing as this truism may be, it is still true; without war to sustain it, the Declaration of Independence would be a forgotten, abortive manifesto.

Writing about an earlier revolutionary war, Thomas Hobbes rammed home the point when he said that "covenants without swords are but words."

But the cynicism of Hobbes can too easily mask a second, equally important truism, perhaps best expressed a century later by David Hume. "As force is always on the side of the governed," Hume wrote, "the governors have nothing to support them but opinion." For all their peculiar aggressiveness, even human beings do not kill and risk death for no reason. Beneath the raw irrationality of violence lies motive—some psychic web spun from logic, belief, perception, and emotion that draws people to commit terrible acts and to hazard everything they possess. . . . If Hobbes—like all his fellow cynics down through history—is right in believing that public opinion is a fairly fragile flower which can seldom survive the hot wind of violence, Hume reminds us that no one, not even a soldier, uses force without somehow being moved to do so.

John Adams put his finger on this matter of motivation when he said that the real American Revolution, the revolution that estranged American hearts from old British loyalties and readied American minds to use (and to withstand) massive violence, was over before the war began. But Adams also opined that a third of the American people supported the Revolutionary cause, another third remained more or less loyal to Britain, and that the rest were neutral or apathetic. Clearly, Adams conceded that not all hearts and minds had been permanently affected in the same way. Many British observers thought that the real American Revolutionaries were the religious Dissenters, Congregationalists and Presbyterians who had always been secretly disloyal to the Crown because they rejected the whole Anglican Establishment, whose head was the king; and that these Revolutionaries persuaded poor Irishmen, who poured into the American colonies in great numbers during the middle third of the eighteenth century, to do most of the dirty business of actual fighting. American Whigs, on the other hand, generally assumed that all decent, sane people supported the Revolution, and that those who did not could be categorized as timid, vicious, corrupt, or deluded. . . .

Like these stock opinions, we have two standard images of the popular response to the Revolutionary War. One is of whole towns springing to arms as Paul Revere carried his warning to them in the spring of 1775. The other is of a tiny, frozen, naked band of men at Valley Forge, all that are left when everyone else went home in the winter of 1778. Which is the true picture? Both, evidently. But that answer is of no use at all when we ask whether the Revolution succeeded only by the persistence of a very small group of people, the intervention of France, and great good luck; or whether the Revolution was—or became—unbeatable because the mass of the population simply would not give up the struggle, and the British simply could not muster the force and the resolution to kill them all or break their will or sit on all or even any large proportion of them. This problem posed by the motivation for violence breaks down into more specific questions: Who actually took up arms and why? How strong was the motivation to serve, and to keep serving in spite of defeat and other adversities? What was the intricate interplay and feedback between attitude and behavior, events and attitude? Did people get war weary and discouraged, or did they become adamant toward British efforts to coerce them? If we could answer these questions with confidence, not only would we know why the rebels won and the government lost, but we would also know important things about the American society that emerged from seven years of armed conflict. . . .

The essential difficulty in answering these questions lies less in the lack of evidence than in the nature of the subject. Violence, with all its ramifications, remains a great mystery for students of human life, while the deeper motivational sources of human behavior—particularly collective behavior under conditions of stress—are almost equally mysterious. . . .

A suitably humble approach to these difficult questions lies at hand in a book written by Peter Oliver, who watched the Revolution explode in Boston. Oliver descended from some of the oldest families of Massachusetts Bay, he was a distinguished merchant and public official, and he became a bitter Tory. His book, *The Origin and Progress of the American Rebellion,* . . . is a fascinatingly unsympathetic version of the Revolution, and in it Oliver makes an attempt to answer some of our questions. . . . Oliver asked a wounded American lieutenant, who had been captured at Bunker Hill, how he had come to be a rebel. The American officer allegedly replied as follows:

> The case was this Sir! I lived in a Country Town; I was a Shoemaker, & got my Living by my Labor. When this Rebellion came on, I saw some of my Neighbors get into Commission, who were no better than myself. I was very ambitious, & did not like to see those Men above me. I was asked to enlist, as a private Soldier. My Ambition was too great for so low a Rank; I offered to enlist upon having a Lieutenants Commission; which was granted. I imagined my self now in a way of Promotion: if I was killed in Battle, there would an end of me, but if my Captain was killed, I should rise in Rank, & should still have a Chance to rise higher. These Sir! were the only Motives of my entering into the Service; for as to the Dispute between great Britain & the Colonies, I know nothing of it; neither am I capable of judging whether it is right or wrong.

Now the lieutenant was not a figment of Oliver's embittered imagination. His name is given by Oliver as Scott, and American records show that Lieutenant William Scott, of Colonel Paul Sargent's regiment, was indeed wounded and captured at Bunker Hill. Scott turns out, upon investigation, to have been an interesting character. Perhaps the first thing to be said about him is that nothing in the record of his life down to 1775 contradicts anything in Oliver's account of the interview. Scott came from Peterborough, New Hampshire, a town settled in the 1730s by Irish Presbyterians. Scott's father had served in the famous Rogers' Rangers during the French and Indian War. At the news of the outbreak of fighting in 1775, a cousin who kept the store in Peterborough recruited a company of local men to fight the British. Apparently the cousin tried to enlist our William Scott—known to his neighbors as "Long Bill," thus distinguishing him from the cousin, "Short Bill." But "Long Bill"—our Bill—seems to have declined serving as a private, and insisted on being a lieutenant if cousin "Short Bill" was going to be a captain. "Short Bill" agreed. So far the stories as told by Oliver and as revealed in the New Hampshire records check perfectly. Nor is there any reason to think that "Long Bill" had a deeper understanding of the causes of the Revolution than appear in Oliver's version of the interview.

What Peter Oliver never knew was the subsequent life history of this battered yokel, whose view of the American rebellion seemed so pitifully naive. When the British evacuated Boston, they took Scott and other American prisoners to Halifax,

Nova Scotia. There, after more than a year in captivity, Scott somehow managed to escape, to find a boat, and to make his way back to the American army just in time for the fighting around New York City in 1776. Captured again in November, when Fort Washington and its garrison fell to a surprise British assault, Scott escaped almost immediately, this time by swimming the Hudson River at night—according to a newspaper account—with his sword tied around his neck and his watch pinned to his hat. He returned to New Hampshire during the winter of 1777 to recruit a company of his own; there, he enlisted his two eldest sons for three years or the duration of the war. Stationed in the Boston area, he marched against Burgoyne's invading army from Canada, and led a detachment that cut off the last retreat just before the surrender near Saratoga. Scott later took part in the fighting around Newport, Rhode Island. But when his light infantry company was ordered to Virginia under Lafayette in early 1781, to counter the raiding expedition led by Benedict Arnold, Scott's health broke down; long marches and hot weather would make the old Bunker Hill wounds ache, and he was permitted to resign from the army. After only a few months of recuperation, however, he seems to have grown restless, for we find him during the last year of the war serving as a volunteer on a navy frigate.

What would Scott have said if Oliver had been able to interview him again, after the war? We can only guess. Probably he would have told Oliver that his oldest son had died in the army, not gloriously, but of camp fever, after six years of service. Scott might have said that in 1777 he had sold his Peterborough farm in order to meet expenses, but that the note which he took in exchange turned into a scrap of paper when the dollar of 1777 became worth less than two cents by 1780. He might also have said that another farm, in Groton, Massachusetts, slipped away from him, along with a down payment that he had made on it, when his military pay depreciated rapidly to a fraction of its nominal value. He might not have been willing to admit that when his wife died he simply turned their younger children over to his surviving elder son, and then set off to beg a pension or a job from the government. Almost certainly he would not have told Oliver that when the son—himself sick, his corn crop killed by a late frost, and saddled with three little brothers and sisters— begged his father for help, our hero told him, should all else fail, to hand the children over to the selectmen of Peterborough—in short, to put them on welfare.

In 1792, "Long Bill" Scott once more made the newspapers: he rescued eight people from drowning when their small boat capsized in New York harbor. But heroism did not pay very well. At last, in 1794, Secretary of War Henry Knox made Scott deputy storekeeper at West Point; and a year later General Benjamin Lincoln took Scott with him to the Ohio country, where they were to negotiate with the Indians and survey the land opened up by Anthony Wayne's victory at Fallen Timbers. At last he had a respectable job, and even a small pension for his nine wounds; but Lincoln's group caught something called "lake fever" while surveying on the Black River, near Sandusky. Scott, ill himself, guided part of the group back to Fort Stanwix, New York, then returned for the others. It was his last heroic act. A few days after his second trip, he died, on September 16, 1796.

Anecdotes, even good ones like the touching saga of "Long Bill" Scott, do not make history; . . . yet the story of his life leads us directly—and at the level of ordinary people—toward crucial features of the process.

Peterborough, New Hampshire, in 1775 had a population of 549. Town, state, and federal records show that about 170 men were credited to Peterborough as performing some military service during the Revolution. In other words, almost every adult male, at one time or another, carried a gun in the war. But of these 170 participants, less than a third performed extensive service; that is, service ranging from over a year up to the whole eight years of the war. And only a fraction of these—less than two dozen—served as long as Bill Scott. In Scott we are not seeing a typical participant, but one of a small "hard core" of revolutionary fighters—the men who stayed in the army for more than a few months or a single campaign. As we look down the list of long-service soldiers from Peterborough, they seem indeed to be untypical people. A few, like Scott and his cousin "Short Bill" and James Taggart and Josiah Munroe, became officers or at least sergeants, and thereby acquired status and perhaps some personal satisfaction from their prolonged military service. But most of the hard core remained privates, and they were an unusually poor, obscure group of men, even by the rustic standards of Peterborough. Many—like John Alexander, Robert Cunningham, William Ducannon, Joseph Henderson, Richard Richardson, John Wallace, and Thomas Williamson—were recruited from outside the town, from among men who never really lived in Peterborough. Whether they lived *anywhere*—in the strict legal sense—is a question. Two men—Zaccheus Brooks and John Miller—are simply noted as "transients." At least two—James Hackley and Randall McAllister—were deserters from the British army. At least two others—Samuel Weir and Titus Wilson—were black men, Wilson dying as a prisoner of war. A few, like Michael Silk, simply appear, join the army, then vanish without a documentary trace. Many more reveal themselves as near the bottom of the socioeconomic ladder: Hackley, Benjamin Allds, Isaac Mitchell, Ebenezer Perkins, Amos Spofford, Jonathan Wheelock, and Charles White were legal paupers after the Revolution, Joseph Henderson was a landless day-laborer, Samuel Spear was jailed for debt, and John Miller was mentally deranged.

We can look at the whole Peterborough contingent in another way, in terms of those in it who were, or later became, prominent or at least solid citizens of the town. With a few exceptions, like "Short Bill" Scott and "Long Bill"'s son John, who survived frost-killed corn and a parcel of unwanted siblings to become a selectman and a leader of the town, these prominent men and solid citizens had served in the war for only short periods—a few months in 1775, a month or two in the Burgoyne emergency of 1777, maybe a month in Rhode Island or a month late in the war to bolster the key garrison of West Point. The pattern is clear, and it is a pattern that reappears wherever the surviving evidence has permitted a similar kind of inquiry. Lynn, Massachusetts; Berks County, Pennsylvania; Colonel Smallwood's recruits from Maryland in 1782; several regiments of the Massachusetts Line; a sampling of pension applicants from Virginia—all show that the hard core of Continental soldiers, the Bill Scotts who could not wrangle commissions, the soldiers at Valley Forge, the men who shouldered the heaviest military burden, were something *less* than average colonial Americans. As a group, they were poorer, more marginal, less well anchored in the society. Perhaps we should not be surprised; it is easy to imagine men like these actually being attracted by the relative affluence, comfort, security, prestige, and even the chance for satisfying human relationships offered by the Continental army. Revolutionary America may have been a middle-class society, happier and more prosperous than any other in its time, but it contained a large and growing number of fairly poor people, and many of them did much of the actual fighting and suffering between 1775 and 1783: A very old story.

The large proportion of men, from Peterborough and other communities, who served only briefly might thus seem far less important to our subject than the disadvantaged minority who did such a large part of the heavy work of revolution. This militarily less active majority were of course the militiamen. One could compile a large volume of pithy observations, beginning with a few dozen from Washington himself, in which the military value of the militia was called into question. The nub of the critique was that these part-time soldiers were untrained, undisciplined, undependable, and very expensive, consuming pay, rations, clothing, and weapons at a great rate in return for short periods of active service. . . .

To understand the Revolutionary militia and its role, we must go back to the year before the outbreak of fighting at Lexington and Concord. Each colony, except Pennsylvania, had traditionally required every free white adult male, with a few minor occupational exceptions, to be inscribed in a militia unit, and to take part in training several times a year. . . . Their real function might be described as a hybrid of draft board and modern reserve unit—a modicum of military training combined with a mechanism to find and enlist individuals when they were needed. But the colonial militia did not simply slide smoothly into the Revolution. Militia officers, even where they were elected, held royal commissions, and a significant number of them were not enthusiastic about rebellion. Purging and restructuring the militia was an important step toward revolution, one that deserves more attention than it has had.

When the news reached America that Parliament would take a very hard line in response to the Boston Tea Party, and in particular had passed a law that could destroy, economically and politically, the town of Boston, the reaction in the colonies was stronger and more nearly unanimous than at any time since the Stamp Act. No one could defend the Boston Port Act; it was an unprecedented, draconian law, the possible consequences of which seemed staggering. Radicals, like Samuel Adams, demanded an immediate and complete break in commercial relations with the rest of the Empire. Boycotts had worked effectively in the past, and they were an obvious response to the British hard line. More moderate leaders, however, dreaded a hasty confrontation that might quickly escalate beyond their control, and they used democratic theory to argue that nothing ought to be done without a full and proper consultation of the popular will. Like the boycott, the consultative congress had a respectable pedigree, and the moderates won the argument. When Congress met in September 1774 there were general expectations in both Britain and America that it would cool and seek to compromise the situation.

Exactly what happened to disappoint those expectations is even now not wholly clear; our own sense that Congress was heading straight toward revolution and independence distorts a complex moment in history, when uncertainty about both ends and means deeply troubled the minds of most decision-makers. Congress had hardly convened when it heard that the British had bombarded Boston. For a few days men from different colonies, normally suspicious of one another, were swept together by a wave of common fear and apprehension. Though the report was quickly proved false, these hours of mutual panic seem to have altered the emotional economy of the Congress. Soon afterward it passed without any serious dissent a resolution in favor of the long-advocated boycott, to be known as the Association. Local committees were to gather signatures for the Association, and were to take necessary steps to enforce its provisions. The Association was the vital link in transforming the colonial militia into a revolutionary organization. . . .

In some places, like Peterborough, the same men who were enrolled in the militia became the strong right arm of the local committee; reluctant militia officers were ignored because, after all, not the militia as such but a voluntary association of militia members was taking the action. . . . The new Revolutionary militia might look very much like the old colonial militia, but it was, in its origins, less a draft board and a reserve training unit than a police force and an instrument of political surveillance. Although the boycott could be defended to moderate men as a constitutional, nonviolent technique, its implementation had radical consequences. Adoption by Congress gave it a legitimacy and a unity that it could have gained in no other way. . . .

It is difficult to overestimate the importance of what happened in 1775 to engage mass participation on the side of the Revolution. The new militia, which repeatedly denied that it was in rebellion and proclaimed its loyalty to the Crown, enforced a boycott intended to make Britain back down; Britain did not back down, but the attempt drew virtually everyone into the realm of politics. Enlistment, training, and occasional emergencies were the means whereby dissenters were identified, isolated, and dealt with. Where the new militia had trouble getting organized, there, Revolutionary activists could see that forceful intervention from outside might be needed. Connecticut units moved into the New York City area; Virginia troops moved into the Delmarva peninsula; in Pennsylvania, men from Reading and Lancaster marched into Bucks County. Once established, the militia became the infrastructure of revolutionary government. It controlled its community, whether through indoctrination or intimidation; it provided on short notice large numbers of armed men for brief periods of emergency service; and it found and persuaded, drafted or bribed, the smaller number of men needed each year to keep the Continental army alive. After the first months of the war, popular enthusiasm and spontaneity could not have sustained the struggle; only a pervasive armed organization, in which almost everyone took some part, kept people constantly, year after year, at the hard task of revolution. While Scott and his sons, the indigent, the blacks, and the otherwise socially expendable men fought the British, James and Samuel Cunningham, Henry Ferguson, John Gray, William McNee, Benjamin Mitchell, Robert Morison, Alexander and William Robbe, Robert Swan, Robert Wilson, and four or five men named Smith—all militiamen, but whose combined active service hardly equalled that of "Long Bill" Scott alone—ran Peterborough, expelling a few Tories, scraping up enough recruits for the Continental army to meet the town's quota every spring, taking time out to help John Stark destroy the Germans at the battle of Bennington.

The mention of Tories brings us, briefly, to the last aspect of our subject. . . . Peterborough had little trouble with Tories; the most sensational case occurred when the Presbyterian minister, the Rev. John Morrison, who had been having difficulties with his congregation, deserted his post as chaplain to the Peterborough troops and entered British lines at Boston in June 1775. But an informed estimate is that a half million Americans can be counted as loyal to Britain. Looking at the absence of serious Loyalism in Peterborough, we might conclude that Scotch-Irish Presbyterians almost never were Tories. That, however, would be an error of fact, and we are impelled to seek further for an explanation. What appears as we look at places like Peterborough, where Tories are hardly visible, and at other places where Toryism was rampant, is a pattern—not so much an ethnic, religious, or ideological pattern, but a pattern of raw power. Wherever the British and their allies were strong enough to penetrate in force—along the seacoast, in the Hudson, Mohawk, and lower Delaware valleys, in Georgia, the Carolinas, and the transappalachian West—there Toryism flourished. But geographically less exposed areas, if population density made self-defense feasible—most of New England, the Pennsylvania hinterland, and piedmont Virginia—where the enemy hardly appeared or not at all, there Tories either ran away, kept quiet, even serving in the rebel armies, or occasionally took a brave but hopeless stand against Revolutionary committees and their gunmen. After the war, of course, men remembered their parts in the successful Revolution in ways that make it difficult for the historian to reconstruct accurately the relationship between what they thought and what they did.

The view here presented of how armed force and public opinion were mobilized may seem a bit cynical—a reversion to Thomas Hobbes. True, it gives little weight to ideology, to perceptions and principles, to grievances and aspirations, to the more admirable side of the emergent American character. Perhaps that is a weakness; perhaps I have failed to grasp what really drove Bill Scott. But what strikes me most forcibly in studying this part of the Revolution is how much in essential agreement almost all Americans were in 1774, both in their views of British measures and in their feelings about them. What then is puzzling, and thus needs explaining, is why so many of these people behaved in anomalous and in different ways. Why did so many, who did not intend a civil war or political independence, get so inextricably involved in the organization and use of armed force? Why did relatively few do most of the actual fighting? Why was a dissenting fifth of the population so politically and militarily impotent, so little able to affect the outcome of the struggle? Answers to these questions cannot be found in the life of one obscure man, or in the history of one backwoods town. But microscopic study does emphasize certain features of the American Revolution: the political structuring of resistance to Britain, the play of social and economic factors in carrying on that resistance by armed force, and the brutally direct effects on behavior, if not on opinions, of military power.

The Strengths and Weaknesses of the Militia

DON HIGGINBOTHAM

"There, my lads, are the Hessians! Tonight our flag floats over yonder hill, or Molly Stark is a widow." Those were the famous words of General John Stark to his militiamen on the eve of the Battle of Bennington, and thanks to them Molly Stark did not lose her vain and volatile husband. For on August 16, 1777, Stark's New Hampshire and Vermont followers smashed a column of Germans from General John Burgoyne's British army, a little gem of a triumph with far-reaching consequences.

Before we sing Stark's praises, other more sobering facts are in order. The Continental Congress had recently rebuked Stark for failing to unite his band with the

Reconsiderations on the Revolutionary War, Don Higginbotham. Copyright © 1978 by Don Higginbotham. Reproduced with permission of Greenwood Publishing Group, Inc., Westport, CT.

American northern army and place himself under the jurisdiction of its commander. If we are inclined to agree with the historian who commented that this was one occasion when insubordination achieved splendid results, we might look ahead to October 7 of that same year: within minutes of General Horatio Gates's climactic battle of the Saratoga campaign against Burgoyne, Stark departed from Gates's camp with his entire militia because their enlistments had expired. These episodes illustrate the complexity of analyzing the performance of militia in the War of Independence.

My purpose in examining the militia is several-fold: to put in historical perspective the approach of previous generations to this subject and, more importantly, to weave together recent strands of scholarship and to add something of my own—to achieve, all told, a kind of overview. . . .

There is a decidedly negative image of the militia in most of our historical literature. Taking as a prime case in point Stark's irresponsibility at Saratoga, C. H. Van Tyne, in his Pulitzer Prize–winning account of the war, declared that "few events . . . so proved the utter failure of the militia system."

When did this view originate? One must commence with Washington and his generals of the Continental Army who labored strenuously and for the most part futilely to secure a long-term professional army modeled in important respects after contemporary European systems. Only such a formidable, well-structured military arm could exchange blow for blow with the legions of Gage, Howe, and Clinton. The militia were seen as poorly trained, ill-disciplined, and unreliable. They were, complained General Nathanael Greene, "people coming from home with all the tender feelings of domestic life" and "not sufficiently fortified with natural courage to stand the shocking scenes of war. To march over dead men, to hear without concern the groans of the wounded, I say few men can stand such scenes unless steeled by habit or fortified by military pride."

The temporary soldiers were wasteful of supplies and weapons. General John Lacey of Pennsylvania, himself a state-level officer, conceded in 1777 that departing militia "had left their camp equipage strewed everywhere—Muskets, Cartouchboxes, Camp kettels, and blankets—some in and some out of the huts the men had left, with here and there a Tent—some standing and some fallen down." Local units made off with so many Continental weapons that Washington implored "that every possible means may be used to recover them [for] the public and no more delivered to Militia."

Small wonder, given these attitudes, that serious friction erupted between Continentals and militia. To Joseph Reed, president of the Executive Council of Pennsylvania, "the jealousy which has taken place in this State, between the Continental troops and them, very much" resembled "the behaviour of the [British] Regulars and our Provincials" in the French and Indian War. Reed cautioned Nathanael Greene that, if the Rhode Island general had in fact been guilty of criticizing militia (as was reported in Philadelphia), he might be more guarded in his future comments. More openly contemptuous was a Colonel Jackson of the Continental line, who, in sending a detachment of regulars to Dorchester, Massachusetts, in 1777, instructed the captain in charge to take no orders from Colonel Thomas Crafts of the militia. . . .

. . . Jackson was scarcely the only Continental colonel who looked askance at taking orders from a militia general. "I have the fullest confidence that you will not put me in a Situation to be commanded by General Herkimer" of the militia, pleaded Colonel Goose Van Schaick, a regular, to Governor George Clinton of New York in 1777. These sentiments were echoed in 1780 by Colonel Daniel Morgan of the Continentals, who warned General Gates that he would find it humiliating to take orders from Virginia militia brigadiers.

Such condescension seemed so well founded that in the postwar years the militia were all but totally excluded from a rightful place in the Revolutionary firmament. Histories of the period focused upon the Continental Army, commanded by Washington, who quite understandably drew the spotlight to events associated with him. Furthermore, the narrator's task was simplified by staying center stage, avoiding the briars and brambles of the wings or peripheral areas where the militia usually operated. Finally, much of our military history was penned by professional soldiers, like Emory Upton, with an ax to grind for a professional military establishment. In our day, however, this traditionally harsh portrait of Revolutionary militia is being challenged. The impact of guerrilla or irregular warfare in the post-1945 world has spawned a desire to understand the place of nonregulars in the winning of independence.

Let us now turn to three somewhat interrelated questions. Who were the militia? What were their functions in the war? And which of those functions did they handle best? The first query sounds easier than it really is. To be sure, the English colonies had included most free white males within the militia structure, and this near universal requirement did not change in 1775 or 1776. Several current researchers have stated or implied that the actual composition of the state militias and the Continental Army was considerably different; that the productive citizens preferred service in the local military outfit, which would normally remain fairly close to home; that the Continentals came substantially from the lower echelons of American society—indentured servants, paid substitutes, farm laborers, unemployed persons, and transients, to say nothing of Blacks and British deserters.

These configurations have led to the conclusion that the long-suffering Continentals at Valley Forge and elsewhere were, rather than freedom fighters, mercenaries not much unlike those in European armies. Perhaps so; there is no need to sugarcoat our history. Still, if enlistees counted the monetary features of shouldering muskets as the overwhelming attraction, why were American armies always so short of manpower? . . .

Undoubtedly motivation for service—both militia and Continentals—must be examined in several contexts, including time and place. The patriotic response early in the war tended to be enthusiastic, especially that of the New England militia; but at the same time the Continental rifle companies to be raised in the frontier counties from Virginia to Pennsylvania were quickly filled, with many would-be volunteers left behind. Recruiting for Continental and state establishments as well probably suffered in areas—Philadelphia and parts of Maryland, for example—where the dominant political elites were unpopular and where class divisions worsened as a result of economic friction over war profiteering and the hoarding of goods.

Militia officers too are worth some analysis. Colonial Americans had actively sought commissions in the militia, as much for reasons of prestige as anything else. Even Jefferson, of all people, was a county lieutenant in Virginia. Whereas in New

England there was a tradition of electing militia officers, the conflict with Britain saw the extension of that practice, especially below field grade, to New York, New Jersey, Pennsylvania, Maryland, and southward. The demand for officers was infinitely greater than ever—than for any of the colonial wars or, quite obviously, for the periods of peace, since militia organizations had deteriorated or become virtually extinct between imperial conflicts. Then, too, some former officers declined to serve in the revamped patriot forces because they were loyalists; while others, accused of being on the king's side, were squeezed out. Consequently, the officer ranks were opened dramatically, as in Maryland. . . .

Expanding the social range of militia officers had significant democratic implications in Maryland and elsewhere. Because local tensions engendered uneven support for the war, Maryland officers at times found their men extremely difficult to control, and officers themselves, willingly or through duress, took positions held by the rank and file. On the other hand, in New England, with its strong whig fervor, militia companies not only picked their officers, but sometimes members of a company adopted a document—a kind of covenant—stating their concerns and principles, their rules of behavior, and their limits or restrictions upon their officers' authority. "What you have," writes Alfred F. Young, "is not quite Cromwell's soldiers debating around the campfires (although maybe some of that) but a democratic soldiery with all the implications of that word."

The election of officers scarcely ever resulted in elevating the ablest men to leadership positions. Thus the New York provincial congress urged in December 1775 that militia officers be picked subsequently "according to their true merit and ability to serve the public." Few newly chosen officers were as self-effacing as a Mr. Beeker of Tryon County, New York, who, it was reported, "modestly declined" appointment to command a company, "alleging his want of education and experience for a station involving so much responsibility." Instead, Beeker proposed a Mr. Luke, who evidently had some military background and who was then "elected by a large majority." Once the training began, so our informant continues, French and Indian War veterans "were particularly engaged in giving instruction and advice," as was also true in Philadelphia and elsewhere. . . .

Officers with the most extensive experience in earlier wars often accepted Continental commissions. Later the leadership of the militia was bolstered by officers who resigned from the regular army, returned home, and took rank in the militia. . . .

But, for the most part, such individuals came home to continue their military careers in the state constabularies. And that, not infrequently, brought political gain from their militia exploits. . . .

When Virginians replaced Jefferson as the state's chief executive in 1781, they tapped General Thomas Nelson, head of the militia since 1777; and Nelson was elevated principally because of his military reputation. Another governorship appears to bear militia-versus-Continental overtones: the 1777 election in New York of Brigadier General George Clinton of the militia over Major General Philip Schuyler of the Continental line, with Clinton projecting the image—synonymous with the militia—of being a man of the people, militantly anti-tory.

Now for our second question: the function of the militia in the War of Independence. It is abundantly clear what that institution could not do: namely, carry the brunt of the conflict. Militia units, John Shy reminds us, had done relatively little fighting as regular formations in the colonial wars. Their previous responsibilities were more "a hybrid of draft board and modern reserve unit—a modicum of military training combined with a mechanism to find and enlist individuals when they were needed." Therefore, the Continental Congress opted to wage war by means of a Continental army, whose general favored minimal reliance upon militia. From the army's camp at Cambridge in 1775, Nathanael Greene asserted, "With regard to the Militia we have no occasion for them. We have here as many of the Province Militia as we know what to do with." Greene's feelings had not changed, only deepened, when he vowed some months later that "all the force in America should be under one Commander raised and appointed by the same Authority, subjected to the same Regulations and ready to be detacht where ever Occasion may require."

Even if Congress and the states responded by raising a formidable army, Washington was a realist; his own forces would hardly be able to contest British regulars and to defend the colonies against their internal enemies as well. "The Militia," he counseled, in explaining his unwillingness to respond to various local crises, should be "more than competent to all purposes" of internal security. Actually, he probably intended to alert colony leaders that they would have to fend for themselves against loyalists, potentially hostile blacks in their midst, and Indians on their frontiers. To scatter his regiments, to be at all places at all times, would have reduced the Virginian to small-unit operations. Unable to openly contend with General William Howe and his successors, Washington would have had no alternative to guerrilla warfare, or what was known then as partisan war, or *la petite guerre*.

Washington instead advocated a response to the enemy that, in modern terminology, is known as the principle of concentration, or mass. "It is of the greatest importance to the safety of a Country involved in a defensive war," he explained, "to endeavor to draw their Troops together at some post at the opening of a Campaign, so central to the theater of War that they may be sent to the support of any part of the Country [that] the Enemy may direct their motions against."

His thinking made sense. To divide his own army would invite his adversaries to defeat it in detail. Besides, a guerrilla conflict had other disadvantages. One might harass and annoy the enemy effectively without its being beaten decisively or driven from the country. That kind of aggressiveness was a tall order, but Congress wanted it. The lawmakers wished the army to stand and fight; and Washington was combative by instinct, although after 1776 he became more cautious, endeavoring to choose the moment and the place that would provide him the greatest advantage and the smallest risk. Then, too, a guerrilla struggle would pose internal dangers to the cause: such physical destruction, such savagery and bloodletting, that the internal institutions of the country, along with the political and legal processes, might fall sacrifice to the war. And in the main, the Revolution's leaders were conservative in both political and military outlook; their principal aims were to preserve and build rather than to tear down and destroy. Finally, the presence of the Continental Army intact offered Americans a symbol of unity and an object of national feeling, just as it was to the outside world—where the patriots hoped to get tangible support—a sign of conventional military strength.

So, in Washington's view, the Continentals and militia had separate, although mutually supportive, roles to play. To improve the militia's effectiveness and to create a degree of uniformity everywhere, Congress made recommendations to the colonies as to the size and organization of regiments. If these proposals were disregarded, they were still definitely in order; for although the patriot militias were to resemble closely their colonial predecessors, the Americans encountered problems in reviving that military instrument. Initial laws were enacted in such haste that they had to be amended or superseded with more comprehensive statutes.

Maryland is a case in point. In December 1774, the Maryland convention passed a resolution for establishing "a well regulated" militia. While the convention instructed the inhabitants between the ages of sixteen and fifty to form themselves into sixty-eight-man companies and to elect their officers, it made no provision for the machinery of mobilization, for officers of field grades, or for specific civil oversight. Was the militia to receive orders only from the convention, the colony-wide council, or the local committees of observation—or might all exercise a controlling and perhaps overlapping and conflicting hand? Following Lexington and Concord, the convention provided the answers and called for artillery units and minute companies. Minute companies there and elsewhere did not work out in actual practice to be satisfactory, and after a time many simply faded out of the picture or, as in New Jersey and New York, were expressly abolished. . . .

As an institution . . . the militia proved deficient. The law-making bodies of the colony-states were never able to bring these military organizations up to meeting their responsibilities. The reason in part is that, as time passed, those responsibilities were vastly enlarged—to the point of embracing just about everything of a military nature. If we are mindful of this all-encompassing role they were asked to play, then we can better understand their limitations and their failures. If, as Washington said, the militia were best suited to control the home front, the problem was that the pressures of the war never allowed them to so restrict themselves.

Only initially, in the first year or so, were the militias able to confine the scope of their duties—to enforce the 1774 Continental Association of Congress on non-importation, to compel people to take sides, to put down loyalist uprisings, to seize military stores from royal governors, and to keep the slave population under control. Increasingly thereafter the state forces were involved in repelling Indian incursions, taking the offensive against the tribesmen, and engaging British coastal raiding parties. Besides, wartime demands, especially the manpower deficiencies of the Continental Army, prompted drafts—usually of short-term duration—to flesh out the ranks of the regulars; they also resulted in drafts, on a large scale, from existing militia units, which then were reorganized into new regiments; and, unlike the trend of the colonial wars, already established militia regiments were sometimes thrust into service. All of these various contingents were not infrequently asked to fight next to Washington's soldiers in formalized engagements. When required to stay for extended lengths in the field far from home, when mixed closely with sizable bodies of Continentals, and when performing against redcoats in open combat—the militia were at their worst. Nothing in their modest training, not to mention their normally deficient equipment and supplies, prepared them for these duties.

If Washington against his better judgment had to throw militia on the front lines with Continentals, there were also situations when part-time defenders had to oppose the enemy alone, particularly when British raiding parties descended upon the coast of a state and, now and then, penetrated inland. So it was in Virginia, which between 1779 and 1781 reeled from a succession of blows. British Generals Edward Mathew, Alexander Leslie, Benedict Arnold, William Phillips, and Lord Cornwallis roamed and pillaged over sections of the tidewater and even into the piedmont. Time and time the counties were urged to turn out their militia, of whom—wailed Jefferson—"there is not a single man who has ever seen the face of an Enemy." Simultaneously, the state's resources were being drained southward, for it was serving as a troop-and-supply center for American operations in the Carolinas.

The greenness of the defenders and the repeated demands upon their services, combined with shortages of weapons, equipment, and transportation in an overwhelmingly rural, agricultural society, made it impossible to keep the militia in the field for protracted periods. . . . Even so, in Pennsylvania, New Jersey, New York, and other states the civilian leadership made repeated efforts to make the militia more resilient. No one labored harder at this task than Virginia's Governor Thomas Nelson in 1781. Nelson advocated for some of the militia "constant training, notwithstanding the expense." Here was the notion of a kind of "standing" militia, well trained and ready to go anywhere on sudden notice. Nelson's scheme never gained acceptance, but as chief executive he received from the legislature an enlargement of the governor's powers over the militia. With the consent of his council, the governor could assemble as many of the militia as he thought necessary and could hasten them to any part of the state; he could also employ them to impress supplies and to act in various other ways. Deserters could now receive the death penalty, while others who failed to come forward could be given six months' additional service.

In a more limited way, both Washington and Congress sought to invigorate the militia without appreciably weakening the regular forces. The most common form of succor was to detach Continental officers for duty with the militia in their home states in times of alarm, as, for example, when Generals George Weedon and Peter Muhlenberg returned to Virginia in 1780. North Carolina's only active brigadier general during the last three years of the conflict, Jethro Sumner, directed the state's militia in harassing the enemy. To keep the militia in arms at crucial moments Congress might even offer to pay the militia and maintain their upkeep, as it did for New York detachments garrisoning Fort Schuyler.

All these endeavors did not dramatically change the performance of the militia. When we seek to find what was revolutionary about the American Revolution, as scholars have done since the days of J. F. Jameson, there is no reason to look to the militia, which institutionally remained very similar to what it had been in the colonial period. Yet, as we have seen, its duties in a sense were revolutionary: it was expected to perform virtually every military function imaginable. Indeed, for this very reason—that so much was demanded of the local contingents—I believe the overall impression of the militia should be one of admiration, not derision.

Where specifically did the militia earn their highest marks? We find that answer in their own backyards, in operations within their own immediate districts, and sometimes in colony- or state-wide endeavors. These activities were always exceedingly important, but in the months before and after the outbreak of hostilities at Lexington and Concord they were absolutely essential to the launching and the continuation of the Revolution as a war. The militia's use of muscle guaranteed that the patriots would maintain control of the political and law-enforcing machinery in every colony. Therefore, from a military point of view, these months were quite likely the most crucial period of the Revolution. If one result of this militia-backed takeover was that the loyalists were to remain permanently on the defensive, surely another consequence was that virtually everywhere British armies landed they encountered a hostile environment. That circumstance helps explain why enormous quantities of supplies and provisions for royal regiments had to come from the mother country, 3,000 miles away, rather than from the mainland colonies. . . .

Both propositions invite closer scrutiny, although the first one has been expressed on several occasions of late. It was probably Walter Millis in 1956 who initially stressed the local role of the militia in the opening rounds of the struggle: "the much despised and frequently unwarlike" militia's choking off any chance of a loyalist "counter-revolution," as he phrased it. Whatever their methods—and they ranged from intimidation to violence—these home guards did the job. Most of those who publicly spoke or acted against the edicts of the community committees, provincial congresses, or Continental Congress were punished or else they recanted, as did Robert Davis of Anne Arundel County in Maryland. When whig militiamen sought to interrogate him, he shouted from behind closed doors, "You damned rebel sons of bitches—I will shoot you if you come any nearer." When his tormentors prepared to storm his house, Davis's threats turned to hollow rhetoric. He meekly consented to come before the committee of safety, where he apologized for his verbal indiscretion.

The second proposition, concerning the British army's inhospitable surroundings, needs more extended commentary. British columns, except for Burgoyne's, usually advanced relatively unimpeded from one fixed point to another. But the redcoats and their loyalist allies had minimal accomplishments outside or beyond those fixed points, which were the cities and occasional towns and fortified geographical locations. One accomplishment that historians, however grudgingly, have conceded to the militia as irregulars is their hit-and-run activity against British patrols and outposts *behind the lines,* with the South Carolina trio of Marion, Sumter, and Pickens receiving most of the limelight. But, as the observation about fixed points suggests, the areas of effective British control were scarcely expansive enough for the expression *behind the lines* to have much meaning. In any event, we might well examine more closely sectors that are clearly *between the lines:* broadly speaking, between the contending armies or not completely in the hands of either side. It was there that the loyalists were most aggressive; there, too, that the British sought to obtain supplies, with forage generally the most sought-after commodity. In seeking to checkmate the enemy in these broad zones, the American militia made a most substantial contribution, second only in magnitude to their sustaining local and provincial whig governmental machinery at the onset of the Revolution. (And we may add, because of their early strong-armed tactics, which were repeated later in the war whenever necessary, there was generally a somewhat secure, stable behind-the-lines region for Continental armies.)

There were whig-tory clashes large and small between the lines, so many, in fact—they number in the hundreds—that the London-published *Annual Register* predicted that "by such skirmishes . . . the fate of America must be necessarily decided." Sizable, well-publicized encounters included Moore's Creek Bridge in 1776, where 1,400 North Carolinians killed or captured virtually an entire force of roughly the same strength, and King's Mountain in 1780, where again the opposing bands numbered over a thousand and again scarcely a soul among the king's friends escaped. Lesser known struggles also involved numerous participants, such as Kettle Creek near the Georgia-Carolina border in 1779, where 700 tories scattered before a much smaller whig party, or Ramsour's Mill in North Carolina in 1780, where another 700 loyalists were dispersed, although there were heavy casualties on both sides.

For illustrative purposes these encounters merit further comment. In all four instances the crown's followers, previously cowed by threats from local patriots, had mustered their courage because they foresaw the protection of British regulars. Moore's Creek Bridge was such a devastating setback for England in North Carolina (the loyalists had come forth in the belief they were to be aided by a royal expedition on the coast) that the tories kept their peace for over four years, that is, until they again saw the prospect of a British invasion of the state in 1780, when Lord Cornwallis's troops appeared in upper South Carolina. But after their premature rising and reversal at Ramsour's Mill, only thirty of them united with His Lordship at Camden. Also important were the results at Kettle Creek; most of the tories of the upper Savannah River region were fearful of showing their true colors for over a year, until the British capture of Charleston in 1780. And as for King's Mountain, the royalist defeat was a blow from which the cause of Britain in the western Carolinas never recovered.

If these battles were all in the South, there were obviously others above the Mason-Dixon line, most of which were less spectacular and involved fewer numbers, a remark that holds true for between-the-lines skirmishing during the British occupation of New York and Philadelphia. Describing "a five-year war of neighbors" across from Manhattan Island in the Hackensack Valley (of Bergen County, New Jersey, and lower Orange County, New York), a local historian declared that while the "militia daily risked brushes with . . . raiders from New York," all too many Continentals remained in their cold-weather encampments and "did not hear a gun fired in battle from one year to the next."

The statement, if exaggerated, is not without some validity, although militia units themselves were often dazed and demoralized by initial British invasions. Yet they did revive, particularly after the crimson-clad regiments settled into winter quarters or congregated at fixed points. . . .

British and German diarists say not only that the rebel militia harassed and bloodied the tories, but that the American amateurs made it necessary for their foraging parties combing the countryside to be escorted by anywhere between several hundred and several thousand regulars. It was such a scavenging expedition—detached from Burgoyne's army in search of food and horse—that was crushed by Stark at Bennington. The preponderance of these encounters were only skirmishes; but to the British they were nasty affairs, expensive in time and matériel and successful in limiting the effectiveness of the foragers. British Lieutenant Colonel Charles Stuart complained that the conflict over forage "kept the army the whole winter [of 1776–1777] in perpetual harassment, and upon a modest computation has lost us more men than the last campaign."

To John Ewald, a German officer serving in the middle states, this "partisan war," as he termed it, "was carried on constantly in full force." The finest troops were deployed against the whig marauders, whom he variously described as "the country people" and "uncivilized mountaineers." But the best—"the Jäger Corps, the light infantry, and the Queen's Rangers"—were themselves bedeviled by the intruders, were compelled to get their rest at midday "because rest can seldom be enjoyed at night and in the morning."

What of a remedy for these raids, ambushes, and nocturnal intrusions? Ewald felt that when the British entered an area, large segments of the army, not just the light units, should be sent out: search and destroy missions, in the language of recent warfare, against roving rebel bands. That was a doubtful cure. In any case, a solution was never found, not by Howe or Clinton in the North, not by Cornwallis in the South. "I will not say much in praise of the militia of the Southern Colonies," confided Cornwallis, "but the list of British officers and soldiers killed and wounded by them . . . proves but too fatally that they are not wholly contemptible." . . .

Outside of New York and Pennsylvania the part-time soldiers held their own against the Indians. In 1776, state-supported columns from Virginia and the Carolinas devastated the settlements of the Cherokee, who were never again a serious threat. And the expeditions of George Rogers Clark, if they did not win the West as his biographers have claimed, did save Kentucky. Even in standardized confrontations with British veterans, the militia occasionally provided much needed help: at Princeton, Savannah, Cowpens, Eutaw Springs, and Springfield. Why did militia stand tall in some battles and not in others? It depended on how they were employed and how they were led. There is an old axiom that civilian-soldiers would go just as far on the battlefield as their officers would take them. Officers like Daniel Morgan and Andrew Pickens would take them quite a distance.

Today, quite properly, the pendulum has swung back toward a more favorable image of the militia and their contributions to American independence. But we may wish to halt its movement before it swings too far, before it denies Washington's Continentals their just desserts. John Shy has accurately spoken of the "triangularity of the struggle," of two armed forces contending "less with each other than for the support and control of the civilian population." Generally . . . I think the Continentals did a reasonably good job—better than the British army—of behaving with propriety, even sensitivity, toward the noncombatant elements. Generals like Washington, Greene, Gates, Schuyler, and Lincoln recognized this delicate dimension to the conflict.

Not so the militia. Nothing so reminds us that the Revolution was also a civil war as certain activities of the home-front defenders. Their very éclat as a constabulary and enforcer of conformity posed a threat. As the war dragged on and as animosities increased, the ruthlessness of the whig militia—and their careless lack of discrimination between friend and foe—to say nothing of their dabbling in local politics—alarmed both state and congressional authorities. The Reverend James Caldwell of Springfield, New Jersey, a staunch patriot whose wife was killed in a British raid, was himself shot down by a trigger-happy militiaman; the minister had gone into enemy-controlled country to bring out a young woman and was returning under a flag of truce when his senseless death occurred. Pennsylvania's General Lacey acknowledged the destructiveness of his own men and agreed with a friend who complained that "Numbers of the Inhabitants begin to be more afraid of our own [militia] than the Army of General Howe." General Greene in the South was equally concerned about the extreme retribution that whig civilian-soldiers inflicted upon tories and alleged royalist sympathizers, fearing it would alienate myriad potential friends. . . .

Greene's concern elicits another observation. Continental officers not only sought to hold down militia atrocities in day-to-day military campaigning; they additionally may have had a strong hand in persuading the patriot inhabitants to accept the loyalists back into the American fold as the war slowly drew to an end. The process of reassimilation, having never received more than passing investigation, warrants careful scrutiny. For despite the deep bitterness in both camps, the patriots, however grudgingly, allowed most of the tories to return to their own communities. . . .

The experiences of the Revolution indicated that a strong dose of central control was required to upgrade the militias of the states. Although reforms such as those proposed by Washington, Steuben, and others failed to impress the Confederation government of the 1780s, the military provisions of the Constitution appeared to represent a triumph of those ideas. The new political instrument contained authority for a radically different kind of militia system. The Congress, in the language of the Constitution, "shall have Power" to call "forth the Militia [of the states] to execute the Laws of the Union, suppress Insurrections and repel Invasions." These passages recognized the wide range of militia endeavors in the recent war; but now they might be carried out under federal rather than state control. Whereas the training of the Revolutionary militia had been sorely deficient, Congress was to have the power "to provide for organizing, arming, and disciplining the Militia," although "reserving to the States, respectively, the appointment of the Officers, and the Authority of training the Militia according to the discipline prescribed by Congress." . . .

Whatever the later vicissitudes of the militia, that institution, for all its frailties, made its finest contributions to the nation in the Revolution. Seldom has an armed force done so much with so little—providing a vast reservoir of manpower for a multiplicity of military needs, fighting (often unaided by Continentals) in the great majority of the 1,331 land engagements of the war. Surely in retrospect we can be as charitable toward the militia as Joseph Reed, who had watched the semi-soldiers throughout the war and who declared, "In short, at this time of day, we must say of them as [of the] Price of a wife: Be to their faults a little blind, And to their virtues very kind. "

F U R T H E R   R E A D I N G

Samuel Flagg Bemis, *The Diplomacy of the American Revolution* (1935)

George Athan Billias, ed., *George Washington's Opponents: British Generals and Admirals in the American Revolution* (1969)

R. Arthur Bowler, *Logistics and the Failure of the British Army in America, 1775–1783* (1975)

Richard Buel, Jr., *Dear Liberty: Connecticut's Mobilization for War* (1980)

E. Wayne Carp, *To Starve the Army at Pleasure: Continental Army Administration and American Political Culture, 1775–1783* (1984)

Stephan Conway, *The War of American Independence, 1775–1783* (1995)

Jeffrey Crow, and Larry Tise, eds., *The Southern Experience in the American Revolution* (1978)

Jonathan R. Dull, *A Diplomatic History of the American Revolution* (1985)

———, *The French Navy and American Independence: A Study of Arms and Diplomacy* (1975)

William M. Fowler, Jr., *Rebels Under Sail: The American Navy During the Revolution* (1976)

Alfred Grant, *Our American Brethren: A History of Letters in the British Press During the American Revolution 1775–1781* (1995)

Robert A. Gross, *The Minutemen and Their World* (1976)

Ira D. Gruber, *The Howe Brothers and the American Revolution* (1972)

Don Higginbotham, *War and Society in Revolutionary America: The Wider Dimensions of the Conflict* (1988)

———, *The War of American Independence: Military Attitudes, Policies, and Practice, 1763–1789* (1971)

Ronald Hoffman, and Peter J. Albert, eds., *Arms and Independence: The Military Character of the American Revolution* (1984)

———, *Diplomacy and Revolution: The Franco-American Alliance of 1778* (1981)

Ronald Hoffman, Thad W. Tate, and Peter J. Albert, eds., *An Uncivil War: The Southern Backcountry During the American Revolution* (1985)

James H. Hutson, *John Adams and the Diplomacy of the American Revolution* (1980)

Richard H. Kohn, *Eagle and Sword: The Beginnings of the Military Establishment in America* (1975)

Piers Mackesy, *The War for America, 1775–1783* (1964)

James Kirby Martin, and Mark E. Lender, *A Respectable Army: The Military Origins of the Republic* (1982)

Richard B. Morris, *The Peacemakers: The Great Powers and American Independence* (1965)

Jan Willem Schulte Nordholt, *The Dutch Republic and American Independence* (1982)

Stephen E. Patterson, *Political Parties in Revolutionary Massachusetts* (1973)

Howard H. Peckham, ed., *The Toll of Independence: Engagements and Battle Casualties of the American Revolution* (1974)

Hugh F. Rankin, *The North Carolina Continentals* (1971)

Eric Robson, *The American Revolution in Its Political and Military Aspects* (1955)

Steven Rosswurm, *Arms, Country, and Class: The Philadelphia Militia and the "Lower Sort" During the American Revolution* (1987)

Charles Royster, *A Revolutionary People at War: The Continental Army and American Character* (1979)

John E. Selby, *The Revolution in Virginia, 1775–1783* (1988)

John Shy, *A People Numerous and Armed: Reflections on the Military Struggle for American Independence* (1976)

Marshall Smelser, *The Winning of Independence* (1972)

Jack M. Sosin, *The Revolutionary Frontier, 1763–1783* (1967)

William C. Stinchcombe, *The American Revolution and the French Alliance* (1969)

Gerald Stourzh, *Benjamin Franklin and American Foreign Policy,* 2d ed. (1969)

Willard M. Wallace, *Appeal to Arms: A Military History of the Revolution* (1951)

Outsiders and Enemies: Native Americans and the Loyalists

Most Americans today view the Revolution as a heroic, triumphant episode. The independent nation it created, with its representative system of government and its unusually broad access to economic and social opportunity, has commanded the allegiance and admiration of generations of Americans since the era of George Washington. The Revolution was painful, and, yes, it demanded great sacrifices, but most of us believe that it turned out well in the end. This is the history of the Revolution from the perspective of the winners.

Some Americans, however, regarded the Revolution as a catastrophe—an unrelieved disaster. The liberty of native Americans, for example, was threatened, not bolstered, by the patriots' victory. Native Americans cared little about the colonists' conflict with Britain except insofar as it led the United States and Britain to interfere with the status quo. Although both sides urged neutrality on the woodland peoples and formally encouraged them to stay aloof from the imperial quarrel, in actuality both sides sought a "benevolent" neutrality that would allow them to move troops freely through native American lands. Moreover, when particular disputes over trade and territorial issues led to physical conflicts, native Americans were drawn into the fighting, usually on the British side. Consequently, when Britain lost, the native Americans also lost. Moreover, after the war, because of the growing white population's irrepressible appetite for land, and it sense of racial and cultural superiority, the national and state governments offered scant protection to native Americans, even those who had fought on behalf of the United States. Although the Revolutionaries did not aim to ravage the peoples of the eastern woodlands, at the least, American independence accelerated their destruction and displacement, and opened the way for western settlement.

The other conspicuous losers in the Revolution were the active loyalists. In contrast to the native Americans, the loyalists rightly understood the Revolution as their own quarrel, and as partisans they stood to gain or lose according to the success of British arms. Thousands of them fought for the King and Parliament, and thousands more evacuated their homes to seek shelter in British-occupied *strongholds like New York City or in Britain, Canada, West Florida, or the West Indies. Castigated in the 1770s by their patriot enemies, subsequently they have often been ignored. As a result, we have mistakenly tended to think of the Revolution not as a civil war, but as a consensus movement against British rule that displaced only a tiny imperial elite. In fact, however, loyalty to Britain commanded substantial support in the colonies, generated bloody battles, and loyalists expressed ideas that set them apart from the patriots. Understanding who they were and what they did and believed enables us to grasp more accurately the character of the Revolution, as both a political movement and a social experience.*

Examining the loyalists also invites us to consider the path not taken in the eighteenth century and to wonder whether the competitive, individualistic, and antiauthoritarian aspects of post-Revolutionary American society would have flourished without the ouster (between 1775 and 1783) of leaders who promoted paternalistic, conservative principles. What seems evident from the experiences of native Americans and loyalists in the Revolution is not only that some people gained while others lost but also that the direction of American society and culture was significantly affected by these victories and defeats.

D O C U M E N T S

Document 1, the Oneida address to Connecticut and the New England colonies, declares the Oneida desire to remain at peace through neutrality. John Adams' report on Congress's strategy reveals that Congress, too, would prefer that native Americans keep out of the conflict, partly owing to its perception of the Indians as "savages." Document 3, the Chickasaw message of 1783, points to some of the many challenges facing Indians after the war ended, and their immediate need for supplies as well as peace.

Documents 4, 5, and 6 express common Patriot sentiments toward Loyalists, or Tories as they were known, both early in the war and later. Document 7, ex-Governor Hutchinson's attack on the Declaration of Independence, illustrates that, from a Loyalist perspective, the sacred American text was just a false propaganda piece. The Loyalists plea to King, Parliament, and Britons, Document 8, reveals Loyalist views of defeat and victimhood. Their case warrants comparison with the Indians. In Document 9, the Philadelphia physician and signer of the Declaration, Benjamin Rush, offers his wartime analysis of who became a patriot and who became a Loyalist.

1. Oneida Indians Declare Neutrality, 1775

We more immediately address you, our brother, the Governour and the Chiefs of *New-England.*

Brothers! We have heard of the unhappy differences and great contention betwixt you and the old *England.* We wonder greatly, and are troubled in our minds.

Brothers! Possess your minds in peace respecting us *Indians.* We cannot intermeddle in this dispute between two brothers. The quarrel seems to be unnatural; you are two brothers of one blood. We are unwilling to join on either side in such a contest, for we bear an equal affection to both of you, *Old* and *New-England.*

"Oneida Indians Declare Neutrality." As found in Peter Force, *American Archives* (Washington, DC: M. St. Clair and Peter Force, 1837–1853).

Should the great King of *England* apply to us for our aid, we shall deny him. If the Colonies apply, we will refuse. The present situation of you two brothers is new and strange to us. We *Indians* cannot find nor recollect in the traditions of our ancestors the like case or a similar instance.

Brothers! For these reasons possess your minds in peace, and take no umbrage that we *Indians* refuse joining in the contest; we are for peace.

Brothers! Was it an alien, a foreign Nation, which struck you, we should look into the matter. We hope, through the wise government and good pleasure of *God,* your distresses may soon be removed, and the dark cloud be dispersed.

Brothers! As we have declared for peace, we desire you will not apply to our *Indian* brethren in *New-England* for their assistance. Let us *Indians* be all of one mind, and live in peace with one another, and you white people settle your own disputes betwixt yourselves.

Brothers! We have now declared our minds; please write to us that we may know yours.

We, the sachems, warriors, and female governesses of *Oneida,* send our love to you, brother Governour, and all the other chiefs in *New-England.*

Signed by	*William Sunoghsis,*	
	Viklasha Watshaleagh,	
	William Kanaghquassea,	
	Peter Thayehcase,	
	Germine Tegayavher,	
	Nickhes Ahsechose,	Chief Warriors
	Thomas Yoghtanawca,	of *Oneida.*
	Adam Ohonwano,	
	Quedellis Agwerondongwas,	
	Handerchiko Tegahpreahdyen,	
	Johnks Skeanender,	
	Thomas Teorddeatha.	

Caughnawaga, June 19, 1775.

Interpreted and wrote by *Samuel Kirkland,* Missionary.

2. John Adams Reports on Congress's Strategy Toward the Native Americans, 1775

Phyladelphia June 7. 1775

Dear Sir

We have been puzzled to discover, what we ought to do, with the Canadians and Indians. . . .

Whether We Should march into Canada with an Army Sufficient to break the Power of Governor [of Quebec Guy] Carlton, to overawe the Indians, and to protect

"John Adams Reports on Congress's Strategy Toward the Native Americans, 1775." Material appears in John Adams, *Papers of John Adams,* ed. Robert J. Taylor (Cambridge: Harvard University Press, 1977–1996), vol. 3, p. 17.

the French has been a great Question. It Seems to be the general Conclusion that it is best to go, if We can be assured that the Canadians will be pleased with it, and join.

The Nations of Indians inhabiting the Frontiers of the Colonies, are numerous and warlike. They seem disposed to Neutrality. None have as yet taken up the Hatchet against us; and We have not obtained any certain Evidence that Either Carlton or [Guy] Johnson [superintendent of Indians in the northern department] have directly attempted to persuade them to take up the Hatchet. Some Suspicious Circumstances there are.

The Indians are known to conduct their Wars, So entirely without Faith and Humanity, that it would bring eternal Infamy on the Ministry throughout all Europe, if they should excite these Savages to War. The French disgraced themselves last War, by employing them. To let loose these blood Hounds to scalp Men, and to butcher Women and Children is horrid. Still it [is] Such Kind of Humanity and Policy as we have experienced, from the Ministry.

3. Chickasaw Indians Seek Help, July 1783

"Brother,

When our great father the King of England called away his warriors, he told us to take your People by the hand as friends and brothers. Our hearts were always inclined to do so & as far as our circumstances permitted us, we evinced our good intentions as Brothers the Virginians can testify—It makes our hearts rejoice to find that our great father, and his children the Americans have at length made peace, which we wish may continue as long as the Sun and Moon, And to find that our Brothers the Americans are inclined to take us by the hand, and Smoke with us at the great Fire, which we hope will never be extinguished.

Brother,

Notwithstanding the Satisfaction all these things give us we are yet in confusion & uncertainty. The Spaniards are sending talks amongst us, and inviting our young Men to trade with them. We also receive talks from the Governor of Georgia to the same effect—We have had Speeches from the Illinois inviting us to a Trade and Intercourse with them—Our Brothers, the Virginians Call upon us to a Treaty, and want part of our land, and we expect our Neighbors who live on Cumberland River, will in a Little time Demand, if not forcibly take part of it from us, also as we are informed they have been marking Lines through our hunting grounds: we are daily receiving Talks from one Place or other, and from People we Know nothing about. We Know not who to mind or who to neglect. We are told that the Americans have 13 Councils Compos'd of Chiefs and Warriors. We Know not which of them we are to Listen to, or if we are to hear some, and Reject others, we are at a loss to Distinguish those we are to hear. We are told that you are the head Chief of the Grand Council, which is above these 13 Councils: if so why have we not had Talks

"Chickasaw Message to Congress, July 1783." As found in *Calendar of Virginia State Papers* (New York: Kraus Reprint Corp., 1968), vol. 3, pp. 515–517.

from you,—We are head men and Chiefs and Warriors also: and have always been accustomed to speak with great Chiefs & warriors—We are Likewise told that you and the Great men of your Council are Very Wise—we are glad to hear it, being assured that you will not do us any Wrong, and therefore we wish to Speak with you and your Council, or if you Do not approve of our so Doing, as you are wise, you will tell us who shall speak with us, in behalf of all our Brothers the Americans, and from whare and whome we are to be supplyed with necessarries in the manner our great father supplied us—we hope you will also put a stop to any encroachments on our lands, without our consent, and silence all those People who sends us Such Talks as inflame & exasperate our Young Men, as it is our earnest desire to remain in peace and friendship with our Br: the Americans for ever.

Brother,

The King our Common father always left one of his beloved Men among us, to whom we told anything we had to say, and he soon obtained an answer—and by him our great Father, his Chiefs & headmen spoke to us.

Our great father always gave him goods to cover the nakedness of our old men who could not hunt, our women and our children, and he was as one mouth, and one tongue between us, and was beloved of us all. Such a man living among us particularly at this time, would rescue us from the darkness and confusion we are in. By directing us to whom we should speak, and putting us in the right Path that wc should not go wrong.

We have desired our Br. Mr. Donne, who brought talks from General Clark, and has been some time among us, to deliver this talk to you, and speak it in our behalf to your Grand Council, that you may know our want, and as you are wise, that you may direct us what to do for the best. He has Promised, at our desire to take it to your great council fire & to bring as your answer, that you may be no more in the dark—believe what he tells you from us; we have told him all that is in our hearts.

Brothers, we are very poor for necessaries, for Amunition particularly. We can supply ourselves from the Spaniards but we are averse to hold any intercourse with them, as our hearts are always with our Brothers the Americans. We have advised our young men to wait with patience for the answer to this talk, when we rest assured of having supplies, and every thing so regulated that no further confusion may ensue. We wish that this land may never again be stained with the blood of either white or Red men, that piece may last forever and that both our women and children may sit down in safety under their own shade to enjoy without fear or apprehension the Blessing which the good Spirit enriches them with. Brother, we again desire you and your cheifs to Listen to what we say that we shall not have to Repeat it again, and as you are all Wise, you will know what to do.

Done at Chuck-ul-issah our Great Town the 28th Day of July, 1783.

> MINGHOMA,
> PYAMATHAHAW,
> KUSHTHAPUTHASA,
> PYAMINGOE of Christhautra,
> PYAMINGO of Chuckaferah."

4. Patriots Intimidate a New Jersey Loyalist, 1775

The 6th of December, at Quibble Town, Middlesex County, Pisquata Township, New Jersey, Thomas Randolph, Cooper, who had publicly proved himself an enemy to his country, by reviling and using his utmost endeavors to oppose the proceedings of the Continental and Provincial Conventions and Committees, in defence of their rights and liberties; and he being adjudged a person of no consequence enough for a severer punishment, was ordered to be stripped naked, well coated with tar and feathers, and carried in a wagon publicly round the town—which punishment was accordingly inflicted; and as he soon became duly sensible of his offence, for which he earnestly begged pardon, and promised to atone as far as he was able, by a contrary behavior for the future, he was released and suffered to return to his house in less than half an hour. The whole was conducted with that regularity and decorum, that ought to be observed in all public punishments.

5. A Patriot Urges Congress to Execute Loyalists, 1776

Northampton, July 17, 1776.

Dear Sir:

I have often said that I supposed a Declaration of Independence would be accompanied with a declaration of high treason. Most certainly it must immediately, and without the least delay, follow it. Can we subsist—did any State ever subsist, without exterminating traitors? . . . Our whole cause is every moment in amazing danger for want of it. The common understanding of the people, like unerring instinct, has long declared this; and from the clear discerning which they have had of it, they have been long in agonies about it. They expect that effectual care will now be taken for the general safety, and that all those who shall be convicted of endeavouring, by overt act, to destroy the State, shall be cut off from the earth.

6. A Newspaper Attack on Loyalists, 1779

Among the many errors America has been guilty of during her contest with Great Britain, few have been greater, or attended with more fatal consequences to these States, than her lenity to the Tories. At first it might have been right, or perhaps political; but is it not surprising that, after repeated proofs of the same evils resulting therefrom, it should still be continued? We are all crying out against the depreciation of our money, and entering into measures to restore it to its value; while the Tories,

---

"Patriots Intimidate a New Jersey Loyalist, 1775." As found in Margaret W. Willard, ed., *Letters on the American Revolution, 1774–1776* (Port Washington, NY: Kennikat Press, 1968).

"A Patriot Urges Congress to Execute Loyalists, 1776." As found in Peter Force, *American Archives* (Washington, DC: M. St. Clair and Peter Force, 1837–1853).

"A Newspaper Attack on Loyalists, 1779." As found in Albert B. Hart, ed., *American History Told by Contemporaries* (New York: Macmillan, 1912).

who are one principal cause of the depreciation, are taken no notice of, but suffered to live quietly among us. We can no longer be silent on this subject, and see the independence of the country, after standing every shock from without, endangered by internal enemies. Rouse, America! your danger is great—great from a quarter where you least expect it. The Tories, the Tories will yet be the ruin of you! 'Tis high time they were separated from among you. They are now busy engaged in undermining your liberties. They have a thousand ways of doing it, and they make use of them all. Who were the occasion of this war? The Tories! Who persuaded the tyrant of Britain to prosecute it in a manner before unknown to civilized nations, and shocking even to barbarians? The Tories! Who prevailed on the savages of the wilderness to join the standard of the enemy? The Tories! Who have assisted the Indians in taking the scalp from the aged matron, the blooming fair one, the helpless infant, and the dying hero? The Tories! Who advised and who assisted in burning your towns, ravaging your country, and violating the chastity of your women? The Tories! Who are the occasion that thousands of you now mourn the loss of your dearest connections? The Tories! Who have always counteracted the endeavors of Congress to secure the liberties of this country? The Tories! Who refused their money when as good as specie, though stamped with the image of his most sacred Majesty? The Tories! Who continue to refuse it? The Tories! Who do all in their power to depreciate it? The Tories! Who propagate lies among us to discourage the Whigs? The Tories! Who corrupt the minds of the good people of these States by every specie of insidious counsel? The Tories! Who hold a traitorous correspondence with the enemy? The Tories! Who daily sends them intelligence? The Tories! Who take the oaths of allegiance to the States one day, and break them the next? The Tories! Who prevent your battalions from being filled? The Tories! Who dissuade men from entering the army? The Tories! Who persuade those who have enlisted to desert? The Tories! Who harbor those who do desert? The Tories! In short, who wish to see us conquered, to see us slaves, to see us hewers of wood and drawers of water? The Tories!

And is it possible that we should suffer men, who have been guilty of all these and a thousand other calamities which this country has experienced, to live among us! To live among us, did I say? Nay, do they not move in on our assemblies? Do they not insult us with their impudence? Do they not hold traitorous assemblies of their own? Do they not walk the streets at noon day, and taste the air of liberty? In short, do they not enjoy every privilege of the brave soldier who has spilt his blood, or the honest patriot who has sacrificed his all in our righteous cause? Yes—to our eternal shame be it spoken—they do. . . . 'Tis time to rid ourselves of these bosom vipers. An immediate separation is necessary. I dread to think of the evils every moment is big with, while a single Tory remains among us. . . . Awake, Americans, to a sense of your danger. No time to be lost. Instantly banish every Tory from among you. Let America be sacred alone to freemen.

Drive far from you every baneful wretch who wishes to see you fettered with the chains of tyranny. Send them where they may enjoy their beloved slavery to perfection—send them to the island of Britain; there let them drink the cup of slavery and eat the bread of bitterness all the days of their existence—there let them drag out a painful life, despised and accursed by those very men whose cause they have had the wickedness to espouse. Never let them return to this happy land—never let them taste the sweets of that independence which they strove to prevent. Banishment, perpetual banishment, should be their lot.

7. Thomas Hutchinson Criticizes the Declaration of Independence, 1776

My Lord,

The last time I had the honour of being in your Lordships company, you observed that you was utterly at a loss to what facts many parts of the Declaration of Independence published by the Philadelphia Congress referred, and that you wished they had been more particularly mentioned, that you might better judge of the grievances, alledged as special causes of the separation of the Colonies from the other parts of the Empire. This hint from your Lordship induced me to attempt a few Strictures upon the Declaration. Upon my first reading it, I thought there would have been more policy in leaving the World altogether ignorant of the motives to this Rebellion, than in offering such false and frivolous reasons in support of it; and I flatter myself, that before I have finished this letter, your Lordship will be of the same mind. But I beg leave, first to make a few remarks upon its rise and progress.

I have often heard men (who I believe were free from party influence) express their wishes, that the claims of the Colonies to an exemption from the authority of Parliament in imposing Taxes had been conceded; because they had no doubts that America would have submitted in all other cases; and so this unhappy Rebellion, which has already proved fatal to many hundreds of the Subjects of the Empire, and probably will to many thousands more, might have been prevented.

The Acts for imposing Duties and Taxes may have accelerated the Rebellion, and if this could have been foreseen, perhaps, it might have been good policy to have omitted or deferred them; but I am of opinion, that if no Taxes or Duties had been laid upon the Colonies, other pretences would have been found for exception to the authority of Parliament. The body of the people in the Colonies, I know, were easy and quiet. They felt no burdens. They were attached, indeed, in every Colony to their own particular Constitutions, but the Supremacy of Parliament over the whole gave them no concern. They had been happy under it for an hundred years past: They feared no imaginary evils for an hundred years to come. But there were men in each of the principal Colonies, who had Independence in view, before any of those Taxes were laid, or proposed, which have since been the ostensible cause of resisting the execution of Acts of Parliament. Those men have conducted the Rebellion in the several stages of it, until they have removed the constitutional powers of Government in each Colony, and have assumed to themselves, with others, a supreme authority over the whole. . . .

Their first attempt was against the Courts of Admiralty, which they pronounced unconstitutional, whose judgments, as well as jurisdiction, they endeavoured to bring into examen before the Courts of Common Law, and a Jury chosen from among the people: About the same time, a strong opposition was formed against Writs of Assistants, granted to the Officers of the Customs by the Supreme Courts, and this opposition finally prevailed in all the Colonies. . . .

Thomas Hutchinson's Strictures Upon the Declaration of the Congress at Philadelphia, in a Letter to a Noble Lord, & c. (London, 1776), 5–9, 29–30.

It does not, however, appear that there was any regular plan formed for attaining to Independence, any further than that every fresh incident which could be made to serve the purpose, by alienating the affections of the Colonies from the Kingdom, should be improved accordingly. One of these incidents happened in the year 1764. This was the Act of Parliament for granting certain duties on goods in the British Colonies, for the support of Government, &c. . . . The Assembly of Massachuset's Bay, therefore, was the first that took any publick notice of the Act, and the first which ever took exception to the right of Parliament to impose Duties or Taxes on the Colonies, whilst they had no representatives in the House of Commons. This they did in a letter to their Agent in the summer of 1764, which they took care to print and publish before it was possible for him to receive it. And in this letter they recommend to him a pamphlet, wrote by one of their members, in which there are proposals for admitting representatives from the Colonies to sit in the House of Commons.

I have this special reason, my Lord, for taking notice of this Act of the Massachuset's Assembly; that though an American representation is thrown out as an expedient which might obviate the objections to Taxes upon the Colonies, yet it was only intended to amuse the authority in England; and as soon as it was known to have its advocates here, it was renounced by the Colonies, and even by the Assembly of the Colony which first proposed it, as utterly impracticable. In every stage of the Revolt, the same disposition has always appeared. No precise, unequivocal terms of submission to the authority of Parliament in any case, have ever been offered by any Assembly. A concession has only produced a further demand, and I verily believe if every thing had been granted short of absolute Independence, they would not have been contented; for this was the object from the beginning. . . .

To carry them to effect, Confederacies were formed by the chiefs of the revolters in each Colony; and Conventions were held by Delegates when judged necessary: Subjects for controversy in opposition to Government were sought for in each of the Colonies, to irritate and inflame the minds of the people, and dispose them to revolt: Dissentions and commotions in any Colony, were cherished and increased, as furnishing proper matter to work upon: For the same purpose, fictitious letters were published, as having been received from England, informing of the designs of ministry, and even of Bills being before the Parliament for introducing into the Colonies arbitrary Government, heavy Taxes and other cruel oppressions: Every legal measure for suppressing illicit trade was represented as illegal and grievous; and the people were called upon to resist it: A correspondence was carried on with persons in England, promoters of the revolt, whose intelligence and advice from time to time were of great use: Persons in England of superior rank and characters, but in opposition to the measures of administration, were courted and deceived, by false professions; and the real intentions of the revolters were concealed: The tumults, riots, contempt and defiance of law in England, were urged to encourage and justify the like disorders in the Colonies, and to annihilate the powers of Government there.

Many thousands of people who were before good and loyal subjects, have been deluded, and by degrees induced to rebel against the best of Princes, and the mildest of Governments.

Governors, and other servants of the Crown, and Officers of Government, with such as adhered to them, have been removed and banished under pretence of their being the instruments of promoting ministerial tyranny and arbitrary power; and finally the people have subjected themselves to the most cruel oppressions of fifty or sixty Despots. . . .

They have, my Lord, in their late address to the people of Great Britain, fully avowed these principles of Independence, by declaring they will pay no obedience to the laws of the Supreme Legislature; they have also pretended, that these laws were the mandates or edicts of the Ministers, not the acts of a constitutional legislative power, and have endeavoured to persuade such as they called their British Brethren, to justify the Rebellion begun in America; and from thence they expected a general convulsion in the Kingdom, and that measures to compel a submission would in this way be obstructed. These expectations failing, after they had gone too far in acts of Rebellion to hope for impunity, they were under the *necessity* of a separation, and of involving themselves, and all over whom they had usurped authority, in the distresses and horrors of war against that power from which they revolted, and against all who continued in their subjection and fidelity to it.

Gratitude, I am sensible, is seldom to be found in a community, but so sudden a revolt from the rest of the Empire, which had incurred so immense a debt, and with which it remains burdened, for the protection and defence of the Colonies, and at their most importunate request, is an instance of ingratitude no where to be parallelled.

Suffer me, my Lord, before I close this Letter, to observe, that though the professed reason for publishing the Declaration was a decent respect to the opinions of mankind, yet the real design was to reconcile the people of America to that Independence, which always before, they had been made to believe was not intended. This design has too well succeeded. The people have not observed the fallacy in reasoning from the *whole* to *part;* nor the absurdity of making the *governed* to be *governors.* From a disposition to receive willingly complaints against Rulers, facts misrepresented have passed without examining. Discerning men have concealed their sentiments, because under the present *free* government in America, no man may, by writing or speaking, contradict any part of this Declaration, without being deemed an enemy to his country, and exposed to the rage and fury of the populace.

8. Loyalists Plead Their Cause to the King, Parliament, and the British People, 1782

We, his majesty's most dutiful and faithful subjects, the loyal inhabitants of America, . . . animated with the purest principles of duty and allegiance to his majesty and the British parliament, beg leave, with the deepest humility and reverence, on the present calamitous occasion of public and national misfortune, in the surrender of lord Cornwallis, and the army under his lordship's command, at York-Town, humbly to entreat that your majesty, and the parliament, would be graciously pleased to permit us to offer this renewed testimony of loyalty and attachment to our most gracious sovereign, and the British nation and government; and thus

"Loyalists Plead Their Cause to the King, Parliament, and the British People, 1782." As found in *Principles and Acts of the Revolution in America,* ed. Hezekiah Niles (Baltimore: W. O. Niles, 1822), 393–397.

publicly to repeat our most heart-felt acknowledgments for the infinite obligations we feel ourselves under for the heavy expenses that have been incurred, and the great national exertions that have been made, to save and rescue us, and your American colonies, from impending ruin, and the accumulated distresses and calamities of civil war. . . . We revere, with a kind of holy enthusiasm, the ancient constitution of the American colonies; and that we cannot but lament every event, and be anxiously solicitous to remove every cause or suspicion, that might have the most distant tendency to separate the two countries, or in any remote degree to lessen the claim we have to the present aid and continued exertions of Great Britain; especially if it should arise from any misrepresentation or distrust, either of our fidelity or numbers, to entitle us to the future countenance and protection of that sovereign and nation, whose government and laws, we call God to witness, that, in the integrity of our souls, we prefer to all others. . . .

Unhappy, indeed, for ourselves, and we cannot but think unfortunately too for Great Britain, the number of well affected inhabitants in America to the parent country, cannot, for obvious reasons, be exactly ascertained. . . . The penalty under which any American subject enlists into his majesty's service, is no less than the immediate forfeiture of all his goods and chattels, lands and tenements; and if apprehended, and convicted by the rebels, of having enlisted, or prevailed on any other person to enlist into his majesty's service, it is considered as treason, and punished with death: Whereas, no forfeiture is incurred, or penalty annexed, to his entering into the service of congress; but, on the contrary, his property is secured, and himself rewarded.

In the former case, he withdraws himself from his family and relations, without any possibility of receiving any assistance from, or affording any relief to either. In the latter, he is subject to no such peculiar self-denials, and real distresses. . . .

The desultory manner also in which the war has been carried on, by first taking possession of Boston, Rhode Island, Philadelphia, Portsmouth, Norfolk, in Virginia, Wilmington, in North Carolina, &c. &c. and then evacuating them, whereby many thousand inhabitants have been involved in the greatest wretchedness, is another substantial reason why more loyalists have not enlisted into his majesty's service, or openly espoused and attached themselves to the royal cause; yet, notwithstanding all these discouraging circumstances, there are *many more men in his majesty's provincial regiments, than there are in the continental service.* Hence it cannot be doubted but that there are more loyalists in America than there are rebels; and also, that their zeal must be greater, or so many would not have enlisted into the provincial service, under such very unequal circumstances. Other reasons might be enumerated, why many more have not enlisted into his majesty's provincial service, if we were not prevented from it by motives of delicacy and tenderness to the character of the person to whose management the business of that department was principally committed. . . .

If it should be said, if such is the number and disposition of the loyalists in America, how comes it to pass that they have not been of more importance to his majesty's service? We answer, might it not with equal propriety be enquired, why his majesty's forces have not more fully answered the just expectations of the nation?— And might not the question with greater propriety be put to his majesty's commanders in America? A due deference to whom, we trust, will be thought the most decent apology for our waving the mention of many more of the true and undeniable causes which we have it in our power to assign. And permit us to add, that it is only from modesty, and a wish to avoid both the appearance and imputation of selfish ostentation, that we decline entering into a particular enumeration of such proofs of allegiance and fidelity, from the conduct and sufferings of American loyalists, as have never been equalled by any people, in any age, or in any country. We cannot, however, refrain from hinting at some incontestible advantages the loyalists have been of, in affording supplies to the royal army,—by acting as guides and pilots, and (independent of those employed in the provincial line) as militia and partizan troops. As corps of Refugees, they have been too often distinguished by the zeal and gallantry of their behavior, to need the mention of any particular instance; if they did, we might refer to the affair of the Block-house, opposite Fort Knyphausen, where captain Ward, with about 70 Refugees, withstood and repulsed the attack of general Wayne, at the head of three chosen brigades of continentals. As a militia, acting by themselves (for we take no notice of the many thousands that, at different times, particularly in Georgia and South Carolina, have attached themselves to the royal army) a small party, some time ago, under the command of one Bunnion, went from Long Island to Connecticut, and there surprised and took prisoner a rebel major general, named Silliman, and several other officers.

A party of militia also not long ago went from Wilmington, in North Carolina, 60 or 70 miles into the country, and took major general Ashe, with two or three field officers, and some other persons, and brought them prisoners to his majesty's garrison at Wilmington. Another party of militia lately went near 200 miles up into the country from Wilmington, to a place called Hillsborough, and with a body of 6 or 700 militia, attacked a party of rebel troops, who were there as a guard to the rebel legislature, then sitting at that place, and took the rebel governor, Mr. Burke, several of his council, 11 continental officers, and about 120 of the troops prisoners, whom the militia delivered to major Craig, who commanded the king's troops at Wilmington. Other more voluntary alerts, performed by the loyalists in South Carolina and elsewhere, might be mentioned without number. Surely such are not *timid friends!* . . .

Relying with the fullest confidence upon national justice and compassion to our fidelity and distresses, we can entertain no doubts but that Great Britain will prevent the ruin of her American friends, at every risk short of certain destruction to herself. But if compelled, by adversity or misfortune, from the wicked and perfidious combinations and designs of numerous and powerful enemies abroad, and more criminal and dangerous enemies at home, an idea should be formed by Great Britain of relinquishing her American colonies to the usurpation of congress, we thus solemnly call God to witness, that we think the colonies can never be so happy or so free as in a constitutional connexion with, and dependence on Great Britain; convinced, as we are, that to be a British subject, with all its consequences, is to be the happiest and freest member of any civil society in the known world—we, therefore, in justice to our members, in duty to ourselves, and in fidelity to our posterity, must not, cannot refrain from making this public declaration and appeal to the faithful subjects of every government, and the compassionate sovereign of every people, in every nation and kingdom of the world, that our principles are the principles of the virtuous and free; that our sufferings are the sufferings of unprotected loyalty, and persecuted fidelity; that our cause is the cause of legal and constitutional government, throughout the world; that, opposed by principles of republicanism, and convinced, from recent observation, that brutal violence, merciless severity, relentless cruelty, and discretionary outrages are the distinguished traits and ruling principles of the present system of congressional republicanism, our aversion is unconquerable, irreconcileable.—That we are attached to monarchical government, from past and happy experience—by duty, and by choice. That, to oppose insurrections, and to listen to the requests of people so circumstanced as we are, is the common interest of all mankind in civil society. That to support our rights, is to support the rights of every subject of legal government; and that to afford us relief, is at once the duty and security of every prince and sovereign on earth. Our appeal, therefore, is just; and our claim to aid and assistance is extensive and universal. But if, reflecting on the uncertain events of war, and sinking under the gloomy prospect of public affairs, from the divisions and contests unhappily existing in the great councils of the nation, any apprehensions should have been excited in our breasts with respect to the issue of the American war, we humbly hope it cannot, even by the most illiberal, be imputed to us as an abatement of our unshaken loyalty to our most gracious sovereign, or of our unalterable predilection in favor of the British nation and government, whom may God long protect and preserve, if, in consequence thereof, we thus humbly implore that your majesty, and the parliament, would be graciously pleased, in the tenderness of our fears, and in pity to our distresses, to solicit, by your ambassadors at the courts of foreign sovereigns, the aid of such powerful and good allies, as to your majesty and parliament, in your great wisdom and discretion, may seem meet. Or if such a measure should in any manner be thought incompatible with the dignity and interest of our sovereign and the nation, we most humbly and ardently supplicate and entreat, that, by deputies or ambassadors, nominated and appointed by your majesty's suffering American loyalists, they may be permitted to solicit and obtain from other nations that interference, aid and alliance, which, by the blessing of Almighty God, may, in the last fatal and ultimate extreme, save and deliver us, his majesty's American loyalists, who, we maintain, in every one of the colonies, compose a great majority of the inhabitants, and those too the first in point of opulence and consequence, from the ruinous system of congressional independence and republican tyranny, detesting rebellion as we do, and preferring a subjection to any power in Europe, to the mortifying debasement of a state of slavery, and a life of insult, under the tyranny of congressional usurpation.

9. Benjamin Rush Contrasts Loyalists and Patriots, 1777*

. . . Tories and Whigs were actuated by very different motives in their conduct, or by the same motives acting in different degrees of force. . . . There were Tories (1) from an attachment to power and office. (2) From an attachment to the British commerce which the war had interrupted or annihilated. (3) From an attachment to kingly

---

* Drawing on notes composed in 1777, Rush made this analysis in his later *Autobiography*.

"Benjamin Rush Contrasts Loyalists and Patriots, 1777." As found in Benjamin Rush, *The Autobiography of Benjamin Rush: His "Travels Through Life" Together With His Commonplace Book from 1789–1813,* ed. George W. Corner (Princeton: American Philosophical Society, 1948), 117–119.

government. (4) From an attachment to the hierarchy of the Church of England, which it was supposed would be abolished in America by her seperation from Great Britain. This motive acted chiefly upon the Episcopal clergy, more especially in the Eastern states. (5) From a dread of the power of the country being transferred into the hands of the Presbyterians. This motive acted upon many of the Quakers in Pennsylvania and New Jersey, and upon the Episcopalians in several of those states where they had been in possession of power, or of a religious establishment.

It cannot be denied, but that private and personal consideration actuated some of those men who took a part in favor of the American Revolution. There were Whigs (1) from a desire of possessing, or at least sharing, in the power of our country. It was said there were Whigs (2) from an expectation that a war with Great Britain would cancel all British debts. There certainly were Whigs (3) from the facility with which the tender laws enabled debtors to pay their creditors in depreciated paper money. (4) A few men were Whigs from ancient or hereditary hostility to persons, or families who were Tories. But a great majority of the people who took part with their country were Whigs (5) from a sincere and disinterested love of liberty and justice.

Both parties differed as much in their conduct as they did in the motives which actuated them. There were (1) furious Tories who had recourse to violence, and even to arms, to oppose the measures of the Whigs. (2) Writing and talking Tories. (3) Silent but busy Tories in disseminating Tory pamphlets and news papers and in circulating intelligence. (4) Peaceable and conscientious Tories who patiently submitted to the measures of the governing powers, and who shewed nearly equal kindness to the distressed of both parties during the war.

The Whigs were divided by their conduct into (1) Furious Whigs, who considered the tarring and feathering of a Tory as a greater duty and exploit than the extermination of a British army. These men were generally cowards, and shrunk from danger when called into the field by pretending sickness or some family disaster. (2) Speculating Whigs. These men infested our public councils, as well as the army, and did the country great mischief. A colonel of a regiment informed a friend of mine that he had made a great deal of money by buying poor horses for his waggon, and selling them again for a large profit after he had fattened them at the public expense. (3) Timid Whigs. The hopes of these people rose and fell with every victory and defeat of our armies. (4) Staunch Whigs. These were moderate in their tempers, but firm, inflexible, and persevering in their conduct. There was, besides these two classes of people, a great number of persons who were neither Whigs nor Tories. They had no fixed principles and accommodated their conduct to their interest, to events, and to their company. They were not without their uses. They protected both parties in many instances from the rage of each other, and each party always found hospitable treatment from them.

Perhaps the inhabitants of the United States might have been divided nearly into three classes, viz. Tories, Whigs, and persons who were neither Whigs nor Tories. The Whigs constituted the largest class. The 3rd class were a powerful reinforcement to them after the affairs of America assumed a uniformly prosperous appearance. . . .

[M]any of the children of Tory parents were Whigs; so were the Jews in all the States. . . .

Professor Gregory Evans Dowd, of the University of Notre Dame, recounts the impact of the Revolutionary War for native Americans of the Ohio region in the first essay. Through Dowd's explanation of the interplay of warfare and diplomacy, it becomes apparent that there was only a narrow range of options for the Indians, none of them particularly effective. The treaties of 1763 and 1783 combined to create a half-century or more of instability and ultimate decline for the Indians of the trans-Appalachian region. The second essay, by Professor Robert M. Calhoon of the University of North Carolina, Greensboro, considers the Loyalist dimension of the fighting, which, like the Indian warfare, brought death and destruction to large areas.

There Was No Winning Strategy for the Indians

GREGORY EVANS DOWD

Only one group of Upper Ohio country Indians would hold out for friendship with the emerging republic for most of the Revolutionary War: the inhabitants of the polyglot cluster of villages surrounding Coshocton. All others had taken arms against the United States by the fall of 1777. Established as the opening shots of the Revolution were fired in the East, Coshocton with its environs became a refuge for Indians of the region who sought to stand apart from the widespread pattern of hostility toward the Anglo-American rebels. Although the village leaders, who favored neutrality, were Unami-speaking Delawares, Coshocton also sheltered Munsee Delawares and Shawnees. Coshocton's Shawnees, members of a people often portrayed as adamantly militant, reveal that forces other than simple tribal or ethnic loyalty were at work in dividing Indians during the early years of the American republic's expansion. Instead of joining close relatives in battle against the United States, these nonmilitant Shawnees had decided to dwell among a like-minded faction of Delawares.

The movement for pan-Indian unity was cut against such factions. It cannot be fully understood without some inquiry into the opinions, policies, and failures of Indians who stood against it. The Shawnees and Delawares of Coshocton did just that. While north and south of the Ohio River religiously minded nativists joined supply-minded advocates of accommodation in an alliance with Great Britain, the Coshocton villagers sought peace with the United States. Alone in the Upper Ohio between 1777 and 1779, they were not alone on the continent; factions among the Six Nations, Catawbas, Cherokees, Creeks, Chickasaws, Potawatomis, Piankashaws, and others also sought cooperation, tolerance, and harmony with the Anglo-American settlers. Like the Coshoctons, many of these peoples would ultimately meet bitter disappointment.

Because of the proximity of Coshocton of Moravian missions, of an active American frontier garrison at Fort Pitt, of the British garrison at Detroit, and of Britain's agents operating along Lake Erie, we have good records concerning such

Dowd, *A Spirited Resistance: The North American Indian Struggle for Unity, 1745–1815,* pp. 65–87.
© 1992 by Johns Hopkins University Press.

divisions in the Ohio country during the revolutionary era. The history of Coshocton reveals not only the complex divisiveness of Indian politics and diplomacy but also the intractable difficulties, often anchored stubbornly in the thickening sediments of Anglo-American hatred, that borderland Indians faced when they looked to the east for peace. . . .

Accommodation in Coshocton, 1775–1779

The Delaware leaders who consistently advocated good relations with the United States were White Eyes and Killbuck. They lived near the cluster of Moravian mission towns of Schönbrunn, Gnadenhutten, and Salem. Neither had converted to Christianity, but the most outspoken neutralist, White Eyes, consistently opposed nativists who threatened the missions. White Eyes had been proposing a Delaware partnership with Anglo-America since 1773. . . .

White Eyes had two aims for his people. First, he sought to gain Congress's recognition of Delaware possession of lands north of the Ohio. Second, he sought Anglo-American instruction. He sought both landed autonomy and active economic cooperation under the direction of white teachers. Once achieved, the two ends would bring security of title and the benefits, as he saw them, of an economy productive of material goods. They would also win back the Christian neophytes, or at least provide for their continued place among the Delawares. . . .

The revolutionary Americans, even when pressed to keep Indian war parties off their borders, would not ratify any treaty that implied Delaware possession. They did not wish to offend the still largely neutral Six Nations, on whose spurious claim to much of the trans-Appalachian west many of the colonial purchases had been made, including, for example, the Kentucky cession disputed by the Shawnees in Dunmore's War. American support for the Six Nation's claims to the Ohio country, against those of the Shawnees and Delawares, hindered attempts by the Shawnee neutralist Cornstalk and the Delaware neutralist White Eyes to increase support for their peaceful policies. If White Eyes' hopes for American recognition of Delaware possessions went unsatisfied in the early years of the war, his desire for economic acculturation ran up against even more formidable barriers.

The neutralist vision of economic and technological transformation unfolds suggestively in a set of documents from the negotiations of the treaty council at Fort Pitt, September 1778. According to the terms of the treaty, negotiated largely by White Eyes, the Delawares of the village of Coshocton and the neutral Mequashake Shawnees should "become the same people." In strong opposition to nativist notions of the separateness of Anglo-Americans and Indians, White Eyes desired that "young men" of Coshocton and the United States "may be made acquainted with one another & that there may be no distinction between them." The representatives of Congress promised to send schoolmasters to the Coshoctons to teach their children. The most radical American suggestion, never implemented by Congress, guaranteed the Delawares' possession of all their claimed lands and suggested, audaciously, that the Ohio Indians still in friendship with the United States might "form a state whereof the Delaware Nation shall be the head, and have a representation in Congress: Provided, nothing in this article to be considered as conclusive until it meets with the approbation of Congress." It is inconceivable that such a proposal was accepted, in good faith, by even the most broad-minded of the commissioners, but it certainly illustrates the lengths American agents were willing to run and the lies they were willing to spin in order to achieve Delaware neutrality.

Neutral Delaware leaders Killbuck and White Eyes were serious enough about peace with the United States to send three of their loved ones—George White Eyes (White Eyes' eight-year-old son), John Killbuck (Killbuck's sixteen-year-old son), and Thomas (Killbuck's eighteen-year-old half brother)—deep into Anglo-America, to Princeton, New Jersey, to live in the home of Indian agent Colonel George Morgan. There they attended the local schools, including the college.

More indicative of his willingness to cooperate with the United States was White Eyes' intention to have an American garrison established near Coshocton to protect his people against the rising opposition of his militant Indian neighbors. The fort was to provide the Coshoctons with "Provisions and Ammunition," as well as with protection. This did not mean military alliance. The Delawares were not ready to combine their request for a fort with a pledge to give active support to the Americans, at least not in 1778. . . .

The American promise to build a fort as both a supply base and a possible defensive haven for the Delawares and an American plan for the capture of Detroit combined to produce Fort Laurens, an isolated, poorly supplied garrison that failed to secure any of its intended ends. Harsh Indian raids prevented the Congress from undertaking an assault on Detroit, and poverty prevented the Americans from adequately supplying the little garrison or, through it, the Indians. So ragged was the American army at Fort Laurens that when its commander warned the Delawares to support American actions lest they suffer the enmity of the United States, the Indians met his threat with "a General Laugh."

Supplies

Laughter can be deep testimony, and at Fort Laurens it spoke of an important reason for the eventual demise of Delaware and Shawnee neutrality: the United States failed to supply the Delawares in the late 1770s with the goods they needed to survive. Colonel George Morgan believed in 1776 that Indian friendship could be bought, but he feared that the British were able to supply the Indians with goods "at a price greatly inferior to those exacted by our Traders." Two years later, Edward Hand, then commander of Pittsburgh, desperately requested that "If there is not a possibility of obtaining lead, I wish we might be indulged with a cargo of bows and arrows, as our people are not yet expert enough at the sling of kill Indians with pebbles." No lead for Hand's army meant no lead for Hand's Indian neighbors.

The lack of supplies debilitated the neutralist Delawares. In Philadelphia in May 1779, a delegation of Coshoctons reminded Congress that the United States had promised to establish a trade, supplying the Delawares with goods, "School Masters and Mistresses," craftsmen, and "Husband-men to instruct the Youth of their Nation in useful Arts." It reminded Congress that at every treaty the promise had been renewed, "without ever having been complied with in any degree, whereby the said Delaware Nations have become poor & naked."

Congress itself, however, remained too poor and its own troops too naked to send goods to the Indians. The members also doubted that "the People in the Back

Counties" would allow an Indian supply train to pass unmolested, "so violent are the Prejudices against the Indians." Even the Delaware carrot of certain land cessions failed to raise the necessary supplies. . . .

Britain, meanwhile, did its best to keep the other northern Indians in cloth, powder, and ball. The British knew they had the advantage in Indian relations. General Frederick Haldimand wrote Major Arrent de Peyster in 1780 that "the Indians in general, wish to protract the War." Added to the danger of Anglo-American settlement, Indians generally favored the British because "it is impossible they can draw resources from the Rebels & they absolutely depend upon us for every Blanket they are covered with. Game remained scarce, trade was disrupted by war, and winters in the Ohio country could be fierce. The Indians needed blankets. It was a simple need, but if it could not be met in trade with the Anglo-Americans it had to be met somehow. Even for Indians who distrusted militant nativists, who put no faith in pan-Indianism, British supplies were *one* reason to take arms against the Anglo-Americans. . . .

They did so particularly in the wake of American raids. In the South, the raids of 1776 had driven the Cherokee nation proper to neutrality, but in the North, circumstances differed, and American raids only increased Indian hostilities. The Senecas suffered from the most serious northern invasions in 1779. The Shawnees were greatly exposed to Kentucky raiders and suffered three invasions: Colonel John Bowman's raid in May 1779, which destroyed the town of Chillicothe; and George Rogers Clark's invasions of August 1780 and November 1782, each of which destroyed several militant Shawnee villages. Clark's raids, conducted when the growing season was well under way, not only destroyed the Indians' stores but deprived them of their next season's food. Far from crushing Shawnee or Seneca militancy, however, the raids actually strengthened it. The raids may have accomplished the objective of delaying Shawnee incursions into Kentucky, but they resulted in few Shawnee or Seneca warriors' deaths. Also, unlike the Cherokees of 1776, the Shawnees could retreat for assistance and protection to Detroit or to the villages of other militants, and the Senecas could retreat to Niagara. As a result, the raids did not force militants among either people into neutrality. If anything, they fed Shawnee militancy by forcing the displaced Indians to rely on support from the British and the militant northern nations.

Murdering Neutrality, 1777–1779

For all its importance, the availability of British supplies did not by itself induce neutrality-minded Indians to join militants in the late years of the Revolution. Equally important was the murderous hatred for Indians that had developed during years of warfare among the inhabitants of western Pennsylvania, Maryland, and Virginia. Hatred became as established an article of backcountry commerce as was Indian land, and though not uncontested by Indians or by American individuals, it combined with a land hunger to inspire a series of killings that ruined the Coshoctons' chances for accommodation with the United States. As early as March 1777, George Morgan of Fort Pitt worried that his neighboring citizens were ready and anxious "to massacre our known [Indian] friends at their hunting camps as well as Messengers on Business to me." . . .

Later that year, several murders seriously eroded Ohioan Indian neutrality. In September, a party of neutral Senecas on its way to the annual autumn treaty at Pittsburgh came under rebel fire. Morgan found it necessary to have the Indian delegates bunk in his personal quarters. the "horrid murders" of Indians prevented a treaty council from taking place that month. They also turned many Senecas against the Americans.

The horrid murders were mere preliminaries to the first decisive act, the murder of Cornstalk, the leading Shawnee exponent of neutrality. By the time of his assassination, many of his people had already rejected his neutralist arguments. Shawnee parties had struck Anglo-American settlements in Virginia and Kentucky throughout the early years of the war, and the militia garrison of Fort Randolph, a Virginian outpost on the site of Point Pleasant, grew deeply embittered against the Shawnees.

On September 19, Fort Randolph's commander, Matthew Arbuckle, took two Shawnees prisoner. . . . By November 7, "satisfied the Shawanese are all our enemies," Arbuckle had taken prisoner two more visiting Shawnee chiefs, the once-nativist Red Hawk and the neutralist Cornstalk himself. Cornstalk's detention sent ripples of concern throughout the Ohio country. . . .

Fort Randolph, meanwhile, lost a soldier to an Indian raid outside its walls. In revenge, the garrison turned its guns on the unarmed prisoners within, murdering Cornstalk, Red Hawk, and all their fellows. Denunciations of Virginian treachery accompanied news of the act throughout the Indian villages of the North. The erstwhile Shawnee neutralist Nimwha became at once an enemy of the United States. He would later both capture Daniel Boone and lead a withering assault on American Fort Laurens. General Hand wrote east that if there had been any chance for peace with the Shawnees, "it is now Vanished." In the murders' wake, remaining neutrals among the Mingos and Senecas had taken up the war club; of the Coshocton Delawares, Hand remained uncertain.

American officials struggled to maintain neutralist factions among the Shawnees and Delawares at Coshocton. A month after the murders, Hand wrote to Patrick Henry that he knew, "it would be vain for me to bring the perpetrators of this horrid act to justice," but by April, several Anglo-Americans stood trail for the crimes at the Rockbridge County Court. It is almost needless to say that all were acquitted; no citizen would testify against them. . . .

Another series of killings compounded the effect on the Delawares of Cornstalk's murder. In February 1778, General Hand left Fort Pitt with five hundred militia in order to destroy a cache of British arms on the Cuyahoga River. Spring flooding hampered their march, but before abandoning it the patriots found and killed six Delawares at Beaver Creek. The victims of the five hundred Americans consisted of an old man and a woman from the Unamis, and three women and a boy from the Munsees. The outrage profoundly deranged Delaware neutrality. The Coshocton council sent word to the Americans that it had lost credibility among its neighbors. It had long boasted among the northern nations of the advantages of peace. In return, complained a member of the council, the Americans drove "the Tomahawk in my head, of which the others will be glad and mock at me." . . .

White Eyes and Killbuck remained opposed to war, despite the grave episode. They argued among their people that war against the white settlers simply could not be won. Unlike most northerners, they believed that even the combined forces of the northern Indians and the British could not overpower prolific, expansionist, and armed Americans. White Eyes and Killbuck accordingly allowed the Beaver Creek affair to pass and worked to tighten their relations with the United States. . . .

White Eyes, as we have seen, had no intention of fighting beside the Americans, but he was willing to guide them, to allow them to establish posts within Delaware territory, and to negotiate for them with their Indian enemies, if possible. He was also willing to carry messages over the dangerous terrain between the two new posts and Fort Pitt. Performing a like service for the Americans in November 1778, the neutralist met his death. The Americans, fearing the effect of the news on Coshocton, announced that he had died of smallpox. George Morgan, much later, related that he had been bushwacked by American militiamen. Given the tenor of feeling, Morgan's story rings true, and so it is most generally given.

White Eyes rode horseback at the time of the killing, at least that is suggested by the full saddlebag, saddlecloth, saddle, and bridle listed among his personal belongings. The "Inventory of Sundry Movables" taken after his death discloses a mixture of European and Delaware goods fit for a leader interested in Anglo-American ways. With his pair of scarlet "Breeches" he carried a buckskin pair of pants, buckskin leggings, and two breech cloths. With his four jackets (one of them scarlet, silk, and laced with gold trimmings) were a fur cap and a beaver hat. He hunted and fought with a rifle, walked in shoes (he had three pairs), sported buckles and a silver medal etches with a portrait of George III, warmed himself in one of his two green coats, painted his face, smoked from a pipe-tomahawk, treated with a belt of wampum in his hand, and saw the world (or perhaps only his close work) through the lenses of his spectacles. By frontier standards—both sides of the frontier—he had been traveling well clothed. His possessions indicate not only his material dependence on Western goods, but also the importance, economically, of his position as a broker with the Americans. If he could get goods from them, he could pass them on to his people.

Despite the cover-up of White Eyes' murder, Delaware-American relations continued to sour in the heat of other murders and murderous plots throughout 1779. In June, Colonel Broadhead informed his Indian "Brothers" at Pittsburgh that "some wicked person" in the neighborhood had mortally wounded a Delaware whom Broadhead professed to love "as my Son." . . . By the end of 1779, the murders had driven many, but not all, Coshocton Delawares and Shawnees into the arms of the militants, and the erstwhile neutral ground disintegrated in civil conflict.

Polarization and Realignment, 1779–1781

The Coshocton-area Delawares, led by White Eyes and Killbuck, and the neutral factions of Shawnees, led by Cornstalk and Nimwha, had kept the peace in the early years. By 1777, the Coshocton Delawares had gathered into their village and its environs 400 of the 500 Unami Delaware "Fighting Men," 20 of the 90 Munsee Delaware warriors, and after Cornstalk's murder, 50 of the 300-odd Shawnee gunmen, most of them Mequashakes. Coshocton, the bastion of neutrality, thus contained some 470 neutralist men, and, we can assume, their families. If men of fighting age constitute a fourth or a fifth of the entire population, greater Coshocton probably supported some 2,000 people: a respectable size for a community on either side of the frontier.

Militant Delawares and Shawnees constituted, at the beginning of the war, a slight minority of the combined Delaware Shawnee populations. One hundred Unami Delaware gunmen had migrated west, as fighting broke out, to join up with the militant Wyandots and Miamis; about 70 Munsee fighters had placed themselves among both the militant Unamis and the Mingos; and most of the 250 Shawnee warriors remaining in the Upper Ohio region had also sided with the militants. Over the course of the war, these militants would see their own numbers rise at the expense of their Coshocton compatriots, as escalating disaffection from the Americans propelled erstwhile neutralists away from the Pennsylvania and Virginia frontier. But until the completion of neutralist alienation from the United States, militant attitudes toward Coshocton heated.

The differences among the Ohio Indians reached their emotional peak in 1779, a year in which the Coshocton Delawares came to actual blows with their anti-American kinsmen. The year would see one of the few instances, since the Seven Years' War, of Upper Ohio country Indians firing at each other in battle. This abandonment of neutrality by Killbuck and his followers would represent no community consensus; it would tear at divisions within the shrinking Coshocton community. Things would go so badly for the Coshoctons over the next two years that by early 1781 most of them would recoil from the policy of friendship with the rebels and would join their kinsmen in a war against the United States.

As 1779 opened, shortly after news of White Eyes' death reached Coshocton, villagers expressed their commitment to neutrality. . . . Although in the year's early months the Delawares would not fight for the Americans, they did, like the neighboring Moravian mission towns, render valuable assistance to the garrison at Fort Laurens in two significant ways. First, they warned the garrisons at Laurens and Pittsburgh that a concerted Indian force, including some Shawnees and Delawares, had gathered at Detroit to plan an assault on Laurens. Along the same lines, they informed Pittsburgh of the progress of the siege of Fort Laurens once it had begun. Second, they helped to raise that siege, persuading, in a series of councils that ended around March 12, 1779, the enemies of the United States to depart. It was after these meetings, after most of the attackers had already withdrawn, that reinforcements relieved the wretched garrison. Morgan credited the Coshocton Delawares with having "saved Fort Laurens."

In the process of winning accolades from an American commander, Killbuck—now, after White Eyes' death and Pipe's withdrawal, Coshocton's most important voice—incurred the wrath of the northern Indians. Killbuck found it impossible to maintain a friendly neutrality with both the United States and its northwestern enemies. . . .

Toward the end of June, pro-American Coshoctons crossed the Rubicon, shedding the blood of their militant relatives. A young Delaware, Nonowland (George Wilson), scouted for twenty militiamen in a raid toward the Seneca country, encountering a party of Senecas and Munsees. Nonowland joined in the fighting himself, and his party took a Munsee Delaware scalp. When the warriors returned with the expedition to Pittsburgh, they presented the hair to visiting Coshocton delegates. These carried the scalp back toward their village, still a home to neutral Munsees. Coshocton had only recently lost a warrior to the Indian-haters on the white frontier. Now one of its number had killed someone closely connected to some of its inhabitants. Killbuck's support for Nonowland's act earned him the militant Munsees' enduring disgust.

Nevertheless, on July 12, Killbuck and the Coshocton Council pledged to become firm allies of the United States. Soon another Indian scalp came in with a party of Delawares and Americans, and on August 11, 1779, 8 of the Coshocton warriors joined Broadhead's 628 men in an attack on the western flank of the Seneca Nation. . . . Broadhead reached the abandoned Seneca towns, destroyed eight of them, and put houses and corn to the torch, forcing the Seneca refugees into greater reliance on Britain. In response, northern Indian opposition to Coshocton mounted. . . .

At this point, barely 10 Coshoctons had actually undertaken hostilities against their kinsmen and neighbors to the north and west. In mid-September 1779, on Broadhead's return to Pittsburgh, 30 more Coshoctons (including some Mequashake Shawnees) sought to accompany the Americans in arms. But Broadhead lacked the supplies with which to pay them, and he had to turn them away. They returned to Coshocton, poorly armed and clothed. Their town lay open to enemy strikes.

Broadhead's inability to secure supplies continued throughout 1780. Without any goods, he could barely maintain a defensive posture in Pittsburgh, much less supply warriors for an expedition against Detroit. When abandoning Fort Laurens in the summer of 1779, he had promised the Coshoctons that he would reestablish the fort to protect them. By the fall of 1780, it was clear that he could not do so. . . . [A]t the time of Broadhead's expedition of 1779, it had appeared likely that the Americans would crush the Indian militants to the north and west. By 1780, it was clear that the militants were stronger and more vigorous than ever. The Coshocton people had risked their reputations among their strengthening kinsmen and had gained little thereby. By early 1781, a faction opposing Killbuck seized control, and Coshocton policy turned abruptly about.

Broadhead got word of the coup in January. He absorbed the depressing news that the reliable Killbuck not only no longer led the Coshoctons, but now sought to live with the Moravians and was considering "becoming a Christian." The deposed leader, Broadhead learned, felt isolated and did not believe that either Broadhead "or the Council of Cooshockung [were] at any loss about me." Killbuck persisted in his personal alliance with the United States, turning further against his own people. He kept Broadhead abreast of Delaware plans, for he still had sources. . . .

It was in this wrathful season that Broadhead decided to undertake a rapid strike against his ally, the Coshocton Delaware community. It stands as a mark of Killbuck's thorough alienation from his own people that Broadhead secured his and his followers' assistance. On April 7, 1781, Broadhead and his 150 Continentals descended the Ohio to Wheeling, where the militia doubled his force. The combined 300, guided by pro-American Coshocton refugee warriors, advanced northward to overwhelm and raze Coshocton.

If Killbuck had any remaining illusions about the militia's attitudes toward Indians, they may have been exposed when the invaders summarily executed fifteen captured Coshocton warriors. And if that was not enough, American Martin Wetzel murdered an enemy envoy who had been promised safe conduct, while five neutral Moravian Indians who had been visiting fled homeward under militia fire. But Killbuck and his loyal followers now had no choice but to risk it with the Americans, lest they incur a heavy penalty from the northern Indians. Under the unsteady protection of the United States, he and his warriors returned with the Continentals to Fort Pitt.

Like most of the American expeditions against Native American villages during the Revolution, Broadhead's attack had harassed, injured, and dispossessed the Coshoctons, but it did little to interfere with their new militancy. The Coshoctons fled, "half naked," to Sandusky, where they were taken in by militant Delawares and Wyandots and where they were supplied by the British. From there, they joined in the heavy raids of 1781, the most alarming attacks yet witnessed by the Anglo-American inhabitants of the revolutionary frontier.

"Two Angry Spirits"

Among the targets of northern Indian raiding was the Moravian mission. . . .

The northern Indians captured the missionaries and delivered them to the British at Detroit. The spared the inhabitants, but plundered the homes, threatened the leaders, and killed much of the livestock, "not only from hunger, but from caprice." . . .

Although Moravian cooperation with the Americans was the main reason for both the capture of the ministers and the disruption of the Moravian Indian towns in that late summer of 1781, the nativistic hostility of many of the northerners toward the Christian communities also played a role. . . . The suspicion that the Moravians harbored witches . . . had plagued the mission throughout its history.

Indian opponents of the Christian mission, despite their seizure of the ministers in 1781, did not deliver the heaviest blow to the mission; that came from the rebels the mission had done so much to protect. In the most gruesome assault on neutrals in the Coshocton area, eighty to ninety Long Knives [Anglo-Americans] under Colonel David Williamson coldly and methodically killed the inhabitants of two Moravian towns, Salem and Gnadenhutten, in March 1782. In all, the militiamen murdered ninety-six unarmed men, women, and children, whom they had gathered at Gnadenhutten. Most of the victims were Munsees, some Unamis, possibly a few were not Delawares but Shawnees. So shameful was the action that, over a century later, a most-partisan advocate of United States expansion, the scholarly Theodore Roosevelt, concluded his narrative of the event with a condemnation of Williamson and his party: "It is impossible not to regret that fate failed to send some strong war party of savages across the path of these inhuman cowards, to inflict on them the punishment they so richly deserved."

Williamson's attack was no spontaneous outbreak of frontier frenzy. Almost a year before, three hundred militiamen had planned an assault on the Moravians. Colonel John Gibson of Fort Pitt had opposed that earlier scheme, writing to Governor Thomas Jefferson of Virginia, "The Moravians have always given us the most convincing proofs of their attachment to the cause of America, by always giving us intelligence of every party that came against the frontiers; & on the late expedition they furnished Col. Broadhead & his party with a large quantity of provisions when they were starving." But by 1782, with the missionaries themselves captive in Detroit, and with the Pennsylvania, Maryland, and Virginia back countries reeling under effective Indian assaults, American affection for the Moravian Indians of Ohio, who had done them such service, had vanished.

The depth of backcountry hostility for all Indians was not lost on the few Coshocton Delawares who had, following Killbuck, allied with the Americans and sought refuge at Fort Pitt. When Captain Williamson and his band returned from their genocidal mission, the proceeded to kill members of Killbuck's party. Most escaped, but the American cause among the Delawares, already lost, had reached its pitiful epilogue. Congress's inability to supply necessities and the intensified Indian-hating on the Anglo-American side of the frontier had combined with the strength of the northern militants and the attractiveness of the British alliance to finish the Coshoctons' experiment in peace with the new nation. . . .

Killbuck himself survived the militia's fury and remained at Fort Pitt until 1785; on no day, Zeisberger later reported, could Killbuck be "sure of his life, on account of the militia." In the late 1780s, with enemies among the whites and among the northern Indians, this poor advocate of accommodation with Anglo-American joined the Moravian community in Loyalist Upper Canada. There he lived under the threat of Indian retaliation. His story is emblematic of the hopelessness of Ohioan Indian cooperation with the United States between the outbreak of the Revolution and the final defeat of the Ohioan militants in 1794. Grasping that hopelessness is important to any understanding of the widespread success of pan-Indian diplomacy both during the Revolutionary War and in the decade that followed its formal end. Both neutrality and cooperation with the United States had been and would continue to be ruled out, in most instances, by the intensity of hatred and the conflict over land along the frontier. Indian conflict with the new nation would become the norm. In missionary David Zeisberger's words, as good for the neutral Coshoctons as for the Moravian Indians, the world between the militants and Anglo-Americans had grown "already too narrow."

The Loyalists Confront Civil, Revolutionary, and Partisan Warfare

ROBERT M. CALHOON

The loyalists are a perplexing element in the history of the War for Independence. . . . In the more sparsely settled parts of the middle and southern colonies much of the population was inclined to acquiesce to whatever regime could maintain order and security. In this context, John Shy suggests, the British and patriots were competing for the allegiance and respect of a sizable, uncommitted segment of the population which was loyalist, neutral, inoffensive, or disaffected, depending on an observer's immediate perspective. . . . Seeking to place loyalists in a broad social context, historians have used the terms civil, partisan, and revolutionary to define the kinds of social conflicts which generated and fueled the War for Independence. Civil war implies two conventional armies arising within the same populace; partisan war refers

Robert M. Calhoon, "Civil, Revolutionary, or Partisan: The Loyalists and the Nature of the War for Independence," in *The Loyalist Perception and Other Essays,* pp. 147–162. Copyright © 1989. Reprinted by permission of the University of South Carolina Press.

to the resort to decentralized, guerilla fighting by at least one side; and revolutionary wars are grand upheavals against existing institutions.

This paper will show how useful these terms can be in examining the factual record of loyalist military activity, especially in the first half of the war. However, another concept, "internal war," must be used if one is to see the later stages of the war through loyalist eyes and to understand the psychological impact which the war had on those loyalists who brooded over the military dilemma confronting them and the British.

From Lexington and Concord in April 1775, . . . and onward into the Howe and Burgoyne offensives of 1777, the advent of war in America was a ragged, chaotic affair. No simple formula can account for the nearly 10,000 loyalists who bore arms during the first half of the war. There were roughly five categories of impulses that drew loyalists to arms. In the first place, some loyalists in arms simply represented Britain's natural assets in America (recently arrived British emigrants, those tied by interest to the British army in New York City or in Albany, or to the Indian Superintendents); second, other loyalists entered the fray in moments of rage, confusion, or fear; third, still others believed themselves to be strategically situated to unleash terrible vengeance on the rebels and acted from a combination of calculation and impulse; fourth, others responded to the need for organized pacification and reconciliation by supporters of the Crown; and fifth, a few groups of armed loyalists were agrarian radicals in conflict with aristocratic patriot elites. Clearly these categories overlap, dissolve into one another, and describe shifting behavior in different circumstances. . . .

The mere presence of large numbers of persons disaffected from the Revolution reflected and aggravated social instability which inhibited either side from exploiting its best opportunities. New Jersey was the classic case of Britain's inability to translate military predominance into political advantage. The Revolutionary regime disintegrated in that province as the British occupied New Jersey after the seizure of New York City in the autumn and early winter of 1776. Nearly 2,500 New Jersey volunteers drawn from a pool of some 13,000 loyalist sympathizers provided ample manpower to pacify a conquered province. . . . Yet even in this promising setting pacification proved impossible. Plundering by Hessian and British troops and numerous acts of personal vengeance and cruelty by armed loyalists mocked British pretentions to be protecting the King's friends in the middle colonies. Even after the British were forced to retreat to isolated beachheads at Amboy and New Brunswick, turmoil in New Jersey at first presented the British command in New York City with the opportunity to make inroads and then pulled the miragelike advantages away. The community of Jersey exiles in New York City continually undermined the British commanders by their penchant for unauthorized terrorist activities.

Garrison towns like New York City gave the British secure bases and havens for loyalist refugees. Garrison towns also were unstable, abnormal communities filled with violent, rootless men. St. Augustine in East Florida and Pensacola in West Florida were refuges for more than 15,000 loyalists driven from the southern colonies. In order to organize these bloated wartime communities the British distributed lavish new land grants and assured refugees that British rule in the Floridas would be perpetual. In East Florida large numbers enlisted into a loyalist provincial corps, the East Florida Rangers, which became a pawn in a vicious power struggle between Colonel Alexander Prevost and Governor Patrick Tonyn. Tonyn appointed the irrepressible South Carolina backcountry partisan, Thomas Brown, commander of the Rangers. First used to patrol the border between East Florida and Georgia, the Rangers increasingly carried out raids into Georgia to steal cattle and slaves.

Ambitious to recapture Georgia on his own initiative and constantly fearful that rebel militia and regulars would swoop down on St. Augustine, Tonyn expected Prevost to function as a subordinate. Tonyn also tried to undercut Indian Superintendent John Stuart's careful management of the Creeks and Choctaws. The impetuous governor expected Stuart to arrange massive Indian support for the reconquest of Georgia and for the periodic reinforcement of St. Augustine. He could not comprehend Stuart's view that Indian support was a precious commodity that required careful bargaining and prudent use. For his part, Thomas Brown knew that there were thousands of potential loyalists still living in the Georgia and South Carolina backcountry and in pockets of the lowcountry as well. With Tonyn's support he committed the Rangers to a dangerous role as spearhead of the reconquest of the backcountry. Tonyn's and Brown's efforts to instill energy, purpose, and zeal into the loyalist exile community in East Florida were just the sort of energetic civil-military policy so badly lacking elsewhere in America in 1776–77, but these efforts came at a high price. Incursions into Georgia, attempts to use Indians as shock troops, and the resort to savage, irregular warfare awakened the dissipirited and chaotic Revolutionary governments of South Carolina and Georgia to the magnitude of the threat which the war posed for their society.

The most thorough and competent effort to pacify Revolutionary America and to reinstitute British authority was, of course, Joseph Galloway's administration as Superintendent of Police and of Exports and Imports in occupied Philadelphia from his appointment in December 1777, until British evacuation the following June. Galloway successfully expanded a subordinate job in the military bureaucracy into that of a powerful administrative overseer of British policy in the city. Since his flight to refuge in New York City in December 1776, Galloway had labored to persuade Howe to move against Philadelphia. He even arranged for pilots familiar with the Delaware River to rendezvous with the British attack force. . . .

Disdainful of Howe's languid movement into the city, Galloway assumed the role of civilian overlord of the region as soon as British troops landed. . . . He appointed a large staff of assistants and undertook systematic collection of intelligence, certification of loyalists, exposure of suspected rebel sympathizers, acquisition of food, establishment of hospital administration, and the issuance of regulations on curfews, garbage collection, tavern licenses, relief for the poor, and other local government functions. At his own expense he organized two companies of loyalist refugees and directed a number of guerilla agents and spies who exhibited great discipline and loyalty. Reestablishing civil government in all but name was for Galloway one essential precondition for reconciliation; the other was constitutional reform along the lines of his 1774 Plan of Union.

Bitterly disappointed by Howe's failure to move aggressively, Galloway in 1779 was the star witness in a Parliamentary inquiry into Howe's conduct of the war. His ludicrous assertion that 80 percent of the population was loyal to the Crown has tended to discredit his assessment of the war. Actually Howe and Galloway shared many of the same assumptions about the nature of the war and of the requirements for pacification. Howe believed that the mass of the population would begin to adhere to the Crown as soon as they saw the Continental Army forced to retreat from centers of population and unable to resist the steady, methodical occupation of territory by British regulars. Galloway predicted that if the loyalist majority of the population was given an opportunity to support pacification, they would respond in large numbers, provided that they were cajoled, coaxed, and assured of safety and security. . . .

. . . [T]he middle colonies contained many pockets of desperate men willing to risk their safety and security to vent their hostility toward the Revolutionary regime. In the Hudson Valley and on the eastern shore of Maryland these groups were populist rebels hostile to social hierarchy and anxious to disperse political power much more widely than prevailing whig oligarchs in New York and Maryland would tolerate.

In the Hudson Valley, where tenant unrest had smoldered for a decade, tenants on Livingston Manor, the baronial holdings of the great whig family of the name, seized the opportunity in 1775 to petition for redress of their own grievances. Some four hundred tenants took up arms for the King in 1776; the militia was riddled with disaffection. Finally in 1777 news of Burgoyne's offensive triggered a premature uprising which was crushed swiftly by militia loyal to Livingstons. On Maryland's Eastern Shore the war accentuated sharp economic and social grievances in a region where the Revolutionary regime lacked the institutions and lines of direct political control and influence. Some slaves in the region responded to Lord Dunmore's appeal to blacks to abandon their masters; the first three slaves caught attempting to flee to the British were publicly hanged, decapitated, and quartered. White loyalists were more numerous and more difficult to handle. Local committees of observation and the state Council of Safety lacked the practical power or the political strength to impose severe penalties on avowed British sympathizers. Thirty-four percent of Eastern Shore residents indicted for political offenses during the Revolution were landless, and popular pressure forced judges and juries to deal mildly with them. The militia was paralyzed by demands that officers be locally elected instead of centrally appointed. In salt riots groups of armed men summarily appropriated scarce supplies of that commodity from wealthy whig merchants. In numerous instances whig officials were beaten, cursed, and otherwise abused with impunity.

These isolated cases of violent, lower-class loyalist insurgency did not constitute a real threat to the success of the Revolution, but they manifested an important characteristic of the social order: the presence of a sizable minority of groups who, in William H. Nelson's apt phrase, "felt weak and threatened" and "had interests they felt needed protection from an American majority." These included pacifist and pietist groups, Mohawk Valley Indian and white settlers alike who looked to the Indian Superintendent for the northern tribes for leadership and protection, and newcomers to the southern backcountry. The presence and attitudes of these groups did not mean that Britain could have won the war if she had only tapped this asset; it does mean that Britain's strongest resource could be mobilized only at a price which the Mother Country could not afford to pay—the dispatch of enough troops to occupy the large regions where fearful, insecure subjects of the Crown resided and thereby to overcome the sense of weakness which immobilized these defensive people. This confused ebb and flow of loyalist military initiatives helps to define more precisely the nature of the partisan, civil, and revolutionary aspects of the war. Partisan war is irregular war which often involves terror inflicted by informal bands of insurgents. Partisan war occurs when the military and political institutions of one or more of the contending sides have ceased to function in part of the contested territory of the war. A leadership vacuum is created to be filled by men uninhibited by prudence, human-ity, or obedience to duly constituted superiors. Irregular war does not replace conven-tional main force combat, but is occurs on the periphery of conventional combat in areas where neither side can restore stable administration with the use of regular troops. Although it occurs on the periphery of conventional operations, irregular war is destabilizing in that it empowers a relatively small number of men to upset the bal-ance of power previously established between the contending parties. . . .

Civil wars are protracted hostilities between irreconcilably antagonistic seg-ments of society within the same country who intend to exclude one another from political power and social advantage and to extirpate one another's beliefs and principles. By several standards the War for Independence was a civil war. Nine-teen thousand loyalists bore arms at one time or another. But civil war was often important as a potential, rather than as an actual, condition. When individual loyal-ists beseeched the British to concentrate force in a given region—the Delaware Valley, around the Chesapeake Bay, the Hudson Valley, the Ohio Valley, southeast-ern Pennsylvania—in order to release the energies of numerous loyalist inhabi-tants, these self-appointed strategic advisors were really saying that civil war was an imminent possibility. Such a war, they reasoned, would be based upon rival loyal and rebel zones of control. It would occur as soon as the British took the necessary risks and expended sufficient manpower and resources to establish secure zones on the colonial map where loyalist and passive adherents to the Crown could reside.

A revolutionary war is the hardest to define because, strictly speaking, the terms applies to a society in the midst of a radical redistribution of wealth and op-portunity or to a society shifting abruptly from one life style to another—conditions which do not entirely obtain in the case of the American Revolution. The rejection of British authority and the advent of republican government aroused strong pas-sions which approximated those of a revolutionary war. Moreover, the volatile mixture of civil and partisan war which occurred spasmodically during the War for Independence made that conflict potentially revolutionary because it raised the spectre of a descent into barbarism.

From such a perspective the War for Independence was partisan on its periphery, civil only when Britain threatened to gain secure control over a large territorial area, and revolutionary in discontinuous moments when the prospect of American victory portended social changes which were terrifying to cohesive and self-conscious loyal-ist and neutralist constituencies. This provisional model does not rigidly separate civil, partisan, and revolutionary warfare. Residents of the Mohawk Valley, for ex-ample, felt that they were involved in a continuous civil war, but only the period of the St. Leger offensive conforms to a precise definition of civil war: two rival, con-ventional armies faced one another and Britain nearly gained regional dominance. Mohawk depredations against pro-American Oneida villages during this period, however, marked the threshold of partisan warfare by Mohawk warriors and by Butler's raiders against patriot white settlers and Indians alike.

That very kind of difficulty, however, has impelled political theorists like Harry Eckstein to develop the model of "internal war" to deal with the whole range of conflicts including social revolution, struggles for national liberation, wars of secession, and internal conflicts which accompany political modernization—"any resort to violence within a political order to change its constitution, rulers, or policies." . . . Loyalist writings about the last half of the War for Independence dealt with increasing urgency and cogency with the problem of internal war, with the sources of counterrevolutionary activity which lay hidden in the recesses of the social order.

These loyalist writings on the nature of the war may not be accurate objective accounts of military realists, but they reveal the harsh impact of the war on the human spirit and imagination, especially on people suddenly convinced that they were victims of both American cruelty and British incompetence. Conceiving of the war as an instrument of punishment was to recognize the immense complexity of the military dilemma facing the British and the loyalists. Colonel Robert Gray, South Carolina loyalist provincial officer, former whig, and backcountry native, recognized a yearning for order and fear of social disintegration in occupied South Carolina in the summer of 1780. "The conquest of the province was complete," he wrote; "the loyal . . . inhabitants, . . . one third" of the population "and . . . by no means the wealthiest, readily took up arms to maintain the British government and others enrolled themselves in the [loyalist] militia, partly because they believed the war to be at an end in the southern provinces and partly to ingratiate themselves with the conquerors. They fondly hoped they would enjoy a respite from the calamities of war and that the restoration of the King's government would restore to them the happiness they enjoyed before the war began. With these views [prevailing] on both sides, the Whigs and Tories seemed to vie with each other in giving proof of the sincerity of their submission" to British authority "and a most profound calm succeeded."

Far from being an advantage to the British, this state of stability was quicksand. Rebels who took an oath of submission returned to their farms and commerce in Charlestown revived. Caught up in this economic bustle, people were outraged by the British army's confiscation of horses, cattle and supplies. The sudden prominence of loyalists in the civil and military establishment afflicted former whig officials with "pangs of disappointed ambition." When notorious rebels were captured, "ignorant" British officers paroled them to their plantations and in a few days they broke parole and sought revenge on the loyalist militiamen who had assisted in their capture. In this fluid situation, which oscillated unpredictably between benumbed submission and furious retaliation, the loyalist militia lost their cohesion as fighting units—"officers not able to inspire their followers with the confidence necessary for soldiers" and British regulars contemptuous "of a militia among a people differing so much in custom and manners from themselves." The destruction of Ferguson's loyalist force at Kings Mountain and the increasingly brutal treatment of loyalists captured in the South Carolina backcountry combined to shatter the tenuous control which the Crown enjoyed in the province. "The unfortunate Loyalist on the frontiers found the fury of the whole war let loose upon him. He was no longer safe to sleep in his house. He hid himself in the swamps." Because the British refused to impose execution on rebel insurgents captured by frontier loyalists, Gray believed, many loyalists were forced into collaboration with the rebels in order to be "safe to go to sleep without . . . having his throat cut before morning." Other loyalists simply resorted to the brutal guerilla tactics familiar to survivors of the Cherokee War—ambush, summary execution of helpless captives, decapitation of victims. "In short, the whole province resembled a piece of patch work" in which "the inhabitants of every settlement . . . united in sentiment" took up "arms for the side it liked best" and made "continual inroads into one another's settlements."

Both their keen perception of the strengths and weaknesses of the Revolutionary social order and their fixation upon the use of conventional and irregular violence to undermine that order induced the loyalists during the last half of the war to conceive of the conflict as an instrument of punishment, vengeance, and retribution and as a technique of social control. The Revolutionary social order, however, evaded punishment. Understandably frustrated and angered, the loyalists who dealt with the military situation became increasingly petulent and meddlesome. As a result their fundamental concern with the war as punishment has been neglected. Central to their viewpoint was the assumption that in 1778–1779 the Revolution was about to collapse and their belief that deft, purposeful British pressure could bring this process to fruition: "the rebel currency is tottering on the very brink of annihilation, if not allowed to recover; . . . the people in general are becoming indifferent if not averse" to a government which has brought them only distress and regimentation; "the enthusiasm which at first enabled the Americans without funds, arrangements, or visible resources to act with such success is now lost in disgust and disappointment . . . and in place of that general union and concert which then prevailed there now remains only a faction and a very limited and artificial army, neither of which are of the people." These were the conclusions which leading loyalist refugees in New York City asked Major Patrick Ferguson to convey to General Clinton in November 1779. . . .

The erosion of popular support for the Revolution and the artificial nature of the rebel regime, Ferguson told Clinton, provided the keys for a successful British prosecution of the war. Once the rebels realized that they could not drive the British from Georgia and once the fickle French fleet departed American waters, Britain would be free to undertake a campaign of retribution "distressing the countryside," seizing and punishing rebel leaders, and "living off of plunder." At this point Washington would have to do battle or suffer humiliating retreat, the currency would collapse, Congress would forfeit all capacity to punish deserters, and the people would "see no end of their fruitless sufferings." This scenario required Britain to employ "the only common, justifiable . . . modes of coercion, . . . destroying their resources," confiscating the property of anyone who impeded the suppression of the rebellion.

Joseph Galloway's trusted subordinate, Isaac Ogden, made much the same assessment a year earlier. "The rebellion hangs by a slender thread," he assured Galloway in November, 1778. . . .

Ogden and Ferguson both acknowledged that the rebellion was an authentic social movement. This implied that Congress and the Army, initially at least, had been "of the people" and that "enthusiasm" had for a time taken the place of money, bureaucracy, and leadership. Until British actions dramatically demonstrated the futility of resistance to large segments of the populace, both men conceded, the movement would not die, and to this extent they were acknowledging its indigenous social roots. Ogden and Ferguson further seemed to sense that the rebellion's indigenous character provided the key to its suppression. By carrying the war to the whole society, by using plunder and destruction as psychological weapons, in short, by threatening to precipitate complete social chaos, Britain could convert disspirited rebels into desperate and disillusioned advocates of peace and submission. John Goodrich of Virginia proposed to Clinton a pincer attack on Williamsburg, "the metropolis of infamy," from the James and York rivers. "I know the genesus of the Virginians," he explained; "an example of devastation would have a good effect, the minds of the people struck with a panic would expect the whole country to share the same fate. Offer rewards for bringing to justice the active rebels, let them be proportioned to their rank and consequence . . . , make proper examples, countenance and protect the inoffensive and honest farmers. This done, every rebel will suspect his neighbor, all confidence will cease, the guilty in crowds will retire to the back country without a possibility of removing provisions for their subsistence, hunger will make them desperate and open their eyes, they will fall on their destructive leaders, peace and submission, of course, must follow." . . .

The loyalists' determination from 1778 through 1781 to use warfare in order to scourge and punish American society for its sins of ingratitude and disobedience was the same kind of curious mixture of political sagacity and moral absolutism which characterized whig ideology. The loyalist conception of military reality was a caricatured mirror image of the Spirit of '76.

F U R T H E R   R E A D I N G

Native Americans

Colin G. Calloway, *The American Revolution in Indian Country: Crisis and Diversity in Native American Communities* (1995)

David H. Corkran, *The Creek Frontier, 1540–1783* (1967)

Gregory Evans Dowd, *A Spirited Resistance: the North American Indian Struggle for Unity, 1745–1815* (1992)

Barbara Graymont, *The Iroquois in the American Revolution* (1972)

Eric Hinderaker, *Elusive Empires: Constructing Colonialism in the Ohio Valley, 1673–1800* (1997)

Reginald Horsman, *Expansion and American Indian Policy* (1967)

Francis Jennings, *Empire of Fortune: Crowns, Colonies, and Tribes in the Seven Years' War* (1988)

Isabel Thompson Kelsay, *Joseph Brant, 1743–1807: Man of Two Worlds* (1984)

William G. McLoughlin, *Cherokee Renascence in the New Republic* (1986)

James H. O'Donnell III, *Southern Indians in the American Revolution* (1973)

Francis Paul Prucha, *American Indian Policy in the Formative Years: The Indian Trade and Intercourse Acts, 1780–1834* (1962)

Daniel K. Richter and James H. Merrell, eds., *Beyond the Covenant Chain: The Iroquois and Their Neighbors in Indian North America* (1987)

Loyalists

Robert S. Allen, ed., *The Loyal Americans: The Military Role of Loyalist Provincial Corps and Their Settlement in British North America, 1775–1784* (1983)

Bernard Bailyn, *The Ordeal of Thomas Hutchinson* (1974)

Carol Berkin, *Jonathan Sewall: Odyssey of an American Loyalist* (1974)

Wallace Brown, *The Good Americans: The Loyalists in the American Revolution* (1969)

————, *The King's Friends: The Composition and Motives of the American Loyalist Claimants* (1965)

Robert M. Calhoon, *The Loyalist Perception and Other Essays* (1989)

————, *The Loyalists in Revolutionary America, 1760–1781* (1973)

M. Thomas Hatley, *The Dividing Paths: Cherokees and South Carolinians through the Revolutionary Era* (1993)

Elizabeth P. McCaughey, *From Loyalist to Founding Father: The Political Odyssey of William Samuel Johnson* (1980)

William H. Nelson, *The American Tory* (1961)

Mary Beth Norton, *The British-Americans: The Loyalist Exiles in England, 1774–1789* (1972)

William Pencak, *America's Burke: The Mind of Thomas Hutchinson* (1982)

Janice Potter, *The Liberty We Seek: Loyalist Ideology in Colonial New York and Massachusetts* (1983)

Philip Ranlet, *The New York Loyalists* (1986)

Paul H. Smith, *Loyalists and Redcoats: A Study in British Revolutionary Policy* (1964)

James W. St. G. Walker, *The Black Loyalists: The Search for a Promised Land in Nova Scotia and Sierra Leone, 1783–1870* (1976)

Ellen Gibson Wilson, *The Loyal Blacks* (1976)

Esther Clark Wright, *The Loyalists of New Brunswick* (1955)

Anne Y. Zimmer, *Jonathan Boucher: Loyalist in Exile* (1978)

Are All Men Equal?
The African-American
Challenge

"We hold these truths to be self-evident, that all men are created equal," Congress proclaimed, "that they are endowed by their Creator with certain unalienable rights, that among these are life, liberty, and the pursuit of happiness." Where did Congress's declaration leave African Americans, virtually all of whom were enslaved on July 4, 1776? For the most part, the Revolution left them as it found them, in slavery. Whatever their private sentiments may have been, Thomas Jefferson, John Adams, Benjamin Franklin, and their colleagues had no intention of applying principles of natural equality and rights to the Africans and African Americans in their midst. The irony of this contradiction struck Samuel Johnson, the English essayist, who quipped: "How is it we hear the loudest yelps for liberty among the drivers of Negroes?"

In fact, in the open society of Revolutionary America such a powerful, soul-stirring idea as natural liberty could not be contained. Inadvertently, Congress subverted age-old customs and institutions with its radical language, and Samuel Johnson was not the only one who noticed. Already in 1775, slaves in the Chesapeake had escaped to freedom in response to Lord Dunmore's promise to free those who would take up arms for Britain; and in New England free African Americans had served in the battles of Lexington and Concord as well as Bunker Hill. The human rights rhetoric of the preceding decade had led many whites without a stake in the slave system to question it, and had provided legitimacy to the efforts of the small but growing number of slaves and free blacks who asserted their right to liberty. By the war's end the new nation possessed a small but significant free black population, and in the northern states, beginning with Vermont and Massachusetts, a powerful movement was taking hold that would abolish slavery either immediately or gradually. But in the south there was vociferous resistance to such efforts; and the net effect of Revolutionary era reforms would be the preservation of the slave system for one half of the nation and its abolition for the other half.

The readiness of colonial slaves, assisted by sympathetic whites, to seize on the rhetoric of liberty is evident in Document 1. Document 2 illustrates how some rural white settlers, people who had no material or political interest in slavery, were ready to overturn it immediately in the name of liberty. Lemuel Haynes's unpublished attack on slavery, Document 3, shows how a free African American, who was a veteran of the Ticonderoga campaign, understood his citizenship role as an advocate for abolition. The Earl of Dunmore's proclamation reveals why the meaning of the Revolutionary War had such different implications for Virginia's whites and blacks in Document 4. The postwar, grassroots defenses of slavery present compelling reasons why whites restricted the ideal of natural rights, equality, and liberty in the south. Where social, political, and material interests were at stake, the sacred rights of property and the legitimacy supplied by scripture provided sufficient arguments to block abolition—beliefs that survived three generations and were only surmounted by Union armies and the pronouncements of President Lincoln. Finally, the Gettysburg Address, although written eighty-seven years after the Declaration of Independence, reasserted that the doctrine of natural equality, which was evaded in the Constitution, should become national policy at last.

1. Massachusetts Slaves Argue for Freedom, 1773

Boston, April 20th, 1773

Sir, The efforts made by the legislative of this province in their last sessions to free themselves from slavery, gave us, who are in that deplorable state, a high degree of satisfaction. We expect great things from men who have made such a noble stand against the designs of their *fellow-men* to enslave them. We cannot but wish and hope Sir, that you will have the same grand object, we mean civil and religious liberty, in view in your next session. The divine spirit of *freedom,* seems to fire every humane breast on this continent, except such as are bribed to assist in executing the execrable plan.

We are very sensible that it would be highly detrimental to our present masters, if we were allowed to demand all that of *right* belongs to us for past services; this we disclaim. Even the *Spaniards,* who have not those sublime ideas of freedom that English men have, are conscious that they have no right to all the services of their fellow-men, we mean the *Africans,* whom they have purchased with their money; therefore they allow them one day in a week to work for themselves, to enable them to earn money to purchase the residue of their time, which they have a right to demand in such portions as they are able to pay for (a due appraizement of their services being first made, which always stands at the purchase money). We do not pretend to dictate to you Sir, or to the Honorable Assembly, of which you are a member. We acknowledge our obligations to you for what you have already done, but as the people of this province seem to be actuated by the principles of equity and justice, we cannot but expect your house will again take our deplorable case into serious consideration, and give us that ample relief which, as *men,* we have a natural right to.

"Massachusetts Slaves Argue for Freedom, 1773." As found in Leslie Fishel and Benjamin Quarles, eds., *Black Americans: A Documentary History* (New York: Morrow, 1970), 45.

But since the wise and righteous governor of the universe, has permitted our fellow men to make us slaves, we bow in submission to him, and determine to behave in such a manner as that we may have reason to expect the divine approbation of, and assistance in, our peaceable and lawful attempts to gain our freedom.

We are willing to submit to such regulations and laws, as may be made relative to us, until we leave the province, which we determine to do as soon as we can, from our joynt labours procure money to transport ourselves to some part of the Coast of *Africa,* where we propose a settlement. We are very desirous that you should have instructions relative to us, from your town, therefore we pray you to communicate this letter to them, and ask this favor for us.

In behalf of our fellow slaves in this province, and by order of their Committee.

Peter Bestes
Sambo Freeman
Felix Holbrook
Chester Joie

2. Worcester County, Massachusetts, Calls for the Abolition of Slavery, 1775

Whereas the Negroes in the counties of Bristol and Worcester, the 24th of March last, petitioned the Committees of Correspondence for the county of Worcester (then convened in Worcester) to assist them in obtaining their freedom. Therefore, In County Convention, June 14th, 1775. Resolved, that we abhor the enslaving of any of the human race, and particularly of the NEGROES in this country. And that whenever there shall be a door opened, or opportunity present, for anything to be done toward emancipating the NEGROES: we will use our influence and endeavor that such a thing may be effected.

3. Lemuel Haynes, a New England Mulatto, Attacks Slavery, 1776

Liberty Further Extended: Or Free thoughts on the illegality of Slave-keeping; Wherein those arguments that Are used in its vindication Are plainly confuted. Together with an humble Address to such as are Concearned in the practise.

> We hold these truths to be self-Evident, that all men are created Equal, that they are Endowed By their Creator with Ceartain unalienable rights, that among these are Life, Liberty, and the pursuit of happyness.

Congress.

. . . Liberty is a Jewel which was handed Down to man from the cabinet of heaven, and is Coaeval with his Existance. And as it proceed from the Supreme Legislature

---

"Worcester County, Massachusetts, Calls for the Abolition of Slavery, 1775." In *Massachusetts Spy* (June 21, 1775): 2.

"Lemuel Haynes, A New England Mulatto, Attacks Slavery, 1776." As found in *William and Mary Quarterly* 40 (1983): 93–105.

of the univers, so it is he which hath a sole right to take away; therefore, he that would take away a mans Liberty assumes a prerogative that Belongs to another, and acts out of his own domain.

One man may bost a superorety above another in point of Natural previledg; yet if he can produse no convincive arguments in vindication of this preheminence his hypothesis is to Be Suspected. To affirm, that an Englishman has a right to his Liberty, is a truth which has Been so clearly Evinced, Especially of Late, that to spend time in illustrating this, would be But Superfluous tautology. But I query, whether Liberty is so contracted a principle as to be Confin'd to any nation under Heaven; nay, I think it not hyperbolical to affirm, that Even an affrican, has Equally as good a right to his Liberty in common with Englishmen. . . .

It hath pleased god to *make of one Blood all nations of men, for to dwell upon the face of the Earth.* Acts 17, 26. And as all are of one Species, so there are the same Laws, and aspiring principles placed in all nations; and the Effect that these Laws will produce, are Similar to Each other. Consequently we may suppose, that what is precious to one man, is precious to another, and what is irksom, or intolarable to one man, is so to another, consider'd in a Law of Nature. Therefore we may reasonably Conclude, that Liberty is Equally as pre[c]ious to a *Black man,* as it is to a *white one,* and Bondage Equally as intollarable to the one as it is to the other: Seeing it Effects the Laws of nature Equally as much in the one as it Does in the other. But, as I observed Before, those privileges that are granted to us By the Divine Being, no one has the Least right to take them from us without our consen[t]; and there is Not the Least precept, or practise, in the Sacred Scriptures, that constitutes a Black man a Slave, any more than a white one.

Shall a mans Couler Be the Decisive Criterion whereby to Judg of his natural right? or Becaus a man is not of the same couler with his Neighbour, shall he Be Deprived of those things that Distuingsheth [Distinguisheth] him from the Beasts of the field? . . . O *Sirs!* Let that pity, and compassion, which is peculiar to mankind, Especially to English-men, no Longer Lie Dormant in your Breast: Let it run free thro' Disinterested Benevolence. then how would these iron yoaks Spontaneously fall from the gauled Necks of the oppress'd! And that Disparity, in point of Natural previlege, which is the Bane of Society, would Be Cast upon the utmost coasts of Oblivion. . . . "O when shall America be consistantly Engaged in the Cause of Liberty!" If you have any Love to yourselves, or any Love to this Land, if you have any Love to your fellow-men, Break these intollerable yoaks, and Let their names Be remembered no more, Least they Be retorted on your own necks, and you Sink under them: for god will not hold you guiltless.

4. Lord Dunmore Promises Freedom to Slaves Who Fight for Britain, 1775

I do, in virtue of the power and authority to *me* given, by his *majesty,* determine to execute martial law, and cause the same to be executed throughout this colony; and to the end that peace and good order may the sooner be restored, I do require every

---

"Lord Dunmore Promises Freedom to Slaves Who Fight for Britain, 1775." In Hezekiah Niles, ed., *Principles and Acts of the Revolution in America* (Baltimore: W. O. Niles, 1822), 375.

person capable of bearing arms to resort to his *majesty's* standard, or be looked upon as traitors to his *majesty's* crown and government, and thereby become liable to the penalty the law inflicts upon such offences; such as forfeiture of life, confiscation of lands, &c. &c. And I do hereby further declare all indented servants, negroes, or others (appertaining to rebels) free, that are able and willing to bear arms, they joining his majesty's troops as soon as may be, for the more speedily reducing this colony to a proper sense of their duty to *his majesty's* crown and dignity....

"Given under my hand, on board the ship William, off Norfolk, the 7th day of November, in the 16th year of his majesty's reign.

"DUNMORE .

"GOD save the KING."

5. Three Virginia Counties Defend Slavery, 1785

To the honourable the General Assembly of Virginia, the Remonstrance and Petition of the Free Inhabitants of Amelia County.

Gentlemen,

When the British Parliament usurped a Right to dispose of our Property without our Consent, we dissolved the Union with our Parent Country, and established a Constitution and Form of Government of our own, that our Property might be secure, in Future. In Order to effect this we risked our Lives and Fortunes, and waded through Seas of Blood. By the favourable Interposition of Providence our Attempt was crowned with Success. We were put in the Possession of our Rights of Liberty and Property: And these Rights as well secured, as they can be by any human Constitution or Form of Government. But notwithstanding this, we understand a very subtle and daring Attempt is made to dispossess us of a very important Part of our Property. An Attempt set on Foot, we are informed, by the Enemies of our Country, Tools of the British Administration, and supported by certain Men among us of considerable Weight, To WREST FROM US OUR SLAVES, by an Act of the Legislature for a general Emancipation of them. An Attempt unsupported by Scripture or sound Policy.

It is unsupported by Scripture. For we find that under the Old Testament Dispensation, Slavery was permitted by the Deity himself. Thus, Leviticus Ch. 25. Ver. 44, 45, 46. "Both thy Bond Men and Bond Maids, which thou shalt have, shall be of the Heathen that are round about you; of them shall ye buy Bond Men and Bond Maids. Moreover, of the Children of the Strangers that do sojourn among you, of them shall ye buy, and of their Families that are with you, which they beget in your Land, and they shall be your Possession, and ye shall take them as an Inheritance, for your Children after you, to inherit them for a Possession; they shall be your Bond-men forever." This Permission to buy and inherit Bond-men and Bond-maids, we have Reason to conclude, continued through all the Revolutions of the

"Three Virginia Counties Defend Slavery, 1785." As found in Fredrika Teute Schmidt and Barbara Wilhelm, "Early Proslavery Petitions in Virginia," *William and Mary Quarterly* 30 (1973): 138–140.

Jewish Government, down to the Advent of our Lord. And we do not find, that either he or his Apostles abridged it. The Freedom promised to his Followers, is a Freedom from the Bondage of Sin and Satan, and from the Dominion of Mens Lusts and Passions; but as to their Outward Condition, whatever that was before they embraced the Religion of Jesus, whether Bond or Free, it remained the same afterwards. This St. Paul expressly asserts 1 Cor. Chap. 7. Ver. 20. where he is speaking directly to this very Point, 'Let every Man abide in the same Calling, wherein he is called'; and Ver. 24. 'Let every Man wherein he is called, therein abide with God.' Thus it is evident the said Attempt is unsupported by Scripture.

It is also exceedingly *impolitic*. For it involves in it, and is productive of Want, Poverty, Distress, and Ruin to the Free Citizen; Neglect, Famine and Death to the black Infant and superannuated Parent; The Horrors of all the Rapes, Murders, and Outrages, which is a vast Multitude of unprincipled, unpropertied, revengeful, and remorseless Banditti are capable of perpetrating; inevitable Bankruptcy to the Revenue, and consequently Breach of public Faith, and Loss of Credit with foreign Nations; and, lastly, sure and final Ruin to this now flourishing free and happy Country.

We therefore, your Petitioners and Remonstrants, do solemnly adjure and humbly pray you that you will discountenance and utterly reject every Motion and Proposal for emancipating our Slaves; that as the Act lately made, empowering the Owners of Slaves to liberate them, hath produced, and is still productive of, very bad Effects, you will immediately and totally repeal it; and that as many of the Slaves, liberated by that Act, have been guilty of Thefts and Outrages, Insolences and Violences, destructive to the Peace, Safety and Happiness of Society, you will make effectual Provision for the due Government of them. . . .

[Amelia County, November 10, 1785, with 22 signatures. Also submitted by Mecklenberg County, November 8, 1785, with 223 signatures, and by Pittsylvania County, November 10, 1785, with 54 signatures.]

6. Abraham Lincoln's Gettysburg Address, 1863

Four score and seven years ago our fathers brought forth on this continent, a new nation, conceived in Liberty, and dedicated to the proposition that all men are created equal.

Now we are engaged in a great civil war, testing whether that nation or any nation so conceived and so dedicated, can long endure. We are met on a great battlefield of that war. We have come to dedicate a portion of that field, as a final resting place for those who here gave their lives that that nation might live. It is altogether fitting and proper that we should do this.

But, in a larger sense, we can not dedicate—we can not consecrate—we can not hallow—this ground. The brave men, living and dead, who struggled here, have consecrated it, far above our poor power to add or detract. The world will little note, nor

"Abraham Lincoln's Gettysburg Address, 1863." As found in Roy P. Basler et al., eds., *The Collected Works of Abraham Lincoln* (New Brunswick, NJ: Rutgers University Press, 1953–1955), vol. 7, p. 23.

long remember what we say here, but it can never forget what they did here. It is for us the living, rather, to be dedicated here to the unfinished work which they who fought here have thus far so nobly advanced. It is rather for us to be here dedicated to the great task remaining before us—that from these honored dead we take increased devotion to that cause for which they gave the last full measure of devotion—that we here highly resolve that these dead shall not have died in vain—that this nation, under God, shall have a new birth of freedom—and that government of the people, by the people, for the people, shall not perish from the earth.

E S S A Y S

Professor Sylvia R. Frey of Tulane University, the leading scholar of African-American experiences in the Revolution, explains the conflicts over slavery and the different meanings of the Revolution generated by the war and its politics. In the second selection, Ira Berlin, a professor at the University of Maryland and author of *Many Thousands Gone: The First Two Centuries of Slavery in North America* (1998), examines African-American experiences during the Revolutionary generation to explain that, notwithstanding powerful white opposition, blacks made significant advances.

Slavery Attacked and Defended

SYLVIA R. FREY

The era of the American Revolution was a time of violent and unpredictable social, economic, and political change. The dislocations of that period were most severely felt in the South. Although historians have tended to view the war in the South in military terms as a bipolarity, in fact it was a complex triangular process involving two sets of white belligerents and approximately four hundred thousand slaves. The environment in which the revolutionary conflict developed in the South was shaped not only by British policies or white southern initiatives but also by African-American resistance.

Actual or potential resistance was a main factor in the development of Britain's southern strategy. Influenced in part by slaves' combative and aggressive behavior, British military leaders and Crown officials seized upon the idea of intimidating independence-minded white southerners with the threat of a slave rising without, however, actually inciting one. In the end the British strategy of manipulating conflict between the races became a rallying cry for white southern unity and impelled the South toward independence. The need to weaken slaves' zeal for service with the British, which threatened to expose the moral absurdity of a society of slaveholders proclaiming the concepts of natural rights, equality, and liberty, formed part of the complex interaction of events that constituted the revolutionary war in

Frey, Sylvia R., *Water from the Rock: Black Resistance in a Revolutionary Age.* Copyright © 1991 by Princeton University Press. Reprinted by permission of Princeton University Press.

the South. To that extent, the American Revolution in the South was a war about slavery, if not a war over slavery. . . .

During the two decades beginning in 1765, slave unrest was more intensive and widespread than in any previous period. In the gathering intensity of the decade beginning in 1765, white Americans in the thirteen English colonies were passing resolutions denouncing Parliament's attempt to "enslave" them by regulating and taxing their property without their consent. . . .

Blacks, slave and free, urban and rural, artisan and field hand, literate and illiterate, were swept up by the force of ideological energy. Northern blacks, who were disproportionately urban, mostly native-born and English speaking, were generally more conversant with the ideology of the Revolution. When asserting their claims to freedom, they frequently invoked the philosophical arguments that white revolutionaries were making in their own fierce struggle against oppression. In the South, were revolutionary ideology was as sincerely affirmed as in the North though the commitment to slavery was much more thorough, the large slave population perceived a change in the coherence and ideology of the master class and tried to take advantage of it. . . .

The slave community had, moreover, the means to maintain a vital oral tradition. The close physical proximity and the communality, which had disappeared among the white upper classes by the late eighteenth century, continued in a modified form among poor whites and slaves, most of whom lived in communal quarters of ten or more people. With the development of larger slave quarters and the creation of a common language, a complex communication system emerged. Table talk listened to by domestic slaves, conversations overheard by slave attendants or musicians, was quickly carried back to the slave quarters and was rapidly disseminated through the cross-quarter underground to other plantations, even to other colonies. Indeed, as Archibald Bullock and John Houston, two of Georgia's delegates to the Continental Congress, confided to John Adams, the slave network could carry news "several hundreds of miles in a week or fortnight."

Whether or not slaves were impelled by the subsuming power of the ideas of liberty and equality, their actions show that they did follow the progress of the war, and they fully appreciated its implications for their own lives. Slaves tried, for example, to take advantage of the confusion generated by the Stamp Act crisis in 1765 to make good their own understanding of revolutionary ideology. In Charleston, South Carolina, they watched with interest as white crowds protested the Stamp Act by parading around the homes of suspected stamp officers shouting "Liberty! Liberty and stamp'd paper." Shortly after, in a move clearly calculated to call attention to their own clanking chains, a group of blacks threw white citizens into panic as they chanted the same cry, "Liberty." . . .

In large measure prerevolutionary slave resistance found its ideology, strategy, and meaning in African patterns of resistance and warfare. As in African slavery, where self-reliance and survival strategies prevailed, the shape and degree of slave resistance was roughly proportional to the possibilities inherent in their situations. Extensive settlement and cultivation had greatly limited the possibilities for maroon types of resistance in the American colonies, particularly in the Chesapeake, where with the exception of the Great Dismal Swamp, which straddled the boundary with North Carolina, the absence of a large wilderness area prevented effective maroon occupation.* The expanse of unsettled frontier and a comparatively large amount of swampland still offered sanctuary for maroonage in the lower South, however. Acutely aware of the strategic possibilities created by the Stamp Act disorders, slaves in Georgia and South Carolina took advantage of the situation to form maroon communities, from which, for a while, they were able to defend themselves against recapture.

At the height of the Stamp Act crisis in Georgia, a group of slave men, women, and children fled to a swamp on the north side of the Savannah River. Like guerrilla fighters they supported themselves by living off the forest and the fruits of their raids on plantations on the south side of the river. Although the Georgia assembly offered a reward of £2s. "For the head of every such Slave making Resistance," the group was apparently sufficiently strong to survive. . . .

At about the same time a group of South Carolina slaves, taking advantage of the Christmas holidays, fled into the swamps. Fearing a general black insurrection, provincial authorities called on the Catawba Indians to "come down and hunt the Negroes." Although Indian tribes sometimes sheltered black runaways, cultural differences and the practice common throughout the South and in the Caribbean of using Indians to crush slave revolts and destroy maroon communities sometimes fomented hostility between Indians and African-Americans. Neither numerous enough nor sufficiently strong to resist successfully, the black fugitives were quickly dispersed or captured by the Indians. . . .

The changing political situation after 1773 exposed the slave population to new motives and greater opportunities for overt resistance. Early in 1773 a group of Boston slaves presented three petitions for freedom to the general court and to General Thomas Gage, British commander in chief in America and governor of Massachusetts Bay. A year later, Gage was presented with two more petitions from "a grate Number of Blacks," as they styled themselves, offering to fight for him if he would arm them and set them free once victory was achieved. In November a group of Virginia slaves met together secretly to select a leader, "who was to conduct them when the English troops should arrive—, which they foolishly thought would be very soon and that by revolting to them they should be rewarded with their freedom." Their plans were, however, discovered and "proper precautions taken to prevent the Infection." In reporting the incident to William Bradford, James Madison cautioned that "it is prudent such things should be concealed as well as suppressed."

Madison's account of the abortive rising and his revealing warning to Bradford expose the dilemma of a slaveholding society about to embark on a war against tyranny: how to prevent their slaves from imbibing the heady notions of liberty and equality, which had become their own rallying cry in the contest with Britain; how to exploit white fears of a slave rebellion to unite the white population behind the patriot cause and at the same time conceal from a watching world that behind the bewitching rhetoric of liberty was the hideous face of slavery. The resolution to the dilemma began to unfold a month later in Georgia, when the prospect of black rebellion threatened to become actual. On December 7, 1774, six "new Negro fellows and four wenches," who belonged to a Captain Morris of St. Andrew parish, killed

---

* "Maroon" refers to communities formed by escaped slaves in peripheral locations that harbor other escapees and may serve as centers for resistance and liberation.

their overseer, went to his house and murdered his wife, and "dangerously wounded a carpenter named Wright" and a boy who died the next day. They then marched to a neighboring plantation and seriously wounded the owner, Angus McIntosh. From there they proceeded to the house of Roderick M'Leod, "wounded him very much," and killed his son before they were taken. Their leader and McIntosh's slave, "a sensible fellow" who had joined the rebels, were burned alive. . . .

In the meantime, British military leaders and Crown officials viewed with intense interest the aggressive behavior of slaves and the apprehension it excited in their owners. Although the motives of the London government were complex, from the beginning of the conflict the North ministry was tempted by the idea of using the slave population in some capacity to crush southern resistance. Early in January 1775, news reached the southern colonies that an extraordinary proposal had been recently introduced into the House of Commons. Aimed at "humbling the high aristocratic spirit of Virginia and the southern colonies," it called for the general emancipation of slaves. The measure failed to win the necessary support in the Commons, but the idea of recruiting slaves as a disruptive tactic gained support as war with the colonies became imminent. . . .

The complex triangularity of events is increasingly apparent in the events leading up to independence. In April 1775, shortly after John Murray, fourth earl of Dunmore and royal governor of Virginia, seized the colony's store of gunpowder from the magazine at Williamsburg, "some Negroes (by one of his servants) had offered to join him and take up arms," thus anticipating by several months Dunmore's famous proclamation. Dunmore ordered them "to go about their business," and "threatened them with his severest resentment, should they presume to renew their application." Slaveholders were, however, suspicious. Convinced that Dunmore "designed, by disarming the people to weaken the means of opposing an insurrection of the slaves," a group of citizens armed themselves and demanded that the powder be returned to the magazine. "Exceedingly exasperated," Dunmore threatened to "declare freedom to the slaves and reduce the City of Williamsburg to ashes" and boasted that in the event of war "he should have . . . people and all the Slaves on the side of Government."

The situation grew steadily more explosive following the actual commencement of hostilities at Lexington and Concord on April 19, 1775. On May 1, Dunmore wrote to William Legge, second Earl of Dartmouth and secretary of state for the colonies, informing him of his plan "to arm all my own Negroes and receive all others that will come to me whom I shall declare free." Properly armed, he boasted, his force would soon "reduce the refractory people of this colony to obedience." Dunmore's threat to recruit slaves and the arrival on May 3 of a letter from Arthur Lee, the American correspondent in London, to Henry Laurens, confirming "that a plan was laid before Administration, for instigating the slaves to insurrection," brought the racial issue to the forefront of public consciousness and gave an entirely new character to the conflict in the South. . . .

The growing identification of slave militancy and British plots to incite slaves as part of its American policy—always a factor in the relations of Britain and her southern colonies—became increasingly important in the spring of 1775. The "dread of instigated Insurrections," a popular euphemism for a British-inspired slave revolt, was particularly acute in South Carolina because of its unique racial demography. In May, a report that slaves would be set free on the arrival of the new governor, Lord William Campbell, and that the sloop of war carrying Campbell was also bearing fourteen thousand stand of weapons became "common talk" among slaves throughout the province and "occasioned impertinent behaviour in many of them." The discovery of an insurrection plot, planned to coincide with the British arrival, threw the white citizenry of Charleston into panic. . . .

When the second session of the First Provincial Congress, the patriots' legislative body, convened June 1, the new president, Henry Laurens, justified the session on the grounds that the outbreak of fighting in Massachusetts, the possibility of an invasion of Charleston, or a slave uprising either independently or in conjunction with a British invasion warranted defense preparations. He called on the Congress to establish a provincial military force, to form an association of patriots, and to create a council of safety to exercise day-to-day executive power. The Provincial Congress responded by approving the formation of an association of defense to which all patriots would subscribe. The test of the association placed the onus squarely on Britain for "The actual Commencement of Hostilities against this Continent—the threats of arbitrary impositions from abroad—& the dread of instigated Insurrections at home." The Provincial Congress also decided to establish three regiments of troops for a dual-purpose described by the Charleston merchant, Josiah Smith: "to keep those mistaken creatures in awe, as well as to oppose any Troops that may be sent among us with coercive Orders." With white fears running high in Charleston, the Congress also ordered three companies of militia to patrol the city's streets, one by day and two at night, "to guard against any hostile attempts that may be made by our domesticks," the jittery Smith wrote to a friend in London. . . .

Determined to quash the slaves' "high notions of liberty," the Provincial Congress also appointed a special committee to investigate the reports of black insurrections and to form further plans for the "public security." In June hearings were held by the committee, and on the twenty-second of the month freeholders were summoned to try the first suspects under the provisions of the Negro Act of 1740, article 17 of which dealt with homicide and insurrection. Two of the plotters were ordered to be "Severely flogged and banished." The alleged leader, a free black man named Thomas Jeremiah, was brought to trial August 11 before a court of two justices of the peace and five freeholders on charges of plotting an insurrection and threatening to assist the royal navy over the bar in Charleston harbor when it arrived, presumably to assist slaves in gaining freedom. Jeremiah, a fisherman and pilot who, according to Henry Laurens, was "puffed up by prosperity, ruined by Luxury and debauchery and grown to an amazing pitch of vanity and ambition," was convicted of intended sedition by a unanimous decision of the judges. On August 18 he was hanged and burned to death in Charleston.

During the trial, which dispensed with most of the legal niceties, a slave named Sambo testified that two or three months earlier Jeremiah had told him that "there was a great War coming soon." When Sambo, a waterman, asked Jeremiah "what shall we poor Negroes do in a schooner," Jeremiah replied that they should "set the schooner on fire, jump on shore and join the soldiers," because "the War was come to help the poor Negroes." Despite the concerted effort of slaveowners to suppress any information that was likely to cause unrest, Jeremiah's message, that slaves had a powerful ally in the British, enjoyed wide credence among slaves—from the swampy rice plantations of South Carolina, to the small tobacco farms hacked out of the thick pine forests of North Carolina, to the great tobacco plantations that lined

Virginia's majestic tidal rivers. During the summer of 1775, the conflict in the South increasingly took on a racial polarity. Rumors of British plans to free slaves excited slave resistance while slave militancy provided the dynamic for British "tampering." The simultaneous operation of the two fostered the feeling among slaveholders that they were beset by foes from within and without. The conviction that their society was in a great crisis contributed to the growing alienation from Britain.

Although by southern standards North Carolina had relatively few slaves, they were heavily concentrated in counties east of the fall line. The rumors of insurrections that spread across the Carolinas in the summer of 1775 caused a frenzy of action throughout the East. Upon receiving a report "that the Negroes mean to take advantage of the times," the frightened citizens of Edenton, in the heart of the tobacco-growing Northeast, "raised up a guard of Eight men in the Town every night, in the Country, the same precaution is taking." . . .

Despite all their precautions, the political excitement stirred by rumors of emancipation produced an actual insurrection attempt. . . . The plot projected July 8 as the day for all slaves "to fall on and destroy the family where they lived, then to proceed from House to House (burning as they went) until they arrived in the Back Country where they were to be received with open arms by a number of Persons there appointed and armed by Government for their Protection, and as a further reward they were to be settled in a free government of their own." By nightfall the revolt, which rumor had it was encouraged by John Collet, military commander of Fort Johnston and by Governor Josiah Martin, had been crushed. Patrollers from the three counties involved, who had been given discretionary power to "shoot any Number of Negroes above four, who are off their Masters Plantations, and will not submit," had killed one slave and arrested nearly forty others. Before dark five of them had been severely whipped and had "both Ears crap'd" [sic] before a crowd of spectators. For several days the interrogations and the "scourgings" continued. During the crucial period political differences were temporarily set aside and the white community closed ranks against the slaves. . . .

Although several issues peculiar to North Carolina were influencing provincial leaders toward revolution, the insurrection scare of 1775, and the belief that Governor Martin and other Crown officials were "spiriting up the back counties, and perhaps the Slaves," were contributing factors to the growing alienation from Britain. As part of the British effort to return the southern colonies to allegiance to the Crown, the London government decided to send a small expedition to the Cape Fear region. The plan was to restore royal government to the control of loyalists and then to withdraw British troops to the north. Governor Martin was charged with responsibility for raising provincial troops, which he would lead as a provincial colonel. During the month of June, rumors began to circulate that the British plan also called for inciting the slaves to revolt, which indeed had some basis in fact. . . .

Thoroughly antagonized, provincial leaders were spurred to action. Local militia companies were hurriedly raised and trained, slaves were disarmed, and patrols were organized to keep them under control. Fearing for his life, Martin sent his pregnant wife to New York, spiked the palace cannon and buried the ammunition in the cellar before fleeing to For Johnston on Cape Fear. His efforts to strengthen the garrison prompted the Wilmington Committee of Safety to raise a force of militia and minutemen to attack the fort. The "savage and audacious mob," led by Colonel Robert Howe, announced their intention to remove the guns from the fort in a letter to Martin from "The People." Listed among the reasons for the attack was Martin's "base encouragement of Slaves eloped from their Masters, feeding and employing them, and his atrocious and horrid declaration that he would incite them to an Insurrection."

Martin's subsequent efforts to subjugate the colony with a force of loyalists supported by slaves, acting in conjunction with British troops, culminated in defeat in the Moore's Creek Bridge campaign. . . .

Events in South Carolina were also pushing that province toward revolution. After a brief period of comparative calm following the trial and sentencing of Thomas Jeremiah, another insurrection scare occurred. . . . The scene of the South Carolina conspiracy was St. Bartholomew parish. The plotters confessed to the court of freeholders convened to try them during the first week of July that they had planned a general insurrection "to take the Country by killing the whites." The St. Bartholomew scare was, however, different in one remarkable respect: its leaders included several black preachers, two of whom were women whose owners were prominent Cheraw planters, Francis Smith, William Smith, John Wells, Thomas Hutchinson, and George Austin. With the exception of Austin, who was an absentee owner, during the war all of the planters either served in the Cheraw District militia or were active supporters of the patriot cause.

Trial testimony revealed that the insurrection had been planned at secret religious meetings held in the woods or some other secluded place, usually on one of the Austin plantations, whose day-to-day operations were left in the hands of an overseer and black driver, which probably gave the slaves greater freedom from close supervision. The meetings, which violated the law prohibiting slaves meeting for religious worship before sunrise or after sunset, were begun some two years previously by a Scottish preacher named John Burnet, who insisted that his only motive was "the salvation of those poor ignorant Creatures." After Burnet was warned that "his conduct was extremely Obnoxious to the People," he withdrew, but self-appointed black preachers began conducting services on their own. Burnet's professed efforts "to reconcile them to that Lot in Life in which God had placed them," and to teach them "the Duty of Obedience to their Masters,"clearly miscarried because, according to one trial witness, the black preachers offered their own distinct rendition of Christian theology. George, the slave of Francis Smith and one of the leaders of the insurrection, told "the Great crowds of Negroes in the Neighborhood of Chyhaw" who attended the meetings in defiance of the law, that "the old King had reced a Book from our Lord by which he was to Alter the World (meaning to set the Negroes free) but for his not doing so, was now gone to Hell, and punishment—That the Young King, meaning our Present One, came up with the Book, & was about to alter the World, & set the Negroes Free." After some deliberation the court decided on "the disagreeable necessity to cause Exemplary punishments" and sent George to the gallows. Although no complicity could be established, Burnet was ordered out of the province.

The exodus motif also made its appearance in Savannah and created deep anxieties among white Georgians, particularly because it came from a black preacher named David. Invited to preach to a gathering of whites and blacks, David "dropped some unguarded expressions, such as, that he did not doubt, but 'God would send Deliverance to the Negroes, from the power of their Masters, as he freed the Children of Israel from Egyptian Bondage.'" . . . Used by Christian slaveholders to rationalize the brutality of slavery, the exodus motif was appropriated by Christian slaves to justify their own struggles for freedom. The theme continued to resonate through the church-associated revolts of the postrevolutionary era. . . .

The waves of unrest that swept the South during the tumultuous summer of 1775 crested in Virginia with the so-called Dunmore rising. . . . Dunmore declared martial law and on November 7, 1775, issued his proclamation from on board the *William,* which he had seized from local merchants and fitted out for war.

Although it was viewed on both sides of the Atlantic as a threat to the very foundations of slavery, Dunmore's intention was neither to overthrow the system nor to make war on it. Directed principally at "all indented servants, Negroes, or others, (appertaining to Rebels), that are able and willing to bear Arms," the proclamation was designed to encourage the defection of useful blacks without provoking a general rebellion and to disrupt the psychological security of whites without unleashing the full military potential of blacks. Practical rather than moral, it was rooted in expediency rather than humanitarian zeal. That is not, however, how it was perceived in the South.

The Continental Congress meeting in Philadelphia represented Dunmore's offer of freedom to slaves as "tearing up the foundations of civil authority and government" in Virginia, and called on the colony to establish a government that would produce happiness and secure peace. In a vain effort to prevent word of it from reaching Maryland's slave population, the provisional government there prohibited all correspondence with Virginia, either by land or water. But in Dorchester County on Maryland's Eastern Shore, an area already troubled by persistent rumors of insurrectionist activities among slaves and lower class whites, the committee of safety reported new signs of slave militancy: "The insolence of the Negroes in this county is come to such a height, that we are under a necessity of disarming them which we affected [sic] on Saturday last. We took about eighty guns, some bayonets, swords, etc." In neighboring North Carolina, Howe's Continentals and the Edenton Minute Men were ordered . . . to prevent a rumored attempt by Dunmore to march into North Carolina and to apprehend agents of Dunmore who were allegedly working to incite slaves. . . .

Nervous whites on the unsettled coast of South Carolina saw an ominous connection between Dunmore's activities and the massing of runaways on Sullivan's Island. Acting with British complicity, the runaways made nightly sorties to rob and harrass the seacoast of Christ-Church. The first reports reached the Council of Safety in Charleston on December 6, 1775. . . . On December 10, the Council received an alarming report [that] . . . the runaways were not "inticed" to desert by the British but "came as freemen, and demanding protection; that he could have had near 500 who had offered; that we were all in actual rebellion," and that he had orders "to distress Americans by every means in his power."

Now fully alarmed, the Council of Safety cut off all supplies and provisions to the king's ships and ordered an immediate attack on the Sullivan's Island refuge. . . . Although most of the fugitives had already escaped with the aid of boats from the British warship *Cherokee,* four blacks were killed and eleven people were captured, including three crew members from the *Cherokee.* Destruction of the runaway haven and the summary justice meted out to them "will serve to humble our Negroes in general," the relieved Charleston Council predicted.

Two of Georgia's delegates to the Continental Congress, Archibald Bullock and John Houston, were far less sanguine. Eager to seize upon any outside encouragement, Georgia slaves were, they confided to John Adams, waiting for the chance to rise. If, the two predicted, "one thousand regular troops should land in Georgia, and their commander be provided with arms and clothes enough, and proclaim freedom to all the negroes who would join his campaign, twenty thousand would join it from [Georgia and South Carolina] in a fortnight." The presence of British war vessels at the mouth of the Savannah River early in January 1776, spurred a rash of slave desertions from Georgia plantations. Although the vessels were there to purchase provisions and not to liberate slaves, the Georgia Council of Safety initiated defensive preparations. The militia was ordered out to protect Savannah against any hostile attempt by the British and coastal areas were advised to increase their vigilance. Slave patrols were sent to search Negro houses throughout the province, including those on the South Carolina side of the Savannah River as far north as Purrysburg, for arms and ammunition. As an added precaution Georgia's last royal governor, Sir James Wright, and the members of his council were arrested and required to give their paroles not to leave the city or to communicate with the British vessels. In February when more British ships arrived, Governor Wright and several of his councillors broke their paroles and fled Savannah "to avoid the rage and violence of the rebels." While the HMS *Scarborough* rode at anchor off Cockspur Island at the entrance to the Savannah River, between two and three hundred slaves presented themselves to Governor Wright, declaring "they were come for the King." For another month while British warships remained in the area, slaves continued to flee from the farms and plantations along the high bluffs of the Savannah River.

The defection of hundreds of slaves produced a powerful defensive response from white leaders. When Colonel Stephen Bull arrived with reinforcements from South Carolina early in March, he learned that some two hundred black fugitives were massed on Tybee Island. Reasoning that if they were successful in joining the British it would "only enable an enemy to fight against us with our own money or property," Bull recommended to Henry Laurens, president of the Council of Safety of Charleston, a campaign of eradication: "It is far better for the public and the owners, if the deserted negroes on Tybee Island . . . be shot, if they cannot be taken." To "deter other negroes from deserting," and to "establish a hatred or aversion between the Indians and negroes," Bull asked permission to employ a party of Creek Indians to carry out the distasteful mission. . . .

Even without access to interministerial discussions it seems clear that the slaveholders' fear of a servile rising and the groundswell of slave resistance that both preceded and accompanied the development of Dunmore's experiment with armed blacks were precipitating factors in the shaping of Britain's Southern strategy. On October 15, 1775, one month before Dunmore's Proclamation, Lord North had recommended to the King an "immediate expedition against the Southern Provinces in North America." The claims of crown officials there that loyalist forces could be raised to restore royal government and pacify the South were "the more to be credited," North told the King, "as we all know the perilous situation of three of them from the great number of their negro slaves, and the small proportion of white inhabitants." Although the strategy was several years away from implementation, the North ministry continued to advance the idea of employing slaves as an ingredient of military policy.

On October 26, 1775, William Henry Lyttleton, former royal governor of South Carolina (1775–1760) and of Jamaica (1760–1766) and a consistent supporter of Lord North, introduced into the House of Commons "something like a proposal for encouraging the negroes in that part of America to rise against their masters, and for sending some regiments to support and encourage them, in carrying the design into execution." Lyttleton's comparison of America to a chain, the upper part, or northern colonies, of which was strong, populous, and capable of resistance, the lower part, or southern colonies, of which was weak "on account of the number of negroes in them," reveals a keen awareness of southern vulnerability. If a few regiments were sent to the South, Lyttleton predicted, "the negroes would rise, and embrue their hands in the blood of their masters." In an acrimonious debate that continued until 4:30 A.M., Lyttleton was "most severely reprehended from the other side, and the scheme totally reprobated, as being too black, horrid and wicked, to be heard of, much less adopted by any civilized people." Lyttleton's motion was defeated by a vote of 278 to 108. One month later Dunmore issued his proclamation.

Impressed by reports coming from southern refugees and exiled governors of the material advantages to be gained by the employment of slaves, British officials were reluctant to cast aside the weapon of a black force. Several of the proposals urged the home government to ride the wave of fear created in Chesapeake by the active hostility of slaves during Dunmore's operations and by the seething discontent of the lower classes, particularly on Maryland's Eastern Shore. In a daring proposal designed to capitalize on local fears of united action by Maryland's slaves and poor whites, Sir John Dalrymple recommended that levies of indentured servants be raised on the Pennsylvania side of the Delaware Bay and in major cities, such as Alexandria, Fredericksburg, Baltimore, and Annapolis, along with "the bravest and most ingenious of the black Slaves whom He may find all over the Bay of Chesapeake," The effect, Dalrymple confidently predicted, would be "to throw the Estates on the Delaware Bay in waste, because the Masters will carry off the Servants from their Estates upon hearing what is happening in Chesapeake Bay." . . .

Proposals to arm slaves and the actual attempt to do so in the Chesapeake provoked an outburst of indignation in and out of Parliament. Merchants and traders in London and Bristol, where the British slave trade was centered, resolutely condemned the idea. . . . In a letter to a friend in Philadelphia one Londoner denounced the North ministry as "worse than barbarians" for its "thoughts of declaring all your negroes free, and to arm them."

The use of slave labor in military capacity was also common among European powers since the seventeenth century, particularly in the Caribbean and Brazil, where shortages of manpower forced colonial nations to recruit slaves for various military functions. The dangerous expedient of arming slaves was, however, generally eschewed until 1795, when the problem of West Indian defense forced the British government to organize black companies. The fact that the government's efforts to arm slaves ran counter to the weight of tradition caused concern in many quarters that the national honor would be impugned. . . . "This measure of emancipating the negroes," the *Register* regretfully reported on July 8, 1776, has been "received with the greatest horror in all the colonies, and has been severely condemned elsewhere."

Critical to British concern over world reaction was the fear of retaliation. Should "the Ministry act in that way," one Londoner predicted, "the *Americans* would march (the slaves) back, and perhaps arm them all that they could trust."

Driven by the same fear, Burke warned the Commons that "when we talk of enfran-chisement, do we not perceive that the American master may enfranchise too; and arm servile hands in defense of freedom?" Although American slaveowners proved to be more reluctant than the British to put weapons into the hands of slaves, a few, including the diplomat Silas Deane, recognized that considerable psychological advantages were to be gained by threatening to do so. . . .

Deane's calculated suggestion is a reminder that events were being played on an international stage, which forced England to take an international view of the matter of arming slaves. Burke's recollection that "other people have had recourse more than once, and not without success," to that expedient, called to mind the Caribbean region, where recurring warfare among European powers frequently provoked slave risings. . . .

The knowledge that British Caribbean colonies were susceptible to the spread-ing influence of slave revolts focused public discussion on two additional questions: Could an alliance with slaves succeed? and Might it succeed too well? Like many of his contemporaries Burke believed that slaves were by nature too servile to make good soldiers. . . . Repeating the commonly held notion that slaves actually pre-ferred bondage to freedom, Burke concluded that "It is sometimes as hard to per-suade slaves to be free, as it is to compel freemen to be slaves; and in this auspicious scheme, we should have both these pleasing tasks on our hands at once."

Even if slavery had not dulled their desire for freedom, Burke wondered, might not blacks be skeptical of "an offer of freedom from that very nation which has sold them to their present masters? . . .

The most important argument against the arming of slaves as a war measure was that it involved a social revolution that went far beyond the aim of disciplining the rebellious colonies. "This measure of emancipating the negroes," the *Annual Register* grimly warned its readers, had momentous implications. It threatened the existing social order. Whereas the conventional practice of relegating slaves to menial tasks had confirmed the validity of the social order, the plan to encourage "African negroes" to appear in arms against white men and to encounter them upon an equal footing in the field, weakened the traditional system of social relations, which turned on social discrimination and a sense of race. . . .

But the gravest risk was to the slave system itself. Prior to the American Revolu-tion the military employment of slaves was usually aimed at preserving the institu-tion of slavery. The various proposals for arming slaves during the revolutionary war generally implied its destruction, an issue few English leaders were prepared to de-bate in 1776. Since the seventeenth century, Englishment, like other Europeans, had considered black peoples different. That perception of difference formed the basis for the traditional justification for slavery: a belief in the Negroes' cultural and racial inferiority, often interwoven with arguments for the utility of slave labor. Reinforced by Christian theology, which continued to distinguish between the spiritual equality of God's children and worldly enslavement, slavery enjoyed general acceptance. . . .

White attitudes toward blacks ranged widely from the virulent negro-phobia of Edward Long, a Jamaican planter who represented West Indian interests in Lon-don, to the vociferous abolitionism of Granville Sharp, who led the fight for the emancipation of black slaves in Britain. General domestic British feeling seems to have been that blacks were, if not sub-human, at least a peculiar and inferior type of human being. . . .

A strong crosscurrent was developing, of course, as economic changes intersected with radical intellectual and cultural developments to begin to transform European attitudes toward slavery. . . . Montesquieu's argument that slavery was forbidden by natural law constituted the most influential intellectual attack on slavery in the eighteenth century. Its most extraordinary impact was on the Scottish philosophers, including James Beattie, Francis Hutcheson, and to a lesser extent, David Hume. Although their specific concern was not with slavery, they uniformly deplored the brutality of slavery. Their notions of morality and justice in turn directly influenced Adam Smith's utilitarian arguments.

. . . At the same time, the emergence of British Protestantism, especially Quakerism and the Methodist movement within the Church of England, exposed the obvious contradictions between the Christian teaching of human equality and slavery. . . .

. . . [T]he national interest was still served by slavery . . . as the *Register* duly noted: "For however founded distinctions with respect to colour may appear, when examined by the tests of nature, reason, or philosophy, while things continue in their present state, while commerce, luxury, and avarice, render slavery a principal object in the political system of every European power that possesses dominion in America, the ideas of a preeminence must always be cherished, and considered as a necessary policy." The only alternative to white dominion and social order was further discord and violence. Above all else, perhaps, it was an irrational fear of the uncontrolled behavior of freed slaves that Englishmen, like their American counterparts, most dreaded.

Debates in the House of Commons in 1778 over the North ministry's conduct of the war exposed the deepest anxieties. In Parliament, the Opposition, which frequently used government's handling of American affairs to attract public support, launched a full-scale attack on the fitful efforts to develop a general slave policy. As chief spokesman on this issue, Edmund Burke introduced a motion condemning the military employment of Indians and slaves. During the debate . . . Burke denounced the government for its deliberate employment of Indians and for its efforts to provoke a slave insurrection. With hyperbolic generalization he warned his colleagues in Commons of "the horrible consequences that might ensue from constituting 100,000 fierce barbarian slaves, to be both the judges and executioners of their masters." With the examples in mind of the Stono Rebellion in South Carolina in 1739 and the massive risings in Berbice and Jamaica in the 1760s, he conjured up images of murders, rapes, and "horrid enormities of every kind," which he insisted "had ever been acknowledged to be the principal objects in the contemplations of all negroes who had meditated an insurrection." The same apocalyptic imagery resonates through the *Register's* account of Dunmore's efforts to arm slaves in Virginia and Maryland. The idea of emancipating slaves was generally repudiated "as tending to loosen the bands of society, to destroy domestic security, and encourage the most barbarous of mankind, to the commission of the most horrible crimes, and the most inhuman cruelties."

It is highly doubtful that the North ministry ever intended to effect a general emancipation of slaves. More likely the policy represented an effort to exploit slave militancy and coerce support from their owners. . . . At any rate, clearly on the defensive, North weakly defended Dunmore's Proclamation on the grounds that "it did not call on them to murder their masters . . . but only to take up arms in defense of their sovereign." Hoping to lay the matter to rest, he volunteered that "Lord Dunmore's proclamation should be laid on the table, that, if reprehensible, it might be attended to." Despite North's public disavowal of attempts to incite a slave insurrection, the temptation to employ slaves in some capacity remained, particularly in the South, whose huge black population made slaves a potentially powerful political, psychological, and military weapon.

Aware of the dangers inherent in such a plan, and with the memory of the public controversy still fresh in mind, the government proceeded cautiously. But the British path toward the military employment of slaves was smoothed by the decision of Americans to accept volunteered slaves for military service. . . .

At the outbreak of the American Revolution several colonies, all of them in the North, accepted blacks in militia units. Blacks were with the patriot forces at Lexington and Concord and at Bunker Hill. Several served with Connecticut units during the Boston campaign. At the time of the Lexington engagement, however, rumors that slaves were mobilizing to massacre the citizens left defenseless when the militia marched off to fight caused such panic among white citizens that the Massachusetts Committee of Safety decided in May to prohibit the enlistment of slaves in any of the colony's armies. Five days after he was appointed commander in chief of the Continental Army, George Washington, the Virginia slaveholder, issued orders against enlisting blacks, although those already in the army were allowed to remain. In a move that suggests the degree to which white attitudes toward slavery had hardened as a result of British "tampering" and escalating slave resistance, Edward Rutledge, who represented South Carolina at the Continental Congress, moved that all blacks, whether slave or free, be discharged from the Continental Army; although the motion was "strongly supported" by southern delegates, it failed. The actuality of black insurrection in Virginia, however, gave the delegates second thoughts and on November 12, 1775, the Continental Congress formally declared all blacks, slave or free, ineligible for military service. Similar policies were subsequently approved by the other northern states.

But the weight of common sense and military necessity compelled the abandonment of the policy. Despite his own repugnance for using slaves as soldiers, Washington was among the first to recognize that slavery had become a military weakness because of the willingness of slaves to fight for the enemy. Dunmore must be crushed instantly, he earnestly urged his countrymen, "otherwise, like a snowball, in rolling, his army will get size." Convinced that the outcome of the war hinged "on which side can arm the Negroes the faster," Washington publicly advocated the recruitment of blacks into the Continental Army, otherwise "they may seek employ in the ministerial army." His great influence in support of the military employment of blacks persuaded the cautious Continental Congress to agree to allow the enrollment of free blacks, although the exclusion of slaves from American armies continued.

Although Dunmore had not created slave rebellion but merely exploited it, the crisis created by his reception and use of black soldiers worked by no means entirely to the disadvantage of America. By blaming Dunmore for inciting slaves to rebellion, colonists found a strong stick with which to beat their opponents. The "dread of instigated Insurrections" combined with the hardening of attitudes after Lexington and Concord were, even to a moderate like Henry Laurens, "causes sufficient to drive an oppressed People to the use of Arms." Paradoxically, white Americans found as well a rationalization for their own incorporation of slaves, rendered necessary by a rapidly developing manpower shortage. When in 1777 Congress began to impose troop quotas on the states, a number of New England towns and state governments began quietly enrolling blacks, although their enlistment was not yet legally sanctioned. . . . Rhode Island, with a population of little better than fifty-one thousand whites and the British in possession of most of the state, including the capital city of Newport, had difficulty in filling its quota. . . . Prompted by the seeming hopelessness of the situation, the legislature approved slave enlistments. Promised freedom in return for service during the duration of the war, some two hundred and fifty slaves joined Rhode Island's black battalion. Similar problems . . . led Connecticut to form an all-black company. . . . By the end of 1777 free blacks and slaves were serving in mixed regiments in a number of states, most of them in the North.

Eager to escape blame for having first resorted to the use of slaves, Lord North later claimed that it was the American decision to enlist blacks that forced Britain to follow suit. In fact the precipitating factor was the decision made in 1778 to shift the seat of the war to the South. During the revolutionary war, Britain pursued a variety of strategies for ending the rebellion: by subduing New England; by securing the Middle Colonies; by pacifying the South. Although the shifting strategies were often marked by confusion, by 1778 operations in the southern colonies clearly occupied the principal place in British planning. Britain's Southern strategy finally emerged with three crucial components: to enlist the help of loyalists to defeat the rebels and to hold territory once it was liberated by British regular forces; to weaken rebel resistance by depriving the South of its labor force and by cutting off southern resources, such as tobacco, rice and indigo, the exportation of which helped attract foreign capital and thus sustained the rebellion; to exploit pro-British Indian tribes along the southern frontiers and the tens of thousands of slaves concentrated in the tidewater and the low country. The groundswell of slave resistance that both preceded and accompanied the gradual crystallization of the strategy, played an instrumental role in Britain's decision to gamble on the dangerous expedient of recruiting slaves for military service as well as in the American decision for independence.

The Revolution in Black Life

IRA BERLIN

The years between 1770 and 1810 were a formative period for Afro-American culture. The confluence of three events—freedom for large numbers of blacks with the abolition of slavery in the North and large-scale manumission in parts of the South; the maturation of a native-born Afro-American population after more than a century of American captivity; and a new, if short-lived, flexibility in white racial attitudes— made these years the pivot point in the development of black life in the United States. The social patterns and institutions established during the revolutionary era

From Alfred F. Young, ed., *Beyond the American Revolution: Explorations in the History of American Radicalism,* 1976, pp. 351–363, 369–377. Copyright © 1976 by Northern Illinois University Press. Used by permission of the publisher.

simultaneously confirmed the cultural transformation of the preceding century and shaped black life well into the twentieth century. In many ways, the revolutionary era, far more than the much studied Reconstruction period, laid the foundation for modern Afro-American life.

The events and ideas of the revolutionary years radically altered the structure of black society and the substance of Afro-American culture. The number of blacks enjoying freedom swelled under the pressure of revolutionary change, from a few thousand in the 1760s to almost two-hundred thousand by the end of the first decade of the nineteenth century. Freedom even within the limited bounds of white domination, enhanced black opportunities by creating new needs and allowing blacks a chance to draw on the rapidly maturing Afro-American culture to fulfill them. But the revolution in black life was not confined to those legally free. The forces unleashed by the American Revolution soon reached beyond the bounds of free black society and deeply influenced the course of slave life in the critical years before the great migration to the Lower South. Most importantly, the revolution in black life created new and enlarged older regional distinctions between the black populations, free and slave, of the North, the Upper South, and the Lower South. In each of these regions, differences in the size, character, and dynamics of development of the free and slave black populations bred distinctive patterns of relations with whites and among blacks, shaping the development of black life and American race relations during the nineteenth century and beyond.

The growth of the free Negro population was one of the most far reaching events of the revolutionary era. Before the Revolution only a tiny fraction of the black population enjoyed liberty in English mainland North America. A 1755 Maryland census, one of the few enumerations of colonial freemen, counted slightly more than 1,800 free Negroes, who composed about 4 percent of the colony's black population and less than 2 percent of its free population. Moreover, over 80 percent of these freemen were of mixed racial origin, and more than one-fifth were cripples or old folk deemed "past labour." Few full-blooded Africans found their way to freedom. . . . Although colonial freemen demand further study, it appears that Maryland's free Negroes typified those found throughout the mainland English colonies. . . .

Although few in number and much like whites in appearance, free Negroes raised white fears of subversion. During the colonial years, lawmakers steadily gnawed at the freemen's liberty, taxing them with numerous proscriptions on their civil, political, and social rights. On the eve of the Revolution, few whites, even those who opposed slavery, showed any inclination to increase the number of Negro freemen. But the events of the revolutionary years moved in unpredictable and uncontrollable ways. As the war dragged on, military necessity forced the British and then, more reluctantly, Americans to muster black slaves into their armies by offering them freedom in exchange for their services.

The British. who had no direct interest in slavery, first offered the exchange. In November 1775, Lord Dunmore, the royal governor of Virginia, declared martial law and freed all slaves that were able and willing to bear arms in His Majesty's service. Even though this declaration shook colonial Virginians, it came as no surprise. Dunmore and other British officials had been threatening such action for several months. Slaves, ever alive to the possibilities of liberty, quickly picked up these first rumblings of freedom. Some months earlier, a group of blacks had visited Dunmore and offered to join him and take up arms. At that time, Dunmore brusquely dismissed them. But the blacks would not be put off, and when Dunmore officially tendered the promise of liberty, they flocked to British headquarters in Norfolk harbor.

Defeat deflated Dunmore's promise of liberty. In December, about a month after his proclamation, patriot troops routed Loyalist forces, including a large number of blacks wearing sashes emblazoned with the words "Liberty to Slaves." The loss broke the back of Dunmore's attempt to discipline rebellious Virginians. . . .

The manpower shortage that forced Dunmore to use black troops worsened as the war dragged on. British commanders, despite popular opposition in England, increasingly followed Dunmore's lead and recruited slaves. When the war turned south in 1778, thousands of blacks flocked to the British standard. General Henry Clinton, the British commander-in-chief, officially promised liberty to all slaves who deserted their masters for British service. In the years that followed, British reliance on black manpower increased, and the proponents of utilizing black military might on a massive scale grew ever more vocal. . . .

Colonial commanders and policymakers were considerably more chary about accepting slave recruits. Many were large slaveholders who had much to lose from any disruption of slavery. Most feared that a servile revolt or a mass defection of slaveholders would follow the arming of blacks. Although blacks had occasionally served in colonial militias and distinguished themselves in the first battles of the Revolution, the Continental Congress, at South Carolina's instigation, barred them from the Continental army. But patriots proved no more immune to the exigencies of war than the British. As the struggle for independence lengthened and manpower grew critically short, the patriot policy shifted. The northern states, led by New England, began to solicit black recruits, and Rhode Island created a black regiment. When the war moved south, Upper South states grudgingly adopted a similar course of action, in spite of their larger black populations and greater dependence on slave labor. Maryland authorized slave enlistments and eventually subjected free Negroes to the draft. Virginia allowed black freemen to serve in its army and navy, and Delaware and North Carolina, following Virginia, occasionally permitted slaves to stand as substitutes for their masters. In the Lower South, however, white resistance to arming blacks stiffened. The numerical superiority of blacks in the lowland rice swamps, the large numbers of newly arrived African slaves, and the commonplace absenteeism bred an overpowering fear of slave rebellion. Despite the pleas of the Continental Congress and the urgings of commanders in the field, South Carolina and Georgia rejected the hesitant measures adopted in the Upper South. . . .

Almost everywhere, the war widened opportunities for blacks to gain their liberty. When the British left America at the end of the war, they carried thousands of blacks to freedom in Great Britain, the West Indies, Canada, and, eventually, Africa. Hundreds, perhaps thousands, of others that were freed by British wartime policy eluded their masters and remained in the United States. There is "reason to believe," petitioned angry white Virginians in 1781, "that a great number of slaves which were taken by the British Army are now passing in this Country as free men." Many blacks who fought with the patriots also secured their liberty. Some grateful masters freed their slaves, and occasionally state legislatures liberated individual bondsmen by special enactment. . . .

Whatever the effects of official British and American policy, the chaos created by rampaging armies did even more to expand a slave's chances for liberty. The actions of soldiers of both belligerents, and the often violent disputes between patriot and Tory militiamen, created near anarchic conditions, revealed the limits of slaveholder authority, and encouraged slaves to take their freedom. Runaways, previously few in number, increased rapidly in the confusion of the war. This was especially true in the Upper South, where the nature of agriculture had allowed second and third generation Afro-Americans to gain broad familiarity with the countryside. At war's end, these fugitives also passed into the growing free black population.

The war did not last long enough to destroy slavery, but the libertarian ideology that patriots used to justify their rebellion continued to challenge it when the war ended. If all men were created equal, why were some men still slaves? . . .

Slavery fell first in New England, where blacks were few in number and never an important part of the labor force or a threat to white dominance. In the Middle Atlantic states, where blacks were more numerous and bondage more deeply entrenched than in New England, slavery proved more resistant to revolutionary change. But an influx of white immigrant workers assured employers of an adequate supply of labor, and undermined the most persuasive argument against abolition. By 1804, every northern state had provided for eventual emancipation.

Still, slavery died hard. In 1810, almost 30,000 blacks—almost a quarter of the region's black population—remained in chattel bondage. Although that number fell dramatically in succeeding decades, slavery continued. There were over 1,000 bondsmen in the "free" states in 1840. Moreover, in many of the new northern states, slaveholders and their allies tried to overthrow the antislavery provisions of the Northwest Ordinance and reinstate the peculiar institution. Failing that, they enacted various forms of long-term indentureships, which allowed chattel bondage to flourish covertly until the Civil War. Nevertheless, slavery was doomed, and the mass of Northern black people had been freed.

South of Pennsylvania, emancipation faced still greater obstacles, and, in the long run, these difficulties proved insuperable. But the Christian equalitarianism unleashed by the evangelical revivals of the mid-eighteenth century complemented and strengthened the idealism of the Revolution in many parts of the South. Like revolutionary ideology, the religious awakenings transcended sectional boundaries. Methodists and Baptist evangelicals crisscrossed the southern states and, in hundreds of camp meetings, made thousands of converts. Propelled by the revolutionary idea that all men were equal in the sight of God, they frequently accepted black and white converts with equal enthusiasm. The equality of the communion table proved contagious, and some evangelicals broke the confines of other-worldly concerns to make the connection between spiritual and secular equality. Methodists, Baptists, and other evangelical sectarians joined with Quakers to become the mainstays of the southern antislavery movement. Like their northern counterparts, they organized antislavery societies, petitioned legislatures, and aided freedom suits.

Economic changes in the Upper South, especially in Maryland, Delaware, and northern Virginia, offered emancipationists an opening wedge. Beginning in the 1760s, the increased worldwide demand for foodstuff encouraged planters to expand cereal production. Dislocations in mercantile ties, resulting from the war and the depression that accompanied independence, further speeded the shift from tobacco to cereal agriculture in many parts of the Chesapeake region. This change reduced the demand for slaves, since wheat culture on small units under the existing technology thrived on free labor. Many farmers found themselves burdened with a surplus of slaves. Moreover, the agricultural transformation and the resultant establishment of new methods of processing and development of new patterns of marketing quickened the pace of commerce, stimulated the growth of light industry, and swelled urban centers. Baltimore, Richmond, Fredericksburg, and Petersburg grew as never before. In all, changes in the agricultural landscape increased commercial activity, and nascent urbanization and industrialization profoundly altered the region. Many Americans believed that the Upper South would follow the pattern of development exemplified by Pennsylvania, and not the states farther south. As the price of slaves sagged under the weight of these changes, the future of slavery became an open question. . . .

The economic transformation of the Upper South supported freedom in other less direct ways. The growing number of tenant farmers and independent tradesmen in the region, often in need of an extra hand and rarely in a position to purchase slaves, frequently employed blacks, with few questions asked. The ability to find a safe haven, even for a few days, could make the difference between a successful flight and a return to bondage. The success of many fugitives, like relatively indiscriminate manumission, not only enlarged the free black population, but darkened it as well. The larger, darker-skinned free Negro population camouflaged fugitives, increased their chances of success, and encouraged still other blacks to make their way from slavery to freedom. The increase in runaways begun during the tumult of the Revolution continued into the postwar years.

Slavery easily survived the increase of manumissions and runaways, recovered its balance, and in most places continued to grow. But the social changes of the revolutionary era profoundly altered the size and character of the free Negro population in the Upper South, and sent reverberations of liberty into the region's slave quarters.

The growth of the free Negro population can be most clearly viewed in Maryland. Between 1755 and 1790, the number of free Negroes in that state increased almost 350 percent, to about 8,000, and in the following decade it again more than doubled. By 1810, almost a quarter of Maryland's blacks were free, numbering nearly 34,000. Although not immediately apparent, slavery in Maryland had been dealt a mortal blow.

Free Negroes registered similar gains throughout the Upper South. In 1782, the year Virginia legalized private manumissions, St. George Tucker estimated the number of freemen in his state at about 2,000. By 1790, Virginia's free Negroes had increased to 12,000. Ten years later, Negro freemen numbered 20,000, and by 1810, the total stood at over 30,000. During the twenty years between 1790 and 1810, the free Negro population of Virginia more than doubled. In all, the number of Negro freemen in the Upper South grew almost 90 percent between 1790 and 1800, and another 65 percent in the following decade, so that freemen now composed more than 10 percent of the region's black population. . . .

The social forces that transformed black society in the North and in the Upper South met stern resistance in the Lower South. There, economic and demographic

Free Negro Population, 1790–1810

	1790	1800	1810
United States	59,466	108,395	186,466
North	27,109	47,154	78,181
South	32,357	61,241	108,265
Upper South	30,158	56,855	94,085
Lower South	2,199	4,386	14,180*

* Increase in the Lower South between 1800 and 1810 is largely due to the accession of Louisiana.
Source: *Population of the United States in 1860* (Washington, DC, 1864), pp. 600–601.

considerations countered the ideology of the Revolution and the great revivals. . . . Following the war, Lower South whites imported thousands of slaves from the states to the north and, in 1803, South Carolina reopened the slave trade with Africa. Not until the 1790s, when the successful black revolution in Saint Domingue sent hundreds of light-skinned *gens de couleur* fleeing for American shores, did the number of free Negroes increase significantly in the Lower South. Thus, unlike northern and Upper South freemen, Lower South free people of color remained a tiny mulatto fragment of the larger black population.

In transforming the structure of black society, the events of the revolutionary years created new, and enlarged older, regional distinctions between the black populations of the North, the Upper South, and the Lower South. By the end of the century, northern whites had committed themselves to emancipation, and the great majority of blacks enjoyed freedom. Upper South slavery, on the other hand, withstood the challenges of the revolutionary years, but its free black population expanded rapidly during the period, so that better than one black in ten was free by 1800. Slavery in the Lower South, although greatly disrupted by the war, never faced the direct emancipationist pressures present in the North or even the Upper South. It stood almost unchallenged throughout the postwar period, quickly recouped its wartime losses, and entered into a period of its greatest expansion. Lower South free people of color remained as they had been in the colonial era, a small appendage to a rapidly increasing slave population. . . . These regional distinctions in the structure of both slave and free black societies reflected and influenced white racial attitudes and shaped the development of black life in the years to come. . . .

Structural and cultural changes in black society profoundly influenced white attitudes and behavior. In the long run, they stiffened white racism. With so many blacks in possession of freedom, whites could no longer rely on their status alone to distinguish themselves from a people they despised. They began to grope for new ways to subordinate Negro freemen and set themselves apart from all blacks. Thus as the free Negro population grew, whites curbed their mobility, limited their economic opportunities, all but obliterated many of their political rights, and schemed to deport freemen from the country. Yet, the Revolution, with its emphasis on equality, forced whites to reconsider their racial values. This reconsideration produced a new flexibility in the racial attitudes of some whites and a brief recession in the color line. The liberalization of manumission codes, the passage of antikidnapping laws, the increased number of free Negroes, and the challenge to slavery all reflected small, but real, changes in white racial attitudes. These changes allowed blacks some room to maneuver in a society that was often hostile to their very being. Nevertheless, racism remained a potent force in revolutionary America. The society and culture that emerged from this first attempt to remake black life in America represented an easing of white racial hostility within a system of continued racial oppression.

The cumulative impact of freedom, cultural maturation, and the new flexibility in white attitudes unleashed the creative energies of black people. Newly freed blacks moved at once to give meaning to their freshly won liberty and form to the cultural transformation of black life in America. They took new names, established new residential and occupational patterns, reconstructed their family life, chose the first recognizable leadership class, and developed new institutions and modes of social action. . . .

Although accompanied by proscription and exclusion, freedom also created new opportunities, often for slaves as well as freemen. It allowed some blacks to attain positions from which all blacks previously had been barred. Suddenly blacks took the role of a painter, poet, author, astronomer, minister, and merchant. The almanacs of Benjamin Banneker, the poems of Phillis Wheatly and Jupiter Hammon, and the portraits of Joshua Johnston stand not only as tributes to the achievements of talented men and women, but also as symbols of the cultural transformation of the revolutionary era.

The new opportunities of freedom also allowed some freemen to accumulate property and achieve a modicum of economic security. William Flora, a revolutionary veteran, purchased several lots in Portsmouth, Virginia, soon after his discharge from the army. Later he opened a livery stable, served Portsmouth for thirty years, and willed his property to his son. In 1783, James McHenry, a Maryland shoemaker, purchased his freedom, and four years later rented a farm for £35 a year and had "a house and other stock more than sufficient for his farm." Henry Carter, a Virginia freeman, was similarly successful. He was emancipated in 1811, and within six years not only had "funds sufficient to purchase his wife Priscilla but some other property, personal & real." Throughout the nation the growth of a black property-holding class followed the growth of the free Negro population. In some places, freemen controlled sizable businesses. The striking success of sea captain Paul Cuffee of New Bedford, Massachusetts, sail manufacturer James Forten of Philadelphia, and merchant Robert Sheridan of Wilmington, North Carolina, suggests how quickly blacks took advantage of the expanding, if still limited, opportunities created by freedom. Although most blacks remained, as in slavery, poor and propertyless, some freemen rose to modest wealth and respectability.

Slowly, a new black elite emerged: Prince Hall in Boston, Richard Allen in Philadelphia, Daniel Coker in Baltimore, Christopher McPherson in Richmond, Andrew Bryan in Savannah, and a host of others in black communities throughout the new republic. Born in the decade before the Revolution, these men came of age with the emergence of the free Negro population and the maturation of Afro-American culture. Many of them owed their liberty to the changes unleashed by the American Revolution, and they shared the optimism and enthusiasm that accompanied freedom. Wealthier and better educated than most blacks, they moved easily into positions of leadership within the black community and pressed whites to expand black liberty. Pointing to the ideas of the Declaration of Independence, the new black elite provided the leadership in petitioning Congress and state legis-latures to abolish slavery and relieve free blacks of the disabilities that prevented them from enjoying their full rights as citizens. Norfolk freemen, in a typical action, requested that they be allowed to testify in court against whites so they could prove their accounts. Boston blacks demanded an equal share of the city's school fund so they might educate their children. South Carolina's free Negroes petitioned for re-lief from a special head tax that pushed them into a condition "but small removed from Slavery." And from Nashville, Tennessee, came a plea that free Negroes "ought to have the same opportunities of doing well that any Person being a citizen & free . . . would have, and that the door ought not be kept shut against them more than any other of the Human race." In the North, blacks, themselves but recently liberated, urged an end to the slave trade and the establishment of a universal emancipation. Occasionally, a few bold southern freemen like Baltimore's Daniel Coker added their voices to this public condemnation of slavery. These freemen protested in vain. Even the most restrained pleas led to harsher repression, further anchoring them to the bottom of free society. . . .

Frustrated by unyielding white hostility, freemen took two divergent courses. Some turned away from slaves in an effort to ingratiate themselves with whites, by trying to demonstrate they were more free than black. This strategy was especially evident in—although not limited to—the Lower South, where ties between freemen and slaves had never been strong and where many of the newly arrived *gens de couleur* had suffered heavy losses at the hands of the Haitian slave rebels. During the 1790s, the free people of color in Charleston established the Brown Fellowship Society, an organization limited to free brown people, and one which remained a symbol of mulatto exclusiveness throughout the antebellum period.

Most freemen, especially in the North and Upper South, took a different course. Increasingly, they turned inward and worked to strengthen the black community—free and slave. Freemen, frequently joined by slaves, established institutions where blacks might pray, educate their children, entertain, and protect themselves. African churches, schools, and fraternal societies not only served the new needs of the much expanded free Negro population and gave meaning to black liberty, but they also symbolized the emergence of Afro-American culture and represented the strongest effort to unite the black community.

Yet, even while they shouldered the new responsibilities of freedom, blacks did not immediately form separate institutions. The development of the African church, for example, was not merely a product of the emergence of the free Negro population. At first, most blacks looked to the white-dominated evangelical churches, which made acceptance of the gospel the only criterion for salvation and welcomed blacks into the fold. Free Negroes, along with slaves and poor whites, found this open membership policy, the emotional sermons, and the generous grants of self-expression an appealing contrast to the icy restrictiveness of the older, more staid denominations. Although racially mixed congregations were often forced to meet at odd hours to avoid hostile sheriffs and slave patrols, black member-ship in these churches grew rapidly. By the end of the eighteenth century, thousands of blacks, free and slave, had joined Methodist and Baptist churches.

The newness of the evangelical denominations together with their Christian equalitarianism fostered new racial patterns. In many such churches, blacks and whites seated themselves indiscriminately. It was not unusual for black churchmen to attend synods and association meetings with whites. In 1794, when one Virginia church called this practice into question, the Portsmouth Baptist Association firmly announced that "it saw nothing in the Word of God nor anything contrary to the rules of decency to prohibit a church from sending as a delegate, any male member they shall choose." Sometimes blacks served as preachers to a mixed congregation. John Chavis, a black Presbyterian circuit rider, enjoyed his greatest success among whites; Fayetteville whites regarded Henry Evans, a black Methodist, as the "best preacher of his time in that quarter"; and when Richard Allen looked down from his Philadelphia pulpit he saw "Nearly . . . as many Whites as Blacks."

Yet the old racial patterns had remarkable resilience. Christian equalitarianism momentarily bent the color line, but could not break it. In most churches, membership did not assure blacks of equal participation. Indeed, whites usually placed blacks in a distant corner or gallery and barred them from most of the rights of church members. One Virginia congregation painted some of its benches black to avoid any possibility of confusion.

As blacks found themselves proscribed from white churches or discriminated against in mixed churches, they attempted the difficult task of forming their own religious institutions. In doing so, blacks not only lacked the capital and organizational experience, but they frequently faced fierce white opposition. This was especially true in the South, where whites identified freemen with slaves and seemed to see every meeting of free blacks, no matter how innocuous, as an insurrectionary plot. The abolition of slavery in the North, in large measure, had freed whites from this fear, allowing blacks greater organizational opportunities. Northern whites frequently took a benign view of black institutions and believed, along with Benjamin Rush, that it would "be much cheaper to build churches for them than jails."

Regional differences in white attitudes allowed blacks to act more openly in the North. While northern freemen quickly established their own churches and schools, southern free blacks, frequently joined by slaves, continued to meet intense opposition. . . . Despite the rising pitch of white opposition, the number of black churches increased steadily throughout the 1780s and 1790s. . . . The rank discrimination of white-dominated churches fostered black separatism, but some blacks welcomed the split. It allowed them, for the first time, full control over their own religious life. By the end of the century, black communities from Boston to Savannah boasted their own African churches. . . .

During the early years of the nineteenth century, blacks continued to establish new African churches in the northern and border slave states. In 1816, leading black churchmen from various parts of these regions joined together to form the first independent black denomination, the African Methodist Episcopal (AME) Church. But if the African church flourished in the North, it fell upon hard times in the South. While the abolition of slavery had freed northern whites from the fear of insurrection, those anxieties grew among white southerners. In 1800, when Gabriel Prosser's aborted insurrection in Virginia nearly transformed the worst fears of southern whites into a dreadful reality, the African church came under still greater pressure. Hysterical whites shut many black churches and forced black ministers to flee the South. Even white churchmen found themselves under attack for proselytizing blacks. When a white circuit rider tried to preach to a mixed congregation in Richmond in 1802, he was threatened with the lash and driven out of the city. Charleston Methodists similarly found themselves "watched, ridiculed, and openly assailed" for allowing blacks to attend their meetings. The growth of the African church in the South was abruptly halted during the first years of the nineteenth century. Later it would revive under very different conditions.

The early development of African schools followed the same tortuous path as that of the independent black churches. In the years immediately following the Revolutionary War, the momentary respite in racial hostility encouraged some freemen and sympathetic whites to establish integrated academies throughout the North and even in some border states. But the emotions and ideals that united poor whites and blacks in evangelical churches were absent from the founding of schools. Schools were middle- and upper-class institutions, and class distinctions alone doubtless excluded most free blacks. Handicapped by a lack of funds and surrounded by increasingly hostile whites, integrated schools languished. By the turn of the century, the ebbing of revolutionary equalitarianism forced those few remaining integrated schools to close their doors or segregate their classrooms. The support of black schools fell largely on black communities. African schools, usually attached to black churches, continued to meet in the North, and in some places increased in size and number. But in the South, they faced intense opposition from whites, who viewed them as nurseries of subversion. . . .

The dismantling of African churches and schools suggests the intensity of white opposition to the development of independent black institutions wherever slavery continued to exist. Yet, even as whites closed black churches and schools and slapped new proscriptions on black liberty in order to freeze blacks into a place of permanent social inferiority, they could not erase all the gains made in the first flush of freedom. In the North, African churches and schools continued to grow and occasionally flourish, and even in the South some of these institutions limped on, although often forced to accept white supervision or meet clandestinely.

On the surface, African churches and schools and allied benevolent and fraternal societies were but a weak imitation of those of the larger society. Often they reflected white values and mimicked the structure of their white counterparts. But, on closer inspection, they embodied an Afro-American culture that was over a century in the making. Whites who visited black church meetings or attended black funerals almost uniformly observed the striking difference between them and their own somber rituals. It was no accident that blacks called their churches African churches, their schools African schools, and their benevolent societies African benevolent societies.

These organizations provided an institutional core for black life throughout the nineteenth century and well into the twentieth. In African churches and schools, black people baptized their children, educated their youth, and provided for the sick, aged, and disabled. African churches strengthened black family life by insisting that marriages be solemnized, by punishing adulterers, and occasionally by reuniting separated couples. Leaders of these institutions, especially ministers, moved into dominant positions in the black community, and African churches, in turn, provided a means of advancement for ambitious black youth. More than this, these institutions gave the black community a sense of solidarity and common purpose.

At no time was this more evident than in the postrevolutionary era, when slaves and freemen joined together to re-form black society and give shape to the cultural transformation of the preceding century. Later, free Negroes and slaves would drift apart, and many of the institutions formed during this earlier era would become identified with the free blacks and urban slave artisans who placed them at the center of black life in the North and urban South. But the new social and institutional forms established during the years after the Revolution were not lost for the mass of enslaved black people. The changes set in motion by the Revolution permeated slave life in ways that are only barely recognized now. The new occupational, religious, and familial patterns and the new social roles and modes of social action established by the convergence of changes in Afro-American and Anglo-American life during the revolutionary era continued to inform slave society, as the great cotton boom pulled slaves out of the seaboard states and into the Lower South. The revolution in black life spread across the continent. On the rich, loamy soils of the cotton South, slaves reshaped the cultural legacy of the revolutionary era to meet the new needs of plantation life. And with the Civil War, the Emancipation Proclamation, and the Thirteenth Amendment, the transformed institutional and cultural legacy of the revolutionary era emerged once again and stood at the center of black life.

F U R T H E R   R E A D I N G

Ira Berlin, *Many Thousands Gone: The First Two Centuries of Slavery in North America* (1998)

———, *Slaves Without Masters: The Free Negro in the Antebellum South* (1974)

——— and Ronald Hoffman, eds., *Slavery and Freedom in the Age of the American Revolution* (1983)

Philip D. Curtin, *The Atlantic Slave Trade: A Census* (1969)

David Brion Davis, *The Problem of Slavery in the Age of Revolution, 1770–1823* (1975)

James Essig, *Bonds of Wickedness: American Evangelicals Against Slavery, 1770–1808* (1982)

Paul Finkelman, *Slavery and the Founders: Race and Liberty in the Age of Jefferson* (1996)

Lorenzo J. Greene, *The Negro in Colonial New England, 1620–1776* (1942)

A. Leon Higginbotham, Jr., *In the Matter of Color: Race and the American Legal Process, the Colonial Period* (1978)

James Oliver Horton and Lois E. Horton, *In Hope of Liberty: Culture, Community, and Protest Among Northern Free Blacks, 1700–1860* (1997)

James Hugo Johnston, *Race Relations in Virginia and Miscegenation in the South, 1776–1860* (1970)

Winthrop D. Jordan, *White over Black: American Attitudes Toward the Negro, 1550–1812* (1968)

Sidney Kaplan and Emma Nogrady Kaplan, *The Black Presence in the Era of the American Revolution*, rev. ed. (1989)

Allan Kulikoff, *Tobacco and Slaves: The Development of Southern Cultures in the Chesapeake, 1680–1800* (1986)

Robert McColley, *Slavery and Jeffersonian Virginia* (1964)

Duncan J. MacLeod, *Slavery, Race, and the American Revolution* (1974)

Joanne Pope Melish, *Disowning Slavery: Gradual Emancipation and "Race" in New England, 1780–1860* (1998)

Edmund S. Morgan, *American Slavery, American Freedom: The Ordeal of Colonial Virginia* (1975)

Donald G. Nieman, "With Liberty for Some: The Old Constitution and the Rights of
    Blacks, 1776–1846," in Nieman, *Promises to Keep: African-Americans and the Con-
    stitutional Order, 1776 to the Present* (1991), 3–29.
Benjamin Quarles, *The Negro in the American Revolution* (1961)
James A. Rawley, *The Transatlantic Slave Trade: A History* (1981)
Donald L. Robinson, *Slavery in the Structure of American Politics, 1765–1820* (1971)
Mechal Sobel, *The World They Made Together: Black and White Values in Eighteenth-
    Century Virginia* (1987)
Jean R. Soderlund, *Quakers and Slavery: A Divided Spirit* (1985)
James W. St. G. Walker, *The Black Loyalists: The Search for a Promised Land in Nova Scotia
    and Sierra Leone, 1783–1870* (1976)
William M. Wiecek, *The Sources of Antislavery Constitutionalism in America, 1760–1848*
    (1977)
Garry Wills, *Lincoln at Gettysburg: The Words that Remade America* (1992)
Ellen Gibson Wilson, *The Loyal Blacks* (1976)
Arthur Zilversmit, *The First Emancipation: The Abolition of Slavery in the North* (1967)

Gender and Citizenship in a Revolutionary Republic

The same challenge that natural rights ideals posed for slavery, they also posed for patriarchy and the widespread denial of rights to women. But instead of there being general recognition of the contradiction, as in the case of slavery versus liberty, most Americans—male and female of all races (except certain Native American groups)—believed that women's subjection to men was a matter of natural law and therefore legitimate. When the contradiction was explicitly asserted, however, most denied the need to extend full equality and citizenship rights to women, arguing that men were naturally the best guardians or custodians of women. God, they agreed, had appointed domestic roles for women, beginning with childbearing.

Under these circumstances the few women, and even fewer men, who challenged this orthodoxy faced powerful obstacles. Although in several states the issue of women's rights was raised and patriarchy was questioned as it applied to the home, the church, and the community, it was almost impossible to bring women's rights into the political arena. Yet Americans did discuss the subject of gender—that is, socially constructed roles based on sex—a discussion that became transatlantic in scope after the publication in London of Mary Wollstonecraft's Vindication of the Rights of Women (1792). Men continued to assert their patriarchal authority—prescribing women's reading and education, controlling children and property, and shutting women out of much public life. But in spite of this "gentlemen's agreement" to stop the contagion of liberty from reaching into their homes or public affairs, egalitarian thinking and female activism began to undermine patriarchal assumptions in the generations leading to the assertion of women's equality in the 1840s.

DOCUMENTS

Document 1, by Thomas Paine, argues against men's tyranny over women. However, it is based on the premise that women's roles are naturally domestic, and Paine seems to propose only a kinder, more considerate patriarchy rather than equality. Document 2, a series of letters written by Abigail and John Adams and the Massachusetts patriot James Sullivan in 1776 before independence, reveal the profound challenge that the Revolution posed for conventional modes of thought and behavior. The revolutionary movement questioned customary political roles, as illustrated in Document 3, "An American Woman Asserts Women's Rights," published in 1780. The full realization of Revolutionary ideology is brilliantly expounded in the final selection, the Declaration of Sentiments, issued by the women's rights convention that met in 1848 in Seneca Falls, New York. Foreshadowing Lincoln's Gettysburg Address fifteen years later, this declaration employed the logic of the equality of natural rights as expressed in the Declaration of Independence.

1. Thomas Paine Admits Women Have Some Rights

> O Woman! lovely Woman!
> Nature made thee to temper man,
> We had been Brutes without you.
>
> *Otway.*

If we take a survey of ages and of countries, we shall find the women, almost—without exception—at all times and in all places, adored and oppressed. Man, who has never neglected an opportunity of exerting his power, in paying homage to their beauty, has always availed himself of their weakness. He has been at once their tyrant and their slave.

Nature herself, in forming beings so susceptible and tender, appears to have been more attentive to their charms than to their happiness. Continually surrounded with griefs and fears, the women more than share all our miseries, and are besides subjected to ills which are peculiarly their own. They cannot be the means of life without exposing themselves to the loss of it; every revolution which they undergo, alters their health, and threatens their existence, Cruel distempers attack their beauty—and the hour, which confirms their release from those, is perhaps the most melancholy of their lives. It robs them of the most essential characteristic of their sex. They can then only hope for protection from the humiliating claims of pity, or the feeble voice of gratitude.

Society, instead of alleviating their condition, is to them the source of new miseries. More than one half of the globe is covered with savages; and among all these people women are completely wretched. Man, in a state of barbarity, equally cruel and indolent, active by necessity, but naturally inclined to repose, is acquainted with little more than the physical effects of love. . . .

The women among the Indians of America are what the Helots were among the Spartans, a vanquished people, obliged to toil for their conquerors. Hence on the banks of the Oroonoko, we have seen mothers slaying their daughters out of compassion, and smothering them in the hour of their birth. They consider this barbarous pity as a virtue. . . .

Among the nations of the East we find another kind of despotism and dominion prevail—the Seraglio, and the domestic servitude of woman, authorised by the

Thomas Paine, "An Occasional Letter on the Female Sex," *Pennsylvania Magazine* (August, 1775). As found in Daniel E. Wheeler, ed., *The Life and Writings of Thomas Paine* (New York: V. Parke, 1908), vol. 2, pp. 186–194.

manners and established by the laws. In Turkey, in Persia, in India, in Japan, and over the vast empire of China, one half of the human species is oppressed by the other. . . .

. . . Even in countries where they may be esteemed most happy, constrained in their desires in the disposal of their goods, robbed of freedom of will by the laws, the slaves of opinion, which rules them with absolute sway, and construes the slightest appearances into guilt; surrounded on all sides by judges, who are at once tyrants and their seducers, and who, after having prepared their faults, punish every lapse with dishonour—nay, usurp the right of degrading them on suspicion! Who does not feel for the tender sex? Yet such I am sorry to say, is the lot of woman over the whole earth. Man with regard to them, in all climates, and in all ages has been either an insensible husband or an oppressor; but they have sometimes experienced the cold and deliberate oppression of pride, and sometimes the violent and terrible tyranny of jealousy. When they are not beloved they are nothing; and, when they are, they are tormented. They have almost equal cause to be afraid of indifference and of love. Over three quarters of the globe nature has placed them between contempt and misery. . . .

Even among people where beauty received the highest homage, we find men who would deprive the sex of every kind of reputation: "The most virtuous woman," says a celebrated Greek, "is she who is least talked of." That morose man, while he imposes duties upon women, would deprive them of the sweets of public esteem, and in exacting virtues from them, would make it a crime to aspire at honour.

If a woman were to defend the cause of her sex, she might address him in the following manner:

"How great is your injustice? If we have an equal right with you to virtue, why should we not have an equal right to praise? The public esteem ought to wait upon merit. Our duties are different from yours, but they are not therefore less difficult to fulfil, or of less consequence to society: They are the fountains of your felicity, and the sweetness of life. We are wives and mothers. 'T is we who form the union and the cordiality of families: 'T is we who soften that savage rudeness which considers everything as due to force, and which would involve man with man in eternal war. We cultivate in you that humanity which makes you feel for the misfortunes of others, and our tears forewarn you of your own danger. Nay, you cannot be ignorant that we have need of courage not less than you: More feeble in ourselves, we have perhaps more trials to encounter. Nature assails us with sorrow, law and custom press us with constraint, and sensibility and virtue alarm us with their continual conflict. Sometimes also the name of citizen demands from us the tribute of fortitude. When you offer your blood to the State think that it is ours. In giving it our sons and our husbands we give more than ourselves. You can only die on the field of battle, but we have the misfortune to survive those whom we love most. Alas! while your ambitious vanity is unceasingly labouring to cover the earth with statues, with monuments, and with inscriptions to eternize, if possible, your names, and give yourselves an existence, when this body is no more, why must we be condemned to live and to die unknown? Would that the grave and eternal forgetfulness should be our lot. Be not our tyrants in all: Permit our names to be sometimes pronounced beyond the narrow circle in which we live: Permit friendship, or at least love, to inscribe its emblems on the tomb where our ashes repose; and deny us not that public esteem which, after the esteem of one's self, is the sweetest reward of well doing."

2. Abigail and John Adams Debate Women's Rights, 1776

Abigail Adams to John Adams

Braintree March 31 1776

. . . I long to hear that you have declared an independancy—and by the way in the new Code of Laws which I suppose it will be necessary for you to make I desire you would Remember the Ladies, and be more generous and favourable to them than your ancestors. Do not put such unlimited power into the hands of the Husbands. Remember all Men would be tyrants if they could. If perticuliar care and attention is not paid to the Laidies we are determined to foment a Rebelion, and will not hold ourselves bound by any Laws in which we have no voice, or Representation.

That your Sex are Naturally Tyrannical is a Truth so thoroughly established as to admit of no dispute, but such of you as wish to be happy willingly give up the harsh title of Master for the more tender and endearing one of Friend. Why then, not put it out of the power of the vicious and the Lawless to use us with cruelty and indignity with impunity. Men of Sense in all Ages abhor those customs which treat us only as the vassals of your Sex. Regard us then as Beings placed by providence under your protection and in immitation of the Supreem Being make use of that power only for our happiness.

John Adams to Abigail Adams

Ap. 14. 1776

. . . As to your extraordinary Code of Laws, I cannot but laugh. We have been told that our Struggle has loosened the bands of Government every where. That Children and Apprentices were disobedient—that schools and Colledges were grown turbulent—that Indians slighted their Guardians and Negroes grew insolent to their Masters. But your Letter was the first Intimation that another Tribe more numerous and powerfull than all the rest were grown discontented.—This is rather too coarse a Compliment but you are so saucy, I wont blot it out.

Depend upon it, We know better than to repeal our Masculine systems. Altho they are in full Force, you know they are little more than Theory. We dare not exert our Power in its full Latitude. We are obliged to go fair, and softly, and in Practice you know We are the subjects. We have only the Name of Masters, and rather than give up this, which would compleatly subject Us to the Despotism of the Peticoat, I hope General Washington, and all our brave Heroes would fight. . . . I begin to think the Ministry as deep as they are wicked. After stirring up Tories, Landjobbers, Trimmers, Bigots, Canadians, Indians, Negroes, Hanoverians, Hessians, Russians, Irish Roman Catholicks, Scotch Renegadoes, at last they have stimulated the [text missing] to demand new Priviledges and threaten to rebell.

"Abigail and John Adams Debate Women's Rights, 1776." As found in *Adams Family Correspondence,* ed. L. H. Butterfield et al. (Cambridge: Harvard University Press, 1963), vol. 1, pp. 369–370, 381–383, 401–403.

Abigail Adams to John Adams

B[raintre]e May 7 1776

. . . I can not say that I think you very generous to the Ladies, for whilst you are proclaiming peace and good will to Men, Emancipating all Nations, you insist upon retaining an absolute power over Wives. But you must remember that Arbitrary power is like most other things which are very hard, very liable to be broken—and notwithstanding all your wise Laws and Maxims we have it in our power not only to free ourselves but to subdue our Masters, and without voilence throw both your natural and legal authority at our feet—

> Charm by accepting, by submitting sway
> Yet have our Humour most when we obey.

I thank you for several Letters which I have received since I wrote Last. They alleviate a tedious absence, and I long earnestly for a Saturday Evening, and experience a similar pleasure to that which I used to find in the return of my Friend upon that day after a weeks absence. The Idea of a year dissolves all my Phylosophy. . . .

Johnny and Charls have the Mumps, a bad disorder, but they are not very bad. Pray be kind enough to remember me at all times and write as often as you possibly can.

John Adams to James Sullivan

Philadelphia May. 26. 1776

Dear Sir

. . . Our worthy Friend, Mr. Gerry has put into my Hand, a Letter from you, of the Sixth of May, in which you consider the Principles of Representation and Legislation, and give us Hints of Some Alterations, which you Seem to think necessary, in the Qualification of Voters. . . .

It is certain in Theory, that the only moral Foundation of Government is the Consent of the People. But to what an Extent Shall We carry this Principle? Shall We Say, that every Individual of the Community, old and young, male and female, as well as rich and poor, must consent, expressly to every Act of Legislation? No, you will Say. This is impossible. How then does the Right arise in the Majority to govern the Minority, against their Will? Whence arises the Right of the Men to govern Women, without their Consent? Whence the Right of the old to bind the Young, without theirs.

But let us first Suppose, that the whole Community of every Age, Rank, Sex, and Condition, has a Right to vote. This Community, is assembled—a Motion is made and carried by a Majority of one Voice. The Minority will not agree to this. Whence arises the Right of the Majority to govern, and the Obligation of the Minority to obey? from Necessity, you will Say, because there can be no other Rule. But why exclude Women? You will Say, because their Delicacy renders them unfit for Practice and Experience, in the great Business of Life, and the hardy Enterprizes of War, as well as the arduous Cares of State. Besides, their attention is So much engaged with the necessary Nurture of their Children, that Nature has made them fittest for domestic Cares. And Children have not Judgment or Will of their own. True. But will not these Reasons apply to others? Is it not equally true, that Men in general in every Society, who are wholly destitute of Property, are also too little acquainted with public Affairs to form a Right Judgment, and too dependent upon other Men to have a Will of their own? If this is a Fact, if you give to every Man, who has no Property, a Vote, will you not make a fine encouraging Provision for Corruption by your fundamental Law? Such is the Frailty of the human Heart, that very few Men, who have no Property, have any Judgment of their own. They talk and vote as they are directed by Some Man of Property, who has attached their Minds to his Interest. . . .

Harrington has Shewn that Power always follows Property. This I believe to be as infallible a Maxim, in Politicks, as, that Action and Re-action are equal, is in Mechanicks. Nay I believe We may advance one Step farther and affirm that the Ballance of Power in a Society, accompanies the Ballance of Property in Land. The only possible Way then of preserving the Ballance of Power on the side of equal Liberty and public Virtue, is to make the Acquisition of Land easy to every Member of Society: to make a Division of the Land into Small Quantities, So that the Multitude may be possessed of landed Estates. If the Multitude is possessed of the Ballance of real Estate, the Multitude will have the Ballance of Power, and in that Case the Multitude will take Care of the Liberty, Virtue, and Interest of the Multitude in all Acts of Government. . . .

The Same Reasoning, which will induce you to admit all Men, who have no Property, to vote, with those who have, for those Laws, which affect the Person will prove that you ought to admit Women and Children: for generally Speaking, Women and Children, have as good Judgment, and as independent Minds as those Men who are wholly destitute of Property: these last being to all Intents and Purposes as much dependent upon others, who will please to feed, cloath, and employ them, as Women are upon their Husbands, or Children on their Parents.

As to your Idea, of proportioning the Votes of Men in Money Matters, to the Property they hold, it is utterly impracticable. There is no possible Way of Ascertaining, at any one Time, how much every Man in a Community, is worth; and if there is, So fluctuating is Trade and Property, that this State of it, would change in half an Hour. The Property of the whole Community, is Shifting every Hour, and no Record can be kept of the Changes.

Society can be governed only by general Rules. Government cannot accommodate itself to every particular Case, as it happens, nor to the Circumstances of particular Persons. It must establish general, comprehensive Regulations for Cases and Persons. The only Question is, which general Rule, will accommodate most Cases and most Persons.

Depend upon it, sir, it is dangerous to open So fruitfull a Source of Controversy and Altercation, as would be opened by attempting to alter the Qualifications of Voters. There will be no End of it. New Claims will arise. Women will demand a Vote. Lads from 12 to 21 will think their Rights not enough attended to, and every Man, who has not a Farthing, will demand an equal Voice with any other in all Acts of State. It tends to confound and destroy all Distinctions, and prostrate all Ranks, to one common Levell.

3. An American Woman Asserts Women's Rights, 1780

On the commencement of actual war, the Women of America manifested a firm resolution to contribute as much as could depend on them, to the deliverance of their country. Animated by the purest patriotism, they are sensible of sorrow at this day, in not offering more than barren wishes for the success of so glorious a Revolution. They aspire to render themselves more really useful; and this sentiment is universal from the north to the south of the Thirteen United States. Our ambition is kindled by the fame of those heroines of antiquity, who have rendered their sex illustrious, and have proved to the universe, that, if the weakness of our Constitution, if opinion and manners did not forbid us to march to glory by the same paths as the Men, we should at least equal, and sometimes surpass them in our love for the public good. I glory in all that which my sex has done great and commendable. I call to mind with enthusiasm and with admiration, all those acts of courage, of constancy and patriotism, which history has transmitted to us: The people favoured by Heaven, preserved from destruction by the virtues, the zeal and the resolution of Deborah, of Judith, of Esther! The fortitude of the mother of the Macchabees, in giving up her sons to die before her eyes: Rome saved from the fury of a victorious enemy by the efforts of Volumnia, and other Roman Ladies: So many famous sieges where the Women have been seen forgetting the weakness of their sex, building new walls, digging trenches with their feeble hands, furnishing arms to their defenders, they themselves darting the missile weapons on the enemy, resigning the ornaments of their apparel, and their fortune, to fill the public treasury, and to hasten the deliverance of their country; burying themselves under its ruins; throwing themselves into the flames rather than submit to the disgrace of humiliation before a proud enemy.

Born for liberty, disdaining to bear the irons of a tyrannic Government, we associate ourselves to the grandeur of those Sovereigns, cherished and revered, who have held with so much splendour the scepter of the greatest States, The Batildas, the Elizabeths, the Maries, the Catharines, who have extended the empire of liberty, and contented to reign by sweetness and justice, have broken the chains of slavery, forged by tyrants in times of ignorance and barbarity. . . .

. . . We are at least certain, that he cannot be a good citizen who will not applaud our efforts for the relief of the armies which defend our lives, our possessions, our liberty? . . . And shall we hesitate to evidence to you our gratitude? Shall we hesitate to wear a cloathing more simple; hair dressed less elegant, while at the price of this small privation, we shall deserve your benedictions. Who, amongst us, will not renounce with the highest pleasure, those vain ornaments, when she shall consider that the valiant defenders of America will be able to draw some advantage from the money which she may have laid out in these. . . . The time is arrived to display the same sentiments which animated us at the beginning of the Revolution, when we renounced the use of teas, however agreeable to our taste, rather than receive them from our persecutors; when we made it appear to them that we placed

Anonymous, *The Sentiments of an American Woman* (Philadelphia: John Dunlap, 1780), 79–82.

former necessaries in the rank of superfluities, when our liberty was interested; when our republican and laborious hands spun the flax, prepared the linen intended for the use of our soldiers; when [as] exiles and fugitives we supported with courage all the evils which are the concomitants of war. Let us not lose a moment; let us be engaged to offer the homage of our gratitude at the altar of military valour, and you, our brave deliverers, while mercenary slaves combat to cause you to share with them, the irons with which they are loaded, receive with a free hand our offering, the purest which can be presented to your virtue, BY AN AMERICAN WOMAN.

4. The Declaration of Sentiments of the Seneca Falls Convention, 1848

When, in the course of human events, it becomes necessary for one portion of the family of man to assume among the people of the earth a position different from that which they have hitherto occupied, but one to which the laws of nature and of nature's God entitle them, a decent respect to the opinions of mankind requires that they should declare the causes that impel them to such a course.

We hold these truths to be self-evident: that all men and women are created equal; that they are endowed by their Creator with certain inalienable rights; that among these are life, liberty, and the pursuit of happiness; that to secure these rights governments are instituted, deriving their just powers from the consent of the governed. Whenever any form of government becomes destructive of these ends, it is the right of those who suffer from it to refuse allegiance to it, and to insist upon the institution of a new government, laying its foundation on such principles, and organizing its powers in such form, as to them shall seem most likely to effect their safety and happiness. Prudence, indeed, will dictate that governments long established should not be changed for light and transient causes; and accordingly all experience hath shown that mankind are more disposed to suffer, while evils are sufferable, than to right themselves by abolishing the forms to which they were accustomed. But when a long train of abuses and usurpations, pursuing invariably the same object evinces a design to reduce them under absolute despotism, it is their duty to throw off such government, and to provide new guards for their future security. Such has been the patient sufferance of the women under this government, and such is now the necessity which constrains them to demand the equal situation to which they are entitled.

The history of mankind is a history of repeated injuries and usurpations on the part of man toward woman, having in direct object the establishment of an absolute tyranny over her. To prove this, let facts be submitted to a candid world.

He has never permitted her to exercise her inalienable right to the elective franchise.

He has compelled her to submit to laws, in the formation of which she had no voice.

He has withheld from her rights which are given to the most ignorant and degraded men—both natives and foreigners.

"The Declaration of Sentiments of the Seneca Falls Convention, 1848." In Elizabeth Cady Stanton, Susan B. Anthony, Matilda J Gage, eds., *The History of Woman Suffrage* (New York: Arno, 1969), vol. 1, pp. 70–76.

Having deprived her of this first right of a citizen, the elective franchise, thereby leaving her without representation in the halls of legislation, he has oppressed her on all sides.

He has made her, if married, in the eye of the law, civilly dead.

He has taken from her all right in property, even to the wages she earns.

He has made her, morally, an irresponsible being, as she can commit many crimes with impunity, provided they be done in the presence of her husband. In the covenant of marriage, she is compelled to promise obedience to her husband, he becoming, to all intents and purposes, her master—the law giving him power to deprive her of her liberty, and to administer chastisement.

He has so framed the laws of divorce, as to what shall be the proper causes, and in case of separation, to whom the guardianship of the children shall be given, as to be wholly regardless of the happiness of women—the law, in all cases, going upon a false supposition of the supremacy of man, and giving all power into his hands.

After depriving her of all rights as a married woman, if single, and the owner of property, he has taxed her to support a government which recognizes her only when her property can be made profitable to it.

He has monopolized nearly all the profitable employments, and from those she is permitted to follow, she receives but a scanty remuneration. He closes against her all the avenues to wealth and distinction which he considers most honorable to himself. As a teacher of theology, medicine, or law, she is not known.

He has denied her the facilities for obtaining a thorough education, all colleges being closed against her.

He allows her in Church, as well as State, but a subordinate position, claiming Apostolic authority for her exclusion from the ministry, and, with some exceptions, from any public participation in the affairs of the Church.

He has created a false public sentiment by giving to the world a different code of morals for men and women, by which moral delinquencies which exclude women from society, are not only tolerated, but deemed of little account in man.

He has usurped the prerogative of Jehovah himself, claiming it as his right to assign for her a sphere of action, when that belongs to her conscience and to her God.

He has endeavored, in every way that he could, to destroy her confidence in her own powers, to lessen her self-respect, and to make her willing to lead a dependent and abject life.

Now, in view of this entire disfranchisement of one-half the people of this country, their social and religious degradation—in view of the unjust laws above mentioned, and because women do feel themselves aggrieved, oppressed, and fraudulently deprived of their most sacred rights, we insist that they have immediate admission to all the rights and privileges which belong to them as citizens of the United States.

In entering upon the great work before us, we anticipate no small amount of misconception, misrepresentation, and ridicule; but we shall use every instrumentality within our power to effect our object. We shall employ agents, circulate tracts, petition the State and National legislatures, and endeavor to enlist the pulpit and the press in our behalf. We hope this Convention will be followed by a series of Conventions embracing every part of the country.

E S S A Y S

Linda Kerber, author of the first essay, is May Brodbeck Professor in the Liberal Arts at the University of Iowa, and has published major studies of women in the Revolution and early republic. The analysis included here shows how deeply unsettling the Revolution was for the politics of the sexes and the home. In Kerber's view, the fact that the Revolution did not swiftly alter women's rights and public roles should not be taken to mean that the conflict did not affect women's rights. Similarly, Professor Jan Lewis of Rutgers University, Newark, explains that women's citizenship was indeed recognized in the Constitution, although that recognition was subsequently compromised. The Revolution, she suggests, opened a path toward equality for women and African Americans that was later closed.

The Revolution and Women's Rights

LINDA K. KERBER

. . . Like all revolutions, the American Revolution had a double agenda. Patriots sought to exclude the British from power: this task was essentially physical and military. Patriots also sought to accomplish a radical psychological and intellectual transformation: "Our principles, opinions, and manners," Benjamin Rush argued, would need to change to be congruent with "the forms of government we have adopted." As Cynthia Enloe has remarked, a successful revolutionary movement establishes new definitions of "what is valued, what is scorned, what is feared, and what is believed to enhance safety and security."

In America this transformation involved a sharp attack on social hierarchies and a reconstruction of family relationships, especially between husbands and wives and between parents and children. Military resistance was enough for rebellion; it was the transformation of values—which received classic expression in Thomas Paine's *Common Sense*—that defined the Revolution. Both tasks were intertwined, and both tasks—resistance and redefinition—involved women as supporters and as adversaries far more than we have understood.

If the army is described and analyzed solely from the vantage point of central command, the women and children will be invisible. To view it from the vantage point of the foot soldier and the thousands of women who followed the troops is to emphasize the marginality of support services for both armies, and the penetrability of the armies by civilians, especially women and children. From the women's perspective, the American army looks far less professional, far more disorganized, than it appears to be in most scholarly studies of the war of the Revolution.

Women were drawn into the task of direct military resistance to a far greater extent than we have appreciated. Along with the French Revolution, the American Revolution was the last of the early modern wars. As they had since the sixteenth century, thousands of women and children traveled with the armies, functioning as nurses, laundresses, and cooks. Like the emblematic Molly Pitcher, they made themselves

---

Excerpted from Linda K. Kerber, "History Can Do It No Justice: Women and the Reinterpretation of the American Revolution," in *Women in the Age of the American Revolution,* ed. Ronald Hoffman and Peter J. Albert (Charlottesville: University Press of Virginia for the United States Capitol Historical Society, 1989), pp. 3–42. Copyright © 1989 by the Rectors and Visitors of the University of Virginia. Reprinted by permission of Georges Borchardt, Inc., for the author and the University Press of Virginia.

useful where they could—hauling water for teams that fired cannon, bringing food to men under fire. In British practice, with which the colonists had become familiar during the Seven Years' War, each company had its own allocation of women, usually but not always soldiers' wives and occasionally mothers; when the British sailed, their women sailed with them. . . . [I]n the original complement of eight regiments that the British sent to put down the American rebellion, each regiment had 677 men and 60 women, a ratio of approximately 10 to 1. . . . Burgoyne's army of 7,200 troops was followed by 2,000 women. American women attached themselves to the troops and followed the armies because they feared to lose track of men with whom they had developed relationships or by whom they were pregnant, or because they feared to stay on in a loyalist area after it had returned to patriot control.

Patriots were skeptical about giving women official status in the army; Washington objected to a fixed quota of women. But the women followed nevertheless, apparently for much the same reasons as the British and German women did. By the end of the war, Washington's General Orders established a ratio of one woman for every fifteen men in a regiment. . . . Extrapolating from this figure, Linda Grant De Pauw offers the high estimate that in the course of the war some "20,000 individual women served as women of the army on the American side." . . . [M]ost women who followed the armies were impoverished. Wives and children who had no means of support when their husbands and fathers were drawn into service—whether by enthusiasm or in the expectation of bounties—followed after and cared for their own men, earning their subsistence by nursing, cooking, and washing for the troops in an era when hospitals were marginal and the offices of quartermaster and commissary were inadequately run. Perhaps the most mythologized of these women is Mary Hayes, of Carlisle, Pennsylvania, who followed her husband when he enlisted as an infantryman. She seems to have spent the winter of 1777–78 at Valley Forge; at the Battle of Monmouth she not only carried water for his gun crew (apparently a standard task for women) but joined the crew and continued the firing when he was disabled. Both stayed on with the army until the end of the war, although he died shortly thereafter. After a brief second marriage, "Molly Pitcher" lived out her life in Carlisle, "doing nursing and menial work" until her death in 1832. "In this last month of her life," writes her memorist, "Pennsylvania recognized her as a veteran" and gave her a pension, which she did not live to enjoy.

The women of the army made Washington uncomfortable. He had good reason to regard them with skepticism. Although they processed food and supplies by cooking and cleaning, they were also a drain on these supplies in an army that never had enough. Even the most respectable women represented something of a moral challenge; by embodying an alternate loyalty to family or lover, they could discourage reenlistment or even encourage desertion in order to respond to private emotional claims. They were a steady reminder to men of a world other than the controlled one of the camp; desertion was high throughout the war, and no general needed anyone who might encourage it further. Most importantly, perhaps, the women of the army were disorderly women who could not be controlled by the usual military devices and who were inevitably suspected of theft and spying for the enemy. As a result, Washington was constantly issuing contradictory orders. Sometimes the women of the army were to ride in the wagons so as not to slow down the troops; at other times they were to walk so as not to take up valuable space in the wagons. But always they were there, and Washington knew they could not be expelled. These women drew rations in the American army; they brought children with them, who drew half rations. American regulations took care to insist that "sucking babes" could draw no rations at all, since obviously they couldn't eat. "The very rules that denied a place in the army to all women sanctioned a place for some." . . .

It is true that cooking, laundering, and nursing were female skills; the women of the army were doing in a military context what they had once done in a domestic one. But we ought not discount these services for that reason, or visualize them as taking place in a context of softness and luxury. "One observer of American troops . . . attributed their ragged and unkempt bearing to the lack of enough women to do their washing and mending; the Americans, not being used to doing things of this sort, choose rather to let their linen, etc., rot upon their backs than to be at the trouble of cleaning 'em themselves." . . .

Women who served such troops were performing tasks of the utmost necessity if the army were to continue functioning. John Shy has remarked that the relative *absence* of women among American troops put Americans at a disadvantage in re-lation to the British; women maintained "some semblance of cleanliness." They did not live in gentle surroundings in either army, and the conditions of their lives were not pleasant. Although they were impoverished, they were not inarticulate. The most touching account of Yorktown I know is furnished by Sarah Osborn, who cooked for Washington's troops and delivered food to them under fire because, as she told Washington himself, "it would not do for the men to fight and starve too." At the end she watched the British soldiers stack their arms and then return "into town again to await their destiny." . . .

In 1786 Benjamin Rush made a famous distinction between the "first act" of the "great drama" of the Revolution, a war accomplished by armies, and the revolution in "principles, opinions and manners so as to accommodate them to the forms of government we have adopted." The dichotomy applies to women's roles as well as the more general aspects of life that he had in mind. Women had been embedded in the military aspects of the war against Britain, but their roles were politically in-visible. American literally lacked a language to describe what was before their eyes. On the other hand, women were visible, even central, to the Revolution and to the patriot effort to transform political culture. That transformation was crucial if the Americans were to sustain the claim that they were doing more than refusing to pay their fair share of taxes. Americans claimed both implicitly and explicitly that they were creating a new kind of politics, a democracy in which the people acted as con-stituent power, in which every adult citizen had an obligation to play an intelligent and thoughtful role in shaping the nation's destiny. . . . It was this cultural transfor-mation that Americans had in mind when they referred, as they frequently did, to the "new era" that political mobilization would usher in.

A dramatic feature of pre-Revolutionary political mobilization was the con-sumer boycott. The boycott was central to the effort to change values, to undermine psychological as well as economic ties to England, and to draw apolitical people into political dialogue. Although consumer boycotts seem to have been devised by men, they were predicated on the support of women, both as consumers—who would make distinctions on what they purchased as between British imports and goods of domestic origin—and as manufacturers, who would voluntarily increase their level of household production. . . .

Women who had thought themselves excused from making political choices now found that they had to align themselves politically, even behind the walls of their own homes. The loyalist Peter Oliver complained that "Mr. Otis's black Regiment, the dissenting Clergy, were also set to Work, to preach up Manufacturers instead of Gospel." Many middle-class women spun in the context of service to the church, presenting their skeins to ministers, and leaving blurred the distinction between what they did politically and what they did in the name of religion. . . . As they decided how much spinning to do, whether to set their slaves to weaving homespun, or whether to drink tea or coffee, men and women devised a political ritual congruent with women's understanding of their domestic roles and readily incorporated into their daily routines. . . .

The boycotts were an occasion for instruction in collective political behavior, formalized by the signing of petitions and manifestos. In 1767 both men and women signed the Association, promising not to import du?ed items. Five years later, when the Boston Committee of Correspondence circulated the Solemn League and Covenant establishing another boycott of British goods, they demanded that both men and women sign. The manifesto of the women of Edenton, North Carolina, against imported tea is perhaps the best known of these collective statements. Collective petitions would serve women as their most usable political device deep into the nineteenth century. . . .

Nowhere can the dependence of rebellion on the transformation of values be seen more clearly than in the continuing struggle for recruitment into the army of militia. . . . In every state except Pennsylvania, militias inscribed every able-bodied free white man in their rolls, and drew those men together in the public exercises of training day. There was no counterpart for women of a training day as a bonding experience that simultaneously linked men to each other, to the local community, and at the same time to the state.

Training day underscored men's and women's different political roles; military training was a male ritual that excluded women. Women, in turn, castigated it as an arena for antisocial behavior. When peacetime drill turned into actual war, women logically complained that they had been placed at risk without their consent. . . . [R]eligiously believing women were deeply skeptical of a military culture that encouraged drink as indispensable to the display of courage and was unperturbed by those who broke the third commandment.

In this context patriots needed to find an alternative to women's traditional skepticism and resistance of mobilization. . . . [T]he alternative role involved sending sons and husbands to battle. The *Pennsylvania Evening Post* offered the model of "an elderly grandmother of Elizabethtown, New Jersey" in 1776: "My children, I have a few words to say to you, you are going out in a just cause, to fight for the rights and liberties of your country; you have my blessings. . . . Let me beg of you . . . that if you fall, it may be like men; and that your wounds may not be in your back parts." . . .

Women who thrust their men to battle were displaying a distinctive form of patriotism. They had been mobilized by the state to mobilize their men; they were part of the moral resources of the total society. Sending men to war was in part their expression of surrogate enlistment in a society in which women did not fight. This was their way of shaping the construction of the military community. They were *shaming* their men into serving the interests of the state; indeed shaming would become in the future the standard role of civilian women in time of war. . . .

The third way in which women transformed what was valued and what was scorned involved crowd behavior that was both disorderly and ritualized—sometimes at one and the same time. Working-class women, who spent much of their lives on the streets as market women or shopkeepers, surely were part of these crowds. . . .

The organizers of the Revolutionary crowds were male, and the bulk of the participants seem to have been young artisans. The rhetorical devices of the great Pope's Day crowds, with their violent battles centered on the effigies of Pope, Devil, and Pretender, were couched in male emblem and male language. In these tableaux, women seem to have been marginal. But women devised their own roles in public ritual. They formed part of . . . the great public funerals for the victims of the Boston Massacre and for the martyred child Christopher Seider.

Women also invented their own public rituals. Most noteworthy of these was the effort of Hannah Bostwick McDougall in New York in April 1770. When her patriot husband Alexander McDougall, was arrested for publishing a seditious broadside, his wife "led a parade of ladies from Chapel Street to the jail, entertaining them later at her home." . . .

Better known is the house-to-house campaign of the patriot women of Philadelphia, led by Esther Reed and Deborah Franklin Bache, to raise money for Washington's soldiers and to get women of other states to do the same, accompanied by an explicit political broadside and by intimidating fund raising. "I fancy they raised a considerable sum by this extorted contribution," sneered Quaker loyalist Anna Rawle, "some giving solely against their inclinations thro' fear of what might happen if they refused."

Bringing ritual resistance to Britain out of the household and into the streets shaded into violence. . . . Perhaps the most violent act of resistance we know is that of the New York woman who was accused of incendiarism in the Great Fire when the British entered the city in 1776. She received her eulogy from Edmund Burke on the floor of the House of Commons:

> Still is not that continent conquered; witness the behaviour of one miserable woman, who with her single arm did that, which an army of a hundred thousand men could not do—arrested your progress, in the moment of your success. This miserable being was found in a cellar, with her visage besmeared and smutted over, with every mark of rage, despair, resolution, and the most exalted heroism, buried in combustibles, in order to fire New-York, and perish in its ashes;—she was brought forth, and knowing that she would be condemned to die, upon being asked her purpose, said, "to fire the city!" and was determined to omit no opportunity of doing what her country called for. Her train was laid and fired; and it is worthy of your attention, how Providence was pleased to make use of those humble means to serve the American cause, when open force was used in vain.

. . . Boycotting imports, shaming men into service, disorderly demonstration—all were ways in which women obviously entered the new political community created by the Revolution. It was less apparent what that entrance might mean. There followed a struggle to define women's political role in a modern republic. The classic roles of women in wartime were two: both had been named by the Greeks, both positioned women as critics of war. . . . Antigone upholds decency.

Cassandra, who foresees the tragic end of the Trojan War, expresses generalized anxiety and criticism.

In America an evangelical version of Cassandra flourished. Many, perhaps most, women were unambivalently critical of the war and offered their criticism in religious terms. . . . In 1787, when the delegates to the Philadelphia Convention were stabilizing a Revolutionary government and embodying their understanding of what the Revolution had meant in the Federal Constitution, there appeared the classic text of the alternative perspective: an anonymous pamphlet called *Women Invited to War.* The author defined herself as a "Daughter of America" and addressed herself to the "worthy women, and honourable daughters of America." She acknowledged that the war had been a "valiant . . . defense of life and liberty," but discounted its ultimate significance. The *real* war, she argued, was not against Great Britain, or Shaysites, but against the Devil. . . .

. . . Then the "Daughter of America" assumed an unusual voice, the voice of the minister, speaking to the special responsibilities of women and articulating the murmur that men were more prone to sin than were women: "But perhaps some of you may say, there are some very heinous sins, which our sex are not so commonly guilty of, as the men are; in particular the vile sin of drinking to excess, and also prophane swearing and cursing, and taking the great and holy name of God in vain, are practiced more by men than by women." . . .

In a few pages the author had moved from the contemplation of women in war emergencies to the argument that women ought to conduct their wars according to definitions that were different from men's; that the main tasks that faced the republic were spiritual rather than political, and that in these spiritual tasks women could take the lead; indeed that they had a special responsibility to display "mourning and lamentation."

In the aftermath of the Revolutionary war, many women continued to define their civic obligations in religious terms. They way to save the city, argued the "Daughter of America," was to purify one's behavior and pray for the sins of the community. By the early nineteenth century, women flooded into the dissenting churches of the Second Great Awakening, bringing their husbands and children with them and asserting that their claim to religious salvation made possible new forms of assertive behavior—criticizing sinful conduct of their friends and neighbors, sometimes traveling to new communities and establishing new schools, sometimes widening in a major way the scope of the books they read. Churches also provided the context for women's benevolent activity. Despairing that secular politics would clear up the shattered debris of the war, religious women organized societies for the support of widows and orphans in a heretofore unparalleled collective endeavor. If women were to be invited to war, they would join their own war and on their own terms. . . .

Between 1775 and 1777 statutory language moved from the term *subject* to *inhabitant, member,* and finally, *citizen.* By 1776 patriots were prepared to say that all loyal inhabitants, men and women, were citizens of the new republic, no longer subjects of the king. But the word *citizen* still carried overtones inherited from antiquity and the Renaissance, when the citizen made the city possible by taking up arms on its behalf. In this way or reasoning, the male citizen "exposes his life in defense of the state and at the same time ensures that the decision to expose it can not be taken without him; it is the possession of arms which makes a man a full citizen." This mode of thinking, this way of relating men to the state, had no room in it for women except as something to be avoided. . . .

Many aspects of American political culture reinforced the gender-specific character of citizenship. First, and most obvious, men were linked to the republic by military service. Military service performed by the women of the army was not understood to have a political component. Second, men were linked to the republic by the political ritual of suffrage, itself an expression of the traditional link between political voice and ownership of property deeply embedded in Lockean political theory. By the late eighteenth century most jurisdictions permitted male owners of land, of movable property of a set value, or men who paid taxes to exercise the franchise; in each case it was understood that control of property was connected with independence of judgment. . . . If the ownership of property, was requisite to political independence, very few women—even in wealthy families—could make that claim. . . . Women of the laboring poor were of course particularly vulnerable. Like all married women, they were legally dependent on their husbands; as working people the range of economic opportunities open to them was severely restricted. Apprenticeship contracts, for example, reveal that cities often offered a wide range of artisanal occupations to boys but limited girls to housekeeping and occasional training as a skilled seamstress. Almshouse records display a steady pattern: most residents were women and their children; most "outwork" was taken by women. Their lack of marketable skills must have smoothed the path to prostitution for the destitute. The material dependency of women was well established in the early republic. . . .

Finally, men were linked to the Revolutionary republic psychologically, by their understanding of self, honor, and shame. These psychological connections were gender-specific and therefore unavailable to women. Thus in his shrewd analysis of the psychological prerequisite for rebellion, Tom Paine linked independence from the empire to the natural independence of the grown son. The image captured the common sense of the matter for a wide range of American men, who made *Common Sense* their manifesto. . . .

The promise of fame was positive reinforcement for physical courage. The army had negative reinforcements as well. For cowardice there were courts-martial and dismissal from service. There was also humiliation, which, observes historian Charles Royster, might take the form of "being marched out of camp wearing a dress, with soldiers throwing dung at him." Manliness and honor were thus sharply and ritually contrasted with effeminacy and dishonor. It is not accidental that dueling entered American practice during the Revolution. Usually "British and French aristocrats" are blamed for its introduction, but that does not explain American receptivity; . . . the duel fit well with officers' needs to define their valor and to respond to their anxieties about shame.

All these formulations of citizenship and civic relations in a republic were tightly linked to men and manhood: it was men who offered military service, men who sought honor, men who dueled in its defense. . . . [H]onor, like fame, was psychologically male. The language of citizenship for women had to be freshly devised. . . .

For the earliest extended American attempt to locate women in the larger political community, we must turn to the fund-raising broadside that Bache and Reed devised for their campaign and sent to Washington along with their contributions.

That revealing document is an ambivalently worded expression of their political self-concept, meandering from third person to first person and back again. Sometimes its authors speak in emphatic collective voice, claiming that only relatively trivial "opinions & manners" forbade them "to march to glory by the same paths as the Men." Otherwise, "we should at least equal, and sometimes surpass them in our love for the public good." Sometimes they offered only the humble viewpoint of an individual excluded from the center of action: "The situation of our soldiery has been represented to me." Their ambiguity reflects the oxymoronic quality of the conception of the woman citizen in the early republic.

Women were assisted in their effort to refine the idea of the woman citizen by changes in male understanding of the role. "The people" of Revolutionary broadsides had clearly been meant to include a broader sector of the population than had been meant by the citizenry of Renaissance Florence; how much more inclusive American citizenship ought to be was under negotiation. It seemed obvious that it had to include more than those who actually took up arms. . . .

But the nature of citizenship remained gendered. Behind it still lurked old republican assumptions, beginning with the obvious one that men's citizenship included a military component and women's did not. The classical republican view of the world had been bipolar at its core, setting reason against the passions, virtue against a yielding to the vagaries of fortune, restraint against indulgence, manliness against effeminacy. The first item in each of these pairs was understood to be a male attribute. The second was understood to be characteristic of women's nature; when displayed by men it was evidence of defeat and failure. The new language of independence and individual choice (which would be termed *liberal*) welcomed women's citizenship; the old language of republicanism deeply distrusted it.

Between 1770 and 1800 many writers, both male and female, articulated a new understanding of the civic role of women in a republic. This understanding drew on some old ingredients but rearranged them and added new ones to create a gendered definition of citizenship that attempted (with partial success) to resolve these polarities. The new formulation also sought to provide an image of female citizenship alternative to the passivity of Cassandra or the crisis-specificity of Antigone. The new formulation had two major—and related—elements. The first, expressed with extraordinary clarity by Judith Sargent Murray in America and Mary Wollstonecraft in England, stressed women's native capability and competence and offered these as preconditions of citizenship. "How can a being be generous who has nothing of its own? or virtuous who is not free?" asked Wollstonecraft. Murray offered model women who sustained themselves by their own efforts, including one who ran her own farm. . . .

By claiming civic virtue for themselves, women undermined the classical polarities. Their new formulation of citizenship reconstructed general relations, politicizing women's traditional roles and turning women into monitors of the political behavior of their lovers, husbands, and children. The formulation claimed for women the task of stopping the historical cycle of achievement followed by inevitable degeneration; women would keep the republic virtuous by maintaining the boundaries of the political community. . . . Thus Lockean childrearing was given a political twist; the bourgeois virtues of autonomy and self-reliance were given extra resonance by the Revolutionary experience.

Men, even young men, seem to have recognized, even encouraged, this new women's role. "Yes, ye fair, the reformation of a world is in your power," conceded a Columbia College commencement speaker. Considering women in the "dignified character of patriots and philanthropists" who aim at "the glory of their country and the happiness of the human race," he maintained that women displayed their patriotism and philanthropy in the context of courtship, marriage, and motherhood. In courtship, they can exclude "libertines and coxcombs" from their society, influencing suitors "to a sacred regard for truth, honour, candour, and a manly sincerity in their intercourse with her sex." In marriage, the wife could "confirm virtuous habits" in her husband, and "excite his perseverance in the paths of rectitude."

But it was when he reached the role of mother that his paean to the republican woman waxed most enthusiastic. It was, after all, in her role as mother that the republican woman entered historical time and republican political theory, implicitly promising to arrest the cycle of inevitable decay by guaranteeing the virtue of subsequent generations. . . . He concluded by welcoming women's new political responsibilities: "Contemplate the rising glory of confederated America. Consider that your exertions can best secure, increase, and perpetuate it. The solidity and stability of the liberties of your country rest with you, since Liberty is never sure, till Virtue reigns triumphant. . . . While you thus keep our country virtuous, you maintain its independence and ensure its prosperity."

As the comments of the Columbia commencement speaker suggest, the construction of the role of the woman of the republic marked a significant moment in the history of gender relations. What it *felt* like to be a man and what if *felt* like to be a woman had been placed under considerable stress by war and revolution; when the war was over, it was easy to see that it had set in motion a revised construction of gender roles. Wars that are not fought by professional armies almost always force a renegotiation of sex roles, if only because when one sex changes its patterns of behavior the other sex cannot help but respond. In this the American Revolution was not distinctive. The Revolution does seem to have been distinctive, however, in the permanence of the newly negotiated roles, which took on lives of their own, infusing themselves into Americans' understanding of appropriate behavior for men and for women deep into the nineteenth and even twentieth centuries.

Some of the change in men's roles was intentional: republicans had in mind an explicit revision of the relationship of individual men to the state. Furthermore, the independence that the state had claimed for itself against Great Britain was understood to be appropriately echoed in the self-assertiveness of individual men. . . . Some of the change in men's roles was unexpected. . . . Hierarchical relationships were disrupted. Thousands who had intimidated stamp tax collectors, or invaded the homes of loyalist elite like Gov. Thomas Hutchinson, or mutinied within the army for back pay would never be deferential again. College students rebelled against ancient restrictions, slaves ran away with the British, or, as in the case of Quock Walker, successfully claimed their natural rights under the new constitutions.

Revolutionary ideology had no place in it for the reconstruction of women's roles. But these roles could not help but change under the stress of necessity and in response to changes in men's behavior. Dependence and independence were connected in disconcerting ways. For example, the men of the army were dependent on the services of the women of the army. . . . And, paradoxically, although men were "defenders" and women "protected" in wartime, the man who left his wife or mother to "protect" her by joining the army might actually place her at greater physical risk. Even those most resistant to changed roles could not help but respond to the changed reality of a community in which troops were quartered or from which supplies were commandeered. Women's survival strategies were necessarily different from those of men. It ought not surprise us that women would also develop different understandings of their relationship to the state. In the years of the early republic, middle- and upper-class women gradually asserted a role for themselves in the republic that stressed their worthiness of the lives that had been risked for their safety, their service in maintaining morals and ethical values, and their claim to judge fathers, husbands, and sons by the extent to which these men lived up to the standards of republican virtue they professed. Seizing the idea of civic virtue, women made it their own, claiming for themselves the responsibility of committing the next generation to republicanism and civic virtue, and succeeding so well that by the antebellum years it would be thought to be distinctively female and its older association with men largely forgotten. Virtue would become for women what honor was for men: a private psychological stance laden with political overtones.

Those who did most to construct the ideology of republican womanhood—like Judith Sargent Murray and Benjamin Rush—had reflected Revolutionary experience authentically, but also selectively. They drew on Revolutionary ideology and experience, emphasizing victimization, pride, decency, and the maintenance of ritual and self-respect. But they denied the most frightening elements of that experience. There was no room in the new construction for the disorderly women who had emptied their pisspots on stamp tax agents, intimidated hoarders, or marched with Washington and Greene. There was no room for the women who had explicitly denied the decency and appropriateness of the war itself. There was no room for the women who had despaired and who had contributed to a war-weary desire for peace at any price in 1779–81. There was no room for the women who had fled with the loyalists; no room, in short, for women who did not fit the reconstructed expectations. Denial of disorder was probably connected to the institutionalization of the Revolution in the federal republic. The women of the army were denied as the Shaysites were denied; to honor and mythologize them would have been to honor and mythologize the most disconcerting and threatening aspects of rebellion. . . .

. . . When we write, at last, an authentic, holistic history of the Revolution, . . . [it] will be disconcerting; its author will have the ability to render multiple perspectives simultaneously.

. . . [T]he Revolution will be understood to be more deeply radical than we have heretofore perceived it because its shock reached into the deepest and most private human relations, jarring not only the hierarchical relationships between ruler and ruled, between elite and yeoman, between slave and free, but also between men and women, husbands and wives, mothers and children. But the Revolution will also be understood to be more deeply conservative than we have understood, purchasing political stability at the price of backing away from the implications of the sexual politics implied in its own manifestos, just as it backed away from the implications of its principles for changed race relations. The price of stabilizing the Revolution was an adamant refusal to pursue its implications for race relations and for the relations of gender, leaving to subsequent generations to accomplish what the Revolutionary generation had not.

Women Were Recognized in the Constitution

JAN LEWIS

It is commonly believed that women are nowhere mentioned in the American Constitution. Although the absence of women from the Constitution has seemed quite clear, scholars have not known what to make of this silence. Some argue that the authors of the Constitution intentionally framed it in a gender-neutral language so that women might be encompassed by its provisions, perhaps at some future date if not just then. It is no accident, such scholars suggest, that the Constitution repeatedly uses such words as "persons," "inhabitants," and "citizens" instead of "men." Other scholars believe that the omission of women, if not intentional, reflected the patriarchal assumptions of the Founders and their belief that women had no role to play in government. These debates go to the heart of a larger question, which is the relationship of women to the liberal state that the Constitution created. Is there a place for women within liberalism? Or have they always stood outside it, excluded from its inception?

. . . [T]he Framers have left us a hint, in an amendment that James Wilson suggested to the resolutions then being debated in the Philadelphia Convention in the summer of 1787. . . . Although these words require careful interpretation, once they are placed in the context of contemporary thinking about representation and about women, it becomes evident that the Constitution does include women, although the role it set out for them was different than the one designed for most men.

. . . The issue before the convention was who should vote for each branch of the proposed federal legislature. . . . It was in this context, a debate about whether representation should be based upon population or wealth, which would include slaves, that Pennsylvania's James Wilson suggested language that would make clear that representation in the lower house would be "in proportion to the whole number of white & other free Citizens & inhabitants of every age sex & condition including those bound to servitude for a term of years and three fifths of all other persons not comprehended in the foregoing description, except Indians not paying taxes, in each state." This wording was voted upon, approved, and incorporated into the resolutions that the group would continue to debate and refine throughout the summer. Wilson's wording, only slightly modified, but with the words of interest to us here—"of every age, sex, and condition"—was included in the resolutions referred to the Committee of Style. . . .

The Committee of Style . . . compressed Wilson's language into the words that actually appear in the Constitution. The relevant clause—now the third paragraph in Article I, Section 2—specified that both representatives and direct taxes were to be "apportioned among the several states . . . according to their respective numbers, which shall be determined by adding to the whole number of free persons, including those bound to servitude for a term of years, and excluding Indians not taxed, three-fifths of all other persons." This change in the wording seems to have been purely stylistic, rather than a change in meaning. The delegates voted many times

Reprinted by permission from the *Journal of the Early Republic,* 15 (Fall 1995), 359–387. Copyright ©
1995 Society for Historians of the Early American Republic.

over the course of the summer to change particular wordings. . . . Presumably, then, when the Committee of Style dropped the words "of every age, sex, and condition," neither they nor the delegates who accepted the revision thought that the meaning of the clause had been changed.

In fact, if we follow the debate on this clause, we can see that throughout the deliberations the delegates assumed that women, as well as children, were to be included whenever the question came up of who should be counted for purposes of apportionment. Wilson's original wording was part of the resolutions that the Convention was considering. . . . But . . . they rendered Wilson's words in a kind of shorthand. . . . [T]he language was modified . . . to "number of inhabitants; according to the provisions hereafter mentioned," hence leaving aside for the moment the question of how to count slaves.

. . . The term "inhabitants"—later changed to "free persons"—now included women and children. Thus we can see what the Committee of Style probably had in mind when it dropped Wilson's original wording about age and sex. Women, then, certainly were considered by the Constitutional Convention, and although Wilson's reference to "sex" was ultimately excised, it seems clear that the Framers intended that women be included among those who were to be represented by the new government. The Constitution included women.

Because no one objected to Wilson's insertion of the work "sex," and because women seem so readily to have been comprehended by the other delegates in the terms "inhabitants" and "person," we might be tempted to think that Wilson was simply inserting words that reflected the common practice of the day. Even though no one raised an objection to Wilson's terminology, it seems to have represented a genuine innovation, and because so few have noticed since, the genuine radicalism of the Constitution's doctrine of representation has been obscured. Although, as J. R. Pole and others have shown, in the revolutionary period democrats were beginning to insist that persons, not property were the proper basis for representation, not until the Federal Constitution had any government based representation upon inhabitants rather than taxpayers or adult men. . . . In fact, none of the new state constitutions enacted at the time of the Revolution numbered women and children as among those who were to be represented. Similarly, the Northwest Ordinance of 1787 specified that representation was to be based upon the number of "free male inhabitants, of full age."

To include female inhabitants when apportioning representatives, then, was a significant extension of democratic trends that were reshaping representation in the states. Wilson took this logic further than others had taken it until now and, in fact, further than those who would frame state constitutions in the near future would be willing to go. Kentucky's constitution of 1792 based representation on "an enumeration of free male inhabitants above twenty-one years of age," and Tennessee's, framed four years later, on "an enumeration of the taxable inhabitants." But because Wilson's additional language about sex was uncontested, it is not immediately clear what he and the other delegates intended by their innovation. . . .

Even before he suggested the wording about "age, sex, and condition," Wilson had developed before the delegates his own theory of representation. . . . Representation should be based upon population; "as all authority was derived from the people, equal numbers of people ought to have an equal no. of representatives, and different numbers of people different numbers of representatives." It was only two days later than he introduced his amendment to add the additional words, including the terms "of every age sex and condition," as well as the three-fifths clause. In this context, then, it seems evident that Wilson intended women to be included among the people, from whom "all authority was derived." In Wilson's mind, at least, women were included in the "We the People" who authorized the Constitution.

At this particular moment in the deliberations, Wilson was engaged in a debate about whether representation in the lower house should be based upon wealth or population. Hence, Massachusetts' Elbridge Gerry immediately objected to Wilson's amendment, addressing the three-fifths clause and asking, "Why then shd. the blacks, who were property in the South, be the rule of representation more than the Cattle & horses of the North." Gerry did no, however, contest Wilson's suggestion that women should be included among the people who were to be represented.

Nor did any of the other delegates who would argue about the proper basis for representation. Pierce Butler of South Carolina would continue to argue that "property was the only just measure of representation. This was the great object of Governt: the great cause of war, the great means of carrying it on." Although conservative nationalists such as New York's Gouverneur Morris agreed that "property was the main object of Society," he was troubled by the South Carolinians' desire to include slaves as part of the population. He thought that the Three Fifths Compromise was "an incoherence. If Negroes were to be viewed as inhabitants . . . they ought to be added in their entire number, and not in the proportion of 3/5." If instead, slaves were being counted as a measure of wealth, then the delegates should acknowledge that representation was being based upon population and property both.

Wilson recognized the contradiction that Morris pointed out. He could not "see on what principle the admission of blacks" for purposes of representation "could be explained. Are they admitted as Citizens? Then why are they not admitted on an equality with White Citizens? Are they admitted as property? then why is not other property admitted into the computation?" Earlier New Jersey's William Paterson had made the same point even more explicitly. . . . Although women could vote only in New Jersey, and children were not admitted to the polls anywhere, Paterson made no objection to including them in the basis for representation. In some clear, if unspecified way, women were members of political society in ways that slaves simply were not.

While Wilson recognized the inconsistency of counting slaves, he was willing to compromise on this issue for the sake of the federal union. He would never concede, however, that "property was the sole or the primary object of Governt. & Society." To the contrary, "the cultivation & improvement of the human mind was the most noble object. With respect to this object, as well as to other *personal* rights, numbers were surely the natural & precise measure of Representation." Now we can see what Wilson had in mind when he added the words "age sex & condition" to the resolutions the delegates were debating. If the purpose of government and society was not property, but the improvement of the human mind and the protection of other personal rights, then surely women must be included.

Although Wilson's intent seems clear enough, the delegates never commented upon Wilson's wording or the place of women in the government that they were creating. We may infer from their silence, however, a general acceptance of Wilson's reasoning, if not an understanding of its practical application. These delegates were alert to—and spent a long summer debating—the subtlest shifts of meaning; surely, then, someone would have noted and objected to Wilson's formulation had it seemed problematic for the purposes at hand. . . .

In none of these discussions was it argued that slaves, free blacks, women, or children should vote, although in some states free blacks and in one women were exercising the franchise. Instead democrats such as Wilson and Madison believed that all free inhabitants were part of the "imagined community" that they called the United States. They drew a distinction between being a member of the nation or community, which they called civil society, and voting. Every state in the new nation restricted the suffrage on the basis not only age, sex, race, and freedom, but also wealth as well. Not even all adult white men could vote. According to the tenets of republicanism, participation in the republic, and not simply voting, should have been restricted only to those who held enough property to secure a stake in the community and maintain their independence. Nascent liberals such as Wilson and Madison thought of the nation in much more expansive terms. Every free person who inhabited it was, in fact, a citizen, deserving of its protection and entitled to representation in the halls of government. In this context, women, who explicitly were to be represented but who just as explicitly were not permitted to represent themselves, became the touchstone of the modern, liberal state. By construing women as interested citizens incapable of representing themselves, liberalism provided a justification for the state: protecting those who could not protect themselves.

. . . James Wilson's suggestion that persons "of every age sex & condition" should be counted was never, of course, an accurate description of social practices in the new nation. But it was also more than a Constitutional mechanism for apportioning representatives in the national government. It was also a close enough rendering of the public sphere that had emerged in American society in the eighteenth century to make it the sketch from which a more inclusive social and political vision might be imagined. Departing as it did from traditional formulas for representation, James Wilson's words made a radical and hopeful statement about what the new nation might be.

That vision of a broadly inclusive society and a government that worked always on its behalf was not realized then, nor has it been since. From the outset, female citizenship had been defined in relationship not so much to white male citizenship, but to that of blacks, both slave and free. Originally, women were the paradigmatic citizens of liberalism; that is, they constituted society, enjoyed its rights, and demanded its protection. Increasingly however, women came to stand for those who were members of society but who did not enjoy full political rights and could not represent themselves. At the same time, free blacks would come to stand for those who enjoyed, nominally at least, complete political rights, but who were excluded from full membership in society. In this manner, the gap between politics and society, which had narrowed considerable in the Revolutionary period as liberal theories of government and society were brought to bear, was forced wider. As gender has been used to construct the political and social practices of race, and race to construct the practices of gender, the fleeting vision of a wide public sphere open to persons of every age, sex, race and condition has faded, leaving barely a trace.

FURTHER READING

Mary Sumner Benson, *Women in Eighteenth-Century America: A Study of Opinion and Social Usage* (1935)

Ruth H. Bloch, "The Gendered Meanings of Virtue in Revolutionary America," *Signs,* 13 (Autumn 1987), 37–58.

Joy Day Buel and Richard Buel, Jr., *The Way of Duty: A Woman and Her Family in Revolutionary America* (1984)

Nancy F. Cott, "Divorce and the Changing Status of Women in Eighteenth-Century Massachusetts," *William and Mary Quarterly,* 3d Ser., 33 (1976), 586–614.

———, *The Bonds of Womanhood: "Women's Sphere" in New England, 1780–1835* (1977)

Cornelia Hughes Dayton, *Women Before the Bar: Gender, Law and Society in Connecticut, 1639–1789* (1995)

Jay Fliegelman, *Prodigals and Pilgrims: The American Revolution Against Patriarchal Authority* (1982)

Joan R. Gundersen. "Independence, Citizenship, and the American Revolution," *Signs,* 13 (Autumn 1987), 59–77.

———, *To Be Useful in the World: Women in Revolutionary America* (1996)

Ronald Hoffman and Peter J. Albert, eds., *Women in the Age of the American Revolution* (1989)

Janet Wilson James, *Changing Ideas About Women in the United States, 1776–1825* (1981)

Joan M. Jensen, *Loosening the Bonds: Mid-Atlantic Farm Women, 1750–1850* (1986)

Susan Juster, *Disorderly Women: Sexual Politics and Evangelicalism in Revolutionary New England* (1994)

Linda K. Kerber, *No Constitutional Right to Be Ladies: Women and the Obligations of Citizenship* (1998)

———, *Women of the Republic: Intellect and Ideology in Revolutionary America* (1980)

Mary Beth Norton, *Liberty's Daughters: The Revolutionary Experience of American Women, 1750–1800* (1980)

Marylynn Salmon, *Women and the Law of Property in Early America* (1986)

Julia Cherry Spruill, *Women's Life and Work in the Southern Colonies* (1938)

C H A P T E R
10

Toleration Versus Religious
Freedom in a Protestant
Republic

During the past generation, as historians have paid increased attention to the
Revolution's social dimensions, the place of religion in public life—like the place
of women and blacks, the subjects of the previous two chapters—has attracted
renewed scrutiny. Moreover, because church-state relations are controversial in
present-day politics, the historical record on religion is especially relevant. Congress
and the Supreme Court make policy based on interpretation of the Constitution's
First Amendment, which deals with church-state relations explicitly. In short, this
branch of Revolutionary history has exceptional influence because of its direct,
practical consequences.

    In the Revolutionary era, as today, virtually everyone believed in religious
liberty. But then, as now, there were significant differences of opinion as to what
religious liberty meant exactly. While most voters believed that the vitality of religion was good for the country, they could not agree as to whether government
power should be used to assist religion directly. In certain states, among them
Massachusetts, a majority favored some form of public assistance to churches. In
other states, including Virginia, the belief prevailed that neither religion nor liberty
was safe when government—a secular, majority-controlled agency—took a hand
in religion. The government should enable churches to operate on their own—but
should do nothing more.

    Until the advent of the Constitution in 1787–1788, these debates over relig-
ious issues occurred primarily at the state level, because no one supposed that the
United States government, as weak and limited as it was, had any voice in the
matter. The relationship of church and state became a national question only when
Antifederalists voiced fears that the new national government, which they associated with an elite political establishment, might also create a religious establishment. The history of religious establishments in Britain and many of the colonies
convinced the Antifederalists that such a development was a real possibility. As a
result of Antifederalist arguments, Congress adopted the First Amendment, using

language that served immediate political needs but that also allowed for different interpretations later.

Americans worked out the relations between church and state in their new, experimental republic in a revolutionary way. Their solutions gave the United States a radical degree of religious freedom while providing a foundation for religion to flourish. American policies, as we shall see, were not entirely consistent, but they did convey the continuing power of the "contagion of liberty."

D O C U M E N T S

Documents 1, 2, 3, and 4—Toleration Can Be Joined to Religious Establishment (1776), the Massachusetts Declaration of Rights (1780), and the comments of Boston and Ashby (an inland country town)—reveal how complex the issue of religious freedom was and how divided Protestants were concerning the role of the government. In Massachusetts the ideal of religious freedom was compatible with compulsory support for churches. The enlightened clergyman and Yale college president Ezra Stiles, who delivered the annual sermon to the Connecticut legislature in 1783, which is reprinted as Document 4, articulated the prevailing New England view that the American republic must also become a reformed Christian republic. He saw the well-being of the United States and of Presbyterianism as one.

The difficulty posed by applying such an outlook on a national scale is illustrated by the next three documents, drawn from Pennsylvania and Virginia. When Philadelphia's Jews objected to their exclusion from officeholding under Pennsylvania's 1776 Constitution, they raised the question of whether it was legitimate for government to prefer Christians over others who believed in God. James Madison's remonstrance against religious taxes and Thomas Jefferson's Virginia Statute of Religious Liberty express the radical implications of Revolutionary ideas for separating church and state. The final document, the First Amendment to the Constitution, short enough to memorize easily, requires far more learning to interpret.

1. Toleration Can Be Joined to Religious Establishment, 1776

. . . In a well regulated state, it will be the business of the Legislature to prevent sectaries of different denominations from molesting and disturbing each other; to ordain that no part of the community shall be permitted to perplex and harrass the other for any supposed heresy, but that each individual shall be allowed to have and enjoy, profess and maintain his own system of religion, provided it does not issue in *overt acts* of treason against the state undermining the peace and good order of society.

To allow one part of a society to lord it over the faith and consciences of the other, in religious matters is the ready way to set the whole community together by the ears. It is laying a foundation for persecution in the abstract; for (as the judicious MONTESQUIEU observes) "it is a principle that every religion which is persecuted, becomes itself persecuting; for as soon as by some accidental turn it arises from persecution, it attacks the religion that persecuted it; not as a religion but as a tyranny."

"Worcestriensis Defends Religious Liberty and Congregational Preference, 1776." In *Massachusetts Spy* (September 4, 1776). As found in Charles S. Hyneman and Donald S. Lutz, eds., *American Political Writing During the Founding Era, 1760–1805* (Indianapolis: Liberty Fund, 1983), vol. 1, pp. 449–454.

It is necessary then that the laws require from the several religions, not only that they shall not embroil the State, but that they shall not raise disturbances among themselves. A citizen does not fulfill the laws by not disturbing the government; it is requisite that he should not trouble any citizen whomever. . . .

Perhaps some sticklers for establishments, requiring conformity to the prevailing religion, may now enquire whether, upon the principles above laid down, any legal establishment at all can take place? and if any, what? In answer to such querists, I would say that if by an establishment they intend the enacting and ordaining laws obliging dissenters from any certain religion to conform thereto, and, in case of nonconformity, subjecting them to pains, penalties and disabilities, in this sense there can and ought to be none. The establishment contended for in this disquisition, is of a different kind, and must result from a different legal Procedure.

It must proceed only from the benign frames of the legislature from an encouragement of the GENERAL PRINCIPLES of religion and morality, recommending free inquiry and examination of the doctrines said to be divine; using all possible and lawful means to enable its subjects to discover the truth, and to entertain good and rational sentiments, and taking mild and parental measures to bring about the design; these are the most probable means to bring about that establishment of religion which is recommended, and a settlement on an immoveable BASIS. It is lawful for the directors of a state to give preference to that profession of religion which they take to be true, and they have right to inflict penalties on those who notoriously violate the laws of natural religion, and thereby disturb the public peace. The openly profane come within their penal jurisdiction. There is no stronger cement of society than a sacred regard to OATHS; nothing binds stronger to the observation of the laws, therefore the public safety, and the *honor* of the SUPREME BEING require that public *profaneness*, should bring down the public vengeance upon those who dare hurl profanities at the throne of OMNIPOTENCE, and thereby *lessen* the reverence of the people for oaths, and solemn appeals to almighty God, and so shaking the foundation of good order and security in society. The same may be said of all Profaneness, and also of debauchery, which strike a fatal blow at the root of good regulation, and the well-being of the state.

And now with regard to the positive interposition of civil magistracy in behalf of religion, I would say, that what has been above suggested with respect to *toleration,* will not disprove the right of the legislature to exert themselves in favor of one religious profession rather than another, they have a right of private judgment as well as others, and are BOUND to do their *utmost* to propagate *that* which they esteem to be true. This they are to do by providing *able* and *learned* TEACHERS, to instruct the people in the knowledge of what they deem the truth, maintaining them by the public money, though at the same time they have no right in the least degree to endeavor the depression of professions of any religious denomination. Nor let it be said (in order to a perfect toleration) that all religious denominations have an equal right to public countenance, for this would be an evident infringement on the right of private judgment in the members of the legislature.

If the greatest part of the people, coincide with the public authority of the State in giving the prefference to any one religious system and creed, the dissenting few, though they cannot conscientiously conform to the prevailing religion, yet ought to acquiesce and rest satisfied that their religious Liberty is not *diminished.* . . .

I would add, that our Legislature of the last year have declared that "a Government so popular can be supported only by universal Knowledge and VIRTUE, in the body of the people."

In addition to this, I shall produce the opinion of the above cited *Montesquieu* (a great *authority!*) and so conclude this number.

"Religion may support a state, when the laws themselves are incapable of doing it.

"Thus when a kingdom is frequently agitated by civil wars, religion may do much by obliging one part of the state to remain always quiet.

"A prince who loves and fears religion, is a lion, who stoops to the hand that strokes or to the voice that appeases him. He who fears and hates religion, is like the savage beast, that growls and bites the chain which prevents his flying on the passenger. He who has no religion at all, is that terrible animal; who perceives his liberty only when he tears in pieces, and when he devours."

2. The Massachusetts Declaration of Rights, 1780

Art. I. All men are born free and equal, and have certain natural, essential, and unalienable rights; among which may be reckoned the right of enjoying and defending their lives and liberties; that of acquiring, possessing, and protecting property; in fine, that of seeking and obtaining their safety and happiness.

II. It is the right as well as the duty of all men in society, publicly, and at stated seasons, to worship the SUPREME BEING, the great creator and preserver of the universe. And no subject shall be hurt, molested, or restrained, in his person, liberty, or estate, for worshipping GOD in the manner and season most agreeable to the dictates of his own conscience; or for his religious profession or sentiments; provided he doth not disturb the public peace, or obstruct others in their religious worship.

III. As the happiness of a people, and the good order and preservation of civil government, essentially depend upon piety, religion and morality; and as these cannot be generally diffused through a community, but by the institution of the public worship of GOD, and of public instructions in piety, religion and morality: Therefore, to promote their happiness, and to secure the good order and preservation of their government, the people of this Commonwealth have a right to invest their legislature with power to authorize and require, and the legislature shall, from time to time, authorize and require, the several towns, parishes, precincts, and other bodies politic, or religious societies, to make suitable provision, at their own expense, for the institution of the public worship of GOD, and for the support and maintenance of public protestant teachers of piety, religion and morality, in all cases where such provision shall not be made voluntarily.

And the people of this Commonwealth have also a right to, and do, invest their legislature with authority to enjoin upon all the subjects an attendance upon the instructions of the public teachers aforesaid, at stated times and seasons, if there be any on whose instructions they can conscienciously and conveniently attend.

"The Massachusetts Declaration of Rights, 1780. As found in Robert J. Taylor, ed., *Massachusetts, Colony to Commonwealth* (Chapel Hill, NC: The University of North Carolina Press, 1961), 129–130.

Provided notwithstanding, that the several towns, parishes, precincts, and other bodies politic, or religious societies, shall, at all times, have the exclusive right of electing their public teachers, and of contracting with them for their support and maintenance.

And all monies paid by the subject to the support of public worship, and of the public teachers aforesaid, shall, if he require it, be uniformly applied to the support of the public teacher or teachers of his own religious sect or denomination, provided there be any on whose instructions he attends; otherwise it may be paid towards the support of the teacher or teachers of the parish or precinct in which the said monies are raised.

And every denomination of christians, demeaning themselves peaceably, and as good subjects of the Commonwealth, shall be equally under the protection of the law; And no subordination of any one sect or denomination to another shall ever be established by law.

3. Boston Supports Religion for the Sake of Order, 1780

The only Article now to be attended to is the third in the Decleration of Rights, which Asserts that Piety, Religion and morality are essential to the happiness, Peace and Good order of a People and that these Principles are diffused by the Publick Worship of God, and by Publick Instructions &c—and in Consequence makes provision for their support. The alterations proposed here which you will Lay before the Convention were designed to Secure the Reights of Consience and to give the fullest Scope to religious Liberty In support of the proposition it urged that if Publick Worship and Publick teaching, did certainly (as was allowed) defuse a general Sence of Duty & moral Obligations, and, so secured the safety of our Persons and Properties, we ought chearfully to pay those from whose agency we derived such Advantages. But we are Attempting to support (it is said) the Kingdom of Christ; It may as well be said we are supporting the Kingdom of God, by institution of a Civil Goverment, which Declared to be an Ordinance to the Deity, and so refuse to pay the civil magistrate. What will be the consequence of such refusal— The greatest disorders, if not a Dissolution of Society. Suspend all provision for the inculation of Morality, religion and Piety, and confusion & every evil work may be justly dreaded; for it is found that with all the Restraints of religion induced by the Preaching of Ministers, and with all the Restraints of Goverment inforced by civil Law, the World is far from being as quiet an abode as might be wished. Remove the former by ceasing to support Morality, religion and Piety and it will be soon felt that human Laws were feble barriers opposed to the uninformed lusts of Passions of Mankind. But though we are not supporting the kingdom of Christ may we not be permitted to Assist civil society by an addoption, and by the teaching of the best set of Morals that were ever offered to the World. To Object to these Morrals, or even to the Piety and Religion we aim to inculcate, because they are drawn from the Gospel, must appear very singular to an Assembly generally professing themselves

---

"Boston's View of Religious Freedom, 1780." As found in Robert J. Taylor, ed., *Massachusetts, Colony to Commonwealth* (Chapel Hill, NC: The University of North Carolina Press, 1961), 149–150.

Christians. Were this really our intention, no Objection ought to be made to it provided, as in fact the case that equal Liberty is granted to every religious Sect and Denomination Whatever, and it is only required that every Man should pay to the support of Publick Worship In his own way. But should any be so Conscientious that they cannot pay to the support of any of the various denominations among us they may then alott their Money to the support of the Poor.

4. Ashby, Massachusetts, Opposes Religious Establishment, 1780

... The third Article lays a restraint: for those who cannot Concientiously or Convenantly attend upon any publick teachers are under restraint as to their Estates & so injurd as to their Liberty and property—

Reason 3. Religeous Societys as such have no voice in Chusing the Legeslature, the Legeslature therefore have no right to make Law binding on them as such; every religeous Society, as such, is intirely independant on any body politick, the Legeslature therefore have no more right to make Laws Binding on them, as such, then the Court of Great Britton have to make Laws binding on the Independant states of America— ...

Reason 6. The Rivers of blood which has ran from the Veins of Marters! and all the torment which they have indured in the flames! was ocationed by the authority of Legeslature over religeous Society in consequence of the authority of the Legeslature or the authority arising from the authority of the Legeslature, the Feet of Paul & Silas where made fast in the stocks, the three Children Cast into the Furnace of fire, Daniel into the Lions Den, and many other such instances might be inumerated—

Reason 7. the third Article says the people of this common wealth have a right to invest their Legeslature with power to make Laws that are binding on religeous Society as (as we understand them) which is as much as to say we will not have Christ to reign over us that the Laws of this Kingdom are not sufficient to govern us, that the prosperity of his Kingdom is not eaqualy important with the Kingdoms of this world and that the Ark of God stands in need of Uzza's band to keep it from falling to the ground, butt lett us attend sereously to this important Truth that I will build my Church upon this Rock, and the Gates of Hell shall not prevail against it, now where resides this power in Christ only? or in the Legeslature?—it may be Objected against the Reasons here given that it leaves people two Louse and does not ingadge them to there duty & therby all religion will fall to the ground and this Objection indeed is very plausable because it may flow from an outward zeal for a form of Godliness without the power butt is it not founded upon this Supposition that men are not sufficiently ingadged to the practice of their Duty unless they doe somthing that God never required of them—

He that made us reasonable Creatures and Conferd upon us the Blessing of the Gospell has by this frame and situation laid us under the strongest Obligation

---

"Ashby, Massachusetts Opposes Religious Establishment, 1780." As found in Oscar and Mary F. Handlin, eds., *The Popular Sources of Political Authority: Documents on the Massachusetts Constitution of 1780* (Cambridge: Harvard University Press, 1966), 633–634.

to the practice of Piety, Religeon, and Morality that can posibly be conceived, & if this wont impress our minds to doe our Duty nothing will[.]

5. Rev. Ezra Stiles, America Will Sustain Christian Truth, 1783

He will then "make them high above all nations which he hath made, in praise, and in name, and in honor, and they shall become a holy people unto the Lord their God." . . .

I have assumed the text only as introductory to a discourse upon the political welfare of God's American Israel, and as allusively prophetic of the future prosperity and splendor of the United States. We may, then, consider—

I. What reason we have to expect that, by the blessing of God, these States may prosper and flourish into a great American Republic, and ascend into high and distinguished honor among the nations of the earth. "To make thee high above all nations which he hath made, in praise, and in name, and in honor."

II. That our system of dominion and civil polity would be imperfect without the true religion; or that from the diffusion of virtue among the people of any community would arise their greatest secular happiness: which will terminate in this conclusion, that holiness ought to be the end of all civil government. "That thou mayest be a holy people unto the Lord thy God."

The United States will embosom all the religious sects or denominations in Christendom. Here they may all enjoy their whole respective systems of worship and church government complete. Of these, next to the Presbyterians, the Church of England will hold a distinguished and principal figure. They will soon furnish themselves with a bishop in Virginia and Maryland, and perhaps another to the northward, to ordain their clergy, give confirmation, superintend and govern their churches,—the main body of which will be in Virginia and Maryland. . . . The *Unitas Fratrum* for above thirty years past have had Moravian bishops in America. . . . The Baptists, the Friends, the Lutherans, the Romanists, are all considerable bodies in all their dispersions through the states. The Dutch and Gallic and German Reformed or Calvinistic churches among us I consider as Presbyterian, differing from us in nothing of moment save in language. There is a considerable body of these in the states of New York, Jersey, Pennsylvania, and at Ebenezer, in Georgia. There is a Greek Church, brought from Smyrna; but I think it falls below these states. There are Westleians, Mennonists, and others, all which make a very inconsiderable amount in comparison with those who will give the religious complexion to America, which for the southern parts will be Episcopal, the northern, Presbyterian. All religious denominations will be independent of one another; . . . and having, on account of religion, no superiority as to secular powers and civil immunities, they will cohabit together in harmony, and, I hope, with a most generous catholicism

"Rev. Ezra Stiles on the Place of Religion in the United States." In Ezra Stiles, *The United States Elevated to Glory and Honor. A Sermon Preached Before His Excellency Jonathan Trumbull and the Honorable General Assembly of the State of Connecticut, Convened at Hartford, at the Anniversary Election, May 8th, 1783* (New Haven: Thomas & Samuel Green, 1783), 403–404, 467–472, 485–495, 505, 519.

and benevolence. The example of a friendly cohabitation of all sects in America, proving that men may be good members of civil society and yet differ in religion. . . .

Removed from the embarrassments of corrupt systems, and the dignities and blinding opulence connected with them, the unfettered mind can think with a noble enlargement, and, with an unbounded freedom, go wherever the light of truth directs. Here will be no bloody tribunals, no cardinal's inquisitors-general, to bend the human mind, forcibly to control the understanding, and put out the light of reason, the candle of the Lord, in man,—to force an innocent Galileo to renounce truths demonstrable as the light of day. Religion may here receive its last, most liberal, and impartial examination. Religious liberty is peculiarly friendly to fair and generous disquisition. Here Deism will have its full chance; nor need libertines more to complain of being overcome by any weapons but the gentle, the powerful ones of argument and truth. Revelation will be found to stand the test to the ten thousandth examination.

There are three coetaneous events to take place, whose futurition is certain from prophecy,—the annihilation of the pontificate, the reassembling of the Jews, and the fulness of the Gentiles. That liberal and candid disquisition of Christianity which will most assuredly take place in America, will prepare Europe for the first event, with which the other will be connected, when, especially on the return of the Twelve Tribes to the Holy Land, there will burst forth a degree of evidence hitherto unperceived, and of efficacy to convert a world. . . .

When we look forward and see this country increased to forty or fifty millions, while we see all the religious sects increased into respectable bodies, we shall doubtless find the united body of the Congregational, consociated, and Presbyterian churches making an equal figure with any two of them. . . . There is the greatest prospect that we shall become thirty out of forty millions. . . . In this country, out of sight of mitres and the purple, and removed from systems of corruption confirmed for ages and supported by the spiritual janizaries of an ecclesiastical hierarchy, aided and armed by the secular power, religion may be examined with the noble Berean freedom, the freedom of American-born minds. And revelation, both as to the true evangelical doctrines and church polity, may be settled here before they shall have undergone a thorough discussion, and been weighed with a calm and unprejudiced candor elsewhere. Great things are to be effected in the world before the millennium, which I do not expect to commence under seven or eight hundred years hence; and perhaps the liberal and candid disquisitions in America are to be rendered extensively subservient to some of the most glorious designs of Providence, and particularly in the propagation and diffusion of religion through the earth, in filling the whole earth with the knowledge of the glory of the Lord. A time will come when six hundred millions of the human race shall be ready to drop their idolatry and all false religion, when Christianity shall triumph over superstition, as well as Deism, and Gentilism, and Mohammedanism. They will then search all Christendom for the best model, the purest exemplification of the Christian church, with the fewest human mixtures. . . . And thus the American Republic, by illuminating the world with truth and liberty, would be exalted and made high among the nations, in praise, and in name, and in honor. I doubt not this is the honor reserved for us.

6. Philadelphia Jews Seek Equality Before the Law, 1783

To the honourable the Council of Censors, assembled agreeable to the Constitution of the State of Pennsylvania. The Memorial of . . . the Synagogue of the Jews at Philadelphia, . . . in behalf of themselves and their brethren Jews, residing in Pennsylvania,

Most respectfully showeth,

That by the tenth section of the Frame of Government of this Commonwealth, it is ordered that each member of the general assembly of representatives of the freemen of Pennsylvania, before he takes his seat, shall make and subscribe a declaration, which ends in these words, "I do acknowledge the Scriptures of the old and new Testament to be given by divine inspiration," to which is added an assurance, that "no further or other religious test shall ever hereafter be required of any civil officer or magistrate in this state."

Your memorialists beg leave to observe, that this clause seems to limit the civil rights of your citizens to one very special article of the creed; whereas by the second paragraph of the declaration of the rights of the inhabitants, it is asserted without any other limitation than the professing the existence of God, in plain words, "that no man who acknowledges the being of a God can be justly deprived or abridged of any civil rights as a citizen on account of his religious sentiments." But certainly this religious test deprives the Jews of the most eminent rights of freemen, solemnly ascertained to all men who are not professed Atheists.

May it please your Honors,

Although the Jews in Pennsylvania are but few in number, yet liberty of the people in one country, and the declaration of the government thereof, that these liberties are the rights of the people, may prove a powerful attractive to men, who live under restraints in another country. Holland and England have made valuable acquisitions of men, who for their religious sentiments, were distressed in their own countries.—And if Jews in Europe or elsewhere, should incline to transport themselves to America, and would, for reason of some certain advantage of the soil, climate, or the trade of Pennsylvania, rather become inhabitants thereof, than of any other State; yet the disability of Jews to take seat among the representatives of the people, as worded by the said religious test, might determine their free choice to go to New York, or to any other of the United States of America, where there is no such like restraint laid upon the nation and religion of the Jews, as in Pennsylvania.— Your memorialists cannot say that the Jews are particularly fond of being representatives of the people in assembly or civil officers and magistrates in the State; but with great submission they apprehend that a clause in the constitution, which disables them to be elected by their fellow citizens to represent them in assembly, is a stigma upon their nation and religion, and it is inconsonant with the second paragraph of the said bill of rights; otherwise Jews are as fond of liberty as their religious societies can be, and it must create in them a displeasure, when they perceive that

"Philadelphia Jews Seek Equality Before the Law, 1783." As found in Anson Phelps, ed., *Church and State in the United States* (New York: Harper and Row, 1963), 287–289.

for their professed dissent to doctrine, which is inconsistent with their religious sentiments, they should be excluded from the most important and honourable part of the rights of a free citizen.

Your memorialists beg further leave to represent, that in the religious books of the Jews, which are or may be in every man's hands, there are no such doctrines or principles established as are inconsistent with the safety and happiness of the people of Pennsylvania, and that the conduct and behaviour of the Jews in this and the neighbouring States, has always tallied with the great design of the Revolution; that the Jews of Charlestown, New York, New-Port and other posts, occupied by the British troops, have distinguishedly suffered for their attachment to the Revolution principles; and their brethren at St. Eustatius, for the same cause, experienced the most severe resentments of the British commanders. The Jews of Pennsylvania in proportion to the number of their members, can count with any religious society whatsoever, the Whigs among either of them; they have served some of them in the Continental army; some went out in the militia to fight the common enemy; all of them have cheerfully contributed to the support of the militia, and of the government of this State; they have no inconsiderable property in lands and tenements, but particularly in the way of trade, some more, some less, for which they pay taxes; they have, upon every plan formed for public utility, been forward to contribute as much as their circumstances would admit of; and as a nation or a religious society, they stand unimpeached of any matter whatsoever, against the safety and happiness of the people.

And your memorialists humbly pray, that if your honours, from any consideration than the subject of this address, should think proper to call a convention for revising the constitution, you would be pleased to recommend this to the notice of that convention.*

7. James Madison Protests Religious Taxes, 1785

To the Honorable the General Assembly of the Commonwealth of Virginia. A Memorial and Remonstrance.

We, the subscribers, citizens of the said Commonwealth, having taken into serious consideration, a Bill printed by order of the last Session of General Assembly, entitled "A Bill establishing a provision for Teachers of the Christian Religion," and conceiving that the same, if finally armed with the sanctions of a law, will be a dangerous abuse of power, are bound as faithful members of a free State, to remonstrate against it, and to declare the reasons by which we are determined. We remonstrate against the said Bill,

---

* When Pennsylvania revised its constitution in 1789–1790, the religious test was modified to accommodate Jews on an equal basis. Now the relevant passage stated: "That no person, who acknowledges the being of a God and a future state of rewards and punishments, shall, on account of his religious sentiments, be disqualified to hold any office or place of trust or profit under this commonwealth."

"James Madison Protests Religious Taxes, 1785." In James Madison, *The Writings of James Madison,* vol. 2, ed. Gaillard Hunt (New York, London: C. P. Putnam, 1901), 183–191.

1. Because we hold it for a fundamental and undeniable truth, "that Religion or the duty which we owe to our Creator and the Manner of discharging it, can be directed only by reason and conviction, not by force or violence." The Religion then of every man must be left to the conviction and conscience of every man; and it is the right of every man to exercise it as these may dictate. This right is in its nature an unalienable right. It is unalienable; because the opinions of men, depending only on the evidence contemplated by their own minds, cannot follow the dictates of other men: It is unalienable also; because what is here a right towards men, is a duty towards the Creator. It is the duty of every man to render to the Creator such homage, and such only, as he believes to be acceptable to him. This duty is precedent both in order of time and degree of obligation, to the claims of Civil Society. . . . True it is, that no other rule exists, by which any question which may divide a Society, can be ultimately determined, but the will of the majority; but it is also true, that the majority may trespass on the rights of the minority.

2. Because if religion be exempt from the authority of the Society at large, still less can it be subject to that of the Legislative Body. . . . The preservation of a free government requires not merely, that the . . . bounds which separate each department of power may be invariably maintained; but more especially, that neither of them be suffered to overleap the great Barrier which defends the rights of the people. The Rulers who are guilty of such an encroachment, exceed the commission from which they derive their authority, and are Tyrants. The People who submit to it are governed by laws made neither by themselves, nor by an authority derived from them, and are slaves.

3. Because, it is proper to take alarm at the first experiment on our liberties. We hold this prudent jealousy to be the first duty of citizens, and one of [the] noblest characteristics of the late Revolution. The freemen of America did not wait till usurped power had strengthened itself by exercise, and entangled the question in precedents. They saw all the consequences in the principle, and they avoided the consequences by denying the principle. We revere this lesson too much, soon to forget it. Who does not see that the same authority which can establish Christianity, in exclusion of all other Religions, may establish with the same ease any particular sect of Christians, in exclusion of all other Sects? That the same authority which can force a citizen to contribute three pence only of his property for the support of any one establishment, may force him to conform to any other establishment in all cases whatsoever?

4. Because, the bill violates that equality which ought to be the basis of every law, and which is more indispensible, in proportion as the validity or expediency of any law is more liable to be impeached. If "all men are by nature equally free and independent," all men are to be considered as entering into Society on equal conditions; as relinquishing no more, and therefore retaining no less, one than another, of their natural rights. Above all are they to be considered as retaining an "*equal* title to the free exercise of Religion according to the dictates of conscience." Whilst we assert for ourselves a freedom to embrace, to profess and to observe the Religion which we believe to be of divine origin, we cannot deny an equal freedom to those whose minds have not yet yielded to the evidence which has convinced us. If this freedom be abused, it is an offence against God, not against man: To God, therefore, not to men, must an account of it be rendered. As the Bill violates equality

by subjecting some to peculiar burdens; so it violates the same principle, by granting to others peculiar exemptions. Are the Quakers and Menonists the only sects who think a compulsive support of their religions unnecessary and unwarantable? Can their piety alone be intrusted with the care of public worship? Ought their Religions to be endowed above all others, with extraordinary privileges, by which proselytes may be enticed from all others? We think too favorably of the justice and good sense of these denominations, to believe that they either covet preeminencies over their fellow citizens, or that they will be seduced by them, from the common opposition to the measure.

5. Because the bill implies either that the Civil Magistrate is a competent Judge of Religious truth; or that he may employ Religion as an engine of Civil policy. The first is an arrogant pretension falsified by the contradictory opinions of Rulers in all ages, and throughout the world: The second an unhallowed perversion of the means of salvation.

6. Because the establishment proposed by the Bill is not requisite for the support of the Christian Religion. To say that it is, is a contradiction to the Christian Religion itself; for every page of it disavows a dependence on the powers of this world: it is a contradiction to fact; for it is known that this Religion both existed and flourished, not only without the support of human laws, but in spite of every opposition from them; and not only during the period of miraculous aid, but long after it had been left to its own evidence, and the ordinary care of Providence: Nay, it is a contradiction in terms; for a Religion not invented by human policy, must have pre-existed and been supported, before it was established by human policy. It is moreover to weaken in those who profess this Religion a pious confidence in its innate excellence, and the patronage of its Author; and to foster in those who still reject it, a suspicion that its friends are too conscious of its fallacies, to trust it to its own merits.

7. Because experience witnesseth that ecclesiastical establishments, instead of maintaining the purity and efficacy of Religion, have had a contrary operation. During almost fifteen centuries, has the legal establishment of Christianity been on trial. What has been its fruits? More or less in all places, pride and indolence in the Clergy; ignorance and servility in the laity; in both, superstition, bigotry and persecution. . . .

8. Because the establishment in question is not necessary for the support of Civil Government. If it be urged as necessary for the support of Civil Government only as it is a means of supporting Religion, and it be not necessary for the latter purpose, it cannot be necessary for the former. If Religion be not within [the] cognizance of Civil Government, how can its legal establishment be said to be necessary to civil Government? What influence in fact have ecclesiastical establishments had on Civil Society? In some instances they have been seen to erect a spiritual tyranny on the ruins of Civil authority; in many instances they have been seen upholding the thrones of political tyranny; in no instance have they been seen the guardians of the liberties of the people. Rulers who wished to subvert the public liberty, may have found an established clergy convenient auxiliaries. A just government, instituted to secure & perpetuate it, needs them not. Such a government will be best supported by protecting every citizen in the enjoyment of his Religion with the same equal hand which protects his person and his property; by neither invading the equal rights of any Sect, nor suffering any Sect to invade those of another.

9. Because the proposed establishment is a departure from that generous policy, which, offering an asylum to the persecuted and oppressed of every Nation and Religion, promised a lustre to our country, and an accession to the number of its citizens. What a melancholy mark is the Bill of sudden degeneracy? Instead of holding forth an asylum to the persecuted, it is itself a signal of persecution. It degrades from the equal rank of Citizens all those whose opinions in Religion do not bend to those of the Legislative authority. Distant as it may be, in its present form, from the Inquisition it differs from it only in degree. The one is the first step, the other the last in the career of intolerance. . . .

10. Because, it will have a like tendency to banish our Citizens. The allurements presented by other situations are every day thinning their number. To superadd a fresh motive to emigration, by revoking the liberty which they now enjoy, would be the same species of folly which has dishonoured and depopulated flourishing kingdoms.

11. Because, it will destroy that moderation and harmony which the forbearance of our laws to intermeddle with Religion, has produced amongst its several sects. Torrents of blood have been spilt in the old world, by vain attempts of the secular arm to extinguish Religious discord, by proscribing all difference in Religious opinions. Time has at length revealed the true remedy. Every relaxation of narrow and rigorous policy, wherever it has been tried, has been found to assuage the disease. The American Theatre has exhibited proofs, that equal and compleat liberty, if it does not wholly eradicate it, sufficiently destroys its malignant influence on the health and prosperity of the State. If with the salutary effects of this system under our own eyes, we begin to contract the bonds of Religious freedom, we know no name that will too severely reproach our folly. At least let warning be taken at the first fruits of the threatened innovation. The very appearance of the Bill has transformed that "Christian forbearance, love and charity," which of late mutually prevailed, into animosities and jealousies, which may not soon be appeased. What mischiefs may not be dreaded should this enemy to the public quiet be armed with the force of a law?

12. Because, the policy of the bill is adverse to the diffusion of the light of Christianity. The first wish of those who enjoy this precious gift, ought to be that it may be imparted to the whole race of mankind. Compare the number of those who have as yet received it with the number still remaining under the dominion of false Religions; and how small is the former! Does the policy of the Bill tend to lessen the disproportion? No; it at once discourages those who are strangers to the light of [revelation] from coming into the Region of it; and countenances, by example the nations who continue in darkness, in shutting out those who might convey it to them. Instead of levelling as far as possible, every obstacle to the victorious progress of truth, the Bill with an ignoble and unchristian timidity would circumscribe it, with a wall of defence, against the encroachments of error.

13. Because attempts to enforce by legal sanctions, acts obnoxious to so great a proportion of Citizens, tend to enervate the laws in general, and to slacken the bands of Society. If it be difficult to execute any law which is not generally deemed necessary or salutary, what must be the case where it is deemed invalid and dangerous? and what may be the effect of so striking an example of impotency in the Government, on its general authority.

14. Because a measure of such singular magnitude and delicacy ought not to be imposed, without the clearest evidence that it is called for by a majority of citizens: and no satisfactory method is yet proposed by which the voice of the majority in this case may be determined, or its influence secured. "The people of the respective counties are indeed requested to signify their opinion respecting the adoption of the Bill to the next Session of Assembly." But the representation must be made equal, before the voice either of the Representatives or of the Counties, will be that of the people. Our hope is that neither of the former will, after due consideration, espouse the dangerous principle of the Bill. Should the event disappoint us, it will still leave us in full confidence, that a fair appeal to the latter will reverse the sentence against our liberties.

15. Because, finally, "the equal right of every citizen to the free exercise of his Religion according to the dictates of conscience" is held by the same tenure with all our other rights. If we recur to its origin, it is equally the gift of nature; if we weigh its importance, it cannot be less dear to us; if we consult the Declaration of those rights which pertain to the good people of Virginia, as the "basis and foundation of Government," it is enumerated with equal solemnity, or rather studied emphasis. Either then, we must say, that the will of the Legislature is the only measure of their authority; and that in the plenitude of this authority, they may sweep away all our fundamental rights; or, that they are bound to leave this particular right untouched and sacred: Either we must say, that they may controul the freedom of the press, may abolish the trial by jury, may swallow up the Executive and Judiciary Powers of the State; nay that they may despoil us of our very right of suffrage, and erect themselves into an independant and hereditary assembly: or we must say, that they have no authority to enact into law the Bill under consideration. We the subscribers say, that the General Assembly of this Commonwealth have no such authority: And that no effort may be omitted on our part against so dangerous an usurpation, we oppose to it, this remonstrance; earnestly praying, as we are in duty bound, that the Supreme Lawgiver of the Universe, by illuminating those to whom it is addressed, may on the one hand, turn their councils from every act which would affront his holy prerogative, or violate the trust committed to them: and on the other, guide them into every measure which may be worthy of his [blessing, may re]dound to their own praise, and may establish more firmly the liberties, the prosperity, and the Happiness of the Commonwealth.

8. Thomas Jefferson's Virginia Statute of Religious Liberty, 1786

I. Whereas Almighty God hath created the mind free; that all attempts to influence it by temporal punishments or burthens, or by civil incapacitations, tend only to beget habits of hypocrisy and meanness, and are a departure from the plan of the Holy author of our religion, who being Lord both of body and mind, yet chose not to propagate it by coercions on either, as was in his Almighty power to do; that the impious

"Thomas Jefferson's Virginia Statute of Religious Liberty, 1786." In William Waller Hening, ed., *Statutes at Large of Virginia* (Richmond: AMS Press, 1809–1823), vol. 12, pp. 84–86.

presumption of legislators and rulers, civil as well as ecclesiastical, who being themselves but fallible and uninspired men, have assumed dominion over the faith of others, setting up their own opinions and modes of thinking as the only true and infallible, and as such endeavouring to impose them on others, hath established and maintained false religions over the greatest part of the world, and through all time; that to compel a man to furnish contributions of money for the propagation of opinions which he disbelieves, is sinful and tyrannical; that even the forcing him to support this or that teacher of his own religious persuasion, is depriving him of the comfortable liberty of giving his contributions to the particular pastor whose morals he would make his pattern, and whose powers he feels most persuasive to righteousness, and is withdrawing from the ministry those temporary rewards, which proceeding from an approbation of their personal conduct, are an additional incitement to earnest and unremitting labours for the instruction of mankind; that our civil rights have no dependence on our religious opinions, any more than our opinions in physics or geometry; that therefore the proscribing any citizen as unworthy the public confidence by laying upon him an incapacity of being called to offices of trust and emolument, unless he profess or renounce this or that religious opinion, is depriving him injuriously of those privileges and advantages to which in common with his fellow-citizens he has a natural right, that it tends only to corrupt the principles of that religion it is meant to encourage, by bribing with a monopoly of worldly honours and emoluments, those who will externally profess and conform to it; that though indeed these are criminal who do not withstand such temptation, yet neither are those innocent who lay the bait in their way; that to suffer the civil magistrate to intrude his powers into the field of opinion, and to restrain the profession or propagation of principles on supposition of their ill tendency, is a dangerous fallacy, which at once destroys all religious liberty, because he being of course judge of that tendency will make his opinions the rule of judgment, and approve or condemn the sentiments of others only as they shall square with or differ from his own; that it is time enough for the rightful purposes of civil government, for its officers to interfere when principles break out into overt acts against peace and good order; and finally, that truth is great and will prevail if left to herself, that she is the proper and sufficient antagonist to error, and has nothing to fear from the conflict, unless by human interposition disarmed of her natural weapons, free argument and debate, errors ceasing to be dangerous when it is permitted freely to contradict them.

II. *Be it enacted by the General Assembly,* that no man shall be compelled to frequent or support any religious worship, place or ministry whatsoever, nor shall be enforced, restrained, molested, or burthened in his body or goods, nor shall otherwise suffer on account of his religious opinions or belief; but that all men shall be free to profess, and by argument to maintain, their opinion in matters of religion, and that the same shall in no wise diminish, enlarge or affect their civil capacities.

III. And though we well know that this assembly, elected by the people for the ordinary purposes of legislation only, have no power to restrain the acts of succeeding assemblies, constituted with powers equal to our own, and that therefore to declare this act to be irrevocable would be of no effect in law; yet as we are free to declare, and do declare, that the rights hereby asserted are of the natural rights of mankind, and that if any act shall hereafter be passed to repeal the present, or to narrow its operation, such act will be an infringement of natural right.

9. The First Amendment to the United States Constitution, 1791

Congress shall make no law respecting an establishment of religion, or prohibiting the free exercise thereof; or abridging the freedom of speech, or of the press; or the right of the people peaceably to assemble, and to petition the government for a redress of grievances.

E S S A Y S

Taking cognizance of a generation or more of previous scholarship, Professor Jon Butler of Yale University argues that, although the Revolution was informed by religious beliefs and had major consequences for religious organizations, it was primarily a secular episode. In the first essay, drawn from *Awash in a Sea of Faith* (1990), his history of religion in America, Butler takes issue with scholars who have claimed a causal link between the Great Awakening and the Revolution. William G. McLoughlin, a professor at Brown University before his death in 1992, was the leading scholar of the Baptists and of religious dissent in early America. His analysis in the second essay places religion in a more central role in the Revolution, which, he argues, harnessed Protestantism to the national mission.

Was There a Revolutionary Millennium?

JON BUTLER

British colonists wrought momentous changes in America between 1760 and 1800. They confronted, then overthrew, the government they had known since colonization began. They established new governments and, some hoped, a new society as well. They were not wrong to trumpet their handiwork as "the new order of the ages." Nor were they wrong to worry about what they had accomplished. Benjamin Franklin warned his countrymen in 1776 that their republic would survive "if you can keep it." Part of the challenge, perhaps the most important part, lay in determining what kind of republic Americans intended. . . .

At its heart, the Revolution was a profoundly secular event. The causes that brought it into being and the ideologies that shaped it placed religious concerns more at its margins than at its center. Yet organized religion not only survived the revolutionary era but probably prospered from it, both because of the nature of the crisis and because of the deft way the denominations handled it. Despite their early hesitation and continuing anxiety about the process, the churches lent their weight to the American cause in a way that paid immense dividends in coming decades.

"The First Amendment to the United States Constitution." As found in Edward S. Corwin, ed., *The Constitution of the United States of America: Analysis and Interpretation* (Washington, DC: US Government Printing Office, 1953, 39–41).

Reprinted by permission of the publisher from *Awash in a Sea of Faith* by Jon Butler, Cambridge, MA: Harvard University Press. Copyright © 1990 by the President and Fellows of Harvard College.

Later, as new tensions arose in the new configuration of politics, society, and religion, the denominations moved to sacralize independence. . . .

Religion has not always interested historians of the American Revolution. Both David Ramsay and George Bancroft saw the Revolution as a thoroughly secular event, and their views represented the dominant opinion of their time. Antebellum revivalism and the approaching Civil War prompted some change in this perspective, though largely among historians of religion. . . .

More dramatic claims for religion's importance in the Revolution emerged a century later. Carl Bridenbaugh's *Mitre and Sceptre* (1962) drew attention to the "bishop question," in which Dissenters denounced alleged Anglican plots to install a colonial bishop while colonial assemblies were fighting off taxes and the escalation of imperial authority. Alan Heimert's seminal *Religion and the American Mind from the Great Awakening to the Revolution* (1966) substituted Calvinist evangelicalism for theological liberalism as the Revolution's principal theoretical foundation. Since then many historians—Gary Nash on the colonial cities, Rhys Isaac on eighteenth-century Virginia, Harry S. Stout on the New England sermon, Patricia Bonomi on denominational antiauthoritarianism—have stressed the importance of evangelical "style" in shaping the Revolution. In these accounts, evangelicalism underwrote economic discontent, fostered new modes of public address, and provoked confrontations with the standing order that eroded public confidence in the established government and played a substantial role in turning protest into rebellion. In the main, however, these accounts' view of the principal religious force that might have shaped the Revolution is unnecessarily narrow in their focus on evangelicalism. They bypass other religious issues and traditions that influenced revolutionary political discourse, exaggerate religion's general importance to the Revolution, and slight the difficulties that the Revolution posed for the American churches and that they ultimately overcame.

The Declaration of Independence provides clear-cut evidence of the secondary role that religion and Christianity played in creating the revolutionary struggle. The religious world invoked in the Declaration was a deist's world, at best; at worst, the Declaration was simply indifferent to religious concerns and issues. The god who appears in the Declaration is the god of nature rather than the God of Christian scriptural revelation, as when Jefferson wrote of "the laws of nature and nature's God." In other allusive appearances this god emerged as "the Supreme Judge of the world," to whom Americans would appeal "for the rectitude of our intentions," and as "Divine Providence," on whom they would rely for protection. Elsewhere, all was secular: taxes, troops, tyranny. Despite its length, not a single religious issue, including the dispute over the Anglican bishop, found a place in the "history of repeated injuries and usurpations" that closed the Declaration and that established the Revolution's most authoritative list of offensive British actions in America.

Yet the Declaration's remarkable silence on religious issues should not obscure the importance of religion in secondary issues. The bishop question, for example, carried significant long-term implications for revolutionary discontent because it undermined trust in British politicians and their motives. The dispute actually acknowledged the institutional progress that Anglicans had made in the eighteenth century. Dissenters feared a bishop, traditionally required for a full presence of the

Church of England anywhere, precisely because they knew how well Anglicans had fared without one. When Dissenters counted, they found Anglican congregations in astonishing numbers: there were some four hundred by 1776. They knew all too well that these congregations were important not only in the colonial cities, where their presence had been visually commanding for many years, but especially in the countryside, where most colonists lived. . . .

The Anglican-Dissenter contest over a bishop for America escalated transatlantic political tensions for years. The controversy first appeared in the 1710s, abated until it flared in the 1750s, then flared again in 1761 when Anglicans purchased an extraordinarily large home in Cambridge, Massachusetts, which Dissenters gleefully named the "bishop's palace." After 1763 the Dissenters' argument was joined to the colonial protests against taxes and other English efforts at imperial centralization, and it climaxed in protests against the Quebec Act of 1774, through which the English government recognized the Catholic church in the conquered French territories of Canada.

The Quebec Act called forth another image: secret Catholicism, associated with every attempt at tyranny in England since the 1640s—the reigns of Charles I and James 11 and the rise of the Pretender in Scotland in 1745. The charges resonated clearly in a society where anti-Catholicism had been a staple crop for two centuries, even among Anglicans. Paul Revere expressed those fears in a superbly crafted engraving in 1774. In it the Devil, Anglican bishops, and England's most notorious politicians, Lord North and Lord Bute, form a cabal to effect their ultimate and long secret objective—Catholicizing the American colonies.

Protestant Christianity also reinforced the Whig political convictions that lay behind early revolutionary rhetoric. Whig sentiment extended throughout the colonies, where it was descended from eighteenth-century English political culture generally rather than from more narrow sources in revivalism or New England Calvinism. Religious support for the Whigs was thus not limited to New England or to evangelical Dissenters. The basic Whig texts—Locke's *Second Treatise of Government,* Benjamin Hoadley's *Origin and Institution of Civil Government Discussed,* and John Trenchard and Thomas Gordon's *Cato's Letters*—were disseminated throughout the colonies, and reached more than evangelicals. . . .

Political Whiggism appeared in colonial sermons in two especially important ways. First, the sermons reinforced the emphasis on virtue and morality that pervaded secular political discussion in eighteenth-century colonial and English society. Indeed, it was the very breadth and perfunctoriness of clerical allusions to politics that made the sermons useful in the political debates of the era. Listeners and clergy together, in a vast number of denominations and congregations, *assumed* that liberty proceeded from a virtuous citizenry. It was the ministers' duty to make sure that this virtue was a Christian virtue, of course. . . .

The clerics' constant emphasis on virtue, responsibility, and, especially, morality helped make sense of revolutionary rhetoric about corruption and evil among English politicians and society. The French and Indian War of 1758–1763 offered some Americans all too intimate a view of that immorality. The behavior of British "regulars" sent from England to fight in America repelled John Cleaveland, who witnessed their antics when he served as chaplain to Massachusetts's Third Regiment. "Profain swearing seems to be the naturalized language of the regulars," he wrote. Their "gaming, Robbery, Thievery, Whoring, bad-company-keeping, etc.," epitomized the evils he and other ministers lamented Sunday after Sunday. . . .

Second, as protest escalated, some ministers discussed Revolution politics specifically. . . . Both ironically (in view of the Revolution's frequent appeals to liberty) and surprisingly (in view of historians' recent emphasis on evangelical Dissent), the most common denominator among pro-Revolution ministers was a state church pulpit. . . . Though virtually all Anglican ministers in the northern and middle colonies, where Anglicans often had to act the role of "dissenters," became loyalists, a third of the Anglican clergy in Virginia and Maryland, where Anglicans held tax-supported pulpits, backed the Revolution. Elsewhere, prorevolutionary sentiment among ministers also coincided with a legally established, tax-supported ministry. In most colonies the Revolution pitted a colonial political establishment against an expanding imperial administration, and the colonial clergy often owed more to the former than to the latter, even if the clergy involved were Anglican. The kind of politically active colonists who led protest against British policy after 1763 usually supported the locally established congregation in colonies with state church systems; the established, tax-supported minister supported the Revolution. Moreover, like the colonial political elites who used local government as a base from which to launch revolutionary-era protest and rebellion, ministers in the state churches used their fast and thanksgiving day sermons in the war against British policies. In this way establishmentarian coercion, rather than Dissenting anti-authoritarian voluntarism, underwrote much of the American ministerial promotion of liberty and attack on Toryism. Most colonial ministers, however, remained silent about politics during the upheavals of the 1760s and 1770s. . . .

Most Presbyterian ministers simply did not participate in revolutionary politics. . . . The demand for obedience was as strong among colonial Presbyterians as it was among Anglicans, and the Presbyterian commitment had been tested only shortly before the Revolution. During the so-called Regulator Movement in North and South Carolina in the late 1760s, backcountry Presbyterian ministers, supported by German Lutheran and Anglican pastors, had not hesitated to use their pulpits to denounce rebellion against colonial governments dominated by tidewater planter elites and to cite the traditional Pauline texts in doing so. . . .

In their 1775 [pastoral] letter the members of the Philadelphia synod ultimately both instructed the Presbyterian laity on loyalty to George III and voiced support for Whig political principles. They expressed their "attachment and respect to our sovereign King George"; they also expressed their regard for "the revolution principles by which his august family was seated on the British throne." Still, as violence swirled around them, obedience preceded rebellion. The ministers explicitly upheld their allegiance to "the person of the prince," not merely to monarchy in the abstract. They believed that he may have been misled, but they also rejected "such insults as have been offered to the sovereign" by American protesters.

The Presbyterian statement suggested why loyalism so frequently had a dual religious foundation and extended beyond the ranks of Church of England ministers, two-thirds of whom departed for England after the Revolution began. One reason concerned the traditional emphasis on authority and obedience in colonial preaching. Loyalist clergymen could be found in every colonial denomination. . . .

A second reason centered on religious discrimination. The political elites who guided the Revolution in so many places also had frequently mistreated religious minorities in earlier times. . . . Some groups, like the Virginia Baptists, supported the Revolution anyway. But backcountry Presbyterians, German Lutheran and German Reformed settlers, and middle and northern colony Anglicans often found themselves drawn to loyalism not only out of political and religious principle but because of antagonisms with settlers who had earlier used the government and the law against them. . . .

The Revolution also shaped American religion, of course, and it did so in complex ways. This complexity emerges even in the story of Christian denominational decline and growth. The most serious erosion occurred in the Anglican congregations, which were often most numerous where other denominations were weakest and whose members had initiated the resurgence of public Christian worship at the beginning of the century. In parish after parish, Anglican ministers left because they openly supported the Crown, because they could not endure abuse by local patriots, or because they were no longer being paid by either the SPG [English Society for the Propagation of the Gospel] or their vestries. Fifty Anglican priests were working in Pennsylvania, New York, and New England before the Revolution; only nine remained afterward. About 100 of the 150 priests in the southern colonies also fled to England. As a result 75 percent of the Church of England parishes, built up so carefully in the previous half century, lost their clergymen and, with them, their principal leadership in sustaining public Christian worship. . . .

. . . The physical destruction loosed on Anglican churches was reminiscent of sixteenth-century English anti-Catholic depredation. In parish after parish supporters of the Revolution stripped Anglican churches of their royal coats of arms, although usually they left the buildings and other fittings intact. . . .

Other dangers came from within patriot society. Clergymen who had struggled for a half century to advance Christian adherence could see much of their work lost in the turmoil of war. The Philadelphia synod continuously appointed fasts to relieve the "low and declining state of religion among us." Its letters spoke of "gross immoralities," "increasing decay of vital piety," "degeneracy of manners," even "want of public spirit." This feeling was not confined to English-speaking Americans or to the old middle colonies. German Reformed ministers, largely from western Pennsylvania, complained that the Revolution increased citizens' "vanity" and decreased their humility; they "indulge[d], without shame and decency, in the most abominable vices." Baptists in Virginia and South Carolina decried advancing sin and immorality amid the Revolution, and Isaac Backus worried deeply about morality in New England, something he too attributed to decline rather than to more persistent indifference to things moral and religious.

The religious tensions generated by the Revolution appeared with special force in the revolutionary army, where chaplains and soldiers were forced to reconstruct their lives and their religion outside of their normal settings. Chaplains were a traditional part of British military and political culture in both England and America. Colonial militias and British troops appointed chaplains during the French and Indian War, and some of these men served again during the Revolution. From a military perspective, chaplains were present primarily to promote discipline and only secondarily to preserve faith. During the French and Indian War, George Washington described a good chaplain as a "gentlemen of sober, serious and religious deportment, who would improve morale and discourage gambling, swearing, and drunkenness." Washington and other revolutionary commanders expected chaplains to serve the same ends, and the Continental Congress quickly approved chaplains for the army when it designated Washington commander-in-chief. . . .

Between the signing of the Declaration of Independence in 1776 and George Washington's death in 1799, American church and denominational leaders renewed efforts to stamp Christian values and goals on a now independent society. Three of these attempts proved especially important: powerful Christian explanations of the Revolution and of the proper political order that ought to govern American society; attacks on irreligion, especially on skepticism and deism; and the creation of new religious groups, which evinced principles that for the first time might be called distinctively American.

The association of society and government with Christianity was traditional in colonial political culture. But the Revolution strengthened the demand to associate society with Christianity in several ways—by revealing the previously shallow foundations of the association, by stressing a particular form of "republicanism" in government and society, and by stimulating a strong sense of cultural optimism that fitted certain religious themes, particularly American millennialism.

Dark concerns about America's religious future extended far beyond the chaplains working in the army camps. The destruction of church buildings, the interruption of denominational organization, the occasional decline in congregations and membership, the shattering of the Anglican church, and the rise of secular pride in revolutionary accomplishments all weighed on American religious leaders. Even as the Revolution advanced, denominational leaders often bemoaned rather than celebrated America's moral fiber. . . .

Republican political ideology heightened concern for moral and religious foundations. Republican principles had enormous importance for American religion because, though they were often vague and elusive, they placed great authority in the very laypeople with whom the clergy had long struggled. . . .

Contemporaries agreed that a successful republican society and government, by definition, depended on "a virtuous people." This sentiment did not take root in a reborn Puritanism but in more modern eighteenth-century principles. . . . The whole of society, not merely some of its parts, constituted the bedrock of the future. The contrast was particularly noticeable in Massachusetts. John Winthrop's Puritan society had been ordered by means of hierarchical responsibilities assigned among the people, "some highe and eminent in power and dignitie; others meane and in subjection." The 1780 Massachusetts constitution, however, rested order on a broader foundation: "The happiness of a people, and the good order and preservation of civil government, essentially depend upon piety, religion, and morality." It did not mention the "highe and eminent" or "others meane and in subjection."

Optimism fueled the new republic. . . . Progressive conceptions of time rooted in a secular, rather than a supernatural, view of life underwrote much of the new American optimism. . . . [Sermons], like those given with almost universal occurrence on July 4, simultaneously celebrated victory and independence. Fast and thanksgiving day sermons continued and even increased. Everywhere a torrent of ministers' words proclaimed American independence and Christianity together. . . .

Millennialist rhetoric predicting Christ's return to earth also expanded. . . . Yet the very ubiquity of such predictions produced a bewildering variety of styles. No single millennialist vision emerged in the early national period. As Ruth Bloch has noted, proponents variously predicted the coming of true liberty and freedom, a rise in piety, American territorial expansion, and even freedom from hunger. Many propagandists hedged their predictions, just as their predecessors had done in the 1740s and 1750s. The few who provided definite dates for specific events usually developed different and sometimes exotic chronologies. As Americans experienced political, social, and economic setbacks after independence had been won, others turned to darker visions of the world and the new nation's place in it. New Hampshire's Samuel MacClintock warned against "luxury, and those other vices." New Jersey's Jacob Green foresaw "contentions, oppressions, and various calamities." New York's "Prophet Nathan" wrote that crop failure resulted from Americans' greed and disunity.

Despite, or perhaps because of, its inconsistencies, millennialist rhetoric performed important functions in revolutionary society. Above all, Christian millennialism played a significant role in rationalizing popular secular optimism, which it transformed more often than it confronted. Rather than make extensive critiques of secular optimism, millennialist propagandists offered a vision of optimistic progress that was made more understandable by Christian teleology. This progress took root not in man, whose imperfections were all too visible even amid the Revolution, but in God, whose perfection was highlighted by invisibility.

At the same time, apocalyptic thinking generally declined in the revolutionary period. . . . The Revolution was an event whose character and outcome seemed to have signaled the beginning of Christ's thousand-year reign, thus making the apocalypse either history or irrelevant.

Millennialism also had important political implications. Millennialist rhetoric secured an unwilling and often perplexed society to the Christian plow with the harness of Christian time. It demanded lay adherence in a society where the people were now sovereign. When New Englanders sought a unicameral legislature and an elected executive on the ground that "the voice of the people is the voice of God" (the view of the *New England Chronicle*), the rhetoric largely benefited the advancement of Christianity: a legislature that spoke for God should also listen to those who articulated Christian theology, morals, and ethics.

The millennialist incorporation of secular optimism in the revolutionary period was paralleled by equally adamant campaigns against irreligion in its intellectual disguises of skepticism, atheism, and deism. . . . But skepticism survived nonetheless, as American clergymen knew all too well. Its most prominent representatives—Franklin, Jefferson, Madison, and Washington, among others—seemed the apotheosis of the Enlightenment. Their support for Enlightenment discourse revealed a tolerance of skepticism, perhaps even irreligion, altogether dangerous in a new republic.

Deism became a chief object of attack in the war against irreligion. The choice proved particularly clever, not least because it clothed a familiar specter in new dress. . . . Most important, deism offered extraordinary opportunities to its critics to demonstrate the need for real religion, meaning orthodox Christianity, in the new republic. This was possible because, to its critics, deism was the epitome of hypocrisy. It masqueraded as religion but was thoroughly irreligious. Deists admitted the justice of religious claims, but they made religion irrelevant to contemporary life. The deists' god was dead. At best, signs of his existence were found only in the distant past, not in the present.

As Americans turned from war making to nation making, clergymen turned to deism to explain their postrevolutionary failures and crises. Deism served as a new and dangerous label under which a broad list of evils, old and new, could be assembled. Thomas Paine's *Age of Reason,* published in 1794, was denounced far more than it was read. In 1798 Jedidiah Morse described why the deism Paine promoted should be so feared: "The existence of a God is boldly denied. Atheism and materialism are systematically professed. Reason and Nature are deified and adored. The Christian religion, and its divine and blessed author, are not only disbelieved, rejected and contemned, but even abhorred." . . .

Thomas Jefferson's try for the presidency in 1800 brought out a second antideist campaign. It was particularly important because it focused on the potentially intimate relationship between a president's personal religious views and the fate of the American republic. Jefferson's actual religious views were complex. He was, indeed, a deist, and he also expressed a quiet regard for Christ and Christian ethics. But he rejected Christ's divinity and criticized religious coercion with a vigor that made some suspicious of his real religious views, despite the fact that evangelicals had long supported him for his efforts on behalf of religious freedom. Federalists linked Jefferson to anticlericalism and atheism in the by then notorious French Revolution; in their vocabulary, "Jacobin" meant atheist as well as democrat. Many ministers denounced Jefferson from their pulpits and decried the fate of the nation in the hands of a red-haired deist, an obvious agent of the Devil.

The campaign to advance Christianity after American independence was not wholly negative. Amid the anger directed against deism, skepticism, and rationalism, other Americans again sought religious renewal, reform, and revival. The most immediately impressive form of that quest emerged from rationalist liberal circles. Developed largely from what Henry May calls the "moderate Enlightenment" and centered in what would come to be called the Universalist and Unitarian movements, rationalist liberalism found itself an early beneficiary of the kind of revolution that had already reshaped American political life. Its principal doctrines— a largely positive view of man, universal salvation, rejection of the Trinity, fascination with science, and a trend toward systematization—closely fitted the political optimism of the times. Among a people simultaneously sweeping away the encrustations of the past and forging new constitutions to bring new states and a nation into being, an emphasis on simple, universal religious principles held considerable appeal. Religious reformers sought to locate Christianity's essentials in a few themes and doctrines, to dispense with the excess baggage of historical theology, and to embrace the new science, all in order to advance mankind and Christianity in a new society and a new age. . . .

Emotion-laden revivals also emerged in postrevolutionary America. . . . The late eighteenth-century revivals exhibited three important characteristics linked to the Revolution. One was a marked tendency toward a reductionism and antitheologicalism, if not anti-intellectualism, which paralleled Unitarian rationalism but not Unitarian spiritual aloofness. . . . Second, revolutionary and postrevolutionary American revivalism had a tendency to involve dreams, visions, apparitions, and physical manifestations of divine intervention seen in some earlier eighteenth-century revivalism. The best-known example was that of the Shakers. Jesus had first appeared to Ann Lee, their apparent founder (and second manifestation of Christ on earth), and her associates in England, and in 1772 visions prompted them to emigrate to New England as the site of Christ's second kingdom. They arrived in New York in 1774. The Revolution only enhanced their millennialist visions, and the rightness of their celibacy came "to be transparent in their ideas in the bright and heavenly visions of God." For Shakers as well as for American revolutionaries, heaven began on earth.

The Shaker emphasis on dreams and visions was commonplace, not unique. [The Freewill Baptist] Benjamin Randel confirmed religious truth through out-of-body experiences and dreams: "I never could tell whether I was in the body or not . . . I saw a white robe brought down and put over me, which covered me, and I appeared as white as snow." Freeborn Garrettson and James Horton, Methodist itinerants, unashamedly shared accounts of their own divine dreams with their listeners, who in turn described equally compelling occurrences. . . .

In all, Christianity recovered from the American Revolution with remarkable alacrity. The churches, though buffeted by a revolution whose battlefield and army camp experiences exposed the tenuousness of popular Christian adherence and reinforced the vigorous secularity of its political principles, emerged with renewed vigor in the 1780s. They sought to sacralize the Revolution and American society through a Christian rhetoric that pulled secular optimism within a Christian orbit. They experienced surprising growth in the 1780s and even greater growth in the 1790s. They found increasingly indigenous resonances in new religious movements, ranging from Unitarian rationalism to Baptist, Methodist, and Shaker ecstasy. In less than two decades, they demonstrated that religious groups that had not initiated the Revolution could nevertheless survive it. In the next half century, they would begin to master the new American environment by initiating a religious creativity that renewed spiritual reflection and perfected institutional power, all to serve Christian ends.

The Role of Religion in the Revolution

WILLIAM G. McLOUGHLIN

The role of religion in the American Revolution cannot be understood apart from its role *before* and *after* the Revolution. If we define religion as the philosophical outlook, the set of fundamental assumptions, ideals, beliefs, and values about man's relationship to his neighbors, his environment, and his future, that provides the cultural cohesion for a community, then the Revolution was both a culmination and a beginning of the process that produced American cultural cohesion. In this sense the Revolution was a religious as well as a political movement.

"The Role of Religion in the Revolution: Liberty of Conscience and Cultural Cohesion in the New Nation" by William G. McLoughlin from *Essays on the American Revolution,* edited by Stephen G. Kurtz and James H. Hutson. Published for the Institute of Early American History and Culture, Williamsburg, Virginia. © 1973 The University of North Carolina Press. Reprinted by permission.

The salient religious development of the Revolution has variously been referred to as disestablishment, the rise of religious liberty, the adoption of voluntaryism, or the separation of church and state (not all the same thing, but all closely related). From a moderately long-range view, this was an irreversible development in America from the time of the Great Awakening and reached one of its logical conclusions a century later with the final abolition of the system of compulsory religious taxes in Massachusetts. An even longer-range view would push the development back to Roger Williams, the Scrooby Separatists, or the Anabaptists of the Reformation and forward to today's problems over federal aid to parochial schools. In the more common and short-range view disestablishment began with George Mason's article on religious liberty in the Virginia Declaration of Rights in 1776 and was "substantially" complete, as J. Franklin Jameson said, by 1800, with the passage of the First Amendment and the abolition of religious tests for officeholding in most state constitutions.

I have chosen in this essay to take the moderately long-range view, concentrating upon the efforts to work out the principles and practical definitions of voluntaryism in the original states from 1776 to the middle of the nineteenth century. But this obliges me to begin with at least a cursory glance at the development of religious and political liberty in the period from 1740 to 1776.

As I see it, the Great Awakening, sometimes seen as a religious reaction to Arminianism and sometimes as the upthrust of the Enlightenment in the colonies, was really the beginning of America's identity as a nation—the starting point of the Revolution. The forces set in motion during the Awakening broke the undisputed power of religious establishments from Georgia to the District of Maine, but more than that, the Awakening constituted a watershed in the self-image and conceptualization of what it meant to be an American. The old assumptions about social order and authority that underlay colonial political economy and produced cultural cohesion dissolved. The corporate and hierarchical ideal of society began to yield to an individualistic and egalitarian one. While the medieval concept of a Christian commonwealth lingered, its social foundations crumbled.

A description of the complex forces that led to the breakdown of the old order and hastened the modernization of American institutions (of which the Revolution was the modus operandi) cannot be attempted here. Nor have I space to trace the subtle theological shifts that sustained this social reformation. But, in essence, between 1735 and 1790 the American colonists redefined their social principles into a cohesive structure sufficiently radical to necessitate a political break with the Old World and sufficiently conservative to sustain a new nation.

The historian of religion would stress three interrelated intellectual strands that gave the pattern to the new national consciousness: the new emphasis in evangelical Calvinism (the prevalent religious commitment of the people), stressing the individual's direct, personal, experiential relationship to God; the general acceptance of the deistic theory of inalienable natural rights and contractual self-government; and the resurgence of the radical whig ideology with its fear of hierarchical tyranny (the united despotism of church and state) epitomized in John Adams's *Dissertation on the Canon and Feudal Law*.

Before the Awakening most individuals gladly yielded their judgment and conscience to the superior claims and knowledge of their "betters," the ruling elite in church and state, who derived their authority from God and as his vicegerents administered the ordinances of government for the good of the people. After the Awakening this order of things became reversed: the state and church were considered by increasing numbers of Americans to be the creatures of the people and subject to their authority. Prior to the Awakening the king, his bishops, judges, and governors interpreted the will of God, and deference was their due. Afterwards the people considered themselves better able than any elite to interpret God's will and expected their elected officials to act as *their* vicegerents under God. The channel of authority no longer flowed from God to the rulers to the people but from God to the people to their elected representatives. State and church were henceforth to serve the needs of the people as defined by the people—or rather, by the people's interpretation of God's will. Intermediaries were dispensed with; every individual was assumed to be in direct relationship to God and responsible only to him, and therefore their collective will was God's will. Or so, in its extreme and logical form, this theory evolved by the time of Thomas Paine's *Common Sense* and came into practice by the age of Jackson. . . .

The religious and political establishments did not fall under these first radical onslaughts of pietistic individualism. But their authority eroded steadily before the rising tide of alienation. The Congregational establishments in New England, always under a measure of popular control, responded to the challenge by altering their posture—yielding power to the New Lights within the structure and granting greater religious liberty to those without. But the Anglican establishments turned more strongly than ever to authoritarian control, and that meant reliance upon the power of kings and bishops across the sea and insistence upon the need for bishops in America. Once the Revolution started, Anglican authority and power immediately ceased.

The Revolution—an essentially irrational impulse despite the eloquent rationalizations provided for it—combined this popular spirit of pietistic self-righteousness with a new commitment to inalienable natural rights (fostered by the Enlightenment). Both fed upon the heady fruits of a long-brewing commonwealth radicalism to produce an ecstatic enthusiasm for national self-assertion. Ostensible rationalists fervently upheld the innate, God-given rights of Englishmen and mankind against a despotic George III; evangelical pietists zealously insisted that Christ died, not for the divine right of kings or hierarchies, but for the Christian liberty of his saints. Both relied ultimately upon their own heartfelt judgments, for which God, but no one else, could hold them responsible. And when, in the final "appeal to heaven" after 1775, God judged for the patriots and pietists, it seemed proof positive that whatever divine right once existed within the British Empire had been corrupted beyond redemption. The power of crown and mitre had passed to the people, and the future site of the millennium had once again moved westward toward its final, and probably imminent, fulfillment. The Peace of Paris brought from the pietists cries of "Come quickly, Lord Jesus" and from the rationalists the belief that the United States of America were "God's last best hope" for mankind. . . .

Once the Rubicon was crossed and the break with Britain made, a new set of circumstances brought political and religious forces into conjunction. Rhetoric had to be put into practice in the construction of bills of rights and state constitutions. Undertaken in the midst of the struggle for independence, these formulations of the social contract required mutual give-and-take if harmony were to be maintained and the needs of all religious persuasions fairly met. The opportunity—the need—to do away with the old established churches necessitated cooperation in the creation of new religious structures in each state.

Having put the ideals of religious liberty into bills of rights, constitutions, and statutes, Americans had then to work them out in practice. Here the pragmatic temper of a frontier people, combined with the multiplicity of sects and a decentralized system of government, enabled a host of different ways of working out the frictions of religious pluralism. . . .

Ultimately the Revolution brought the dissenting sects out of their apolitical pietistic shells and within the pale of political power. Ceasing to be outgroups, they entered the mainstream of the nation as participating partners. The favored status of one Protestant denomination gave way to the equal status of all Protestants. In addition, as colonial boundaries broke down and the nation united, denominations formed interstate or national bodies and sometimes joined formally with other denominations in evangelistic or benevolent activities. Parochialism gave way to wider national horizons. Becoming respected and respectable, dissenters found men of rank and position willing now to join their churches. In the southern states Baptists, Methodists, and Presbyterians rapidly became the dominant denominations not only in numbers but in power and wealth.

These are only the most obvious and general ways in which the Revolution, by breaking the cake of custom and opening new opportunities, interacted with the ideals, the hopes, and the allegiances of all religious groups, uniting individual, sectarian, and local interests to those of the nation at large. . . . Under the urgent need to create one out of many, even Roman Catholics and Jews, the most extreme outsiders, found themselves included in the new nation. Many even talked as though Buddhists and Mohammedans would have been equally welcome.

Yet the harmony was deceptive. Beneath the abstract rhetoric and universal ideals of the Revolution—sufficiently powerful to break the vital bonds to the mother country—there yet remained assumptions, beliefs, and values that were far from universal or absolute. Americans did not cease at once to think like Englishmen, and their cultural heritage and homogeneity produced a very relativistic and ethnocentric definition of religious liberty. The Protestant establishment of the nineteenth century, so obvious to Tocqueville and Lord Bryce, may seem a betrayal of the Revolution if one thinks of Thomas Jefferson as its spokesman or if one reads the religious clauses of the bills of rights and the First Amendment with the deistic gloss that the Supreme Court has applied to them in the twentieth century. But, as I hope to indicate below, Americans were clearly committed to the establishment of a Protestant Christian nation. Religious liberty was to be granted to all, but the spiritual cement that was to hold the nation together had to be Protestant. . . .

The ambiguity of the Revolutionary generation toward religious duties (which were to be enforced) and religious liberty (which was to be untrammeled) has so often been noted that it hardly bears summary: laws requiring respect for the Sabbath and even church attendance were passed but seldom enforced; clergymen were admitted to state office despite prohibitions against it; Jefferson, Madison, and John Leland opposed the payment of federal and state chaplains although many Baptists and other evangelicals proudly accepted such posts; the Northwest Ordinance and

Southwest Ordinance utilized federal funds for religious purposes despite the First Amendment; "In God We Trust" was placed on the coins but not in the Constitution; tax exemption was granted to all church property and often to ministers; national days of fasting, thanksgiving, and prayer were regularly proclaimed by some presidents and governors but objected to strenuously by others; and laws against gambling, dueling, theatergoing, and intemperance were debated with varying degrees of religious intensity in various parts of the country for the next century. . . . Heated arguments took place in the age of Jackson over the right of the state to deliver the mail on Sunday. Courts prosecuted citizens for blaspheming against the Christian religion until 1836, and most jurists throughout the nineteenth century believed that Christianity was part of the common law, Jefferson notwithstanding. . . .

The heart of these indecisions, inconsistencies, and contradictions lay in precisely what kinds of "friendly aids" the political fathers might give to the cause of Christianity. And, logically enough, the first great debate about the proper relationship of church and state in the new nation concerned a general assessment for the support of religion. The essence of this debate was encapsulated in the contrast between Jefferson's assertion in the preamble to his act for religious liberty "that even the forcing [a citizen] to support this or that teacher of his own religious persuasion is depriving him of the comfortable liberty of giving his contribution to the particular pastor whose morals he would make his pattern," and George Washington's negative reply to Madison's "Remonstrance": "I must confess that I am not amongst the number of those who are so much alarmed at the thoughts of making people pay toward the support of that which they profess. . . ."

According to the general-assessment concept every citizen would be required to pay a tax in proportion to his wealth for the support of religion (specifically for some form of Protestantism), but each taxpayer could specify to which particular church or minister he wished his religious assessment allocated (presumably to the church or minister he attended upon). Nothingarians, atheists, Roman Catholics, Jews, and other non-Protestants were equally responsible for paying such taxes, but sometimes in order to preserve their rights of conscience various alternatives were suggested for the allocation of their monies. In Virginia one general-assessment plan stated that the non-Protestant might allocate his money to the support of the poor, while another said his taxes would be allocated to public education; the Maryland plan exempted any Jew or Mohammedan who made a declaration of his belief before two justices; in Massachusetts those who did not attend any church had their taxes allocated to the oldest church in their parish (invariably the Congregational church—a fact that led many to assert that the Massachusetts general-assessment plan favored the old establishment). . . .

In view of the defeat of all efforts at general-assessment plans in the southern states, it has frequently been inferred that New England was backward and out of touch with the prevailing current for religious liberty and equality. But seen in the broader context the old Puritan states were going through precisely the same debate and on precisely the same terms. The reasons why the balance tipped in favor of the general-assessment system in New England can be attributed more to historical tradition and practice than to any significant difference of public opinion regarding the importance of compulsory tax support for religion. . . .

Other factors may also account for New England's willingness to try the general-assessment plan. First of all, there were far fewer dissenters in New England, probably less than a fifth in 1780; hence they did not have the votes or the influence to defeat it. Second, the New England Congregational system was a solid and thriving one that, despite the separations during the Great Awakening, remained in firm control of almost every parish. Third, the Congregational clergy, having been staunch supporters of the Revolution, attained increased respect and allegiance during that crisis. And finally, the rulers of Connecticut and Massachusetts may have been somewhat more fearful of social disruption than those of Virginia, where the upper class felt sufficiently secure to accept the dissolution of an ecclesiastical system that had never been very effective anyway. . . .

The avowed commitment of Americans to religious equality gradually produced a kind of tolerated status for Roman Catholics and Jews within the prevailing establishment (similar to that of Presbyterians in colonial Virginia or Anglicans in colonial Massachusetts), [but] Americans were unable to stretch their concept of religious liberty to include such extremes as Mormonism, the American Indian religions, Mohammedanism, or the various Oriental religions. The last two were prevented even from entering the country by one means or another (sometimes called "gentlemen's agreements") on the grounds that they were so outlandish as to be "unassimilable." The Mormons and Indians were forced to conform, the former by a combination of mob, martial, and judicial law, the latter by being treated as incompetent wards of the state whose education was turned over to the various denominations.

If religion in America, institutionalized as incorporated voluntaryism and the Protestant ethic, became so culture-bound as to constitute by the mid-nineteenth century a new form of official establishment, this does not mean that religion became one of the less important aspects of American life. If the American Revolution was a revival, the new nation became a church. Far from being an opiate, religion was an incredible stimulus to the American people.

FURTHER READING

Sidney E. Ahlstrom, *A Religious History of the American People* (1972)

John F. Berens, *Providence and Patriotism in Early America, 1640–1815* (1978)

Ruth H. Bloch, *Visionary Republic: Millennial Themes in American Thought, 1756–1800* (1985)

Patricia U. Bonomi, *Under the Cope of Heaven: Religion, Society, and Politics in Colonial America* (1986)

Carl Bridenbaugh, *Mitre and Sceptre: Transatlantic Faiths, Ideas, Personalities, and Politics, 1689–1775* (1962)

Thomas E. Buckley, *Church and State in Revolutionary Virginia, 1776–1787* (1977)

Jon Butler, *Awash in a Sea of Faith: Christianizing the American People* (1990)

Thomas J. Curry, *The First Freedoms: Church and State in America to the Passage of the First Amendment* (1986)

Peter S. Field, *The Crisis of the Standing Order: Clerical Intellectuals and Cultural Authority in Massachusetts, 1780–1833* (1998)

Nathan O. Hatch, *The Sacred Cause of Liberty: Republican Thought and the Millennium in Revolutionary New England* (1988)

——, *The Democratization of American Christianity* (1989)

Alan Heimert, *Religion and the American Mind from the Great Awakening to the Revolution* (1966)

Ronald Hoffman and Peter Albert, eds., *Religion in a Revolutionary Age* (1994)

Rhys Isaac, *The Transformation of Virginia, 1740–1790* (1982)

Susan Juster, *Disorderly Women: Sexual Politics and Evangelicalism in Revolutionary New England* (1994)

David S. Lovejoy, *Religious Enthusiasm in the New World: Heresy to Revolution* (1985)

William G. McLoughlin, *New England Dissent, 1630–1833: The Baptists and the Separation of Church and State* (1971)

Stephen A. Marini, *Radical Sects of Revolutionary New England* (1982)

Sidney E. Mead, *The Old Religion in the Brave New World: Reflections on the Relation Between Christendom and the Republic* (1977)

William Lee Miller, *The First Liberty: Religion and the American Republic* (1986)

Richard W. Pointer, *Protestant Pluralism and the New York Experience: A Study of Eighteenth-Century Religious Diversity* (1988)

Robert A. Rutland, *The Birth of the Bill of Rights, 1776–1791* (1955)

Charles B. Sanford, *The Religious Life of Thomas Jefferson* (1984)

Bernard Schwartz, *The Great Rights of Mankind: A History of the American Bill of Rights* (1977)

Sally Schwartz, *A Mixed Multitude: The Struggle for Toleration in Colonial Pennsylvania* (1987)

Harry S. Stout, *The New England Soul: Preaching and Religious Culture in Colonial New England* (1986)

Donald Weber, *Rhetoric and History in Revolutionary New England* (1988)

Peacetime Government Under the Articles of Confederation

While Americans were confronting some of the unexpected social implications of their revolution, such as the place of women, African-Americans, and religion in the new republic, the mundane affairs of peacetime government went on. Commercial and foreign policy, public finance, and western land all demanded attention. In Congress, now sitting under the mandate of the Articles of Confederation (whose ratification was completed in 1781), all of these issues were addressed by delegates representing different interests and viewpoints. Although substantial obstacles, both political and structural, impeded their work, they made some headway in the formulation of national policy, especially in relation to western lands.

The history of this Confederation era, once called the critical period, has been dominated by the Federalist belief that the Articles of Confederation were a failure and that the Constitution of 1787 rescued the nation. Indeed, celebrating the Constitution is part of the national culture of the United States, whereas the Articles are widely forgotten, resurrected for praise mostly by champions of states' rights or critics of national policies. But the fact that the Articles of Confederation laid the foundation for the later Constitution and that the national government began during its tenure should lead to the recognition that this earlier blueprint for a national government shared much in common with the Constitution and was by no means its opposite. During the Constitution-ratification controversy and subsequently, it has been convenient rhetorically to picture the two frames of government as polar opposites: the Articles as weak, divided, and consensual; the Constitution as strong, united, and majoritarian. But in this case, the rhetoric clouds precise understanding.

In reality, strong continuities ran through the two governments. Consideration of the text of the Articles of Confederation, and of the politics surrounding government land policy, reveals the political principles and the practical realities of national government in the new republic of the 1780s. Complaints of frustration were certainly part of an open, representative government, but so was the noteworthy achievement of the Northwest Ordinance.

Yet neither state nor national government ran smoothly during the 1780s. Frustrations at the national level led to genuine alarm when state governments faltered. In Massachusetts, a civil war erupted in 1786 that became known as Shays's Rebellion, named for one of its leaders, Daniel Shays. Lasting for about eight months, Shays's Rebellion began with peaceful county conventions in the summer of 1786 and ended in the first months of 1787 with thousands of armed soldiers, pitched battles, and bloodshed. Because Massachusetts possessed the most fully developed state constitution, drafted by John Adams and ratified by popular vote in 1780, this was a crucial test for republican government. The Massachusetts constitution gave the governor veto power and carefully articulated the separation of powers among the executive, legislature, and judiciary. The state not only had literate voters but featured a broad, relatively equal distribution of property when compared to states like New York and Virginia. Truly, Massachusetts faced a crisis, one that seemed emblematic for the United States as a whole. If republican self-government failed in Massachusetts, where would it succeed?

The issues in Massachusetts, which pitted debtors against creditors and re- volved around taxation, currency, and public finances, were problems throughout the new nation. Although they led to warfare only in Massachusetts, the interests of farmers and merchants came into conflict in nearly all the states. In the midst of this turmoil, the United States Congress under the Articles of Confederation could offer no remedies. In fact, congressional vitality ebbed as the various state govern- ments, not Congress, became the arenas for resolving political problems. It was this realization—the sense that the national interest was failing and that a vigorous national government could reverse the direction of American politics—that led nationalists like James Madison to press for constitutional reform.

DOCUMENTS

Document 1, the Articles of Confederation, is a landmark in American constitutional history. Drafted by the Pennsylvanian John Dickinson (author of the *Farmer's Letters*) at the direction of Congress in 1777, the frame of government was finally ratified in 1781, after Maryland successfully insisted that states with western land claims cede them to the national govern- ment. Although the whole Confederation plan differs in some essential ways from the Consti- tution, several of its articles were brought into the later document almost intact. Moreover, the principle of majority rule, not unanimous consensus, was clearly established in the plan.

Documents 2 and 3 treat the disposition of western lands. The plan Congress established in 1785 has had a powerful impact on the settlement history, human ecology, and natural en- vironment of the entire United States. The Northwest Ordinance of 1787, which follows, was the last major achievement of the Confederation. This document not only provided for the admission of future states on an equal basis with the old ones, it also excluded slavery from much of the country while assuring its protection elsewhere by a provision for the return of fugitive slaves. But Congress's success with western lands did not arrest its overall decline, as is evident in Document 4, Charles Pinckney's letter to the New Jersey legislature in 1786, and in the complaints of congressional delegates in 1787 reprinted as Document 5.

All was not well in the states either. As the Massachusetts farmers' complaints show in Document 6, they believed their state government had failed them. Calling themselves "regulators" not "rebels," they sought to win general support in the fall of 1786. But as Document 7 illustrates, the eastern Massachusetts elite which led the legislature was not persuaded. They saw regulator arguments as ill-informed and wrong-headed, and they replied to the people of their state with a lecture on political economy and citizenship.

1. The Articles of Confederation and Perpetual Union, 1781

Articles of Confederation and Perpetual Union Between the States of New Hampshire, Massachusetts Bay, Rhode Island and Providence Plantations, Connecticut, New York, New Jersey, Pennsylvania, Delaware, Maryland, Virginia, North Carolina, South Carolina, and Georgia

Article One

The style of this Confederacy shall be "The United States of America."

Article Two

Each State retains its sovereignty, freedom, and independence, and every power, jurisdiction, and right, which is not by this Confederation expressly delegated to the United States in Congress assembled.

Article Three

The said States hereby severally enter into a firm league of friendship with each other, for their common defence, the security of their liberties, and their mutual and general welfare, binding themselves to assist each other against all force offered to, or attacks made upon them, or any of them, on account of religion, sovereignty, trade, or any other pretence whatever.

Article Four

The better to secure and perpetuate mutual friendship and intercourse among the people of the different States in this Union, the free inhabitants of each of these States, paupers, vagabonds, and fugitives from justice excepted, shall be entitled to all the privileges and immunities of free citizens in the several States, and the people of each State shall have free ingress and regress to and from any other State, and shall enjoy therein all the privileges of trade and commerce, subject to the same duties, impositions, and restrictions as the inhabitants thereof respectively, provided that such restrictions shall not extend so far as to prevent the removal of property imported into any State, to any other State of which the owner is an inhabitant; provided also, that no imposition, duties, or restriction shall be laid by any State, on the property of the United States, or either of them.

If any person guilty of or charged with treason, felony, or other high misdemeanor in any State, shall flee from justice, and be found in any of the United States, he shall, upon demand of the governor or executive power of the State from which he fled, be delivered up and removed to the State having jurisdiction of his offence.

"The Articles of Confederation and Perpetual Union, 1781." As found in *American State Papers* (Chicago: Encyclopedia Britannica, 1952), 6–9.

Full faith and credit shall be given in each of these States to the records, acts, and judicial proceedings of the courts and magistrates of every other State.

Article Five

For the more convenient management of the general interests of the United States, delegates shall be annually appointed in such manner as the legislature of each State shall direct, to meet in Congress on the first Monday in November, in every year, with a power reserved to each State to recall its delegates, or any of them, at any time within the year, and to send others in their stead, for the remainder of the year.

No State shall be represented in Congress by less than two, nor by more than seven members; and no person shall be capable of being a delegate for more than three years in any term of six years, nor shall any person, being a delegate, be capable of holding any office under the United States for which he or another for his benefit receives any salary, fees, or emolument of any kind.

Each State shall maintain its own delegates in a meeting of the States, and while they act as members of the committee of the States.

In determining questions in the United States, in Congress assembled, each State shall have one vote.

Freedom of speech and debate in Congress shall not be impeached or questioned in any court or place out of Congress, and the members of Congress shall be protected in their persons from arrests and imprisonments, during the time of their going to or from, and attendance on, Congress, except for treason, felony, or breach of the peace.

Article Six

No State, without the consent of the United States in Congress assembled, shall send any embassy to, or receive any embassy from, or enter into any conference, agreement, alliance, or treaty with, any king, prince, or state; nor shall any person holding any office of profit or trust under the United States, or any of them, accept of any present, emolument, office, or title of any kind whatever from any king, prince, or foreign state; nor shall the United States in Congress assembled, or any of them, grant any title of nobility.

No two or more States shall enter into any treaty, confederation, or alliance whatever between them, without the consent of the United States in Congress assembled, specifying accurately the purposes for which the same is to be entered into, and how long it shall continue.

No State shall lay any imposts or duties, which may interfere with any stipulations in treaties entered into by the United States in Congress assembled, with any king, prince, or state, in pursuance of any treaties already proposed by Congress, to the courts of France and Spain.

No vessels of war shall be kept in time of peace by any State, except such number only as shall be deemed necessary by the United States in Congress assembled, for the defence of such State or its trade; nor shall any body of forces be kept up by any State, in time of peace, except such number only as in the judgment of the United States in Congress assembled shall be deemed requisite to garrison the forts necessary for the defence of such State; but every State shall always keep up a well regulated and disciplined militia, sufficiently armed and accoutred, and shall provide and constantly have ready for use, in public stores, a due number of field-pieces and tents, and a proper quantity of arms, ammunition, and camp equipage.

No State shall engage in any war without the consent of the United States in Congress assembled, unless such State be actually invaded by enemies, or shall have received certain advice of a resolution being formed by some nation of Indians to invade such State, and the danger is so imminent as not to admit of a delay till the United States in Congress assembled can be consulted; nor shall any State grant commissions to any ships or vessels of war, nor letters of marque or reprisal, except it be after a declaration of war by the United States in Congress assembled, and then only against the kingdom or state, and the subjects thereof, against which war has been so declared, and under such regulations as shall be established by the United States in Congress assembled, unless such State be infested by pirates, in which case vessels of war may be fitted out for that occasion, and kept so long as the danger shall continue, or until the United States in Congress assembled shall determine otherwise.

Article Seven

When land forces are raised by any State for the common defense, all officers of or under the rank of colonel shall be appointed by the legislature of each State respectively, by whom such forces shall be raised, or in such manner as such State shall direct; and all vacancies shall be filled up by the State which first made the appointment.

Article Eight

All charges of war and all other expenses that shall be incurred for the common defence or general welfare, and allowed by the United States in Congress assembled, shall be defrayed out of a common treasury, which shall be supplied by the several States, in proportion to the value of all land within each State, granted to or surveyed for any person, and such land and the buildings and improvements thereon shall be estimated according to such mode as the United States in Congress assembled shall from time to time direct and appoint.

The taxes for paying that proportion shall be laid and levied by the authority and direction of the legislatures of the several States within the time agreed upon by the United States in Congress assembled.

Article Nine

The United States in Congress assembled shall have the sole and exclusive right and power of determining on peace and war, except in the cases mentioned in the sixth article—of sending and receiving ambassadors—entering into treaties and alliances, provided that no treaty of commerce shall be made whereby the legislative power of the respective States shall be restrained from imposing such imposts and duties on foreigners as their own people are subjected to, or from prohibiting the exportation or importation of any species of goods or commodities whatsoever—of establishing rules for deciding, in all cases, what captures on land or water shall be legal, and in what manner prizes taken by land or naval forces in the service of the United States shall be divided or appropriated—of granting letters of marque and reprisal in times of peace—appointing courts for the trial of piracies and felonies committed on the high seas, and establishing courts for receiving and determining finally appeals in all cases of captures, provided that no member of Congress shall be appointed a judge of any of the said courts.

The United States in Congress assembled shall also be the last resort on appeal in all disputes and differences now subsisting or that hereafter may arise between two or more States concerning boundary, jurisdiction, or any other cause whatever; which authority shall always be exercised in the manner following:—Whenever the legislative or executive authority or lawful agent of any State in controversy with another shall present a petition to Congress stating the matter in question and praying for a hearing, notice thereof shall be given by order of Congress to the legislative or executive authority of the other State in controversy, and a day assigned for the appearance of the parties by their lawful agents, who shall then be directed to appoint, by joint consent, commissioners or judges to constitute a court for hearing and determining the matter in question; but if they cannot agree, Congress shall name three persons out of each of the United States, and from the list of such persons each party shall alternately strike out one, the petitioners beginning, until the number shall be reduced to thirteen; and from that number not less than seven nor more than nine names, as Congress shall direct, shall, in the presence of Congress, be drawn out by lot, and the persons whose names shall be so drawn, or any five of them, shall be commissioners or judges, to hear and finally determine the controversy, so always as a major part of the judges who shall hear the cause shall agree in the determination; and if either party shall neglect to attend at the day appointed, without showing reasons, which Congress shall judge sufficient, or, being present, shall refuse to strike, the Congress shall proceed to nominate three persons out of each State, and the Secretary of Congress shall strike in behalf of such party absent or refusing; and the judgment and sentence of the court to be appointed, in the manner before prescribed, shall be final and conclusive; and if any of the parties shall refuse to submit to the authority of such court, or to appear or defend their claim or cause, the court shall nevertheless proceed to pronounce sentence or judgment, which shall in like manner be final and decisive, the judgment or sentence and other proceedings being in either case transmitted to Congress, and lodged among the acts of Congress for the security of the parties concerned: provided that every commissioner, before he sits in judgment, shall take an oath, to be administered by one of the judges of the Supreme or Superior Court of the State where the cause shall be tried, *"well and truly to hear and determine the matter in question according to the best of his judgment, without favor, affection, or hope of reward,"* provided also that no State shall be deprived territory for the benefit of the United States.

All controversies concerning the private right of soil, claimed under different grants of two or more States, whose jurisdictions as they may respect such lands and the States which passed such grants are adjusted, the said grants or either of them being at the same time claimed to have originated antecedent to such settlement of jurisdiction, shall, on the petition of either party to the Congress of the United States, be finally determined as near as may be in the same manner as is before prescribed for deciding disputes respecting territorial jurisdiction between different States.

The United States in Congress assembled shall also have the sole and exclusive right and power of regulating the alloy and value of coin struck by their own authority, or by that of the respective States—fixing the standard of weights and measures throughout the United States—regulating the trade and managing all affairs with the Indians, not members of any of the States, provided that the legislative right of any State within its own limits be not infringed or violated—establishing and regulating post-offices from one State to another, throughout all the United States, and exacting such postage on the papers passing through the same as may be requisite to defray the expenses of the said office—appointing all officers of the land forces in the service of the United States, excepting regimental officers—appointing all the officers of the naval forces, and commissioning all officers whatever in the service of the United States—making rules for the government and regulation of the said land and naval forces, and directing their operations.

The United States in Congress assembled shall have authority to appoint a committee, to sit in the recess of Congress, to be denominated "A Committee of the States," and to consist of one delegate from each State; to appoint such other committees and civil officers as may be necessary for managing the general affairs of the United States under their direction; and to appoint one of their number to preside, provided that no person be allowed to serve in the office of president more than one year in any term of three years—to ascertain the necessary sums of money to be raised for the service of the United States, and to appropriate and apply the same for defraying the public expenses—to borrow money, or emit bills on the credit of the United States, transmitting every half-year to the respective States an account of the sums of money so borrowed or emitted—to build and equip a navy—to agree upon the number of land forces, and to make requisitions from each State for its quota, in proportion to the number of white inhabitants in such State; which requisition shall be binding, and thereupon the legislature of each State shall appoint the regimental officers, raise the men, and clothe, arm, and equip them in a soldier-like manner, at the expense of the United States, and the officers and men so clothed, armed, and equipped shall march to the place appointed, and within the time agreed on by the United States in Congress assembled; but if the United States in Congress assembled shall, on consideration of circumstances, judge proper that any State should not raise men, or should raise a smaller number than its quota, and that any other State should raise a greater number of men than the quota thereof, such extra number shall be raised, officered, clothed, armed, and equipped in the same manner as the quota of such State, unless the legislature of such State shall judge that such extra number cannot be safely spared out of the same, in which case they shall raise, officer, clothe, arm, and equip as many of such extra number as they judge can be safely spared: and the officers and men, so clothed, armed, and equipped shall march to the place appointed, and within the time agreed on, by the United States in Congress assembled.

The United States in Congress assembled shall never engage in a war, nor grant letters of marque and reprisal in time of peace, nor enter into any treaties or alliances, nor coin money, nor regulate the value thereof, nor ascertain the sums and expenses necessary for the defence and welfare of the United States, or any of them, nor emit bills, nor borrow money on the credit of the United States, nor appropriate money, nor agree upon the number of vessels of war to be built or purchased, or the number of land or sea forces to be raised, nor appoint a commander-in-chief of the army or navy, unless nine States assent to the same; nor shall a question on any other point, except for adjourning from day to day, be determined, unless by the votes of a majority of the United States in Congress assembled.

The Congress of the United States shall have power to adjourn to any time within the year, and to any place within the United States, so that no period of adjournment be for a longer duration than the space of six months, and shall publish the journal of their proceedings monthly, except such parts thereof relating to treaties, alliances, or military operations, as in their judgment require secrecy, and the yeas and nays of the delegates of each State on any question shall be entered on the journal, when it is desired by any delegate; and the delegates of a State, or any of them, at his or their request, shall be furnished with a transcript of the said journal, except such parts as are above excepted to lay before the legislatures of the several States.

Article Ten

The Committee of the States, or any nine of them, shall be authorized to execute, in the recess of Congress, such of the powers of Congress as the United States in Congress assembled, by the consent of nine States, shall from time to time think expedient to vest them with: provided that no power be delegated to the said Committee, for the exercise of which, by the Articles of Confederation, the voice of nine States in the Congress of the United States assembled is requisite.

Article Eleven

Canada, acceding to this Confederation, and joining in the measures of the United States, shall be admitted into and entitled to all the advantages of this Union; but no other colony shall be admitted into the same, unless such admission be agreed to by nine States.

Article Twelve

All bills of credit emitted, moneys borrowed, and debts contracted by or under the authority of Congress, before the assembling of the United States in pursuance of the present Confederation, shall be deemed and considered as a charge against the United States, for payment and satisfaction whereof the said United States and the public faith are hereby solemnly pledged.

Article Thirteen

Every State shall abide by the determinations of the United States in Congress assembled, on all questions which by this Confederation are submitted to them. And the Articles of this Confederation shall be inviolably observed by every State, and the Union shall be perpetual; nor shall any alteration at any time hereafter be made in any of them, unless such alteration be agreed to in a Congress of the United States, and be afterwards confirmed by the legislatures of every State.

AND WHEREAS it hath pleased the Great Governor of the world to incline the hearts of the legislatures we respectfully represent in Congress to approve of and to authorize us to ratify the said Articles of Confederation and perpetual Union, Know Ye, That we, the undersigned delegates, by virtue of the power and authority to us given for that purpose, do by these presents, in the name and in behalf of our respective constituents, fully and entirely ratify and confirm each and every of the said Articles of Confederation and perpetual Union, and all and singular the matters and things therein contained: and we do further solemnly plight and engage the faith of our respective constituents that they shall abide by the determinations of the United States in Congress assembled, on all questions which by the said Confederation are submitted to them. And that the Articles thereof shall be inviolably observed by the States we respectively represent, and the Union shall be perpetual.

2. Congress Passes an Ordinance on Western Lands, 1785

An Ordinance for Ascertaining the Mode of Disposing of Lands in the Western Territory, May 20, 1785

Be it ordained by the United States in Congress assembled, that the territory ceded by individual States to the United States, which has been purchased of the Indian inhabitants, shall be disposed of in the following manner: . . .

The Surveyors, as they are respectively qualified, shall proceed to divide the said territory into townships of six miles square, by lines running due north and south, and others crossing these at right angles, as near as may be, unless where the boundaries of the late Indian purchases may render the same impracticable, and then they shall depart from this rule no farther than such particular circumstances may require; and each surveyor shall be allowed and paid at the rate of two dollars for every mile, in length, he shall run, including the wages of chain carriers, markers, and every other expense attending the same.

The first line, running north and south as aforesaid, shall begin on the river Ohio. . . .

The plats of the townships respectively, shall be marked by subdivisions into lots of one mile square, or 640 acres, in the same direction as the external lines, and numbered from 1 to 36; . . .

As soon as seven ranges of townships, and fractional parts of townships, in the direction from south to north, shall have been surveyed, the geographer shall transmit plats thereof to the board of treasury, who shall record the same, with the report, in well bound books to be kept for that purpose. . . . The Secretary at War shall have recourse thereto, and shall take by lot therefrom, a number of townships, . . . as will be equal to one seventh part of the whole of such seven ranges . . . for the use of the late continental army. . . . The board of treasury shall, from time to time,

---

"Congress Passes an Ordinance on Western Lands." As found in Edmund C. Burnett, ed., *Letters of Members of the Continental Congress* (Washington, DC: The Carnegie Institute of Washington, 1936), vol. 8, pp. 95–97, 129–131.

cause the remaining numbers, as well those to be sold entire, as those to be sold in lots, to be drawn for, in the name of the thirteen states respectively, according to the quotas in the last preceding requisition on all the states . . . provided, that none of the lands . . . be sold under the price of one dollar the acre, to be paid in specie, or loan office certificates, reduced to specie value . . .

There shall be reserved for the United States out of every township, the four lots, being numbered 8, 11, 26, 29 . . . for future sale. There shall be reserved the lot N 16, of every township, for the maintenance of public schools, within the said township; also one third part of all gold, silver, lead and copper mines, to be sold, or otherwise disposed of as Congress shall hereafter direct.

3. The Northwest Ordinance, 1787

An Ordinance for the Government of the Territory of the United States Northwest of the River Ohio

Section 1. Be it ordained by the United States in Congress assembled, That the said territory, for the purposes of temporary government, be one district, subject, however, to be divided into two districts, as future circumstances may, in the opinion of Congress, make it expedient. . . .

Sec. 3. Be it ordained by the authority aforesaid, That there shall be appointed, from time to time, by Congress, a governor, whose commission shall continue in force for the term of three years, unless sooner revoked by Congress; he shall reside in the district, and have a freehold estate therein in one thousand acres of land, while in the exercise of his office.

Sec. 4. There shall be appointed from time to time, by Congress, a secretary, whose commission shall continue in force for four years, unless sooner revoked; he shall reside in the district, and have a freehold estate therein, in five hundred acres of land, while in the exercise of his office. . . . There shall also be appointed a court, to consist of three judges, any two of whom to form a court, who shall have a common-law jurisdiction, and reside in the district, and have each therein a freehold estate, in five hundred acres of land, while in the exercise of their offices; and their commissions shall continue in force during good behavior.

Sec. 5. The governor and judges, or a majority of them, shall adopt and publish in the district such laws of the original States, criminal and civil, as may be necessary, and best suited to the circumstances of the district, and report them to Congress from time to time, which laws shall be in force in the district until the organization of the general assembly therein, unless disapproved of by Congress; but afterwards the legislature shall have authority to alter them as they shall think fit.

Sec. 6. The governor, for the time being, shall be commander-in-chief of the militia, appoint and commission all officers in the same below the rank of general officers; all general officers shall be appointed and commissioned by Congress.

"The Northwest Ordinance, 1887." In Francis N. Thorpe, ed., *Federal and State Constitutions: Colonial Charters, and Other Organic Laws of the States, Territories, and Colonies, Now or Heretofore Forming the United States of America* (Washington, DC: US Government Printing Office, 1909) vol. 2, pp. 957–964.

Sec. 7. Previous to the organization of the general assembly the governor shall appoint such magistrates, and other civil officers, in each county or township, as he shall find necessary for the preservation of the peace and good order in the same. After the general assembly shall be organized the powers and duties of the magistrates and other civil officers shall be regulated and defined by the said assembly; but all magistrates and other civil officers, not herein otherwise directed, shall, during the continuance of this temporary government, be appointed by the governor. . . .

Sec. 9. So soon as there shall be five thousand free male inhabitants, of full age, in the district, upon giving proof thereof to the governor, they shall receive authority, with time and place, to elect representatives from their counties or townships, to represent them in the general assembly: Provided, That for every five hundred free male inhabitants there shall be one representative, and so on, progressively, with the number of free male inhabitants, shall the right of representation increase, until the number of representatives shall amount to twenty-five; after which the number and proportion of representatives shall be regulated by the legislature: Provided, That no person be eligible or qualified to act as a representative, unless he shall have been a citizen of one of the United States three years, and be a resident in the district, or unless he shall have resided in the district three years; and, in either case, shall likewise hold in his own right, in fee-simple, two hundred acres of land within the same: Provided, also, That a freehold in fifty acres of land in the district, having been a citizen of one of the States, and being resident in the district, or the like freehold and two years' residence in the district, shall be necessary to qualify a man as an elector of a representative.

Sec. 10. The representatives thus elected shall serve for the term of two years; and in case of the death of a representative, or removal from office, the governor shall issue a writ to the county or township, for which he was a member, to elect another in his stead, to serve for the residue of the term.

Sec. 11. The general assembly, or legislature, shall consist of the governor, legislative council, and a house of representatives. The legislative council shall consist of five members, to continue in office five years, unless sooner removed by Congress. . . . And the governor, legislative council, and house of representatives shall have authority to make laws in all cases for the good government of the district, not repugnant to the principles and articles in this ordinance established and declared. And all bills, having passed by a majority in the house, and by a majority in the council, shall be referred to the governor for his assent; but no bill, or legislative act whatever, shall be of any force without his assent. The governor shall have power to convene, prorogue, and dissolve the general assembly when, in his opinion, it shall be expedient.

Sec. 12. The governor, judges, legislative council, secretary, and such other officers as Congress shall appoint in the district, shall take an oath or affirmation of fidelity, and of office; the governor before the President of Congress, and all other officers before the governor. As soon as a legislature shall be formed in the district, the council and house assembled, in one room, shall have authority, by joint ballot, to elect a delegate to Congress who shall have a seat in Congress, with a right of debating, but not of voting, during this temporary government.

Sec. 13. And for extending the fundamental principles of civil and religious liberty, which form the basis whereon these republics, their laws and constitutions, are erected; to fix and establish those principles as the basis of all laws, constitutions, and governments, which forever hereafter shall be formed in the said territory; to provide, also, for the establishment of States, and permanent government therein, and for their admission to a share in the Federal councils on an equal footing with the original States, at as early periods as may be consistent with the general interest:

Sec. 14. It is hereby ordained and declared, by the authority aforesaid, that the following articles shall be considered as articles of compact, between the original States and the people and States in the said territory, and forever remain unalterable, unless by common consent, to wit:

Article I

No person, demeaning himself in a peaceable and orderly manner, shall ever be molested on account of his mode of worship, or religious sentiments, in the said territories.

Article II

The inhabitants of the said territory shall always be entitled to the benefits of the writ of habeas corpus, and of the trial by jury; of a proportionate representation of the people in the legislature, and of judicial proceedings according to the course of common law. All persons shall be bailable, unless for capital offences, where the proof shall be evident, or the presumption great. All fines shall be moderate; and no cruel or unusual punishments shall be inflicted. No man shall be deprived of his liberty or property, but by the judgment of his peers, or the law of the land, and should the public exigencies make it necessary, for the common preservation, to take any person's property, or to demand his particular services, full compensation shall be made for the same. And, in the just preservation of rights and property, it is understood and declared, that no law ought ever to be made or have force in the said territory, that shall, in any manner whatever, interfere with or affect private contracts, or engagements, bona fide, and without fraud previously formed.

Article III

Religion, morality, and knowledge being necessary to good government and the happiness of mankind, schools and the means of education shall forever be encouraged. The utmost good faith shall always be observed towards the Indians; their lands and property shall never be taken from them without their consent; and in their property, rights, and liberty they never shall be invaded or disturbed, unless in just and lawful wars authorized by Congress; but laws founded in justice and humanity shall, from time to time, be made, for preventing wrongs being done to them, and for preserving peace and friendship with them.

Article IV

The said territory, and the States which may be formed therein, shall forever remain a part of this confederacy of the United States of America, subject to the Articles of Confederation, and to such alterations therein as shall be constitutionally made;

and to all the acts and ordinances of the United States in Congress assembled, conformable thereto. . . .

Article V

There shall be formed in the said territory not less than three nor more than five States. . . . And whenever any of the said States shall have sixty thousand free inhabitants therein, such State shall be admitted, by its delegates, into the Congress of the United States, on an equal footing with the original States, in all respects whatever; and shall be at liberty to form a permanent constitution and State government: Provided, The constitution and government, so to be formed, shall be republican, and in conformity to the principles contained in these articles, and, so far as it can be consistent with the general interest of the confederacy, such admission shall be allowed at an earlier period, and when there may be a less number of free inhabitants in the State than sixty thousand.

Article VI

There shall be neither slavery nor involuntary servitude in the said territory, otherwise than in the punishment of crimes, whereof the party shall have been duly convicted: Provided always, That any person escaping into the same, from whom labor or service is lawfully claimed in any one of the original States, such fugitive may be lawfully reclaimed, and conveyed to the person claiming his or her labor or service as aforesaid. . . .

4. Congressman Charles Pinckney Admonishes the New Jersey Legislature, 1786

Mr. Speaker,

The united states in congress assembled, have been informed, that this house had, on the 20th ultimo, resolved that they could not, consistently with their duty to their constituents, assent to the requisition of September last, for federal supplies. . . .

When these states united, convinced of the inability of each to support a separate system, and that their protection and existence depended on their union—policy, as well as prudence, dictated the necessity of forming one GENERAL and Efficient Government, which, while it protected and secured the whole, left to the several states, those rights of INTERNAL SOVEREIGNTY, it was not necessary to delegate, and which could be exercised without injury to the federal authority. In them were placed all the essential powers which constitute a nation—such are, the exclusive rights of peace and war; of sending and receiving embassies; of forming treaties and alliances; and equipping and raising fleets and armies. To

"Congressman Charles Pinckney Admonishes the New Jersey Legislature, 1786." As found in Edmund C. Burnett, ed., *Letters of Members of the Continental Congress* (Washington, DC: The Carnegie Institute of Washington, 1936), vol. 8, pp. 322–328.

them, also, was delegated the power of obtaining loans on the faith of the united states; and of apportioning to the several members of the union, their quotas of the public expences. . . .

The states having thus by their voluntary act, formed one government as essential to the protection of the whole—and placed in a supreme controuling power the administration of its general concerns, and to which they were to look up for support—each state is bound, according to its abilities, to furnish a proportion of the expences; and the whole are jointly and severally pledged for the public engagements, foreign and domestic. . . . New Jersey has not only assented to the mode by which she is rated, but furnished the returns on which the assessment could be made with exactness: she certainly cannot, therefore, complain of bearing an undue proportion. She will not, I trust, upon reflection, suppose she can, either consistently with her duty to the union, or with safety to its welfare, refuse to comply with the requisition. If she has been over-rated, upon stating the excess in evidence to congress, she will always receive the relief she may be justly entitled to. If, on the other hand, she conceives herself unequally situated, or that she does not participate in those common benefits which the general government was expected to dispense to all its members—if she thinks, with me, that its powers are inadequate to the ends for which it was instituted, and that they should be increased—there can be no doubt of the conduct she ought to pursue. She ought immediately to instruct her delegates in congress, to urge the calling of a general convention of the states, for the purpose of revising and amending the federal system. In this constitutional application, she will meet with all the attention and support she can wish. I have long been of opinion, that it was the only true and radical remedy for our public defects; and shall with pleasure assent to, and support, any measure of that kind, which may be introduced, while I continue a member of that body. . . .

It is certainly more the interest of the small, than it can be of the large states, to preserve the confederation upon its present principles. We are aware of the necessity which compelled the latter to confederate upon terms allowing each state an equal vote in the national councils. Had the system been formed in a time of peace— when no common danger pressed—when deliberation was unaccompanied with apprehension, and the large states preferred conceding the point of proportionable representation, however important, to the greater evil of being again reduced to the power of Great Britain—can it be thought that any union would have been formed upon principles so unequal and oppressive as the present?

Let us for a moment suppose the confederation dissolved, and an assembly of the states convened for the purpose of adopting a system calculated to render the general government firm and energetic—is it not to be reasonably expected, that the large states would contend and insist upon a greater influence than they at present possess? Would they again consent to unite upon principles which should allow states not contributing a twelfth part of their quotas to the public expences, an equal vote with themselves! It is not even to be hoped. It ought, therefore, to appear exceedingly important to the small states to maintain a system so advantageous to their particular interests, when they reflect that in the event of another confederation, they cannot expect to be placed in a situation, to which they are neither entitled by common justice, or an equal attention to the rights of the other members of the union.

Though our present disorders must be attributed, in the first instance, to the weakness and inefficacy of the general government, it must still be confessed they have been precipitated by the refractory and inattentive conduct of the states; most of whom have neglected altogether the performance of their federal duties; and, whenever their state policy or interests prompted, used their retained rights to the injury and disgrace of the federal head.

5. Delegates Report from a Demoralized Congress, 1787

Stephen Mix Mitchell to Jeremiah Wadsworth

NEW YORK Jany. 24th, 1787

Dear Sir,

Whether I am to tell you we have a Congress or no, I cannot tell.

The Situation of Congress is truely deplorable. no one seems willing to contribute a Mite to extricate us from the mire into which we are fallen.

Pensylvania in answer to Messrs. King and Monro, have so far declared in favor of dividing the Debt, as to say, they will pay their own Citizens only.

I cannot see there remains any necessity for keeping up a Representation in Congress. in our present Situation, all we can possibly do, is to recommend, which is an old, stale device and no better than the wish of a few Individuals relative to publick Concerns.

Our Eyes at present are turn'd to Masachusetts and expect by Saturday's post, to hear of feats of Chivalry. We are told that Genl. Lincoln and Mr. Shays are this week to take feild to try the Title for Empire in the feild of Mars; whether Good or ill is to be produced, futurity must discover.

James Madison to George Washington

NEW YORK Feby. 21, 1787

Dear Sir,

Some little time before my arrival here a quorum of the States was made up and Genl. Sinclair put in the Chair. . . . The objects now depending and most immediately in prospect, are 1. The Treaty of peace. . . . 2. a recommendation of the proposed Convention in May. Cong's have been much divided and embarrassed on the question whether their taking an interest in the measure would impede or

"Delegates Report from a Demoralized Congress." As found in Edmund C. Burnett, ed., *Letters of Members of the Continental Congress* (Washington, DC: The Carnegie Institute of Washington, 1936), vol. 8, pp. 531, 545–548

promote it. . . . Our latest information from Mass'ts gives hopes that the mutiny or as the Legislature there now style it, the Rebellion is nearly extinct. If the measures however on foot for disarming and disfranchising those concerned in it should be carried into effect, a new crisis may be brought on. I have not been here long enough to gather the general sentiments of leading characters touching our affairs and prospects. I am inclined to hope that they will gradually be concentered in the plan of a thorough reform of the existing system. Those who may lean towards a Monarchial Govt. and who I suspect are swayed by very indigested ideas, will of course abandon an unattainable object whenever a prospect opens of rendering the Republican form competent to its purposes. Those who remain attached to the latter form must soon perceive that it can not be preserved at all under any modification which does not redress the ills experienced from our present establishments.

James Madison to Edmund Pendleton

NEW YORK, Feby. 24, 1787

Dear Sir,

. . . The only step of moment taken by Cong's, since my arrival has been a recommendation of the proposed meeting in May for revising the federal articles. Some of the States, considering this measure as an extra constitutional one, had scruples agst. concurring in it without some regular sanction. By others it was thought best that Cong's should remain neutral in the business, as the best antidote for the jealousy of an ambitious desire in them to get more powers into their hands. This suspense was at length removed by an instruction from this State to its delegates to urge a Recommendatory Resolution in congress which accordingly passed a few days ago. . . . In general I find men of reflection much less sanguine as to the new than despondent as to the present System. Indeed the Present System neither has nor deserves advocates; and if some very strong props are not applied will quickly tumble to the ground. No money is paid into the public Treasury; no respect is paid to the federal authority. Not a single State complies with the requisitions, several pass them over in silence, and some positively reject them. The payments ever since the peace have been decreasing, and of late fall short even of the pittance necessary for the Civil list of the Confederacy. It is not possible that a Government can last long under these circumstances. If the approaching convention should not agree on some remedy, I am persuaded that some very different arrangement will ensue. The late turbulent scenes in Mass'ts and infamous ones in Rhode Island, have done inexpressible injury to the republican character in that part of the U. States; and a propensity towards Monarchy is said to have been produced by it in some leading minds. The bulk of the people will probably prefer the lesser evil of a partition of the Union into three more practicable and energetic Governments. The latter idea I find after long confinement to individual speculations and private circles, is beginning to shew itself in the Newspapers. But tho' it is a lesser evil, it is so great a one that I hope the danger of it will rouse all the real friends of the Revolution to exert themselves in favor of such an organization of the confederacy, as will perpetuate the Union, and redeem the honor of the Republican name.

6. Hampshire County, Massachusetts, Farmers Call for Help, 1786

Petition from the Town of Greenwich, Massachusetts
16 January 1786

To the Honourable Senate and the House of Representatives in General Court assembled att their next session:

A Petition of the Subscribers humbly sheweth—

That in the time of the late war, being desirous to defend secure and promote the wrights and liberties of the people, we spared no pains but freely granted all that aid and assistance of every kind that our civel fathers required of us.

We are sencable also that a great debt is justly brought upon us by the war and are as willing to pay our shares towards itt as we are to injoy our shars in independancy and constatutional priviledges in the Commonwealth, if itt was in our power. And we beleve that if prudant mesuers ware taken and a moderate quantety of medium to circulate so that our property might sel for the real value we mite in proper time pay said debt.

But with the greatest submittion we beg leave to informe your Honours that unles something takes place more favourable to the people, in a little time att least, one half of our inhabitants in our oppinion will become banckerupt—how can itt be otherwise—the constables are dayly vandering [vendering, i.e., selling] our property both real and personal, our land after itt is prised by the best judges under oath is sold for about one third of the value of itt, our cattle about one half the value, the best inglesh [English] hay thirteen shilings per tone, intervale [native] hay att six shilings per tone, and other things att the same rate. And we beg leave further to informe your honours that sutes att law are very numerous and the atturneys in our oppinion very extravigent and oppressive in their demands. And when we compute the taxes laid upon us the five preceeding years: the state and county, town and class taxes,* the amount is equil to what our farms will rent for. Sirs, in this situation what have we to live on—no money to be had; our estates dayly posted and sold, as above described. What can your honours ask of us unles a paper curancy or some other medium be provided so that we may pay our taxes and debts. Suerly your honours are not strangers to the distresses of the people but doe know that many of our good inhabitants are now confined in gole for det and for taxes: maney have fled, others wishing to flee to the State of New York or some other State; and we believe that for two years past four inhabitants have removed from this State to some other State to one that has come from some other State to settle in this State.

Honoured Sirs, are not these imprisonments and fleeing away of our good inhabitants very injurious to the credit or honour of the Commonwealth? will not the people in the neighbouring States say of this State: altho' the Massachusets bost of

---

"Hampshire County, Massachusetts, Farmers Call for Help, 1786." In George Richards Minot, *The History of the Insurrections in Massachusetts in the Year MDCCLXXXVI, and the Rebellion Consequent Thereon* (Worcester, MA: Isaiah Thomas, 1788), 83–84.

* A wartime tax used to pay enlistment bounties to soldiers.

their fine constatution, their government is such that itt devours their inhabitents? Notwithstanding all these distresses, we hear of no abatement of sallerys, but his Excellency the Governor must be paid eleven hundred a year out of the moneys collected as before mentoned, and other sallerys and grants to other gentlemen, as your honours very well know. Iff these things are honest, just and rite, we sincearly wish to be convinced of itt: but we honestly confess itt is beyond our skill to reconsile these sallerys and grants with the principles of our Constatution (viz.) piaty, justice, moderation, temperance, etc. . . .

[Signed by 60 men]

7. Regulators Call for Popular Support, 1786

To the Printer of the Hampshire Herald

Sir,

It has some how or other fallen to my lot to be employed in a more conspicuous manner than some others of my fellow citizens, in stepping forth in defence of the rights and privileges of the people, more especially of the county of Hampshire.

Therefore, upon the desire of the people now at arms, I take this method to publish to the world of mankind in general, particularly the people of this Commonwealth, some of the principal grievances we complain of, and of which we are now seeking redress, and mean to contend for, until a redress can be obtained, which we hope, will soon take place; and if so, our brethren in this Commonwealth, that do not see with us as yet, shall find we shall be as peaceable as they be.

In the first place, I must refer you to a draught of grievances drawn up by a committee of the people, now at arms, . . . which is heartily approved of; some others also are here added, viz.

1st. The General Court, for certain obvious reasons, must be removed out of the town of Boston.

2d. A revision of the constitution is absolutely necessary,

3d. All kinds of governmental securities, now on interest, that have been bought of the original owners for two shillings, three shillings, four shillings, and the highest for six shillings and eight pence on the pound, and have received more interest than the principal cost the speculator who purchased them—that if justice was done, we verily believe, nay positively know, it would save this Commonwealth thousands of pounds.

4th. Let the lands belonging to this Commonwealth, at the eastward, be sold at the best advantage, to pay the remainder of our domestick debt.

5th. Let the monies arising from impost and excise be appropriated to discharge the foreign debt.

6th. Let that act, passed by the General Court last June, by a small majority of only seven, called the Supplementary Aid, for twenty five years to come, be repealed.

"Regulators Call for Popular Support, 1786." In George Richards Minot, *The History of the Insurrections in Massachusetts in the Year MDCCLXXXVI, and the Rebellion Consequent Thereon* (Worcester, MA: Isaiah Thomas, 1788), 85–87.

7th. The total abolition of the Inferiour Court of Common Pleas and General Sessions of the Peace.

8th. Deputy Sheriffs totally set aside, as a useless set of officers in the community; and Constables who are really necessary, be empowered to do the duty, by which means a large swarm of lawyers will be banished from their wonted haunts, who have been more damage to the people at large, especially the common farmers, than the savage beasts of prey.

To this I boldly sign my proper name, as a hearty wellwisher to the real rights of the people.

Thomas Grover
Worcester, December 7, 1786.

8. The Massachusetts Legislature Advises Thrift, Virtue, and Patience, 1786

An Address from the General Court, to the People of the Commonwealth of Massachusetts

At a period, when grievances are complained of, in divers counties of the State; when the symptoms of discontent are manifest and alarming, and individuals resort to arms, to support their disaffection, and oppose the Courts of Justice; it becomes the duty of the Legislature, to investigate, and, as far as may be, to remove the grounds of complaint; to undeceive those, who are misguided by false representation; and if lenient means are ineffectual, to vindicate by vigorous and decisive measures, the honor of government, and provide for the security of the State. . . .

We have no doubt, that endeavours are used by evil and designing men, to alienate the affections of the people in general, from those who are concerned in the administration of government; but conscious of the rectitude of our intentions, we are convinced, that if the public measures are examined with candour, the confidence you lately reposed in us, will not be lessened. . . .

As we apprehend a great part of the uneasiness in the State, has arisen from misinformation, we shall in the first place subjoin a state of the public debt, as well the particular debt of this Commonwealth, as this State's proportion of the national or Continental debt. . . . [Here follows a detailed accounting of the several kinds of debt.]

Although from the foregoing statement, it appears that a large debt is due, yet when our resources, and the manner in which payment can be made, are considered; we think the inhabitants of the Commonwealth will be satisfied, not only that they are able to pay the debt; but that it may be discharged without greatly distressing them.

The particular debt of this Commonwealth is almost wholly due to its citizens; the payment therefore will not weaken the State by draining it of its property.

"The Massachusetts Legislature Advises Thrift, Virtue, and Patience, 1786." In Massachusetts General Court, *An Address from the General Court to the People of the Commonwealth of Massachusetts* (Boston: Adams & Nourse, 1786), 3–4, 8–11, 24–29, 31–40.

Considerable sums are expected from the sale of lands in the easterly part of the State, and every measure that prudence will admit, is taken for the speedy sale of those lands. . . .

If an individual is involved in debt, both prudence and honesty require him to be frugal, and pay his debt as soon as may be. By a long and expensive war, we incurred a large public debt, tho' far less than that, which our enemies incurred; but instead of using every effort to pay it, divers persons have employed themselves in devising methods to get rid of it, without payment; many indeed have employed much more time and money to this end, than (if better employed) might have purchased their whole proportion of the public securities; they alledge, that many of the first possessors have been obliged to sell them, for little more than one third of their amount, and therefore that the present holders ought to receive no more; but we should do well to remember, that the public has received the full value of all the notes they have issued; they were made transferable by law, and many of them have been sold; but if we had paid them as we promised, very few would have been sold; and shall we take no measures to pay them now, because we have omitted the payment so long? . . .

The sitting of the General Court in Boston, has occasioned uneasiness; doubtless it would be more convenient for a part of the State, if it was holden at some other place; but the interest and wishes of a part, are not to be considered alone: Boston has long been thought the most convenient place: some of the General Court have supposed otherwise; but the major part were against a removal, and must the minor part therefore rise against the government? Because they could not have every thing as they wished, could they be justified in resorting to force? Such a principle would destroy all society. Attention, however, has been paid to the instruction of many towns respecting the removal of the General Court out of the town of Boston, and a Committee consisting of a member from each county, has been appointed to consider the subject and report.

It never can be the case, that the whole community shall be of the same opinion; in a republican government the major part must govern: if the minor part governs, it becomes an aristocracy: if every one opposes at his pleasure, it is no government, it is anarchy and confusion.

In some parts of the Commonwealth, it is frequently said, if our Representative goes to Court, he will do us no service; for the measures he is in favour of, will not be adopted: but why will they not be adopted? Every measure that is proposed, is attended to, and considered; and if finally rejected, it is because the majority think it inexpedient; and how absurd and contradictory would the proceedings of the Court be, if every proposition should be acceeded to.

The complaints in different parts of the State are repugnant, and petitions from different places, request measures directly opposite; it is impossible therefore, that all should be gratified: what then shall be done? Unless we submit to be controuled by the greater number, the Commonwealth must break in pieces. . . .

It is even said by some, that a new constitution is necessary; and although the sentiments of the persons, who complain, are opposite on this point, the subject may demand some attention. . . .

We have but lately heard that the Senate has been thought by any one to be a grievance; if it has been so considered, we think it must have been owing to inattention; for we are convinced that every judicious man who attends to the nature of our government, will consider that as an important and necessary branch of the Legislature. . . .

The constitution is as free and popular as the preservation of society will admit; and indeed some have feared, it is more so: it has been highly applauded by foreigners and approved by the people: all persons employed in the legislative or executive parts of government, depend annually upon the people for their choice; if the people are dissatisfied with their conduct, they have an opportunity yearly to appoint others, in whom they can more fully confide. Can there be any necessity then, of resorting to irregular, or violent measures, to obtain redress of grievances?

That the people are overburthened with taxes is said to be a grievance: the taxes have indeed been very great; perhaps the General Court have misjudged of the abilities of their constituents, but it may be that those who complain, if they knew the state of the public debt, and the motives of the Legislature, would be satisfied. . . .

Public credit is one of the most important trusts committed to the Legislature; in proportion as that declines, the State is weakened and in danger. It is of the same importance to a community, as a character for truth is to individuals. The want of a paper currency has been complained of as a grievance; but . . . a little attention to the subject, we conceive, must satisfy every intelligent and unprejudiced mind, that the emission of such a currency would be exceedingly prejudicial. If it could be carried into circulation, the solid coin would be exported, the morals of the people would become more depraved, designing men would practice innumerable frauds; and if it should ever afterwards be redeemed, it would plunge the State in deeper distress: If it should not be redeemed, it would cause the ruin of many individuals, and brand the State with infamy. And upon whom would that ruin fall? Not upon the artful and unprincipled, they would gain by the fraud; not upon the prudent and discerning, they would be guarded against it; but the loss would chiefly happen to the widow and the orphan, the simple and unwary; the most innocent and defenceless part of the community; that part, whose interests the Legislature ought to defend with peculiar attention. The widow and orphan are the special charge of the Supreme Being, and all are enjoined to exercise vigilance and tenderness for their welfare. This injunction every man, possessed of natural affections, must feel the force of; for who can tell how soon his wife and his children may fall a prey to sharpers and speculators, if a paper money system shall be adopted. . . .

We feel in common with our neighbours the scarcity of money; but is not this scarcity owing to our own folly? At the close of the war, there was no complaint of it; since that time, our fields have yielded their increase, and heaven has showered its blessings on us, in uncommon abundance; but are we not constrained to allow, that immense sums have been expended, for what is of no value, for the gewgaws imported from Europe, and the more pernicious produce of the West-Indies; and the dread of a paper currency impedes the circulation of what remains: It is said however, that such a currency would give us present relief; but like the pleasure of sin, it would be but for a season; and like that too, it would be a reproach to the community, and would produce calamities without end. . . .

Within a few years the habits of luxury have exceedingly increased, the usual manufactures of the country have been little attended to. That we can buy goods cheaper than we can make them, is often repeated, and is even become a maxim in economy, altho' a most absurd and destructive one. . . .

Without a reformation of manners, we can have little hope to prosper in our public or private concerns. At the close of the war we greedily adopted the luxurious modes of foreign nations. Although our country abounds with all the necessaries of life, the importations from abroad, for our own consumption, have been almost beyond calculation; we have indulged ourselves in fantastical and expensive fashions and intemperate living; by these means our property has been lessened and immense sums in specie have been exported. Government is complained of, as if they had devoured them; and the cry of many persons now is, make us paper money. This request is next in point of imprudence, to that of the Israelites to Aaron, to make them a calf; and a compliance would be but a little more honorable or advantageous, in the one case, than it was in the other.

As the difficulty in paying debts increased, a disregard to honesty, justice and good faith, in public and private transactions become more manifest. That virtue, which is necessary to support a Republic, has declined; and as a people, we are now in the precise channel, in which the liberty of States has generally been swallowed up. But still our case is not desperate; by recurring to the principles of integrity and public spirit, and the practice of industry, sobriety, economy, and fidelity in contracts, and by acquiescing in laws necessary for the public good, the impending ruin may be averted, and we become respectable and happy.—By such means, we may falsify the invidious predictions our enemies, that we should crumble to pieces, and should be too corrupt to maintain republican freedom. In such a cause we may hope, that the God of our fathers, who has defended us hitherto, will prosper the work of his own hands, and save the fair structure of American liberty from falling into ruin. . . .

When the people are distressed with the conduct of any government, it may at least deserve a reflection, whether the difficulty is not with themselves. At the last election in this State, perhaps a greater number of new Members were returned, than at any former period; they came together with a fixed design, to gratify their constituents, in every thing which the interest of the community would permit; and they never lost sight of that object; notwithstanding which, greater dissatisfaction with public measures is expressed at this time, than ever before since the revolution. The Legislature have attended to all the petitions that have been presented, and all the complaints that have been made; so far as justice will allow, they will comply with the requests in those petitions and remove the grounds of those complaints. . . .

The General Court have heard with inexpressible concern, of the insurrections in several counties of the State. The pretence that the Court of Common Pleas, is a grievance, affords but a wretched excuse for such outrageous proceedings; that Court, except a small alteration in the name, has existed time immemorial; no complaints were heard against it in former times; no application has been made to the Legislature before this session to abolish it. . . . But if the Court of Common Pleas has been by any supposed unnecessary, how surprizing then, the idea, that any persons could think themselves justified, in opposing by force, an ancient institution, without taking a single step to obtain redress in a regular method. But not content with obstructing the Courts of Common Pleas, the disaffected have taken arms to prevent the sitting of the Supreme Judicial Court, against which, not a single complaint has been uttered. These proceedings are the more alarming, as they can be accounted for, only on the supposition, that the instigators wish to subvert all order and government, and reduce the Commonwealth, to the most deplorable state of wretchedness and contempt.

In this view, our situation appears exceedingly alarming; sufficiently so, to arrest the most serious attention, and summon the united efforts, of all orders in the State. Some persons have artfully affected to make a distinction between the government and people, as though their interests were different and even opposite; but we presume, the good sense of our constituents will discern the deceit and falsity of those insinuations. Within a few months the authority delegated to us will cease, and all the citizens will be equally candidates in a future election; we are therefore no more interested to preserve the constitution and support the government, than others; but while the authority given us continues, we are bound to exercise it for the benefit of our constituents. And we now call upon persons of all ranks and characters to exert themselves for the public safety. Upon the Ministers of religion, that they inculcate upon the minds of their people, the principles of justice and public virtue; that they earnestly endeavour to impress them with sentiments of reverence to the Deity and benevolence to men, and convince them of the ruinous effects of luxury and licentiousness. Upon the officers of every denomination, that they endeavour to inform the ignorant; and by their examples of economy, to induce others to the practice of the same virtue; and that they use their utmost efforts to suppress the insurrections of such lawless and violent men, as may wish to pull down the fabric of law and government, and level it with the dust. And upon the whole body of the people, that they provide for the instruction of the rising generation; that they practice all those virtues which are the ornament and strength of society, and abstain from those vices and follies, that weaken the State, and have a tendency to its ruin; and especially that they oppose with fortitude and perserverance, all attempts to impede the course of justice and render their own lives and property insecure.

Many who disapprove insurrections against the government, neglect to afford their aid, in suppressing them; but to stand still, inactive spectators in such case, is like a man who when his house is in flames, should stand with folded arms, and console himself with this, that he did not set it on fire.

We persuade ourselves, that the far greater part of those who have been concerned in the late dangerous tumults, have been deluded by the false representations of men who go about to deceive; and we wish them to reflect how fatal such proceedings may prove in the issue, to themselves and their children; that they must increase the public burthens, and embarrass the measures calculated for relief; that it is their own constitution and laws they are endeavouring to overthrow; that this constitution and these laws were formed for the safety of every member of the State; and that the man who attempts to subvert those laws, and that constitution, does in effect make an attempt upon the life, liberty and property of every member of the community; and we conjure them, by all that they hold dear and sacred, forthwith to desist from such ruinous pursuits.

Perhaps there are some, who deaf to the voice of reason, and lost to all sense of justice and virtue, may resolve to continue in their dangerous course; but let them be assured, although they flatter themselves that the considerations of friendship and affinity, may delay the time of recompence; yet the vengeance of an injured community, must one day, pursue and overtake them.

The first essay in this section by the Pulitzer Prize–winning Stanford University professor, Jack N. Rakove, analyzes the national political issues of the 1780s. In the article, Rakove explains why reformers turned from piecemeal, incremental reform of the Articles of Confederation to their replacement by a new constitutional scheme. He emphasizes the false starts and frustrations of national politics in the 1780s that led reformers, who were more pragmatic than ideological, to their eventual Constitutional convention strategy. The second essay, by Professor John L. Brooke of Tufts University, tackles local and state politics during the 1780s in Massachusetts. Questions of Congress, western lands, and overseas trade were much less important to Massachusetts citizens than access to local public officials and a responsive state tax and justice system. Although Massachusetts people ultimately resolved their problems themselves, the unrest that climaxed in Shays's Rebellion was an important catalyst for constitutional reform.

American Federalism Before the Constitution

JACK N. RAKOVE

At the close of the Revolutionary War, many problems and prospects confronted Americans eager to redirect their attention to private pursuits too long constrained by the burdens of a protracted war—to the restoration of old line of commerce and the opening of new markets, to the extension of settlements both north and south of the Ohio River, and to a host of other concerns. But few of these matters constituted an agenda, unfinished or otherwise, in any strict sense of the term, a docket of proposals awaiting action by responsible authorities or concerned parties. . . . After eight years of war and economic dislocation, Americans were too exhausted to do much more than put their own affairs, too long neglected, in order.

The one area in which the literal concept of an agenda does have an obvious relevance, however, [was] . . . the amendment of the Articles of Confederation. For from 1781 on, those who actively sought to strengthen the national government were forced to think in quite specific terms about just which further powers Congress needed, and which ones it was most likely to obtain. They had to ask, too, how the adoption or rejection of one proposal would affect the fate of other. Above all, they had to calculate how best to surmount the two obstacles that stood in the way of the adoption of any amendment: the preliminary hurdle of creating a substantial consensus within Congress, and the greater barrier of securing unanimous ratification by the states. Far more than was the case at the state level of politics, where the task of correcting the errors incorporated in the first constitutions seemed open-ended, reform of the confederation could proceed only through the pursuit of a carefully delineated agenda. So at least it seemed to James Madison, the most thoughtful and eventually the most influential of these reformers, and to the relatively small circle of like-minded men who shared his interest in national political problems.

From Jack P. Greene, ed., *The American Revolution: Its Character and Limits,* pp. 80–103. Copyright © 1987. Reprinted by permission of New York University Press.

But did the agenda that they were pursuing in the mid-1780s anticipate the transformation of the federal system that would begin to unfold with the Constitutional Convention of 1787? Since many leading Federalists had been seeking to amend the Articles of Confederation for some time, much of the historiography of the Revolution has treated the events of 1787–88 as the culmination of a struggle that had begun a decade earlier, when "radical" proponents of state sovereignty had vanquished "conservative" supporters of effective national power in the drafting of the first state constitutions and the Articles of Confederation. That criticisms of the Articles were being voiced even before they were finally ratified certainly implies that they received less than a fair trial. . . . No sooner did the Articles go into operation than Congress began appointing a series of committees charged with considering what additional amendments and powers were necessary to discharge its responsibilities effectively. Madison himself was a member of the first of these committees, whose report proposed authorizing the union to use force against states that failed to meet their "federal engagements" for men, money, and supplies. Six years later, he was still agonizing over the same issue.

Other telling similarities seem to link the various amendments discussed in the early 1780s and the actual changes the framers of the Constitution either effected or at least contemplated. The idea of holding a constitutional convention was itself broached as early as 1780. Even more striking, many historians believe, is the connection between the financial measures that Robert Morris urged Congress to adopt in 1782–83, and the comprehensive program that Hamilton later pursued, with greater success, as Secretary of the Treasury. This nationalist upsurge failed when heavy-handed tactics and the coming of peace prevented the adoption of the Morris proposals. But in 1787, with the economic dislocations of the mid-1780s and Shays' Rebellion providing a convenient foil, the Federalists won the final round.

Certainly there is much to be said for attempting to identify which leaders and which groups would have favored or opposed a stronger national government at any point after 1776. Yet this emphasis on continuity in alignments makes it difficult to perceive the abrupt shifts in both tactics and goals that distinguished the gradual and modest amendments considered before 1786 from the radical measures pursued in 1787. It also ignores the enormous intellectual leap that enabled the framers of the Constitution to link the familiar problems of federalism with more complex and open-ended questions about republican government in general. Now and again, in the surviving records of these earlier years, one can find a document that foreshadows the full range of concerns that would preoccupy the framers in 1787. But the historian who compares the actual debates at the Federal Convention with both the public and private discussions of the mid-1780s will be struck far more by their disparities than their similarities. By 1787, the framers of the Constitution could plausibly assume that their labors were meant to cure not only the palpable shortcomings of the Articles, but also the weaknesses of republican government within the states; many, like Madison and Hamilton, were even so bold as to believe that "we were now to decide for ever the fate of Republican Government." . . . Only in 1787 did it become possible to believe that the movement to strengthen the confederation might address issues more fundamental than the mere augmentation of the powers of Congress.

What happened in 1787, then, was that one agenda was abandoned and another, both more innovative and expansive, substituted in its place. This transformation did not require the framers of the Constitution to cast themselves as the belated victors in a long struggle against their less enlightened predecessors, but it was a transformation nonetheless. One of the great challenges inherent in explaining the making of the Constitution is thus to understand how the prosaic debates of the mid-1780s could give way to the enthusiasms of 1787–88. . . .

At the close of the Revolutionary War, the allocation of authority between Congress and the states constituted an unfinished agenda in at least two senses of the term. The first and more obvious set of problems arose from gaps between the broad responsibilities that had been delegated to Congress and the circumscribed powers with which it had to exercise its duties. Its most conspicuous weaknesses had become apparent during the final years of the war, when the states had proved incapable of raising the full quotas of men, money, and supplies that Congress had requisitioned. . . . The first years of peace revealed comparable problems in the realm of foreign affairs and in the management of the national domain, over which Congress had acquired effective title by 1784. National defense, foreign relations, and the development of the West were the three great responsibilities that were generally conceded to belong to Congress. . . . Yet in each of these areas the actual authority that Congress could exercise fell well short of what it needed. Most of the additional Articles that were proposed or merely discussed before 1786 were designed not to enhance its role but simply to enable it to operate within its alloted sphere.

But the federal agenda was unfinished in a second and more basic sense. In 1783, few were prepared to say just what additional functions could be safely or appropriately delegated to a national government. Would a confederation originally framed to deal with the exigencies of a revolutionary war prove adequate for a nation that, having gained its independence, was now evidently poised for a process of internal development and westward expansion? In 1777, more than a few members of Congress may have privately agreed, with Thomas Burke, that the drafting of the Articles was best delayed until war's end. But other considerations had compelled them to complete a recognizably imperfect plan of confederation. Few then would have claimed that the Articles had been framed with an eye turned to the long-term development of the republic. Political exigencies had led its framers to establish a fairly simple division of authority between Congress and the states. Congress was given broad control over the conduct of war and foreign affairs, while the states were left responsible for almost everything that could be lumped under the broad heading of "internal police." Efforts to vest Congress with broad constitutional authority over Western lands had been decisively turned back by a bloc of "landed" states, led by Virginia, anxious to preserve their claims to vast expanses of territory lying beyond the existing perimeter of settlement. Congress received nothing more than the most carefully hedged authority over territorial matters, even though leaders of both landed and landless states understood that federal regulation of the American interior would ultimately prove necessary. In other matters of domestic concern—most notably commerce—the powers of Congress were so circumscribed as to be rendered nugatory.

Suppose, then, that the members of Congress had sat down in the summer of 1783. . . .

What items would have appeared under the first heading of "unfinished business"? The principal federal concern in the summer of 1783, without doubt, was to see the states adopt the revenue plan that Congress had approved on April 18, 1783, following months of furious politicking marked by the threats and cajolings of Superintendent of Finance Morris and rumors of unrest (and worse) emanating from the army. . . . The comprehensive plan of April 1783 had three major elements: an impost lasting twenty-five years, to be collected by officials appointed by the states; a call upon the states to appropriate supplemental taxes for the payment of federal obligations; and a revision in Article 8 of the Confederation, altering the formula for apportioning the common expenses of the war among the states.

Robert Morris had sought far more. For almost a year he had conducted an aggressive campaign to convince Congress and interested parties "out-of-doors" that the union should be vested with authority to levy poll, land, and excise taxes as well as an impost. A few delegates, like the ideologue Arthur Lee of Virginia and David Howell of Rhode Island, opposed these measures—and the final compromise—out of a mixture of personal emnity against Morris and staunchly Whiggish convictions that liberty would be endangered if Congress enjoyed its own powers of taxation. "[N]o one who had ever opened a page or read a line on the subject of liberty," Lee declaimed, "could be insensible to the danger of surrendering the purse into the same hand which held the sword." . . .

The more telling objections against the Morris program were, in any case, political rather than ideological. Amendments to the Articles required the unanimous approval of the states, and after watching the original impost proposal of 1781 founder upon the lone opposition of Rhode Island, the delegates had no choice but to treat this condition with the utmost respect. A carefully framed compromise commanding the support of a substantial majority within Congress stood some reasonable chance of adoption by the states; a bolder and more controversial measure did not.

The idea that the states might be coaxed into approving a balanced and carefully explained compromise was not unrealistic. For in the second great item of unfinished business confronting Congress at war's end—the creation of a national domain northwest of the Ohio River—the delegates could have found some precedent for hoping that enlightened appeals could lead to the amicable adjustment of national and state interests. By agreeing to give Congress control over so vast an expanse of land, the states had indicated that it was not the financial autonomy of the union they objected to, but only a national power of taxation. Indeed, the same delegates who were most opposed to the idea of federal taxation on ideological grounds were first to exaggerate the windfall Congress would receive from the national domain. Transported by visions of the sale of millions of acres of land, they believed that its speedy exploitation would render schemes of taxation superfluous. . . . When Congress belatedly accepted the conditions that Virginia, the key landed state, had attached to its cession, the completion of this arduous process at last seemed at hand.

Read in this way, then, the tortuous politics of the Western lands issue seemed to provide a great and hopeful lesson in the possibilities of interstate cooperation. More than that . . . it illuminated what might be called necessities of federal government itself. For what the territorial controversies of the 1770s and 1780s revealed was that the individual states were hardly capable of exercising the panoply of sovereign rights with which they were presumably vested under both the Articles of Confederation and their own constitutions. They could neither secure their territorial limits—a minimal criterion of statehood—nor command the loyalty of all the communities lying within their claimed boundaries. Far from being the primordial sovereign units of which the union was composed, the individual states were themselves fragile governments whose authority was little less precarious than that of Congress. Individual states could hope to establish their legitimacy . . . only through a process of mutual recognition that presupposed the existence of a federal union. Federalism was thus the logical solution not only to problems involving demonstrably common interests, but also to the debilities of statehood itself.

That was not, however, the only way the controversy over Western lands could be read. Its value as a precedent for the resolution of other difficult issues was unclear. Key advantages that Congress had enjoyed in bringing this dispute to an acceptable conclusion might not be replicable on other issues. The creation of a national domain had required neither the unanimous acquiescence of the states nor approval of a formal amendment to the Confederation. Instead, Congress had proceeded *politically,* seeking individual cessions from the states with claims to the land in question. . . . In the end, the creation of the national domain was the result of a consensus to which the various parties to this dispute could subscribe. Whether similar agreement could be reached on other issues was, however, far from certain.

Revenue and land, then, were the two issues that headed the congressional agenda in 1783 and 1784. The relation between them was embarrassingly reciprocal. Congress was anxious to develop the national domain precisely because it saw the sale of these millions of acres of lands as a panacea for its financial woes, but its bankruptcy severely undermined its ability to settle the territory across the Ohio River in an orderly fashion. Congress was too poor both to maintain enough troops to restrain the frontiersmen who began spilling across the Ohio at war's end, and to afford to extinguish Indian claims to the lands in question through fair purchase. Instead, at the dictated treaties of Fort Stanwix (October 1784) and Fort McIntosh (January 1785), federal commissioners—including the intemperate Arthur Lee— followed congressional instructions and invoked a theory of conquest to justify dispossessing the four hostile tribes of the Iroquois and their allies to the west of their rights to the desired territory. These negotiations marked the beginning of the ill-advised policies that would lead to the Indian wars of the early 1790s.

North of the Ohio River, Congress had only itself to blame for the deteriorating relations with the Indian tribes. Further south its intentions were better, but here the course of Indian relations provided a revealing case study in the "defects" of the Articles of Confederation. No clause of the Articles appeared more baffling than that which pertained to Indian affairs. Article IX gave Congress the "sole and exclusive right and power of . . . regulating the trade and managing all affairs with the Indians, not members of any of the States, provided that the legislative right of any States within its own limits be not infringed or violated." A broad grant of authority was thus immediately compromised by two substantial qualifications. In 1783 and 1784, the ambiguity of this clause had sparked brief jurisdictional disputes between Congress and the states of New York and Pennsylvania, but once Congress acquired title to the Indian lands it sought, which lay beyond the claimed boundaries of either state, the basis for conflict evaporated. But there was no national domain south of the Ohio. Here North Carolina and Georgia were pursuing extremely aggressive policies designed to divest the Cherokees and Creeks of as much land as possible, and by adhering to a geographical definition of Indian "membership," they could plausibly claim to be exercising a valid "legislative right." Congress attempted to brake their policy in the Hopewell treaties of 1785–86, but by the summer of 1787, when war seemed imminent along the Southern frontier, Secretary of War Henry Knox and a congressional committee were forced to admit that effective federal jurisdiction could be created only if the Southern states completed cessions comparable to those that had led to the creation of the national domain.

Of course, by the summer of 1787, the state of Indian affairs either north or south provided little more than an incidental illustration of the "imbecility" of Congress and the shortcomings of the Articles of Confederation. Well before then, additional and more disturbing items had begun to appear on the agenda of unfinished business, as the pervasive transition from war to peace allowed state and regional interests to be asserted with a new candor. . . .

The most serious doubts about the adequacy of the Articles of Confederation arose within the realm of foreign affairs. Indeed, it was the inability of Congress to frame and implement adequate foreign policies in the mid-1780s that originally provided nationally minded politicians with the most compelling set of reasons for contemplating major constitutional reform. Whatever uncertainty might have existed about the domestic responsibilities of Congress, there was general agreement that the conduct of foreign relations was a federal concern. Because this was the case, the emerging foreign policy dilemmas of the mid-1780s were doubly disturbing. . . .

Within a year of the conclusion of peace, Congress confronted three external challenges to the national welfare. American merchants, eager to restore pre-Revolutionary patterns of commerce, found early cause for disappointment in the measures that Britain quickly took to close both home island and West Indian ports to American shipping. At the same time, a stream of British ships sailed into American harbors, bringing goods that had been sorely missed during the wartime years of deprivation. In theory, the United States should have pursued a retaliatory strategy of limiting British access to American ports until British harbors were opened to American shipping. But such a policy stood to fail on two counts. Lacking authority to regulate interstate or foreign commerce, Congress could neither devise nor impose a uniform set of restrictions on British ships. This *constitutional* debility in turn diminished whatever prospects there might have been for advancing American trading interests through the negotiation of a satisfactory commercial treaty with Britain: what privileges could John Adams, the American minister, offer that British merchants did not already enjoy?

The second great issue of foreign relations was an outgrowth of the Treaty of Paris that had brought the Revolutionary War to a close. Article IV of the treaty provided that "creditors on either side shall meet with no lawful impediment" to the recovery of debts previously contracted in good faith. Under Article V, Congress was required to *recommend* that the states similarly permit British subjects and American Loyalists to sue for the recovery of confiscated property. Both articles placed Congress in the awkward position of guaranteeing what it lacked the constitutional authority to deliver: the compliance of state legislatures and courts with a national commitment made to a foreign power. When individual states, not unexpectedly, failed to abide by the terms of the treaty, Britain used their noncompliance as a pretext for retaining the Northwestern forts (Oswego, Niagara, and Detroit) whose surrender had also been part of the treaty of peace. This in turn further jeopardized the entire congressional policy for the national domain, since a continued British presence in the Northwest encouraged the hostile Western tribes to resist American encroachments on their lands.

The future of westward expansion was also implicated in the third major problem of foreign policy to arise with the coming of peace. In April 1784, Spain closed New Orleans and the lower Mississippi River to American navigation, in effect preventing frontier settlers living west to the mountain barrier from shipping their produce to the Gulf of Mexico and thence to other markets. This action, coupled with abortive separatist efforts to establish new states in Kentucky and what would become Tennessee, threatened to deprive the United States of the generous territorial settlement accorded by the Treaty of Paris. Should the weakness of the union force Western settlers to accommodate themselves to Spain, control of the regions lying between the mountains and the Mississippi would be lost to the United States. Furthermore, since the region below the Ohio was commonly viewed as an outpost of *Southern* expansion, acquiescence in the Spanish action threatened to exacerbate sectional tensions within Congress. Southern leaders grew particularly outraged in 1786, when John Jay, the secretary of foreign affairs, went so far as to propose that the United States abjure its navigational rights in exchange for a commercial treaty with Spain. Jay's proposal evoked a sharp and bitter sectional division within Congress, giving sudden validity to hitherto vague speculations about the eventual devolution of the United States into two or three regional confederacies. . . .

Revenue, Western land, the protection of American commerce, and state violations of the Treaty of Paris: these were principal concerns of the relatively small group of leaders who supported the movement to strengthen the Articles of Confederation. Their ideas of what was desirable in theory did not transcend their awareness of what they hoped might prove feasible in practice. Their thoughts centered naturally on the specific additional powers that Congress would need if national interests were to be effectively asserted and national responsibilities effectively discharged. What was largely missing from their discussions and proposals was the larger array of concerns that we associate with the debates at the Constitutional Convention, with the Federalism of 1787–88, and with the central theory that even today arguably provides the dominant paradigm of American political science: James Madison's conception of the extended republic.

For the reformers of the mid-1780s were not thinking of using the amendment of the Confederation as a means for curing the vices of republican government within the states. Nor did their discussions more than incidentally consider the relevance of such aspects of constitutional theory as the separation of powers or the nature of representation to the existing problems of the union. The various amendments to the Articles that were proposed during these years did not anticipate the theoretical concerns that would acquire so prominent a place in the debates of 1787. They were designed, first and foremost, to free Congress from its dependence on the states, to enable it to resolve problems that fell within its existing sphere of responsibility. The improved conduct of national affairs, it was hoped, would gradually elevate the character of public life within the states as well, but that would be a secondary and deferred benefit. Concerns about what might be called the internal efficiency of Congress were similarly relegated for later consideration. . . .

It was not, of course, a lack of imagination or interest in issues of constitutional theory that discouraged efforts to conceive of the problem of federalism in terms that went beyond identifying the specific additional powers that Congress needed. Rather, all such matters were rendered merely speculative by the requirement that amendments to the Articles receive the unanimous ratification of the states. This was the first and dominant condition to which the supporters of a stronger federal union had to accede. Instead of contemplating the calling of a general convention, they pursued a prudent strategy of proposing discrete and limited amendments in the hope that their piecemeal adoption and implementation would make Americans less wary of the dangers of a more efficient national government. The desultory and ultimately fruitless histories of *all* the amendments that Congress had requested since 1781 indicated that proposals envisioning a more radical transfer of power from states to union stood little if any chance of adoption. . . .

To say that the nationally minded reformers of the mid-1780s had little reason to anticipate the larger theoretical problems that would confront the Federal Convention of 1787 does not mean, however, that such issues were not being considered in a different context. For at a lower level of politics, questions about the proper distribution of power among the branches of government and the obligations of representatives were becoming subjects of thoughtful controversy during these years. The experience of republican government within the states was indeed leading many to reconsider the validity of the assumptions of 1776. The most important and novel lessons that brought James Madison to fashion his doctrine of the extended republic were not, after all, those he had learned during his four years at Congress, but rather the result of the three succeeding years of frustration in the Virginia legislature. The basis for rethinking basic principles of republican government was being laid within the states; what was missing, until late 1786, was an occasion for recognizing that these lessons could be usefully or realistically applied to the problem of federalism.

This transposition became possible only when the abortive Annapolis Convention of September 1786 left the reformers with no other option than the risky gamble of a general constitutional assembly. The Annapolis meeting marked a final effort to salvage the strategy of piecemeal, gradual reform. It was called to consider the sole issue of commerce, and convened under the authority of the states to avoid the taint that would henceforth afflict any amendment emanating from Congress itself. The hopes underlying that strategy were exploded when the Annapolis Convention failed to muster the quorum needed to bestow weight on the amendment it was expected to propose. Rather than adjourn and admit that this final tactic had proved bankrupt, the handful of delegates present agreed to issue a call for a plenary convention to assemble the following spring. Their act was the work not of a group of political conspirators stealing a march on their slumbering opponents, but of likeminded men who had now realized that further caution carried no prospect of victory. The call issued by the Annapolis delegates was the result more of political desperation than anything else.

Desperation, it turned out, had its rewards. Now that the other alternatives for reform had been discredited—and once it became clear that a majority of states were responding favorably to the call—the very fact of the Convention became significant in its own right. With good reason, skeptics still doubted whether such a body could reach agreement on any set of proposals that stood a realistic chance of adoption. But others, especially those leaders aware of the extent of sectional tensions within Congress, sensed that they could no longer count upon enjoying an indefinite period of time for amending the Articles. During the nine months that separated the dispersion from Annapolis and the gathering at Philadelphia, it at last became both politically and intellectually possible to link the debilities of the union with the vices of republican government within the states.

No one illustrates this transition more dramatically or significantly than James Madison. Throughout the mid-1780s, Madison had been deeply committed to the strategy of piecemeal reform. In 1785 he had warned James Monroe, his replacement at Congress, against pursuing the idea of a general convention. By 1786, recognizing that any amendment emanating from Congress itself would be fatally tainted, he changed his mind and placed his hope in the meeting at Annapolis, but in doing so he still insisted on the need for gradual reform. Now, however, he set himself to the task of rethinking the entire problem of federal government, and in the paper he distilled from his researches—his pre-Convention memorandum on "The Vices of the Political System"—he forged an explicit link between federalism and republicanism. . . . [T]he establishment of an extended federal republic could serve to secure the great object of protecting individual liberty against the dangers it faced within the states. It would do so, first, by obstructing the formation of factious majorities intent on pursuing private interests in the guise of the public good, and second, by encouraging power to pass from the demagogues dominant at the state level of politics into the hands of a better class of men.

Some historians resist according so great an importance to the merely intellectual labors of Madison. Certainly had Shays's Rebellion and its aftermath in the Massachusetts elections of 1787 not provided impressive evidence in support of his thesis, his argument, by itself, might well have proved unavailing. Nor should we treat the Convention itself as a sort of referendum on Madison's theory; were we to do so, it would be difficult to claim that its logic had carried the day. Yet it would be wrong to dismiss the theory of the extended republic solely as a text in political philosophy. In at least one vital sense, its aims were immediate, pragmatic, and consciously designed to influence the politics of the Convention.

Madison had made it possible to cast the agenda of national reform in terms that went well beyond anything that had been seriously considered before the spring of 1787. . . . The Virginia Plan—which arguably was the next extension of his thought—did not assume that the Convention had to begin its work by identifying which additional powers the union needed. Instead, it presumed that the national government would receive a general grant of legislative authority, and moved ahead to ask how that government should be designed. It thus diverted the attention of the delegates away from the stock concerns of the mid-1780s, and forced them to begin to confront a range of issues that hitherto had not seemed pertinent to the context of national politics. Now lessons drawn from the experience of the states could be applied to the problems of the union, and serve, at the same time, as a generalized commentary on how a republican government, at any level of the polity, should be constituted. During the opening weeks of the Convention, it seemed less important to determine what role the federal government was actually to play in American life than to decide how it was to be organized and (of course) whom and what it would represent.

The irony of this situation is that the Convention could never have succeeded had contemporaries been able to grasp just how easily or sweepingly the standing agenda of the mid-1780s could be altered, had they foreseen just how far the Convention would be prepared to go. . . . Even Madison—the best prepared of the delegates—did not begin to pull his specific ideas together until March 1787; while the actual preparation of the Virginia Plan was only made possible by the failure of the Convention to muster a quorum on the appointed date of May 14, which gave the Virginians the time to frame their proposals. Against such a background, the intellectual task of bridging the gap between the limited proposals of the mid-1780s and the Federalist platform of 1787 proved too difficult for parochial leaders to perform—even if Patrick Henry did smell a rat. It was because the delegates came to Philadelphia largely unencumbered by instructions or binding positions that they were able to accept the Virginia Plan, in its full scope, as an appropriate framework for discussion.

There was, however, a second irony that would require decades rather than months to unveil. The shift in perspective that led the framers to focus on the architecture of government rather than its functions was, in a sense, a distraction. The Convention may well have come to believe that the entire future of republican government hinged on its debates. But the original concerns of the mid-1780s remained intact; at the core of the new government's powers one would still find the pre-eminent worries of the immediate postwar years: foreign affairs, commerce, and the disposition of Western lands. Whether it would have significant duties beyond these familiar areas seemed, by the later weeks of the Convention, to be very much of an open question. The rhetoric of the earlier weeks of conflict between the small and large states had led partisans on both sides to project the responsibilities of the new regime in exaggerated terms: if the new government were to be so powerful, one could argue with equal plausibility either that justice to the large states required a system of proportional representation in both houses, or that the security of the small states warranted giving them an equal vote in at least one chamber. Yet once this issue was surmounted, and passions had begun to cool, many delegates were even prepared to admit that the new government might not, after all, have that much to do. . . .

No one observing the operations of the federal government during much of the next century could have concluded that the Convention had in fact established a political leviathan. In the realm of what might be called public policy, its principal business remained consistent with the concerns that had comprised the unfinished agenda of national politics at the close of the Revolution; at the more prosaic level of daily activity, its most vital service, arguably, was the delivery of the mail. In many ways, the United States was not much less of a confederation in 1836, when Madison, the last of the framers, passed away, than it had been half a century earlier. The federal government remained, in John Murrin's phrase, "a midget institution in a giant land'—an establishment in which . . . "there were more people making the law than enforcing it." . . .

One is left to wonder whether the adoption of the Constitution owed more to the contingent political factors operating in 1786–88 than to any great structural imperatives demanding the establishment of a stronger union. Indeed, had the requirement of unanimous state ratification not obstructed every effort at reform, a good case could be made that the adoption of even one amendment to the Articles might have rendered the gradual process to which Madison and others were originally committed workable, permitting the United States to remain a confederation in name as well as substance. But the failure of all previous efforts at amendment, coupled with a sense of approaching crisis evoked by such events as Shays' Rebellion and the debate over the Mississippi, concentrated the minds of the delegates wonderfully, preparing them to entertain ides that might have been dismissed as either absurd or at least impracticable only months earlier.

In Massachusetts All Politics Was Local in the 1780s

JOHN L. BROOKE

The twin problems of public debt and a North Atlantic credit crisis made civil unrest inevitable throughout the Confederation. The stringent measures adopted by the Massachusetts General Court, at the insistence of creditor-merchant interests, made it likely that such unrest would be particularly intense in Massachusetts. However, while people throughout the commonwealth were concerned about the pressure of public and private debt, open rebellion against public institutions broke out only in certain places, most especially in Hampshire County. . . . [I]t was the collapse of institutional legitimacy, rather than simply high levels of economic distress, that provided the context for rebellion against the courts in that county in the 1780s. In turn, Hampshire's experience with conventions and armed insurgency in 1782 and 1783, rooted in prior revolutionary experience, established the precedent for the greater uprising against constitutional government in 1786. In short, the roots of Shays's Rebellion lay in great part in a failure of a revolutionary settlement of civil institutions unique to Hampshire County.

Most fundamentally, a revolution involves the transformation of governing regimes; the stable structure of constitutional framework and civil institutions that is the outcome of such a transformation may be termed a revolutionary settlement. To endure, such a settlement must be accepted as legitimate and noncontroversial. In the American Revolutionary experience, the appeal to popular sovereignty in the constitution-making process, building on political traditions that had developed over the colonial era, required that this legitimacy rest, not in raw power, but in a broad consensus concerning the authority of institutions. The concept of a revolutionary settlement shaped contemporary views and historical interpretations of the entire period between 1776 and 1789 and into the early republic. Most obviously, the dissatisfaction with the Articles of Confederation among a broad coalition fueled demands for an overarching national revolutionary settlement, resulting in the

John L. Brooke, "In Massachusetts All Politics Was Local in the 1780s." Reprinted by permission of *William and Mary Quarterly*.

Constitutional Convention of 1787. Despite widespread suspicions of the convention and its product, the federal Constitution rapidly became the ground for the national revolutionary settlement that endured for seven decades before it collapsed under the contradictions posed by the existence of chattel slavery.

But in 1782 there was no such national framework; revolutionary settlements resided in the various state constitutions and governments, most dramatically manifested in the states' separate responsibilities for the war debt. And as the events of the 1780s in Hampshire County clearly suggest, revolutionary settlements also depended on more local circumstances. The conclusion of the revolutionary process, and the restoration of the routine operation of institutions, also required the minimal fulfillment of popular expectations regarding the transformation of local structures of power and authority.

Such expectations were deeply rooted in the provincial experience of Massachusetts. The men who marched with Samuel Ely and Daniel Shays were acting out of conflict of institutions that had lurked just below the surface of Massachusetts politics since the establishment of the 1691 charter. . . . In both 1782 and 1786, insurgents drew upon the example of the formative events of the Revolutionary crisis of 1774, when the demands of county conventions that the royal courts be closed were executed by militias throughout the province. During the crises of the 1780s the configuration of economy, civil institutions, and ideology that had shaped Revolutionary beginnings was still very much in place. People in Massachusetts towns wanted justice from local, rather than distant, courts; neighbors holding state commissions could act in judicial capacities at far less cost than county magnates. Corruption and ruin had been feared in 1774; in 1782 and 1786 they seemed a reality. Anxieties about "slavery" and "lordships" that had been so powerful in 1774 reappeared in the language of the Regulators. In 1774, 1782, and 1786 there was the same fear that an unaccountable provincial bureaucracy reaching down into the county courts would be the agent of impoverishment, stratification, and a progressive erosion of household independence, the social basis of the republican experiment.

In many places the events of the 1770s reshaped and relegitimized the institutional fabric of the county courts. But these years brought no viable countywide revolutionary settlement to the broad valley and hills of Hampshire, and progress toward such a settlement was only halting and selective during the 1780s. The failure of such a settlement was a primary cause of the civil unrest that culminated in Shays's Rebellion. To the west and east, Berkshire and Worcester counties achieved settlements that deflected popular unease under proportionately greater burdens of public or private debt, and mitigated the confrontation of men and institutions in Shays's Rebellion, when armed uprisings spread far beyond the bounds of Hampshire County. Furthermore, these distinct revolutionary histories and settlements of county institutions played a central role in the politics of the federal constitutional ratifying convention and the first elections for federal representatives. Paradoxically, the partial resolution of Hampshire County's institutional problems in a section of the western hill towns ensured the critical margin for ratification at the Massachusetts constitutional convention in 1788; here the uneven progress of a county revolutionary settlement played a pivotal role in the broader national settlement. [E]xamining the local circumstances of political mobilization in these three counties from the 1760s through

1789 . . . may encourage historians to temper their use of broad, regional categories with some attention to the specific local arenas, compounded of class, institutions, and political tradition, which shaped the civil life of the young republic.

The first obvious signs of Hampshire County's controversy with the common-wealth were two county conventions in the spring of 1782, . . . [the first convention complained] of the governor's salary and the cost of the courts. . . . [T]he convention advocated the transferal of a host of administrative functions from the county courts to the towns. The convention's final resolve was its most controversial: it requested that "the laws in civil matters," with the exception of those relating to taxation, be suspended until the people were "redressed relative to the foregoing grievances." A more moderate convention of thirty-seven towns meeting in Hatfield on the following April 9 rejected this resolve, . . . but this convention nonetheless voted that the Court of General Sessions was a wasteful expense and should be dissolved. . . . The votes against the courts by the Hadley and Hatfield conventions provided the authority for [Samuel] Ely's insurrection against the Court of Common Pleas at Northampton. On April 4, 1782, Ely sent a circular letter through the Hampshire towns declaring that "the court was going contrary to the mind of the convention" and summoning the people to action. Eight days later, he led a crowd against the court, with threats to knock off the justices' gray wigs and "send them out of the World in an instant."

For the next two months Hampshire County endured civil war, as bodies of militia and Regulators parried, hostages were exchanged, and court and jail at Northampton were besieged. . . . While the courts attempted to meet under the constitution, conventions of town committees criticized the courts' procedures and their very existence. On the authority of those conventions, towns raised militias to regulate the courts. The direct action of the people out-of-doors, in conventions and armed assemblies led by local notables, was substituted for an unresponsive legislative process. Representing an alternative sovereignty to the constituted government of Massachusetts, the conventions and assemblies gave evidence that the Revolution was not over in Hampshire County. Four years later, Ely's Rebellion would be replicated on a grander scale in Shays's Rebellion, when, across the three counties of western Massachusetts, as well as Middlesex and Bristol to the east, conventions would draw up petitions that set the stage for Regulators to close the courts as a means of forcing a legislative redress of grievances. In both episodes, the institutions of constituted government clashed with the institutions of a corporate politics of "the body of the people."

The disturbances in Hampshire County in 1782 and the years following were not paralleled in the other two western Massachusetts counties. . . . Conventions of towns met in Hampshire on at least twenty occasions between 1781 and 1786, and Shays's Rebellion began in Northampton, when 1,500 men closed the Court of Common Pleas on August 29 [1786]. It was on Hampshire's model of the preceding four years that Regulators in Berkshire, Worcester, Middlesex, and Bristol challenged their county courts. The following January, Hampshire County was the scene of the most dramatic moments of the rebellion, as state troops at the Springfield arsenal fired on the Regulators led by Daniel Shays. . . .

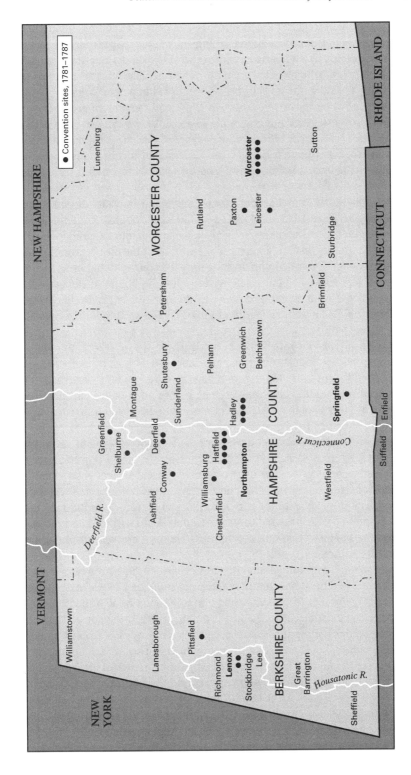

Convention sites, 1781–1787

However, with regard to the critical issues of public and private debt, the circumstances of unrest and rebellion in Hampshire County seem curious on close examination, at least by comparison with some of the other counties. . . . [A]nalysis of the . . . cases of debt appealed from the common pleas where the debtor failed to appear—suggests that the level of private debt in Hampshire County was only half that of either Worcester or Middlesex in 1782, and the pattern grew stronger over the following years. . . . [F]igures for the cases prosecuted in the Court of Common Pleas between 1784 and 1786 similarly suggest that the burden of debt was far heavier in Worcester than in Hampshire. . . . None of this economic evidence provides obvious reasons for Hampshire County's role in the civil disturbances leading up to the Regulation of 1786.

Thus debt alone cannot account for the particular intensity of unrest in Hampshire County between 1782 and 1786 or for the local patterns of mobilization in the western counties. . . . The failure to arrive at an acceptable reconfiguration of town and county authority, in combination with the crisis of the post-Revolutionary economy, set the stage for armed uprisings against the constitutional order. As much as the pervasive pressure of public and private debt, the failure to achieve an acceptable revolutionary settlement of county institutions in Hampshire played a critical role in shaping the tumultuous politics of the 1780s in western Massachusetts.

Before we can consider revolutionary settlements, we must look to revolutionary beginnings, and before that to provincial political traditions. If revolutionary settlements shaped the response to the economic crisis, they in turn were shaped by very different political traditions developed long before the Revolution, and by the very different ways in which these Massachusetts counties moved from royal to popular authority in and after 1774.

Two provincial political cultures cast long shadows over the Revolutionary struggle in western Massachusetts. The Popular party had a powerful presence in the Worcester countryside, but it was virtually absent to the west, where the old Court-faction elite dominated the courts, legislative politics, and the mercantile economy. The Popular tradition provided the ground for a smooth transition from royal to popular sovereignty in Worcester County and facilitated a satisfactory revolutionary settlement of county institutions. Things were very different in Hampshire and Berkshire. . . .

The roots of Worcester Popular tradition lay in the currency disputes of the 1730s, manifested most concretely in the Land Bank of 1740–1741. A scheme advanced by the Popular leadership in Boston to base an issue of private bank notes on mortgaged lands, the Land Bank was enthusiastically supported in agricultural towns of Popular inclinations, most especially in Worcester County. . . . Popular party men outnumbered Court adherents by twenty-two to nine among the thirty-one Worcester deputies who either voted on partisan issues in the General Court in the 1760s. . . . In 1763, the government revived the bitter politics of currency by publishing a list of delinquent Land Bank mortgagees; Worcester had three times as many per population as the rest of the province. . . . The sons and nephews of Land Bankers served in the county conventions and provincial congresses in 1774 and 1775 and in the minute companies in April 1775.

Thus the Popular politics of currency shaped the patterns of Revolutionary mobilization in Worcester County. But when the crisis came to an end, the county courts were reestablished with little trouble by a block of experienced men. Of the twenty-two Popular partisans of the 1760s, seven were appointed to the reconstituted county court system in the winter of 1775. Four of these new justices drawn from the old Popular men, including Artemas Ward, had served as royal justices; few in number, they were symptomatic of broader patterns, and they provided a key element of institutional and political continuity across the Revolutionary transition.

Such a group was utterly missing . . . in old Hampshire and Berkshire counties. The Connecticut Valley had long been under the political and economic domination of an intermarried cluster of great families known as the River Gods, closely tied to the Court interest, who began to extend their power . . . in the 1730s in what in 1761 became Berkshire County. In the partisan sparring of the 1760s, four Popular men were outnumbered by nineteen Court adherents among the representatives serving from Hampshire and Berkshire. . . . Two Country partisans from . . . Hampshire County played a role in the establishment of Revolutionary government, serving in the 1774 house and the provincial congresses, and receiving appointments to the judiciary in the winter of 1775–1776. But neither of these men had served among the royal justices, and they were counterbalanced among the Revolutionary placeholders by two royal justices who had stood with the Court in the 1760s. . . . The absence of a group of leaders with experience in the Popular tradition in Berkshire and Hampshire would have profound consequences.

The key to the local power of the Court party gentry of provincial Hampshire lay in their monopoly of judicial placeholding "in the form of a close corporation." . . . [A]lmost three-quarters of the county officials serving in Hampshire between 1731 and 1760 were close relations of one of a half dozen River God families. Equally important, the placeholders were highly concentrated along the Connecticut River and in the Housatonic Valley, severely limiting access to relatively cheap local justice for the people of the outlying towns. In 1774, roughly 65 percent of the people of Hampshire County and 45 percent of Berkshire County lived in towns without a resident justice of the peace. In sharp contrast, even though Worcester County had a roughly similar ratio of justices to population, its placeholders were far more widely distributed; in 1774 only 25 percent of the county's people lived in towns without a local justice.

Here, then, lay the markings of an early and satisfactory revolutionary settlement in Worcester County and the failure of such a settlement in Hampshire and Berkshire. Except for the removal of the small group of elite tory placeholders, Worcester moved through the Revolutionary transition with remarkable stability. By contrast, neither Hampshire nor Berkshire experienced such continuity. . . .

In short, the Revolution came to Worcester County in an orderly fashion, led by old Popular men and by the county convention. To the west the Revolution brought chaos; with the old Court elite splintered and broken, no effective group of leaders emerged from the conventions of 1774 and 1775. These histories diverged still more sharply and strikingly in 1775 and 1776, when county courts were reestablished by the General Court.

In Worcester County the process was again a smooth one; fifteen of the thirty-one new justices had served under royal commissions, and eighteen had served in the county convention or the provincial congresses. The sitting of the Worcester courts was adjourned by the legislature in 1778 but otherwise never challenged until September 1786. . . .

In Berkshire County, events followed a strikingly different path toward a roughly similar outcome. . . . Inspired by a Lockean natural rights rhetoric drawn from the writings of Thomas Paine and Richard Price, and articulated by the Reverend Thomas Allen of Pittsfield, the people of central Berkshire rose to stop the Court of Quarter Sessions in February 1776. The 1778 plan for the legislature to write a constitution further fueled the Constitutionalist cause. Berkshire voted in convention to keep the courts closed and to demand a constitutional convention. In 1779 a crowd acting on the authority of another county convention stopped the Superior Court session planned for Great Barrington. In all, four conventions met in Berkshire between December 1775 and May 1779 to ratify popular opposition to the courts and demands for a popular constitution.

The Lockean politics of Constitutionalism was rooted in Berkshire's relative lack of history and tradition. Berkshire was a new frontier; its people were for the most part indifferent to the established traditions of provincial Massachusetts. Sparsely populated by the 1760s along the Housatonic River, the county grew by 500 percent between 1765 and 1776. The old placeholding elite was located in southern towns settled before the French and Indian War; the Constitutionalists dominated in the newly settled but very fertile towns of the upper valley. . . . [L]eading Constitutionalists were not poor, struggling debtors. Rather, they were an emergent elite for whom the Revolution was an opportunity to destroy the power of the Court party gentry of the south county towns. Many of Berkshire's people were recent arrivals from Connecticut and Rhode Island who had no particular allegiance to the Massachusetts charter; they were often inclined toward religious dissent. . . . Constitutionalism in Berkshire sprang from conscious hostility to ancient ways in Massachusetts.

The Berkshire Constitutionalists were successful in keeping the courts closed until 1780. With the establishment of a new framework of authority, their leadership moved to gain control of the court system. . . . And in a dramatic move, unique in confederation-era Massachusetts, the Constitutionalists managed to have the town of Lenox established as the county seat, superseding the older south county towns of Stockbridge and Great Barrington. With this coup, the Constitutionalists moved to reshape the county's institutional geography and to establish the symbolic basis of a new political order.

As in Worcester County, the number of justices elected to the legislature in the 1780s indicates the success of Berkshire's revolutionary settlement and an acceptance of the newly legitimized county institutions. . . . Berkshire sent the highest proportion of justices of all three western counties. In this electoral endorsement of the county's justices, Berkshire County arrived at a revolutionary settlement on the surface not unlike that of Worcester.

Things were significantly different in Hampshire. . . . The share of Hampshire justices in town representation was the lowest of the three western counties, and roughly half that of Berkshire, an indication that they had not achieved the public acceptance that their counterparts enjoyed in the other two counties.

The dwindling role of Hampshire's placeholders as representatives was an important symptom of a public crisis specific to that county. In both Worcester and Berkshire the action of conventions, articulating the priorities of Popular and Constitutionalist politics, brought accommodation between elites and broad segments of the county electorate. But no such accommodation was reached in Hampshire. . . .

Discontent with the court system was expressed throughout the returns of the Hampshire towns to the proposed state constitutions of 1778 and 1780. In particular, the towns wanted local control of the justices of the peace. . . . Greenwich suggested the annual election of justices in each town, with town recording the probates and deeds. Ashfield in 1780 held that local election of justices was "the Natural Right of the Commonwealth." In 1778 Belchertown argued that such local control of the justices was "agreeable to the spirit of Liberty". . . .

Belchertown's formula reflected a widespread concern with the continuing inaccessibility of justice in the Hampshire court system. . . . By the mid-1780s the ratio of justices to population in Hampshire County had risen only slightly and placeholders were still strikingly concentrated: just under 50 percent of the people lived in towns without resident justices, especially in the towns of the eastern hills. In sharp contrast, the judicial system was becoming more accessible in Berkshire and Worcester. The population per justice ratio in these two counties was dropping, quite dramatically in Berkshire, and only 13 percent of each county's population lived in towns lacking resident justices. . . . Hampshire saw nothing like the accommodation of people and institutions evident in Worcester and Berkshire.

The economic crisis that preceded Shays's Rebellion was rooted in a disordered revolutionary economy. . . .

The people of western Massachusetts responded to this economic pressure in very different ways. Rather than expressing the sentiments of a single, coherent region, the local initiatives, convention politics, and legislative voting of the late 1770s and early 1780s all reflected the sharply divergent provincial traditions and Revolutionary histories of the western counties. Worcester County stood out in its consistent and sophisticated attention to the complex fiscal affairs that dominated the state's politics. Rooted in a Popular tradition running back to the 1730s, Worcester's united opposition to the creditor interests in convention and legislature built a consensus between leadership and electorate that survived the turmoil of the rebellion of 1786. In Berkshire, the workings of Lockean Constitutionalism militated against a corporate politics of conventions, and the county's representatives sided not with the opposition but with the creditor forces in the General Court. The result was a growing division within the county and a particularly bitter confrontation in 1786. In Hampshire, a proliferation of conventions focused on the problems of local institutions, in some cases directly challenging the courts, in others seeking reform. . . .

The point should be plain: the smooth continuity of Worcester County's early Revolutionary settlement carried with it a deeply rooted county tradition of support for paper money, economic regulation, and public accountability. This was a tradition nurtured among a broad stratum of county leaders in the Popular faction in the decade before the Revolution. Far from being backward-looking subsistence farmers, they were men with an eye to commercial possibilities. But neither were they rural embodiments of Adam Smith; they would have utterly rejected a vision of an economy of disassociated private interests. Their world view was structured by traditional expectations of corporate mutuality and obligation. . . . This Popular tradition of public meetings, fiscal oversight, and paper money provided a common ground for public debate and discourse in Worcester that was utterly absent in the counties to the west. The action in this common political arena, combined with a relatively acceptable court system, worked to contain civil unrest in the county with the highest rate of public and private debt in the entire commonwealth.

The convention politics in Hampshire County had a drastically different character. Rather than the issues of currency and expenditure that dominated the agenda in Worcester County, the Hampshire conventions were overwhelmingly concerned with the structure of county institutions. . . .

Time and again, . . . Hampshire conventions complained about the jurisdiction of the Court of General Sessions and the operation of the registry of deeds and the probate court. . . . Overall, before the August 1786 convention at Hatfield, which may well have been influenced by the attention to fiscal matters so prominent in Worcester, the Hampshire conventions voted roughly twice as many resolves regarding county institutions as fiscal issues.

Berkshire County had significantly higher levels of actions for personal debt, and discontent was brewing below the surface, as indicated in the bitter language of Robert Karson, a Richmond yeoman convicted in 1782 for cursing the court as a "damned pack of rascals" and swearing that he wanted "to kill a Judge or a Lawyer." Yet neither legislative nor convention politics provided any outlet for rising tensions. . . . The county's leading men took seriously the contractual theory of society and government. In their thinking, the county had acted legitimately in convention during the state of nature lasting from the Declaration of Independence in 1776 to the ratification of the state constitution in 1780. But now that the constitution had restored a state of society, the Constitutionalists' Lockean political culture worked to discourage traditional meetings of the people in their corporate capacity.

When rebellion erupted in the fall of 1786, triggered by a new round of taxes, it was shaped and conditioned by these three county histories, these very different movements through the Revolutionary experience. Suppressing any corporate politics, liberal Berkshire County was a powder keg waiting to explode; here the Regulation was a desperate class war between haves and have nots. In Hampshire, divisions between the county elite and the discontented were rooted in the proliferation of conventions rather than their absence, and reflected the overarching problem of a failed revolutionary settlement. Here a continuing interaction between conventions and Regulators between 1782 and 1786 structured the core of the county's opposition. In Worcester, the Popular tradition fed both moderation and mediation when rebellion finally broke out in the most heavily burdened county in the commonwealth.

With few conventions meeting, and the county's representatives voting as often as not with the creditor forces in the legislature, Berkshire had few public outlets for political opposition during the 1780s. Similarly, when a convention did meet in

Lenox in August 1786 to consider the impending crisis, it voiced decidedly pro-government opinions, supporting the current tax system and the grants made to the Congress, opposing any paper money proposal, and pledging to support the courts. With the friends of government firmly in control of public forums, Berkshire's Regulators were politically isolated: the rebellion there took on an especially violent, polarized character. . . . [I]t resembled an extended guerrilla war, particularly in the Regulators' winter march from New Lebanon, New York, through Stockbridge, sacking the mansions of the old Court party gentry, to the final skirmish in Sheffield. Even after this showdown, insurgents staged hit-and-run raids on the property of county notables—real social banditry—and as late as October 1787 a crowd ran through Great Barrington cheering for Shays.

Court records indicate that the Berkshire insurgents lacked support among men of local standing and that the courts hounded them unmercifully. Among men listed in state warrants, imprisoned, or formally indicated for insurrection by the Supreme Judicial Court, fewer than 20 percent in Berkshire County were gentlemen or militia officers, as compared to 60 percent in subsequently Antifederalist Worcester towns and more than 90 percent in Antifederalist Hampshire towns. While the courts in Hampshire and Worcester aimed at men of some local stature, the Berkshire courts indicted large numbers of laborers and yeomen. . . . It is telling that the only executions in the wake of the rebellion—the hangings of John Bly and Charles Rose for burglary at Lenox in December 1787—took place in Berkshire. Witnessed by hundreds of assembled militiamen, including some from Regulator hilltowns, these executions were a means by which a shaken Berkshire elite attempted to reassert its newly established—and violently challenged—public authority.

By contrast, conventions and Regulation were fundamentally linked in Hampshire County. . . . Conventions there were increasingly the domain of men of local experience and the vehicle of protest against a highly self-conscious valley elite. They were intertwined with Regulator mobilization, first with the Hadley and Hatfield conventions of 1782, second in the Springfield court closing of 1783, and most dramatically in the events of August 1786. Almost 40 percent of the convention delegates from Antifederalist towns can be identified as supporting the Regulation. . . . There was also a continuity between the crowd actions of 1782–1783 and participation in Shays's Rebellion. At least a third of the men indicted for rioting against the courts in Hampshire in 1782–1783 later were to be found among the Shaysite ranks.

In Worcester County there was a different line of demarcation, expressed most succinctly by Josiah Walker of Sturbridge when he refused his election as captain of the Regulators in 1786 because "he was a Convention man." There appears to have been a distinct division between two levels of leadership in Worcester—a county gentry who served in the legislature and the conventions, and a group of town leaders who would lead the Regulators. The delegates to the conventions of 1781–1784 at Worcester typically had experience in the legislature but were far less likely to be drawn into the Regulation. As in Hampshire, the Regulator leaders in Worcester were men of more local experience; they were often selectmen or militia officers but few had served as representatives. The Worcester Regulator leadership was thus broadly similar to it counterparts in Hampshire and seems to have followed their example. . . .

While civil violence did break out in Worcester County, it was at least miti- gated by the Popular tradition and the county's revolutionary settlement. This county political culture was manifested in the Regulators' tolerance of Artemas Ward's speech at the Worcester court closing in September and again in the Regu- lators' restraint in Worcester that December, when, in sharp contrast to the "plun- dering insurgents" of Berkshire, they strictly avoided commandeering supplies while occupying the court town. At the same time, county gentry of Popular and convention experience made strenuous efforts to mediate between the Regulators and the government force commanded by Gen. Benjamin Lincoln. . . .

Levels of public and private debt certainly played a role in the mobilization of 1786, but political contexts were equally important. The Regulation gained the strongest support in places, particularly in Hampshire County, where there were few local justices and, more generally, where the population had been effectively disfranchised in the late provincial period. Lacking the right of direct representa- tion, the people of these towns had to defer to the authority of the Court faction placeholders in the dominant towns in their region; their political experience above the level of the town was truncated and stifled. In Hampshire County, their Revolu- tionary experience had been one of continuing struggle with an unresponsive court system and of resort to the direct action of convention and riot for political expres- sion. This political mode was well established in Pelham, the town that gained the reputation of being the center of the Regulation. . . . Pelham had a long history of civil violence against the county elite, rioting against a sheriff in 1762, marching on Hatfield in February 1775 to smoke Justice Israel Williams into submission, and the next day threatening to give the same treatment to Solomon Stoddard of Northampton, son of Justice John Stoddard and a leading creditor in the county. Action against the courts in 1786 was thus part of a continuous tradition of direct action among a people for whom the provincial public culture manifested in place- holding and representation had been alien and inaccessible.

Within the broader pattern of Regulator mobilization in outlying districts in old Court party regions, the revolutionary settlement in the west Hampshire hills provides the exception that proves the rule. Here the expansion of the judicial sys- tem seems to have turned a region that might well have been a Regulator strong- hold decisively toward the government. In Hampshire County, Regulator towns were concentrated in the eastern hills and in towns where justices had not been ap- pointed by 1786. But in the western hills there were a surprising number of towns where militia captains were able to raise small companies to defend the courts. In 1786, these conflicted western towns differed from the Regulator towns of the east- ern hills less in their level of overdue taxes (64 percent vs. 87 percent) than in the presence of local justices (64 percent vs. 25 percent). In 1776 many of these western hilltowns had voted to keep the courts closed, acting on the encouragement of Con- stitutionalist Thomas Allen. But by 1782 almost two-thirds of these towns had been granted local justices, and their delegates voted in the Hatfield convention of April 1782 against closing the courts. It was in these same towns that militia cap- tains were able to raise companies for the government in 1786–1787. By contrast, in eight of the older hilltowns to the east where no resident justices had been appointed by 1782, no such pro-government notables emerged; including Shays's hometown of Pelham, these towns composed the epicenter of the Regulation. The progress toward a revolutionary settlement in the west Hampshire hilltowns would have even more dramatic results over the next two years.

The final episodes in this political drama were acted out in the state convention called to ratify the federal Constitution in January 1788 and in the first election of federal representatives, which began the following December. These events brought the closure of the national revolutionary settlement and the beginning of a routine national politics. Once again, the pattern of sentiment expressed in this convention and this election reflected the distinct political histories of the three counties and was decisively conditioned by local revolutionary outcomes.

Worcester's Popular consensus reemerged after Shays's Rebellion and left its permanent record at the ratifying convention. The county's delegates cast an overwhelming 86 percent vote (forty-three to seven) against ratification, the strongest Antifederalist vote in the commonwealth. Men of the Revolutionary generation and of countywide stature led this majority, in sharp contrast to the still-divided counties to the west. Seven of the eight Worcester delegates who had served in the Provincial Congress of 1774–1775 voted against ratification, the exact opposite of Hampshire delegates. Justices and "esquires" from Worcester County opposed the Constitution, six to two; those from the west favored it, twelve to three. All three states senators from Worcester opposed ratification; every senator from Berkshire and Hampshire voted for it. One of the Worcester senators at the convention was Amos Singletary of Sutton, long a leading figure in a town where the Popular tradition was deeply rooted, a Land Bank stronghold, and the storm center of convention politics from 1777 through 1786. Warning the convention that "moneyed men" intended "to be managers of this Constitution" and "swallow up all us little folks, like the great leviathan," Singletary's speech against federal powers of taxation has survived as the essential voice of grass-roots Antifederalism. . . .

To the west, roughly two-thirds of the towns in Berkshire and Hampshire opposed the Constitution. Berkshire's vote apparently hinged on a reaction to the efforts to suppress the Regulation, because its 68 percent Antifederalist vote (fifteen to seven) was a significant departure from its legislative voting record of most of the preceding decade. Very obscure men were elected delegates in a number of important towns, and the protests from Williamstown, Great Barrington, and Sheffield against the procedures by which Federalist delegates were elected may have turned men against ratification. Such was the case in Hampshire County, where the delegates from Deerfield and Conway announced after the convention that they had planned to vote in favor of the Constitution but had voted with the opposition to protest "insults" to Antifederalist delegates. Nonetheless, the 63 percent vote for the Constitution by Hampshire delegates (thirty-three to nineteen) was decisive to its passage.

Delegates from the older Hampshire towns along the river voted predictably for ratification, but the critical margin came from the western hilltowns. To a startling degree, Massachusetts's ratification of the Constitution depended on the gradual progress of a revolutionary settlement of county institutions in these hinterland localities. This story centered in the town of Chesterfield, which had taken the lead in the Constitutionalist initiatives of 1776, voting with a narrow majority against the justices acting under a commission in the king's name. Among the men active on committees in the years following, Benjamin Mills was appointed justice of the peace by 1778, Luke Bonney, a Baptist and the town's delegate to the constitutional convention of 1779, raised a government company in January 1787, and his brother Benjamin, another committeeman, drew pay as a colonel. Benjamin Bonney chaired the August 1786 Hatfield convention and issued the call for the convention that met that November in Hadley—a convention that, among all the problems confronting the state, resolved only that the location of the probate courts was a grievance. This complaint had been voiced by Samuel Ely, by the 1782 Hadley convention, and by numerous town resolves, and it finally received attention. It was addressed the following March, when the General Court established four registries of deeds and four sittings of the probate court at Deerfield, Northampton, Hadley, and Springfield. Ten months later, Benjamin Bonney and nine other delegates from small towns in the west Hampshire hills voted to ratify the Constitution.

If these towns had followed the example of their neighbors in Deerfield and Conway, of the east Hampshire hill towns, or of Worcester County, the Constitution might well not have been ratified in Massachusetts. As it was, the Federalists won by a margin of only nineteen votes, 187 to 168. If the ten Federalist delegates from the west Hampshire hills had turned against the Constitution, the vote would have stood at 177 to 178. Given the crucial position of the Massachusetts vote in the entire ratification process, it may fairly be said that the selective settlement of county institutions in Hampshire County played a decisive role in the far grander national revolutionary settlement. The pace of this settlement of county institutions meant that Massachusetts stood poised between two very different outcomes. On the one hand, a more rapid appointment of local justices in the 1770s and early 1780s might well have diffused some of the discontent among local notables that resulted in conventions and regulation. On the other, a slower process might have meant that fewer pro-government leaders would have emerged in the west Hampshire hills, that the Regulation would have been less contested in this region, and that the vote on the Constitution would have been far closer, perhaps even reversed. . . .

The interweaving of local circumstance and national revolutionary process outlined here was by no means unique to western Massachusetts. The history of the confederated states in the 1770s and 1780s was a compound of hundreds of such dramas, as the workings of revolutionary settlements in neighborhoods, towns, and counties established the ground for a decision on the final national settlement of 1787–1788. Some of the more critical of these local dramas are well known. . . . [F]our critical votes for the razor-thin (thirty to twenty-seven) ratification of the federal Constitution in New York State were cast by delegates from the freeholding sections of Dutchess County, popular whig leaders who had played a mediating role between the opposing coalitions of a conservative Livingston faction and the former tenants of dispossessed tory landlords. In Virginia, Baptist insurgency against the establishment, culminating in the disestablishment of the Anglican church in 1785 and a powerful revival in 1787–1789, decisively shaped the call for a federal Bill of Rights. In the same years the county courts in Virginia, long a bastion of traditional gentry authority, were reformed by the legislature under the leadership of James Madison. In Orange County, Madison's long-term support of dissenters' rights must have played an important role in his election to the ratifying convention; it certainly was critical to his election to the first United States Congress. If Virginia saw a negotiated revolutionary settlement and relatively little civil violence in the 1780s, Pennsylvania's oddly convulsive constitutional history contributed to its western counties' challenge to the national constitutional settlement in the Whiskey Rebellion of 1793–1794. The rapidity with which the Federalists moved on the Constitution sparked a riot in Carlisle and provoked western Antifederalists to meet in convention in Harrisburg to protest the powers of new federal inferior courts. In Westmoreland County a committee of correspondence mobilized sentiment against the Constitution; five years later, men throughout Westmoreland and neighboring Washington counties rose against the new government's excise and the authority of its distant courts.

The unique element in western Massachusetts's passage through the revolutionary process was the degree to which the settlement of state and county institutions was challenged by civil disorder in the 1780s. Certainly, economic conflict shaped this political crisis. But mobilization in legislature, convention, regulation, and election was powerfully conditioned by the specific political and institutional histories of the western counties. These histories, compounded of provincial traditions, Revolutionary beginnings, and revolutionary settlements, shaped the public arenas in which people engaged in political discourse and action. These public arenas, which determined the circumstances of everyday economic life, were contested territories, but contested in very different ways. In each county a different history shaped a different mosaic of relations among placeholders, legislators, convention delegates, local notables of town and neighborhood, and ordinary householders—a mosaic that responded in quite different ways to the growing pressure of public and private debt. In Berkshire, a fragile settlement based on liberal Lockean principles was shattered; in Worcester, an ongoing process of communication within a well-established political tradition mitigated the crisis; in Hampshire, the failure of elites to accommodate popular expectations for revolutionary change brought a collapse of institutional legitimacy. Local men, responding to popular grievances, mobilized in a manner that challenged the sovereign power of the new state. As nowhere else in the newly sovereign states in the 1780s, revolutionary expectations in Hampshire County clashed with persistent elite formations. But everywhere in these newly sovereign states, local histories of conflict and accommodation, flowing from varying compounds of political culture and structural circumstance, linked locality to the national revolutionary settlement.

FURTHER READING

Willi Paul Adams, *The First American Constitutions: Republican Ideology and the Making of the State Constitutions in the Revolutionary Era* (1980)

Richard Beeman, Stephen Botein, and Edward C. Carter II, eds., *Beyond Confederation: Origins of the Constitution and American National Identity* (1987)

John L. Brooke, *The Heart of the Commonwealth: Society and Political Culture in Worcester County, Massachusetts, 1713–1861* (1989)

Christopher Clark, *The Roots of Rural Capitalism: Western Massachusetts, 1780–1860* (1990)

Jacob Ernest Cooke, *Alexander Hamilton* (1982)

Edward Countryman, *A People in Revolution: The American Revolution and Political Society in New York, 1760–1790* (1981)

Philip A. Crowl, *Maryland During and After the Revolution: A Political and Economic Study* (1943)

Elisha P. Douglas, *Rebels and Democrats: The Struggle for Equal Political Rights and Majority Rule During the American Revolution* (1955)

James E. Ferguson, *The Power of the Purse: A History of American Public Finance, 1776–1790* (1961)

Robert A. Gross, ed., *In Debt to Shays: The Legacy of an Agrarian Rebellion* (1991)

———, *The Minutemen and Their World* (1976)

Van Beck Hall, *Politics Without Parties: Massachusetts, 1780–1791* (1972)

H. James Henderson, *Party Politics in the Continental Congress* (1974)

Ronald Hoffman and Peter J. Albert, eds., *Sovereign States in an Age of Uncertainty* (1982)

Reginald Horsman, *The Frontier in the Formative Years, 1783–1815* (1970)

Merrill Jensen, *The New Nation: A History of the United States During the Confederation, 1781–1789* (1950)

Ralph Ketcham, *James Madison: A Biography* (1971)

Leonard W. Levy and Dennis J. Mahoney, eds., *The Framing and Ratification of the Constitution* (1987)

Donald S. Lutz, *Popular Consent and Popular Control: Whig Political Theory in the Early State Constitutions* (1980)

McCormick, *Experiment in Independence: New Jersey in the Critical Period, 1781–1789* (1950)

Forrest McDonald, *E Pluribus Unum: The Formation of the American Republic, 1776–1790* (1965)

———, *Novus Ordo Seclorum: The Intellectual Origins of the Constitution* (1985)

[Michael McGiffert, ed.], "The Creation of the American Republic, 1776–1787: A Symposium of Views and Reviews," *William and Mary Quarterly,* 3d Ser., 44 (1987), 549–640.

Andrew C. McLaughlin, *The Confederation and the Constitution, 1783–1789* (1905)

Jackson Turner Main, *Political Parties Before the Confederation* (1973)

———, *The Social Structure of Revolutionary America* (1965)

———, *The Sovereign States, 1775–1783* (1973)

———, *The Upper House in Revolutionary America* (1967)

James R. Morrill, *The Practice and Politics of Fiat Finance: North Carolina in the Confederation, 1783–1789* (1969)

Richard B. Morris, *The Forging of the Union, 1781–1789* (1987)

Allan Nevins, *The American States During and After the Revolution, 1775–1789* (1924)

Peter S. Onuf, *The Origins of the Federal Republic: Jurisdictional Controversies in the United States, 1775–1787* (1983)

———, "Reflections on the Founding: Constitutional Historiography in Bicentennial Perspective," *William and Mary Quarterly,* 3d Ser., 46 (1989), 341–375.

———, *Statehood and Union: A History of the Northwest Ordinance* (1987)

Jack N. Rakove, *The Beginnings of National Politics: An Interpretive History of the Continental Congress* (1979)

John Philip Reid, *Constitutional History of the American Revolution: The Authority of Rights* (1986)

Malcolm J. Rohrbough, *The Trans-Appalachian Frontier: People, Societies, and Institutions, 1775–1850* (1978)

Charles Page Smith, *James Wilson, Founding Father, 1742–1798* (1956)

David P. Szatmary, *Shays's Rebellion: The Making of an Agrarian Insurrection* (1980)

Alan Taylor, *Liberty Men and Great Proprietors: The Revolutionary Settlement on the Maine Frontier, 1760–1820* (1990)

Robert J. Taylor, *Western Massachusetts in the Revolution* (1954)

Alfred F. Young, *The Democratic-Republicans of New York: The Origins, 1763–1797* (1967)

Gordon S. Wood, *The Creation of the American Republic, 1776–1787* (1969)

CHAPTER
12

Making the
Constitution of 1787

The United States Constitution of 1787 is the oldest operating written constitution in
the world. It has been so often and so genuinely celebrated, and for so many generations, that it possesses the stature of a sacred text. In American civic culture, reverence
for the Constitution is a fundamental dogma that sustains the document's vitality.
For unlike a king or a military dictator, the Constitution commands no armies; it
compels obedience to its doctrines only through the force of public allegiance.

Veneration for the men who created the Constitution is a corollary of this positive preconditioning and is expressed in our designation of them as the founding
fathers. As with the document itself, it has been difficult to achieve a realistic and
balanced assessment of these political leaders. During much of the twentieth century,
ever since the publication in 1913 of Charles A. Beard's Economic Interpretation
of the Constitution, historians and textbooks have debated the heroic myth and
an unheroic antimyth. In the Beardian or Progressive interpretation, as in its neo-
Progressive successors, the Constitution has been described as the creation of practical, even selfish, politicians, men bent on forming a government to defend a
system of wealth and privilege in which they shared. Although this debate has
subsided in recent decades, it has taught us to recognize—as did the delegates to
the convention—that interests, especially those concerning money and power,
were ever present forces in politics, then as now. In addition, we have learned that
acknowledging the play of interests in the formation of the Constitution does not
deny the reality of public spirit and commitment to ideals of liberty. The mingling
of interests and idealism was critical to the Constitution's success.

Moreover, we have come to recognize that the design of the Constitution was a
contingent event. Not only was it not designed in heaven or by a band of demigods;
it was not even the preconceived plan of any one delegate or set of delegates. The
Constitution that the framers sent on to Congress in September 1787 resulted from
a three-month negotiation and debate in which possibilities were tested, rejected,
and then revised and adjusted according to the changing perspectives of various
delegates. No one who signed the Constitution saw it as perfect, but all hoped that
it would be good enough to serve the material and political interests of their own
state and region, as well as the United States.

D O C U M E N T S

James Madison was the most important individual in shaping the collective achievement known as the Constitution of 1787. The thirty-six-year-old Virginia delegate made an influential analysis of the defects of the Confederation and its interaction with the state governments in a private memorandum that he circulated among his colleagues and that appears below as Document 1. In his essay "Vices of the Political System of the United States," Madison offered a view of the problem that supplied the starting point for the Virginia Plan. This plan, which is reproduced here as Document 2, was presented to the convention by the more senior Edmund Randolph, the Virginia governor. The plan became the foundation on which, with alterations, the delegates constructed the Constitution.

The Virginia Plan, which called for a national government that linked population and power, was challenged directly by the New Jersey Plan, Document 3. This plan offered a more limited revision of the Articles, one that retained the principle of equality among the states. The delegates debated these two plans (see Document 4) for a few days before laying aside the New Jersey Plan. Thereafter, they debated a wide range of topics. The selections comprising Document 5 treat democracy and the legislature, sectional interests and legislative apportionment, the qualifications for voters, and slavery and slave imports, and they provide only a sample of what went on. The fact that the debates were closed to the public—secret in fact—enabled the delegates to speak freely on controversial subjects. Document 6, the Constitution, is the product of all of the delegates.

1. James Madison on the Vices of the Political System of the United States, 1787

1. Failure of the States to Comply with the Constitutional Requisitions

This evil has been so fully experienced both during the war and since the peace, results so naturally from the number and independent authority of the States and has been so uniformly examplified in every similar Confederacy, that it may be considered as not less radically and permanently inherent in, than it is fatal to the object of, the present System.

2. Encroachments by the States on the Federal Authority

Examples of this are numerous and repetitions may be foreseen in almost every case where any favorite object of a State shall present a temptation. Among these examples are the wars and Treaties of Georgia with the Indians—The unlicensed compacts between Virginia and Maryland, and between Pena. & N. Jersey—the troops raised and to be kept up by Massts.

"James Madison on the Vices of the Political System of the United States, 1787." In James Madison, *The Writings of James Madison,* ed. Gaillard Hunt (New York, 1900–1910), vol. 2, pp. 361–369.

3. Violations of the Law of Nations and of Treaties

From the number of Legislatures, the sphere of life from which most of their members are taken, and the circumstances under which their legislative business is carried on, irregularities of this kind must frequently happen. Accordingly not a year has passed without instances of them in some one or other of the States. The Treaty of peace—the treaty with France—the treaty with Holland have each been violated. The causes of these irregularities must necessarily produce frequent violations of the law of nations in other respects. . . .

4. Trespasses of the States on the Rights of Each Other

These are alarming symptoms, and may be daily apprehended as we are admonished by daily experience. See the law of Virginia restricting foreign vessels to certain ports—of Maryland in favor of vessels belonging to her own citizens—of N. York in favor of the same.

Paper money, instalments of debts, occlusion of Courts, making property a legal tender, may likewise be deemed aggressions on the rights of other States. As the Citizens of every State aggregately taken stand more or less in the relation of Creditors or debtors, to the Citizens of every other States, Acts of the debtor State in favor of debtors, affect the Creditor State, in the same manner, as they do its own citizens who are relatively creditors towards other citizens. . . .

The practice of many States in restricting the commercial intercourse with other States, and putting their productions and manufactures on the same footing with those of foreign nations, though not contrary to the federal articles, is certainly adverse to the spirit of the Union, and tends to beget retaliating regulations, not less expensive & vexatious in themselves, than they are destructive of the general harmony.

5. Want of Concert in Matters Where Common Interest Requires It

This defect is strongly illustrated in the state of our commercial affairs. How much has the national dignity, interest, and revenue suffered from this cause? Instances of inferior moment are the want of uniformity in the laws concerning naturalization & literary property; of provision for national seminaries, for grants of incorporation for national purposes, for canals and other works of general utility, wch. may at present be defeated by the perverseness of particular States whose concurrence is necessary.

6. Want of Guaranty to the States of Their Constitutions and Laws Against Internal Violence

The confederation is silent on this point and therefore by the second article the hands of the federal authority are tied. According to Republican Theory, Right and power being both vested in the majority, are held to be synonimous. According to fact and experience a minority may in an appeal to force, be an overmatch for the majority. 1. If the minority happen to include all such as possess the skill and habits of military life, & such as possess the great pecuniary resources, one third only may conquer the remaining two thirds. 2. One third of those who participate in the choice of the rulers, may be rendered a majority by the accession of those whose poverty excludes them from a right of suffrage, and who for obvious reasons will be more likely to join the standard of sedition than that of the established Government. 3. Where slavery exists the republican Theory becomes still more fallacious.

7. Want of Sanction to the Laws, and of Coercion in the Government of the Confederacy

A sanction is essential to the idea of law, as coercion is to that of Government. The federal system being destitute of both, wants the great vital principles of a Political Cons[ti]tution. Under the form of such a Constitution, it is in fact nothing more than a treaty of amity of commerce and of alliance, between so many independent and Sovereign States. . . . It is no longer doubted that a unanimous and punctual obedience of 13 independent bodies, to the acts of the federal Government, ought not be calculated on. Even during the war, when external danger supplied in some degree the defect of legal & coercive sanctions, how imperfectly did the States fulfil their obligations to the Union? In time of peace, we see already what is to be expected. . . .

8. Want of Ratification by the People of the Articles of Confederation

In some of the States the Confederation is recognized by, and forms a part of the constitution. In others however it has received no other sanction than that of the Legislative authority. From this defect two evils result: 1. Whenever a law of a State happens to be repugnant to an act of Congress, particularly when the latter is of posterior date to the former, it will be at least questionable whether the latter must not prevail; and as the question must be decided by the Tribunals of the State, they will be most likely to lean on the side of the State.

2. As far as the Union of the States is to be regarded as a league of sovereign powers, and not as a political Constitution by virtue of which they are become one sovereign power, so far it seems to follow from the doctrine of compacts, that a breach of any of the articles of the confederation by any of the parties to it, absolves the other parties from their respective obligations, and gives them a right if they chuse to exert it, of dissolving the Union altogether.

9. Multiplicity of Laws in the Several States

In developing the evils which viciate the political system of the U.S. it is proper to include those which are found within the States individually, as well as those which directly affect the States collectively, since the former class have an indirect influence on the general malady and must not be overlooked in forming a compleat remedy. Among the evils then of our situation may well be ranked the multiplicity of laws from which no State is exempt. . . .

10. Mutability of the Laws of the States

This evil is intimately connected with the former yet deserves a distinct notice as it emphatically denotes a vicious legislation. We daily see laws repealed or superseded, before any trial can have been made of their merits; and even before a knowledge of them can have reached the remoter districts within which they were to operate. In the regulations of trade this instability becomes a snare not only to our citizens but to foreigners also.

11. Injustice of the Laws of States

If the multiplicity and mutability of laws prove a want of wisdom, their injustice betrays a defect still more alarming: more alarming not merely because it is a greater evil in itself, but because it brings more into question the fundamental principle of republican Government, that the majority who rule in such Governments, are the safest Guardians both of public Good and of private rights. To what causes is this evil to be ascribed?

These causes lie

1. in the Representative bodies.
2. in the people themselves.

1. Representative appointments are sought from three motives. 1. ambition, 2. personal interest, 3. public good. Unhappily the two first are proved by experience to be most prevalent. Hence the candidates who feel them, particularly, the second, are most industrious, and most successful in pursuing their object: and forming often a majority in the legislative Councils, with interested views, contrary to the interest, and views, of their Constituents, join in a perfidious sacrifice of the latter to the former. A succeeding election it might be supposed, would displace the offenders, and repair the mischief. But how easily are base and selfish measures, masked by pretexts of public good and apparent expediency? How frequently will a repetition of the same arts and industry which succeeded in the first instance, again prevail on the unwary to misplace their confidence?

How frequently too will the honest but unenligh[t]ened representative be the dupe of a favorite leader, veiling his selfish views under the professions of public good, and varnishing his sophistical arguments with the glowing colours of popular eloquence?

2. A still more fatal if not more frequent cause lies among the people themselves. All civilized societies are divided into different interests and factions, as they happen to be creditors or debtors—Rich or poor—husbandmen, merchants or manufacturers—members of different religious sects—followers of different political leaders—inhabitants of different districts—owners of different kinds of property &c &c. In republican Government the majority however composed, ultimately give the law. Whenever therefore an apparent interest or common passion unites a majority what is to restrain them from unjust violations of the rights and interests of the minority, or of individuals? Three motives only 1. a prudent regard to their own good as involved in the general and permanent good of the Community. This consideration although of decisive weight in itself, is found by experience to be too often unheeded. It is too often forgotten, by nations as well as by individuals that honesty is the best policy. 2dly. respect for character. However strong this motive may be in individuals, it is considered as very insufficient to restrain them from injustice. In a multitude its efficacy is diminished in proportion to the number which is to share the praise or the blame. Besides, as it has reference to public opinion, which within a particular Society, is the opinion of the majority, the standard is fixed by those whose conduct is to be measured by it. The public opinion without the Society, will

be little respected by the people at large of any Country. Individuals of extended views, and of national pride, may bring the public proceedings to this standard, but the example will never be followed by the multitude. Is it to be imagined that an ordinary citizen or even an assemblyman of R. Island in estimating the policy of paper money, ever considered or cared in what light the measure would be viewed in France or Holland; or even in Massts or Connect.? It was a sufficient temptation to both that it was for their interest: it was a sufficient sanction to the latter that it was popular in the State; to the former that it was so in the neighbourhood. 3dly. will Religion the only remaining motive be a sufficient restraint? It is not pretended to be such on men individually considered. Will its effect be greater on them considered in an aggregate view? quite the reverse. The conduct of every popular assembly acting on oath, the strongest of religious Ties, proves that individuals join without remorse in acts, against which their consciences would revolt if proposed to them under the like sanction, separately in their closets. When indeed Religion is kindled into enthusiasm, its force like that of other passions, is increased by the sympathy of a multitude. But enthusiasm is only a temporary state of religion, and while it lasts will hardly be seen with pleasure at the helm of Government. Besides as religion in its coolest state, is not infallible, it may become a motive to oppression as well as a restraint from injustice. Place three individuals in a situation wherein the interest of each depends on the voice of the others, and give to two of them an interest opposed to the rights of the third? Will the latter be secure? The prudence of every man would shun the danger. The rules & forms of justice suppose & guard against it. Will two thousand in a like situation be less likely to encroach on the rights of one thousand? The contrary is witnessed by the notorious factions & oppressions which take place in corporate towns limited as the opportunities are, and in little republics when uncontrouled by apprehensions of external danger. If an enlargement of the sphere is found to lessen the insecurity of private rights, it is not because the impulse of a common interest or passion is less predominant in this case with the majority; but because a common interest or passion is less apt to be felt and the requisite combinations less easy to be formed by a great than by a small number. The Society becomes broken into a greater variety of interests, of pursuits, of passions, which check each other, whilst those who may feel a common sentiment have less opportunity of communication and concert. It may be inferred that the inconveniences of popular States contrary to the prevailing Theory, are in proportion not to the extent, but to the narrowness of their limits.

The great desideratum in Government is such a modification of the Sovereignty as will render it sufficiently neutral between the different interests and factions, to controul one part of the Society from invading the rights of another, and at the same time sufficiently controuled itself, from setting up an interest adverse to that of the whole Society. In absolute Monarchies, the prince is sufficiently neutral towards his subjects, but frequently sacrifices their happiness to his ambition or his avarice. In small Republics, the sovereign will is sufficiently controuled from such a Sacrifice of the entire Society, but is not sufficiently neutral towards the parts composing it. As a limited Monarchy tempers the evils of an absolute one; so an extensive Republic meliorates the administration of a small Republic.

An auxiliary desideratum for the melioration of the Republican form is such a process of elections as will most certainly extract from the mass of the Society the purest and noblest characters which it contains; such as will at once feel most strongly the proper motives to pursue the end of their appointment, and be most capable to devise the proper means of attaining it.

12. Impotence of the Laws of the States

[Madison's memorandum ends here.]

2. Edmund Randolph Presents the Virginia Plan, 1787*

Mr. Randolph then opened the main business. . . .

He then commented on the difficulty of the crisis, and the necessity of preventing the fulfilment of the prophecies of the American downfall.

He observed that in revising the federal system we ought to inquire (1) into the properties which such a government ought to possess, (2) the defects of the Confederation, (3) the danger of our situation, and (4) the remedy.

1. The character of such a government ought to secure (1) against foreign invasion; (2) against dissentions between members of the Union, or seditions in particular States; (3) to procure to the several States various blessings, of which an isolated situation was incapable; (4) to be able to defend itself against incroachment; and (5) to be paramount to the State Constitutions.

2. In speaking of the defects of the Confederation he professed a high respect for its authors, and considered them as having done all that patriots could do, in the then infancy of the science of constitutions and of confederacies. . . .

He then proceeded to enumerate the defects: (1) that the Confederation produced no security against foreign invasion; Congress not being permitted to prevent a war nor to support it by their own authority. . . . (2) That the fœderal government could not check the quarrels between States, nor a rebellion in any, not having constitutional power nor means to interpose according to the exigency. (3) That there were many advantages which the United States might acquire, which were not attainable under the Confederation—such as a productive impost, counteraction of the commercial regulations of other nations, pushing of commerce ad libitum, etc., etc. (4) That the fœderal government could not defend itself against incroachments from the States. (5) That it was not even paramount to the State Constitutions, ratified, as it was in many of the States.

3. He next reviewed the danger of our situation, and appealed to the sense of the best friends of the United States—the prospect of anarchy from the laxity of government everywhere; and to other considerations.

4. He then proceeded to the remedy; the basis of which he said must be the republican principle.

He proposed as conformable to his ideas the following resolutions, which he explained one by one.

---

* From James Madison's notes.

"Edmund Randolph Proposes the Virginia Plan, 1787." As found in Max Farrand, ed., *The Records of the Federal Convention of 1787* (New Haven: Yale University Press, 1937), vol. 1, pp. 20–23.

[Virginia Plan]

1. Resolved, that the Articles of Confederation ought to be so corrected and enlarged as to accomplish the objects proposed by their institution; namely, "common defence, security of liberty and general welfare."

2. Resolved therefore, that the rights of suffrage in the National Legislature ought to be proportioned to the quotas of contribution, or to the number of free inhabitants, as the one or the other rule may seem best in different cases.

3. Resolved, that the National Legislature ought to consist of two branches.

4. Resolved, that the members of the first branch of the National Legislature ought to be elected by the people of the several States every [blank] for the term of [blank]; to be of the age of [blank] years at least, to receive liberal stipends by which they may be compensated for the devotion of their time to the public service; to be ineligible to any office established by a particular State, or under the authority of the United States, except those peculiarly belonging to the functions of the first branch, during the term of service, and for the space of [blank] after its expiration; to be incapable of re-election for the space of [blank] after the expiration of their term of service, and to be subject to recall.

5. Resolved, that the members of the second branch of the National Legislature ought to be elected by those of the first, out of a proper number of persons nominated by the individual Legislatures, to be of the age of [blank] years at least; to hold their offices for a term sufficient to ensure their independence; to receive liberal stipends, by which they may be compensated for the devotion of their time to the public service; and to be ineligible to any office established by a particular State, or under the authority of the United States, except those peculiarly belonging to the functions of the second branch, during the term of service, and for the space of [blank] after the expiration thereof.

6. Resolved, that each branch ought to possess the right of originating Acts; that the National Legislature ought to be impowered to enjoy the legislative rights vested in Congress by the Confederation, and moreover to legislate in all cases to which the separate States are incompetent, or in which the harmony of the United States may be interrupted by the exercise of individual legislation; to negative all laws passed by the several States, contravening, in the opinion of the National Legislature the articles of Union; and to call forth the force of the Union against any member of the Union failing to fulfil its duty under the articles thereof.

7. Resolved, that a National Executive be instituted; to be chosen by the National Legislature for the term of [blank] years, to receive punctually at stated times, a fixed compensation for the services rendered, in which no increase nor diminution shall be made so as to affect the magistracy, existing at the time of increase or diminution, and to be ineligible a second time; and that besides a general authority to execute the national laws, it ought to enjoy the executive rights vested in Congress by the Confederation.

8. Resolved, that the Executive and a convenient number of the National Judiciary, ought to compose a Council of Revision with authority to examine every Act of the National Legislature before it shall operate, and every Act of a particular Legislature before a negative thereon shall be final; and that the dissent of the said Council shall amount to a rejection, unless the Act of the National Legislature be

again passed, or that of a particular Legislature be again negatived by [blank] of the members of each branch.

9. Resolved, that a National Judiciary be established to consist of one or more supreme tribunals, and of inferior tribunals to be chosen by the National Legislature, to hold their offices during good behaviour; and to receive punctually at stated times fixed compensation for their services, in which no increase or diminution shall be made so as to affect the persons actually in office at the time of such increase or diminution. That the jurisdiction of the inferior tribunals shall be to hear and determine in the first instance, and of the supreme tribunal to hear and determine in the dernier resort, all piracies and felonies on the high seas, captures from an enemy, cases in which foreigners or citizens of other States applying to such jurisdictions may be interested, or which respect the collection of the national revenue; impeachments of any National officers, and questions which may involve the national peace and harmony.

10. Resolved, that provision ought to be made for the admission of States lawfully arising within the limits of the United States, whether from a voluntary junction of government and territory or otherwise, with the consent of a number of voices in the National Legislature less than the whole.

11. Resolved, that a republican government and the territory of each State, except in the instance of a voluntary junction of Government and territory, ought to be guarantied by the United States to each State.

12. Resolved, that provision ought to be made for the continuance of Congress and their authorities and privileges, until a given day after the reform of the articles of Union shall be adopted, and for the completion of all their engagements.

13. Resolved, that provision ought to be made for the amendment of the Articles of Union whensoever it shall seem necessary, and that the assent of the National Legislature ought not to be required thereto.

14. Resolved, that the legislative, executive and judiciary powers within the several States ought to be bound by oath to support the articles of Union.

15. Resolved, that the amendments which shall be offered to the Confederation by the Convention, ought at a proper time or times, after the approbation of Congress, to be submitted to an assembly or assemblies of representatives recommended by the several Legislatures to be expressly chosen by the people, to consider and decide thereon.

3. William Patterson Proposes the New Jersey Plan, 1787

Mr. Patterson, laid before the Convention the plan which he said several of the deputations wished to be substituted in place of that proposed by Mr. Randolph. . . :

1. Resolved, that the articles of Confederation ought to be so revised, corrected & enlarged, as to render the federal Constitution adequate to the exigencies of Government, & the preservation of the Union.

"William Patterson Proposes the New Jersey Plan, 1787." As found in Max Farrand, ed., *The Records of the Federal Convention of 1787* (New Haven: Yale University Press, 1937), vol. 1, pp. 242–246.

2. Resolved, that in addition to the powers vested in the U. States in Congress, by the present existing articles of Confederation, they be authorized to pass acts for raising a revenue, by levying a duty or duties on all goods or merchandizes of foreign growth or manufacture, imported into any part of the U. States, by Stamps on paper, vellum or parchment, and by a postage on all letters or packages passing through the general post-office, to be applied to such federal purposes as they shall deem proper & expedient; to make rules & regulations for the collection thereof; and the same from time to time, to alter & amend in such manner as they shall think proper: to pass Acts for the regulation of trade & commerce as well with foreign nations as with each other: provided that all punishments, fines, forfeitures & penalties to be incurred for contravening such acts rules and regulations shall be adjudged by the Common law Judiciaries of the State in which any offence contrary to the true intent & meaning of such Acts rules & regulations shall have been committed or perpetrated, . . . subject nevertheless, for the correction of all errors, both in law & fact in rendering Judgment, to an appeal to the Judiciary of the U. States.

3. Resolved, that whenever requisitions shall be necessary, instead of the rule for making requisitions mentioned in the articles of Confederation, the United States in Congress be authorized to make such requisitions in proportion to the whole number of white & other free citizens & inhabitants of every age sex and condition including those bound to servitude for a term of years & three fifths of all other persons not comprehended in the foregoing description, except Indians not paying taxes; that if such requisitions be not complied with, in the time specified therein, to direct the collection thereof in the non complying States & for that purpose to devise and pass acts directing & authorizing the same; provided that none of the powers hereby vested in the U. States in Congress shall be exercised without the consent of at least [blank] States, and in that proportion if the number of Confederated States should hereafter be increased or diminished.

4. Resolved, that the U. States in Congress be authorized to elect a federal Executive to consist of [blank] persons, to continue in office for the term of [blank] years, to receive punctually at stated times a fixed compensation for their services, in which no increase or diminution shall be made so as to affect the persons composing the Executive at the time of such increase or diminution, to be paid out of the federal treasury; to be incapable of holding any other office or appointment during their time of service and for [blank] years thereafter; to be ineligible a second time, & removeable by Congress on application by a majority of the Executives of the several States; that the Executives besides their general authority to execute the federal acts ought to appoint all federal officers not otherwise provided for, & to direct all military operations; provided that none of the persons composing the federal Executive shall on any occasion take command of any troops, so as personally to conduct any military enterprise as General or in other capacity.

5. Resolved, that a federal Judiciary be established to consist of a supreme Tribunal the Judges of which to be appointed by the Executive, & to hold their offices during good behaviour, to receive punctually at stated times a fixed compensation for their services in which no increase or diminution shall be made, so as to affect the persons actually in office at the time of such increase or diminution; that the Judiciary so established shall have authority to hear & determine in the first instance on all impeachments of federal officers, & by way of appeal in the dernier resort in all

cases touching the rights of Ambassadors, in all cases of captures from an enemy, in all cases of piracies & felonies on the high Seas, in all cases in which foreigners may be interested, in the construction of any treaty or treaties, or which may arise on any of the Acts for regulation of trade, or the collection of the federal Revenue: that none of the Judiciary shall during the time they remain in office be capable of receiving or holding any other office or appointment during their time of service, or for [blank] thereafter.

6. Resolved, that all Acts of the U. States in Congress made by virtue & in pursuance of the powers hereby & by the articles of Confederation vested in them, and all Treaties made & ratified under the authority of the U. States shall be the supreme law of the respective States so far forth as those Acts or Treaties shall relate to the said States or their Citizens, and that the Judiciary of the several States shall be bound thereby in their decisions, any thing in the respective laws of the Individual States to the contrary notwithstanding; and that if any State, or any body of men in any State shall oppose or prevent the carrying into execution such acts or treaties, the federal Executive shall be authorized to call forth the power of the Confederated States, or so much thereof as may be necessary to enforce and compel an obedience to such Acts, or an observance of such Treaties.

7. Resolved, that provision be made for the admission of new States into the Union.

8. Resolved, the rule for naturalization ought to be the same in every State.

9. Resolved, that a Citizen of one State committing an offense in another State of the Union, shall be deemed guilty of the same offense as if it had been committed by a Citizen of the State in which the offense was committed.

4. Congress Debates the New Jersey and Virginia Plans, 1787

Mr. Lansing called for the reading of the 1st resolution of each plan, which he considered as involving principles directly in contrast; that of Mr. Patterson says he sustains the sovereignty of the respective States, that of Mr. Randolph distroys it: the latter requires a negative on all the laws of the particular States; the former, only certain general powers for the general good. The plan of Mr. R. in short absorbs all power except what may be exercised in the little local matters of the States which are not objects worthy of the supreme cognizance. He grounded his preference of Mr. P.'s plan, chiefly on two objections against that of Mr. R. 1. want of power in the Convention to discuss & propose it. 2. the improbability of its being adopted.

1. He was decidedly of opinion that the power of the Convention was restrained to amendments of a federal nature, and having for their basis the Confederacy in being. The Act of Congress The tenor of the Acts of the States, the Commissions produced by the several deputations all proved this. And this limitation of the power to an amendment of the Confederacy, marked the opinion of the States, that

"The Convention Debates the New Jersey and Virginia Plans, 1787." As found in Max Farrand, ed., *The Records of the Federal Convention of 1787* (New Haven: Yale University Press, 1937), vol. 1, pp. 121–129.

it was unnecessary & improper to go farther. He was sure that this was the case with his State. N. York would never have concurred in sending deputies to the convention, if she had supposed the deliberations were to turn on a consolidation of the States, and a National Government.

2. was it probable that the States would adopt & ratify a scheme, which they had never authorized us to propose? and which so far exceeded what they regarded as sufficient? . . . The States will never feel a sufficient confidence in a general Government to give it a negative on their laws. The Scheme is itself totally novel. There is no parallel to it to be found. The authority of Congress is familiar to the people, and an augmentation of the powers of Congress will be readily approved by them.

Mr. Patterson, said as he had on a former occasion given his sentiments on the plan proposed by Mr. R. he would now avoiding repetition as much as possible give his reasons in favor of that proposed by himself. He preferred it because it accorded 1. with the powers of the Convention, 2. with the sentiments of the people. If the confederacy was radically wrong, let us return to our States, and obtain larger powers, not assume them of ourselves. . . . Our object is not such a Government as may be best in itself, but such a one as our Constituents have authorized us to prepare, and as they will approve. If we argue the matter on the supposition that no Confederacy at present exists, it can not be denied that all the States stand on the footing of equal sovereignty. All therefore must concur before any can be bound. If a proportional representation be right, why do we not vote so here? If we argue on the fact that a federal compact actually exists, and consult the articles of it we still find an equal Sovereignty to be the basis of it. He reads the 5th art: of the Confederation giving each State a vote—& the 13th declaring that no alteration shall be made without unanimous consent. This is the nature of all treaties. . . . It is urged that two branches in the Legislature are necessary. Why? for the purpose of a check. But the reason for the precaution is not applicable to this case. Within a particular State, where party heats prevail, such a check may be necessary. In such a body as Congress it is less necessary, and besides, the delegations of the different States are checks on each other. Do the people at large complain of Congress? No, what they wish is that Congress may have more power. If the power now proposed be not eno', the people hereafter will make additions to it. With proper powers Congress will act with more energy & wisdom than the proposed National Legislature; being fewer in number, and more secreted & refined by the mode of election. The plan of Mr. R will also be enormously expensive. Allowing Georgia & Delaware two representatives each in the popular branch the aggregate number of that branch will be 180. Add to it half as many for the other branch and you have 270. members coming once at least a year from the most distant as well as the most central parts of the republic. In the present deranged state of our finances can so expensive a system be seriously thought of? By enlarging the powers of Congress the greatest part of this expence will be saved, and all purposes will be answered. At least a trial ought to be made.

Mr. [James] Wilson [Pennsylvania] entered into a contrast of the principal points of the two plans so far he said as there had been time to examine the one last proposed. These points were 1. in the Virginia plan there are 2 & in some degree 3 branches in the Legislature: in the plan from N.J. there is to be a single legislature only—2. Representation of the people at large is the basis of the one:—the State Legislatures, the pillars of the other—3. proportional representation prevails in one:—equality of suffrage in the other—4. A single Executive Magistrate is at the head of the one:—a plurality is held out in the other.—5. in the one the majority of the people of the U. S. must prevail:—in the other a minority may prevail. 6. the National Legislature is to make laws in all cases to which the separate States are incompetent &-:—in place of this Congress are to have additional power in a few cases only—7. A negative on the laws of the States:—in place of this coertion to be substituted—8. The Executive to be removeable on impeachment & conviction;—in one plan: in the other to be removeable at the instance of a majority of the Executives of the States—9. Revision of the laws provided for in one:—no such check in the other—10. inferior national tribunals in one:—none such in the other. 11. In the one jurisdiction of National tribunals to extend &c—; an appellate jurisdiction only allowed in the other. 12. Here the jurisdiction is to extend to all cases affecting the National peace & harmony: there, a few cases only are marked out. 13. finally the ratification is in this to be by the people themselves:—in that by the legislative authorities according to the 13 art: of the Confederation.

With regard to the power of the Convention, he conceived himself authorized to conclude nothing, but to be at liberty to propose any thing. In this particular he felt himself perfectly indifferent to the two plans.

With regard to the sentiments of the people, he conceived it difficult to know precisely what they are. Those of the particular circle in which one moved, were commonly mistaken for the general voice. He could not persuade himself that the State Governments & Sovereignties were so much the idols of the people, nor a National Government so obnoxious to them, as some supposed. . . . Where do the people look at present for relief from the evils of which they complain? Is it from an internal reform of their Governments? no, Sir. It is from the National Councils that relief is expected. For these reasons he did not fear, that the people would not follow us into a national Government and it will be a further recommendation of Mr. R.'s plan that it is to be submitted to them, and not to the Legislatures, for ratification.

Proceeding now to the 1st point on which he had contrasted the two plans, he observed that anxious as he was for some augmentation of the federal powers, it would be with extreme reluctance indeed that he could ever consent to give powers to Congress he had two reasons either of which was sufficient. 1. Congress as a Legislative body does not stand on the people. 2. it is a single body. 1. He would not repeat the remarks he had formerly made on the principles of Representation. he would only say that an inequality in it, has ever been a poison contaminating every branch of Government. . . . The Impost, so anxiously wished for by the public was defeated not by any of the larger States in the Union. 2. Congress is a single Legislature. Despotism comes on Mankind in different Shapes, sometimes in an Executive, sometimes in a Military, one. Is there no danger of a Legislative despotism? Theory & practice both proclaim it. If the Legislative authority be not restrained, there can be neither liberty nor stability; and it can only be restrained by dividing it within itself, into distinct and independent branches. In a single House there is no check, but the inadequate one, of the virtue & good sense of those who compose it.

On another great point, the contrast was equally favorable to the plan reported by the Committee of the whole. It vested the Executive powers in a single Magistrate. The plan of N. Jersey, vested them in a plurality. In order to controul the Legislative authority, you must divide it. In order to controul the Executive you must unite it. One man will be more responsible than three. Three will contend among themselves till one becomes the master of his colleagues. In the triumvirates of Rome first Caesar, then Augustus, are witnesses of this truth. The Kings of Sparta, & the Consuls of Rome prove also the factious consequences of dividing the Executive Magistracy. . . .

Mr. [Charles] PINKNEY [South Carolina], the whole comes to this, as he conceived. Give N. Jersey an equal vote, and she will dismiss her scruples, and concur in the National system. He thought the Convention authorized to go any length in recommending, which they found necessary to remedy the evils which produced this Convention. . . .

5. Congress Debates the Issues, 1787
*Democracy and the Lower House**

In committee of the whole on Mr. Randolph's propositions.

The 3d Resolution "that the National Legislature ought to consist of two branches" was agreed to without debate or dissent, except that of Pennsylvania, given probably from complaisance to Doctor Franklin, who was understood to be partial to a single House of legislation.

Resolution 4, first clause "that the members of the first branch of the National Legislature ought to be elected by the people of the several States" being taken up,

Mr. Sherman [Conn.] opposed the election by the people, insisting that it ought to be by the State Legislatures. The people, he said, immediately should have as little to do as may be about the government. They want information, and are constantly liable to be misled.

Mr. Gerry [Mass.]. The evils we experience flow from the excess of democracy. The people do not want virtue, but are the dupes of pretended patriots. In Massachusetts it had been fully confirmed by experience that they are daily misled into the most baneful measures and opinions by the false reports circulated by designing men, and which no one on the spot can refute. One principal evil arises from the want of due provision for those employed in the administration of government. It would seem to be a maxim of democracy to starve the public servants. He mentioned the popular clamour in Massachusetts for the reduction of salaries and the attack made on that of the Governor, though secured by the spirit of the Constitution itself. He had he said been too republican heretofore: he was still however republican, but had been taught by experience the danger of the levilling spirit.

Mr. Mason [Va.] argued strongly for an election of the larger branch by the people. It was to be the grand depository of the democratic principle of the Government. It was, so to speak, to be our House of Commons. It ought to know and sympathise with every part of the community; and ought therefore to be taken not only from different parts of the whole republic, but also from different districts of the larger members of it, which had in several instances, particularly in Virginia, different interests and views arising from difference of produce, of habits, etc., etc.

"The Convention Debates the Issues, 1787." As found in Max Farrand, ed., *The Records of the Federal Convention of 1787,* rev. ed., (New Haven: Yale University Press, 1937), vol. 1, pp. 47–50 (May 31, 1787), 578–588 (July 11, 1787); vol. 2, pp. 199–205 (August 7, 1787), 369–374 (August 22, 1787), 415–416 (August 25, 1787).

* Madison's notes for May 31, 1787.

He admitted that we had been too democratic, but was afraid we should incautiously run into the opposite extreme. We ought to attend to the rights of every class of the people. He had often wondered at the indifference of the superior classes of society to this dictate of humanity and policy; considering that however affluent their circumstances, or elevated their situations might be, the course of a few years not only might but certainly would distribute their posterity throughout the lowest classes of society. Every selfish motive, therefore, every family attachment, ought to recommend such a system of policy as would provide no less carefully for the rights and happiness of the lowest than of the highest orders of citizens.

Mr. Wilson [Penn.] contended strenuously for drawing the most numerous branch of the Legislature immediately from the people. He was for raising the federal pyramid to a considerable altitude, and for that reason wished to give it as broad a basis as possible. No government could long subsist without the confidence of the people. In a republican government this confidence was peculiarly essential. . . .

Mr. Madison considered the popular election of one branch of the National Legislature as essential to every plan of free government. He observed that in some of the States one branch of the Legislature was composed of men already removed from the people by an intervening body of electors. That if the first branch of the general legislature should be elected by the State Legislatures, the second branch elected by the first, the Executive by the second together with the first; and other appointments again made for subordinate purposes by the Executive, the people would be lost sight of altogether; and the necessary sympathy between them and their rulers and officers, too little felt. He was an advocate for the policy of refining the popular appointments by successive filtrations, but thought it might be pushed too far. . . .

Mr. Gerry did not like the election by the people. . . . Experience he said had shewn that the State legislatures drawn immediately from the people did not always possess their confidence. . . . He seemed to think the people might nominate a certain number out of which the State legislatures should be bound to choose.

Mr. Butler [S. C.] thought an election by the people an impracticable mode.

On the question for an election of the first branch of the National Legislature by the people:

Mass. ay. Conn. div. N.Y. ay. N.J. no. Penn. ay. Del. div. Va. ay. N.C. ay. S.C. no. Geo. ay.

Sectional Interests and Legislative Apportionment*

Mr. Randolph's motion requiring the Legislature to take a periodical census for the purpose of redressing inequalities in the representation, was resumed.

Mr. Sherman [Conn.] was against shackling the Legislature too much. We ought to choose wise and good men, and then confide in them.

Mr. Mason [Va.] The greater the difficulty we find in fixing a proper rule of representation, the more unwilling ought we to be, to throw the task from ourselves, on the General Legislature. He did not object to the conjectural ratio which was to prevail in the outset; but considered a revision from time to time according to some permanent and precise standard as essential to the fair representation

---

* Madison's notes for July 11, 1787.

required in the first branch. According to the present population of America, the northern part of it had a right to preponderate, and he could not deny it. But he wished it not to preponderate hereafter when the reason no longer continued. From the nature of man we may be sure that those who have power in their hands will not give it up while they can retain it. On the contrary we know they will always when they can rather increase it. If the southern States therefore should have three-quarters of the people of America within their limits, the Northern will hold fast the majority of representatives. One quarter will govern the three-quarters. The southern States will complain: but they may complain from generation to generation without redress. Unless some principle therefore which will do justice to them hereafter shall be inserted in the Constitution, disagreeable as the declaration was to him, he must declare he could neither vote for the system here, nor support it in his State. . . . He urged that numbers of inhabitants, though not always a precise standard of wealth, was sufficiently so for every substantial purpose.

Mr. Williamson [N.C.] was for making it the duty of the Legislature to do what was right and not leaving it at liberty to do or not do it. He moved that Mr. Randolph's proposition be postponed in order to consider the following: "that in order to ascertain the alterations that may happen in the population and wealth of the several States, a census shall be taken of the free white inhabitants and three-fifths of those of other descriptions on the first year after this Government shall have been adopted, and every [blank] year thereafter; and that the representation be regulated accordingly."

Mr. Randolph agreed that Mr. Williamson's proposition should stand in the place of his. . . .

Mr. Butler [S.C.] and General [C. C.] Pinckney [S.C.] insisted that blacks be included in the rule of representation, equally with the whites: and for that purpose moved that the words "three-fifths" be struck out.

Mr. Gerry [Mass.] thought that three-fifths of them was . . . the full proportion that could be admitted.

Mr. Gorham. [Mass.] This ratio was fixed by Congress as a rule of taxation. Then it was urged by the delegates representing the States having slaves that the blacks were still more inferior to freemen. At present when the ratio of representation is to be established, we are assured that they are equal to freemen. The arguments on the former occasion had convinced him that three-fifths was pretty near the just proportion, and he should vote according to the same opinion now.

Mr. Butler insisted that the labour of a slave in South Carolina was as productive and valuable as that of a freeman in Massachusetts, that as wealth was the great means of defence and utility to the nation they were equally valuable to it with freemen; and that consequently an equal representation ought to be allowed for them in a government which was instituted principally for the protection of property, and was itself to be supported by property.

Mr. Mason could not agree to the motion, notwithstanding it was favorable to Virginia, because he thought it unjust. It was certain that the slaves were valuable, as they raised the value of land, increased the exports and imports, and of course the revenue; would supply the means of feeding and supporting an army, and might in cases of emergency become themselves soldiers. As in these important respects they were useful to the community at large, they ought not to be excluded from the estimate of representation. He could not, however, regard them as equal to freemen, and could not vote for them as such. He added as worthy of remark, that the southern States have this peculiar species of property, over and above the other species of property common to all the States.

Mr. Williamson [N.C.] reminded Mr. Gorham that if the southern States contended for the inferiority of blacks to whites when taxation was in view, the eastern States on the same occasion contended for their equality. He did not, however, either then or now, concur in either extreme, but approved of the ratio of three-fifths.

On Mr. Butler's motion for considering blacks as equal to whites in the apportionment of representation.

Mass. no. Conn. no. [N.Y. not on floor.] N.J. no. Pa. no. Del. ay. Md. no. Va. no. N.C. no. S.C. ay. Geo. ay. . . .

Mr. Rutledge contended for the admission of wealth in the estimate by which representation should be regulated. The western States will not be able to contribute in proportion to their numbers; they should not therefore be represented in that proportion. The Atlantic States will not concur in such a plan. He moved that "at the end of [blank] years after the first meeting of the Legislature, and of every [blank] years thereafter, the Legislature shall proportion the Representation according to the principles of wealth and population." . . .

Mr. Gouverneur Morris. . . . He could not persuade himself that numbers would be a just rule at any time. The remarks of [Mr. Mason] relative to the western country had not changed his opinion on that head. Among other objections, it must be apparent they would not be able to furnish men equally enlightened, to share in the administration of our common interests. The busy haunts of men, not the remote wilderness, was the proper school of political talents. If the western people get the power into their hands, they will ruin the Atlantic interests. The back members are always most averse to the best measures. He mentioned the case of Pennsylvania formerly. The lower part of the State had the power in the first instance. They kept it in their own hands, and the country was the better for it. Another objection with him against admitting the blacks into the census, was that the people of Pennsylvania would revolt at the idea of being put on a footing with slaves. They would reject any plan that was to have such an effect. . . .

Mr. Madison [Va.]. . . . To reconcile the gentleman with himself, it must be imagined that he determined the human character by the points of the compass. The truth was that all men having power ought to be distrusted to a certain degree. The case of Pennsylvania had been mentioned, where it was admitted that those who were possessed of the power in the original settlement, never admitted the new settlements to a due share of it. England was a still more striking example. The power there had long been in the hands of the boroughs, of the minority; who had opposed and defeated every reform which had been attempted. Virginia was in a less degree another example. With regard to the western States, he was clear and firm in opinion that no unfavorable distinctions were admissible either in point of justice or policy. He thought also that the hope of contributions to the Treasury from them had been much underrated. . . . He could not agree that any substantial objection lay against fixing numbers for the perpetual standard of Representation. It was said that Representation and taxation were to go together; that taxation and wealth ought to go together, that population and wealth were not measures of each other. He admitted that in different climates, under different forms of Government, and in different stages of civilization, the inference was perfectly just. He would admit that in no situation numbers of inhabitants were an accurate measure of wealth. He contended however that in the United States it was sufficiently so for the object in contemplation. Altho' their climate varied considerably, yet as the governments, the laws, and the manners of all were nearly the same, and the intercourse between different parts perfectly free, population, industry, arts, and the value of labour, would constantly tend to equalize themselves. . . .

On the question on the first clause of Mr. Williamson's motion as to taking a census of the free inhabitants, it passed in the affirmative. Mass. ay. Cont. ay. N.J. ay. Pa. ay. Del. no. Md. no. Va. ay. N.C. ay. S.C. no. Geo. no.

The next clause as to three-fifths of the negroes being considered,

Mr. King [Mass.], being much opposed to fixing numbers as the rule of representation, was particularly so on account of the blacks. He thought the admission of them along with whites at all, would excite great discontents among the States having no slaves. . . .

Mr. Wilson did not well see on what principle the admission of blacks in the proportion of three-fifths could be explained. Are they admitted as citizens? then why are they not admitted on an equality with white citizens? are they admitted as property? then why is not other property admitted into the computation? These were difficulties however which he thought must be overruled by the necessity of compromise. He had some apprehensions also from the tendency of the blending of the blacks with the whites, to give disgust to the people of Pennsylvania as had been intimated by his colleague. But he differed from him in thinking numbers of inhabitants so incorrect a measure of wealth. He had seen the western settlements of Pennsylvania, and on a comparison of them with the city of Philadelphia could discover little other difference, than that property was more unequally divided among individuals here than there. Taking the same number in the aggregate in the two situations he believed there would be little difference in their wealth and ability to contribute to the public wants.

Mr. Gouverneur Morris was compelled to declare himself reduced to the dilemma of doing injustice to the southern States or to human nature, and he must therefore do it to the former. For he could never agree to give such encouragement to the slave trade as would be given by allowing them a representation for their negroes, and he did not believe those States would ever confederate on terms that would deprive them of that trade.

On the question for agreeing to include three-fifths of the blacks:

Mass. no. Cont. ay. N.J. no. Pa. no. Del. no. Md. no. Va. ay. N.C. ay. S.C. no. Geo. ay.*

Qualifications for voters†

Mr. Gouverneur Morris [Pa.] moved to . . . restrain the right of suffrage to freeholders.

Mr. Fitzsimons [Penn.] seconded the motion.

Mr. Williamson [N.C.] was opposed to it.

---

* Later this provision was passed.
† Madison's notes for August 7, 1787.

Mr. Wilson [Pa.] . . . It was difficult to form any uniform rule of qualifications for all the States. Unnecessary innovations he thought too should be avoided. It would be very hard and disagreeable for the same persons at the same time to vote for Representatives in the State Legislature and to be excluded from a vote for those in the National Legislature.

Mr. Gouverneur Morris. Such a hardship would be neither great nor novel. The people are accustomed to it and not dissatisfied with it in several of the States. In some the qualifications are different for the choice of the Governor and of the Representatives; in others for different houses of the Legislature. . . .

Mr. Ellsworth [Conn.] thought the qualifications of the electors stood on the most proper footing. The right of suffrage was a tender point, and strongly guarded by most of the State Constitutions. The people will not readily subscribe to the National Constitution if it should subject them to be disfranchised. The States are the best judges of the circumstances and temper of their own people.

Col. Mason [Va.]. The force of habit is certainly not attended to by those gentlemen who wish for innovations on this point. Eight or nine States have extended the right of suffrage beyond the freeholders; what will the people there say if they should be disfranchised? A power to alter the qualifications would be a dangerous power in the hands of the Legislature.

Mr. Butler [S.C.]. There is no right of which the people are more jealous than that of suffrage. Abridgments of it tend to the same revolution as in Holland where they have at length thrown all power into the hands of the Senates, who fill up vacancies themselves, and form a rank aristocracy.

Mr. Dickinson [Pa.] had a very different idea of the tendency of vesting the right of suffrage in the freeholders of the country. He considered them as the best guardians of liberty; and the restriction of the right to them as a necessary defence against the dangerous influence of those multitudes without property and without principle with which our country like all others, will in time abound. As to the unpopularity of the innovation, it was in his opinion chimerical. The great mass of our citizens is composed at this time of freeholders, and will be pleased with it.

Mr. Ellsworth. How shall the freehold be defined? Ought not every man who pays a tax, to vote for the representative who is to levy and dispose of his money? Shall the wealthy merchants and manufacturers, who will bear a full share of the public burdens, be not allowed a voice in the imposition of them? Taxation and representation ought to go together.

Mr. Gouverneur Morris. He had long learned not to be the dupe of words. The sound of aristocracy, therefore, had no effect on him. It was the thing, not the name, to which he was opposed, and one of his principal objections to the Constitution as it is now before us, is that it threatens this country with an aristocracy. The aristocracy will grow out of the House of Representatives. Give the votes to people who have no property, and they will sell them to the rich who will be able to buy them. We should not confine our attention to the present moment. The time is not distant when this country will abound with mechanics and manufacturers who will receive their bread from their employers. Will such men be the secure and faithful guardians of liberty? Will they be the impregnable barrier against aristocracy? He was as little duped by the association of the words "taxation and representation."

The man who does not give his vote freely is not represented. It is the man who dictates the vote. Children do not vote. Why? because they want prudence, because they have no will of their own. The ignorant and the dependent can be as little trusted with the public interest. He did not conceive the difficulty of defining "freeholders" to be insuperable. Still less, that the restriction could be unpopular. Nine-tenths of the people are at present freeholders, and these will certainly be pleased with it. As to merchants, etc., if they have wealth and value the right, they can acquire it. If not, they don't deserve it.

Col. Mason. We all feel too strongly the remains of antient prejudices, and view things too much through a British medium. A freehold is the qualification in England, and hence it is imagined to be the only proper one. The true idea in his opinion was that every man having evidence of attachment to and permanent common interest with the society ought to share in all its rights and privileges. Was this qualification restrained to freeholders? Does no other kind of property but land evidence a common interest in the proprietor? Does nothing besides property mark a permanent attachment? Ought the merchant, the monied man, the parent of a number of children whose fortunes are to be pursued in his own country, to be viewed as suspicious characters, and unworthy to be trusted with the common rights of their fellow citizens?

Mr. Madison [Va.] The right of suffrage is certainly one of the fundamental articles of republican government, and ought not to be left to be regulated by the Legislature. A gradual abridgment of this right has been the mode in which aristocracies have been built on the ruins of popular forms. Whether the Constitutional qualification ought to be a freehold, would with him depend much on the probable reception such a change would meet with in States where the right was now exercised by every description of people. In several of the States a freehold was now the qualification. Viewing the subject in its merits alone, the freeholders of the country would be the safest depositories of Republican liberty. In future times a great majority of the people will not only be without landed, but any other sort of, property. These will either combine under the influence of their common situation; in which case, the rights of property and the public liberty will not be secure in their hands: or what is more probable, they will become the tools of opulence and ambition, in which case there will be equal danger on another side. . . .

Dr. Franklin [Pa.] It is of great consequence that we should not depress the virtue and public spirit of our common people; of which they displayed a great deal during the war, and which contributed principally to the favorable issue of it. . . . He did not think that the elected had any right in any case to narrow the privileges of the electors. . . . He was persuaded also that such a restriction as was proposed would give great uneasiness in the populous States. The sons of a substantial farmer, not being themselves freeholders, would not be pleased at being disfranchised, and there are a great many persons of that description.

Mr. Mercer [Md.] The Constitution is objectionable in many points, but in none more than the present. He objected to the footing on which the qualification was put, but particularly to the mode of election by the people. The people can not know and judge of the characters of candidates. The worst possible choice will be made. . . .

Mr. Rutledge [Va.] thought the idea of restraining the right of suffrage to the freeholders a very unadvised one. It would create division among the people and make enemies of all those who should be excluded.

Slavery and the Importation of Slaves*

Mr. Sherman [Conn.] . . . disapproved of the slave trade; yet as the States were now possessed of the right to import slaves, as the public good did not require it to be taken from them, and as it was expedient to have as few objections as possible to the proposed scheme of government, he thought it best to leave the matter as we find it. He observed that the abolition of slavery seemed to be going on in the United States, and that the good sense of the several States would probably by degrees compleat it. He urged on the Convention the necessity of despatching its business.

Col. Mason [Va.] This infernal trafic originated in the avarice of British merchants. The British Government constantly checked the attempts of Virginia to put a stop to it. The present question concerns not the importing States alone but the whole Union. The evil of having slaves was experienced during the late war. Had slaves been treated as they might have been by the enemy, they would have proved dangerous instruments in their hands. . . . Maryland and Virginia he said had already prohibited the importation of slaves expressly. North Carolina had done the same in substance. All this would be in vain if South Carolina and Georgia be at liberty to import. The western people are already calling out for slaves for their new lands, and will fill that country with slaves if they can be got thro' South Carolina and Georgia. Slavery discourages arts and manufactures. The poor despise labor when performed by slaves. They prevent the immigration of whites, who really enrich and strengthen a country. They produce the most pernicious effect on manners. Every master of slaves is born a petty tyrant. They bring the judgment of Heaven on a country. As nations cannot be rewarded or punished in the next world, they must be in this. By an inevitable chain of causes and effects, Providence punishes national sins, by national calamities. He lamented that some of our eastern brethren had from a lust of gain embarked in this nefarious traffic. As to the States being in possession of the right to import, this was the case with many other rights, now to be properly given up. He held it essential in every point of view that the General Government should have power to prevent the increase of slavery.

Mr. Ellsworth [Conn.] As he had never owned a slave could not judge of the effects of slavery on character: he said, however, that if it was to be considered in a moral light we ought to go farther and free those already in the country. As slaves also multiply so fast in Virginia and Maryland that it is cheaper to raise than import them, whilst in the sickly rice swamps foreign supplies are necessary; if we go no farther than is urged, we shall be unjust towards South Carolina and Georgia. Let us not intermeddle. As population increases, poor laborers will be so plenty as to render slaves useless. Slavery in time will not be a speck in our country. Provision is already made in Connecticut for abolishing it, and the abolition has already taken place in Massachussets. As to the danger of insurrections from foreign influence, that will become a motive to kind treatment of the slaves.

---

* Madison's notes for August 22, 25, 1787.

Mr. Pinckney [S.C.] If slavery be wrong, it is justified by the example of all the world. He cited the case of Greece, Rome, and other antient States; the sanction given by France, England, Holland, and other modern States. In all ages one half of mankind have been slaves. If the southern States were let alone they will probably of themselves stop importations. He would himself as a citizen of South Carolina vote for it. An attempt to take away the right as proposed will produce serious objections to the Constitution, which he wished to see adopted.

General Pinckney [S.C.] declared it to be his firm opinion that if himself and all his colleagues were to sign the Constitution and use their personal influence, it would be of no avail towards obtaining the assent of their constituents. South Carolina and Georgia cannot do without slaves. As to Virginia, she will gain by stopping the importations. Her slaves will rise in value, and she has more than she wants. It would be unequal to require South Carolina and Georgia to confederate on such unequal terms. He said the royal assent before the Revolution had never been refused to South Carolina as to Virginia. He contended that the importation of slaves would be for the interest of the whole Union. The more slaves, the more produce to employ the carrying trade, the more consumption also; and the more of this, the more of revenue for the common treasury. . . .

Mr. Dickinson [Pa.] considered it as inadmissible on every principle of honor and safety that the importation of slaves should be authorised to the States by the Constitution. The true question was whether the national happiness would be promoted or impeded by the importation, and this question ought to be left to the National Government, not to the States particularly interested. . . .

Mr. Rutledge [Va.]. If the Convention thinks that North Carolina, South Carolina, and Georgia will ever agree to the plan, unless their right to import slaves be untouched, the expectation is vain. The people of those States will never be such fools as to give up so important an interest. . . .

Mr. Gouverneur Morris wished the whole subject to be committed, including the clauses relating to taxes on exports and to a navigation act. These things may form a bargain among the northern and southern States. . . .

General Pinckney moved to strike out the words "the year eighteen hundred" as the year limiting the importation of slaves, and to insert the words "the year eighteen hundred and eight".

Mr. Gorham seconded the motion.

Mr. Madison. Twenty years will produce all the mischief that can be apprehended from the liberty to import slaves. So long a term will be more dishonorable to the national character, than to say nothing about it in the Constitution.

On the motion; which passed in the affirmative.

N.H. ay. Mass. ay. Conn. ay. N.J. no. Pa. no. Del. no. Md. ay. Va. no. N.C. ay. S.C. ay. Geo. ay. . . .

The first part of the report was then agreed to, amended as follows,

> The migration or importation of such persons as the several States now existing shall think proper to admit, shall not be prohibited by the Legislature prior to the year 1808.

N.H. Mass. Conn. Md. N.C. S.C. Geo.: ay
N.J. Pa. Del. Va.   .   .   .   .   no

6. The Constitution of the United States of America, 1787

We, the people of the United States, in order to form a more perfect union, establish justice, insure domestic tranquillity, provide for the common defense, promote the general welfare, and secure the blessings of liberty to ourselves and our posterity, do ordain and establish this Constitution for the United States of America.

Article One

Section 1. All legislative powers herein granted shall be vested in a Congress of the United States, which shall consist of a Senate and House of Representatives.

Section 2. The House of Representatives shall be composed of members chosen every second year by the people of the several States, and the electors in each State shall have the qualifications requisite for electors of the most numerous branch of the State legislature.

No person shall be a Representative who shall not have attained to the age of twenty five years, and been seven years a citizen of the United States, and who shall not, when elected, be an inhabitant of that State in which he shall be chosen.

Representatives and direct taxes shall be apportioned among the several States which may be included within this Union, according to their respective numbers, which shall be determined by adding to the whole number of free persons, including those bound to service for a term of years, and excluding Indians not taxed, three-fifths of all other persons. The actual enumeration shall be made within three years after the first meeting of the Congress of the United States, and within every subsequent term of ten years, in such manner as they shall by law direct. The number of Representatives shall not exceed one for every thirty thousand, but each State shall have at least one Representative; and until such enumeration shall be made, the State of New Hampshire shall be entitled to choose three, Massachusetts eight, Rhode Island and Providence Plantations one, Connecticut five, New York six, New Jersey four, Pennsylvania eight, Delaware one, Maryland six, Virginia ten, North Carolina five, South Carolina five, and Georgia three.

When vacancies happen in the representation from any State, the executive authority thereof shall issue writs of election to fill such vacancies.

The House of Representatives shall choose their Speaker and other officers, and shall have the sole power of impeachment.

Section 3. The Senate of the United States shall be composed of two Senators from each State, chosen by the legislature thereof, for six years; and each Senator shall have one vote.

Immediately after they shall be assembled in consequence of the first election, they shall be divided as equally as may be into three classes. The seats of the Senators of the first class shall be vacated at the expiration of the second year; of the

---

"The Constitution of the United States of America." As found in Edward S. Corwin, ed., *The Constitution of the United States of America: Analysis and Interpretation* (Washington, DC: US Government Printing Office, 1953), 19–35.

second class, at the expiration of the fourth year, and of the third class, at the expiration of the sixth year, so that one-third may be chosen every second year; and if vacancies happen by resignation or otherwise during the recess of the legislature of any State, the executive thereof may make temporary appointments until the next meeting of the legislature, which shall then fill such vacancies.

No person shall be a Senator who shall not have attained to the age of thirty years, and been nine years a citizen of the United States, and who shall not, when elected, be an inhabitant of that State for which he shall be chosen.

The Vice-President of the United States shall be President of the Senate, but shall have no vote, unless they be equally divided.

The Senate shall choose their other officers, and also a President pro tempore in the absence of the Vice-President, or when he shall exercise the office of President of the United States.

The Senate shall have the sole power to try all impeachments. When sitting for that purpose, they shall be on oath or affirmation. When the President of the United States is tried, the Chief Justice shall preside: and no person shall be convicted without the concurrence of two-thirds of the members present.

Judgment in cases of impeachment shall not extend further than to removal from office, and disqualification to hold and enjoy any office of honor, trust, or profit under the United States; but the party convicted shall, nevertheless, be liable and subject to indictment, trial, judgment, and punishment, according to law.

Section 4. The times, places, and manner of holding elections for Senators and Representatives shall be prescribed in each State by the legislature thereof; but the Congress may at any time by law make or alter such regulations, except as to the places of choosing Senators.

The Congress shall assemble at least once in every year, and such meeting shall be on the first Monday in December, unless they shall by law appoint a different day.

Section 5. Each house shall be the judge of the elections, returns, and qualifications of its own members, and a majority of each shall constitute a quorum to do business; but a smaller number may adjourn from day to day, and may be authorized to compel the attendance of absent members, in such manner, and under such penalties, as each house may provide.

Each house may determine the rules of its proceedings, punish its members for disorderly behavior, and, with the concurrence of two-thirds, expel a member.

Each house shall keep a journal of its proceedings, and from time to time publish the same, excepting such parts as may in their judgment require secrecy, and the yeas and nays of the members of either house on any question shall, at the desire of one-fifth of those present, be entered on the journal.

Neither house, during the session of Congress, shall, without the consent of the other, adjourn for more than three days, nor to any other place than that in which the two houses shall be sitting.

Section 6. The Senators and Representatives shall receive a compensation for their services, to be ascertained by law and paid out of the Treasury of the United States. They shall, in all cases except treason, felony, and breach of the peace, be privileged from arrest during their attendance at the session of their respective houses, and in going to and returning from the same; and for any speech or debate in either house they shall not be questioned in any other place.

No Senator or Representative shall, during the time for which he was elected, be appointed to any civil office under the authority of the United States, which shall have been created, or the emoluments whereof shall have been increased during such time; and no person holding any office under the United States shall be a member of either house during his continuance in office.

Section 7. All bills for raising revenue shall originate in the House of Representatives; but the Senate may propose or concur with amendments as on other bills.

Every bill which shall have passed the House of Representatives and the Senate shall, before it becomes a law, be presented to the President of the United States; if he approve he shall sign it, but if not he shall return it, with his objections, to that house in which it shall have originated, who shall enter the objections at large on their journal and proceed to reconsider it. If after such reconsideration two-thirds of that house shall agree to pass the bill, it shall be sent, together with the objections, to the other house, by which it shall likewise be reconsidered, and if approved by two-thirds of that house it shall become a law. But in all such cases the votes of both houses shall be determined by yeas and nays, and the names of the persons voting for and against the bill shall be entered on the journal of each house respectively. If any bill shall not be returned by the President within ten days (Sundays excepted) after it shall have been presented to him, the same shall be a law, in like manner as if he had signed it, unless the Congress by their adjournment prevent its return, in which case it shall not be a law.

Every order, resolution, or vote to which the concurrence of the Senate and House of Representatives may be necessary (except on a question of adjournment) shall be presented to the President of the United States; and before the same shall take effect, shall be approved by him, or being disapproved by him, shall be repassed by two-thirds of the Senate and House of Representatives, according to the rules and limitations prescribed in the case of a bill.

Section 8. The Congress shall have power to lay and collect taxes, duties, imposts, and excises, to pay the debts and provide for the common defense and general welfare of the United States; but all duties, imposts, and excises shall be uniform throughout the United States;

To borrow money on the credit of the United States;

To regulate commerce with foreign nations and among the several States, and with the Indian tribes;

To establish an uniform rule of naturalization, and uniform laws on the subject of bankruptcies throughout the United States;

To coin money, regulate the value thereof, and of foreign coin, and fix the standard of weights and measures;

To provide for the punishment of counterfeiting the securities and current coin of the United States;

To establish post-offices and post-roads;

To promote the progress of science and useful arts by securing for limited times to authors and inventors the exclusive right to their respective writings and discoveries;

To constitute tribunals inferior to the Supreme Court;

To define and punish piracies and felonies committed on the high seas and offenses against the law of nations;

To declare war, grant letters of marque and reprisal, and make rules concerning captures on land and water;

To raise and support armies, but no appropriation of money to that use shall be for a longer term than two years;

To provide and maintain a navy;

To make rules for the government and regulation of the land and naval forces;

To provide for calling forth the militia to execute the laws of the Union, suppress insurrections, and repel invasions;

To provide for organizing, arming, and disciplining the militia, and for governing such part of them as may be employed in the service of the United States, reserving to the States respectively the appointment of the officers, and the authority of training the militia according to the discipline prescribed by Congress;

To exercise exclusive legislation in all cases whatsoever over such district (not exceeding ten miles square) as may, by cession of particular States and the acceptance of Congress, become the seat of the Government of the United States, and to exercise like authority over all places purchased by the consent of the legislature of the State in which the same shall be, for the erection of forts, magazines, arsenals, dockyards, and other needful buildings; and

To make all laws which shall be necessary and proper for carrying into execution the foregoing powers, and all other powers vested by this Constitution in the Government of the United States, or in any department or officer thereof.

Section 9. The migration or importation of such persons as any of the States now existing shall think proper to admit shall not be prohibited by the Congress prior to the year one thousand eight hundred and eight, but a tax or duty may be imposed on such importation, not exceeding ten dollars for each person.

The privilege of the writ of habeas corpus shall not be suspended, unless when in cases of rebellion or invasion the public safety may require it.

No bill of attainder or ex post facto law shall be passed.

No capitation or other direct tax shall be laid, unless in proportion to the census or enumeration hereinbefore directed to be taken.

No tax or duty shall be laid on articles exported from any State.

No preference shall be given by any regulation of commerce or revenue to the ports of one State over those of another; nor shall vessels bound to or from one State be obliged to enter, clear, or pay duties in another.

No money shall be drawn from the Treasury but in consequence of appropriations made by law; and a regular statement and account of the receipts and expenditures of all public money shall be published from time to time.

No title of nobility shall be granted by the United States; and no person holding any office of profit or trust under them shall, without the consent of the Congress, accept of any present, emolument, office, or title, of any kind whatever, from any king, prince, or foreign State.

Section 10. No State shall enter into any treaty, alliance, or confederation; grant letters of marque and reprisal; coin money; emit bills of credit; make anything but gold and silver coin a tender in payment of debts; pass any bill of attainder, ex post facto law, or law impairing the obligation of contracts, or grant any title of nobility.

No State shall, without the consent of Congress, lay any imposts or duties on imports or exports, except what may be absolutely necessary for executing its inspection laws; and the net produce of all duties and imposts, laid by any State on imports or exports, shall be for the use of the Treasury of the United States; and all such laws shall be subject to the revision and control of the Congress.

No State shall, without the consent of Congress, lay any duty of tonnage, keep troops or ships of war in time of peace, enter into any agreement or compact with another State or with a foreign power, or engage in war, unless actually invaded or in such imminent danger as will not admit of delay.

Article Two

Section 1. The executive power shall be vested in a President of the United States of America. He shall hold his office during the term of four years, and together with the Vice-President, chosen for the same term, be elected as follows:

Each State shall appoint, in such manner as the legislature thereof may direct, a number of electors, equal to the whole number of Senators and Representatives to which the State may be entitled in the Congress; but no Senator or Representative, or person holding an office of trust or profit under the United States, shall be appointed an elector.

[The electors shall meet in their respective States and vote by ballot for two persons, of whom one at least shall not be an inhabitant of the same State with themselves. And they shall make a list of all the persons voted for, and of the number of votes for each; which list they shall sign and certify, and transmit sealed to the seat of the government of the United States, directed to the President of the Senate. The President of the Senate shall, in the presence of the Senate and House of Representatives, open all the certificates, and the votes shall then be counted. The person having the greatest number of votes shall be the President, if such number be a majority of the whole number of electors appointed; and if there be more than one who have such majority, and have an equal number of votes, then the House of Representatives shall immediately choose by ballot one of them for President; and if no person have a majority, then from the five highest on the list the said House shall in like manner choose the President. But in choosing the President the votes shall be taken by States, the representation from each State having one vote; a quorum for this purpose shall consist of a member or members from two-thirds of the States, and a majority of all the States shall be necessary to a choice. In every case, after the choice of the President, the person having the greatest number of votes of the electors shall be the Vice-President. But if there should remain two or more who have equal votes, the Senate shall choose from them by ballot the Vice-President.*

The Congress may determine the time of choosing the electors and the day on which they shall give their votes, which day shall be the same throughout the United States.

No person except a natural-born citizen, or a citizen of the United States at the time of the adoption of this Constitution, shall be eligible to the office of President; neither shall any person be eligible to that office who shall not have attained to the age of thirty-five years, and been fourteen years a resident within the United States.

In case of the removal of the President from office, or of his death, resignation, or inability to discharge the powers and duties of the said office, the same shall

---

* This procedure was changed by the Twelfth Amendment.

devolve on the Vice-President, and the Congress may by law provide for the case of removal, death, resignation, or inability, both of the President and Vice-President, declaring what officer shall then act as President, and such officer shall act accordingly until the disability be removed or a President shall be elected.

The President shall, at stated times, receive for his services a compensation, which shall neither be increased nor diminished during the period for which he shall have been elected, and he shall not receive within that period any other emolument from the United States or any of them.

Before he enter on the execution of his office he shall take the following oath or affirmation:

"I do solemnly swear (or affirm) that I will faithfully execute the office of President of the United States, and will to the best of my ability preserve, protect, and defend the Constitution of the United States."

Section 2. The President shall be Commander-in-chief of the Army and Navy of the United States, and of the militia of the several States when called into the actual service of the United States; he may require the opinion, in writing, of the principal officer in each of the executive departments, upon any subject relating to the duties of their respective offices, and he shall have power to grant reprieves and pardons for offenses against the United States, except in cases of impeachment.

He shall have power, by and with the advice and consent of the Senate, to make treaties, provided two-thirds of the Senators present concur; and he shall nominate, and, by and with the advice and consent of the Senate, shall appoint ambassadors, other public ministers and consuls, judges of the Supreme Court, and all other officers of the United States, whose appointments are not herein otherwise provided for, and which shall be established by law; but the Congress may by law vest the appointment of such inferior officers, as they think proper, in the President alone, in the courts of law, or in the heads of departments.

The President shall have power to fill up all vacancies that may happen during the recess of the Senate, by granting commissions which shall expire at the end of their next session.

Section 3. He shall from time to time give to the Congress information of the state of the Union, and recommend to their consideration such measures as he shall judge necessary and expedient; he may, on extraordinary occasions, convene both houses, or either of them, and in case of disagreement between them with respect to the time of adjournment, he may adjourn them to such time as he shall think proper; he shall receive ambassadors and other public ministers; he shall take care that the laws be faithfully executed, and shall commission all the officers of the United States.

Section 4. The President, Vice-President, and all civil officers of the United States shall be removed from office on impeachment for and conviction of treason, bribery, or other high crimes and misdemeanors.

Article Three

Section 1. The judicial power of the United States shall be vested in one Supreme Court, and in such inferior courts as the Congress may from time to time ordain and establish. The judges, both of the supreme and inferior courts, shall hold their offices during good behavior, and shall, at stated times, receive for their services a compensation which shall not be diminished during their continuance in office.

Section 2. The judicial power shall extend to all cases, in law and equity, arising under this Constitution, the laws of the United States, and treaties made, or which shall be made, under their authority; to all cases affecting ambassadors, other public ministers, and consuls; to all cases of admiralty and maritime jurisdiction; to controversies to which the United States shall be a party; to controversies between two or more States; between a State and citizens of another State; between citizens of different States; between citizens of the same State claiming lands under grants of different States, and between a State, or the citizens thereof, and foreign States, citizens, or subjects.

In all cases affecting ambassadors, other public ministers and consuls, and those in which a State shall be a party, the Supreme Court shall have original jurisdiction. In all the other cases before mentioned the Supreme Court shall have appellate jurisdiction, both as to law and fact, with such exceptions and under such regulations as the Congress shall make.

The trial of all crimes, except in cases of impeachment, shall be by jury; and such trial shall be held in the State where the said crimes shall have been committed; but when not committed within any State, the trial shall be at such place or places as the Congress may by law have directed.

Section 3. Treason against the United States shall consist only in levying war against them, or in adhering to their enemies, giving them aid and comfort. No person shall be convicted of treason unless on the testimony of two witnesses to the same overt act, or on confession in open court.

The Congress shall have power to declare the punishment of treason, but no attainder of treason shall work corruption of blood or forfeiture except during the life of the person attainted.

Article Four

Section 1. Full faith and credit shall be given in each State to the public acts, records, and judicial proceedings of every other State. And the Congress may by general laws prescribe the manner in which such acts, records, and proceedings shall be proved, and the effect thereof.

Section 2. The citizens of each State shall be entitled to all privileges and immunities of citizens in the several States.

A person charged in any State with treason, felony, or other crime, who shall flee from justice, and be found in another State, shall, on demand of the executive authority of the State from which he fled, be delivered up, to be removed to the State having jurisdiction of the crime.

No person held to service or labor in one State, under the laws thereof, escaping into another, shall, in consequence of any law or regulation therein, be discharged from such service or labor, but shall be delivered up on claim of the party to whom such service or labor may be due.

Section 3. New States may be admitted by the Congress into this Union; but no new State shall be formed or erected within the jurisdiction of any other State; nor any State be formed by the junction of two or more States or parts of States, without the consent of the legislatures of the States concerned as well as of the Congress.

The Congress shall have power to dispose of and make all needful rules and regulations respecting the territory or other property belonging to the United States;

and nothing in this Constitution shall be so construed as to prejudice any claims of the United States or of any particular State.

Section 4. The United States shall guarantee to every State in this Union a republican form of government, and shall protect each of them against invasion, and on application of the legislature, or of the executive (when the legislature cannot be convened), against domestic violence.

Article Five

The Congress, whenever two-thirds of both houses shall deem it necessary, shall propose amendments to this Constitution, or, on the application of the Legislatures of two-thirds of the several States, shall call a convention for proposing amendments, which, in either case, shall be valid to all intents and purposes, as part of this Constitution, when ratified by the Legislatures of three-fourths of the several States, or by conventions in three-fourths thereof, as the one or the other mode of ratification may be proposed by the Congress; provided that no amendment which may be made prior to the Year One thousand eight hundred and eight shall in any manner affect the first and fourth Clauses in the Ninth Section of the first Article; and that no State, without its consent, shall be deprived of its equal suffrage in the Senate.

Article Six

All debts contracted and engagements entered into, before the adoption of this Constitution, shall be as valid against the United States under this Constitution, as under the Confederation.

This Constitution and the laws of the United States which shall be made in pursuance thereof and all treaties made, or which shall be made, under the authority of the United States, shall be the supreme law of the land; and the judges in every State shall be bound thereby, anything in the Constitution or laws of any State to the contrary notwithstanding.

The Senators and Representatives before mentioned, and the members of the several State Legislatures, and all executive and judicial officers, both of the United States and of the several States, shall be bound by oath or affirmation, to support this Constitution; but no religious test shall ever be required as a qualification to any office or public trust under the United States.

Article Seven

The ratification of the Conventions of nine States shall be sufficient for the establishment of this Constitution between the States so ratifying the same.

Done in convention by the unanimous consent of the States present the seventeenth day of September in the year of our Lord one thousand seven hundred and eighty-seven and of the independence of the United States of America the twelfth, in witness whereof we have hereunto subscribed our names.

G. WASHINGTON—President
and deputy from Virginia

✦ E S S A Y S

Professors Lance G. Banning of the University of Kentucky and Jack N. Rakove of Stanford University are two of the leading analysts of James Madison's ideas and of his role in the politics of constitution-writing. Banning sketches the operation of the constitutional convention in the first essay and shows how the division between the large and small states shaped events, leading ultimately to compromise. In the second essay, which analyzes many of the same questions from a different viewpoint, Rakove focuses directly on how the delegates achieved the "Great Compromise" (also called the "Connecticut Compromise") and discusses the profound conflicts regarding federalism that the delegates debated. He also describes Madison's frustrations. Although Madison was an extremely influential individual, it took many delegates, many states, and an arduous process to create the Constitution of 1787.

What Happened at the Constitutional Convention

LANCE G. BANNING

Meeting at the Pennsylvania State House (Independence Hall), the Constitutional Convention found a quorum on May 25 and sat until September 17. Fifty-five delegates participated in its work, though there were seldom more than forty in the room for any single session. Representing every state except Rhode Island, the delegates comprised a good cross-section of the early national elite. Lawyers (34), merchants (7), farmers (27), public creditors (30), and public servants (10), nearly all were wealthy men, and most had taken generally conservative positions in their states. Yet members came from a variety of local factions and from all the major regions of the several states except the west. The nation might have organized an equally impressive meeting from the ranks of leaders who did not attend. John Adams and Thomas Jefferson were representing the United States abroad in 1787. John Jay and Samuel Adams were passed over. Patrick Henry "smelt a rat" and turned down his election. Still, most states attempted to select their most experienced and best, usually with slight regard to factional considerations, and they succeeded well enough that Jefferson described the roster as a gathering of "demigods." George Washington was present. Inevitably, he was quickly chosen to preside.

Among the delegates as well was young James Madison, Jefferson's close friend, an influential member of the Annapolis Convention, and long a leading advocate of national reforms. Madison had led Virginia, which had led the other states, in organizing the convention and selecting delegates whose talents and distinguished reputations signaled a profound commitment to its work. In the weeks before the meeting, he had taken careful notes on ancient and modern confederacies and prepared a formal memorandum on the "Vices of the Political System of the United States," thinking problems through to a degree that no one else had done and urging other members of his delegation to arrive in Philadelphia in time to frame some introductory proposals with which the meeting might begin. Virginia's seven delegates assembled daily while they waited for the full convention to obtain

"The Constitutional Convention" by Lance G. Banning. Abridged from *The Framing and Ratification of the Constitution* edited by Leonard W. Levy and Dennis J. Mahoney. Copyright © 1987 by Macmillan Publishing Company, a Division of Macmillan, Inc.

a quorum, agreeing on a set of resolutions that might serve as a preliminary basis for discussions. Speaking for the delegation as a whole, Governor Edmund Randolph introduced these resolutions on May 29, as soon as the convention had agreed upon its rules. . . .

A solemn sense of high responsibility and urgent, common purpose was indispensable to the Convention's great achievement, not least because most delegates were only partially prepared for the enormous changes sketched by the Virginia Plan. Seizing the initiative for radical reform, Madison's proposals demonstrated an instinctive grasp of several broad, though hazy, understandings that would limit and direct the course of the proceedings. Leaders of a democratic Revolution, including thirty veterans of the war, the delegates had not forgotten the complaints and hopes that had propelled them into independence. Nearly all of them had come to think that an effective central government would have to have, at minimum, an independent source of revenues, authority to regulate the country's trade, and power to compel obedience to its legitimate commands. Nearly all agreed, as well, that powers that the colonies had stubbornly denied to England would have to be accompanied by careful checks against the possibility of their abuse. Many, nonetheless, were far from willing to consent to the specific kinds of checks proposed by the initial resolutions. The Pennsylvanians and Virginians were prepared from the beginning to insist that powers of this sort could be entrusted only to a well-constructed, fully representative republic. Overawed by the Virginia Plan, accepting many of its goals, and unprepared to offer comprehensive counterresolutions, dissenters were uncertain how to counter its proponents in debate. They nevertheless objected from the start that the convention was empowered only to reform the present federal system, not to overturn it. The framing of the Constitution thus became a complicated story of a fundamental conflict that occurred within the context of a common quest. . . .

Between May 30 and June 13, the Committee of the Whole conducted a complete consideration of the Randolph Plan. During these two weeks, with Madison and James Wilson of Pennsylvania at their head, a brilliant group of delegates from larger states developed a compelling case for radical reform. Distinguishing between a "national" government and one "merely federal," Wilson, Madison, Randolph, George Mason (Virginia), Gouverneur Morris (Pennsylvania), and others argued that the fatal weakness of the old confederation was its unavoidable dependence on the thirteen states for revenues and for a host of intermediary actions necessary to enforce its laws and treaties. Lacking independent means to carry its decisions into action, they explained, Congress had been baffled by the states even when its measures were supported by a huge majority and undeniably were within its proper province. Paper grants of new responsibilities would only add new sources of frustration if the states retained the power to ignore or counteract the central government's decisions; and yet a federal power to compel the states might introduce a constant threat of war between the union and its members. The inescapable necessity, the nationalists maintained, was to abandon the unworkable idea of a government over governments, a sovereignty over sovereignties, and give the central government the courts and other independent means to act directly on the individual members of society. Revolutionary principles required, however, that any government possessing the authority to reach the people's lives and purses would have to represent its citizens immediately and fairly. Given the necessity for larger federal powers, the traditional equality between the states would have to be abandoned in order to preserve equality among the people and majority control. . . .

But as the skeleton of the Virginia Plan acquired some flesh and as it grew increasingly more difficult to settle lesser questions while the great ones went unanswered, the confrontation that had loomed from the beginning could no longer be contained. New Jersey's delegates demanded a decision on apportioning the Congress, insisting on June 9 that proportional representation would destroy the smaller states and place the whole confederation at the mercy of a coalition of its largest members: Massachusetts, Pennsylvania, and Virginia. Ten of thirteen states, warned William Paterson, would certainly reject this scheme. If he could not defeat it in the hall, he would oppose it in his state. New Jersey would "never confederate on the plan before the committee."

. . . James Wilson answered Paterson in kind. "If the small states will not confederate on this plan," he assured them, Pennsylvania and some others "would not confederate on any other." The division that would dominate proceedings for the next five weeks had burst into the open. It would prove the clearest, most dramatic, most persistent argument of the convention—the single conflict over which the gathering repeatedly approached collapse.

For all its threatening potential, nevertheless, the clash between the small states and the large cannot explain developments between May 30 and June 13. It was not the only conflict that emerged, nor can an exclusive emphasis on conflicts and divisions properly illuminate the course of the proceedings. The Constitutional Convention was successful, in the end, because its battles almost always raged in multiple dimensions, because the push-and-pull that marked its course was never simply a result of clashing interests, and because the men involved were more than merely clever brokers for their states. . . .

The first two weeks of the convention seem most helpfully described as an initial exploration during which a complicated pattern of divisions rapidly emerged within a framework of evolving, general understandings. Like Madison, most delegates had come to Philadelphia as worried by conditions in the states as by the problems of the union. They readily agreed with the Virginian that the will of unrestrained majorities was often inconsistent with the rights of the minority or long-term public needs, and that the early Revolutionary constitutions had neglected dangers of this sort by trusting too much power to the lower houses of assembly. . . . Everywhere, as Elbridge Gerry phrased it, the country seemed to suffer from "an excess of democracy." Good government appeared to have been sacrificed to revolutionary fears of unresponsive rulers.

Few members of the Constitutional Convention carried their alarm about majority misrule so far as to suggest nostalgia for aristocrats or kings. Most genuinely shared the people's fierce commitment to a democratic system. Yet nearly all were powerfully determined not to replicate the errors they believed had been committed in the early Revolutionary constitutions. Here, again, the resolutions of May 29 successfully defined the boundaries of disagreement. Sound republics, they suggested, must be built upon two legislative houses: one elected by the people; the other chosen in a manner that would shield its members from the whims of the majority and thus assure continuing protection for the rights of the minority and continuing attention to the nation's long-term needs. The legislature should be counterbalanced by a forceful, separate executive, and the judiciary should be independent of them both. Through almost four months of often bitter quarrels, there was never any serious dispute about these fundamental principles of governmental structure. . . .

The Virginia Plan survived its first examination fundamentally intact. . . . Wilson, Madison, and their lieutenants made it clear that what they wanted was to build a wise and energetic central government upon a broadly popular foundation, blending a responsibility to the majority with multiple securities against an overbearing, popularly elected lower house. Impressed by their analysis of the debilities of the existing system, the convention speedily agreed to substitute a complex and authoritative central government for the present, feeble, unicameral regime. Sharing their dissatisfaction with the constitutions of the states, it worked from the beginning to establish genuinely independent, fully countervailing branches.

Through these early days, Madison and Wilson towered over the convention like a team of titans. . . . Still, the nationalist assault by no means carried everything before it. Although the smallest states seemed relatively isolated in the earliest debates and were severely beaten on the matter of the lower house, the fierce resistance vocalized by Paterson and [George] Read [of Delaware] became increasingly imposing as it coalesced with opposition based on different concerns. Three delegates—no more—were rigidly committed to a "merely federal" system, but [Robert] Yates and [John] Lansing could control New York while Luther Martin often managed to divide the Maryland contingent. For each obstructionist, moreover, there were several others for whom the pervasive fear of popular misrule, which made the resolutions of May 29 a universally attractive model for republican reform, could also reinforce a natural reluctance to surrender local powers to a national majority. Although the delegations from Connecticut and South Carolina were especially inclined to be distrustful of a scheme that would erect a stronger central government on greater popular involvement, almost every delegation was composed of men who differed widely in their judgments of the people's competence as well as in their willingness to shift additional responsibilities to federal hands. As the smaller states discovered partial allies, sometimes here and sometimes there, it seemed increasingly unlikely that a national republic could secure approval both from a majority of states and from the representatives of a majority of the people. Even optimistic nationalists resigned themselves to a campaign that promised to extend throughout the summer.

Confronted with so many overlapping fears, the democratic nationalists encountered rising opposition during the convention's first two weeks and suffered one decisive check. The Virginia Plan provided for election of the senate by the lower house from persons nominated by the states. On June 7, over loud objections from Madison and Wilson, majorities in every delegation disapproved this proposition in favor of election of the senate by the legislatures of the states. . . . Many . . . were forcefully impressed by the insistence of John Dickinson (Delaware) and Roger Sherman (Connecticut) that selection by the local legislatures could collect the sense of states as states, assure a federal harmony, and offer firm securities against potential federal usurpations.

Committed nationalists were deeply disappointed. Fearing that selection of the senate by the states would build into the system exactly the flaw that was destroying the confederation, they also rightly sensed that an insistence on a federal role for states as states would reinforce demands for an equality between them. On June 11, just before the crucial votes, Sherman urged that representation in the lower house might be appointed to free population, while every state might retain an equal vote in the senate. By moving to revive an old confederation formula, which counted a slave as three-fifths of a man, Wilson promptly headed off an argument that might have split the large-state coalition. But the overwhelming vote for proportional representation in the lower house was followed by a very close decision on the senate, where Sherman's motion for equality was narrowly rejected, 6 to 5: Connecticut, New York, New Jersey, Delaware, and Maryland, aye; Massachusetts, Pennsylvania, Virginia, North Carolina, South Carolina, and Georgia, no. A combination of concerns had joined to check the nationalist momentum. Two days later the Committee of the Whole reported its amended resolutions to the House, but the convention then immediately adjourned in order to permit opponents to prepare alternatives to the Virginia Plan.

William Paterson's New Jersey Resolutions, introduced on June 15, were thrown together quickly by the coaliton that had voted for an equal senate days before. This coalition was united only by its opposition to the Randolph Plan, and its proposals did not represent the real desires of any of their framers. As Dickinson suggested in a private talk with Madison, many members from the smaller states were not opposed in principle to an effective, "national" system. . . . Under the New Jersey Plan, the general government would still have had the power to impose a stamp tax, postal duties, and an impost, to compel compliance with its requisitions, and to regulate the country's interstate and foreign commerce. Federal laws would still have overridden local legislation. A separate executive and federal courts would still have shared authority with Congress. For Luther Martin and the two New Yorkers, this was clearly rather much. For Dickinson and others, just as clearly, Paterson's proposal that the legislature should remain a single house, in which each state would keep its equal vote, was mainly an attempt to force concessions from the other side. . . .

It soon became apparent that the conflict over representation overshadowed every lesser disagreement. The convention managed, with increasing difficulty, to confirm its preference for a bicameral regime. It voted once again for popular election of the lower house and state election of the upper. It reached agreement on a two-year term for representatives and six years for the senate. At every step, however, members fearful of a wholly national plan attempted to insert provisions that would give the states a larger role in paying or selecting federal officials. Small-state delegates attempted a variety of schemes that might disrupt the large-state coalition. Though Madison and Hamilton insisted that the small states need not fear a combination of the large, because the most important differences within the union were between the North and the South, William Samuel Johnson of Connecticut responded that a general government was being framed for states as well as people and that even Mason had admitted that the states should have some means to guarantee their rights and place within the system.

By the end of June, when the Convention voted 6-4-1 (as usual) for proportional representation in the lower house, the meeting was approaching dissolution. At this point Connecticut again proposed the compromise that Sherman had suggested weeks before, putting the proposal now in the language of an ultimatum.

Remarking that the union might be "partly national," but should continue "partly federal" as well, Oliver Ellsworth said that he was not entirely disappointed that the meeting had approved proportional representation in the lower house, which would conform to national ideas and offer safety to the larger states. But he could see no ground for compromise and no alternative to the collapse of the convention and the union if the larger states would not concede an equal senate. . . .

With the meeting at a deadlock and the large-state coalition showing obvious internal stress, Charles C. Pinckney recommended the appointment of a grand committee to devise a compromise. Only Madison and Wilson disapproved, fearing that the tide was turning irreversibly toward an accommodation—as, indeed, it was. Voting for a member from each state, the meeting chose a grand committee that included Ellsworth, Bedford, Paterson, Yates, and Martin, but not a single member from the larger states who had not hinted at a commitment to conciliation. . . .

To Madison and Wilson, the result was not a compromise at all, but a surrender to the smaller states—and one that seriously marred the symmetry of the evolving system. In exchange for equal representation in the upper house, the smaller states accepted proportional representation in the lower and agreed to give the lower house exclusive authority over money bills. This last provision, Madison and Wilson argued, might rob the senate of the power to restrain the lower house on matters where restraint was needed, but it would not prevent minorities from using their position in the senate to defeat the national will. Pleading with the smaller states to give up their demand for a concession plainly incompatible with democratic principles and larger federal powers, the leading nationalists continued to oppose the compromise throughout the next two weeks. They swam against a swelling current.

During these two weeks, the meeting saw a jumble of confusing motions and appointed two additional committees to distribute seats in the first house of representatives. Regional considerations, which had lurked beneath the early 6-4-1 divisions—in which all the southern states had voted with the large-state bloc—now bubbled to the surface. In arguments about a periodic census and admission of new states, as well as in maneuvers over seats in the lower house, members hostile to the three-fifths rule or fearful of the west confronted Southerners who realized that they would be outnumbered 8 to 5 in the projected senate and insisted on provisions that would guarantee their speedy reinforcement from the west, which was a southern section at that time. The smaller northern states proved willing to concede a little on these points in order to secure their more immediate objective. Meanwhile, it became increasingly apparent that several influential members from the larger states were less and less inclined toward a continued confrontation. Not only did they realize that the convention's work would surely be rejected if the smaller states walked out, but some of them conceded that a senate that would represent the states as states might help maintain a federal equilibrium while standing at a proper distance from the lower house. . . . On July 16, the convention voted 5-4-1 for the committee's compromise proposal: Connecticut, New Jersey, Delaware, Maryland, North Carolina, aye; Pennsylvania, Virginia, South Carolina, Georgia, no; Massachusetts divided.

The decision of July 16, as Randolph quickly noted, was not as narrow as the margin might suggest. New York, New Hampshire, and Rhode Island were unrepresented. All would probably have favored equal representation in at least one house. In addition, several moderates from Georgia, Pennsylvania, and Virginia sympathized with those in Massachusetts, Maryland, and North Carolina, who had voted for the Connecticut plan. The large states held a caucus in the aftermath of the decision. Wilson, Madison, and others still preferred to try to face the small states down. The caucus failed to reach agreement. All the members from the larger states returned to the convention, and the smaller states were satisfied from that point forward that opponents of the compromise would make no serious attempt to countermand the vote.

Randolph also said that the decision of July 16 "embarrassed the business extremely." Every previous decision, he explained, had been directly influenced by the supposition that proportional representation would prevail in both branches of the legislature; all would have to be thought through again in light of this new ruling. The implications, for that matter, were even more profound than the Virginian immediately perceived. With the adoption of the Great (or Connecticut) Compromise, every delegate was forced to make new calculations as to how the actions of the central government might touch his state or section. Assured an equal vote in one part of the Congress, the members from the smaller middle states, as Dickinson had predicted, immediately began to favor ample federal powers. Southerners, by contrast, suddenly became more wary, especially of the enormous powers that the gathering had earlier intended for the senate. . . .

Amazingly, on first appearances at least, the members needed only ten more days to reach agreement on the basic features of the Constitution. As Randolph failed to see, however, the decision that the general government would represent both individuals and states prepared the way for resolution of more than just the conflict over representation. Both the large states and the small, the North together with the South, could now anticipate control of one part of the legislature. With every state and section armed with a capacity to counter threats to its essential interests, every delegate felt freer to address the national ills that none of them denied. . . .

Among remaining difficulties, the most perplexing centered on the powers and selection of the chief executive. From July 17 through July 25, the convention literally revolved around these questions. . . . Madison reviewed the options on the 25th. Election by the legislature, he explained, might introduce intrigues and render the executive incapable of acting as a check on legislative usurpations—plainly so if the executive was eligible for reelection. Election by the local legislatures or the state executives, however, might introduce the influence of the very bodies whose "pernicious measures" the convention still intended to control. Two alternatives remained: election by electors chosen by the people, which had been suggested on July 19 by King and Paterson, but handily defeated; or direct election by the people, which he had come to favor but which seemed to put the smaller states, together with the South, at a considerable disadvantage. Hugh Williamson (North Carolina) suggested that the disadvantage to the smaller states could be corrected if the people were required to vote for more than a single candidate. Morris added that the citizens might cast two ballots, one of which would have to be for someone from another state. Yet, reinforced by Gerry, Mason still insisted that the people were least qualified to make a good selection. On the 26th the meeting came full circle to the proposition with which it had started: selection by the national legislature for a single term.

Few were really satisfied with this "solution." . . . Discontent with state equality, fear of legislative domination, and a wish to make it possible for an experienced executive to succeed himself, which seemed impossible to reconcile with legislative choice, were moving Madison and other large-scale nationalists toward popular election and larger executive powers. Yet fear of an elective monarchy, distrust of popular election, and sheer impatience to complete the meeting's tasks still counterbalanced these considerations. On July 24, the House had chosen a Committee of Detail to put its resolutions into order. Now, the members eagerly agreed to an adjournment until Monday, August 6, in order to allow ten days for this committee to report. . . .

John Rutledge (South Carolina), Edmund Randolph, Nathaniel Gorham (Massachusetts), Oliver Ellsworth, and James Wilson assumed responsibility for much more than a careful ordering of the decisions reached in the convention by July 26. In sessions from which only fragmentary records still survive, the Committee of Detail apparently assumed—without objection from their tiring colleagues—that they were free to make significant contributions of their own. Taking note of nearly everything that had transpired in the course of the deliberations. the committee added numerous details to the convention's resolutions and offered several significant additions. Besides providing more elaborate descriptions of executive and judicial powers, their report advanced a new procedure for resolving arguments among the states and recommended that agreement by two-thirds of Congress should be necessary for admission of new states or passage of commercial regulations. It inserted prohibitions of a tax on exports or on interference with the slave trade, which Pinckney had demanded as conditions for his state's agreement. Most significant of all, it offered an enumeration of the powers of the central government, a matter that the full convention had repeatedly postponed, and introduced a range of prohibitions on the sort of local legislation that Madison had planned to counter by a federal veto on state laws, a power that the full convention had decisively refused. . . .

Complicated, often heated arguments concerning these provisions dominated the convention through the second half of August. Though Madison and Wilson joined with King and Morris to condemn the ban on export taxes, protesting that it would deny the government an easy source of revenues and an important weapon in its efforts to compel the Europeans to relax their navigation laws, the planting states were virtually unanimous in their insistence on this prohibition. Georgia and the Carolinas, though opposed by the Virginians as well as by the antislavery members from the North, were equally insistent on prohibiting congressional restrictions on the slave trade, making this an absolute condition of their states' approval of a plan. On August 21 the compromisers from Connecticut and Massachusetts voted with the Southerners to reaffirm the prohibition of a tax on exports, 7 states to 4 (New Hampshire, New Jersey, Pennsylvania, Delaware, no). Sherman, Gerry, Ellsworth, Gorham, and their colleagues indicated, though, that they expected their conciliatory efforts to be met in kind, that they had voted to accept the South's demands in expectation that the Southerners would now prove willing to protect New England's vital interests. On August 22 Morris moved referral of the slave trade, export taxes, and commercial regulation to another grand committee, where these subjects might provide materials for a "bargain" between the North and the South. Several Southerners approved.

The August compromise between the North and the South, Massachusetts and South Carolina, was second in importance only to the bargain of July 16 to the completion of the Constitution. On August 24 the grand committee chaired by William Livingston of New Jersey reported a proposal to prohibit legislative interference with the slave trade until the year 1800, to reaffirm the ban on export taxes, but to strike the clause requiring two-thirds of Congress for the passage of commercial regulations. On August 25, Pinckney moved extension of the prohibition until 1808, Gorham seconded the motion, and the prohibition carried 7 states to 4 (New Jersey, Pennsylvania, Delaware, Virginia, no). . . . Then, on August 31, on Sherman's motion, the convention voted to refer all postponed questions to still another grand committee. The procedure had become the members' standard strategy for handling issues too complex or too divisive for resolution by the whole.

Chaired by David Brearley of New Jersey, the Committee on Unfinished Business (or on Postponed Parts) untangled the convention's last remaining snarls, the knottiest of which was certainly the long-debated question of a sound executive. . . . Reporting on September 4, . . . the Brearley committee sought to cut this knot by recommending an election for a four-year term by electors chosen in such manner as the local legislatures should direct. Each state would be entitled to as many electors as the total of its seats in Congress, and each elector would cast two ballots, at least one of which would have to be for someone from another state. If a single candidate obtained an absolute majority of the electors' votes, he would be president. If not, the president would be elected by the senate from the five who had the highest totals. (In either case, the person placing second in the voting would become vice-president, an office first suggested and defined by this committee.) Both the cumbersome procedure and the introduction of an officer who was essentially superfluous were carefully contrived to balance the demands of the larger and smaller states. . . .

Some of these details proved problematic. Assuming that the college of electors would seldom show an absolute majority for any single person, most members realized that the committee's plan was meant to give the larger states the largest role in making a preliminary nomination, from which the senate, dominated by the smaller states, would make the final choice. Since the smaller states would have a disproportionate advantage even in the number of electors, several members from the larger states objected. . . . In an excellent example of the way in which the delegates had periodically applied collective wisdom to a common problem, these difficulties were resolved by shifting final choice of the executive from the senate to the house of representatives, which would vote by states on this occasion, and by narrowing to three the individuals from among whom the selection must be made. . . .

September 10 saw final pleas for reconsideration of some features over which several members had become increasingly alarmed. Randolph said that he had introduced "a set of republican propositions" on May 29, but that these resolutions had been so disfigured in the course of the convention that he might "dissent" from the completed plan unless the meeting would provide that state conventions could propose amendments to a second general convention, whose alterations would be final. Sharing Randolph's dread of hazy wording and majority control of commerce, together with his fear that an objectionable senate might combine with a powerful executive to overbalance the people's representatives in the lower house,

Mason argued on September 12 that the convention also ought to add a bill of rights. Gerry readily agreed.

Responding partly to these fears, the members did consent to substitute two-thirds of Congress for the three-fourths previously required to override a presidential veto. But with Sherman pointing out that nothing in the Constitution would repeal state declarations or infringe the liberties that they protected, the states unanimously declined to draft a bill of rights. As the convention speedily considered the report of the Committee of Style—obviously eager to adjourn, repeatedly refusing to consider major changes—the final drama was at hand. Mason failed to win insertion of a clause requiring two-thirds of the Congress for the passage of commercial regulations until 1808 (by which date, he may have hoped, the planting states would get their reinforcements from the west). Randolph moved again for a procedure under which the plan would not be ratified until a second general convention could consider changes recommended by the state conventions, warning that he could not sign without some such provision. Concluding that the finished plan "would end either in monarchy or a tyrannical aristocracy," Mason followed with a similar pronouncement, as did Gerry. Randolph's motion was unanimously defeated. Every delegation present voted to approve the finished Constitution and to order it engrossed. . . . Of the forty-two still present on September 17, . . . all but three felt able to subscribe their names to the completed work. Whereupon, as Washington confided to his diary, "the members adjourned to the City Tavern, dined together, and took a cordial leave," nearly all of them agreeing with the venerated Franklin that the emblem on the chair in which the general had presided over their deliberations—testifying by his presence to the gravity of the occasion and the possibility that great executive authority might be entrusted to great virtue—was, indeed, a rising sun.

Ideas and Interests Drove Constitution-Making

JACK N. RAKOVE

Of all the questions that may be asked about the intentions of the framers of the Constitution, seemingly the least puzzling involve explaining the decision to give the states an equal vote in the Senate. . . . [T]he conflict is readily reducible to a single issue: whether the states would retain an equal vote in one house of the national legislature, or whether schemes of proportional representation would be devised for both upper and lower chambers. . . . When the small-state leaders proved unyielding after seven weeks of struggle, their opponents accepted defeat and began the process of pragmatic accommodation that would characterize the remaining two months of deliberation.

. . . [T]he politics of the Great Compromise [of July 16] nicely reflects the prevailing image of the convention as a cumulative process of bargaining and

Jack N. Rakove, "The Great Compromise: Ideas, Interests, and the Politics of Constitution Making," *William and Mary Quarterly,* 3d Series, Vol. 44, 1987, pp. 424–457. Copyright © 1987. Reprinted by permission of *William and Mary Quarterly.*

compromise in which a rigid adherence to principle was subordinated to the pragmatic tests of reaching agreement and building consensus.

Such an emphasis has obvious advantage. It enable scholars to cast the deliberations of 1787 within the familiar frameworks that we ordinarily use to analyze
legislative politics. Historians and political scientists have thus tended to interpret
the results of the convention in more or less equivalent terms: as the pragmatic work
of "a reform caucus in action" or as reflections of changing alignments among delegations that can be charted by identifying either key bargains or shifts in voting
blocs. Such approaches assume that the Federal Convention, however exceptional
or unprecedented it seemed at the time, was ultimately an assembly not so different
from other deliberative bodies whose actions reflect the play of competing interests
espoused by representatives sharing a well-defined set of fundamental values. . . .

Were the politics of the Federal Convention really quite so conventional? The
major scholarly dissenters from this view have been political theorists who are
concerned to recover both the deep convictions upon which the framers acted and
the principles that the Constitution itself incorporated. . . .

At first glance, these disparate emphases on interests and ideas . . . do not sit
well with one another. . . . But at bottom these approaches are more complementary than elusive.

Accepting that ideas and interests separately deserve credit does not, however,
enable us to assess the elusive interplay between them within the actual context of
the convention's deliberations. . . .

Two sets of considerations justify assessing how appeals to theory affected the
unconventional politics of constitution making. First, the key decision of July 16
cannot be construed simply as a triumph for pragmatism. . . . In the end, the Great
Compromise was a compromise in name only. The small states carried their position by the narrowest margin possible: five states to four, with Massachusetts, by
all rights a member of the large-states bloc, divided by the votes of Gerry and
Caleb Strong. The victors naturally called this decision a compromise. But the
losers rightly saw it as a defeat and continued to deny that the nominal concession
extended to them—the power of the House over money bills—was consequential.

Second, although the vote of July 16 was a breakthrough, it was so long in the
making precisely because the preceding seven weeks of debate were dominated
not by efforts to find common ground but by a campaign designed to break the resistance of the small states by persuasion, rational argument, and appeals to principle. During these weeks, the large-state delegates. . . . attempt[ed] to formulate a
theory of representation superior to that which had prevailed at the outset of the
Revolution, to reconceive the basis upon which individuals and interests alike
could be most appropriately represented in government. In place of the received
view that imagined polity composed of the rulers and ruled, of the few and the many,
or (more to the point) of fictive corporate units, they were struggling to fashion a
more realistic—modern—image of society. . . . In the end, of course, reason did
not prevail against will. But to explain why it did not may illuminate the complex
interplay between ideas and interests that shaped the special nature of constitutional politics. And more than that, a careful reconstruction of this struggle demon-
strates that James Madison's theory of the extended republic was very much at the
center of debate throughout these opening weeks.

No one could have been surprised that the issue of representation became the great sticking point of the convention. It had been, after all, the first questions of substance raised at the First Continental Congress of 1774. Rather than bog down in controversy over this issue, Congress had agreed to give each colony one vote. This precedent held up over the next few years, when Congress haltingly went about the task of framing confederation. Against the withering arguments of a succession of large-state delegates—first Patrick Henry and John Adams, later James Wilson— member from the small states clung to the principle of equal state voting. . . . The critical decisions Congress had to take ultimately called not so much for bare majorities as for consensus and even unanimity, and this in turn made fair apportionments seem less urgent.

Rooted as it was in Revolutionary expediency, the victory that the small states gained in drafting the Articles never carried great intellectual conviction, but its theoretical implications gathered importance as criticism of the Articles mounted in the 1780s. Because the principle of an equal state vote was naturally conducive to an image of a federation of sovereign states joined for specific purposes, it sharply limited the range of additional *powers* that would-be reformers of the Articles could seriously consider bestowing on the union. . . .

In practice, the requirement of unanimous state approval made the adoption of any amendment to the Confederation improbable and a change in the principle of representation inconceivable. . . . Only after they abandoned the tactics of piecemeal reform in the waning months of 1786 did it become not only possible but necessary to restore the issue or representation to the central place it had occupied in the original debates over confederation. "The first step to be taken is I think a change in the principle of representation," Madison wrote Edmund Randolph in early April 1787. . . .

Because of the central role that Madison played at Philadelphia and the commanding position his ideas now occupy in all interpretations of "the founding," one must ask why he insisted upon making a shift to some scheme of proportional representation the "ground-work" upon which all other changes would rest. The current canon of interpretation holds that when Madison considered the problem of representation, his principal concern was to establish "such a process of elections as will most certainly extract from the mass of the Society the purest and noblest characters which it contains." In point of fact, however, Madison's commitment to proportional representation preceded in time and exceeded in clarity the development of his ideas about the electoral mechanisms that would bring the right men into office. . . . In 1787 Madison was prepared to accept whatever electoral systems the states adopted so long as principles of equitable apportionment were vindicated. . . .

Madison addressed the issue of proportional representation most explicitly in his preconvention letters. . . . [T]he starting point of this analysis was the inefficacy of a federal system that made Congress so dependent on the states. As Madison observed in his concurrent memorandum on the vices of the political system, an administration resting on the "voluntary compliance" of the states "will never fail to render federal measures abortive." Madison accordingly concluded that the new government had to be empowered to act not indirectly through the states but directly upon their populations. Stripping the states of what might be called their federal functions, would undermine their major claim to a right of equal representation.

Madison had never doubted the justice of such a change; what was new was his belief that it had now become both "practicable" and necessary. The smallest states would oppose any change, but Madison assumed that, in *regional* terms, apportionment would appeal to both the North, because of "the actual superiority of their populousness," and to the South, because of "their expected superiority." . . .

. . . In fashioning his theory of the extended republic, . . . Madison had two preeminent goals in mind. In the first place, he was certainly intent on refuting the received wisdom that held that stable republican governments could be established only in small, relatively homogeneous societies. He had to demonstrate that a national republic could avoid the "vices" that had produced the "multiplicity," "mutability," and finally the "injustice" of state legislation. Scholarly debate will long continue as to which of two key elements of this theory would matter more and the *natural* level of politics: the obstacles the extended republic would place to the formation of factious majorities in the body politic or the legislature, or the encouragement it would give to the recruitment of a talented and conscientious class of legislators. But both prongs of this argument bent to the same point: to prove that national lawmaking would escape the vicious pressures that prevailed in the state assemblies.

This would cure only half the evil. For in the second place, Madison was also convinced that the injustice of state lawmaking required vesting the national legislature with "a negative *in all cases whatsoever* on the legislative acts of the States, as heretofore exercised by the Kingly prerogative." . . .

Madison's attachment to this proposal had important implications for his ideas about representation. Beyond all the other arguments in favor of both proportional representation and popular election, the need to preserve the device that he had hailed as the solution to "the great desideratum" of republican government reinforced his unwillingness to compromise on the issue of apportionment. Foreseeing that a bicameral veto would prove unwieldy, he early decided that "the negative on the laws might be most conveniently exercised" by the upper chamber of the national legislature. Two conclusions followed from this. First, the large states cold never accept the national veto if it were vested in a senate constituted along the same lines as the existing Congress. Second, the negative would prove ineffective if the members of the upper house were elected by the state legislatures and were thus dependent on their will. . . . [B]ecause Madison viewed the upper house as the single most important institution of government, the question of its composition became even more sensitive.

But what other than a credulous confidence in the good intentions of the large states could lead the small states to entrust either the veto or any other substantial powers to a body in which they would no longer enjoy an equal vote? Their great professed fear was that the relative reduction of their representation would expose them to the rapacious impulses of a putative coalition of the large states. . . .

It was in part to overcome this objection that the most familiar element of Madison's theory was addressed: the recognition that "all civilized societies are divided into different interests and factions, as they happen to be creditors or debtors—Rich or poor—husbandmen, merchants or manufacturers—members of different religious sects—followers of different political leaders—inhabitants of different districts—owners of different kinds of property &c &c." Ordinarily this passage (or the more polished variation in the tenth *Federalist*) is cited in the context of Madison's refutation of the orthodox notion that the stability of a republic rested upon the virtue of its citizens and the similarity of their interests. But in two major respects his realistic image of the actual sources of faction was also directly relevant to the issue of proportional representation. For if, in the first place, Madison would indeed prove that the extension of the republic would work to protect *all* interests against factious majorities, the claims of the small states to equal representation for purposes of security would be sharply undercut. The small states would no longer need an equal vote because the process of national legislation would operate to prevent any majority from trampling upon the rights of any minority. . . .

This part of the argument explained why the small states did not *need* equal representation, but Madison further sought to demonstrate why they did not *deserve* it. To make their case conclusive, spokesmen for the large states had to refute the claim that the states deserved representation as corporate units, as the sovereign constituencies of which the union was originally and immutably composed. This was precisely what the modern image of society that forms the very heart of Madison's theory enabled them to do. Implicit in its logic lay the recognition that states themselves were not real interests deserving representation. As political entities they were mere units of convenience that ultimately embodied only the fictitious legal personality of all corporations. . . .

The connection between the specific claim for proportional representation and the ostensibly more general concerns expressed in Madison's preconvention memorandum on the vices of the political system was thus intimate. . . . What he carried to Philadelphia was not a set of discrete proposals but a comprehensive analysis of the problems of federalism and republicanism. Nor was he inclined to rank the components of his theory in order of importance, discriminating those that were essential from those that were merely desirable. Within this argument there was no room for the "compromise" that would eventually prevail. . . .

Yet comprehensive and even integrated as this theory was, it had critical weaknesses. The most obvious, of course, was the pet scheme of the negative on state laws, which was found vulnerable to a wide range of objections. But at Philadelphia two other problems proved even more threatening. One was the difficulty of devising a satisfactory procedure for electing the upper house, one that could safely deprive the state legislatures of a claim to representation. Here the indefinite character of Madison's ideas served him poorly, especially since his desire to render the Senate independent of both the legislatures and the people made it difficult to specify just what social entities it was representing.

The other problem that Madison had not thought through had more ominous overtones. How well would his favorite image of a society "broken into a greater variety of interests, of pursuits, of passions" work when the convention confronted certain stark conflicts, rooted in specific interests, that cut across state lines? . . .

Madison was the best prepared of the delegates who gathered in Philadelphia in May 1787, but he was not the only one who had pondered just how the deliberations were to be structured. Among his colleagues, the nearest potential competitor may have been John Dickinson of Delaware, who had taken the leading role in preparing the first official draft of the Articles of Confederation eleven years earlier. . . .

Rather than seek agreement on broad principles, he argued, the convention need only agree "that the confederation is defective; and then proceed to the definition of such powers as may be thought adequate to the objects for which it was instituted." . . .

On many other points Dickinson and Madison were in agreement. But in the event it was Madison's notion of the course the deliberations should take that prevailed. Chance as much as foresight made this possible: only the tardy arrival of other delegations enabled the Virginians to draft the plan that Randolph presented on May 29. . . .

The plan had a preemptive intent. It presupposed that the powers of the new central government would be substantial but sought to defer discussion of their precise nature and scope until basic agreement had been reached on the structure and composition of its several branches. Rather than detail the specific functions the government would discharge, Article 6 of the plan merely offered a general statement of the principal powers to be accorded to the legislature. These powers were formidable, extending as they did to "the Legislative Rights vested in Congress by the Confederation," to "all cases to which the separate States are incompetent, or in which the harmony of the United States may be interrupted by the exercise of individual [state] legislation," to a national veto over state laws "contravening . . . the articles of Union," and to the right "to call forth the fore of the Union agst. any member . . . failing to fulfill its duty." The contrast between this open-ended language and the carefully delimited amendments to the Articles proposed hitherto could not have been more striking. Finally, on the critical issue of representation the Virginia Plan called for "suffrage . . . to be proportioned to the Quotas of contribution, or to the number of free inhabitants, as the one or the other rule may seem best in different cases." The sole concession extended to the states as such was to permit their assemblies to nominate the candidates from whom the members of the upper house would be chosen by the lower house, which itself would be popularly elected.

As Madison and his colleagues sought to define the issues, then, the problem of representation had to be resolved first. Because the national government was to be so powerful, justice demanded that its political will—vested in the legislature—embody the real constituent interests of the society, not the artificial claims of the states. . . .

Insistence on this rule of action guided the conduct of the large-state delegates throughout the opening weeks of debate. . . . Only when the convention seemed poised near deadlock in late June did they begin to contemplate even modest compromise, but what is more remarkable is the consistency of the positions, both theoretical and tactical, that they held down to the last summative debate of July 14. . . .

The initial debate on the Virginia Plan followed the lines Madison desired—and not because his opponents were stunned by the scope of the changes envisioned. . . . Dickinson revealed as much in calling for "a more simple mode" of proceeding on May 30 and again three days later when he observed that the conflict over representation "must probably end in mutual concession," in which "each State would retain an equal voice at least in one branch of the National Legislature." . . . The strongest evidence of the resentment that Madison's tactics provoked can be found in an encounter that took place immediately after the reading of the New Jersey Plan on June 15, when an angry Dickinson took Madison aside to make sure the message was clear. "You see the consequence of pushing things too far," he asserted. "Some of the members from the small States . . . are friends to a good

National Government; but we would sooner submit to a foreign power, than submit to be deprived of an equality of suffrage, in both branches of the legislature."

This anger was far from unjustified, for from the outset Madison and his allies evinced a candid determination to reject the claim for an equal state vote. "[W]hatever reason might have existed for the equality of suffrage when the Union was a federal one among sovereign States," Madison observed on May 30, "it must cease when a national Governt. should be put into the place." . . .

What had been largely absent from the debate thus far was any sustained effort to explain exactly how the specific rights and interests of the small states would be either injured or protected should proportional representation be instituted in both houses. The second phase of debate that began with William Paterson's reading of the New Jersey Plan on June 15 brought this issue to the fore. In appearance the New Jersey Plan offered a genuinely confederal alternative to the nationalistic thrust of the Virginia Plan. In the substance of the powers it would have conferred on the union, it resembled the proposals for amending the Confederation that had been discussed during the 1780s. . . .

This was so conspicuously its major weakness that one has to ask whether the New Jersey Plan was meant to be taken seriously on its merits . . . —it simply would not have given the federal government the authority that most delegates believed necessary. This its supporters tacitly conceded when they barely bothered to defend the plan's actual provisions. Instead, their central line of argument ran against the legitimacy, not the merits, of the Virginia Plan. . . .

On its merits, then, the New Jersey Plan had little to commend it, and immediately after Madison spoke, the committee of the whole rejected Paterson's resolutions by a decisive margin of seven states to three, with one divided. . . .

. . . But . . . the New Jersey Plan's advocates . . . had already achieved their point. It was . . . to convince the large states that the scope of change envisioned in the Virginia Plan would never be adopted unless the small states were accorded an equal vote in one house. Should the large states persist in *their* ultimatum, the small states would respond in kind and accept nothing that went much beyond the modest amendments discussed in the mid-1780s. . . .

. . . [I]t was during the final third of June that the great issues between the two contending sides were most clearly drawn and the strengths and weaknesses of the large-state position also became evident. . . .

. . . [T]he defense of the equal state vote was deployed along three parallel lines, any two of which could be abandoned as circumstances dictated. The first and most conspicuous held that the interests of the small states would be entirely ignored or overwhelmed should proportional representation prevail in both houses. A second position asserted that the continued existence of the state governments could not be assured "without allowing them to participate effectually in the Genl. Govt.," and that this in turn required "giving them each a distinct and equal vote for the purpose of defending themselves in the general Councils." Finally, the same logic could be extended to imply that the existence of the states "as political societies"—that is, as self-governing communities—similarly depended on the principle of equal representation in the upper house.

The flaws in each of these positions were easy to detect, and leading speakers from the large states hammered away at them relentlessly. . . .

On what basis "was a combination of the large [states] dreaded?" Madison asked. . . . What "common interest" did Virginia, Massachusetts, and Pennsylvania share that would enable them to coalesce against the other states? His answer amounted, in effect, to a restatement of his theory of faction. "In point of situation they could not have been more effectually separated from each other by the most jealous citizen of the most jealous state," Madison declared. "In point of manners, Religion and the other circumstances, which sometimes beget affection between different communities, they were not more assimilated than the other states." Nor, of course, did they have common economic interests. . . .

Yet the overall weakness of their theoretical arguments did little to impair the political position of the small states. . . . Each narrow defeat their coalition suffered strengthened the claim for compromise. . . . Ellsworth disclosed the logic of this gambit: . . . "He was not sorry on the whole" about the result of "the vote just passed," he declared, for "he hoped it would become a ground of compromise with regard to the 2d. branch." He thereupon moved to give the states an equal vote in the upper house.

Ellsworth justified this proposal in part with the famous image of a union that was "partly national; partly federal"; but the argument he pressed more vigorously was the familiar one of security: "the power of self-defence was essential to the small States." An equal vote in the second house would accord them the same protection the large states enjoyed in the first. "If security be all that the great States wish for," he argued the next day, "the 1st. branch secures them." But security was not in fact what the large states desired, Wilson and Madison replied, nor was it to be equated with justice. The true issue was not protection but legislation—that is, the ability of the national government to act, consistent with the will and interests of whatever majority would be represented in Congress. . . .

It was at this point that Madison injected a new argument, . . . well known for its frank invocation of the danger of sectionalism. Madison agreed

> that every peculiar interest whether in any class of citizens, or any description of States, ought to be secured as far as possible. . . . But he contended that the States were divided into different interests not by their difference of size, but by other circumstances; the most material of which resulted partly from climate, but principally from ⟨the effects of⟩ their having or not having slaves. These two causes concurred in forming the great division of interests in the U. States. It did not lie between the large & small States: it lay between the Northern & Southern. [A]nd if any defensive power were necessary, it ought to be mutually given to these two interests. He was so strongly impressed with this important truth that he had been casting about in his mind for some expedient that would answer the purpose.

. . . If he was now willing to risk all the difficulties that the interjection of the sectional issue raised, it could only have been because he sensed that the tide of debate was turning against his position. For the invocation of sectional conflict could cut in two quite different directions. On the one hand, it could certainly be used to show that the immediate conflict between small and large states was not the major danger the union faced; on the other, by calling attention to fundamental differences not simply between states but between entire regions, it also encouraged every delegation to ask how its constituents might be protected should the balance of power within Congress swing against their particular interests.

If these were the assumptions upon which Madison rested his . . . remarks . . . his expectations were well founded. . . . [D]eadlock itself could provide a sufficient rationale for compromise, regardless of the merits of the arguments on either side. . . . [T]he convention elected a committee to frame a compromise, and its very composition revealed how strong the sentiment for accommodation had become. For while the large states were represented by those delegates whose previous statements augured best for conciliation—Gerry, Franklin, and Mason—the members elected from the small states included its leading partisans: Paterson, Ellsworth, Martin, and Gunning Bedford. Moreover, Madison must have sensed that the opportunity for rational persuasion was evaporating. On the central issue of voting there was little left to say. . . . Controversy centered instead on the precise apportionment of representation within the lower house, and as Madison must have expected, this in turn forced each delegation to assess the question of sectional balance.

The debate over apportionment had both geographical and chronological dimensions. It pitted the northern states not only against the southern states but conceivably also against the future states of the West, whose interest in opening the Mississippi to American navigation might lead them into a natural alliance with the South. And it required determining not only how seats would originally be allocated but also how later decisions about reapportionment would be made. . . . The central consideration that drove the convention to give constitutional sanction to both the three-fifths clause and periodic reapportionment was the need to assure the southern states that their current inferiority would be eased or even reversed by the anticipated movement of population to the west and south. The net result of this debate . . . may plausibly be described as a compromise that, ironically, rested on the mistaken assumption that the southern states would soon control the lower house while the northern states would enjoy at least an initial advantage in the Senate.

Within the context of the larger debate over representation in two houses the sociology of sectionalism had one obvious intellectual advantage. It described objective interests and differences that everyone understood were fated to endure well beyond the adjournment of the convention and that reflected in the most profound terms the underlying characteristics of individuals, states, and entire regions. The same could not be said about the mere size of a state. . . .

Yet the marginal gains to be reaped in this way did not outweigh the costs. The more carefully the question of apportionment in the lower house was examined, the more difficult it became for any delegate to ignore considerations of *regional* security. Rather than treat sectional differences as an alternative and superior way of describing the real interests at play in national politics, the delegates saw them instead as an additional conflict that also had to be accommodated if an enduring union was to be established. In this sense, the apportionment issue reinforced the position that the small states had clung to all along. For it called attention not to the way in which all interests could be protected in an extended and extending republic, but rather to the need to safeguard the most conspicuous interest of North and South. This defensive orientation in turn enabled even some large-state delegates to see virtue as well as necessity in the call for an equal state vote. . . .

In his final comments, Madison echoed his [earlier] conclusions. . . . An equal state vote would not merely give the small states the security they craved; in practice it would also enable them to thwart the majority will. But he then cited one last "serious consideration" that he felt should be opposed to the claim for an equal state vote—and he did so in a way that implicitly called into question much of what he had argued hitherto. "It seemed now to be pretty well understood that the real difference of interests lay, not between the large & small but between the N. & Southn. States," Madison reminded his colleagues, alluding, of course, to the previous days of debate over the apportionment of representation in the lower house. "The institution of slavery & its consequences formed the line of discrimination," with the five states from Maryland south arrayed against the eight from Delaware north. The disparity would remain even should a scheme of proportional representation be adopted for both houses, "but not in the same degree [as] at this time; and every day would tend towards an equilibrium" of sectional power.

Did "equilibrium" as Madison used it here mean anything different from the "security" that Ellsworth had sought for the small states? The debate over apportionment had exposed the central tension—or even contradiction—that lay at the core of the general theory that Madison labored so hard to develop. For the recognition that there was one overriding issue that threatened to establish a great "division of interests" between slave and free states could not be easily rendered compatible with the pluralist imagery of the diverse sources of faction. In both instances, it is true, Madison expressed concern for the protection of minority rights, by which he meant, principally but not exclusively, rights of property. Yet radically different inferences could be drawn from these two attempts to trace the origins of faction. . . .

In the end, . . . the framers could not avoid reverting to the idea that states somehow were the essential constituents elements of the polity and that simple residence in the same state would establish the first and most natural bond of individual political loyalty. Even Madison found it hard to convert his brilliant conception of faction into a more detailed map of the diverse interests that actually existed both among and within the states. . . .

. . . [L]egislative election of senators, for all its faults, was preferred by a decisive majority of the convention. From that point on, Madison found himself having to hope either that the damage could be limited without jeopardizing the cause of proportional representation or that an eventual victory on apportionment could be used to reverse the decision on election. But once the specter of sectional conflict legitimated the small states' appeal to security, that opportunity was lost. With it went not his hopes for a better government but his confidence that the analysis he had framed in the spring would provide the foundation upon which the entire system would rest.

To examine the role that particular arguments played within the overall structure of the debates of 1787 does not require us to conclude that the Federal Convention took the form of a seminar in political theory or of sustained intellectual combat between Madison and the ghost of Montesquieu. But the opening weeks of debate were nevertheless very much concerned with testing the appeal and the merits of the original formulation of the theory of the extended republic that James Madison brought to Philadelphia. All of the major components of his thought figured prominently in the debates leading up to the decision of July 16. That result and the consequences that followed from it cannot be described simply as a referendum on Madison's theory.

But neither can the making of the Constitution be adequately explained unless careful attention is paid both to the range of uses to which Madison and his allies put his ideas and to the difficulties they encountered in defending the broad theory.

F U R T H E R   R E A D I N G

Terence Ball and J. G. A. Pocock, eds., *Conceptual Change and the Constitution* (1988)

Lance Banning, *The Sacred Fire of Liberty: James Madison and the Founding of the Federal Republic* (1995)

Richard Beeman, Stephen Botein, and Edward C. Carter II, eds., *Beyond Confederation: Origins of the Constitution and American National Identity* (1987)

Herman Belz, Ronald Hoffman, and Peter J. Albert, eds., *To Form a More Perfect Union: The Critical Ideas of the Constitution* (1991)

Richard B. Bernstein and Kym S. Rice, *Are We to Be a Nation? The Making of the Constitution* (1987)

George Athan Billias, *Elbridge Gerry: Founding Father and Republican Statesman* (1976)

Catherine Drinker Bowen, *Miracle at Philadelphia: The Story of the Constitutional Convention, May to September, 1787* (1966)

Christopher Collier and James Lincoln Collier, *Decision in Philadelphia: The Constitutional Convention of 1787* (1986)

Jacob Ernest Cooke, *Alexander Hamilton* (1982)

Max Farrand, *The Framing of the Constitution of the United States* (1913)

———, ed., *The Records of the Federal Convention of 1787* (1937)

James H. Hutson, ed., *Supplement to Max Farrand's "The Records of the Federal Convention of 1787"* (1987)

Ralph Ketcham, *James Madison: A Biography* (1971)

Leonard W. Levy and Dennis J. Mahoney, eds., *The Framing and Ratification of the Constitution* (1987)

Elizabeth P. McCaughey, *Government by Choice: Inventing the United States Constitution* (1987)

Forrest McDonald, *E Pluribus Unum: The Foundation of the American Republic, 1776–1790* (1965)

[Michael McGiffert, ed.], "The Creation of the American Republic, 1776–1787: A Symposium of Views and Reviews," *William and Mary Quarterly,* 3d Ser., 44 (1987), 549–640.

Andrew C. McLaughlin, *The Confederation and the Constitution, 1783–1789* (1905)

———, *The Foundation of American Constitutionalism* (1932)

William Lee Miller, *The Business of May Next: James Madison and the Founding* (1992)

Richard B. Morris, *Witnesses at the Creation: Hamilton, Madison, Jay, and the Constitution* (1985)

David E. Narrett and Joyce S. Goldberg, eds., *Essays on Liberty and Federalism: The Shaping of the U.S. Constitution* (1988)

Peter S. Onuf, "Reflections on the Founding: Constitutional Historiography in Bicentennial Perspective," *William and Mary Quarterly,* 3d Ser., 46 (1989), 341–375.

Jack N. Rakove, *Original Meanings: Politics and Ideas in the Making of the Constitution* (1996)

Charles Page Smith, *James Wilson, Founding Father, 1742–1798* (1956)

Gordon S. Wood, *The Creation of the American Republic, 1776–1787* (1969)

Neil L. York, ed., *Toward a More Perfect Union: Six Essays on the Constitution* (1988)

Rosemarie Zagarri, *The Politics of Size: Representation in the United States, 1776–1850* (1987)

Ratification Politics
and the Bill of Rights

Part of the mythology that has grown up surrounding the Constitution is that its adoption was inevitable. Today, it is hard to imagine that after all the labors of the constitutional convention, all the shrewdness, wisdom, and insight that went into its debates, the product—our Constitution—might actually have been rejected and thrown on the scrap heap of history. Yet that was a genuine possibility. The procedure written into the Constitution for its adoption, ratification by nine states, supplied its opponents with abundant opportunities to block it. In the four largest states— Massachusetts, New York, Pennsylvania, and Virginia—the Constitution was hotly contested, and in all of these but Pennsylvania, approval came on a close vote after an uphill struggle. Even if ratification could have been achieved without one or more of these large states—and that is doubtful, because of additional opposition in New Hampshire, North Carolina, and Rhode Island—the new nation would scarcely have been viable. Consequently, the ratification struggle, which was not won until June 1788, marked a crucial episode in the creation of the United States of America.

The debates generated by the ratification process have been especially important; not only have they shaped our understanding of the Constitution, but they also led to the adoption of the first ten amendments, the Bill of Rights. The politics of ratification differed from state to state, owing to local circumstances and the allegiances of state leaders, but the arguments employed to attack the Constitution and to defend it were much the same everywhere. They reflected the several strains of ideology that influenced the Revolution, from the liberal, Lockean belief in individual liberty, to the classical republicanism of civic virtue, to the ideal of a strong nation—in addition to the ideology of thrift and industriousness. Nothing less than the future direction of the United States was at stake.

These debates and the Bill of Rights that resulted from the politics of ratification continue to influence American politics and society. Here the classic American political controversies were articulated: over the power of the central government versus the states; the correct relationship between majority rule and minority rights; the proper nature of representation; and the boundaries between executive, legislative, and judicial power. As in 1788, these subjects remain a contested terrain more than 200 years later.

The history of the drafting and ratification of the Constitution teaches us that in most cases it is vain to suppose that we can discover the original intentions of the founding fathers. Indeed, the whole idea that there was some fixed, original intent is misleading. The delegates were rarely unanimous in their thinking at the Philadelphia convention; and once their Constitution entered the ratifying process, it was subject to myriad interpretations by its friends and its foes. Ratification was a political process. Even the Bill of Rights was crafted pragmatically, as a compromise among contending parties. The constitutional achievements of the founders of the United States, while expressing a revolutionary idealism, were ultimately political.

D O C U M E N T S

The four excerpts composing Document 1 are taken from *The Federalist Papers,* a series of eighty-five essays explaining and defending the Constitution that were authored by James Madison, Alexander Hamilton, and John Jay. First written between October 1787 and May 1788 to influence voters in New York, and printed in New York City newspapers, they circulated widely and supplied Federalists elsewhere with arguments to defend the Constitution. Since 1788 *The Federalist Papers* have come to be regarded less as a political tract than as the classic textbook for expounding the meaning and intentions of the Constitution.

Opponents of the Constitution, called Antifederalists, also used the press to express their views. Their newspaper access was somewhat limited, however, because more newspapers favored ratification than not. Document 2 features three Antifederalist perspectives. Richard Henry Lee of Virginia and James Winthrop of Massachusetts were among the most highly recognized spokespersons for the cause. Mercy Otis Warren of Massachusetts, who concealed her identity under the pseudonym "A Columbian Patriot," published the pamphlet *Observations on the New Constitution,* from which the eighteen reasons are drawn. This work, long believed to have been written by Elbridge Gerry, a Massachusetts delegate who refused to sign the Constitution, illustrates the almost paranoid suspiciousness characteristic of many Antifederalist arguments.

The proceedings in the state ratifying conventions are the focus of Documentary 3. These activities reveal the context of Antifederalist criticism within which the movement for a Bill of Rights emerged. Both the Massachusetts proposals and those of Virginia show the nature of Antifederalist concerns. The actual Bill of Rights appears as the final document. Although distinct from the state proposals, it clearly reflects these influences.

1. *The Federalist* Expounds the Advantages of the Constitution, 1787–1788

Factions and Their Remedy (James Madison, No. 10)

November 22, 1787

To the People of the State of New York:

Among the numerous advantages promised by a well constructed Union, none deserves to be more accurately developed than its tendency to break and control the violence of faction. The friend of popular governments, never finds himself so

---

"*The Federalist* Expounds the Advantages of the Constitution, 1787–1788." As found in Alexander Hamilton, John Jay, James Madison, *The Federalist* (New York: Random House, 1961), nos. 10, 39, 84.

much alarmed for their character and fate, as when he contemplates their propensity to this dangerous vice. . . .

By a faction I understand a number of citizens, whether amounting to a majority or minority of the whole, who are united and actuated by some common impulse of passion, or of interest, adverse to the rights of other citizens, or to the permanent and aggregate interests of the community.

There are two methods of curing the mischiefs of faction: the one, by removing its causes; the other, by controling its effects.

There are again two methods of removing the causes of faction: the one by destroying the liberty which is essential to its existence; the other, by giving to every citizen the same opinions, the same passions, and the same interests.

It could never be more truly said than of the first remedy, that it is worse than the disease. Liberty is to faction, what air is to fire, an aliment without which it instantly expires. But it could not be a less folly to abolish liberty, which is essential to political life, because it nourishes faction, than it would be to wish the annihilation of air, which is essential to animal life, because it imparts to fire its destructive agency.

The second expedient is as impracticable, as the first would be unwise. As long as the reason of man continues fallible, and he is at liberty to exercise it, different opinions will be formed. As long as the connection subsists between his reason and his self-love, his opinions and his passions will have a reciprocal influence on each other; and the former will be objects to which the latter will attach themselves. The diversity in the faculties of men from which the rights of property originate, is not less an insuperable obstacle to a uniformity of interests. The protection of these faculties is the first object of Government. From the protection of different and unequal faculties of acquiring property, the possession of different degrees and kinds of property immediately results: and from the influence of these on the sentiments and views of the respective proprietors, ensues a division of the society into different interests and parties.

The latent causes of faction are thus sown in the nature of man; and we see them every where brought into different degrees of activity, according to the different circumstances of civil society. A zeal for different opinions concerning religion, concerning Government and many other points, as well of speculation as of practice; an attachment to different leaders ambitiously contending for pre-eminence and power; or to persons of other descriptions whose fortunes have been interesting to the human passions, have in turn divided mankind into parties, inflamed them with mutual animosity, and rendered them much more disposed to vex and oppress each other, than to co-operate for their common good. So strong is this propensity of mankind to fall into mutual animosities, that where no substantial occasion presents itself, the most frivolous and fanciful distinctions have been sufficient to kindle their unfriendly passions, and excite their most violent conflicts. But the most common and durable source of factions, has been the various and unequal distribution of property. Those who hold, and those who are without property, have ever formed distinct interests in society. Those who are creditors, and those who are debtors, fall under a like discrimination. A landed interest, a manufacturing interest, a mercantile interest, a monied interest, with many lesser interests, grow up of necessity in civilized nations, and divide them into different classes, actuated by different sentiments and views. The regulation of these various and interfering interests forms the principal task of modern Legislation, and involves the spirit of party and faction in the necessary and ordinary operations of Government.

No man is allowed to be a judge in his own cause; because his interest would certainly bias his judgment, and, not improbably, corrupt his integrity. With equal, nay with greater reason, a body of men, are unfit to be both judges and parties, at the same time; yet, what are many of the most important acts of legislation, but so many judicial determinations, not indeed concerning the rights of single persons, but concerning the rights of large bodies of citizens; and what are the different classes of legislators, but advocates and parties to the causes which they determine? . . .

It is in vain to say, that enlightened statesmen will be able to adjust these clashing interests, and render them all subservient to the public good. Enlightened statesmen will not always be at the helm: Nor, in many cases, can such an adjustment be made at all, without taking into view indirect and remote considerations, which will rarely prevail over the immediate interest which one party may find in disregarding the rights of another, or the good of the whole.

The inference to which we are brought, is, that the causes of faction cannot be removed; and that relief is only to be sought in the means of controling its effects.

If a faction consists of less than a majority, relief is supplied by the republican principle, which enables the majority to defeat its sinister views by regular vote: It may clog the administration, it may convulse the society; but it will be unable to execute and mask its violence under the forms of the Constitution. When a majority is included in a faction, the form of popular government on the other hand enables it to sacrifice to its ruling passion or interest, both the public good and the rights of other citizens. To secure the public good, and private rights, against the danger of such a faction, and at the same time to preserve the spirit and the form of popular government, is then the great object to which our enquiries are directed. . . .

By what means is this object attainable? Evidently by one of two only. Either the existence of the same passion or interest in a majority at the same time, must be prevented; or the majority, having such co-existent passion or interest, must be rendered, by their number and local situation, unable to concert and carry into effect schemes of oppression. If the impulse and the opportunity be suffered to coincide, we well know that neither moral nor religious motives can be relied on as an adequate control. . . .

From this view of the subject, it may be concluded, that a pure Democracy, by which I mean, a Society, consisting of a small number of citizens, who assemble and administer the Government in person, can admit of no cure for the mischiefs of faction. A common passion or interest will, in almost every case, be felt by a majority of the whole; a communication and concert results from the form of Government itself; and there is nothing to check the inducements to sacrifice the weaker party, or an obnoxious individual. Hence it is, that such Democracies have ever been spectacles of turbulence and contention; have ever been found incompatible with personal security, or the rights of property; and have in general been as short in their lives, as they have been violent in their deaths. Theoretic politicians, who have patronized this species of Government, have erroneously supposed, that by reducing mankind to a perfect equality in their political rights, they would, at the same time, be perfectly equalized and assimilated in their possessions, their opinions, and their passions.

A Republic, by which I mean a Government in which the scheme of representation takes place, opens a different prospect, and promises the cure for which we are seeking. Let us examine the points in which it varies from pure Democracy, and we shall comprehend both the nature of the cure, and the efficacy which it must derive from the Union.

The two great points of difference between a Democracy and a Republic are, first, the delegation of the Government, in the latter, to a small number of citizens elected by the rest: secondly, the greater number of citizens, and greater sphere of country, over which the latter may be extended.

The effect of the first difference is, on the one hand to refine and enlarge the public views, by passing them through the medium of a chosen body of citizens, whose wisdom may best discern the true interest of their country, and whose patriotism and love of justice, will be least likely to sacrifice it to temporary or partial considerations. Under such a regulation, it may well happen that the public voice pronounced by the representatives of the people, will be more consonant to the public good, than if pronounced by the people themselves convened for the purpose. On the other hand, the effect may be inverted. Men of factious tempers, of local prejudices, or of sinister designs, may by intrigue, by corruption or by other means, first obtain the suffrages, and then betray the interests of the people. The question resulting is, whether small or extensive Republics are most favorable to the election of proper guardians of the public weal: and it is clearly decided in favor of the latter by two obvious considerations.

In the first place it is to be remarked that however small the Republic may be, the Representatives must be raised to a certain number, in order to guard against the cabals of a few; and that however large it may be, they must be limited to a certain number, in order to guard against the confusion of a multitude. Hence the number of Representatives in the two cases, not being in proportion to that of the Constituents, and being proportionally greatest in the small Republic, it follows, that if the proportion of fit characters, be not less, in the large than in the small Republic, the former will present a greater option, and consequently a greater probability of a fit choice.

In the next place, as each Representative will be chosen by a greater number of citizens in the large than in the small Republic, it will be more difficult for unworthy candidates to practise with success the vicious arts, by which elections are too often carried; and the suffrages of the people being more free, will be more likely to centre on men who possess the most attractive merit, and the most diffusive and established characters.

It must be confessed, that in this, as in most other cases, there is a mean, on both sides of which inconveniencies will be found to lie. By enlarging too much the number of electors, you render the representative too little acquainted with all their local circumstances and lesser interests; as by reducing it too much, you render him unduly attached to these, and too little fit to comprehend and pursue great and national objects. The Federal Constitution forms a happy combination in this respect; the great and aggregate interests being referred to the national, the local and particular, to the state legislatures.

The other point of difference is, the greater number of citizens and extent of territory which may be brought within the compass of Republican, than of Democratic Government; and it is this circumstance principally which renders factious combinations less to be dreaded in the former, than in the latter. The smaller the society, the fewer probably will be the distinct parties and interests composing it; the fewer the distinct parties and interests, the more frequently will a majority be found of the same party; and the smaller the number of individuals composing a majority, and the smaller the compass within which they are placed, the more easily will they concert and execute their plans of oppression. Extend the sphere, and you take in a greater variety of parties and interests; you make it less probable that a majority of the whole will have a common motive to invade the rights of other citizens; or if such a common motive exists, it will be more difficult for all who feel it to discover their own strength, and to act in unison with each other. Besides other impediments, it may be remarked, that where there is a consciousness of unjust or dishonorable purposes, communication is always checked by distrust, in proportion to the number whose concurrence is necessary.

Hence it clearly appears, that the same advantage, which a Republic has over a Democracy, in controling the effects of faction, is enjoyed by a large over a small Republic—is enjoyed by the Union over the States composing it. Does this advantage consist in the substitution of Representatives, whose enlightened views and virtuous sentiments render them superior to local prejudices, and to schemes of injustice? It will not be denied, that the Representation of the Union will be most likely to possess these requisite endowments. Does it consist in the greater security afforded by a greater variety of parties, against the event of any one party being able to outnumber and oppress the rest? In an equal degree does the encreased variety of parties, comprised within the Union, encrease this security. Does it, in fine, consist in the greater obstacles opposed to the concert and accomplishment of the secret wishes of an unjust and interested majority? Here, again, the extent of the Union gives it the most palpable advantage.

The influence of factious leaders may kindle a flame within their particular States, but will be unable to spread a general conflagration through the other States: a religious sect, may degenerate into a political faction in a part of the Confederacy; but the variety of sects dispersed over the entire face of it, must secure the national Councils against any danger from that source: a rage for paper money, for an abolition of debts, for an equal division of property, or for any other improper or wicked project, will be less apt to pervade the whole body of the Union, than a particular member of it; in the same proportion as such a malady is more likely to taint a particular county or district, than an entire State.

In the extent and proper structure of the Union, therefore, we behold a Republican remedy for the diseases most incident to Republican Government.

The Constitution Is National and Federal
(James Madison, No. 39)

To the People of the State of New York: . . .

The first question that offers itself is, whether the general form and aspect of the government be strictly republican. It is evident that no other form would be reconcilable with the genius of the people of America; with the fundamental principles of the Revolution; or with that honorable determination which animates every votary of freedom, to rest all our political experiments on the capacity of mankind for self-government. If the plan of the convention, therefore, be found to depart from the republican character, its advocates must abandon it as no longer defensible.

What, then, are the distinctive characters of the republican form? . . . We may define a republic to be, or at least may bestow that name on, a government which derives all its powers directly or indirectly from the great body of the people, and is administered by persons holding their offices during pleasure, for a limited period, or during good behavior. It is essential to such a government that it be derived from the great body of the society, not from an inconsiderable proportion, or a favored class of it; otherwise a handful of tyrannical nobles, exercising their oppressions by a delegation of their powers, might aspire to the rank of republicans, and claim for their government the honorable title of republic. It is sufficient for such a government that the persons administering it be appointed, either directly or indirectly, by the people; and that they hold their appointments by either of the tenures just specified; otherwise every government in the United States, as well as every other popular government that has been or can be well organized or well executed, would be degraded from the republican character. . . .

On comparing the Constitution planned by the convention with the standard here fixed, we perceive at once that it is, in the most rigid sense, conformable to it. The House of Representatives, like that of one branch at least of all the State legislatures, is elected immediately by the great body of the people. The Senate, like the present Congress, and the Senate of Maryland, derives its appointment indirectly from the people. The President is indirectly derived from the choice of the people, according to the example in most of the States. Even the judges with all other officers of the Union, will, as in the several States, be the choice, though a remote choice, of the people themselves. The duration of the appointments is equally conformable to the republican standard, and to the model of State constitutions. The House of Representatives is periodically elective, as in all the States; and for the period of two years, as in the State of South Carolina. The Senate is elective, for the period of six years; which is but one year more than the period of the Senate of Maryland, and but two more than that of the Senates of New York and Virginia. The President is to continue in office for the period of four years; as in New York and Delaware the chief magistrate is elected for three years, and in South Carolina for two years. In the other States the election is annual. In several of the States, however, no constitutional provision is made for the impeachment of the chief magistrate. And in Delaware and Virginia he is not impeachable till out of office. The President of the United States is impeachable at any time during his continuance in office. The tenure by which the judges are to hold their places, is, as it unquestionably ought to be, that of good behavior. The tenure of the ministerial offices generally, will be a subject of legal regulation, conformably to the reason of the case and the example of the State constitutions.

Could any further proof be required of the republican complexion of this system, the most decisive one might be found in its absolute prohibition of titles of nobility, both under the federal and the State governments; and in its express guaranty of the republican form to each of the latter.

"But it was not sufficient," say the adversaries of the proposed Constitution, "for the convention to adhere to the republican form. They ought, with equal care, to have preserved the federal form, which regards the Union as a Confederacy of sovereign states; instead of which, they have framed a national government, which regards the Union as a consolidation of the States." And it is asked by what authority this bold and radical innovation was undertaken? The handle which has been made of this objection requires that it should be examined with some precision. . . .

First.—In order to ascertain the real character of the government, it may be considered in relation to the foundation on which it is to be established; to the sources from which its ordinary powers are to be drawn; to the operation of those powers; to the extent of them; and to the authority by which future changes in the government are to be introduced.

On examining the first relation, it appears, on one hand, that the Constitution is to be founded on the assent and ratification of the people of America, given by deputies elected for the special purpose; but, on the other, that this assent and ratification is to be given by the people, not as individuals composing one entire nation, but as composing the distinct and independent States to which they respectively belong. It is to be the assent and ratification of the several States, derived from the supreme authority in each State,—the authority of the people themselves. The act, therefore, establishing the Constitution, will not be a national, but a federal act.

That it will be a federal and not a national act, as these terms are understood by the objectors; the act of the people, as forming so many independent States, not as forming one aggregate nation, is obvious from this single consideration, that it is to result neither from the decision of a majority of the people of the Union, nor from that of a majority of the States. It must result from the unanimous assent of the several States that are parties to it, differing no otherwise from their ordinary assent than in its being expressed, not by the legislative authority, but by that of the people themselves. Were the people regarded in this transaction as forming one nation, the will of the majority of the whole people of the United States would bind the minority, in the same manner as the majority in each State must bind the minority. . . . Each State, in ratifying the Constitution, is considered as a sovereign body, independent of all others, and only to be bound by its own voluntary act. In this relation, then, the new Constitution will, if established, be a federal, and not a national constitution.

The next relation is, to the sources from which the ordinary powers of government are to be derived. The House of Representatives will derive its powers from the people of America; and the people will be represented in the same proportion, and on the same principle, as they are in the legislature of a particular State. So far the government is national, not federal. The Senate, on the other hand, will derive its powers from the States, as political and coequal societies; and these will be represented on the principle of equality in the Senate, as they now are in the existing Congress. So far the government is federal, not national. The executive power will be derived from a very compound source. The immediate election of the President is to be made by the States in their political characters. The votes allotted to them are in a compound ratio, which considers them partly as distinct and coequal societies, partly as unequal members of the same society. The eventual election, again, is to be made by that branch of the legislature which consists of the national representatives; but in this particular act they are to be thrown into the form of individual delegations, from so many distinct and coequal bodies politic. From this aspect of the government, it appears to be of a mixed character, presenting at least as many federal as national features. . . .

The proposed Constitution, therefore, is, in strictness, neither a national nor a federal Constitution, but a composition of both. In its foundation it is federal, not national; in the sources from which the ordinary powers of the government are drawn, it is partly federal and partly national; in the operation of these powers, it is national, not federal; in the extent of them, again, it is federal, not national; and, finally, in the authoritative mode of introducing amendments, it is neither wholly federal nor wholly national.

The System of Checks and Balances (Alexander Hamilton or James Madison, No. 51)

To the People of the State of New York:

To what expedient, then, shall we finally resort, for maintaining in practice the necessary partition of power among the several departments, as laid down in the Constitution? The only answer that can be given is, that as all these exterior provisions are found to be inadequate, the defect must be supplied, by so contriving the interior structure of the government as that its several constituent parts may, by their mutual relations, be the means of keeping each other in their proper places. . . .

In order to lay a due foundation for that separate and distinct exercise of the different powers of government, which to a certain extent is admitted on all hands to be essential to the preservation of liberty, it is evident that each department should have a will of its own; and consequently should be so constituted that the members of each should have as little agency as possible in the appointment of the members of the others. . . .

It is equally evident, that the members of each department should be as little dependent as possible on those of the others, for the emoluments annexed to their offices. Were the executive magistrate, or the judges, not independent of the legislature in this particular, their independence in every other would be merely nominal.

But the great security against a gradual concentration of the several powers in the same department, consists in giving to those who administer each department the necessary constitutional means and personal motives to resist encroachments of the others. The provision for defence must in this, as in all other cases, be made commensurate to the danger of attack. Ambition must be made to counteract ambition. The interest of the man must be connected with the constitutional rights of the place. It may be a reflection on human nature, that such devices should be necessary to control the abuses of government. But what is government itself, but the greatest of all reflections on human nature? If men were angels, no government would be necessary. If angels were to govern men, neither external nor internal controls on government would be necessary. In framing a government which is to be administered by men over men, the great difficulty lies in this: you must first enable the government to control the governed; and in the next place oblige it to control itself. A dependence on the people is, no doubt, the primary control on the government; but experience has taught mankind the necessity of auxiliary precautions. . . .

But it is not possible to give to each department an equal power of self-defence. In republican government, the legislative authority necessarily predominates. The remedy for this inconveniency is to divide the legislature into different branches; and to render them, by different modes of election and different principles of action, as little connected with each other as the nature of their common functions and their common dependence on the society will admit. It may even be necessary to guard against dangerous encroachments by still further precautions. As the weight of the legislative authority requires that it should be thus divided, the weakness of the executive may require, on the other hand, that it should be fortified. An absolute negative on the legislature appears, at first view, to be the natural defence with which the executive magistrate should be armed. But perhaps it would be neither altogether safe nor alone sufficient. On ordinary occasions it might not be exerted with the requisite firmness, and on extraordinary occasions it might be perfidiously abused. . . .

There are, moreover, two considerations particularly applicable to the federal system of America, which place that system in a very interesting point of view.

First. In a single republic, all the power surrendered by the people is submitted to the administration of a single government; and the usurpations are guarded against by a division of the government into distinct and separate departments. In the compound republic of America, the power surrendered by the people is first divided between two distinct governments, and then the portion allotted to each subdivided among distinct and separate departments. Hence a double security arises to the rights of the people. The different governments will control each other, at the same time that each will be controlled by itself.

Second. It is of great importance in a republic not only to guard the society against the oppression of its rulers, but to guard one part of the society against the injustice of the other part. Different interests necessarily exist in different classes of citizens. If a majority be united by a common interest, the rights of the minority will be insecure. . . .

In the extended republic of the United States, and among the great variety of interests, parties, and sects which it embraces, a coalition of a majority of the whole society could seldom take place on any other principles than those of justice and the general good.

No Bill of Rights Is Needed (Alexander Hamilton, No. 84)

To the People of the State of New York:

In the course of the foregoing review of the Constitution, I have taken notice of, and endeavored to answer most of the objections which have appeared against it. . . .

The most considerable of the remaining objections is that the plan of the convention contains no bill of rights. Among other answers given to this, it has been upon different occasions remarked that the constitutions of several of the States are in a similar predicament. I add that New York is of the number. And yet the opposers of the new system, in this State, who profess an unlimited admiration for its constitution, are among the most intemperate partisans of a bill of rights. To justify their zeal in this matter, they allege two things: one is that, though the constitution of New York has no bill of rights prefixed to it, yet it contains, in the body of it, various provisions in favor of particular privileges and rights, which, in substance, amount to the same thing; the other is, that the Constitution adopts, in their full extent, the common and statute law of Great Britain, by which many other rights, not expressed in it, are equally secured.

To the first I answer, that the Constitution proposed by the convention contains, as well as the constitution of this State, a number of such provisions.

Independent of those which relate to the structure of the government, we find the following: Article 1, section 3, clause 7—"Judgment in cases of impeachment shall not extend further than to removal from office, and disqualification to hold and enjoy any office of honor, trust, or profit under the United States; but the party convicted shall, nevertheless, be liable and subject to indictment, trial, judgment, and punishment according to law." Section 9, of the same article, clause 2—"The privilege of the writ of habeas corpus shall not be suspended, unless when in cases of rebellion or invasion the public safety may require it." Clause 3—"No bill of attainder or ex-post-facto law shall be passed." Clause 7—"No title of nobility shall be granted by the United States; and no person holding any office of profit or trust under them, shall, without the consent of the Congress, accept of any present, emolument, office, or title of any kind whatever, from any king, prince, or foreign state." Article 3, section 2, clause 3—"The trial of all crimes, except in cases of impeachment, shall be by jury; and such trial shall be held in the State where the said crimes shall have been committed; but when not committed within any State, the trial shall be at such place or places as the Congress may by law have directed." Section 3, of the same article—"Treason against the United States shall consist only in levying war against them, or in adhering to their enemies, giving them aid and comfort. No person shall be convicted of treason, unless on the testimony of two witnesses to the same overt act, or on confession in open court." And clause 3, of the same section—"The Congress shall have power to declare the punishment of treason; but no attainder of treason shall work corruption of blood, or forfeiture, except during the life of the person attainted."

It may well be a question, whether these are not, upon the whole, of equal importance with any which are to be found in the constitution of this State. The establishment of the writ of habeas corpus, the prohibition of ex-post-facto laws, and of Titles of Nobility, to which we have no corresponding provision in our [New York] Constitution, are perhaps greater securities to liberty and republicanism than any it contains. The creation of crimes after the commission of the fact, or, in other words, the subjecting of men to punishment for things which, when they were done, were breaches of no law, and the practice of arbitrary imprisonments, have been, in all ages, the favorite and most formidable instruments of tyranny. . . .

To the second—that is, to the pretended establishment of the common and statute law by the Constitution, I answer, that they are expressly made subject "to such alterations and provisions as the legislature shall from time to time make concerning the same." They are therefore at any moment liable to repeal by the ordinary legislative power, and of course have no constitutional sanction. The only use of the declaration was to recognize the ancient law, and to remove doubts which might have been occasioned by the Revolution. This consequently can be considered as no part of a declaration of rights, which under our constitutions must be intended as limitations of the power of the government itself.

It has been several times truly remarked that bills of rights are, in their origin, stipulations between kings and their subjects, abridgments of prerogative in favor of privilege, reservations of rights not surrendered to the prince. Such was Magna Charta, obtained by the barons, sword in hand, from King John. Such were the subsequent confirmations of that charter by succeeding princes. Such was the *Petition of Right* assented to by Charles I., in the beginning of his reign. Such, also, was the Declaration of Right presented by the Lords and Commons to the Prince of Orange in 1688, and afterwards thrown into the form of an act of parliament called the Bill of Rights. It is evident, therefore, that, according to their primitive signification, they have no application to constitutions, professedly founded upon the power of the people, and executed by their immediate representatives and servants. Here, in strictness, the people surrender nothing; and as they retain every thing they have no need of particular reservations. "We, the people of the United States, to secure the blessings of liberty to ourselves and our posterity, do ordain and establish this Constitution for the United States of America." Here is a better recognition of popular rights. . . .

I go further, and affirm that bills of rights, in the sense and to the extent in which they are contended for, are not only unnecessary in the proposed Constitution, but would even be dangerous. They would contain various exceptions to powers not granted; and, on this very account, would afford a colorable pretext to claim more than were granted. For why declare that things shall not be done which there is no power to do? Why, for instance, should it be said that the liberty of the press shall not be restrained, when no power is given by which restrictions may be imposed? I will not contend that such a provision would confer a regulating power; but it is evident that it would furnish, to men disposed to usurp, a plausible pretence for claiming that power. They might urge with a semblance of reason, that the Constitution ought not to be charged with the absurdity of providing against the abuse of an authority which was not given, and that the provision against restraining the liberty of the press afforded a clear implication, that a power to prescribe proper regulations concerning it was intended to be vested in the national government. This may serve as a specimen of the numerous handles which would be given to the doctrine of constructive powers, by the indulgence of an injudicious zeal for bills of rights.

On the subject of the liberty of the press, as much as has been said, I cannot forbear adding a remark or two: in the first place, I observe, that there is not a syllable concerning it in the constitution of this State; in the next, I contend, that whatever has been said about it in that of any other State, amounts to nothing. What signifies a declaration, that "the liberty of the press shall be inviolably preserved"? What is the liberty of the press? Who can give it any definition which would not leave the utmost latitude for evasion? I hold it to be impracticable; and from this I infer, that its security, whatever fine declarations may be inserted in any constitution respecting it, must altogether depend on public opinion, and on the general spirit of the people and of the government. . . .

There remains but one other view of this matter to conclude the point. The truth is, after all the declamations we have heard, that the Constitution is itself, in every rational sense, and to every useful purpose, A BILL OF RIGHTS. The several bills of rights in Great Britain form its Constitution, and conversely the constitution of each State is its bill of rights. And the proposed Constitution, if adopted, will be the bill of rights of the Union. Is it one object of a bill of rights to declare and specify the political privileges of the citizens in the structure and administration of the government? This is done in the most ample and precise manner in the plan of the convention; comprehending various precautions for the public security, which are not to be found in any of the State constitutions. Is another object of a bill of rights to define certain immunities and modes of proceeding, which are relative to personal and private concerns? This we have seen has also been attended to, in a variety of cases, in the same plan. Adverting therefore to the substantial meaning of a bill of rights, it is absurd to allege that it is not to be found in the work of the convention.

2. Antifederalists Attack the Constitution, 1787–1788

Richard Henry Lee on Why a National Government Will Be Unrepresentative and Despotic

The essential parts of a free and good government are a full and equal representation of the people in the legislature, and the jury trial of the vicinage in the administration of justice—a full and equal representation, is that which possesses the same interests, feelings, opinions, and views the people themselves would were they all assembled—a fair representation, therefore, should be so regulated, that every order of men in the community, according to the common course of elections, can have a share in it—in order to allow professional men, merchants, traders, farmers, mechanics, &c. to bring a just proportion of their best informed men respectively into the legislature, the representation must be considerably numerous—We have about 200 state senators in the United States, and a less number than that of federal representatives cannot, clearly, be a full representation of this people, in the affairs of internal taxation and police, were there but one legislature for the whole union. The representation cannot be equal, or the situation of the people proper for one government only—if the extreme parts of the society cannot be represented as fully as the central—It is apparently impracticable that this should be the case in this extensive country—it would be impossible to collect a representation of the parts of the country five, six, and seven hundred miles from the seat of government. . . .

There are other considerations which tend to prove that the idea of one consolidated whole, on free principles, is ill-founded—the laws of a free government rest on the confidence of the people, and operate gently—and never can extend the influence very far—if they are executed on free principles, about the centre, where the benefits of the government induce the people to support it voluntarily; yet they must be executed on the principles of fear and force in the extremes—This has been the case with every extensive republic of which we have any accurate account.

There are certain unalienable and fundamental rights, which in forming the social compact, ought to be explicitly ascertained and fixed. . . . I do not pay much regard to the reasons given for not bottoming the new constitution on a better bill of rights. I still believe a complete federal bill of rights to be very practicable. . . .

There is no reason to expect the numerous state governments, and their connections, will be very friendly to the execution of federal laws in those internal affairs,

"Richard Henry Lee on Why a National Government Will Be Unrepresentative and Despotic." In Richard Henry Lee, *Observations Leading to a Fair Examination of the System of Government Proposed by the Late Convention; and to Several Essential and Necessary Alterations in It. In a Number of Letters from the Federal Farmer to the Republican* (New York: Thomas Greenleaf, 1787), 202–205.

which hitherto have been under their own immediate management. There is more reason to believe, that the general government, far removed from the people, and none of its members elected oftener than once in two years, will be forgot or neglected, and its laws in many cases disregarded, unless a multitude of officers and military force be continually kept in view, and employed to enforce the execution of the laws, and to make the government feared and respected. . . . Neglected laws must first lead to anarchy and confusion; and a military execution of laws is only a shorter way to the same point—despotic government.

James Winthrop Explains Why a Large Republic Cannot Work

To the People. . . .

. . . It is the opinion of the ablest writers on the subject, that no extensive empire can be governed upon republican principles, and that such a government will degenerate to a despotism, unless it be made up of a confederacy of smaller states, each having the full powers of internal regulation. This is precisely the principle which has hitherto preserved our freedom. No instance can be found of any free government of considerable extent which has been supported upon any other plan. . . . The reason is obvious. In large states the same principles of legislation will not apply to all the parts. The inhabitants of warmer climates are more dissolute in their manners, and less industrious, than in colder countries. A degree of severity is, therefore, necessary with one which would cramp the spirit of the other. We accordingly find that the very great empires have always been despotick. They have indeed tried to remedy the inconveniences to which the people were exposed by local regulations; but these contrivances have never answered the end. The laws not being made by the people, who felt the inconveniences, did not suit their circumstances. . . . To promote the happiness of the people it is necessary that there should be local laws; and it is necessary that those laws should be made by the representatives of those who are immediately subject to the want of them. By endeavouring to suit both extremes, both are injured.

It is impossible for one code of laws to suit Georgia and Massachusetts. They must, therefore, legislate for themselves. Yet there is, I believe, not one point of legislation that is not surrendered in the proposed plan. . . . The idea of an uncompounded republick, on an average one thousand miles in length, and eight hundred in breadth, and containing six millions of white inhabitants all reduced to the same standard of morals, of habits, and of laws, is in itself an absurdity, and contrary to the whole experience of mankind. The attempt made by Great Britain to introduce such a system, struck us with horrour, and when it was proposed by some theorist that we should be represented in parliament, we uniformly declared that one legislature could not represent so many different interests for the purposes of legislation and taxation. This was the leading principle of the revolution, and makes an essential article in our creed. All that part, therefore, of the new system, which relates to the internal government of the states, ought at once to be rejected.

"James Winthrop Explains Why a Large Republic Cannot Work." In James Winthrop, "The Letters of Agrippa," *Massachusetts Gazette* (Boston), December 3, 1787. Also in Paul Leicester Ford, ed., *Essays on the Constitution of the United States, Published During the Discussion by the People, 1787–1788* (Brooklyn, NY: Oliver & Munroe and John Cushing, 1892), 63–65.

Mercy Otis Warren Offers Eighteen Reasons to Reject the Constitution

I will first observe . . . the best political writers have supported the principles of annual elections with a precision, that cannot be confuted, though they may be darkned, by the sophistical arguments that have been thrown out with design, to undermine all the barriers of freedom.

2. There is no security in the profered [sic] system, either for the rights of conscience or the liberty of the Press. . . .

3. There are no well defined limits of the Judiciary Powers, they seem to be left as a boundless ocean. . . .

4. The Executive and the Legislative are so dangerously blended as to give just cause of alarm, and every thing relative thereto, is couched in such ambiguous terms—in such vague and indefinite expression, as is a sufficient ground without any objection, for the reprobation of a system, that the authors dare not hazard to a clear investigation.

5. The abolition of trial by jury in civil causes.—This mode of trial the learned Judge Blackstone observes, "has been coeval with the first rudiments of civil government, that property, liberty and life, depend on maintaining in its legal force the constitutional trial by jury." . . .

6. Though it has been said by Mr. Wilson and many others, that a Standing-Army is necessary for the dignity and safety of America, yet freedom revolts at the idea. . . . Standing armies have been the nursery of vice and the bane of liberty from the Roman legions to the . . . planting of the British cohorts in the capitals of America:—By the edicts of an authority vested in the sovereign power by the proposed constitution, the militia of the country, the bulwark of defence, and the security of national liberty . . . may be sent into foreign countries for the fulfilment of treaties, stipulated by the President and two thirds of the Senate.

7. Notwithstanding the delusory promise to guarantee a Republican form of government to every State in the Union—. . . there are no resources left for the support of internal government, or the liquidation of the debts of the State. Every source of revenue is in the monopoly of Congress. . . .

8. As the new Congress are empowered to determine their own salaries, the requisitions for this purpose may not be very moderate, and the drain for public moneys will probably rise past all calculation. . . .

9. There is no provision for a rotation, nor anything to prevent the perpetuity of office in the same hands for life; which by a little well timed bribery, will probably be done, to the exclusion of men of the best abilities from their share in the offices of government. . . .

10. The inhabitants of the United States, are liable to be draged [sic] from the vicinity of their own country, or state, to answer the litigious or unjust suit of an adversary, on the most distant borders of the Continent: in short the appelate jurisdiction of the Supreme Federal Court, includes an unwarrantable stretch of power over the liberty, life, and property of the subject, through the wide Continent of America.

"Mercy Otis Warren Offers Eighteen Reasons to Reject the Constitution." In Mercy Otis Warren, *Observations on the New Constitution, and on the Federal and State Conventions. By a Columbian Patriot* (Boston, 1788), 7–13.

11. One Representative to thirty thousand inhabitants is a very inadequate representation. . . .

12. If the sovereignty of America is designed to be elective, the circumscribing the votes to only ten electors in this State, and the same proportion in all the others, is nearly tantamount to the exclusion of the voice of the people in the choice of their first magistrate. It is vesting the choice solely in an aristocratic junto, who may easily combine in each State to place at the head of the Union the most convenient instrument for despotic sway.

13. A Senate chosen for six years will, in most instances, be an appointment for life, as the influence of such a body over the minds of the people will be coequal to the extensive powers with which they are vested. . . .

14. There is no provision by a bill of rights to guard against the dangerous encroachments of power in too many instances to be named: . . . The rights of individuals ought to be the primary object of all government, and cannot be too securely guarded by the most explicit declarations in their favor. . . .

15. The difficulty, if not impracticability, of exercising the equal and equitable powers of government by a single legislature over an extent of territory that reaches from the Mississippi to the Western lakes, and from them to the Atlantic Ocean, is an insuperable objection to the adoption of the new system. . . .

16. It is an undisputed fact that not one legislature in the United States had the most distant idea when they first appointed members for a convention, entirely commercial, or when they afterwards authorized them to consider on some amendments of the Federal union, that they would without any warrant from their constituents, presume on so bold and daring a stride, as ultimately to destroy the state governments, and offer a consolidated system, irreversible but on conditions that the smallest degree of penetration must discover to be impracticable.

17. The first appearance of the article which declares the ratification of nine states sufficient for the establishment of the new system, wears the face of dissension, is a subversion of the union of Confederated States. . . .

18. The mode in which this constitution is recommended to the people to judge without either the advice of Congress, or the legislatures of the several states is very reprehensible—it is an attempt to force it upon them before it could be thoroughly understood.

3. Proceedings in the State Ratifying Conventions, 1788

Massachusetts Proposes Amendments to the Constitution

The Convention, having impartially discussed, and fully considered the constitution for the United States of America, reported to Congress, by the Convention of delegates from the United States of America, and submitted to us, by a resolution of the

---

"Massachusetts Proposes Amendments to the Constitution, in Massachusetts Convention, 1788." In Jonathan Elliot, *Debates, Resolutions and Other Proceedings of the Convention of the Commonwealth of Massachusetts . . . on the Decision of the Grand Question* (Boston: Oliver & Munroe and John Cushing, 1808), 222–224.

General Court . . . Do, in the name, and in behalf of the people of the Commonwealth of Massachusetts, assent to and ratify the said constitution for the United States of America.

And, as it is the opinion of this Convention, that certain amendments and alterations in the said constitution would remove the fears and quiet the apprehensions of many of the good people of this commonwealth, and more effectually guard against an undue administration of the federal government, the Convention do therefore recommend that the following alterations and provisions be introduced into the said constitution.

First, That it be explicitly declared, that all powers not expressly delegated by the aforesaid constitution, are reserved to the several states, to be by them exercised.

Secondly, That there shall be one representative to every thirty thousand persons, according to the census mentioned in the constitution, until the whole number of representatives amounts to two hundred.

Thirdly, That Congress do not exercise the powers vested in them by the 4th section of the first article, but in cases when a state shall neglect or refuse to make the regulations therein mentioned, or shall make regulations subversive of the rights of the people to a free and equal representation in Congress, agreeably to the constitution.

Fourthly, That Congress do not lay direct taxes, but when the monies arising from the impost and excise are insufficient for the publick exigencies, nor then, until Congress shall have first made a requisition upon the states, to assess, levy and pay their respective proportion of such requisition, agreeably to the census fixed in the said constitution, in such way and manner as the legislatures of the states shall think best, and in such case, if any state shall neglect or refuse to pay its proportion, pursuant to such requisition, then Congress may assess and levy such state's proportion, together with interest thereon, at the rate of six per cent per annum, from the time of payment prescribed in such requisition.

Fifthly, That Congress erect no company with exclusive advantages of commerce.

Sixthly, That no person shall be tried for any crime, by which he may incur an infamous punishment, or loss of life, until he be first indicted by a grand jury, except in such cases as may arise in the government and regulation of the land and naval forces.

Seventhly, The Supreme Judicial Federal Court shall have no jurisdiction of causes, between citizens of different states, unless the matter in dispute, whether it concern the realty or personalty, be of the value of three thousand dollars at the least; nor shall the federal judicial powers extend to any action between citizens of different states, where the matter in dispute, whether it concerns the realty or personalty, is not of the value of fifteen hundred dollars at the least.

Eighthly, In civil actions between citizens of different states, every issue of fact, arising in actions at common law, shall be tried by a jury, if the parties or either of them, request it.

Ninthly, Congress shall at no time consent, that any person holding an office of trust or profit, under the United States, shall accept of a title of nobility, or any other title or office, from any king, prince, or foreign state.

Patrick Henry of Virginia Denounces the Constitution

Have they said, We, the states? Have they made a proposal of a compact between states? If they had, this would be a confederation. It is otherwise most clearly a consolidated government. The question turns, sir, on that poor little thing—the expression, We, the people, instead of the states, of America. I need not take much pains to show that the principles of this system are extremely pernicious, impolitic, and dangerous. . . . Here is a resolution as radical as that which separated us from Great Britain. It is radical in this transition; our rights and privileges are endangered, and the sovereignty of the states will be relinquished. . . . The rights of conscience, trial by jury, liberty of the press, all your immunities and franchises, all pretensions to human rights and privileges, are rendered insecure, if not lost, by this change. . . . It is said eight states have adopted this plan. I declare that if twelve states and a half had adopted it, I would, with manly firmness, and in spite of an erring world, reject it. You are not to inquire how your trade may be increased, nor how you are to become a great and powerful people, but how your liberties can be secured; for liberty ought to be the direct end of your government.

. . . Is it necessary for your liberty that you should abandon those great rights by the adoption of this system? Is the relinquishment of the trial by jury and the liberty of the press necessary for your liberty? Will the abandonment of your most sacred rights tend to the security of your liberty? Liberty, the greatest of all earthly blessings—give us that precious jewel, and you may take every thing else! . . . We are come hither to preserve the poor commonwealth of Virginia, if it can be possibly done: something must be done to preserve your liberty and mine. The Confederation, this same despised government, merits, in my opinion, the highest encomium: it carried us through a long and dangerous war; it rendered us victorious in that bloody conflict with a powerful nation; it has secured us a territory greater than any European monarch possesses: and shall a government which has been thus strong and vigorous, be accused of imbecility, and abandoned for want of energy? Consider what you are about to do before you part with the government. . . .

How does your trial by jury stand? In civil cases gone—not sufficiently secured in criminal—this best privilege is gone. But we are told that we need not fear; because those in power, being our representatives, will not abuse the powers we put in their hands. I am not well versed in history, but I will submit to your recollection, whether liberty has been destroyed most often by the licentiousness of the people, or by the tyranny of rulers. I imagine, sir, you will find the balance on the side of tyranny. . . . Most of the human race are now in this deplorable condition. . . .

. . . [It] appears that three fourths of the states must ultimately agree to any amendments that may be necessary. Let us consider the consequence of this. . . . To suppose that so large a number as three fourths of the states will concur, is to suppose that they will possess genius, intelligence, and integrity, approaching to miraculous. . . . A trifling minority may reject the most salutary amendments. Is this an easy mode of securing the public liberty? It is, sir, a most fearful situation,

From Jonathan Elliot, ed., *The Debates in the Several State Conventions on the Adoption of the Federal Constitution* (Philadelphia: Lippincott, 1836), vol. 3, pp. 44–54, 56–61, 63, 324–326.

when the most contemptible minority can prevent the alteration of the most oppressive government. . . .

This, sir, is the language of democracy—that a majority of the community
have a right to alter government when found to be oppressive. But how different is
the genius of your new Constitution from this! How different from the sentiments
of freemen, that a contemptible minority can prevent the good of the majority! . . .

A standing army we shall have, also, to execute the execrable commands of
tyranny. . . . Your militia is given up to Congress, also, in another part of this
plan: they will therefore act as they think proper: all power will be in their own
possession. . . .

. . . The distinction between a national government and a confederacy is not
sufficiently discerned. Had the delegates, who were sent to Philadelphia, a power
to propose a consolidated government instead of a confederacy? Were they not
deputed by states, and not by the people? The assent of the people, in their collective capacity, is not necessary to the formation of a federal government. The people
have no right to enter into leagues, alliances, or confederations; they are not the
proper agents for this purpose. . . . This, therefore, ought to depend on the consent
of the legislatures, the people having never sent delegates to make any proposition
for changing the government. . . .

Consider our situation, sir: go to the poor man, and ask him what he does. He
will inform you that he enjoys the fruits of his labor, under his own fig-tree, with
his wife and children around him, in peace and security. Go to every other member
of society,—you will find the same tranquil ease and content; you will find no
alarms or disturbances. Why, then, tell us of danger, to terrify us into an adoption
of this new form of government? And yet who knows the dangers that this new system may produce? They are out of the sight of the common people: they cannot
foresee latent consequences. I dread the operation of it on the middling and lower
classes of people: it is for them I fear the adoption of this system. . . .

The necessity of amendments is universally admitted. . . . I ask, if amendments
be necessary, from whence can they be so properly proposed as from this state?
The example of Virginia is a powerful thing, particularly with respect to North
Carolina, whose supplies must come through Virginia. Every possible opportunity
of procuring amendments is gone, our power and political salvation are gone, if we
ratify unconditionally. . . .

We are told that all powers not given are reserved. . . . The English history is
frequently referred to by gentlemen. Let us advert to the conduct of the people
of that country. The people of England lived without a declaration of rights till
the war in the time of Charles 1. That king made usurpations upon the rights of
the people. . . .

The rights of the people continued to be violated till the Stuart family was banished, in the year 1688. The people of England magnanimously defended their rights,
banished the tyrant, and prescribed to William, Prince of Orange, by the bill of rights,
on what terms he should reign; and this bill of rights put an end to all construction
and implication. Before this, sir, the situation of the public liberty of England was
dreadful. For upwards of a century, the nation was involved in every kind of calamity,
till the bill of rights put an end to all, by defining the rights of the people, and limiting
the king's prerogative. . . . It is alleged that several states, in the formation of their

government, omitted a bill of rights. To this I answer, that they had the substance of a bill of rights contained in their constitutions, which is the same thing. . . .

Of what advantage is it to the American Congress to take away this great and general security? . . . Why is the trial by jury taken away? All the learned arguments that have been used on this occasion do not prove that it is secured. Even the advocates for the plan do not all concur in the certainty of its security. Wherefore is religious liberty not secured? . . . This sacred right ought not to depend on constructive, logical reasoning.

When we see men of such talents and learning compelled to use their utmost abilities to convince themselves that there is no danger, is it not sufficient to make us tremble?

Virginia's Declaration of Rights and Proposed Amendments to the Constitution

Mr. Wythe reported, from the committee appointed, such amendments to the proposed Constitution of government for the United States as were by them deemed necessary to be recommended to the consideration of the Congress which shall first assemble under the said Constitution, to be acted upon according to the mode prescribed . . . as follows:—

That there be a declaration or bill of rights asserting, and securing from encroachment, the essential and unalienable rights of the people, in some such manner as the following:—

1st. That there are certain natural rights, of which men, when they form a social compact, cannot deprive or divest their posterity; among which are the enjoyment of life and liberty, with the means of acquiring, possessing, and protecting property, and pursuing and obtaining happiness and safety.

2d. That all power is naturally invested in, and consequently derived from, the people; that magistrates therefore are their trustees and agents, at all times amenable to them.

3d. That government ought to be instituted for the common benefit, protection, and security of the people; and that the doctrine of non-resistance against arbitrary power and oppression is absurd, slavish, and destructive to the good and happiness of mankind.

4th. That no man or set of men are entitled to separate or exclusive public emoluments or privileges from the community, but in consideration of public services, which not being descendible, neither ought the offices of magistrate, legislator, or judge, or any other public office, to be hereditary.

5th. That the legislative, executive, and judicial powers of government should be separate and distinct; and, that the members of the two first may be restrained from oppression by feeling and participating the public burdens, they should, at fixed periods, be reduced to a private station, return into the mass of the people, and the vacancies be supplied by certain and regular elections, in which all or any

"Virginia's Declaration of Rights and Proposed Amendments to the Constitution." In Jonathan Elliot, ed., *The Debates in the Several State Conventions on the Adoption of the Federal Constitution* (Philadelphia: Lippincott, 1836), vol. 3, pp. 29–34.

part of the former members to be eligible or ineligible, as the rules of the Constitution of government, and the laws, shall direct.

6th. That the elections of representatives in the legislature ought to be free and frequent, and all men having sufficient evidence of permanent common interest with, and attachment to, the community, ought to have the right of suffrage; and no aid, charge, tax, or fee, can be set, rated or levied, upon the people without their own consent, or that of their representatives, so elected; nor can they be bound by any law to which they have not, in like manner, assented, for the public good.

7th. That all power of suspending laws, or the execution of laws, by any authority, without the consent of the representatives of the people in the legislature, is injurious to their rights, and ought not to be exercised.

8th. That, in all criminal and capital prosecutions, a man hath a right to demand the cause and nature of his accusation, to be confronted with the accusers and witnesses, to call for evidence, and be allowed counsel in his favor, and to a fair and speedy trial by an impartial jury of his vicinage, without whose unanimous consent he cannot be found guilty, (except in the government of the land and naval forces;) nor can he be compelled to give evidence against himself.

9th. That no freeman ought to be taken, imprisoned, or disseized of his freehold, liberties, privileges, or franchises, or outlawed, or exiled, or in any manner destroyed or deprived of his life, liberty, or property, but by the law of the land.

10th. That every freeman restrained of his liberty is entitled to a remedy, to inquire into the lawfulness thereof, and to remove the same, if unlawful, and that such remedy ought not to be denied nor delayed.

11th. That, in controversies respecting property, and in suits between man and man, the ancient trial by jury is one of the greatest securities to the rights of the people, and to remain sacred and inviolable.

12th. That every freeman ought to find a certain remedy, by recourse to the laws, for all injuries and wrongs he may receive in his person, property, or character. He ought to obtain right and justice freely, without sale, completely and without denial, promptly and without delay; and that all establishments or regulations contravening these rights are oppressive and unjust.

13th. That excessive bail ought not to be required, nor excessive fines imposed, nor cruel and unusual punishments inflicted.

14th. That every freeman has a right to be secure from all unreasonable searches and seizures of his person, his papers, and property; all warrants, therefore, to search suspected places, or seize any freeman, his papers, or property, without information on oath (or affirmation of a person religiously scrupulous of taking an oath) of legal and sufficient cause, are grievous and oppressive; and all general warrants to search suspected places, or to apprehend any suspected person, without specially naming or describing the place or person, are dangerous, and ought not to be granted.

15th. That the people have a right peaceably to assemble together to consult for the common good, or to instruct their representatives; and that every freeman has a right to petition or apply to the legislature for redress of grievances.

16th. That the people have a right to freedom of speech, and of writing and publishing their sentiments; that the freedom of the press is one of the greatest bulwarks of liberty, and ought not to be violated.

17th. That the people have a right to keep and bear arms; that a well-regulated militia, composed of the body of the people trained to arms, is the proper, natural, and safe defence of a free state; that standing armies, in time of peace, are danger-ous to liberty, and therefore ought to be avoided, as far as the circumstances and protection of the community will admit; and that, in all cases, the military should be under strict subordination to, and governed by, the civil power.

18th. That no soldier in time of peace ought to be quartered in any house without the consent of the owner, and in time of war in such manner only as the law directs.

19th. That any person religiously scrupulous of bearing arms ought to be ex-empted, upon payment of an equivalent to employ another to bear arms in his stead.

20th. That religion, or the duty which we owe to our Creator, and the manner of discharging it, can be directed only by reason and conviction, not by force or violence; and therefore all men have an equal, natural, and unalienable right to the free exercise of religion, according to the dictates of conscience, and that no partic-ular religious sect or society ought to be favored or established, by law, in prefer-ence to others.

Amendments to the Constitution

1st. That each state in the Union shall respectively retain every power, jurisdiction, and right, which is not by this Constitution delegated to the Congress of the United States, or to the departments of the federal government.

2nd. That there shall be one representative for every thirty thousand according to the enumeration or census mentioned in the Constitution, until the whole num-ber of representatives amounts to two hundred: after which, that number shall be continued or increased, as Congress shall direct, upon the principles fixed in the Constitution, by apportioning the representatives of each state to some greater number of people, from time to time, as population increases.

3d. When the Congress shall lay direct taxes or excises, they shall immediately inform the executive power of each state, of the quota of such state, according to the census herein directed, which is proposed to be thereby raised; and if the legis-lature of any state shall pass a law which shall be effectual for raising such quota at the time required by Congress, the taxes and excises laid by Congress shall not be collected in such state.

4th. That the members of the Senate and House of Representatives shall be in-eligible to and incapable of holding, any civil office under the authority of the United States during the time for which they shall respectively be elected.

5th. That the journals of the proceedings of the Senate and House of Representa-tives shall be published at least once in every year, except such parts thereof, relating to treaties, alliances, or military operations, as, in their judgment, require secrecy.

6th. That a regular statement and account of the receipts and expenditures of public money shall be published at least once a year.

7th. That no commercial treaty shall be ratified without the concurrence of two thirds of the whole number of the members of the Senate; and no treaty ceding, contracting, restraining, or suspending, the territorial rights or claims of the United States, or any of them, or their, or any of their rights or claims to fishing in the American seas, or navigating the American rivers, shall be made, but in cases of the most urgent and extreme necessity; nor shall any such treaty be ratified without the concurrence of three fourths of the whole number of the members of both houses respectively.

8th. That no navigation law, or law regulating commerce, shall be passed without the consent of two thirds of the members present, in both houses.

9th. That no standing army, or regular troops, shall be raised, or kept up, in time of peace, without the consent of two thirds of the members present, in both houses.

10th. That no soldier shall be enlisted for any longer term than four years, except in time of war, and then for no longer term than the continuance of the war.

11th. That each state respectively shall have the power to provide for organizing, arming, and disciplining its own militia, whensoever Congress shall omit or neglect to provide for the same. That the militia shall not be subject to martial law, except when in actual service, in time of war, invasion, or rebellion; and when not in the actual service of the United States, shall be subject only to such fines, penalties, and punishments, as shall be directed or inflicted by the laws of its own state.

12th. That the exclusive power of legislation given to Congress over the federal town and its adjacent district, and other places, purchased or to be purchased by Congress of any of the states, shall extend only to such regulations as respect the police and good government thereof.

13th. That no person shall be capable of being President of the United States for more than eight years in any term of sixteen years.

14th. That the judicial power of the United States shall be vested in one Supreme Court, and in such courts of admiralty as Congress may from time to time ordain and establish in any of the different states. The judicial power shall extend to all cases in law and equity arising under treaties made, or which shall be made, under the authority of the United States; to all cases affecting ambassadors, other foreign ministers, and consuls; to all cases of admiralty and maritime jurisdiction; to controversies to which the United States shall be a party; to controversies between two or more states, and between parties claiming lands under the grants of different states. In all cases affecting ambassadors, other foreign ministers, and consuls, and those in which a state shall be a party, the Supreme Court shall have original jurisdiction; in all other cases before mentioned, the Supreme Court shall have appellate jurisdiction, as to matters of law only, except in cases of equity, and of admiralty, and maritime jurisdiction, in which the Supreme Court shall have appellate jurisdiction both as to law and fact, with such exceptions and under such regulations as the Congress shall make: but the judicial power of the United States shall extend to no case where the cause of action shall have originated before the ratification of the Constitution, except in disputes between states about their territory, disputes between persons claiming lands under the grants of different states, and suits for debts due to the United States.

15th. That, in criminal prosecutions, no man shall be restrained in the exercise of the usual and accustomed right of challenging or excepting to the jury.

16th. That Congress shall not alter, modify, or interfere in the times, places, or manner of holding elections for senators and representatives, or either of them, except when the legislature of any state shall neglect, refuse, or be disabled, by invasion or rebellion, to prescribe the same.

17th. That those clauses which declare that Congress shall not exercise certain powers, be not interpreted, in any manner whatsoever, to extend the powers of Congress; but that they be construed either as making exceptions to the specified powers where this shall be the case, or otherwise, as inserted merely for greater caution.

18th. That the laws ascertaining the compensation of senators and representatives for their services, be postponed, in their operation, until after the election of representatives immediately succeeding the passing thereof; that excepted which shall first be passed on the subject.

19th. That some tribunal other than the Senate be provided for trying impeachments of senators.

20th. That the salary of a judge shall not be increased or diminished during his continuance in office, otherwise than by general regulations of salary, which may take place on a revision of the subject at stated periods of not less than seven years, to commence from the time such salaries shall be first ascertained by Congress.

And the Convention do, in the name and behalf of the people of this commonwealth, enjoin it upon their representatives in Congress to exert all their influence, and use all reasonable and legal methods, to obtain a ratification of the foregoing alterations and provisions, in the manner provided by the 5th article of the said Constitution; and, in all congressional laws to be passed in the mean time, to conform to the spirit of these amendments, as far as the said Constitution will admit.

4. The Constitutional Amendments, 1791 (The Bill of Rights)

Article One

Congress shall make no law respecting an establishment of religion, or prohibiting the free exercise thereof; or abridging the freedom of speech, or of the press; or the right of the people peaceably to assemble, and to petition the Government for a redress of grievances.

Article Two

A well-regulated militia being necessary to the security of a free State, the right of the people to keep and bear arms shall not be infringed.

Article Three

No soldier shall, in time of peace, be quartered in any house, without the consent of the owner, nor in time of war but in a manner to be prescribed by law.

"The Constitutional Amendments, 1791 (The Bill of Rights)." As found in Edward S. Corwin, ed., *The Constitution of the United States of America: Analysis and Interpretation* (Washington, DC: US Government Printing Office, 1953), 39–41.

Article Four

The right of the people to be secure in their persons, houses, papers, and effects, against unreasonable searches and seizures, shall not be violated, and no warrants shall issue, but upon probable cause, supported by oath or affirmation, and particularly describing the place to be searched, and the persons or things to be seized.

Article Five

No person shall be held to answer for a capital, or otherwise infamous crime, unless on a presentment or indictment of a Grand Jury, except in cases arising in the land or naval forces, or in the militia, when in actual service in time of war or public danger; nor shall any person be subject for the same offense to be twice put in jeopardy of life or limb; nor shall be compelled in any criminal case to be a witness against himself, nor be deprived of life, liberty, or property, without due process of law; nor shall private property be taken for public use, without just compensation.

Article Six

In all criminal prosecutions the accused shall enjoy the right to a speedy and public trial, by an impartial jury of the State and district wherein the crime shall have been committed, which district shall have been previously ascertained by law, and to be informed of the nature and cause of the accusation; to be confronted with the witnesses against him; to have compulsory process for obtaining witnesses in his favor, and to have the assistance of counsel for his defense.

Article Seven

In suits at common law, where the value of controversy shall exceed twenty dollars, the right of trial by jury shall be preserved, and no fact tried by a jury shall be otherwise reexamined in any court of the United States, than according to the rules of the common law.

Article Eight

Excessive bail shall not be required, nor excessive fines imposed, nor cruel and unusual punishments inflicted.

Article Nine

The enumeration in the Constitution of certain rights shall not be construed to deny or disparage others retained by the people.

Article Ten

The powers not delegated to the United States by the Constitution, nor prohibited by it to the States, are reserved to the States respectively or to the people.

E S S A Y S

Isaac Kramnick, who holds the Richard J. Schwartz Professorship of Government at Cornell University, specializes in eighteenth-century British and American political theory. In the first essay, he addresses a controversy among historians as to whether Lockean liberalism or classical republicanism was the dominant influence in early national political thought. His analysis reveals that more elements are involved and that the either/or dichotomy is not faithful to the ideas that leaders articulated. In the second essay, Leonard W. Levy examines the Bill of Rights and shows how closely connected politically the first ten amendments were to James Madison and to the ratification of the Constitution. Levy is presently a distinguished scholar-in-residence at Southern Oregon State College. Previously Levy was the Andrew W. Mellon professor and chair of the graduate faculty of history at Claremont Graduate School.

The Main Themes of Constitutional Discussion

ISAAC KRAMNICK

Americans, Alexander Hamilton wrote on October 27, 1787, in the New York *Independent Journal,* were "called upon to deliberate on a new Constitution." His essay, *The Federalist* No. 1, pointed out that in doing this Americans were proving that men could create their own governments "from reflection and choice," instead of forever having to depend on "accident and force." These deliberations on the Constitution would by no means be decorous and genteel. Much too much was at stake, and, as Hamilton predicted, "a torrent of angry and malignant passions" was let loose in the "great national discussion." . . .

How does one read that "great national discussion" two centuries later? Most present-day scholars would follow the methodological guidelines offered by J. G. A. Pocock in this respect. . . .

Problematic in this approach is the assumption that there is but one language—one exclusive or even hegemonic paradigm—that characterizes the political discourse of a particular place or moment in time. This was not the case in 1787. In the "great national discussion" of the Constitution Federalists and Antifederalists, in fact, tapped several languages of politics, the terms of which they could easily verbalize. This [selection] examines four such "distinguishable idioms," which co-existed in the discourse of politics in 1787–1788. None dominated the field, and the use of one was compatible with the use of another by the very same writer or speaker. . . . Reading the framers and the critics of the Constitution, one discerns the languages of republicanism, of Lockean liberalism, of work-ethic Protestantism, and of state-centered theories of power and sovereignty.

Civic Humanism and Liberalism in the Constitution and Its Critics

Contemporary scholarship seems obsessed with . . . the omnipresence of neoclassical civic humanism. Dominating eighteenth-century political thought in Britain and America, it is insisted, was the language of republican virtue. Man was a political being who realized his telos only when living in a *vivere civile* with other propertied,

"The 'Great National Discussion:' The Discourse of Politics in 1787" by Isaac Kramnick, *William and Mary Quarterly, 45,* (Jan. 1988). Reprinted by permission of the author.

arms-bearing citizens, in a republic where they ruled and were ruled in turn. Behind this republican discourse is a tradition of political philosophy with roots in Aristotle's *Politics,* Cicero's *Res Publica,* Machiavelli, Harrington, Bolingbroke, and the nostalgic country's virtuous opposition to Walpole and the commercialization of English life. The pursuit of public good is privileged over private interests, and freedom means participation in civic life rather than the protection of individual rights from interference. Central to the scholarly enterprise of republicanism has been the self-proclaimed "dethronement of the paradigm of liberalism and of the Lockean paradigm associated with it."

In response to these republican imperial claims, a group whom Gordon S. Wood has labeled "neo-Lockeans" has insisted that Locke and liberalism were alive and well in Anglo-American thought in the period of the founding. Individualism, the moral legitimacy of private interest, and market society are privileged in this reading over community, public good, and the virtuous pursuit of civic fulfillment. For these "neo-Lockeans" it is not Machiavelli and Montesquieu who set the textual codes that dominated the "great national discussion," but Hobbes and Locke and the assumptions of possessive individualism.

Can we have it both ways? We certainly can if we take Federalist and Antifederalist views as representing a single text of political discourse at the founding. A persuasive case can be made for the Federalists as liberal modernists and the Antifederalists as nostalgic republican communitarians seeking desperately to hold on to a virtuous moral order threatened by commerce and market society. The Federalist tendency was to depict America in amoral terms as an enlarged nation that transcended local community and moral conviction as the focus of politics. The Federalists seemed to glory in an individualistic and competitive America, which was preoccupied with private rights and personal autonomy. This reading of America is associated with James Madison more than with anyone else, and with his writings in the *Federalist.*

Madison's adulation of heterogeneous factions and interests in an enlarged America, which he introduced into so many of his contributions to the *Federalist,* assumed that the only way to protect the rights of minorities was to enlarge the political sphere and thereby divide the community. . . . In *Federalist* No. 10 Madison described the multiplication of regional, religious, and economic interests, factions, and parties as the guarantor of American freedom and justice. He put his case somewhat differently in a letter to Thomas Jefferson: "Divide et impera, the reprobated axiom of tyranny, is under certain conditions, the only policy, by which a republic can be administered on just principles." Pride of place among "these clashing interests," so essential for a just order, went to the economic interests inevitable in a complex market society. They were described in the often-quoted passage from *Federalist* No. 10:

> The most common and durable source of factions has been the various and unequal distribution of property. Those who hold and those who are without property have ever formed distinct interests in society. . . . creditors . . . debtors. . . . A landed interest, a manufacturing interest, a mercantile interest, a moneyed interest. . . . The regulation of these various and interfering interests forms the principal task of modern legislation.

Government for Madison, much as for Locke, was a neutral arbiter among competing interests. Indeed, in *Federalist* No. 43 Madison described the legislative task as providing "umpires"; and in a letter to George Washington he described government's role as a "disinterested & dispassionate umpire in disputes." . . . As it was for Locke—who wrote that "justice gives every Man a Title to the product of his honest Industry"—so, too, for Madison and the Federalists: justice effectively meant respecting private rights, especially property rights.

The commitment in the preamble to the Constitution to "establish justice" meant for the framers that it would protect private rights, which would help it achieve the next objective—to "insure domestic tranquility." . . .

The acceptance of modern liberal society in the Federalist camp went beyond a legitimization of the politics of interest and a conviction that government's purpose was to protect the fruits of honest industry. There was also an unabashed appreciation of modern commercial society. . . . Hamilton, for example, in *Federalist* No. 12, insisted that

> the prosperity of commerce is now perceived and acknowledged by all enlightened statesmen to be the most useful as well as the most productive source of national wealth, and has accordingly become a primary object of their political cares. By multiplying the means of gratification, by promoting the introduction and circulation of the precious metals, those darling objects of human avarice and enterprise, it serves to vivify and invigorate the channels of industry and to make them flow with greater activity and copiousness.

Hamilton was perfectly aware that his praise of private gratification, avarice, and gain flew in the face of older ideals of civic virtue and public duty that emphasized the subordination of private interest to the public good. He turned this very rejection of the republican moral ideal into an argument for the need of a federal standing army. This was a further blow to the ideals of civic virtue, which had always seen professional armies as evil incarnate, undermining the citizen's self-sacrificial participation in the defense of the public realm, which was the premise of the militia. America as a market society could not rely on the militia, according to Hamilton. . . .

In *Federalist* No. 8, another defense of standing armies, Hamilton acknowledged the eclipse of older civic ideals of self-sacrifice and participatory citizenship in commercial America: "The industrious habits of the people of the present day, absorbed in the pursuit of gain and devoted to the improvements of agriculture and commerce, are incompatible with the condition of a nation of soldiers, which was the true condition of the people of those [ancient Greek] republics."

Many of the Antifederalists, on the other hand, were still wedded to a republican civic ideal, to the making of America into what Samuel Adams called "a Christian Sparta." The very feature of pluralist diversity in the new constitutional order that Madison saw as its great virtue, the Antifederalists saw as its major defect. . . . A chorus of Antifederalists insisted that virtuous republican government required a small area and a homogeneous population. Patrick Henry noted that a republican form of government extending across the continent "contradicts all the experience of the world." Richard Henry Lee argued that "a free elective government cannot be extended over large territories." . . .

Montesquieu and others had taught Antifederalists "that so extensive a territory as that of the United States, including such a variety of climates, productions, interests, and so great differences of manners, habits, and customs" could never constitute a moral republic. . . . Antifederalists' fears over the absence of homogeneity in the enlarged republic were as important as the issue of size. . . . Most Antifederalists held that a republican system required similarity of religion, manners, sentiments, and interests. They were convinced that no such sense of community could exist in an enlarged republic, that no one set of laws could work within such diversity. "We see plainly that men who come from New England are different from us," wrote Joseph Taylor, a southern Antifederalist. [James Winthrop], on the other hand, declared that "the inhabitants of warmer climates are more dissolute in their manners, and less industrious, than in colder countries. A degree of severity is, therefore, necessary with one which would cramp the spirit of the other. . . . It is impossible for one code of laws to suit Georgia and Massachusetts."

A just society, for many Antifederalists, involved more than simply protecting property rights. . . . It was expected to promote morality, virtue, and religion. Many Antifederalists, for example, were shocked at the Constitution's totally secular tone and its general disregard of religion and morality. Equally upsetting was the lack of any religious content in Federalist arguments for the Constitution. . . . Antifederalists held that religion was a crucial support of government. . . .

The problem with the Federalist position for many Antifederalists was the inadequacy of its vision of community based on mere interests and their protection. . . . A proper republican community, for these Antifederalists, required a moral consensus, which, in turn, required similarity, familiarity, and fraternity. . . .

Madison and Hamilton understood full well that this communitarian sentiment lay at the core of much of the Antifederalist critique of the new constitutional order. In *Federalist* No. 35 Hamilton ridiculed the face-to-face politics of those "whose observation does not travel beyond the circle of his neighbors and his acquaintances." Madison in No. 10 described two alternative ways of eliminating the causes of factions and thus the politics of interest: one by "destroying the liberty which is essential to its existence; the other by giving to every citizen the same opinions, the same passions, and the same interests." These were both unacceptable. To do either would cut out the very heart of the liberal polity he championed.

Can one go too far in making the case for the Antifederalists as antiliberal communitarians . . . ? Some were, without doubt, but others responded to the enlargement of the federal government and the enhancement of executive power with a call for the protection of private and individual rights through a bill of rights. Even this, however, may be explained by their communitarian bias. If, after all, government was to be run from some city hundreds of miles away, by people superior, more learned, and more deliberative than they, by people with whom they had little in common, then individual rights needed specific protection. . . .

An equally strong case can be made for the Federalists as republican theorists, and here we see full-blown . . . the overlapping of political languages, in 1787. . . . The crucial move in No. 10 that sets Madison firmly within the republican paradigm is his assumption that the representative function in an enlarged republic would produce officeholders who would sacrifice personal, private, and parochial interest to the public good and the public interest. What made the layers of filtration prescribed by the new constitutional order so welcome was their ultimate purpose— producing enlightened public-spirited men who found fulfillment in the quest for public good. . . . The greater number of citizens choosing representatives in a larger republic would reject "unworthy candidates" and select "men who possess the most attractive merit." A large republic and a national government would lead to "the substitution of representatives whose enlightened views and virtuous sentiments render them superior to local prejudices and to schemes of injustice." . . .

The class focus of the Federalists' republicanism is self-evident. Their vision was of an elite corps of men in whom civic spirit and love of the general good overcame particular and narrow interest. Such men were men of substance, independence, and fame who had the leisure to devote their time to public life and the wisdom to seek the true interests of the country as opposed to the wicked projects of local and particular interests. This republicanism of Madison and the Federalists was, of course, quite consistent with the general aristocratic orientation of classical republicanism, which was, after all, the ideal of the independent, propertied, and therefore leisured citizen. . . .

Filtering out mediocrity for Madison went hand in hand with disinterested pursuit of the public good. Many Antifederalists, for their part, saw legislatures as most representative when their membership mirrored the complexity and diversity of society—when, in fact, each geographical unit and social rank was represented. In offering the mirror, not the filter, as the model for representation, Antifederalists seemed to be calling for the representation of every particular interest and thus appear to resemble interest-centered liberals. . . .

Hamilton repudiated the Antifederalist interest theory in *Federalist* No. 35. "The idea of an actual representation of all classes of the people, by persons of each class," so that the feelings and interests of all would be expressed, "is altogether visionary," he wrote. The national legislature, Hamilton recommended, should be composed only of "landholders, merchants, and men of the learned professions." Ordinary people, however much confidence "they may justly feel in their own good sense," should realize that "their interests can be more effectually promoted" by men from these three stations in life.

The confusion of paradigms is further evident when one analyzes in more detail these Federalist and Antifederalist theories of representation. . . . Antifederalists tended to espouse the traditional republican conviction, dominant in most states under the Articles of Confederation, that representatives should be directly responsible to their constituents and easily removable. This, of course, tapped a rich eighteenth-century republican tradition of demanding frequent elections. Implicit in the Federalist notion of filtration, however, was a denial of the representative as mere delegate or servant of his constituents. . . . Madison's legislators of "refined and enlarged public views," seeking "the true interest of their country," ought not to be subject to yearly review by local farmers and small-town tradesmen.

The Language of Virtuous Republicanism

The meaning of virtue in the language of civic humanism is clear. It is the privileging of the public over the private. Samuel Adams persistently evoked the idioms of Aristotle and Cicero. "A Citizen," he wrote, "owes everything to the Commonwealth." He worried that Americans would so "forget their own generous Feelings for the Publick and for each other, as to set private Interest in Competition with that of the great Community." . . . Republican government required "a positive Passion for the public good, the public Interest. . . . Superiour to all private Passions."

This is not all that virtue meant. . . . The values at risk were apolitical and personal. Madison feared for the sobriety, the prudence, and the industry of Americans. His concern was "the industry and morals of the people." . . . Virtuous republican people could, in fact, be described in noncivic, personal terms by the very same men who used the language of civic humanism. John Adams could see the foundation of virtuous government in men who are "sober, industrious and frugal." . . .

The republican tradition had, to be sure, always privileged economy over luxury. . . . But there is more than the all-pervasive paradigm of republicanism at work here. The inclusion of industry in the litany of virtue directs us to another inheritance, to another language in which Americans in the late eighteenth century conceptualized their personal and political universe. Americans also spoke the language of work-ethic Protestantism derived from Richard Baxter, John Bunyan, and the literature of the calling and of "industry." . . .

Central in work-ethic Protestantism was the vision of a cosmic struggle between the forces of industry and idleness. Its texts vibrated less with the dialectic of civic virtue and self-centered commerce than with the dialectic of productive hardworking energy, on the one hand, and idle unproductive sloth, on the other. Its idiom was more personal and individualistic than public and communal. Work was a test of self-sufficiency and self-reliance, a battleground for personal salvation. All men were "called" to serve God by busying themselves in useful productive work that served both society and the individual. . . .

The Protestant language of work and the calling is, of course, complementary to the liberal language of Locke with its similar voluntaristic and individualistic emphasis. . . . Virtuous man is solitary and private man on his own, realizing himself and his talents through labor and achievement; corrupt man is unproductive, indolent, and in the devil's camp. . . .

In this vocabulary, industry, simplicity, and frugality were the signs not only of a virtuous people but also of a free people. As one Rhode Island writer put it, "the industrious and the frugal only will be free." The Boston *Evening-Post* of November 16, 1767, noted that "by consuming less of what we are not really in want of, and by industriously cultivating and improving the natural advantages of our own country, we might save our substance, even our lands, from becoming the property of others, and we might effectually preserve our virtue and our liberty, to the latest posterity." Three weeks later the *Pennsylvania Journal* proclaimed: "Save Your Money and You Will Save Your Country." . . .

Virtue was becoming privatized in the latter part of the eighteenth century. It was being moved from the realm of public activity to the sphere of personal character. The virtuous man partook less and less of that republican ideal that held sway from Aristotle to Harrington—the man whose landed property gave him the leisure necessary for civic commitment in the public arena, be its manifestations political or martial. Property was still important in the Protestant paradigm—not, however, as grantor of leisure but as the rightful fruit of industrious work.

Gordon Wood has noted that Carter Braxton more than any other in the founding generation of Americans sensed the tension between a republicanism based on public virtue—the "disinterested attachment to the public good, exclusive and independent of all private and selfish interests"—and an American polity where in reality most practiced a private virtue in which each man "acts for himself, and with a view of promoting his own particular welfare." Republican privileging of public over private had never been, according to Braxton, the politics of "the mass of the people in any state." In this observation lay Braxton's real insight. Republican virtue was historically the ideal of a circumscribed, privileged citizenry with an independent propertied base that provided the leisure and time for fulfillment in public life through the moral pursuit of public things. . . . From our perspective, we can credit Braxton with perceiving the decline of republican hegemony in the face of the alternative worlds of Lockean liberalism and the Protestant ethic. . . . Citizenship and the public quest for the common good were for some replaced by economic productivity and industrious work as the criteria of virtue. . . . One's duty was still to contribute to the public good, but this was best done through economic activity, which actually aimed at private gain. Self-centered economic productivity, not public citizenship, would become a badge of the virtuous man. At the heart of this shift from republican to Protestant notions of virtue was also a transvaluation of work and leisure. Many Americans in 1787 would have dissented vigorously from the centuries-old republican paradigm set forth in Aristotle's *Politics:* "In the state with the finest constitution, which possesses just men who are just absolutely and not relatively to the assumed situation, the citizens must not live a mechanical or commercial life. Such a life is not noble, and it militates against virtue. Nor must those who are to be citizens be agricultural workers, for they must have leisure to develop their virtue, and for the activities of a citizen."

The Language of Power and the State

Lost today in the legitimate characterization of the Constitution as bent on setting limits to the power exercised by less than angelic men is the extent to which the Constitution is a grant of power to a centralized nation-state. This loss reflects a persistent privileging of Madison over Hamilton in reading the text. While posterity emphasizes the Constitution's complex web of checks and balances and the many institutionalized separations of powers, the participants in the "great national discussion," on whichever side they stood, agreed with Hamilton that the Constitution intended a victory for power, for the "principle of strength and stability in the organization of our government, and vigor in its operations." . . .

In the political discourse of 1787 there was thus a fourth paradigm at work, the state-centered language of power. It, too, reached back into the classical world, to the great lawgivers and founders Solon and Lycurgus, and to the imperial ideal of Alexander and Julius Caesar. Not republican city states but empire and, much later, the nation-state were its institutional units. . . . This language of politics was focused on the moral, heroic, and self-realizing dimensions of the exercise and use of power. . . .

It was the experience of war that shaped the vision of America's state-builders. The war against Britain provided them with a continental and national experience that replaced the states-centered focus of the pre-1776 generation. A remarkable number of framers of the Constitution either served in the Continental army or were diplomats or administrative officials for the Confederation or members of the Continental Congress. Indeed, thirty-nine of the fifty-five delegates to the Constitutional Convention had sat in the Congress. . . . While most of the Antifederalists were states-centered politicians whose heroics took place before 1776, most of the Federalists were shaped by the need to realize the national interest in an international war. Their common bond was an experience that transcended and dissolved state boundaries.

Madison and Hamilton had sat on the same committee of the Continental Congress in 1782–1783, working on the funding of the war and the maintenance of the French alliance. From experiences like this they and their state-building colleagues came to view the thirteen states collectively as a "country," a country among countries. If their country were going to live in a world of nation-states, it needed to become, like the others, a centralized nation-state with sovereign power to tax, regulate trade, coin money, fund a debt, conduct a foreign policy, and organize a standing army. . . .

Hamilton's preoccupation with money and arms as essential for state-building, and his zeal to push aside any intermediate bodies between the state and individuals, while directly relevant for the case he was making on behalf of the Constitution, were also heavily influenced by his perceptive reading of the pattern of state-building in Europe. . . . Equally evident is his sense that the pattern of European development, with the triumph of coercive centralized nation-states, should be reproduced in America under the Constitution. . . . Hamilton was interested less in the limited liberal state than in the heroic state; heroic state-builders like him cannot fear power, for power is the essence of the state. That power is so often abused does not rule out its creative and useful role. . . .

All of the power-centered paradigm's euphemisms for power—"strength," "vigor," "energy"—come together in Hamilton's conception of the presidential office. The presidency was the heart of the new American state for Hamilton, just as the monarch or chief magistrate was for older European nation-states. . . . The president was the energetic builder of an energetic state. In *Federalist* No. 70 Hamilton argued: "Energy in the executive is a leading character in the definition of good government. . . . A feeble executive implies a feeble execution of the government. A feeble execution is but another phrase for a bad execution; and a government ill executed, whatever it may be in theory, must be in practice, a bad government."

Hamilton saw a close relationship between a state with energy and power at home and a powerful state in the world of states. . . . Hamilton was preoccupied with the interrelationship between commerce, state power, and international politics. . . . But Hamilton did not want to build an American state with all that statehood required—a financial and commercial infrastructure, energetic leadership, and powerful military forces—merely to allow America to hold its own in a world system characterized by conflict, competition, and clashing power. He had a grander vision for the American state, a call to greatness. . . . If Americans would only "concur in erecting one great American system," the American state would be "superior to the control of all transatlantic force or influence, and able to dictate the terms of the connection between the old and the new world." In the face of a vigorous American state Europe would cease to be "mistress of the world." America would become ascendant in the Western Hemisphere.

Hamilton's horizons were dazzling. His internationalism transcended the cosmopolitan vision of his fellow Federalists as it transcended the localism of the Antifederalists. The victory of the state center over the American periphery would in Hamilton's fertile imagination catapult America from the periphery of nations to the center of the world system. . . .

We must not lose sight of the other side in the "great national discussion," however. Hamilton's discourse of power with its vision of an imperial American state attracted the fire of Antifederalists like one of Franklin's lightning rods. It was Patrick Henry who most angrily and most movingly repudiated the Federalist state. Henry's American spirit was Tom Paine's. With the Federalist state America would lose its innocence, and "splendid government" would become its badge, its dress. On the ruins of paradise would be built, if not the palaces of kings, then armies and navies and mighty empires. At the Virginia ratifying convention Henry evoked a different language of politics.

> The American spirit has fled from hence; it has gone to regions where it has never been expected; it has gone to the people of France, in search of a splendid government, a strong, energetic government. Shall we imitate the example of those nations who have gone from a simple to a splendid government? Are those nations more worthy of our imitation? What can make an adequate satisfaction to them for the loss they have suffered in attaining such a government, for the loss of their liberty? If we admit this consolidated government, it will be because we like a great, splendid one. Some way or other we must be a great and mighty empire; we must have an army, and a navy, and a number of things. When the American spirit was in its youth, the language of America was different; liberty, sir, was then the primary object.

What was Madison's relationship to the discourse of power and the Hamiltonian state? Madison was a state-builder, too, but his state was quite different from Hamilton's, and upon these differences a good deal of American politics in the next two decades, as well as to this day, would turn. Madison and Hamilton were in agreement on many things. They agreed on the need to establish an effective unified national government. They agreed on the serious threats to personal property rights posed by the state legislatures and on the role that a central government would play in protecting these rights. They agreed on the need to have the central government run by worthy, enlightened, and deliberative men. They agreed on the Constitution as necessary to provide the essential framework for commercial development through the creation of a national market, public credit, uniform currency, and the protection of contract. To be sure, Madison's vision tilted toward agrarian capitalism and Hamilton's toward manufactures and commerce. Where they markedly disagreed, however, was in giving positive, assertive power, "energy," and "vigor" to the state.

Hamilton held the new American state valuable for its own sake as assertive power. He saw the nation-state with its historic and heroic goals, seeking power in a competitive international system of other power-hungry states. Madison saw the nation-state as necessary only to protect private rights and thus ensure justice. Like Locke he saw the need for a grant of power to the state, but a grant of limited power. Madison saw the central government providing an arena for competitive power, where the private bargaining of free men, groups, and interests would take place, and the state would define no goals of its own other than ensuring the framework for orderly economic life. All the state would do was regulate "the various and interfering interests" or, as Madison put it to Washington in straightforward Lockean terms, be an impartial umpire in disputes. Energy in politics for Madison would come from individuals and groups seeking their own immediate goals, not from an energetic state seeking its own heroic ends. . . .

The Federalists triumphed in the "great national discussion" that was the debate over the ratification of the Constitution. But posterity has not remembered simply the victorious advocates of the Constitution in 1787 and 1788. The Antifederalists have lived on in the American imagination as well. Their worst fears were never realized, which proves the glaring exception in a comparison of the American Revolution with other revolutions. The Antifederalists, while losers in 1788, were neither liquidated nor forced to flee. Nor, more significantly, were their ideas extinguished. Their values lived on in America, as they themselves did, and have been absorbed into the larger pattern of American political culture. . . .

Just as there ultimately was no decisive victor in the political and pamphlet battle, so, too, there was none in the paradigm battle. No one paradigm cleared the field in 1788 and obtained exclusive dominance in the American political discourse. There was no watershed victory of liberalism over republicanism. These languages were heard on both sides during the "great national discussion." So, too, were the two other paradigms available to the framers' generation, the Protestant ethic and the ideals of sovereignty and power. So it has remained. American political discourse to this day tends to be articulated in one or another of these distinguishable idioms.

The Politics of the Bill of Rights

LEONARD W. LEVY

The Bill of Rights consists of the first ten amendments to the Constitution of the United States. Congress submitted those amendments to the states for ratification on September 25, 1789, and the requisite number of state legislatures had ratified them by December 15, 1791. The triumph of individual liberty against government power, as epitomized by the Bill of Rights, is one of our history's noblest and most enduringly important themes. Yet James Madison, justly remembered as the "father" of the Bill of Rights, privately referred on August 19, 1789 to the "nauseous project of amendments." He had proposed the Bill of Rights, in part, because "It will kill the opposition everywhere. . . ." In this attitude lies a suggestion that party politics saturated the making of the first ten amendments. . . .

The omission of a bill of rights was a deliberate act of the Constitutional Convention. . . . On September 12, 1787, George Mason of Virginia remarked that he "wished the plan had been prefaced by a Bill of Rights," because it would "give great quiet" to the people. Mason thought that with the states' bills of rights as models, "a bill might be prepared in a few hours." He made no stirring speech for

"The Politics of the Bill of Rights" by Leonard W. Levy. Abridged from *The Encyclopedia of American Political History,* Jack P. Greene, Editor-in-Chief. Vol. 2, pp. 104–125. Copyright © 1984 by Charles Scribner's Sons.

civil liberties in general or any rights in particular. He did not even argue the need for a bill of rights or move the adoption of one, although he offered to second a motion if one were made. Elbridge Gerry of Massachusetts then moved for a committee to prepare a bill of rights, and Mason seconded the motion. Roger Sherman of Connecticut observed that the rights of the people should be secured if necessary, but because the Constitution did not repeal the bills of rights of the states, the Convention need not do anything. Without further debate the delegates, voting by states, defeated the motion 10–0. Two days later, after the states unanimously defeated a motion by Mason to delete from the Constitution a ban on ex post facto laws by Congress, Charles Pinckney of South Carolina, seconded by Gerry, moved to insert a declaration "that the liberty of the Press should be inviolably observed." Sherman laconically replied, "It is unnecessary. The power of Congress does not extend to the Press," and the motion lost 7–4. Three days later the Convention adjourned.

In the Congress of the Confederation, Richard Henry Lee of Virginia moved that a bill of rights, which he had adapted from his own state's constitution, be added to the federal Constitution. Lee was less interested in the adoption of a bill of rights than in defeating the Constitution. Amendments recommended by Congress required ratification by all the state legislatures, not just nine state ratifying conventions. Lee's motion was defeated, but it showed that, from the start of the ratification controversy, the omission of a bill of rights became an Antifederalist mace with which to smash the Constitution. Its opponents sought to prevent ratification and exaggerated the bill-of-rights issue because it was one with which they could enlist public support. Their prime loyalty belonged to states' rights, not civil rights. . . .

Why did the Constitutional Convention omit a bill of rights? No delegate opposed one in principle. As George Washington informed Lafayette, "there was not a member of the Convention, I believe, who had the least objection to what is contended for by the advocates for a Bill of Rights. . . ." All the framers were civil libertarians as well as experienced politicians who had the confidence of their constituents and the state legislatures that elected them. Even the foremost opponents of ratification praised the make-up of the Convention. . . . How could such an "assembly of demigods," as Jefferson called them, neglect the liberties of the people? . . .

The overwhelming majority of the Convention believed, as Sherman succinctly declared, "It is unnecessary." Why was it unnecessary, given the fact that the Convention recommended a new and powerful national government that could operate directly on individuals? The framers believed that the national government could exercise only enumerated powers or powers necessary to carry out those enumerated, and no provision of the Constitution authorized the government to act on any natural rights. A bill of rights would restrict national powers; but, as Hamilton declared, such a bill would be "dangerous" as well as unnecessary because it "would contain various exceptions to powers not granted and, on this very account, would afford a colorable pretext to claim more than were granted. For why declare that things shall not be done which there is no power to do? Why, for instance, should it be said that the liberty of the press shall not be restrained, when no power is given by which restrictions may be imposed?"

Hamilton expressed a standard Federalist position, echoing other framers and advocates of ratification. Excluding a bill of rights from the Constitution was fundamental to the constitutional theory of the framers. . . .

Civil liberties, the supporters of the Constitution believed, faced real dangers from the possibility of repressive state action, but that was a matter to be guarded against by state bills of rights. They also argued, inconsistently, that some states had no bills of rights but were as free as those with bills of rights. They were as free because personal liberty, to Federalist theoreticians, depended not on "parchment provisions," which Hamilton called inadequate in "a struggle with public necessity," but on public opinion, an extended republic, a pluralistic society of competing interests, and a free and limited government structured to prevent any interest from becoming an overbearing majority.

The fact that six states had no bills of rights, and that none had a comprehensive list of guarantees, provided the supporters of ratification with the argument, made by Wilson among others, that an imperfect bill of rights was worse than none at all because the omission of some rights might justify their infringement by implying an unintended grant of government power. The record was not reassuring; the states had very imperfect bills of rights, which proved to be ineffective when confronted by "public necessity," and the state governments did in fact abridge rights that had not been explicitly reserved.

Virginia's Declaration of Rights, for example, did not ban bills of attainder. In 1778 the Virginia assembly adopted a bill of attainder and outlawry, drafted by Jefferson at the instigation of Governor Patrick Henry, against a reputed cutthroat Tory, one Josiah Philips, and some fifty unnamed "associates." By legislative enactment they were condemned for treason and murder, and on failure to surrender were subject to being killed by anyone. At the Virginia ratifying convention, Edmund Randolph, irked beyond endurance by Henry's assaults on the Constitution as dangerous to personal liberties, recalled with "horror" the "shocking" attainder. When Henry defended the attainder, John Marshall, who supported ratification without a bill of rights, declared, "Can we pretend to the enjoyment of political freedom or security, when we are told that a man has been, by an act of Assembly, struck out of existence without a trial by jury, without examination, without being confronted with his accusers and witnesses, without the benefits of the law of the land?"

The framers of the Constitution tended to be skeptical about the value of "parchment barriers" against "overbearing majorities," as Madison said. He had seen repeated violations of bills of rights in every state. Experience proved the "inefficacy of a bill of rights to those occasions when its control is most needed," he said. In Virginia, for example, despite an explicit protection of the rights of conscience, the legislature had favored an establishment of religion, which was averted only because Madison turned the tide of opinion against the bill. As realists the framers believed that constitutional protections of rights meant little during times of popular hysteria; any member of the Constitutional Convention could have cited examples of gross abridgments of civil liberties in states that had bills of rights.

Virginia's bill was imperfect not just because it lacked a ban on bills of attainder. The much vaunted Declaration of Rights of Virginia also omitted the freedoms of speech, assembly, and petition; the right to the writ of habeas corpus; the right to grand jury proceedings; the right to counsel; separation of church and state; and freedom from double jeopardy and from ex post facto laws. The rights omitted were as numerous and important as those included. Twelve states, including Vermont, had framed constitutions, and the only right secured by all was trial by jury in criminal cases. Although all protected religious liberty, five either permitted or provided for an establishment of religion. Two states passed over a free press guarantee. Four neglected to ban excessive fines, excessive bail, compulsory self-incrimination, and general search warrants. Five ignored protections for the rights of assembly, petition, counsel, and trial by jury in civil cases. Seven omitted a prohibition of ex post facto laws. Nine failed to provide for grand jury proceedings, and nine failed to condemn bills of attainder. Ten said nothing about freedom of speech, while eleven were silent on double jeopardy. Whether omissions implied a power to violate, they seemed, in Federalist minds, to raise dangers that could be prevented by avoiding an unnecessary problem entirely: omit a bill of rights when forming a federal government of limited powers.

That the framers of the Constitution actually believed their own arguments purporting to justify the omission of a bill of rights is difficult to credit. Some of the points they made were patently absurd, like the insistence that the inclusion of a bill of rights would be dangerous and, on historical grounds, unsuitable. The last point most commonly turned up in the claim that bills of rights were appropriate in England but not in America. Magna Carta, the Petition of Right of 1628, and the Bill of Rights of 1689 had been grants wrested from kings to secure royal assent to certain liberties, and therefore had "no application to constitutions . . . founded upon the power of the people" who surrendered nothing and retained everything. That argument, made in *Federalist* number 84 and by leading ratificationists as sophisticated as Wilson and Oliver Ellsworth of Connecticut, was so porous that it could persuade no one. . . .

Abroad, two wise Americans serving their country in diplomatic missions coolly appraised the proposed Constitution without the obligation of having to support a party line. John Adams, having received a copy of the document in London, wrote a short letter to Jefferson in Paris. The Constitution seemed "admirably calculated to preserve the Union," Adams thought, and he hoped it would be ratified with amendments adopted later. "What think you," he asked, "of a Declaration of Rights? Should not such a Thing have preceded the Model?" Jefferson, in his first letter to Madison on the subject of the Constitution, began with praise but ended with what he did not like: "First the omission of a bill of rights. . . ." After listing rights he thought deserved special protection, starting with freedom of religion and of the press, Jefferson dismissed as campaign rhetoric Wilson's justification for the omission of a bill of rights and concluded, "Let me add that a bill of rights is what the people are entitled to against every government on earth, general or particular, and what no just government should refuse, or rest on inference." . . .

If it was unnecessary, Antifederalists asked, why did the Constitution protect some rights? The protection of some opened the Federalists to devastating rebuttal. They claimed that because no bill of rights could be complete, the omission of any particular right might imply a power to abridge it as unworthy of respect by the government. That argument, in effect that to include some would exclude all others, boomeranged. The protection of trial by jury in criminal cases, the bans on religious tests, ex post facto laws, and bills of attainder, the narrow definition of treason, and the provision for the writ of habeas corpus, by the Federalists' own reasoning, were turned against them. . . .

Henry cleverly observed that the "fair implication" of the Federalist argument against a bill of rights was that the government could do anything not forbidden by the Constitution. Because the provision on the writ of habeas corpus allowed its suspension when the public safety required, Henry reasoned, "It results clearly that, if it had not said so, they could suspend it in all cases whatsoever. It reverses the position of the friends of this Constitution, that everything is retained which is not given up; for, instead of this, every thing is given up which is not expressly reserved." . . . [Richard Henry] Lee objected to leaving the rights of the people to "logical inferences," because Federalist principles led to the implication that all the rights not mentioned in the Constitution were intended to be relinquished. . . .

In sum, the usually masterful politicians who had dominated the Convention had blundered by botching constitutional theory and making a serious political error. Their arguments justifying the omission of a bill of rights were impolitic and unconvincing. Mason's point that a bill of rights would quiet the fears of the people was unanswerable. Alienating him and the many who agreed with him was bad politics and handed to the opposition a stirring cause around which they could muster sentiment against ratification. The single issue that united Antifederalists throughout the country was the lack of a bill of rights. . . .

In Pennsylvania, the second state to ratify, the minority demanded a comprehensive bill of rights similar to that in their state constitution. Massachusetts, the sixth state to ratify, was the first to do so with recommended amendments. Only two of the recommended amendments, dealing with jury trial in civil suits and grand jury indictment, belonged in a bill of rights. Supporters of the Constitution in Massachusetts had withdrawn a proposed bill of rights on the supposition that Antifederalists would use it as proof that the Constitution endangered liberty. Maryland too would have recommended a bill of rights, but the Federalist majority jettisoned it when the Antifederalists tried to insert curbs on national powers to tax and regulate commerce. Nevertheless, Federalists grudgingly accepted ratification with recommended amendments to ward off conditional ratification or the defeat of the Constitution. New Hampshire, whose approval as the ninth state made ratification an accomplished fact, urged a comprehensive bill of rights for adoption by amendments after the new government went into operation. Virginia and New York, whose ratification was politically indispensable, followed suit. North Carolina was the fourth state to ratify with a model bill of rights among its recommendations. But the states also recommended crippling restrictions on delegated powers.

Thus, the Constitution was ratified only because crucial states, where ratification had been in doubt, were willing to accept the promise of a bill of rights in the form of subsequent amendments to the Constitution. State recommendations for amendments, including those of the Pennsylvania minority, received nationwide publicity, adding to the clamor for a bill of rights. Every right that became part of the first ten amendments was included in state recommendations except the clause in the Fifth Amendment requiring just compensation for private property taken for public use. . . .

Although Madison had periodically apprised Jefferson, in Paris, on ratification developments, he had not answered Jefferson's letter of December 1787 supporting a bill of rights. On October 17, 1788, the eve of his campaign for a House seat,

Madison faced the issue. He [now] favored a bill of rights, he wrote, but . . . also worried about the difficulty of adequately protecting the most important rights; experience proved that a bill of rights was a mere parchment barrier when most needed. Government, after all, was the instrument of the majority, which could endanger liberty. "What use then . . . can a bill of rights serve in popular Governments?" Its political truths, he conceded by way of answer, could educate the people, thereby inhibiting majority impulses.

Jefferson's reply of March 15, 1789, had a profound influence on Madison, as Madison's great speech of June 8 would show. An argument for a bill of rights that Madison had omitted, wrote Jefferson, was "the legal check which it puts into the hands of the judiciary." Jefferson believed that an independent court could withstand oppressive majority impulses by holding unconstitutional any acts violating a bill of rights. The point was not new to Madison, for he himself, when defending a ban on ex post facto laws at the Constitutional Convention, had declared that it would "oblige the Judges to declare [retrospective] interferences null and void." As for the point that the delegated powers did not reach the reserved rights of the people, Jefferson answered that because the Constitution protected some rights but ignored others, it raised implications against them, making a bill of rights "necessary by way of supplement." Moreover, he added, the Constitution "forms us into one state as to certain objects," requiring a bill of rights to guard against abuses of power. As for the point that a bill of rights could not be perfect, Jefferson replied with the adage that half a loaf is better than none; even if all rights could not be secured, "let us secure what we can." Madison had also argued that the limited powers of the federal government and the jealousy of the states afforded enough security, to which Jefferson answered that a bill of rights "will be the text whereby to try all the acts of the federal government." The argument that a bill of rights was inconvenient and not always efficacious did not impress Jefferson. Sometimes, he replied, it was effective, and if it inconveniently cramped the government, the effect was short-lived and remediable, whereas the inconveniences of not having a bill of rights could be "permanent, afflicting, and irreparable." Legislative tyranny, Jefferson explained, would be a formidable dread for a long time, and executive tyranny would likely follow.

Jefferson's arguments, however persuasive, would have been unproductive but for the dangerous political situation, which Madison meant to ameliorate. Four states, including his own and New York, had called for a second convention, whose purpose, Madison feared, would be to "mutilate the system," especially as to the power to tax. Omitting it "will be fatal" to the new federal government. Madison correctly believed that many Antifederalists favored an effective Union on condition that a bill of rights bridled the new government. His strategy was to win them over by persuading the first Congress to adopt protections of civil liberties, thereby alleviating the public's anxieties, providing popularity and stability for the government, and isolating those Antifederalists whose foremost objective was "subverting the fabric . . . if not the Union itself."

In the first Congress, Representative Madison sought to fulfill his pledge of subsequent amendments. His accomplishment in the face of opposition and apathy entitles him to be remembered as "father of the Bill of Rights" even more than as "father of the Constitution." Many Federalists thought that the House had more important tasks, like the passage of tonnage duties and a judiciary bill. The opposition party, which had previously exploited the lack of a bill of rights in the Constitution, realized that its adoption would sink the movement for a second convention and make unlikely any additional amendments that would cripple the substantive powers of the government. They had used the bill-of-rights issue as a smokescreen for objections to the Constitution that could not be dramatically popularized, and now they sought to scuttle Madison's proposals. They began by stalling, then tried to annex amendments aggrandizing state powers, and finally depreciated the importance of the very protections of individual liberty that they had formerly demanded as a guarantee against impending tyranny. Madison meant to prove that the new government was a friend of liberty; he also understood that his amendments, if adopted, would thwart the passage of proposals aggrandizing state powers and diminishing national ones. He would not be put off; he was insistent, compelling, unyielding, and, finally, triumphant.

On June 8, 1789, he made his long, memorable speech before an apathetic House, introducing amendments culled mainly from state constitutions and state ratifying convention proposals, especially Virginia's. All power, he argued, is subject to abuse and should be guarded against by constitutionally securing "the great rights of mankind." . . . The great objective he had in mind, Madison declared, was to limit the powers of government, thus preventing legislative as well as executive abuse, and above all preventing abuses of power by "the body of the people, operating by the majority against the minority." Mere "paper barriers" might fail, but they raised a standard that might educate the majority against acts to which they might be inclined.

To the argument that a bill of rights was not necessary because the states constitutionally protected freedom, Madison had two responses. One was that some states had no bills of rights, others "very defective ones," and the states constituted a greater danger to liberty than the new national government. The other was that the Constitution should, therefore, include an amendment that "No State shall violate the equal rights of conscience, or the freedom of the press, or the trial by jury in criminal cases." This, Madison declared, was "the most valuable amendment in the whole list." To the contention that an enumeration of rights would disparage those not protected, Madison replied that the danger could be guarded against by adopting a proposal of his composition that became the Ninth Amendment. If his amendments were "incorporated" into the Constitution, Madison said, using another argument borrowed from Jefferson, "independent tribunals of justice will consider themselves in a peculiar manner the guardians of those rights; they will be an impenetrable bulwark against every assumption of power in the legislative or executive; they will be naturally led to resist every encroachment upon rights expressly stipulated for in the constitution." . . .

Notwithstanding the support of correspondents, Madison's speech stirred no immediate support in Congress. Indeed, every speaker who followed him, regardless of party affiliation, either opposed a bill of rights or believed that the House should attend to far more important duties. Six weeks later Madison "begged" for a consideration of his amendments, but the House assigned them to a special committee instead of debating them. That committee, which included Madison, reported in a week. It added freedom of speech to the rights protected against state abridgement, deleted Madison's reference to no "unreasonable searches and seizures," made some stylistic revisions, but otherwise recommended the amendments substantially as he had proposed them. The committee's report was tabled, impelling Madison on August 3 to implore its consideration.

On August 13 the House finally began to consider the reported amendments, and in the course of debate it made some significant changes. Madison had proposed to "incorporate" the amendments within the text of the Constitution at appropriate points. He did not recommend their adoption as a separate "bill of rights," although he had referred to them collectively by that phrase. Members objected that to incorporate the amendments would give the impression that the framers of the Constitution had signed a document that included provisions not of their composition. Another argument for lumping the amendments together was that the matter of form was so "trifling" that the House should not squander its time debating the placement of the various amendments. Ironically, Roger Sherman, who still believed that the amendments were unnecessary, deserves the credit for insistently arguing that they should be appended as a supplement to the Constitution instead of being interspersed within it. Thus, what became the Bill of Rights achieved its significant collective form over the objections of its foremost proponent, Madison, and because of the desire of its opponents in both parties to downgrade its importance.

The House recast the free exercise of religion clause and its allied clause banning establishments of religion, improving Madison's original language. The House also confined to criminal cases Madison's broad phrasing that no person should be compelled to give evidence against himself. On the other hand the House restored the extremely important principle against unreasonable searches and seizures, dropped by the committee. In another major decision the House decisively defeated Gerry's motion, for the Antifederalists, to consider not just the committee's report but all amendments that the several states had proposed; the Antifederalists thus failed to intrude crippling political amendments. Finally the House added "or to the people" in the recommendation by Madison that the powers not delegated to the United States be reserved to the states. On the whole the House adopted Madison's amendments with few significant alterations during the course of its ten-day debate on the Bill of Rights. . . .

The Senate, which kept no record of its debates, had deliberated on seventeen amendments submitted by the House. One the Senate killed, the proposal Madison thought "the most valuable": protection against state infringement of speech, press, religion, or trial by jury. The motion to adopt failed to receive the necessary two-thirds vote, although by what margin is unknown. The Senate also weakened the House's ban on establishments of religion. Otherwise the Senate accepted the House proposals, although the Senate combined several, reducing the total number from seventeen to twelve. The first of the twelve dealt with the relation of population to the number of representatives from each state, and the second would have prevented any law going into effect that would have increased the salaries of members of Congress until after the next election.

The House adamantly refused to accept the Senate's version of its ban on establishments. A conference committee of both houses met to resolve differences. The committee, which included Madison, accepted the House's ban on establishments but otherwise accepted the Senate's version. On September 24, 1789, the

House voted for the committee report; on the following day the Senate concurred, and the twelve amendments were submitted to the states for ratification.

Within six months nine states ratified the Bill of Rights, although of the twelve amendments submitted for approval, the first and second were rejected. The four recalcitrant states by mid-1790 were Virginia, Massachusetts, Connecticut, and Georgia. The admission of Vermont to the Union made necessary the ratification by eleven states. Connecticut and Georgia refused to ratify. Georgia's position was that amendments were superfluous until experience under the Constitution proved a need. Connecticut believed that any suggestion that the Constitution was not perfect would add to the strength of Antifederalism.

In Massachusetts, Federalist apathy to the Bill of Rights was grounded on a satisfaction with the Constitution as it was, and the Antifederalists were more interested in amendments that would strengthen the states at the expense of the national government. Nevertheless the Massachusetts lower house adopted all but the first, second, and twelfth amendments, and the upper house adopted all but the first, second, and tenth. Thus both houses of the Massachusetts legislature actually approved what became the First through Seventh Amendments and the Ninth; but a special committee, dominated by Antifederalists, urged that all amendments recommended by Massachusetts should be adopted before the state concurred in any amendments. As a result the two houses never passed a bill promulgating ratification of eight amendments. Jefferson, the secretary of state, believed that Massachusetts, "having been the 10th state which has ratified, makes up the three-fourth [sic] of the legislatures whose ratification was to suffice." He wrote to a Massachusetts official, asking for clarification. The reply was, "It does not appear that the Committee ever reported any bill." In 1939, Massachusetts joined Connecticut and Georgia when they belatedly ratified on the sesquicentennial anniversary of the Constitution.

Ratification of the Bill of Rights by Vermont, in November 1789, left Virginia the last state to act. Its ratification as the eleventh state was indispensable, although the hostility of its Antifederalist leaders presaged a doubtful outcome. . . . The Federalists of Virginia, however, eagerly supported the Bill of Rights in the knowledge that its adoption would appease public fears and stymie the amendments supported by the Antifederalists. . . .

. . . In the end Madison's confidence proved justified. Jefferson made his influence felt on behalf of the Bill of Rights, and the Antifederalists grudgingly gave ground before public opinion. On December 15, 1791, after two years of procrastination, the [state] senate finally ratified without record vote, thereby completing the process of state ratification and making the Bill of Rights part of the Constitution.

F U R T H E R   R E A D I N G

Bernard Bailyn, ed., *The Debate on the Constitution: Federalist and Antifederalist Speeches, Articles, and Letters During the Struggle Over Ratification* (1993)
Richard Beeman, Stephen Botein, and Edward C. Carter II, eds., *Beyond Confederation: Origins of the Constitution and American National Identity* (1987)
Stephen R. Boyd, *The Politics of Opposition: Antifederalists and the Acceptance of the Constitution* (1979)

Robert E. Brown, *Charles Beard and the Constitution: A Critical Analysis of "An Economic Interpretation of the Constitution"* (1956)

Patrick T. Conley and John P. Kaminski, eds., *The Constitution and the States: The Role of the Original Thirteen in the Framing and Adoption of the Federal Constitution* (1988)

Saul Cornell, "Aristocracy Assailed: The Ideology of Backcounty Antifederalism," *Journal of American History,* 76 (March 1990), 1148–1172.

Linda Grant De Pauw, *The Eleventh Pillar: New York State and the Federal Constitution* (1966)

David F. Epstein, *The Political Theory of "The Federalist"* (1984)

Alexander Hamilton, John Jay, and James Madison, *The Federalist Papers* (1788)

Merrill Jensen, et al., eds., *The Documentary History of the Constitution* (1976)

———, *The New Nation: A History of the United States During the Confederation* (1950)

John P. Kaminski and Richard Leffler, *Federalists and Antifederalists: The Debate Over the Constitution,* 2d ed. (1998)

Michael Kammen, *A Machine That Would Go by Itself: The Constitution in American Culture* (1986)

Cecelia M. Kenyon, ed., *The Antifederalists* (1966)

Charles R. Kesler, ed., *Saving the Revolution: "The Federalist Papers" and the American Founding* (1987)

Leonard W. Levy and Dennis J. Mahoney, eds., *The Framing and Ratification of the Constitution* (1987)

Jackson Turner Main, *The Antifederalists: Critics of the Constitution, 1781–1788* (1961)

Forrest McDonald, *We the People: The Economic Origins of the Constitution* (1958)

Edmund S. Morgan, *Inventing the People: The Rise of Popular Sovereignty in England and America* (1988)

David E. Narrett and Joyce S. Goldberg, eds., *Essays on Liberty and Federalism: The Shaping of the U.S. Constitution* (1988)

Peter S. Onuf, "Reflections on the Founding: Constitutional Historiography in Bicentennial Perspective," *William and Mary Quarterly,* 3d Series, 46 (1989), 342–375.

Robert A. Rutland, *The Birth of the Bill of Rights, 1776–1791* (1955)

———, *The Ordeal of the Constitution: The Antifederalists and the Ratification Struggle of 1787–1788* (1966)

Stephen L. Schechter, ed., *The Reluctant Pillar: New York and the Adoption of the Federal Constitution* (1985)

Bernard Schwartz, *The Great Rights of Mankind: A History of the American Bill of Rights* (1992)

Herbert J. Storing, ed., *The Complete Antifederalist* (1981)

———, *What the Antifederalists Were For* (1981)

CHAPTER
14

The Consequences
of the Revolution

How we interpret the Revolution has always been largely influenced by assessments of its aftermath—of its consequences over the long term. Few of us would be content to call it the Revolution if we believed that it left the status quo *of the colonial era in place, though under new management. Moreover, when changes attributed to the Revolution occurred generally across the western world and took place over many generations, it is reasonable to ask whether the movement to secure American independence and to form the United States produced those changes, or whether larger, deeper forces were at work.*

At the opening of the twenty-first century, more than two hundred years after the historical events, there is no consensus among scholars as to how to understand the Revolution. But if no orthodoxy rules and there is no "correct" interpretation of the Revolution, that should not be cause for complaint. Instead, it provides opportunities for creativity and innovation—to think freshly about old topics and to define new ones. In the absence of any ruling orthodoxy, we may consider new possibilities along with old ones, and fashion interpretations that we find persuasive.

E S S A Y S

Contemporary scholars have proposed fresh ways of analyzing the Revolution, and the essays that follow present interesting possibilities. Professor Rosemarie Zagarri of George Mason University argues that the Revolution should be seen as *revolutionary* with respect to citizenship and gender. However, if Zagarri's subtle analysis of post-war women's rights is put into a transatlantic context, and if the extended time span she considers is emphasized, the argument changes. One wonders whether it was the American Revolution that changed relations between the sexes, or whether it was the broader cultural forces of the Enlightenment era that were responsible.

Alfred F. Young's systematic approach—topic by topic consideration of change and continuity associated with the Revolution—offers another viewpoint. In the Northern Illinois University emeritus professor's analysis, the terms by which elites rule, not just whether they survive, is a crucial issue. Young instructs us in the shadings of interpretation, presenting a historical record where meanings are not purely black or white. The final essay, by Professor Edward Countryman of Southern Methodist University, considers the Revolution from yet another perspective—that of the continental contest between the Native Americans and the several imperial powers. In Countryman's view, the Revolution replaced an external colonial regime with an internal one that was determined to control and exploit the continent for the benefit of one set of people and interests. For Countryman, the Revolution becomes a central event in the development of American capitalism, a view that in some respects complements Gordon Wood's interpretation, through resting on very different assumptions and arguments.

Finally, there is no last word in debates such as these. But there is enriched under-standing of how the past influences the future, and how present concerns shape the way we look back as well as forward in time. Students should pick and choose among the examples offered here. Better yet, they can fashion interpretations and arguments that they find most convincing.

The Revolution Advanced Men's and Women's Rights

ROSEMARIE ZAGARRI

On July 4, 1804, a group of young men in Harrisburg, Pennsylvania, offered a series of toasts to commemorate the nation's Independence. Among their testimonials, they offered one to a cherished ideal: "[To] the rights of men, and the rights of women—. May the former never be infringed, nor the latter curtailed." This apparently simple statement provides a tantalizing clue to the complex relationship between politics and gender in the early national era. In one sense, it points to an important change in women's status. The men acknowledged, even celebrated, an innovative and con-troversial idea: women along with men should be regarded as the bearers of rights. In the wake of the American Revolution and especially after the publication of Mary Wollstonecraft's *Vindication of the Rights of Woman* (1792), women gained a dig-nity and an esteem that had hitherto been denied them—though the exact nature of their rights was, as we shall see, a matter still to be determined.

The revelers, however, did something more. They made a pointed distinction between the rights of males and females, a distinction based on sex. The danger to men's rights came from an infringement on their liberties, especially their political liberties, whereas the threat to women's rights came from a curtailment of their privileges, which were nonpolitical in nature. Put simply, men's rights involved liberties that allowed choices, while women's rights consisted of benefits that im-posed duties. Rather than an abstract, universal proposition, rights became a gen-dered variable.

The differentiation of rights on the basis of sex reveals a crucial, but previously overlooked, bifurcation in the evolution of natural rights ideology in the early years of the republic. At the same time Americans were debating the "rights of man," they conducted a parallel discussion about the "rights of woman." The latter debate, however, did not occur within official political institutions, nor was it principally

---

concerned with political rights. To reconstruct this debate, we must broaden our understanding of politics and employ sources not usually considered in the writing of traditional political history. Ladies' magazines, literary periodicals, and prescriptive literature for women provide a glimpse into a world of ideas that had not yet surfaced in the formal political realm.

In addition, scholarly disciplines outside of history can help shape our interpretative framework. In particular, the works of political theorists . . . provide insights into the assumptions behind theories of natural rights, the existence of various natural rights traditions, and the power of "rights talk" in American society. Feminist theorists . . . offer another point of departure. . . . [T]hese scholars argue that the creation of the modern liberal state has necessarily presumed that subordination of women to men. In theory as well as practice, democratic nations from the time of John Locke through the French Revolution to the present have depended for their existence, they say, on a "structural sexism" that excludes women from full participation in the polity.

The historical evidence on women's rights talk in the United States from 1792 to 1825 allows us to test these assertions. In the post-Revolutionary era, Americans attempted to reconcile two conflicting principles: the equality of the sexes and the subordination of women to men. In the process, they came to define the rights of women in contrast to the rights of men. Yet they did not attribute different rights to each sex arbitrarily, merely on the basis of whim or prejudice. Instead, they drew on two separate, preexisting traditions of natural rights, one inherited from Locke and the other from the Scottish Enlightenment. To men, writers applied a Lockean conception of rights that emphasized equality, individual autonomy, and the expansion of personal freedoms. By accentuating the importance of individual liberty, Lockean discourse endowed unfranchised white males with the moral authority to challenge their exclusion from the political process. To women, authors applied a Scottish theory that treated rights as benefits, conferred by God and expressed in the performance of duties to society. The stress on duty and obligation, rather than on liberty and choice, gave women's rights a fundamentally different character from those of men. Women's rights were to be nonpolitical in nature, confined to the traditional feminine role of wife and mother.

While these developments may appear to confirm the feminist interpretation, a close reading of the sources suggests otherwise. Efforts to constrict the meaning of women's rights did not succeed. . . . Once women had attained the status of rights bearers, no formal theory, whether of Scottish or Lockean origins, could contain the radical power of rights talk. Soon after the Revolution, and long before the emergence of the first women's rights movement, rights discourse itself expanded the range of rights that women could and would claim.

Before the publication of *A Vindication of the Rights of Woman* [1792], the concept of women's rights was virtually inconceivable in Anglo-America. During the American Revolution, some individuals began to explore whether ideas of equality and natural rights applied to women as well as to men. In private letters and correspondence, Abigail Adams, Hannah Lee Corbin, Rachel Wells, Mary Willing Byrd, and others discussed the meaning of citizenship for women and objected to their exclusion from political power, yet they seldom made their ideas known publicly or expressed their concerns in print. . . . [L]ater, in 1790, Judith Sargent Murray, writing as "Constantia," published an essay "On the Equality of the Sexes" that exposed the injustice of social and political inequities between men and women. Yet these isolated statements did not initiate a broader public discussion of women's rights.

In fact, historians have convincingly shown that the Revolution produced few concrete changes in the political status of American women. There was neither an organized movement for women's rights nor a systematic effort to alter their political condition. Even in New Jersey, where they briefly enjoyed the right to vote, women apparently voiced no public protests when legislators revoked their franchise of 1807. Even so, the paucity of legal and political changes does not necessarily mean that Americans ignored the effect of the Revolution on women. To the contrary, a vital ongoing discussion about the meaning of women's rights surfaced in the post-Revolutionary era. But where the Revolution raised the question of women's rights only by implication, *A Vindication of the Rights of Woman* raised the issue directly, in a way that people could not avoid. . . .

Wollstonecraft's tract represented the strongest and most reverberant statement of women's rights up to that time. First published in Britain in 1792, American editions appeared shortly thereafter. The title echoed Thomas Paine's sensational work on the French Revolution, *The Rights of Man,* issued in 1791 and 1792. . . .

A Vindication of the Rights of Woman exposed the gendered assumptions behind the term "rights of man." Like Paine, Wollstonecraft asserted the existence of universal human rights; unlike Paine, she explicitly applied the concept to women. "If the abstract rights of man will bear discussion and explanation, those of woman, by parity of reasoning, will not shrink from the same test." Yet while only some men were denied rights, all women had been excluded from their possession, merely on the basis of their sex. "The *rights* of humanity," Wollstonecraft asserted, "have been . . . confined to the male line from Adam downwards," with the result that half of the population was kept from realizing its full human potential. "The tyranny of man" and the perpetuation of a "male aristocracy" oppressed women in all aspects of their lives, retarding the development of their reason, hindering the growth of their virtue, and preventing them from making a full contribution to society.

Wollstonecraft, like Paine, also called for a revolution—but hers was to be a "Revolution in Female Manners" that would open up greater educational and professional opportunities to women. . . . "Contending for the rights of woman," she wrote, "my main argument is . . . that if [woman] be not prepared by education to become the companion of man, she will stop the progress of knowledge and virtue." At only one point in her tract, and then only tentatively, did Wollstonecraft mention the subject of political rights for women. . . .

Wollstonecraft's readers, however, understood that *A Vindication* implied something more than a confirmation of the gender status quo. Despite her vagueness in demanding specific rights, Wollstonecraft portrayed women in a radically new way. She constructed an image of woman as an independent rights bearer, as "having a voice . . . [and] participation in the natural rights of mankind." Pressing her readers to apply the same principles and standards to women as to men, she in effect challenged the exclusion of women from a wide range of educational, professional, and political opportunities. If men refused to acknowledge that women had rights, she wrote, then "by the same rule, their duties vanish, for rights and duties are inseparable." . . .

A *Vindication* quickly won a wide audience in the United States. Excerpts appeared as early as 1792 in the *Ladies Magazine,* published in Philadelphia, and the *Massachusetts Magazine,* published in Boston. By 1795, three American editions had been issued. A modern study finds that treatise in more private American libraries of the period than was Paine's *Rights of Man.* In America as in England, many of the first reviews were laudatory. . . . By the end of the decade, it is true, Wollstonecraft's apparent disdain for conventional norms of sexual behavior and the sanctity of marriage made her the object of vitriolic personal attacks. Nonetheless, her intellectual influence persisted over time.

Wollstonecraft and her work became the enduring symbol and chief referent for the idea of women's rights in the early republic. American magazines brought the terminology of women's rights into widespread usage. Numerous contributions—poetry, fiction, humor, and prescriptive essays—bore the title "The Rights of Woman" (or "Women") or contained allusions to women's rights. The attitudes expressed ranged from highly positive to negative or hostile. . . .

Both male and female authors participated in the discussion of women's rights, although contemporary literary conventions make it difficult to pinpoint the authorship of individual pieces. . . . In addition, articles reprinted from British as well as American sources reveal the existence of a transatlantic dialogue on women's rights. The frequent publication of such pieces indicates a high level of reader interest in women's rights from the 1790s onward. The generation of reformers who came of age in the post-Revolutionary era thus encountered discussions of women's rights long before there was an organized movement to mobilize their sentiments.

In the highly charged political atmosphere of the early republic, when the rights of men were being contested daily, Wollstonecraft challenged the assumption that rights could be considered solely a male prerogative. Popular writers responded by expanding the range of discussion. "The Rights of Women are no longer strange sounds to an American ear," Elias Boudinot proclaimed in 1793. "They are now heard as familiar terms in every part of the United States." Yet Wollstonecraft's tract did something more. Newspapers and magazines picked up her terminology and popularized a new language—the language of rights—by which Americans could understand, refer to, and analyze women. This language had radical implications. "Let the defenders of male despotism answer (if they can) the Rights of Woman, by Miss Wollstonecraft," declared the *National Magazine* in 1800. Just as the rights of man took on new meanings over time—meanings the American Revolutionaries had not anticipated—so, too, did the rights of woman.

The new understanding of women's rights emerged at a time when Americans were working out the implications of Revolutionary ideology for white males. Their thinking drew not on a monolithic concept of natural rights, as is commonly supposed, but on at least two existing theoretical traditions. The more familiar tradition is John Locke's social contract theory, based on ideas of natural rights and equality in a state of nature. The other tradition, transmitted by thinkers of the Scottish Enlightenment, carried very different assumptions and implications. . . .

American Revolutionaries drew heavily on the natural rights philosophy of Locke. . . .

Locke's theory of natural rights provided the basis for his broader understanding of the relations among the individual, society, and polity. According to Locke, men, equals in a state of nature, voluntarily gathered together to form a social compact. Under this agreement, they relinquished some personal freedom in exchange for the government's protection of life, liberty, and property. If the governing authority violated this contract, individuals could withdraw from the compact or renegotiate its terms. In theory, consent implied the performance of corresponding duties. Yet as Americans translated Locke's theory into practice, they tended to minimize the importance of duties and enhance the importance of personal autonomy and individual choice. Political liberty rather than the reciprocal performance of duties came to be the hallmark of Lockeanism in America.

The thinkers of the "conservative" or Scottish Enlightenment offered a different framework for understanding natural rights. Francis Hutcheson, Thomas Reid, and Lord Kames, explicitly rejecting social contract theory, drew heavily on a Protestant natural law tradition. . . . Their work emphasized duty over liberty and custom over contract. Moral obligation and the preservation of social harmony took precedence over individual autonomy. Scottish moral philosophers assumed the existence of a hierarchical society made up of unequals. At the top, God was the ultimate "obligator" who conferred benefits, known as rights, on individuals. These benefits imposed corresponding duties in a much more direct way than in Locke's construct. Rights were a moral power exercised over oneself and one's property; they were "not simply powers granted, but powers granted for a purpose; they have a right use, namely, that of contributing to an overall moral order." . . . Scottish natural rights theory thus had very different implications from its Lockean counterpart. By defining rights in terms of duties, the Scots limited the possibility for the creation of new rights and affirmed the existing social and political order—deflating, in effect, the radical potential of natural rights discourse.

By the early nineteenth century, Scottish moral philosophy had become the standard curriculum in institutions of higher learning throughout the United States. Educated men were schooled in Hutcheson, Reid, and Kames. . . . [L]ibraries frequently contained works by Scottish Enlightenment authors. Ladies' magazines and literary periodicals, as well as popular conduct books . . . also acted as conduits. Thus a broad segment of the reading public encountered the Scottish theory of natural rights.

From the Revolution into the 1790s, Americans witnessed the tremendous power of natural rights ideas to alter the political landscape. As many historians have shown, Jeffersonians invoked the rights of man in their campaigns to expand the franchise, eliminate property qualifications for holding office, and open social and economic opportunities to greater portions of the white male population. Propertyless men, artisans, and mechanics became full members of the political community. Jeffersonians bypassed the Scottish theory of natural rights in favor of the Lockean conception. Articulating a social contract theory of government, they stressed the centrality of individual equality and personal autonomy in the pursuit of public and private aims. . . . The discourse itself tended to expand the range of privileges known as "rights," creating an impulse that could easily be harnessed by broader and broader segments of the population.

Unlike their adversaries, Federalists sought to contain rather than exploit the radical power of natural rights ideas. They preferred to maintain the hierarchical order of society, in which the lower sort deferred to their social and political betters. To this end, Federalists openly attacked the credibility of Lockean social contract theory, questioned the existence of a state of nature, and cast doubt on the whole notion of "natural" rights. . . . "Good order is the foundation of all good things. . . . The body of the people must not find the principles of natural subordination by art rooted out of their minds. They must respect that property, of which they cannot partake." . . .

Because they so feared the "subversive possibilities" of natural rights, some Federalists eschewed rights language altogether. Other's restricted rights language to the Scottish theory of rights. The Scots' emphasis on duty, moral obligation, and the structural inequalities of society fit neatly with the Federalists' conservative views on these subjects. . . . As Federalist congressman Fisher Ames put it, "All our individual rights are to be exercised with due regard to the rights of others; they are tied fast by restrictions, and are to be exercised within certain reasonable limits." . . .

The political controversies of the early national era—the debate over the rights of man and the French Revolution, discussions of the franchise, and attacks on deference—highlighted the divergence between Federalist and Republican views of natural rights. Jeffersonians exploited the subversive potential of Lockean social contract theory and natural rights language to expand the political and economic privileges of white males. . . . Federalists, on the other hand, resisted the radical implications of natural rights ideas. They either shied away from rights talk altogether or gravitated toward a duty-bound definition of rights derived from the Scots. Yet when the question of natural rights shifted from males to females, the gap between Federalist and Republican views narrowed. Members of both parties could agree: women's rights differed fundamentally from those of men.

In the post-Revolutionary era, popular authors who wrote about women faced a dilemma: they were willing to admit women's equality with men, but they also wanted to preserve the notion of inherent differences between the sexes. They wanted to reconcile a new notion—women's rights—with a very old idea, women's subordination to men. Applying natural rights language to women, however, represented a dangerous innovation. Rights discourse could spin out of control and present possibilities that were neither intended nor desired. Just as rights rhetoric had enabled white males to challenge social and political institutions, so, too, might the rhetoric of women's rights undermine an even more basic structure, the gender status quo. . . .

In the early national period, most Americans—women as well as men—could not tolerate the prospect of fundamental change in gender roles. The question of women's rights raised the specter of domestic discontent and rebellion. Discussions of "equality of right," "A Lady" worried, might "excit[e] an insurrection in the female world." The discourse itself opened up new possibilities. If women construed natural rights as a warrant to claim privileges outside their existing station, they might abandon their domestic role or demand exactly the same treatment as men. . . . "If once a man raises his wife to an equality with himself," declared "Ignotus" in 1801, "it is all over, and he is doomed to become a subject for life to the most despotic of government[s]." As a result, commentators came to realize that if they applied rights language to women, they must do so with care. Women's rights must be defined in such a way as to prevent women from exploiting the "subversive possibilities" of rights talk.

One tactic was to focus on equality in the spiritual realm. From time immemorial, Woman had been blamed for the Fall of Man. By the late eighteenth century, however, critics were less inclined to focus on women's culpability. Christ's death, they claimed, had made amends for Eve's transgression and "restored woman to her proper station"; men and women were equal before God. As one man saw it, women are "entitled to the same rights, capable of the same enjoyments, and expectants of the same immortality" as men. Even so, spiritual equality carried with it no expectation of equal rights on earth.

Nor did equal rights in certain areas of life imply equal rights in all areas. For example, women and men were said to share a right to sociability, a freedom to be friends and companions with one another. Earlier societies had segregated women from men, but American society encouraged the mixing and interaction of the sexes. "THE RIGHTS OF WOMEN, as well as OF MEN, are acknowledged," proclaimed the *American Spectator,* "and . . . [women] are caressed as the first and dearest friends of their partners." This equality in no way compelled equal legal or political rights. . . .

Men and women also had no need to receive identical schooling. Females, it was said, had an "equal right" with men to education. Yet "when women carry the idea of their equality with the other sex so far as to insist that there should be *no difference* in their education and pursuits," warned Samuel Miller in 1803, "they mistake both their character, their dignity, and their happiness." The purpose of a woman's education differed fundamentally from a man's. "The proper object of female education," declared the *Mercury and New-England Palladium,* "is to make women rational companions, good wives and good mothers. . . .

Other authors adopted a markedly different strategy with regard to women's rights. Rather than argue that men and women had equal rights, they maintained that the sexes had separate and distinctive rights. A Scottish theory of rights came to pertain to women, while a Lockean understanding became the province of men. The concept of rights, like the concept of virtue, increasingly became a gendered proposition. . . .

Authors thus denied certain kinds of rights to women on the basis of their sex. They condemned real women—such as Mary Wollstonecraft—and fictional caricatures who used rights language in the same way men had: to claim new legal or political powers. . . . Because political rights were considered masculine, women who voted, as they did briefly in New Jersey, or who aspired to political office would become like men. . . .

Women as well as men often assented to the gendered division of rights. "Although [women's] powers of the mind may be equal to the task," commented Hannah Mather Crocker of Boston, "[it] is morally improper and physically very incorrect, for the female character to claim the statesman's berth, or ascend the rostrum to gain the loud applause of men." Political rights threatened to violate women's essential nature and subvert their God-given social roles. Women thus could not and should not aspire to the same status as men.

Yet such observers did not absolutely reject the claim that women had rights. Instead, they asked what particular rights women possessed. . . . Americans . . . accepted the universality of natural rights for both men and women but applied the concept differentially according to the sex of the rights bearer.

Pamphleteers and periodical writers defined women's rights in terms of duties and obligations, not political liberty and personal autonomy. An 1801 article with the evocative title "A Second Vindication of the Rights of Women" declared that women's and men's rights differed in basic ways. . . . Rather than follow Wollstonecraft's mistaken lead, American women should see that the true vindication of their rights arose out of the performance of their traditional feminine duties. . . . "A real friend to the fair sex" elaborated on this notion. Listing twelve rights that belonged to women, he included a woman's "undoubted right to choose a husband"; "a right, in common with her husband, to instruct her children"; "a right to promote frugality, industry, and economy"; and "a right . . . to be neat and decent in her person and family." Notably lacking is any mention of legal or political rights.

Because of its emphasis on the primacy of duties, the Scottish rights conception allowed authors to portray women's rights in a nonpejorative, even a positive, light. Rights were identified so closely with duties that the terms became virtually identical. . . . By performing their God-given role, women laid claim to their appropriate rights; their appropriate rights became synonymous with their womanly duties. In this sense, women's rights could be celebrated, even by authors who were otherwise skeptical of women's claim on Lockean rights. . . .

This approach helped maintain the existing gender hierarchy. Where the Lockean conception of rights allowed white males to expand their political rights and challenge social privilege, the Scottish view tended to legitimate current social arrangements and justify existing power differentials. By conflating rights with duties, it privileged women's domestic role and precluded the possibility of women's direct participation in politics. It enabled Americans to adopt the language of rights for women at the same time it prevented (it was hoped) the expansion of women's rights into the public sphere. Scottish natural rights theory could thus serve conservative ends.

Despite its conservative tenor, even the Scottish conception yielded unintended, beneficial consequences for women. As authors thought about the meaning of women's rights, they began to reexamine women's position in society, the limits of female political authority, and the relationship between the sexes. . . . Rights talk pushed women to exercise their duties—not only in the home but outside the domestic sphere as well. Rights talk further led to consideration of the mutual dependence of men's and women's rights. If women had rights and duties with respect to men, men also had rights and responsibilities toward women. . . . In his *Rights of Women Vindicated,* the Reverend John Hanning, M. D., insisted that men owed women "the respect due to the sex in general." He specifically attacked husbands who failed in their duty to their wives by drinking, gambling, or adultery. Women's rights deserved protection from infringement or usurpation.

Even more important, some writers insisted that women's rights, like men's, should be regarded as inherent and unalienable. An 1802 "Plan for the Emancipation of the Fair Sex" discussed efforts to "re-establish" women "in their rights . . . [and] natural equality." The key term is "re-establish." If women's rights were truly natural (that is, had existed in the state of nature), women were not gaining new rights; they were merely recovering rights they had lost. Although some analysts debated whether political rights should be included as natural rights, they still acknowledged women's unalterable claim to certain basic privileges. William Loughton Smith told a female audience in 1796, "Tho' you are excluded from a participation in our political institutions, yet nature has also assigned to you valuable and salutary rights, which are beyond their [men's] control. To delight, to civilize, and to ameliorate mankind . . . *these are the precious rights of woman!*" The idea of natural rights implied the possession of privileges beyond human delegation or manipulation.

A duty-bound definition of rights was thus not simply or necessarily a diversion. Americans could have decided that women, like slaves, were subhuman or second-class human beings, unworthy to be the possessors of rights. But they did not. They granted women rights, albeit rights that were different from men's, derived from the Scottish rather than the Lockean natural rights tradition. In doing so, however, these writers conceded crucial ground: they acknowledged that women shared the same dignity and moral standing as men—both in the eyes of God, which Christianity has long taught, and because they were human beings whose rights were based in nature and guaranteed by nature's God. Having gained the status of rights bearers, women also acquired something more: the moral authority to claim specific or particular rights. The genie was out of the bottle.

Once women were acknowledged to have rights, whether of the Lockean or Scottish variety, it was hard to restrict the scope and meaning of those rights. Even the limited application of rights language to women raised troubling questions. . . .

Among the real complaints that soon emerged was the women's lack of political rights. Rights talk led to speculation about the possibility of women voting, holding office, or obtaining representation in their legislatures. As early as 1790, the New York *Daily Advertiser* published an anonymous column that declared, "It is certainly unjust to exclude from any share in government one half of those who, considered as equals of the males, are obliged to be subject to laws they have no share in making!" The president of Harvard College, John Thornton Kirkland, admitted in 1798, "Had the new theory of the *Rights of Women* enlightened the world at the period of the formation of our constitution, it is possible that the framers, convinced of its arguments might have set aside the old system of exclusion, upon which the world has always proceded till this reforming age, as illiberal, and tyrannical." The very words, "women's rights" conjured up the prospect of women's political participation.

Even before the feminist movement of the 1830s, some authors imagined the possibility of women holding office. Writing in 1816, "A Lady" commented on what she saw as an important flaw in her government. "It is a curious fact," she remarked, "that a republic which avows equality of right as its first principle, persists in an ungenerous exclusion of the female sex from its executive department." The issue took on greater urgency when a woman, Elizabeth Bartlett, was nominated for the position of register of deeds in Middlesex County, Massachusetts, in 1822. . . . "If a lady is eligible as a Register of Deeds, is she not also as a Governor, Senator, Representative, Overseer of the poor, or other public office? . . . I have some curiosity to know where we are to stop." Long before women publicly agitated for their rights, people . . . understood—though they may not have liked—the implications of natural rights ideas for women.

The most serious discrepancy between men's and women's political rights came to notice as states debated the expansion of the white male franchise. With the elimination of property qualifications for men, it became clear that the main impediment to women's voting was their sex. As early as 1821, a "friend" of the ladies published a jocular petition on the subject to the New York state constitutional convention: "That ev'ry one must have a vote, / Who does not wear a petticoat, / Is generally admitted." While many states by then allowed all kinds of men, even those who had "forfeit[ed] all pretentions / To decency and common sense," into "the birthright of election," women, though "pure as Eden's queen," could "never to election come." Women, it was clear, were excluded simply because they were women—not because they lacked sufficient property, education, or virtue. The author then asked New Yorkers to broaden the franchise beyond white males. "But why should women be denied, / And have their tongues completely tied, / For party broils well fitted." The expansion of male suffrage caused a shift from a property-based to a gender-based prerogative, a shift that only highlighted the injustice of women's systematic exclusion from the political process.

In the post-Revolutionary era, many Americans anticipated the radical consequences of natural rights talk and rejected its implications for women. The denial of political rights to women, in particular, came to represent the defining outer limit of natural rights ideology in the early United States, the line that even the Jeffersonians would not cross in their advocacy of the universal rights of man. Whatever the intent, citizens could not contain the radicalism of rights language for long. The discussion of women's rights had already begun to expose the basic contradictions of an egalitarian polity that denied truly equal rights to women.

This discourse concerning women's rights provides a crucial intellectual link between the Revolutionary era and the first feminist movement of the 1830s and 1840s. More explicitly than "Republican Motherhood," natural rights ideas defined women's relationship to the political community and forced Americans to specify precisely what that relationship should be. During the Revolution, some Americans had begun to explore, mostly in private, the meaning of equality and natural rights of women. Mary Wollstonecraft's *Vindication of the Rights of Woman* appropriated the idea of natural rights and applied it explicitly to women. American periodicals popularized the language of women's rights and raised the question of exactly what kind of rights women should have. This issue generated debate for many years. As early as the 1790s, it was on the table for discussion. Rather than an unquestioned given, women's exclusion from politics now had to be rationalized and justified.

Such exclusion seems, on the face of it, to confirm the feminist critique of the liberal state. Theorists such as Carole Pateman, Nancy Hirschmann, and Joan Landes and historians such as Susan Juster have argued that, from the beginning, democratic states have been "masculinist" in character, depending for their existence on the political exclusion or social marginalization of women. The primary features of a liberal polity—consent, obligation, and choice—have been understood, they argue, as referring exclusively to males and defined so as to preclude women's participation in the public sphere. . . . Juster, looking at changing gender roles in evangelical religious sects, reaches a similar conclusion about the American Revolution. "The democratic revolution," she says, "was . . . constructed *against* not merely *without* women."

The historical evidence adduced here suggests that women's exclusion was contingent rather than essential. From the Revolution onward, at least some Americans realized that the ideals of equality and natural rights could be applied to women as well as to men. In fact, they realized that, unless they could come up with a persuasive rationale to exclude women, the universalistic assumptions of natural rights ideology would compel women's inclusion. But a commitment to rights was at odds with a commitment to the gender hierarchy. As a result, Americans attempted to circumvent the radicalism of natural rights. Drawing selectively on Scottish and Lockean natural rights traditions, they defined men's and women's rights differently. Although women would have rights, they would, by virtue of their fundamental nature, be prevented from claiming the same rights as men. The result was a gendered division of rights and, concurrently, the elaboration of separate spheres ideology.

Rights talk, however, could not be anchored to any particular usage or theory. By acknowledging the existence of women's rights, writers created the possibility that women could exploit rights discourse for themselves. By 1848, the Seneca Falls Declaration would claim, not the separate rights of woman, but the universal rights of all humanity. Women's ability to claim equal rights did not, to be sure, guarantee public recognition of those rights; that struggle would take more than a century. Yet a historical understanding of women's rights talk exposes, not the exclusivity, but the irony, of the liberal, rights-based state. Though nature was invoked to justify women's subordinate status, natural rights ideology subverted the claim. Natural rights represented the turning point, the discursive key that unlocked the possibility of women's social and political equality.

The Revolution Was Radical in Some Ways, Not in Others

ALFRED F. YOUNG

In 1926, J. Franklin Jameson spoke of "the stream of revolution once started [which] could not be confined within thin narrow banks but [which] spread abroad upon the land." And in 1967 Bernard Bailyn saw in the Revolution "a movement of thought, rapid, irreversible and irresistible" which "swept past boundaries few had set out to cross, into regions few had wished to enter." In the "contagion of liberty" "a spark" jumped from Whig political ideology to ignite sentiment for antislavery, religious liberty, and the rejection of deference. All historians use metaphors and Jameson and Bailyn provided evocative physical analogies which, as they often do, allowed little room for human agency. If Jameson was vague in identifying the

Condensed from Alfred F. Young, ed., *Beyond the American Revolution: Explorations in the History of American Radicalism,* 1993, pp. 317–364. Copyright © 1993 by Northern Illinois University Press. Used by permission of the publisher.

dynamic source of change, Bailyn, as David B. Davis has written, "tend[ed] to exaggerate the autonomous power of ideas" to effect change. Who broke the banks of the river? Which people carried the sparks from one tree of liberty to another?

Recent scholarship suggests a number of propositions that might restore agency to this process and moves us toward a synthesis of the origins of radicalism without, however, suggesting a single paradigm:

First, there were deep roots of radicalism in ideas, values, traditions, and customs held by common people long before the Revolution.

Second, as groups played an active role in the Revolution and became aware of their own interests, they invoked their own traditions in addition to appropriating Whig rhetoric.

Third, experiences over an unusually long revolutionary era contributed to radical impulses, not only in the now well-known decade of resistance before 1775, but during the protracted war from 1775 to 1781 and even more from the mid-1780s on, especially through the 1790s, when the impulses of the French Revolution and the successful black revolution in St. Domingue rekindled American radicalism.

Fourth, as antagonisms increased, many groups of common people acquired a heightened consciousness of themselves and their distinct interests which enabled them to become a presence in American life.

Sources of Radicalism

"That each of us may sit down under his own fig-tree
and enjoy the fruits of his own labour"

The first proposition, that there were deep roots of radicalism in ideas, values, traditions, and customs held by common people which they brought to the era of the Revolution, has been analyzed by historians within various frameworks: moral economy, *mentalité,* class ideology, political culture, or "customs in common." . . . Take, for example, the yeoman farmers. . . . A common assumption among early American farmers was that they were entitled to "the fruits of their labor," attained by the "sweat of their brow." . . . This is what informed the long-standing fear, among New England yeomen in particular, of being reduced to "vassals" under "lordships." . . . This is what made yeoman farmers so quick to respond to any threat to the security of their title to land, especially to taxes that threatened to reduce them to the status of debtors, which could lead to the loss of their land. Political leaders like John and Samuel Adams were successful because they were attuned to such fears. This was the social nexus of the agrarian response to Whig political and constitutional rhetoric.

Historians can now pull this red thread through the skein of collective agrarian responses from the late seventeenth century through the prewar Regulator movements, the political conflicts of the 1770s with England, and the Shaysism of the 1780s, to the agrarian rebellions and agrarian politics of the 1790s and early 1800s. This was the radicalism of farmers who were property holders or would-be property holders and believed they had a right to land, tools, and other productive property. These were not necessarily marginal farmers, although many were landowners with uncertain title to their land, tenants with insecure leases, or backcountry squatters. Nor did farmers have to be poverty-stricken to become radical. As often as not, they were landholders with families who worried about becoming impoverished—a fear of falling—or the sons of landholders who feared they would be unable to acquire land and duplicate the success of their fathers. Their goal was personal independence through secure landholding, a goal that merged with the political aspiration for national independence in some regions, making yeoman patriots, and which in other regions decidedly did not, leaving a large number of farmers Tory, neutral, or "disaffected" during the war.

Artisans were imbued with similar values. Also property holders or would-be-property holders, they were men (and sometimes women) who practiced a productive trade as masters ("a man on his own") or as journeymen, working for others who aspired to be masters. They were heirs to the ancient traditions of their trades as well as to a belief in property right tenets long articulated by their forebears among English artisans of the seventeenth and eighteenth centuries. . . . Artisans in the port cities, even more than country folk, lived in fear of becoming dependent, of falling into the poorhouse or becoming recipients of poor relief. Journeymen worried that they might remain wage earners and not rise to the ranks of the independent. Apprentices who ran away had little confidence they could ever climb the ladder into this artisan world.

What values might we expect to find among the free, propertyless wage earners at the bottom? Among merchant seamen, for instance—the largest single group of wage earners in early America? As Admiral Peter Warren testified in 1745 after they fiercely resisted impressment into His Majesty's navy, seamen "have the highest notion of the rights and liberties of Englishmen, and indeed are almost Levellers." Sailors prized their freedom. . . .

Throughout the colonial era, those in servitude, whether African-American slaves, immigrant indentured servants from Great Britain, or native-born apprentices, demonstrated what in 1721 the Reverend Cotton Mather of Boston called a "fondness for freedom." Fifty years later a slave in the same city, the African-born Phillis Wheatley, wrote: "In every human Breast, God has implanted a Principle, which we call Love of Freedom. It is impatient of Oppression, and pants for Deliverance; and by the Leave of our modern Egyptians I will assert, that the same Principle lives in us." . . .

Slaves of the last half of the eighteenth century warrant being identified as African American. . . .

What did slaves aspire to after emancipation? Their lives as workers were a constant reminder that their daily labor was being stolen from them, just as they or their ancestors had been stolen from Africa. The evidence of the revolutionary era, the time of the first emancipation, suggests that no less than white Anglo-American yeomen and artisans they sought the means to secure personal independence. Massachusetts slaves began a 1773 petition with the premise that "they have in common with other men, a natural right to be free, and without molestation, to enjoy such property, as they may accumulate by their industry," moved to a plea that "they may be liberated and made free-men," and ended with the request that they be granted "some part of the unimproved land, belong to this province, for a settlement, that each of us may there quietly sit down under his own-fig-tree, and enjoy the fruits of his own labour." Tens of thousands of slaves fled during the war; many were transported by the British to Nova Scotia in 1783, sought land there, and when they fared poorly made their way back to Africa to the British colony of Sierra Leone in quest of land. In the 1790s, when Robert Carter began to free the five hundred slaves on his Virginia plantation by individual acts of manumission, they sought from him land or the means to pursue a trade they assumed was their right.

This set of beliefs among both free farmers and artisans and unfree slaves, as their language alone suggests, was often rooted in religion, especially in the evangelical dissenting faiths. . . . They were Baptists, New Light Congregationalists, ultra-evangelical Antinomians who sought to bypass a learned clergy in pursuit of direct spiritual encounters." . . .

Religious awakenings reverberated through the revolutionary era. While historians continue to explore the links between the Great Awakening (1739–45) and the Revolution, far more attention is being paid to the waves of enthusiastic religions during and especially after the war. Millennialism, it is now clear, took many forms—charging, for example, the radical protest of an intercolonial backcountry rebel like Herman Husband with his vision of a New Jerusalem in the West as a yeoman's utopia. By the early 1800s the evangelical Baptists and Methodists, on the way to becoming the most numerous of American denominations, contributed not only to . . . "the democratization of American Christianity," but to the democratization of American political life. . . .

Appropriations of Liberty

"Who can have a better right to the land than we
who have fought for it?"

If this commitment to prior source of radical values is valid, it is not hard to argue the second proposition, namely that in the era of the Revolution, as groups of ordinary people played an active role in the Revolution and became aware of their own interests, they invoked their own traditions as well as the Whig rhetoric of lawyers, ministers, planters, and merchants. There was a synthesis of traditional veins of radical thought with newer currents forged in the experiences of the Revolution that scholars are only now analyzing. . . .

Language reveals the synthesis. . . . They held an underlying assumption of a right to land drawn from radical Christian traditions ("God gave the earth to his children") and a sense of a moral economy. ("Wild lands ought to be as free as the common air.") But their military service in the war fortified this claim. ("Who can have a better right to the land than we who have fought for it?") And the fact that the land in dispute was confiscated from England made it all the more common property. ("These lands once belonged to King George. He lost them by the American Revolution & they became the property of the people who defended and won them.")

Other language showed an intricate appropriation of Whig rhetoric. The unfree living in the centers of patriot movements were extraordinarily quick to seize on Whig ideas, especially when patriots shifted the meaning of liberty from traditional English constitutional rights to natural rights, the first transition in the meaning of this keyword that Countryman analyzes. Thus, in Massachusetts, the first petition of slaves for freedom in January 1773 was a plaintive Christian humanitarian plea: "We have no Property! We have no Wives! No Children! We have no City! No Country! But we have a Father in Heaven." The second, in July, spoke of a "natural right to be free" but dwelt on a person's right to his own labor. Even their 1774 petition, in which they spoke of themselves as "a freeborn Pepel [who] have never forfeited this Blessing by aney compact or agreement whatever," continued to blend this Whig theme with Christian values. Not until a 1777 petition, which referred to their patience in presenting "Petition after Petition," did they pick up on their "natural & unalienable right" to freedom. This appropriation was so opportunistic one is tempted to argue that Whig rhetoric was more the occasion than a cause for asserting a claim to liberty.

As individuals picked up ideas that were in the air, they often pushed them far beyond anything intended by patriot leaders. Years later Ebenezer Fox, a Boston-area apprentice . . . who shipped out on a privateering vessel, wrote in his memoirs: "I thought I was doing myself a great injustice by remaining in bondage when I ought to be free; that the time was come, when I should liberate myself from the thraldom of others and set up a government of my own; or in other words, do what was right in the sight of my own eyes." His words reveal the kind of personal Declaration of Independence from all authority that Henry Thoreau would have appreciated, and that would have made John Adams shudder.

The unequals had to make a leap in their thinking to turn the talk of liberty into a demand for equality for themselves; and the leap is better explained by experience than by any logic inherent in the idea. For George Robert Twelves Hewes, a Boston shoemaker who survives in two as-told-to biographies, the experience of participating in the Boston Massacre, the Boston Tea Party, and countless other events of resistance enabled him to cast off deference. He vividly recalled the deference he earlier felt as an apprentice shoemaker when he called on John Hancock, one of the wealthiest merchants in Boston; and then, a decade later, the sense of equality he felt when (as he remembered it) he worked side by side with Hancock throwing the tea overboard in the Tea Party. It is unlikely that Hancock would have risked arrest at so illegal an event, but Hewes could have mistaken another gentleman for him. For the rest of his life Hewes would remember the Revolution's moments of equality—when he was as good a man as his "betters," whether John Hancock, the customs official Hewes defied, or the ship's officer for whom he refused to take his hat off.

We know enough about Abigail Adams to gain insight into what led one woman to make the leap and therefore to speculate about others. In her "remember the Ladies" letter to John in March 1776, she seemed to be raising the demand to end the tyranny of husbands over their wives for the first time. For more than a decade she had been reading or hearing her husband's rhetoric of "tyranny" and "slavery" and "lords and vassals," but it does not seem that she, John, or anyone else in Massachusetts had publicly applied the principle to the status of women.

What were her experiences? Over the decade she had followed the active participation of the women of Boston and the surrounding countryside in the making of the Revolution and referred to herself as a "politician." She may well have drawn inspiration from the black petitioners and alleged conspirators of 1773–74 who, she felt, "have as good a right to freedom as we have." In 1776, only the month before her letter to John, she had read *Common Sense* with its message to begin the world over again. But perhaps most decisive, for almost two years while her husband was intermittently away in Philadelphia, she had taken on new responsibilities outside the traditional "female sphere": she managed the family farm, boasting she had become "quite a farmeriss," and she had become "school mistress" to her three young children. Thus she had a growing consciousness both of her own capacities and her own inadequacies—how ill-educated she was for the task. It was in the context of such experiences that she lifted her voice to John to "remember the Ladies." Similar wartime experiences would lead other women to make such a leap and verbalize a new consciousness.

Sources of Radicalism

Promises Unfulfilled

The third proposition, that experiences shaped radical impulses over a very long revolutionary era that extended through the 1780s, the 1790s, and beyond, is becoming more of a commonplace among historians as they think through the life histories of the revolutionary generation. The Revolution did not end in 1776, in 1783, in 1787, or even in 1801. In writing about the great leaders—Washington, Adams, Hamilton, Jefferson, Madison—historians have no problem dealing with their entire political lives, which often stretched over half a century and more. Why not think the same way of the common people who lived out their lives over the same years? For many, their radicalism was the product of their *cumulative* experience over the entire era. . . .

The experiences of a long war—the longest in American history—generated a variety of radical impulses. . . . Roughly 200,000 men served in the military, about half in the militia, half in the regular army. The Philadelphia militia, whose artisans, journeymen, and laborers were the base of the movement that pushed Pennsylvania to independence and enacted the most radical constitution of any state "carried their egalitarianism with them into the field" and carried it back to the streets of Philadelphia in the campaign for price controls in 1779–80. The militias elsewhere, even when a cross section of their communities, were too democratic in the eyes of elitist officer. Soldiers of the regular army, who after 1776 were drawn from "the very poorest and most repressed persons in Revolutionary society" scholars now agree were no less patriotic for having their aspirations for a better life tied to the promises of land. Tension between enlisted men and officers was endemic and Baron Von Steuben was astute enough to recognize that he had to teach American officers to adapt to the "genius" of individualistic American enlistees and win their "love and respect." "Continentals," who early in the war often expressed their bitterness at the inequities of army life in drunkenness, desertion, and bounty jumping, as they became more disciplined and cohesive, expressed their protest collectively, climaxing in the mutinies of the New Jersey and Pennsylvania lines in 1781. . . .

At sea the rage for privateering gave some 60,000 men (as opposed to a few thousand who served in the Navy) a chance to "make their fortunes and serve their country" as the recruiters beguiled them. It also gave them a taste of legalized privacy, in which captains, like pirate commanders, courted the consent of their crews. And thousands of seamen who were captured, if they survived the horrors of British prisons, had the experience of collective self-government.

In the countryside the Revolution took the character of a civil war for tens of thousands of ordinary Americans . . . especially in parts of the southern backcountry, where it "took on the appearance of a social convulsion." Wherever there was a prior history of intense conflict between colonial elites and common folk—especially in the two Carolinas—patriot elites encountered intense opposition. In Maryland where there was more cohesion, there was still active opposition to large planter leadership by the "disaffected"—poor farmers and tenants. The pattern was similar in New York, where tenants opposed patriot landlords. Even in relatively tranquil Virginia there was opposition, only partially overcome when old elites embraced Patrick Henry. While alignments in the South often produced a patchwork of social classes, the principal experience for many southerners was confronting and thwarting their betters, tidewater or low-country elites.

For slaves the "turbulence of the war . . . rocked the slave system to its foundations." The British army was a magnet to slaves, North and South, with General Clinton repeating in 1780 in South Carolina Lord Dunmore's offer of 1775 in Virginia, although the British never risked a generalized appeal that would alarm their slave-owning supporters. In the North the urgencies of recruiting quotes forced patriots to reverse their ban on slaves, but in the end probably more slaves wielded arms for the British than against them, and even more simply took flight. . . . [I]n the southern low country, Philip Morgan points out, "wartime anarchy created a power vacuum in the countryside that allowed slaves to expand their liberty" or autonomy within the system. . . .

For women the war offered experiences out of the "domestic sphere." As many as 20,000 women attached themselves to the army as cooks, laundresses, and nurses, usually following family members. And when men went off to war, women were called upon to clothe them—a traditional role—but they also assumed male roles, managing the farm or trade, repeating Abigail Adams's experience of 1775–76. While the role of "deputy husband" was time-honored, never had so many women assumed it as a patriotic duty.

The experiences of postwar society spawned a radicalism of disappointment. For those who had served in the Army, the inequities of the settlement left a long-simmering resentment. Officers received pensions; and soldiers who were wounded received some recompense. But ordinary soldiers rarely received the bounty lands promised them on enlistment. The government did not enact a pension for enlisted men until 1818, and then only for those "in reduced circumstances," which produced 40,000 claims, a Domesday book of American poverty. And not until 1832 was this means test eliminated and an unrestricted pension law enacted for those who could give "a very full account" of their service. Twenty thousand applied. Historians have only begun to take the measure of the pain, pride and outrage in the pension applications of these survivors of the Revolution.

The hard times of the Confederation era forged a radicalism of desperation: of farmers imprisoned for debt and faced with the loss of their land and property; of mechanics swamped by the flood of British-manufactured imports or ruined in the collapse of American shipbuilding; of migrants into the backcountry frustrated in their quest for land. Petitions rained on the state legislatures demanding "access to land, debtor relief, and remedies to the burden of heavy and regressive taxes." Shaysism was not confined to one state. Among elites . . . there was an even greater fear that the radicalism of the "people-out-of-doors" would come "indoors," to dominate state legislatures.

Thus by 1787 there is every reason to believe that the "interests" James Madison analyzed in *The Federalist* no. 10 were also perceived by nonelites. Madison wrote of essentially two different sources of "factions." One source lay in substantial propertied interests: "a landed interest, a manufacturing interest, a mercantile interest, a monied interest." But "the most common and durable source of factions" was "the various and unequal distribution of property. Those who hold and those who are without property have ever formed distinct interests in society. Those who are creditors, and those who are debtors, fall under a like discrimination," thus identifying the key conflicts of the 1780s uppermost in elite minds. The creation of the federal Constitution mobilized the substantial commercial interests as never before. The conflict over ratification mobilized a broader array of interests in opposition, inspiring a populist Antifederalism on a scale that is only now being recognized by scholars.

The Hamiltonian economic program of the 1790s, coming on top of the new Constitution, widened the popular perception of a national ruling class . . . rule by the few at the expense of the many. In this context . . . "the astonishing American enthusiasm for the French Revolution" is understandable. Once the French Revolution entered domestic politics in the guise of foreign policy issues—the war between revolutionary republican France and monarchist Britain, the Paineite effort to revolutionize Great Britain, the Federalist accommodation with Britain in 1795 and the half-war with France—it inspired new levels of equalitarianism and millennialism. Thomas Paine's *The Rights of Man* seemed to pose the same issues that *Common Sense* had in 1776. The impulses to radicalism soared. . . .

Popular Consciousness

"Class," "Plebeian" or "Democratic"?

The fourth proposition about the sources of radicalism—namely, that as the antagonisms of the revolutionary era increased, many groups of common people acquired a heightened consciousness of themselves which enabled them to establish a presence in American life—is the the most problematic, not to prove, but to formulate. Historians seem to agree that a new kind of popular consciousness—a sense of "we" and "they"—came into being over the revolutionary era. They do not agree how to conceptualize it. . . .

In the wake of the Revolution the common language of class among nonelites often expressed a polarity of two major divisions in the society. In the debate over ratifying the Constitution, Amos Singletary, a Massachusetts farmer of little formal education, feared that "lawyers, and men of learning, and moneyed men" will "swallow up us little folks." In New York, Melancton Smith, the chief Antifederalist spokesman, a self-made merchant, thought that the proposed new government would fall into the hands of "the few and the great," while excluding "those of the middling class of life." In the debates of the 1790s the language of radicals suggests they drew the dividing line between the productive and nonproductive classes: "those that labour for a living and those who get one without" or "the Many" and "the Few" (William Manning); "the laboring people" against "learned and designing men" or the "idle rich" (Herman Husband); "the people" versus "the aristocracy" (Thomas Paine in *The Rights of Man*). . . .

Clearly, some nonelite groups "discovered themselves" more than others, moving toward a more interest-specific if not class-specific consciousness. . . . At some point in the 1770s, as conservative elites challenged their right to a voice in public affairs, "mechanics" began to wear that term as a badge of pride. In New York City and Philadelphia there were "mechanic" political tickets and Committees of Mechanics. By the mid-1780s in New York they formed a General Society of Mechanics and Tradesmen (the title bridging old and new usage). In Boston The Association of Tradesmen and Manufacturers, a body with delegates from the various trades, addressed written appeals to "their brethren, the mechanics" in other cities, asking them to join in a campaign for the protection of American manufactures. The emblem of the New Yorkers, adopted by societies in other cities, was an upright brawny arm holding a hammer, with a slogan "By Hammer and Hand All Arts Do Stand," a bold assertion of the primacy of the mechanic arts. Mechanics unquestionably became an influence in political life; they knew it, and political leaders knew it. . . .

If such groups "discovered themselves" in conflict, it does not necessarily follow that they remained in constant antagonism with their opponents. On the contrary, because the Revolution was also a war for national liberation, nascent classes formed coalitions with other classes against a common outside enemy. Indeed, the era led to a constant reforming of coalitions, especially in face of a foreign danger that persisted in major crises throughout the era. . . .

Furthermore, nascent classes divided internally. In the countryside with the expansion of a market economy, the distinction . . . between market-embedded commercial farmers and non-market-oriented yeomen helps explain political divisions among farmers, for example, over ratifying the commercially oriented Constitution of 1787. In the cities the mechanic trades also divided according to market orientation. By the late eighteenth century free wage labor was becoming the norm in northern cities: imported indentured servitude was drying up, slavery was fading, and apprenticeship was being transformed into a form of cheap labor. As the market system made its inroads on artisan production the conflict between masters and apprentices and masters and journeymen rent the fabric of mechanic cohesion.

While there undoubtedly was a growing sense of commonality among "the laboring classes" embracing town and countryside, urban mechanics usually failed to support agrarians in insurrections, whether it was the tenant uprising in New York in 1766 or Shays's Rebellion in 1786. . . . "The laboring classes" in countryside and city were female as well as male, but radicals who embraced Paine's *Rights of Man* (1791–92) showed no comparable interest in Mary Wollstonecraft's *Vindication of the Rights of Women* (1791). The laboring classes included blacks—in a greater proportion than at any other time in American history—yet neither agrarian nor mechanic radicals welcomed Gabriel's abortive insurrection in 1800, or the efforts of free blacks in northern cities to forge their own community institutions. And the free blacks of Boston volunteered to put down Shays's Rebellion. Thus the multiple radicalisms of the revolutionary era remained separate.

Taken together, the argument advanced in these four propositions suggests new ways of thinking about the sources of radicalism in the revolutionary era. It posits not a single radicalism but multiple radicalisms. It does not see them stemming from one all-pervasive idea or ideology. It assumes a prior array of radical value systems which came into play at that time. The Revolution was itself an incalculable stimulus to radicalism. . . .

Results of the Revolution

A Framework for Analysis

If recent scholarship has . . . increased our "appreciation" of the many radical movements of the Revolution, it leaves open the question of their success. . . . The retention and expansion of slavery, the maintenance of a patriarchal subordination of women, the destructive inroads of a market economy on the laboring classes in the cities, to say nothing of the destructive impact of national expansion on American Indians, were developments central to post-revolutionary society.

Scholars contrasting such results with the democratization of American politics, the opening of economic opportunity, and the surges of equalitarianism—all gains benefiting principally yeomen and mechanics and then women—often end up using words like "contradiction" or "paradox," which still leave us hanging for an explanation. Other historians, by claiming as does Gordon Wood, for example, that however much the Revolution failed "to abolish slavery and change fundamentally the lot of women, [it] made possible the anti-slavery and women's rights movements of the nineteenth century and in fact all our current egalitarian thinking," essentially evade their responsibility for historical analysis.

. . . [T]here were several ways to measure the success of popular radical movements, short of their achieving power: by their capacity to articulate a distinct ideology, to endure as movements, and especially to influence those in power and shape events. . . .

First, in response to the upsurges of radicalism, elites attempting to make themselves into a national ruling class, divided as to how to confront these threats. In the political sphere their responses ranged on a spectrum from the traditional methods of the English ruling class—force, deference and influence—to negotiation leading to accommodation.

Second, the processes of negotiation were most successful with the middling classes—yeomen and mechanics—who had pushed their way into the political system, establishing a continuing presence that elites could not ignore if they wished to govern successfully.

Third, negotiation was pervasive throughout the society, offering accommodations to groups excluded from the political system—women and slaves—without destroying the subordination on which the social and economic system rested. American Indians, the real outsiders, were powerful enough in certain places and times to force a kind of accommodation on Anglo-Americans that delayed expansion.

And finally, as a result of the process of accommodation which made the political system more democratic, radical popular movements divided as to the means to effect change on a spectrum that ranged from the traditional time-honored, effective, extralegal forms of opposition to working within the new political system.

Framing the analysis of results in this way—as a process of confrontation, negotiation and accommodation occurring on a range of separate spheres—offers the possibility of resolving the so-called contradictions in the outcome of the Revolution. It also leaves room in the analysis for the integration of the complex ways in which the transformations leading the United States toward a capitalist society both stimulated and frustrated radical impulses.

Elites Divide

Accommodation in the Public Sphere

That the would-be ruling classes divided in response to the popular upheavals in the revolutionary era has been established by scholars, state by state. . . . In the colonial era elites varied in their cohesiveness. In many colonies, elite families were ever at each other's throats, often appealing demagogically in elections to artisans or farmers with the vote, uniting only to assert their hegemony over the subordinate classes. The merchant classes were usually fragmented; so were large slaveholders or landlords in the Hudson River Valley. But, in general, elites contained the sporadic threats from below. What was new, from the 1770s on, was a persistent popular democratic presence in politics. How to handle it could divide great aristocratic families within (as with the Carrolls of Maryland) or from their neighbors and kin (as in New York), or divide even the confident ruling gentry (as in Virginia).

The Revolution produced a crisis of confidence among old elites in their capacity to take their chances with democracy (to them, "the rabble" or "the mob") and with the new men responsible to popular constituencies with whom elites now had to compete for power (to them, "upstarts" and "demagogues"). Confidence of this sort was something of a dividing line within elites over the entire revolutionary era: between Whigs and loyalists over separating from Great Britain, among Whigs in state making and constitution making, in the 1790s between Democratic Republicans and Federalists, and after their defeat in 1800, between "old school" and "new school" Federalists.

The metaphors elites used for the threats from below are telling tokens of their different outlooks. Panic-stricken conservatives referred to the people as a beast that had to be driven or as a reptile that would bite. . . . By contrast, Robert R. Livingston, a landlord potentate in New York typical of more risk-taking conservatives, in 1777 used the metaphor of a stream: rulers had to "learn the propriety of Swimming with a Stream which it is impossible to stem"; they should "yield to the torrent if they hoped to direct its course." Thirty years later, Noah Webster scolded his fellow Federalists who had fallen from power because they "attempted to resist the current popular opinion instead of falling into the current with a view to direct it." . . .

What was new was that the Revolution nationalized the threat of radicalism which earlier was localized. Neither Shaysism nor the whiskey uproar was confined to one state. The creation of a national government created a national arena for conflicts. And the increase in the number and frequency of newspapers permitted a more rapid dissemination of opinion. Master mechanics communicated from one city to another. Some fifty Democratic Societies came into being in the backcountry as well as eastern cities. One consequence of this minor revolution in communications was that outside events could have a fairly rapid national influence. Successive events in the French Revolution produced common reactions all over the United States; the news of successful black revolutionaries in the Caribbean invigorated African-American resistance. North and South, alarming slaveholders as well as antislavery advocates.

The torrents of national radicalism required extraordinary skill of the nation's pilots. In the postwar crisis that culminated in the Constitutional Convention of 1787, the elite leaders best able to assume national leadership were men like James Madison, who recognized it as a crisis of "the political system," itself a revealing phrase. Madison was able to negotiate on two fronts: with the conflicting substantial propertied "interests" so well represented in the convention (the haves) and with the radical democratic movements that were a "presence" at the convention, even if they were not present (the have-nots and the have-littles). The framers more or less agreed with Madison that if the Constitution was to last "for the ages," it had to conform to "the genius of the people," a phrase meaning spirit or underlying values. . . . Nathaniel Gorham of Boston, a merchant sensitive to a mechanic constituency, summed it up: "We must consult the rooted prejudices [of the people] if we expect their concurrence in our propositions."

Bold, sophisticated conservatives had learned a lesson from the Revolution— they had to accommodate democratic-minded constituencies in advance. The Federalists of 1787–88 made two grand accommodations usually missing from civics lessons: the first, in the concessions to democratic rule they built into the Constitution itself; the second, during the process of ratification, when they divided the powerful popular opposition who wanted a less centralized and more democratic structure by promising amendments which they later reduced to the Bill of Rights, which left the essential framework intact. The result was a constitution a nationalist-minded radical like Thomas Paine and a localist plebeian democrat like William Manning could fault but accept. . . .

The elites who gained power but had the least long-run success were the Hamiltonian Federalists of the 1790s, who adopted England as a model. Hamilton . . . tried to consolidate a government in the 1790s based on the English system of deference, influence, and force. But deference was on the wane, and any attempt to impose it led to the charge of "aristocracy." Building influence through a funding system and bank produced a backlash against corruption. And force—whether military to put down extralegal opposition . . . or political repression like the Sedition Law of 1798 to imprison legal opposition—misjudged the "genius of the people," ushering the Federalists out of power.

The elites with the greatest capacity for survival coalesced as the Democratic Republicans, under the leadership of Madison and Jefferson. The Virginia leaders had mastered the process in their native state by building alliances with the dissenting religions in a ten-year battle to disestablish the Anglican church. They learned how to accommodate nationally: to build a coalition of southern slave-owning planters, yeomen, northern merchants in search of markets to make them independent of Britain, and mechanics and would-be manufacturers. It is not surprising that their principal northern allies were politicians from New York and Pennsylvania like Robert R. Livingston, who once again was ready to swim with the stream. The interests thus brought together could share a common aim of expanding overseas commercial markets for agricultural produce, expanding to the West, and developing American manufactures.

Democratic Republicans shifted to accommodate radical agrarians to their left. . . . [I]n 1794 Madison and Jefferson . . . were more concerned with eliminating grievances than putting down agrarian rebels. And with the vast public domain as a resource they were prepared to accommodate insistent settler demands for land. Both fought the repressive Sedition Law. They also recognized the importance of the mechanics—"the yeomanry of the cities" to Jefferson. However, they could not accommodate African Americans in slavery, or American Indians, and were indifferent to the new voices among American women.

Negotiations in the Private Sphere

African Americans

All this negotiation was in the public sphere. The work of historians in a variety of fields of social history suggests that negotiation also was underway within private spheres (a distinction from the public sphere that was often dissolving). This seems true among many segments of the laboring classes, especially in the 1790s. . . . Masters and apprentices literally signed a contract expressing reciprocal obligations for living and working under the same roof. As apprentice deference eroded, the master had to mend his ways. . . . At the same time, journeymen in many trades organized on their own to deal with masters, leading to the first pattern of American strikes by journeymen ("turnouts") and lockouts by masters. . . .

In rural areas the armed confrontations between settlers and great proprietors could end in negotiations. In Maine, once the proprietors conceded the right of squatters to acquire land, the conflict could boil down to haggling over the price of land. Leading men in frontier communities often served as middlemen. . . . Here politicians brokered a social conflict, an innovation that in time became a cliché in American politics.

The war enhanced the capacity of slaves to negotiate with their masters. The new scholarship on slavery in the revolutionary era has identified the processes by which slaves won "space" for themselves within an oppressive system. In 1775–76 southern planters clearly were in no position to accommodate the massive upsurge for freedom. Yet during the war they often had no choice; slaves expanded their autonomy within the system, or made good their flight from it. And after the war the low-country blacks, for example, did not readily surrender their wartime gains and "many continued to flaunt their increased autonomy." In the upper South, Maryland and Virginia passed laws that made it easier for individual slaveholders to free their own slaves through manumission, creating the first sizable free black population in the Chesapeake. . . .

In the North, where there were 50,000 slaves on the eve of the Revolution, emancipation on a state-by-state basis . . . dragged out for years. . . . [T]he insistent black pressures for freedom did as much as white antislavery benevolence to bring about this first emancipation. During and after the war northern slaves seized freedom, by fighting with the British or the patriots or by running away; or they purchased their own freedom and that of their families. In the five northern states with the largest slave populations, the legislatures provided only gradual emancipation for children born of slaves after they reached their twenties, which explains why in 1810 there were still 27,000 slaves in the North compared to 50,000 free blacks. Once free, blacks in the northern states faced a continuing struggle against racism for access to schools, the ballot, and civil rights. It was a grudging emancipation.

By 1820 in the country as a whole the number of freed blacks approached 250,000, while the number of slaves had grown to 1.5 million. Thus, as Berlin sums it up, ". . . if the Revolution marked a new birth of freedom, it also launched a great expansion of slavery."

How was this possible? The question is crucial to understanding the Revolution. . . . [David Brian Davis argued in 1975 that] "slavery was of central importance to both the southern and national economies, and thus to the viability of the 'American system.'" Moreover, "a free society was by no means incompatible with dependent classes of workers." . . . Chattel slaves provided the property which defined independence, the long-cherished goal of southern farmers. What accounts for the northern acquiescence to southern slavery? Economic interest, the high priority placed on national union, the devotion to private property in Whig ideology, and the growth of racism as the indispensable justification for continuing slavery in a land of liberty—all these contributed to what was perhaps the most fateful accommodation of the revolutionary era.

Accommodations in the "Domestic Sphere"

Women

This pattern of accommodation within a system of subordination assumed a different shape for women. "We are ready to ask," Linda Kerber writes, "whether and how the social relations of the sexes were renegotiated in the crucible of the Revolution." As a result of women's participation in the prewar resistance and in the war, "how much more inclusive American citizenship should be was under negotiation."

Thought about this way, the oft-cited exchange of letters between Abigail and John Adams in 1776 can be viewed as the opening round of a quintessential negotiation. He would hear nothing of equality of rights, but was receptive to her continuing demands for educational opportunities for women. Out of such exchanges—which we can assume were repeated without written record in countless families of the middling sort—came the accommodation Kerber has called "Republican motherhood," in which mothers were endowed with the patriotic responsibility of raising their sons and daughters as virtuous citizens for the new Republic and therefore required a better education. The "role of Republican motherhood," as Kerber recently reflected, "was a conservative stabilizing one, deflecting the radical potential of the revolutionary experience"; at the same time, it contributed to the expansion of education for women, the principal gain of the decades after 1790.

Thus the literate young women able to read novels . . . were the beneficiaries of the first negotiation. . . . In the long struggle by women for equal rights this may not seem very subversive, but as long as marriage was the chief option open to women, . . . a woman had "an opportunity to work out in the safe context of her imagination just what she wanted from men and from marriage." This in turn very likely contributed to "matrimonial republicanism," another product of the negotiation between the sexes. How widespread were these changes, how far they extended beyond educated middling women is not clear. . . . Scholars have found it easier to measure the absence of change in laws and institutions; they are only beginning to tap sources that measure changes in women's consciousness.

That some women should articulate independence as a goal is not surprising in an era in which personal independence was the heightened goal of every Tom, Dick, and Harry. Mary Wollstonecraft's *Vindication of the Rights of Women* found a receptive readership among educated American women. "In very many of her sentiments," the Philadelphia Quaker Elizabeth Drinker confided to her diary, "she, as some of our friends say, *speaks my mind.* In some others, I do not always coincide with her. I am not for quite so much independence." John Adams thought Abigail was "a perfect disciple of Wollstonecraft." Through the 1790s Judith Sargent Murray, the most vocal American theorist of women's rights, argued for an independence that pushed at the boundaries of republican motherhood. . . . [S]he argued, "marriage should not be presented as the *summum bonum,* or as a certain, or even necessary, event; they should learn to respect a single life, and even regard it as the *most eligible,* except a warm, mutual and judicious attachment has gained the ascendancy in the bosom." . . .

In an era when most white men had access to the means to achieve independence, most women did not; and most men were not prepared to surrender "our masculine systems," as John Adams put it. Why not? Just as the independence of the slaveholder was defined by the dependence of his slaves, or the independence of the artisan defined by the dependence of his apprentices and journeymen, so the independence of a white male, whatever his occupation, was defined by the dependence of his wife and children. . . .

Accommodations

American Indians, Elites, and Frontiersmen

The revolutionary era was a time of unprecedented landed expansion. . . . This expansion produced a triangular confrontation of American Indians, eastern national elites, and western settlers that led to alternating national policies of accommodation and warfare and to deep divisions within native American societies.

The range of accommodation with native Americans was limited by an ethnocentrism that made the most well-meaning Anglo-Americans incapable of coexisting with Indians as they were. During and after the war, in which most Indians fought on the side of the British, their traditional protectors, the dominant attitude among whites . . . [were] encapsulated in such toasts and slogans as "Civilization or death to all American Savages" or "Civilization or extinction." But Anglo-American leaders had not calculated on the Indians' will for independence or their capacity to defend it.

In the decades before and after the war, native American societies had experienced movements of spiritual revitalization . . . that reinforced political and military resistance. . . . The Revolutionary War, which produced "a near unanimity of the trans-Appalachian struggle against the United States," enhanced pan-Indianism. The tactics of Revolutionary War leaders such as the scorched-earth decimation of Iroquois villages (which earned George Washington the reputation among the Iroquois as "town destroyer") put native Americans in no mood to accommodate the victorious United States.

In the peace treaty, the British . . . "passed the card called sovereignty" over Indian land, "a legal fiction," to the new nation. But spokesmen for the Iroquois Confederacy in the north said they were "a free People subject to no Power upon earth," while the southern tribes insisted they had done nothing "to forfeit our Independence and natural Rights." Confronted with Indian power, national political leaders rapidly shifted, recognizing Indian claims to sovereignty, literally negotiating treaties, and promising, in the Northwest Ordinance of 1787, that "the utmost good faith shall always be observed towards the Indians; their land and property shall never be taken from them without their consent."

The corollary of this accommodation was to bring the "blessings of civilization" to American Indians. This meant . . . that "Indian men would adopt plow agriculture, women would abandon the field for the home, and all would give up their heathen ways for Christ." The symbol was engraved on the silver peace medal U.S. presidents bestowed on cooperating chieftains: a native American male throwing a broken arrow to the ground before President Washington, who is in his general's uniform, sword at his side; and in the background, a man, perhaps the same Indian, guiding a plough pulled by two oxen, tilling a field.

The pressures of western agrarians forced a change on national policymakers. . . . The tillers of the soil, whose labor gave it value, were alone entitled to the land. Indians, in the eyes of farmers, did nothing to improve the "howling wilderness." The same class antagonism informed the backcountryman's attitude toward absentee land proprietors and eastern opponents of an aggressive policy toward the Indians. The Tennessee territorial legislature in 1794 reminded Congress that "citizens who live in poverty on the extreme frontiers were as entitled to be protected in their lives, their families and little property, as those who were in luxury, ease and affluence in the great and opulent eastern cities." In the 1790s eastern elites with their own agendas for expansion, bent to these pressures, sanctioning war on a massive scale. . . .

Anglo-American pressures forced people into their own internal processes of accommodation. . . . Tribal societies were divided among those who would accommodate by negotiating away land rights and moving on, those who were willing to adopt the white man's ways, including Christianity and plow agriculture, and those who rejected them or sought selective adaptation of Anglo-American ways. . . . In this context the divisions within Indian societies confronting imperial expansion bear some resemblance to the divisions within the Anglo-American society of the same era.

The Democratic Republicans, once in national power, offered their own mixture of benevolence and belligerence, paving the way for the next step, physical removal from the eastern United States. In 1783, 150,000 Indians lived east of the Mississippi; by 1844, less than one-fourth remained. . . .

Radical Divisions

The process of accommodation in the political system contributed to a division within radical popular movements as to the best means for effecting change. The norm inherited from colonial times was extralegal action: mob actions in the cities and Regulator movements in the countryside. . . .

In the eyes of the common people the success of the Revolution legitimized extralegal action, and the war sanctioned violence, endowing both with the aura of patriotism. . . . If any single act became symbolic of the Revolution as a whole, it may have been the Boston Tea Party.

The democratization of the political culture, the accommodations by elites, combined with a quasi-revolution in communications, undoubtedly had an effect in channeling protest into a now more open political system. Petitioning to state legislatures, which very likely was on a greater scale than in the colonial era, lost the tone of supplication. Yet extralegal action was hardly abandoned; it seemed to run parallel to the legal. In the 1790s in western Pennsylvania, farmers formed Democratic societies, passed resolutions, and sent petitions to the federal government. Simultaneously, they resorted to tar-and-feathering tax collectors, erecting liberty poles, and parading thousands-strong through Pittsburgh to intimidate local elites. They were prepared for military resistance, but confronted by a massive federal mobilization of force, the rebels debated strategy and withdrew.

Resorting to force produced a crisis in confidence within popular movements over achieving their ends within the system, the mirror image of the crisis in confidence among elites over taking their chances with democracy. Clearly, a kind of constitutional democratic radicalism came into being. William Manning, the plebeian democrat who had opposed Shays's Rebellion, would have members of his proposed national laboring society take an oath to support the government against insurrections. The aim of the society was to educate "the Many" to make use of their electoral power to oust "the Few." . . .

. . . [R]espectable mechanics and tradesmen fashioned new, affirmative, non-violent rituals: they paraded in civic festivals, attended Fourth of July ceremonies, and celebrated the victories of the French Revolution at dinners. They also took part in politics, and those qualified to vote—a large proportion of the total—cast ballots in increasing numbers. The ballot box was not the coffin of a plebeian citizen consciousness. The assembly election of 1796 in New York City, Hamilton reported with anguish, "in the eyes of the common people was a question between the rich and the poor." . . .

If by the end of the eighteenth century, African-American slaves in the South had fewer legal paths to freedom, it might be argued they had enlarged their range of illegal options. The war and the rise of free black communities made flight more possible and more successful than ever before. But collective insurrection was now a possibility, inspired variously by the example of successful rebellion in St. Domingue, a new wave of evangelical religion, the emergence of an artisan class among slaves, and the example of the first viable free black communities. There is a temptation to speak of a new cycle of insurrection after the turn of the century.

Gabriel Prosser's failed conspiracy in Richmond, Virginia, in the summer of 1800, which to Gov. James Monroe was "unquestionably the most serious and formidable conspiracy we have ever known of that kind," was led by urban artisans. St. George Tucker, an antislavery Virginian, measured how far black people had come in the quarter of a century since 1775. In response to Lord Dunmore's plea, slaves had acted individually by running away; in 1800 they showed they were capable of "acting in concert"—to a degree Tucker found "astonishing." In 1775 they "fought for freedom merely as a good; now they also claim it as a right." At his trial one rebel said, "I have nothing more to offer than what George Washington would have had to offer, had he been taken by the British and put on trial by them. I have ventured my life in endeavoring to obtain the liberty of my countryman, and am a willing sacrifice in their cause." . . .

Among advocates of women's rights, by contrast, it is difficult to detect a split as to means. There clearly were differences among articulate women. . . . However, that women aired their differences in newspapers, magazines, and novels or privately in correspondence, diaries, and conversations suggests the boundaries of women's activities. . . . [B]y 1800 it is not quite possible to speak of a women's movement much less a women's rights movement.

1776

Twenty-five Years Later

How successful were the multiple radicalisms that emerged in 1775–76 and flourished in the 1780s and 1790s? I have argued that over the long revolution era one of the best tests of the success of radical movements is their impact on the elites. In 1801 the Democratic Republicans, led by the more accommodating of the two national elites, won power. How far did they then carry the processes of accommodation in the different spheres of American life?

Some of the players are the same. Thomas Jefferson characterized his election over John Adams as "the revolution of 1800," and "as real a revolution in the principles of our government as that of 1776 was in its form." . . .

In power the Jeffersonian elite would accommodate only some . . . popular movements. Would-be yeoman farmers hungry for land could anticipate revisions in federal land laws making the public domain available in smaller parcels at lower prices. And when an expansionist president acquired the Louisiana Territory, he could claim to have fulfilled the expectation of his inaugural address of land "for the thousandth generation to come." Mechanics could be optimistic when they submitted to Congress in 1801 a petition for protection for American manufactures with the same wording they had submitted in 1789.

Others had less reason for optimism. The journeymen shoemakers of Philadelphia, a hundred of whom began a long strike in 1799, the first of a half a dozen such strikes that would take place in as many cities in the next decade or so, would be tried and convicted for conspiracy. They drew more opposition than support from local Democratic Republicans. . . .

Nationally Jeffersonians wanted to contain, not accommodate, the radical thrusts for freedom from southern slaves. Jefferson had not published a word of public criticism of slavery since *Notes on Virginia* in the 1780s. His antislavery sentiment, already withering on the vine of his racism, froze with the news of rebellions in St. Dominque, even before Gabriel's conspiracy at home. . . . Confronted as president with the Napoleonic effort to overthrow the successful slave revolutionaries in their West Indies colony, Jefferson consistently "pressed for the devastation and destruction of the black Jacobins."

Women could expect less support from Jefferson than Adams. "Our good ladies," Jefferson rejoiced . . . "have been too wise to wrinkle their foreheads with politics. They are contented to soothe and calm the minds of their husbands returning ruffled from political debate." . . . [O]nly here and there a few maverick Republicans—Benjamin Rush, James Sullivan, Charles Brockden Brown—took a public stand on women' issues.

The limits of Jeffersonian accommodation were soon made clear to the American Indians. To a visiting delegation, the philosopher-scientist expressed the hope that "we shall see your people become disposed to cultivate the earth, to raise herds of the useful animals, and to spin and weave for their food and clothing." To the territorial governor of Ohio, Jefferson revealed his underlying rationale: "Our settlements will gradually circumscribe and approach the Indians & they will in time either incorporate with us as citizens of the U.S. or remove beyond the Mississippi." Inside a velvet glove he kept a mailed fist. "We presume our strength and their weakness is now so visible," he remarked in 1803, "that they must see we have only to shut our hand to crush them." The "empire for liberty" Jefferson envisioned was for white male yeoman farmers and their families.

How radical was the American Revolution? Or, if you prefer, how much transformation was there as a result of the Revolution? The central concept I have advanced of a negotiation among contending groups, "classes," and individuals offers a number of advantages as an analytical tool or as a heuristic principle of investigation. It differs from the old progressive and conflict interpretations, which focused primarily on the political and saw outright victory for one side and defeat for the other. . . . It differs from the old consensus interpretation in analyzing results as the product of conflict. It avoids the weakness of intellectual or ideological interpretations that posit a single cluster of ideas from which all change emanates. It acknowledges the systems or structures that framed what people did, but assigns priority to the agency of people in effecting change and renewing their struggles even in the face of defeat.

It enables us to encompass more of the multiple dimensions of the Revolution: as a colonial struggle for liberation from imperial rule, in which there were coalitions of nascent "classes" in both cooperative and antagonistic relationships, and as a series of internal struggles in separate but often overlapping spheres. It allows us to measure the results of these struggles, not at one stopping point, but as an ongoing process, in which negotiations were often renewed and sometimes faded. It further permits us to measure results in many different spheres of life, private as well as public. And it enables us to recognize that while the Revolution was indeed radical, there is no single answer to the question, How radical was the American Revolution?

The Revolution Rearranged North America's Human Landscape

EDWARD COUNTRYMAN

Between 1965 and 1985 a burst of creative scholarship transformed understanding of the American Revolution. As that burst began, historians' general sense was that the great issues turned on problems of central government and that the prime result was the national liberation of a more or less unified people. By its end, we realized how different it was to be citizens of a republic rather than subjects of a monarch.

"The Revolution Rearranged North America's Human Landscape," by Edward Countryman. *William and Mary Quarterly,* 3d Series, Volume LIII, Number 2, April 1996. Copyright © 1996. Reprinted by permission of the Omohundro Institute of Early American History and Culture.

We understood that political society and political ideology had altered radically. We appreciated the Revolution's popular and disruptive dimensions and how all sorts of people took part in building the new American order. We grasped how the Revolution transformed gender from an unproblematic "distinction of nature" (Thomas Paine's phrase in *Common Sense* [January 1776] into a central element of the American cultural agenda. We saw the Revolution breaking the automatic American connection between enslavement and blackness and turning slavery itself from a general given into a morally and politically troubling sectional peculiarity. By 1985, we had a vastly sharpened sense of how different the late colonies of King George III were from the early republic of President George Washington.

During the same two decades, another discussion was probing the emergence of capitalist society in the young republic. The formation of investment capital and new social classes, the importance of gender both for social experience and as an ideological construct, urbanization, the spread of long-distance market relationships, the problem of free black people,the transformation of law to suit the new society's needs: all these proved fruitful areas of discussion. In the mid-1990s, these separate themes of a revolutionary Revolution and post-Revolutionary capitalist development seem to be converging . . . toward . . . an account of American society through time and across issues that shows shared experiences and an ultimate common identity without homogenizing the diverse American people.

Yet something remains missing. Gordon S. Wood points to the problem when he insists on interpreting Americans' Revolutionary experience in terms of the social reality his subjects knew, and no other. . . . But he misses what is really specific about American society. His fugal three-part invention of monarchy, republicanism, and democracy has almost nothing to say about Revolutionary-era Americans who were not white, free, and mostly northeastern. That slavery persisted and grew, that what whites gained in the great interior was also what Indians lost: these facts may be regrettable, but they are mere sideshows. Yet without considering everybody involved, we cannot appreciate either the Revolution's magnitude or its price.

I attempt a different formulation, reaching westward into Indian country, eastward to the Old World, and linking what developed after Independence to a specifically American version of the eighteenth-century ancien régime. I seek an understanding that brings together all three of the large, racially defined groups of late colonial and early republican American society. I develop that understanding in terms of structures, the patterns of law, power, and expectation that constrain what people do, while recognizing that during the Revolution old patterns came loose and new ones emerged and became set. . . . I also consider the losses that were the price of the young republic's gains and at least sketch the connection that bound all these to the expanded slavery that accompanied the young republic's freedom.

Let us begin with a simple . . . point. During the forty years between the peace of 1763 and the Louisiana Purchase, only one new line of long-term geopolitical importance was drawn upon the North American map. This line separated the eastern United States from Canada in 1783. Throughout the epoch of the Revolution, in other words, the thirteen colonies/United States occupied a single huge quadrilateral, defined by the Atlantic seaboard, the Florida boundary and Gulf Coast, the Mississippi, and the Great Lakes-St. Lawrence basin. What changed geopolitically was relationships within those boundaries. . . . [T]his truism becomes the basis for a fresh understanding of colonial and early republican America in the new scholarship on the early "west."

Thanks to that scholarship, we understand that the eighteenth-century interior was no wilderness. The colonial powers drew lines on maps to mark spheres of influence. . . . The great arcs of fortifications, missions, and settlements that the French cut between Quebec and New Orleans and that Spaniards inscribed through Florida and from Texas to Arizona were thin. But they were just as irremovable from either the map or the landscape as the far thicker arc of English settlements along the Atlantic.

We think of these arcs as the outposts of warring powers. But we might also regard them as the great structural outcome of the European invasion. Together, the Florida, Mississippi/St. Lawrence, and east coast arcs entirely surrounded all of what became the young United States. Everyone within them—whites, whatever language they spoke; Indians, whatever their tribal identity; and slaves, whoever claimed to own them—participated in colonial and early national society. . . .

This argument—that everyone east of the Mississippi participated in "colonial" social relations—is not a matter of applying latter-day concepts that the subjects would not have understood. On the contrary, the people of Iroquoia and trans-Appalachia comprehended their situation. They nominated emissaries to the outside world. . . . These people observed, considered, and took their knowledge back.

Adaptation extended to institutions. Whole tribes took shape as defensive formations under the pressures of disease, trade, and war. The Iroquois supplemented their Great League of Peace, made for their own purposes before any Indian saw an invading white, with a confederacy that let them face the Europeans with flexible unity. They forged their Covenant Chain to define relations both east and west. In the "village world" of the western Great Lakes an enduring accommodation emerged among Indians, métis [mixed-race], and Europeans alike. . . .

Interior Indians wove this entangling network of diplomacy, war, commerce, intermarriage, and residence out of lessons, learned from the seventeenth-century defeat of their fellows along the coast. . . . But few Indians thought the Europeans could be pushed back militarily from whatever ground they had gained, at least very far. They came to realize that building and using their own institutions presented much better possibilities for survival and self-defense than war.

The evidence that Indians coped with the new situation lies in numbers. Historians and anthropologists have dismissed the notion that North America was effectively empty when Europeans and Africans began to arrive. More recently, we have come to understand that the great demographic disaster after contact was not driven solely by biology. Indians responded to the epidemics in terms of social organization as much as in terms of infection and immunity. . . . East of the mountains, numbers did dwindle toward virtual insignificance. In Florida, however, Indians held steady. Cherokees, Creeks, and Chickasaws/Choctaws bottomed out and rebounded, the latter groups numbering well above 10,000 each in 1790. The same appears true in the Great Lakes country. . . .

These numbers do not compare with the burgeoning white and black population along the coastal plain and piedmont. The Indians were still vastly outnumbered. But the figures indicate that their situation was not hopeless. They suggest the absolute importance of institutions and procedures that enabled Indians to protect themselves within a world which they could resist but not escape. . . .

In the late colonial period, European/African society crept westward. In the early republic, it surged. Historians usually attribute the difference to little more than greater pressure of white numbers after Independence than before. The 3,929,214 white and black people counted in the 1790 census did represent a great increase over the roughly 2,200,000 colonists of 1775. But between 1790 and 1800, white and black population density increased only from 4.5 persons to 6.1 persons per square mile. Between 1800 and 1810, with the Louisiana Territory acquired but not yet undergoing settlement, density fell to 4.3 persons per square mile. Before 1776, white colonists stayed east not simply because they were as yet few but also because people west of them had the means to resist. Resistance was not raw, untamed savagery. It was institutional, economic, and political as well as military. Indians had worked out a way of participating in the larger colonial formation on more or less their own terms. For more than a century, that way served them well.

This perspective shifts our sense of the colonial social order and the Revolution that transformed it. In broad terms, two contrasting possibilities for understanding that order have been argued and re-argued. One portrays the mature British colonies as already "modern." It has seen a Revolution that preserved, confirmed, and extended a beneficent order that "Americans" already enjoyed. The other view draws on strictly European notions of an ancien régime. Among white colonial America's gentry, merchants, holders of minor titles, and archaic social practices, it has sought counterparts for the "mediæval rubbish" that Marx saw the French Revolution as sweeping away. Proponents of each approach can adduce ample evidence; proponents of neither can convince people who hold fast to the other. Gordon Wood's recent work attempts a synthesis by arguing both the pervasive organizing power of the metaphor of monarchy and the corrosive energy with which American social practice attacked that power. . . . [H]e has not won general assent.

Both perspectives rest on the unspoken assumption that colonial and Revolutionary America was a "neo-Europe," a place "thousands of miles from Europe" where "the great majority" of people were of European descent, with enormous productivity of foodstuffs and eventually industrial goods. For Massachusetts, Connecticut, and Rhode Island, the idea works. By 1760, their ecology was transformed in European ways. Their native peoples had largely (though not entirely) disappeared. Their black population never rose higher than 3 percent and was lower than that at the eighteenth century's beginning and end. . . .

Outside lower New England, however, that formulation's inadequacy is readily demonstrated. Eighteenth-century Virginia encompassed not only the modern commonwealth but also what are now West Virginia and Kentucky. It claimed a much larger territory, covering much of the Midwest. Planters, yeomen, and politicians were aware of that point, and it was central to their strategies. Expansion was part of how white Virginians lived, both because of what their tobacco did to the soil and because their inheritance practices required ever more land as new generations matured. It will not do to say that Virginia society stopped at the mountains, even in white consciousness.

Though great planters gave themselves a veneer of being English gentry, the reality of their lives was otherwise. . . . African slaves produced not the food-stuffs and livestock of an English estate but rather a strictly colonial staple crop, under conditions that no English estate displayed. . . . If we accept that both slaves and Indians were important components of the colonial formation, neither a the-colonies-were-born-modern perspective nor a the-colonies-were-intrinsically-an-old-order-in-the-European-style perspective does justice to them. To resolve the problem, we need to look west.

Hints of how to approach the trans-Appalachian west's place in the colonial order appear in recent work by Bernard Bailyn and Jack P. Greene. But, like Gordon Wood searching for genuinely American social conditions, neither Bailyn nor Greene goes far enough. Bailyn's studies of the "peopling of America" rightly deny that any absolute western boundary circumscribed "the colonies." Instead, the "interior" sprawled across political lines. Bailyn gives no suggestion that the hemisphere was already well peopled, that a large number of Atlantic migrants came from Africa, or that his own "voyagers to the west" were as much conquerors for greater Britain as refugees from it.

Greene probes the problem another way, drawing explicitly on the question of center and periphery as formulated by Edward Shils. . . .

Borrowing from Shils, Greene develops a notion of "extended polities." The idea is fertile, but for Greene those polities stop at the limits of white settlement. The idea works much better if we extend it to comprehend everyone involved, both before and after the transformation of Independence. . . .

That the Revolution was a disaster for Indians is a commonplace. The point remains true despite [the fact] . . . that Indians fought back and that the disaster was drawn out over half a century. The protraction merely renders it exactly parallel to the half century the Revolution's liberating implications took to work themselves through among whites.

What needs exploring are how the two are intertwined and how the intertwining is linked with the expansion of black American slavery as well as white American freedom. Two different dimensions of the problem present themselves. One is the place of Indians in relation to the self-denied, self-governing, self-sovereign American people that emerged from the Revolution. The other is how the western land that Indians held on their own terms under the old order became the huge trove of free capital that was the basis for the young republic's commercial agricultural expansion, north and south alike.

Though the two problems cannot really be separated, let me deal with the constitutional dimension first. . . . White American colonial freedom had been the uneven tangle of liberties, privileges, and immunities that settlers had imported from England and developed among themselves under what we conventionally call "salutary neglect." White American national freedom was to be the formal equality of citizens, all participating in a shared sovereignty with no authority above them and with powerful institutions to realize their collective will. Here lay the great sociological change (a separate people), the great ideological change (a self-sovereign people), and the great institutional change (a people possessing the instruments of its own power) that the Revolution wrought. . . .

The contrast between what the Revolutionaries achieved and the absolutist phase of the ancien régime [traditional European monarchies] was enormous. *L'état, c'est moi* gave way to *l'état, c'est nous,* and the difference reverberated from the Urals to the Andes. But Blackstone's notion of "a supreme, irresistible, absolute, uncontrolled authority" was enhanced and relocated, not destroyed. By defining themselves as sovereign, the American people were also claiming the power to exclude others or to define others as their subjects, just as they had been subject to the sovereign king. Briefly, that problem was faced even by people on the rapidly expanding edge of white settlement. But in the new order the permanently subordinate, subject others would be Indians, slaves, and free people of color. From their angle, the Revolution did not destroy absolutism at all.

The official language of American self-sovereignty is universalistic and inclusive: "all men are created equal," "one people . . . separate the political bands that have connected them with another," "we the people . . . do ordain and establish this constitution" in order "to secure the blessings of liberty." But practical reality became otherwise. "Cut up every Indian cornfield," ordered South Carolina leader William Henry Drayton in 1776, "and burn every Indian town and every Indian taken shall be the slave and property of the taker and . . . the nation be extirpated and the lands become the property of the public." . . . Justifying the Revolution to the outside world, the Declaration of Independence called Indians "merciless . . . savages, whose known rule of warfare is an undistinguished destruction of all ages, sexes and conditions." The Constitution dismissed them as "Indians not taxed." They were outsiders to the new polity's self-definition.

We should not confuse the sharp shift of principles that the Revolution embodied with actual, immediate reality. . . .

Nor did Indians regard subjection to the new United States as a necessary outcome of whatever the whites did to one another. Many may not have regarded the struggle between Britain and its colonies as a "real event" at all, seeing it instead as just "an unmarked interval in a continuing series of struggles that had begun long before 1776 and would continue after the British surrender at Yorktown." When settlers began pouring into the Ohio Country after Independence, Delawares who were already there tried to copy by behaving as generous hosts, sharing what they had with people in need. The American presidency took on the claim to symbolic fatherhood that the French and British monarchies had originated . . . in the name of the sovereign American people. . . .

By their own lights, the Revolutionaries did not operate from ill motives. Early official policy assumed that as individuals Indians might be fully assimilable. The intermarriage of Indian women and white men, a transformation of gender roles so that Indian men would farm, and the guarantee of fee-simple farmsteads adequate for single families constituted "Jeffersonian philanthropy." This was fully consistent with the dominant vision of a prosperous and virtuous republic based on commercial agriculture. . . .

The fundamental issue was land and its usage. . . .

. . . When New York State confiscated loyalist property in 1779, it declared "the sovereignty of the people of this state in respect of all property within the same." At first glance, the reference might seem to be to the New York City and

Hudson-Mohawk estates the loyalists lost. But a more likely long-term goal—and a certain long-term consequence—was to assert the state's power over Iroquoia. Despite claims by the United States that it alone could regulate Indian affairs, New York negotiated one Iroquois treaty after another, all to acquire land. By 1791, eleven million acres had passed by different routes into white hands. The land became capital, to be bought, sold, and developed on the fastest possible terms.

The Iroquois collapsed so rapidly after having held on so long because the Revolutionary War destroyed their political coherence and their military reputation. Their ceremonial council fire at Onondaga was extinguished in 1779, the same year John Sullivan's expedition demolished their material resources. Other major groups did not collapse nearly so fast. The Cherokee's establishment of themselves as an autonomous republic that was associated with the United States but not subordinate to it was a highly creative adaptation to the new reality. It opened the possibility of Indian participation in a composite American polity, republican rather than monarchical. On a micro scale, the Catawbas became a republican people within South Carolina and survived the era of removal without losing what was left of their land. . . .

Half a century separates the destruction of the Iroquois and the stark choice between dispersal and departure that Georgia gave the Cherokees. It was during those five decades that the national economy of the United States acquired the self-driving capacity to transform itself as well as simply expand. North and south, that capacity sprang from the emergence of market-driven capitalist agriculture as the only workable strategy for rural life. The . . . strategy came not only from the separate states that had public land to dispose but also from the United States as a whole. The policy was enunciated in the three ordinances for the northwest, of 1784, 1785, and 1787. It was continually developed in subsequent legislation to foster public land development.

More than one motive was at stake. Fostering public virtue, rewarding soldiers of the Revolution, and establishing communities all figured among the motivations of the architects of the American land system, especially at the national level. So did paying the national debt without anybody except Indians having to sacrifice. But these coexisted with enormous speculations, from Henry Knox's 500,000 acres in Maine, to Alexander Macomb's 3,500,000 in northern New York, to Georgia's 20,000,000-acre Yazoo grants. None of these projects aimed at creating tenanted seigneurial estates. . . . Speculation, the northwest ordinances, and public land laws all privatized the land and fostered possessive individualism. All turned land into a commodity in commerce, capital in its own right. . . . The way that both would-be wheat farmers north of the Ohio and would-be cotton growers in the expanding Deep South took up public land in rhythm with the surge and decline of prices turned a static blueprint into throbbing, working rural capitalism.

At one level, . . . "America" did not expand at all. . . . [S]ocial relations within the zone defined by the Atlantic coast, the Florida boundary, the Mississippi River, and Great Lakes/St. Lawrence basin changed enormously. There were Indian nations east of the Mississippi in 1803 that controlled what they thought was theirs, on terms that suited themselves. Some continued doing so into the 1820s. But that situation was doomed east of the Mississippi, at least on any basis more significant than occupying a shrunken remnant of land that nobody else wanted anyway. Their own negligibility allowed Iroquois survivors to retain their reservations in New York and the Catawbas theirs in South Carolina through the era of removal.

The legal forms remained unchanged from what had been worked out in the colonial era. Every step of the way, dispossessing and removing an Indian group meant finding someone within it to sign a treaty, until the treaty system itself was abolished in 1871. Even the operations of the Indian Removal Act of 1830 were carried out within a framework of formal diplomacy between two parties. But there was only one object in view for one side: the permanent and total alienation of land, both in the economic sense of possession and the political sense of claiming ultimate power over the conditions of its use and transfer.

This is the sense in which the American version of the ancien régime ceased to be. From the point of view of Indians, it was a monstrous injustice, which a great deal of present-day litigation and protest has aimed to remedy. From the point of view of the new republican American order, the change was total and absolutely beneficial. . . . The triumphant new power . . . moved to . . . an all-encompassing social reality that allowed virtually no room for exceptions or variations. . . . By 1830, the process was complete east of the Mississippi and well advanced beyond the river. Simultaneously, and not coincidentally, the Revolution finally worked through its social process and the United States completed its self-formation as a liberal capitalist society.

In its way, the young United States could claim to be just as much a composite state (as opposed to a unitary one) as any ancien régime monarchy had been. The whole purpose of the dual sovereignty schema that was worked out at the federal Convention was to reconcile state corporate autonomy with necessary central power in a way that had proven impossible against the claims of the centralizing British monarchy during the imperial crisis. Unlike the old order, the new schema allowed only one means for a self-defined people to participate in sovereignty. This was by seeking statehood. In all but a very few instances (Vermont, Kentucky, Tennessee, Maine, Texas, West Virginia, California) acquiring statehood meant following the institutional path through territorial status defined by the Northwest Ordinance of 1787. For all practical purposes, this route could be followed only by whites, carrying with them the expectations and beliefs about public life and economics inherited from their previous experiences of statehood elsewhere. Moreover, once a new state did constitute itself, it could follow the same course against claimants to autonomy within its borders as did New York against the Iroquois or Georgia against the Cherokees.

The composite reality of the United States was to be a matter of ceaseless, self-replication by a more or less uniform sovereign people, rather than one of great variety beneath a sovereign that in some fashion hovered above. The old French and British orders had allowed in practice and in something close to theory for the participation of self-determining, nonwhite, communally focused, custom-driven social entities, meaning Indian tribes. This, much more than the remnants of feudalism that had crossed the Atlantic and prospered in the colonies for a while, is what stood between the East Coast colonists and the full realization of the tendencies toward what would be the actual future that were bursting forth within their own sector of colonial society. In the American social formation, as opposed to its colonial forebear, their sector made itself the only sector that counted.

There was only one enduring exception at the level of state constitution-ality and law—the continuation of French law and traditions in Louisiana. Yet Louisiana's Creoles and Cajuns could count as white, and they enjoyed the pro-tection of the treaty terms of the Louisiana cession. Indians were not white, and they enjoyed no external protection, not the moral protection of an enforceable treaty or the military protection of an ally. As the republic consolidated itself, all potential allies were gone.

One final issue remains—the place of slavery within the great transformation, once the Revolution turned black bondage from a general fact of social life into the South's "peculiar institution." Indians were southern as well as northern. Although the southern Indians took longer than their northern counterparts to be vanquished, their collapse provides the key to slavery's expansion as the Revolution realized itself. What Cherokees, Creeks, Choctaws, and Chickasaws lost during the nine-teenth century's first quarter instantly became the new Deep South, and it required slaves. . . . More than 90,000 enslaved Africans were brought to the United States between Independence and 1808. . . . They composed more than a quarter of the Africans legally brought to the mainland colonies and the United States during the whole slave trade. Their enslavement was not an after-spasm of the trade's main history; it was a primal part of it, even though the enslavers knew their time was almost over. Another 98,000 people endured forced migration to the Deep South out of the overcrowded, worked-out Chesapeake states before 1820. Still more people, perhaps more than 50,000, came in the holds of clandestine slavers after the African trade was legally closed.

These people were essential to turning the land enclosed within the rapidly moving southern frontier into the basis of capitalist cotton-producing agriculture. The cotton the slaves grew, in turn, provided the main material basis for the indus-trial transformation of the northeast. South of the Ohio, Indians lost the land so that slaves could be placed immediately upon it. The fact of total and necessary inter-connectedness among the great racially defined and economically emplaced groups that composed American society had not changed. What changed, as I have been insisting, was the terms of that interconnectedness.

The social processes and structural changes sketched here could have taken place without juridical independence. We can describe them as a shift from external colonialism under the British to "internal colonialism" within the United States. Michael Hechter has used that term to describe the historical relationship between the metropolitan English and their so-called Celtic Fringe. Eugen Weber uses the same concept to show how widely disparate peasants cohered into Frenchmen. E. P. Thompson begins one of his very last essays with the clash of "custom, law, and common right" among the English, moves to the Scottish highlands where "law . . . afforded no shelter to a population evicted from lands which they had sup-posed to be communally owned, from time out of mind, by their clans," and leaps to a global perspective that takes in New England, New Zealand, and India. One of the main participants in India was the very same Lord Cornwallis who surrendered to Washington at Yorktown. In none of these places except the United States was political revolution or the emergence of self-governing republicanism involved. In all of them there was change in roughly the same direction anyway, following roughly the same scenario. . . .

To admit that in principle the change could have happened without the American Revolution is not to refute the claim that in America it was part of the Revolution. The Independence crisis found Indians, the western half of the colonial social formation, in a condition of extreme historical contingency, neither foredoomed to defeat nor guaranteed the future they would have chosen. Instead, the late empire provided them with a means, a context, and an unstable balance point for asserting and protecting themselves. All these would be denied by the young republic, although other possibilities did for a time seem open. The shift was bound up with both the self-constitution of a sovereign American people and that people's redefinition of the appropriate usage for the space where it claimed sovereignty. One social order that had filled the whole of that space gave way to another, vastly more suited than its predecessor to the democratic capitalist energy that we now see as the Revolution's product.

FURTHER READING

Bernard Bailyn, *Faces of Revolution: Personalities and Themes in the Struggle for American Independence* (1990)

———, *The Ideological Origins of the American Revolution* (1967)

Thomas C. Barrow, "The American Revolution Considered as a Colonial War for Independence," *William and Mary Quarterly,* 3d ser., 25 (1968), 452–464.

Richard Buel Jr., "Democracy and the American Revolution: A Frame of Reference," *William and Mary Quarterly,* 3d ser., 21 (1964), 165–190.

Edwin G. Burrows and Michael Wallace, "The American Revolution: The Ideology and Practice of National Liberation," *Perspectives in American History* 6 (1972), 167–306.

Edward Countryman *The American Revolution* (1985)

Jay Fliegelman, *Prodigals and Pilgrims: The American Revolution Against Patriarchal Authority* (1982)

William M. Fowler, Jr. and Wallace Coyle, eds., *The American Revolution: Changing Perspectives* (1979)

Jack P. Greene, ed., *The American Revolution: Its Character and Limits* (1987)

Ronald Hoffman and Peter J. Albert, *The Transforming Hand of Revolution: Reconsidering the American Revolution as a Social Movement* (1995)

Jameson, J. Franklin, *The American Revolution Considered as a Social Movement* (1926)

Merrill Jensen, "The American People and the American Revolution," *Journal of American History* 57 (1970), 5–35.

———, Historians and the Nature of the American Revolution," in *The Reinterpretation of Early American History,* R. A. Billington, ed. (1966)

Stephen G. Kurtz and James H. Hutson, eds., *Essays on the American Revolution* (1973)

Jesse Lemisch, "The American Revolution Seen from the Bottom Up," in *Towards a New Past,* Barton Bernstein, ed. (1968)

Kenneth A. Lockridge, "Social Change and the Meaning of the American Revolution," *Journal of Social History* 4 (1973), 403–439.

[Michael McGiffert, ed.] "Forum: Rethinking the American Revolution," *William and Mary Quarterly,* 3d Ser., 53 (1996), 341–386.

Edmund S. Morgan, *The Challenge of the American Revolution* (1976)

Richard B. Morris, *The American Revolution Reconsidered* (1967)

Gary B. Nash, *The Urban Crucible: Social Change, Political Consciousness, and the Origins of the American Revolution* (1979)

Robert R. Palmer, "The Revolution," in *The Comparative Approach to American History,* C. Vann Woodward, ed. (1968)

Frederick B. Tolles, "The American Revolution Considered as a Social Movement: A Re-Evaluation," *American Historical Review* 60 (1954–55), 1–12.

Gordon S. Wood, *The Radicalism of the American Revolution* (1992)

———, "Rhetoric and Reality in the American Revolution," *William and Mary Quarterly,* 3d ser., 23 (1966), 3–32.

Alfred F. Young, ed., *The American Revolution: Explorations in the History of American Radicalism* (1976)

———, *Beyond the American Revolution: Explorations in the History of American Radicalism* (1993)